Lecture Notes in Computer Science

Lecture Notes in Artificial Intelligence 15712
Founding Editor

Jörg Siekmann

Series Editors

Randy Goebel, *University of Alberta, Edmonton, AB, Canada*
Wolfgang Wahlster, *DFKI, Berlin, Germany*
Zhi-Hua Zhou, *Nanjing University, Nanjing, China*

The series Lecture Notes in Artificial Intelligence (LNAI) was established in 1988 as a topical subseries of LNCS devoted to artificial intelligence.

The series publishes state-of-the-art research results at a high level. As with the LNCS mother series, the mission of the series is to serve the international R & D community by providing an invaluable service, mainly focused on the publication of conference and workshop proceedings and postproceedings.

Thomas Ågotnes · Dragan Doder
Editors

Logic and Argumentation

6th International Conference, CLAR 2025
Taiyuan, China, June 14–16, 2025
Proceedings

Editors
Thomas Ågotnes
University of Bergen
Bergen, Norway

Dragan Doder
Utrecht University
Utrecht, The Netherlands

ISSN 0302-9743　　　　　　　ISSN 1611-3349　(electronic)
Lecture Notes in Artificial Intelligence
ISBN 978-981-96-7955-3　　　ISBN 978-981-96-7956-0　(eBook)
https://doi.org/10.1007/978-981-96-7956-0

LNCS Sublibrary: SL7 – Artificial Intelligence

© The Editor(s) (if applicable) and The Author(s), under exclusive license to Springer Nature Singapore Pte Ltd. 2025

This work is subject to copyright. All rights are solely and exclusively licensed by the Publisher, whether the whole or part of the material is concerned, specifically the rights of translation, reprinting, reuse of illustrations, recitation, broadcasting, reproduction on microfilms or in any other physical way, and transmission or information storage and retrieval, electronic adaptation, computer software, or by similar or dissimilar methodology now known or hereafter developed.
The use of general descriptive names, registered names, trademarks, service marks, etc. in this publication does not imply, even in the absence of a specific statement, that such names are exempt from the relevant protective laws and regulations and therefore free for general use.
The publisher, the authors and the editors are safe to assume that the advice and information in this book are believed to be true and accurate at the date of publication. Neither the publisher nor the authors or the editors give a warranty, expressed or implied, with respect to the material contained herein or for any errors or omissions that may have been made. The publisher remains neutral with regard to jurisdictional claims in published maps and institutional affiliations.

This Springer imprint is published by the registered company Springer Nature Singapore Pte Ltd.
The registered company address is: 152 Beach Road, #21-01/04 Gateway East, Singapore 189721, Singapore

If disposing of this product, please recycle the paper.

Preface

These are the proceedings of The 6th International Conference on Logic and Argumentation (CLAR 2025), which took place at Shanxi University in Taiyuan, China, June 14–16, 2025. The aim of the conference was to highlight recent advances in logic and argumentation and foster interaction in these two areas.

The interplay between logic and argumentation spans different disciplines and historical eras: from ancient philosophy (Socrates' dialectics, Aristotle's logic) to contemporary computer science (dialogues, multiagent systems). Research in logic and argumentation offers formal or semi-formal models that capture reasoning patterns and dialogue activities of diverse kinds. Their applications in artificial intelligence range from law and ethics to linguistics. Established in 2016 as a workshop hosted by Zhejiang University, the CLAR series has been increasingly successful and become an international event and discussion forum in the two areas of logic and argumentation. The aim for CLAR 2025 was to be a platform for the advancement of the existing discussions within each of the areas above, to build bridges between their different traditions, and finally to open argumentation to new applications and other areas in artificial intelligence, such as legal reasoning, explainable AI, ethical dilemmas, reasoning about uncertainty and knowledge representation, etc.

An open call for submissions was issued, inviting contributions from logic, artificial intelligence, philosophy, computer science, linguistics, law, and other areas studying logic and formal argumentation.

We received 38 submissions, which were reviewed by the program committee using a single-blind process. Most papers received three reviews; all papers at least two. One paper was co-authored by one of the PC chairs; the review process was handled separately by the other PC chair. In the end, 22 papers were accepted. They can be found in this volume.

The strong conference program represented the depth and breadth of research in formal logic, formal argumentation, and the intesection between the two. In addition to the contributed papers in this volume, it also contains invited talks by leading international researchers: Ryuta Arisaka on argumentation and logic – a modern and natural connection, Nicholas Asher on investigating reasoning in language models, Zoe Christoff on the majority illusion in social networks, Emiliano Lorrini on preferences in concurrent games, and Nico Potyka on logic and argumentation for explainable AI.

We thank the authors of the submitted papers, the program committee, the invited speakers, and, last but not least, the local organizers at Shanxi University for making CLAR 2025 a success in advancing the state of the art in logic and argumentation.

April 2025   Thomas Ågotnes
                                                                                            Dragan Doder

Organization

Program Committee Chairs

Thomas Ågotnes — University of Bergen, Norway, and Shanxi University, China
Dragan Doder — Utrecht University, the Netherlands

Steering Committee

Beishui Liao — Zhejiang University, China
Huimin Dong — TU Wien, Austria
Thomas Ågotnes — University of Bergen, Norway
Pietro Baroni — University of Brescia, Italy
Christoph Benzmüller — Otto-Friedrich-Universität Bamberg, Germany and Freie Universität Berlin, Germany
Mehdi Dastani — Utrecht University, the Netherlands
Yì N. Wáng — Sun Yat-sen University, China
Leendert van der Torre — University of Luxembourg, Luxembourg

Program Committee

Natasha Alechina — Open Universiteit, the Netherlands
Leila Amgoud — IRIT - CNRS, France
Ofer Arieli — Academic College of Tel-Aviv, Israel
Pietro Baroni — University of Brescia, Italy
Christoph Benzmüller — Otto-Friedrich-Universität Bamberg, Germany and Freie Universität Berlin, Germany
Antonis Bikakis — University College London, UK
Pedro Cabalar — University of A Coruña, Spain
Martin Caminada — Cardiff University, UK
Walter Carnielli — University of Campinas, Brazil
Weiwei Chen — Sun Yat-sen University, China
Mehdi Dastani — Utrecht University, the Netherlands
Huimin Dong — TU Wien, Austria
Sylvie Doutre — IRIT - Université Toulouse Capitole, France
Hein Duijf — Utrecht University, the Netherlands

Federico L. G. Faroldi	Flanders Research Foundation, Belgium
Raul Fervari	Universidad Nacional de Córdoba and CONICET, Argentina
Rustam Galimullin	University of Bergen, Norway
Sujata Ghosh	Indian Statistical Institute, Chennai, India
Massimiliano Giacomin	University of Brescia, Italy
Guido Governatori	Central Queensland University, Australia
Jesse Heyninck	Open Universiteit, the Netherlands
Anthony Hunter	University College London, UK
Fengkui Ju	Beijing Normal University, China
Marie-Christine Lagasquie-Schiex	Université Toulouse 3 – IRIT, France
Hannes Leitgeb	Ludwig Maximilians University Munich, Germany
Beishui Liao	Zhejiang University, China
Yasir Mahmood	Paderborn University, Germany
Jean-Guy Mailly	Université Toulouse Capitole, IRIT, France
Réka Markovich	University of Luxembourg, Luxembourg
Juan Carlos Nieves	Umeå University, Sweden
Hitoshi Omori	Tohoku University, Japan
Valeria de Paiva	Topos Institute, USA
Xavier Parent	TU Wien, Austria
Henry Prakken	Utrecht University, the Netherlands
Carlo Proietti	National Research Council of Italy (CNR) - Institute for Computational Linguistics (ILC), Italy
Revantha Ramanayake	University of Groningen, the Netherlands
R. Ramanujam	Institute of Mathematical Sciences, India
Tjitze Rienstra	Maastricht University, the Netherlands
Antonino Rotolo	University of Bologna, Italy
Olivier Roy	Universität Bayreuth, Germany
Katsuhiko Sano	Hokkaido University, Japan
Chenwei Shi	Tsinghua University, China
Sonja Smets	University of Amsterdam, the Netherlands
Thomas Studer	University of Bern, Switzerland
Geoff Sutcliffe	University of Miami, USA
Matthias Thimm	FernUniversität in Hagen, Germany
Leon van der Torre	University of Luxembourg, Luxembourg
Mauro Vallati	University of Huddersfield, UK
Fernando R. Velázquez-Quesada	University of Bergen, Norway
Emil Weydert	University of Luxembourg, Luxembourg
Stefan Woltran	TU Wien, Austria
Yì Nicholas Wáng	Sun Yat-sen University, China

Wei Xiong	Sun Yat-Sen University, China
Tomoyuki Yamada	Hokkaido University, Japan
Fan Yang	Utrecht University, the Netherlands
Bruno Yun	Université Claude Bernard Lyon 1, France
Antonio Yuste-Ginel	University of Málaga, Spain

Additional Reviewers

Lydia Blümel
Jonas Becker Arenhart
Chen Chen
Zhaoqun Li
Mo Liu
Kamal Lodaya
Valentin Müller
Sunil Simon
Kenneth Skiba
Liuwen Yu

Contents

Interpretable Biomedical Named Entity Recognition via BLSTM
with Talmudic Public Announcement Logic 1
   *Yulin Chen, Beishui Liao, Bruno Bentzen, Bo Yuan, Zelai Yao,
Haixiao Chi, and Dov Gabbay*

Each of Those Eight Coalition Logics is Also Determined by Four Other
Kinds of Models 17
   Zixuan Chen and Fengkui Ju

Incomplete Higher-Order Abstract Argumentation Frameworks 34
   *Sylvie Doutre, Marie-Christine Lagasquie-Schiex, Jean-Guy Mailly,
and Antonio Yuste-Ginel*

Modal Equivalence, n-Bisimulation and Model Comparison Game
for Basic Neighbourhood Logic 53
   Xiaoxuan Fu and Zhiguang Zhao

Preference-Based Extension Enforcement in Argumentation 66
   Nguyen Duy Hung and Van-Nam Huynh

Argumentation Framework with Attitude Classification: A New Approach
to Handle Controversial Arguments, Defeat Cycles and Self-defeating
Arguments 84
   Lehuai Jiang and Wei Chen

Ontology of Autonomous Driving as a Tool for Argumentation
on Responsibility 104
   Piotr Kulicki and Robert Trypuz

A Proposal for the Reconstruction and Evaluation of Multimodal
Argumentation in Print Advertisements 121
   Ting Lan and Jianying Cui

Validity of Attacks Related to Argument Set in Higher-Order
Argumentation Frameworks 139
   Hengfei Li and Jiachao Wu

Deontic Sufficiency in Dyadic Deontic Logic 150
   Xu Li

Reasoning in Coalition Planning 168
  Yanjun Li

The Surprise Exam in Full Modal Fixed-Point Logic 185
  Yanjun Li, Jie Ren, and Thomas Ågotnes

Which One Takes Priority?—Reflections on the Concept of Argument 201
  Runcheng Liang

Argument-Based Belief and the Evidence Topology 217
  John I. Lindqvist and Chenwei Shi

On Pluralistic Methods for Explaining Argument Acceptance in Abstract
Argumentation 235
  Siyi Liu, Ziyi Gao, Beishui Liao, and Chen Chen

Proportional Acceptability of Arguments 254
  Xiaolong Liu and Weiwei Chen

Towards Assumption-Based Argumentation Mining in Hotel Reviews 272
  *Teeradaj Racharak, Watanee Jearanaiwongkul, Jiraporn Pooksook,
  and Kazuki Takashima*

A Dialogical Interpretation of Cut-Elimination and Its Application
to Argumentation Theory 291
  Ryo Takemura

On SCC-Recursiveness in Quantitative Argumentation 309
  Zongshun Wang and Yuping Shen

Six Faces of Or-to-If 327
  Xuefeng Wen

Relevance for Stability of Verification Status of a Set of Arguments
in Incomplete Argumentation Frameworks 343
  Anshu Xiong and Songmao Zhang

The A-BDI Metamodel for Human-Level AI: Argumentation as Balancing,
Dialogue and Inference 361
  Liuwen Yu and Leendert van der Torre

Author Index 381

Interpretable Biomedical Named Entity Recognition via BLSTM with Talmudic Public Announcement Logic

Yulin Chen[1], Beishui Liao[1(✉)], Bruno Bentzen[1], Bo Yuan[1], Zelai Yao[1], Haixiao Chi[2], and Dov Gabbay[3]

[1] Zhejiang University, Hangzhou 310028, China
{yulinchen,baiseliao,bbentzen,byuan,zelai.yao}@zju.edu.cn
[2] Xiamen Medical College, Fujian 361023, China
haixiaochi@zju.edu.cn
[3] King's College London, London 695014, UK
dov.gabbay@kcl.ac.uk

Abstract. Biomedical Named entity recognition (BioNER) is a crucial initial step for biomedical information processing, serving as the cornerstone technology for identifying biomedical entities and their interactions. However, the inherent workings of most BioNER models remain opaque to users, posing a significant challenge in enhancing their interpretability. In this paper, we propose a novel interpretable learning method based on Talmudic Public announcement logic (TPK), which can learn human-readable knowledge from Bi-directional Long Short-Term Memory (BLSTM) models and generate effective explanations in the form of dichotomous TPK trees. Empirical evaluations conducted on the publicly available BioNER dataset, GENIA, demonstrate that our TPK-based deep learning method outperforms the vanilla BLSTM models in low-source settings. Furthermore, the logical reasoning based on TPK models shows how BLSTM handles BioNER tasks in real applications, providing users with rigorous and transparent logical justifications.

Keywords: Biomedical Named entity recognition · Talmudic Public announcement logic · BLSTM · interpretable

1 Introduction

Biomedical Named Entity Recognition (BioNER) constitutes a pivotal research area in applying Natural Language Processing (NLP) techniques to bioinformatics [4]. The primary objective of BioNER tasks is to identify and classify biomedical named entities in unstructured text, such as proteins, DNAs, RNAs, and cells [6]. This process serves as a fundamental component in the development of biomedical Information Extraction (IE) systems [17]. However, BioNER presents a more formidable challenge compared to general NER due to the intricacies inherent in biomedical text, including irregular expressions, indistinct entity boundaries, and the dynamic nature of biomedical terminology. The complexity and significant implications of this task have garnered considerable attention from researchers in the field [21].

Over the past decades, researchers have produced a variety of BioNER techniques, including dictionary-based methods [6], rule-based methods [3], and machine learning methods [12,15]. With the development of artificial intelligence algorithms [22,23], methods based on deep learning have been widely used in the last decade. Among these methods, Bi-directional Long Short-Term Memory (BLSTM) models are widely used due to their ability to establish dependencies in neighboring word [7,18]. However, although methods based on deep learning are more advanced, their inherent black-box nature makes them unable to provide an explanation for decision results, especially those involving ambiguous or polysemous words. In biomedical application areas where NER technology provides extensive life-critical supports, interpretable algorithms and transparent decision systems are critical for system reliability and users' trust [5].

Recently, eXplainable artificial intelligence (XAI) has become a hot research topic, since the decision behaviors of an explainable artificial intelligence model or transparent artificial intelligence model can be easily understood by humans [16,19]. Despite the success of explainable deep learning algorithms in providing explanations for neural networks [8,11,20], there are few explainability efforts for BioNER and BLSTM, although models with explainability are vital for establishing users' trust in biomedical applications [2,9]. When users cannot know how AI algorithms make decisions, it is difficult to believe it. Therefore, based on the existing research work on the interpretability of BioNER and BLSTM, we try to bridge this gap by answering the following research questions:

(i) How to represent the human-readable knowledge implicitly involved in the decision process of AI models and use it for improving performances?
(ii) How to acquire human-readable knowledge from the training process of BLSTM and use it for providing more effective and meaningful explanations in BioNER tasks?

To answer the first question, we need a suitable knowledge representation and reasoning method. Talmudic public announcement logic (TPK) is one of modal logic, used to deal with situations where the outcome of a specific action in the current state is ambiguous and requires future clarification [1].[1] For instance, given a sentence "Harry Potter is a good movie", after the word "movie" appears in the later sentence (in the future) we can know that "Harry Potter" here refers to a movie, not a book or a person. The situation where current decisions depend on future information is represented

---

[1] The perceptive reader will realize that traditional public announcement logic deals with modal possible world semantics of the form $\langle S, R, s_0, s \rangle$ where s_0 is the actual root world and s is the evaluation world, the world we are in. The public announcement takes the form of a wff ϕ, prompting us to throw away from the model all worlds in which ϕ holds subject to the condition that ϕ holds at the evaluation world s, i.e. s is not thrown out. In TPK, the model is a tree with root s_0 and we follow a path from s_0 to the evaluation world s, and the public announcement says that there is an incompatibility problem in the choice of the path from s_0 to the world s in which we currently are, and that we should really be at a different world s', following a different path. Thus, we are prompted to move to a different world s'. So the public announcement is an incompatibility announcement, saying that you are in the wrong world s and you need to jump to another world $s' = \rho(s)$, where ρ is a public announcement function (actually is an incompatibility announcing function) telling you where to jump to.

by a public announcement in TPK. Public announcements are made in a state after an action has taken place [1].[2] More importantly, due to its inherent temporal characteristic, TPK can also represent and obtain the knowledge of sequences, which coincides with the working mechanism of BLSTM in processing sequences. Therefore, we use TPK [1] as a tool to explain the decision process of BioNER and bring transparency to BLSTM, since the reversible and modifiable recognition process in BLSTM is very much in line with the problem that TPK is trying to deal with. By modifying the accessibility relation in a temporal tree structure, the public announcement at a future state will tell which path should be chosen. Thus, it's essential to generate public announcements from BLSTM.

To answer the second question, we propose a new TPK-based deep learning method to learn human-readable knowledge from the training process of BLSTM models, and then generate trustworthy explanations in the form of dichotomous TPK trees. TPK-based deep learning method enables users to understand the inner logical mechanism of BLSTM. For instance, we know how BLSTM makes decisions since it can deal with actions depending on future determination by public announcements, and we can understand the potential semantics of context by reasoning about TPK models. A better understanding of how BLSTM arrives at decisions can also make BLSTM more transparent and facilitate researchers to establish human-dependent models (explainable models) through black-box models (like BLSTM) and human-intelligible (like modal logic models). Empirically, we also evaluate the proposed method on the public BioNER dataset in different settings, and the experimental results demonstrate the advantages of our method.

To summarise, this paper makes the following contributions:

1. We introduce a novel interpretable learning method that represents the human-readable knowledge implicitly involved in the decision process of BioNER models and employ it to improve model performance.
2. We propose a novel TPK-based deep learning method based on the original TPK model to acquire human-readable knowledge from BLSTM, and lay out how BLSTM handles BioNER sequences in the form of TPK trees.
3. Experimental evaluations conducted on a publicly available BioNER dataset demonstrate that our TPK-based BLSTM consistently outperforms the vanilla BLSTM in all settings, highlighting the efficacy of our proposed method.

The rest of this paper is structured as follows. In Sect. 2, we introduce the basic theory of our approach, namely, Talmudic public announcement logic (TPK), and our model checking method. In Sect. 3, we define a dichotomous TPK tree to give explanations and design a new learning method to establish interpretable models for BioNER tasks. In Sect. 4, we present our experimental paradigm, including the dataset, implementation details, and evaluation metrics. In Sect. 5, we discuss the results of the experiments. Based on the global model checking of modal logic, we also advance a new

---

[2] Note that we are not saying here what and why we have incompatibility. We are just describing the mathematics of it in this paper, and the incompatibility in the biomedical named entity recognition is caused by the contextual factors. In Talmudic logic, the incompatibility is taking action under the wrong choice of factual assumption.

semantic analysis of BioNER tasks and present the inner decision logic of BLSTM. Finally, we draw conclusions and future work in Sect. 6.

2 Preliminaries

This section aims to introduce the basic semantic notions used in Talmudic Public Announcement Logic, with special emphasis on the theory of deterministic public announcements, the model it gives rise to, and the model-checking techniques. Readers familiar with TPK may notice that the present exposition of the model differs slightly from the more informal presentation found in [1, §3.3].

2.1 Deterministic Public Announcements

Traditional public announcement logic fails to formally capture the temporal dependency in BLSTM architectures when handling NER tasks, where future token embeddings retroactively influence current-word predictions. TPK addresses this by enabling dynamic determination of the prior states based on future conditions [1]. Herein, we start by explaining the basic idea of a time-action model to clarify the properties of the deterministic public announcements used in TPK. Roughly, the time-action model used in TPK is a tree on a non-empty set of states $S = \{s_0, \ldots, s_n\}$ with root s_0 induced by a non-empty set of actions $A = \{a_1, \ldots, a_m\}$ that take a state to a next one in time. If an action $a \in A$ is deterministic, it will take a state $s \in S$ to a unique successor $s' \in S$. But what gives the model a tree structure is the fact that the action $a \in A$ may be non-deterministic and, at the same time, take the same state $s \in S$ to different successor states $s' \in S$ and $s'' \in S$. In this case, the successor of s is left undetermined at this point in time. But it may be determined by a public announcement that occurs later on.

To be more precise, the trees used in the TPK model are directed, labeled trees. They have to be directed because each edge represents a succession of states at the node level. The edges must be labeled by actions since only actions take states to successor states. Moreover, the edges in every bifurcation must have the same non-deterministic action as their label. In order to deal with all these technical details more rigorously, we provide the following definitions. For convenience, we assume that $s_0 \in S$ is always the case for any set of states S.

Definition 1. (Successor). *Given a set of states S and a set of actions A, we say that $R \subseteq S^2 \times A$ is a successor relation, also denoted as $\rightarrow$ in infix notation, iff the following conditions hold:*

1. *for every $s' \in S$, there exists an $s \in S$ such that $s \xrightarrow{a} s'$, provided $s' \neq s_0$, for some $a \in A$;*
2. *$s \not\xrightarrow{a} s$, for all $a \in A$ and $s \in S$;*
3. *if $s \xrightarrow{a} s'$, then $s' \not\xrightarrow{a} s$, for all $a \in A$ and $s, s' \in S$;*
4. *if $s \xrightarrow{a} s'$ and $s \xrightarrow{a'} s''$ then $a = a'$, for all $a, a' \in A$ and $s, s' \in S$.*

To ensure that R is indeed a tree successor relation, one has to guarantee that it is not transitive and has no cycles, or, in any case, that there exists a unique path from every node to the root. This can be guaranteed with the existence of a function that calculates the distance from the root of every node.

Definition 2. (**Tree successor**). *A successor relation $R \subseteq S^2 \times A$ is said to be a tree successor relation iff there exists a function $D : S \to \mathbb{N}$ such that*

1. $D(s_0) = 0$
2. $D(s') = D(s) + 1$ whenever $s \xrightarrow{a} s'$.

It is henceforth assumed that every successor relation R is also a tree successor. The transitive closure of R, denoted R^* or $\to^*$, is called the accessibility relation. It is worth noting that it is a dichotomous relation that neglects actions, unlike the successor relation. Two states $s, s' \in S$ are said to be equidistant iff $D(s) = D(s')$. What's more, if v is a previous state of s' then $D(v) < D(s)$ holds.

Definition 3. (**Public announcement**). *Given a tree $\langle S, R, s_0 \rangle$, we call a partial function $\rho: S \to S$ a public announcement iff ρ satisfies the following properties:*

(a) *there exists no $x \in S$ such that $\rho(s_0) = x$;*
(b) *$\rho(x) \neq x$ for all $x \in S$;*
(c) *$\rho(s) = s'$ only if s and s' are equidistant;*
(d) *Let $x, y \in S$ and $x \neq y \neq s_0$, if $\rho(x) = y$, then $\rho(y) = x$ doesn't hold.*

The public announcement ρ is said to publicly clarify that s is s' when $\rho(s) = s'$. Now, some remarks about this definition are in order. Condition (a) indicates that only successors can be publicly clarified and (b) ensures that there are no trivial public clarifications. Then (c) indicates that public announcements respect the successor relation in the sense that a state can only be publicly clarified to be another with the same distance from the root. Condition (d) shows the property of function ρ that the original function ρ is not symmetric about $y = x$. Public announcements are deterministic because they clarify previously undetermined actions and the successor of a certain state. In addition, since the accessibility relation is based on a tree with root s_0, every point $s \in S$ determines a unique path backwards to the root after a public announcement occurs.[3]

2.2 Talmudic Public Announcement Logic

Before presenting the definition of a Talmudic public announcement logic (TPK) model, let us introduce the basic language of TPK first. The basic language of TPK is defined using a set of propositions and modal operators $\Box$, $\boxminus$, Y and $\mathbb{Y}$. A TPK formula ϕ is constructed from a set of propositional letters, a functionally complete set of logical

---

[3] It is worth noting that a public announcement in epistemic or dynamic epistemic logic deletes some possible worlds after an announcement, while a deterministic public announcement in this paper simply disregards some accessibility links after an announcement. Technically speaking, these two approaches are similar but not equivalent [1].

connectives, and four modal operators. The minimal syntax for TPK can be specified in Backus–Naur form as follows:

$$\phi ::= p_i \mid \neg\phi \mid \phi \wedge \psi \mid \Box\phi \mid \boxminus\phi \mid Y\phi \mid \mathbb{Y}\phi \tag{1}$$

where p_i is a propositional letter for $i \in \mathbb{N}$, ϕ and ψ are valid TPK formulas. Note that $\Box$ is the standard necessity operator, Y is a yesterday operator for $\Box$, $\boxminus$ is a modal operator corresponding to function ρ, and $\mathbb{Y}$ is a yesterday operator for $\boxminus$. Based on the above language, a TPK model can be defined as follows [1]:

Definition 4. (TPK model). *Given a tree $\langle S, R, s_0 \rangle$ with root s_0, let A be a set of actions and ρ be the public announcement function, a Talmudic public announcement logic (TPK) model is defined as a 5-tuple $\langle S, A, R, \rho, \pi \rangle$, where $\pi : \{p_i \mid i \in \mathbb{N}\} \to \mathcal{P}(S)$ plays the role of the valuation function.*

Let $M = \langle S, A, R, \rho, \pi \rangle$ be a TPK model and $s \in S$. We say that a propositional letter p_i is satisfied at s in M, in symbols, $M, s \vDash p_i$, iff $s \in \pi(p_i)$. The semantics of the modal operators of TPK is given by extending the satisfiability relation as follows:

1. $M, s \vDash \Box\phi$ iff for all $s' \in S$, $s \xrightarrow{a} s'$ implies $M, s' \vDash \phi$, for any $a \in A$;
2. $M, s \vDash Y\phi$ iff for all $s' \in S$, $s' \xrightarrow{a} s$ implies $M, s' \vDash \phi$, for any $a \in A$;
3. $M, s_0 \nvDash Y\phi$;
4. $M, s \vDash \boxminus\phi$ iff for all $s' \in S$, $\rho(s) = s'$ implies $M, s' \vDash \phi$;
5. $M, s \vDash \mathbb{Y}\phi$ iff for all $s' \in S$, $\rho(s') = s$ implies $M, s' \vDash \phi$.

Models are said to be deterministic because ρ leads to at most one successor state when there is a public announcement, i.e., one state should be the unique clarified successor of the state where the public announcement occurs.

2.3 Model Checking

Model checking is used to perform the automatic verification of a TPK model. It is a technique for checking finite-state concurrent systems by traversing the finite state space of the system to verify whether the system satisfies a certain property. Generally speaking, the following two checking tasks can be specified according to the different methods adopted [14]:

- **Global task:** Given a TPK model M and a formula ϕ, determine the set $\{s \in S \mid M, s \vDash \phi\}$ of all states in M that satisfy ϕ.
- **Local task:** Given a TPK model M, a formula ϕ and a state $s \in S$, determine whether s satisfies ϕ.

To explain the prediction of BioNER models, this paper focuses on the global model checking task instead of the local checking task, and we present how to check a TPK model in BioNER tasks in Sect. 3.4.

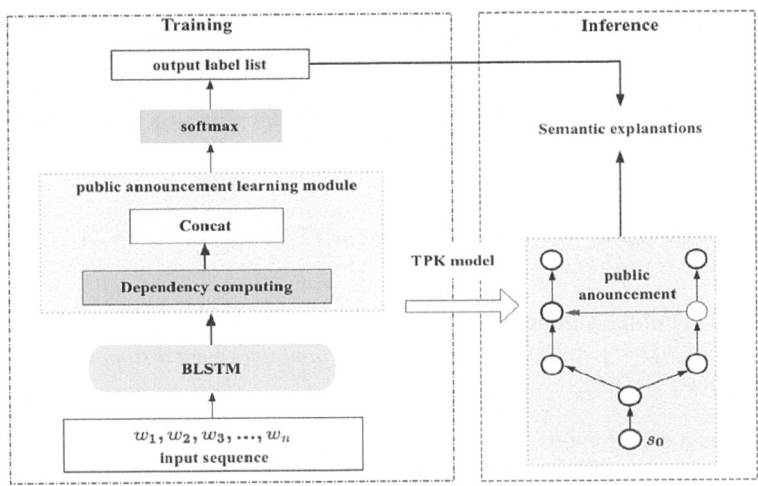

Fig. 1. The illustration of our proposed TPK-based deep learning method.

3 Approach

3.1 Overview

The overall framework is shown in Fig. 1. In the training phase, we focus on learning a TPK-based Bidirectional Long Short-Term Memory (BLSTM) model. Initially, we extract the latent states of the given sequences from the BLSTM, concurrently constructing the pathway of a TPK tree based on these extracted states. Secondly, we learn public announcements of the sequences by calculating the dependency matrix. By integrating the public announcement into the decision-making process through a concatenation layer, we derive the label lists for the input sequence via a softmax layer. During the inference stage, with a well-trained TPK-based BLSTM model, we employ the global model-checking algorithms to generate semantic explanations in the form of dichotomous TPK trees. In the following, we will elaborate on the formal definition of a dichotomous TPK model, the learning steps of TPK-based BLSTM, and the BioNER model-checking task.

3.2 A Dichotomous TPK Model

As mentioned above, TPK logic can represent and acquire knowledge of sequences due to its natural timing characteristics, and this coincides with the working mechanism of BLSTM. For BioNER tasks, there are at most two options for each entity, *i.e.*, forward output and final output, which is much in line with the structure of a dichotomous tree. In addition, it is easier to generate explanations in the form of trees. Therefore, we define a dichotomous TPK model according to Definition 4.

Definition 5. (A dichotomous TPK model). *A successor relation R is dichotomous iff given $s \xrightarrow{a} s'$ and $s \xrightarrow{a} s''$, if $s \xrightarrow{a} n$ then $n = s'$ or $n = s''$. We say a model $M = \langle S, A, R, \rho, \pi \rangle$ is dichotomous if R is dichotomous.*

Note that a dichotomous TPK model is also a dichotomous TPK tree since a TPK model is always a tree. So a dichotomous TPK model will be henceforth called a dichotomous tree. Specifically, nodes are represented by the set of states S, and edges are represented by successor relation R. To explore the structural properties of a dichotomous TPK tree, the height and the public announcement distance of a dichotomous TPK model are defined as below.

Definition 6. (Height). *Given any dichotomous TPK model $M = \langle S, A, R, \rho, \pi \rangle$, the height H of M is $max\{D(s) \mid s \in S\} + 1$.*

Definition 7. (Public Announcement Distance). *If $s \xrightarrow{a} x$ and $\rho(s') = s''$ and $s \rightarrow^* s'$ and $x \rightarrow^* s''$ and $D(s') = D(s'')$, then the public announcement distance D_ρ is defined by $D_\rho = |D(s') - D(s)|$.*

Formally, a dichotomous TPK tree is generated by induction on height $H = 1$, as Fig. 2 shows. Obviously, a tree of height $H = 1$ is a single node s_0, where s_0 is an empty state representing the start of hidden states of BLSTM. We begin to add elements after that, and we write $y \rightarrow x$ to mean that x is the predecessor of y. The inductive steps are as follows: Assume that there is a 2-option dichotomous tree of height $H = n$ ($n \geq 1$), with junction nodes of each height $k < n$, and leaf nodes $x_1, x_2, \ldots, x_m$. As Fig. 2 shows, we have two options to add new nodes above the leaf nodes of Height $H = n+1$ ($n \geq 1$): (1) Not to split: only add one node above each node in $\{x_1, x_2, \ldots, x_m\}$, then $y_1, y_2, \ldots, y_m$ become leaf nodes. (2) To split: add two nodes above each node in $\{x_1, x_2, \ldots, x_m\}$, then $y_1, y_2, \ldots, y_{2m}$ become the leaf nodes of the tree of height $H = n + 1$.

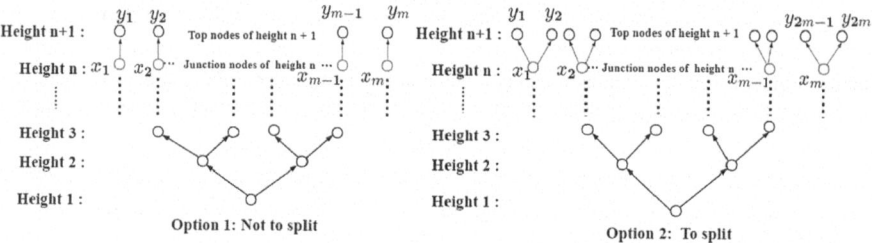

Fig. 2. Two kinds of induction options to add new nodes on height $H = n + 1$ for dichotomous TPK trees

Since TPK models have natural time series characteristics and can represent the relationship between future decisions and current state through public announcements, thus a dichotomous TPK tree can also represent the semantic relationship of sentence data. For instance, let a sentence sequence be $w = (w_1, \ldots, w_k)$, where w_i denotes the ith word in the sentence. If we regard this sentence sequence as a time sequence, then the ith word can represent the ith time step, and the different states in the ith time step correspond to different meanings of the ith word. For each input biomedical sequence, if a junction node is a split junction, it is annotated with several possible labels. In our paper, model compatibility is checked after each action by the BLSTM. Thus the function ρ is activated and makes a public announcement to go to the right path at a certain state. However, there may be wrong public announcements since machines are not as smart as humans in real life. Thus, we apply the model checking method to check whether public announcements are accurate in a TPK model in Sect. 3.4.

Similarly, a TPK model can also extract the potential logical relationship between hidden states in a BLSTM and represent them in the form of a dichotomous TPK tree. To do this, a BLSTM is defined formally as below.

Definition 8. (BLSTM). *A BLSTM B is a graph $\langle S, R \rangle$, where S denotes its hidden states and R denotes the edges of the graph. Importantly, these edges also represent the connections of hidden states of a network.*

3.3 TPK-Based Deep Learning Method

In this paper, we regard BioNER as a sequence labeling problem, whose input includes a set of sequences and labels. For any sequence $W = (w_1, w_2, ..., w_n)$, the corresponding labels are $Y = (y_1, y_2, ..., y_n)$, where w_i denotes a word in the sequence, and y_i comes from BIO (meaning the Beginning, the Inside and the Outside of an biomedical entity, respectively) tagging schema for labeling elements from the sequence. Finally, we have a labeled dataset $D = \{W, Y\}$.

Based on the properties of a TPK model and a BLSTM in the last subsection, the mechanism of a BLSTM can be represented by a dichotomous TPK model $M = \langle S, A, R, \rho, \pi \rangle$. Here, we begin by describing how to represent a BLSTM through the tree structure $\langle S, R, s_0 \rangle$ of a dichotomous TPK model with height $H = n$ ($n \geq 1$), then we elaborate on how to learn public announcements by training the BLSTM, and finally introduce how to obtain the valuation function π and action A. The hidden state (feature vector) associated with each word in the sequence can be found using word-level embedding; as a result, the set of states S and relation R of TPK are given by:

$$\begin{cases} S = \{h_0, h_1, h_2, ..., h_n\} \\ 1 \leq n \leq |R| < |S| * (|S| - 1) \end{cases} \quad (2)$$

where h_i means the hidden state (feature vector) of the ith element w_i in a BLSTM, h_0 denotes the start, which corresponds to the root of a TPK model. $|S|$ is the number of nodes and $|R|$ is the number of edges. H corresponds to the number of elements in a sequence. Unlike standard dichotomous trees, the size $|R|$ is greater than or equal to n because there may be loops in a dichotomous TPK tree, since there exist public announcements in the tree.

The set of public announcements $\varrho = \{\rho_1, \rho_2 ..., \rho_k\}$ in a TPK model is trained by a dependency computing module. Any public announcement ρ_i can also represent the dependency relation between a given entity and the context of a sequence. Suppose that for the input sequence $W = (w_1, w_2, ..., w_n)$, the corresponding (context) labels are $\Lambda = \{l_1, l_2, ... l_n\}$, where w_i denotes the ith element of the sequence and l_i denotes the label of the ith element. Then, the dependency matrix of the input sequence W is calculated by the following equations:

$$score(h_i, h_j) = h_i \cdot tanh(z_1 h_i + z_2 h_j)$$
$$M_d(i,j) = \text{Softmax}(score(h_i, h_j))$$
$$= \frac{exp(score(h_i, h_j))}{\sum_{j=1}^{n} score(h_i, h_j)} \tag{3}$$

where h_i denotes the hidden states of word $w_i \in W$ in BLSTM, z_1 and z_2 are trained parameters and $M_d(i,j)$ denotes the dependency score of word i and the word j. Thus, the possible accessibility relation between words i and j in the TPK model can be denoted as $M_d(i,j)$, where $M_d(i,j)$ ranges from 0 to 1. The higher value of $M_d(i,j)$ means greater impact. For the given entity $w_i \in W$, let $M_d^{w_i}$ denote the possible accessibility relations between the given entity and the context such that $M_d^{w_i} = M_d(i,;)\backslash\{M_d(i,i)\}$. Then, the potential public announcements ϱ_{w_i} for the given entity $w_i \in W$ is given by:

$$\varrho_{w_i} = Maxi(M_d^{w_i}) \tag{4}$$

where $Maxi(\cdot)$ represents a function that gets the maximum element from the given set. Finally, the public announcement distance can be calculated by the following equation:

$$D_\rho = |D(i) - D(j)| \tag{5}$$

According to Definition 7, D_ρ denotes the public announcement distance from word i to j, $D_\rho = 0$ when there is no public announcement.

Algorithm 1. TPK-based deep learning.

Input:
　　Sequences W;
Output:
　　The labels O of the dataset; Potential public announcements ϱ;
1: Embed the input sequence;
2: Extract the hidden states S from a BLSTM on step 1., including forward hidden states and backward hidden states;
3: Generate different paths of TPK trees by S according to Equation (2);
4: Calculate the dependency matrix M_d of the input sequence according to Equation (3);
5: Extract the possible accessibility relations $M_d^{w_i}$ between each given entity $w_i \in W$ and the context according to Equation (4);
6: $C_{M,S} = Concat(M_d, S)$; where $Concat$ is a function based on keras that can concatenate tensors;
7: Calculate the labels of $C_{M,S}$ in Softmax layer, denoted as O;
8: **return** O, ϱ;

The assignment function π determines the true value of each proposition variable and can also represent the information distribution of each word (entity). Assuming that the recognition results of words are denoted by O, then we can obtain π by:

$$\pi = Distribution\{O\} \tag{6}$$

where $Distribution\{O\}$ means the label information distribution of O, and the label information distribution is determined by datasets since different datasets may have different kinds of labels.

As for action sets A, all actions refer to the recognition of entities for BioNER tasks. Although they're important in modal logic, these actions are not the root cause of different states in our tasks, so we do not label actions in a dichotomous TPK tree. The implementation details of learning a dichotomous TPK tree from the BLSTM are shown in Algorithm 1.

3.4 BioNER Model-Checking Task

For the prediction results of each input sequence and the corresponding TPK tree, we can verify the model by a global model-checking method. Different from the traditional model checking method for Kripke models [13], this paper focuses on the logic reasoning process and the checking of predictions. Based on the definition of model checking in Subsect. 2.3 [14], a BioNER model-checking task is defined as below.

Definition 9. (**BioNER model-checking task**). *Assume that the true labels of an input sequence can be represented by a formula ϕ. Given a dichotomous TPK tree $M = \langle S, A, R, \rho, \pi \rangle$ learned from BLSTM and a formula ϕ, this task is to verify whether the states in M satisfy ϕ by traversing the finite state space of the model.*

For example, considering the sequence={I think hemoglobin is one of the most important proteins for human health}; let the proposition letter p represent that the word is recognized as "Protein", proposition letter q represent that the word is recognized as "Others", and s_i denote the state of i-th words in the input sequence. From the semantics of TPK, "hemoglobin" is correctly recognized as "Protein" iff $s_3 \vDash p$. Assume $\phi = p$, then we can check whether the states satisfy ϕ by traversing the finite state space of the given model. As we mentioned before, the key to model checking in TPK is to check public announcements, thus we also consider the functional relation of states in dichotomous TPK trees. The BioNER model-checking (BMC) algorithm is presented in Algorithm 2, and we use P_i ($i \in \mathbb{N}$) to denote a path from the root to a certain state.

Complexity Analysis. As shown in Fig. 2, each entity node in a dichotomous TPK tree may have two leaf nodes, generating 2^k possible worlds for k entity words in an n-length sequence ($H = n$). While this suggests exponential growth in model-checking paths, practical constraints bound $k \leq 10$ for typical named entities (as a named entity with more than 10 words will not generally appear), rendering the worst-case 2^{10} paths computationally tractable. Crucially, the separation of training and reasoning ensures scalability: during training, we exclusively optimize BLSTM parameters and public announcement learning mechanisms, achieving a per-timestep time complexity of $O(W)$ (where W denotes trainable parameters), while deferring model checking to reasoning. Let ϱ denote the number of public announcements, post-training semantic interpretation leverages the BLSTM's bidirectionality to collapse 2^k TPK-based paths into a linear $2k + \varrho$-step resolution via well-trained hidden states. This design preserves theoretical expressiveness while ensuring tractability through bidirectional gradient alignment and finite state checking.

Algorithm 2. Global model-checking algorithm for BioNER tasks.

Input:
　　The TPK model M; The height of $H = n$; Formula ϕ;
Output:
　　The Boolean value MC of model-checking; Public announcement ρ
1: Find all possible paths of M according to the successor relation of states;
2: Traverse all possible paths of M from height 1 to n;
3: If there exists one path that the set of its states satisfy ϕ, $MC = True$; if not, go to the next step;
4: If there exists a public announcement ρ, then traverse the new path (denoted as P_1) generated by the public announcement;
5: If all states in P_1 satisfy ϕ, $MC = True$; return $MC = False$ and ρ;
6: **return** MC and ρ;

4 Experiments

4.1 Dataset

GENIA[4] is a public biomedical named entity recognition dataset [10] including 11 label categories. We extract 1000 train samples and 3856 test samples to test the model performance with low-source settings. We use this dataset to evaluate model performance and explore the semantic explanation of TPK-based BLSTM.

4.2 Setup

In our experiments, we evaluate our method in two settings: vanilla BLSTM and TPK-based BLSTM. We also set up five groups of experiments for the given dataset, specifically, we only select D (200, 400, 600, 800, 1000) sentences from the train set to train models for evaluating performance under limited observational instances. We always keep test datasets unchanged in all experiments. By default, we set $batch\_size = 64$ and $dropout\_rate = 0.4$. Hidden states and embedding dimensions are fixed at 128. We also use 'adam' optimizer and 'sparse_categorical_crossentropy' loss function. As for the BLSTM model, we use 'tanh' as activation function and 'sigmoid' as recurrent activation function. In all experiments, we run 5 times and use the averaged performance with the variance given in the subscripts.

4.3 Evaluation Metrics

In this work, we mainly consider performance at the word level. To provide a comprehensive and balanced measure of model performance, we adopt the weighted average metrics. These metrics consider the proportion of the number of labels in each category of total labels. Specifically, we utilize the weighted average precision (denoted as P), weighted average recall (denoted as R) and weighted average F_1 score (denoted as F_1) to assess the efficacy of our models in recognizing biomedical entities.

---
[4] http://www.geniaproject.org/genia-corpus/term-corpus.

5 Results and Discussion

In this section, we first analyze our experimental results on the public BioNER dataset. Secondly, we give an explanation of real instances in the form of dichotomous TPK trees and show how to generate explanations by TPK-based deep learning method.

Table 1. Evaluation results of the vanilla BLSTM and our method with weighted average metrics on the GENIA dataset, where D denotes the training data size and **bold** denotes the optimal performance in each data setting.

	BLSTM			TPK-based BLSTM		
	Precision	Recall	F_1 score	Precision	Recall	F_1 score
200	$95.22\pm_{1e-32}$	$97.58\pm_{1e-32}$	$96.39\pm_{0e-00}$	$97.45\pm_{1e-32}$	$97.46\pm_{1e-32}$	$\mathbf{97.34}\pm_{0e-00}$
400	$97.49\pm_{3e-7}$	$97.78\pm_{4e-7}$	$97.55\pm_{3e-7}$	$97.67\pm_{5e-7}$	$97.63\pm_{1e-6}$	$\mathbf{97.57}\pm_{9e-7}$
600	$99.76\pm_{5e-7}$	$97.80\pm_{3e-7}$	$97.58\pm_{2e-7}$	$97.81\pm_{6e-7}$	$97.72\pm_{9e-8}$	$\mathbf{97.66}\pm_{2e-7}$
800	$97.68\pm_{4e-7}$	$97.84\pm_{3e-8}$	$97.66\pm_{3e-7}$	$97.80\pm_{2e-7}$	$97.82\pm_{4e-7}$	$\mathbf{97.73}\pm_{3e-7}$
1000	$97.79\pm_{4e-8}$	$97.89\pm_{8e-8}$	$97.74\pm_{5e-8}$	$97.88\pm_{5e-7}$	$97.84\pm_{5e-8}$	$\mathbf{97.80}\pm_{1e-7}$

5.1 Main Results

To investigate how the TPK-based deep learning method performs in practical BioNER tasks, we carry out extensive experiments with the TPK-based BLSTM. The use of limited data in model evaluation is crucial in the context of BioNER, as acquiring large-scale, high-quality annotated biomedical data is often challenging and time-consuming. This limitation necessitates the development of methods that can effectively learn from limited data, making our evaluation particularly practical. The comparisons between vanilla BLSTM and TPK-based BLSTM on the GENIA corpus are presented in Table 1. The results demonstrate that our method achieves significant improvements in the weighted average F_1 score in all experimental settings. Specifically, for $D = 200$, our method yields a boost of 0.95 in the weighted average F_1 score. Even when the dataset size increases to $D = 1000$, our method still achieves a significant improvement of 0.6 in weighted average F_1 score. These results strongly indicate that TPK-based deep learning is a potentially effective method for recognizing biomedical entities from limited data. However, due to sample imbalance, when incorporating public announcement learning, the TPK-based BLSTM tends to focus on a larger proportion of samples, leading to a slight decrease in recall. Nonetheless, in general, our method outperforms the vanilla BLSTM in terms of precision and F_1 score.

5.2 Semantic Ambiguity Explanation

Based on the experimental results, we can generate explanations of biomedical entities using TPK-based deep learning method. Intuitively, the hidden states of BLSTM are hard to understand; however, with explanations of BLSTM decisions mapped to a

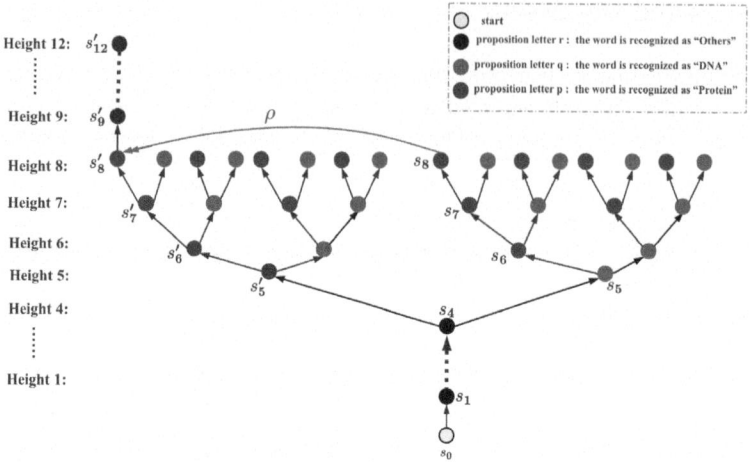

Fig. 3. A dichotomous TPK tree of $task_{378}$, where ρ denotes the public announcement.

dichotomous TPK tree, the public announcement function can illustrate how to go back to a more reasonable state. On this basis, we can show users in which way that BLSTM derives decisions through the Algorithm 1 and the predictions of BLSTM can be illustrated by the Algorithm 2. Generally, the explanation consists of public announcements and a natural language template.

Example 1. Consider the sentence $task_{378}$ = "Biochemical characterization of the NF-Y transcription factor complex during B lymphocyte development".
Question: Why is "NF-Y" recognized as a Protein rather than a DNA? Explanation: Because the "complex" (public announcement) appears in the following words, it is more reasonable to be recognized as "Protein".

In this example, the dichotomous TPK tree is generated by Algorithm 1 and TPK-based logic reasoning (as shown in Fig. 3). Let the proposition letter p denote that the word is recognized as "Protein", proposition letter q denote that the word is recognized as "DNA", and proposition letter r denote that the word is recognized as "Others". According to Definition 9, BMC algorithm checks whether it satisfies the given formula by traversing the state space components (*i.e.*, possible paths) of the TPK tree. According to the semantics of TPK and the true labels of this sequence (*i.e.*, $task_{378}$) in datasets, the biomedical entity "NF-Y transcription factor complex" is correctly recognized iff $(s'_5 \vDash p)$ and $(s'_6 \vDash p)$ and $(s'_7 \vDash p)$ and $(s'_8 \vDash p)$, and all the words of $task_{378}$ are recognized correctly iff $(s_4 \vDash Yr)$ and $(s'_5 \vDash p)$ and $(s'_6 \vDash p)$ and $(s'_7 \vDash p)$ and $(s'_8 \vDash p)$ and $(s'_9 \vDash \Box r)$, where s_i and s'_i denote the states of ith word in the sequence. Based on the complexity analysis in Sect. 3.4, the BMC complexity for checking the entity "NF-Y transcription factor complex" is $2*k+\varrho = 9$ with $k = 4$ and $\varrho = 1$, since the BLSTM's bidirectionality collapses 2^k TPK-based paths into a linear resolution. For full-sequence checking, this expands to $2*k+\varrho+m = 17$, where m denotes the number of deterministic states without public announcements. According to Algorithm 1, we can visualize the mechanism of Bi-LSTM by a dichotomous TPK tree in Fig. 3. Specifically, when the model gets words from s_1 and goes forward to s_8, the path from s_1 to s_8 can be represented as $(s_4 \vDash Yr)$ and $(s_5 \vDash q)$ and $(s_6 \vDash p)$ and $(s_7 \vDash p)$ and $(s_8 \vDash p)$. However, there is a public announcement $\rho(s_8) = s'_8$, so the model will go back to s'_5 and then go forward to the end state s'_{12}, generating a new path. The new path can be denoted by $(s_4 \vDash Yr)$ and $(s'_5 \vDash p)$ and $(s'_6 \vDash p)$ and $(s'_7 \vDash p)$ and $(s'_8 \vDash p)$ and $(s'_9 \vDash \Box r)$, which indicates that "NF-Y transcription factor complex" is a protein entity in $task_{378}$. Furthermore, the relation between s_8 and s'_8 can be represented as $s_8 \twoheadrightarrow s'_8$, which indicates that the word NF-Y is recognized as "Protein" instead of "DNA" because the "complex" (public announcement) appears in the following words. The above reasoning process on a dichotomous TPK tree tells us how BLSTM makes decisions based on future information and derives the final predictions through public announcements.

6 Conclusions and Future Work

In this paper, we propose a novel TPK-based deep learning method to exploit human-readable knowledge in BioNER tasks and further instantiate an interpretable TPK-based BLSTM model. Unlike the existing interpretable methods, TPK-based deep learning method firstly introduces the idea of Talmudic public announcement logic into the training process, and learn public announcements to integrate human-readable knowledge into the text representation explicitly. In this way, we can effectively and logically capture the semantics in the context and generate explanations in the form of TPK trees to show the internal mechanism of BLSTM. Besides, we conduct experimental comparisons using the public BioNER dataset, demonstrating that our TPK-based BLSTM model surpasses vanilla BLSTM in low-resource settings.

For future work, we plan to further improve the interpretability of our method in the following two aspects. On the one hand, we hope to integrate human-readable knowledge in the loss function to guide model learning; on the other hand, we are interested in developing a more generalized modal logical model to provide explanations for other language models like BERT.

Acknowledgements.. The authors are thankful to the three anonymous reviewers for their helpful comments and suggestions. Beishui Liao is financially supported by the National Social Science Foundation Major Project of China (20 & ZD047).

References

1. Abraham, M., Belfer, I., Gabbay, D.M., Schild, U.: Future determination of entities in talmudic public announcement logic. J. Appl. Log. **11**(1), 63–90 (2013)
2. Agarwal, O., Yang, Y., Wallace, B.C., Nenkova, A.: Interpretability analysis for named entity recognition to understand system predictions and how they can improve. Comput. Linguist. **47**(1), 117–140 (2021)
3. Archana, S.M., Prakash, J., Singh, P.K., Ahmed, W.: An effective biomedical named entity recognition by handling imbalanced data sets using deep learning and rule-based methods. SN Comput. Sci. **4**(5), 650 (2023)

4. Chang, L., Zhang, R., Lv, J., Zhou, W., Bai, Y.: A review of biomedical named entity recognition. J. Comput. Methods Sci. Eng. **22**(3), 893–900 (2022)
5. Fu, J., Liu, P., Neubig, G.: Interpretable multi-dataset evaluation for named entity recognition. arXiv preprint arXiv:2011.06854 (2020)
6. Fu, Z., Su, Y., Meng, Z., Collier, N.: Biomedical named entity recognition via dictionary-based synonym generalization. In: Bouamor, H., Pino, J., Bali, K. (eds.) Proceedings of the 2023 Conference on Empirical Methods in Natural Language Processing, EMNLP, pp. 14621–14635. Association for Computational Linguistics (2023)
7. Gajendran, S., Manjula, D., Sugumaran, V.: Character level and word level embedding with bidirectional LSTM - dynamic recurrent neural network for biomedical named entity recognition from literature. J. Biomed. Informatics **112**, 103609 (2020)
8. Hou, B.J., Zhou, Z.H.: Learning with interpretable structure from gated rnn. IEEE Trans. Neural Netw. Learn. Syst. **31**(7), 2267–2279 (2020)
9. Hupkes, D., Veldhoen, S., Zuidema, W.H.: Visualisation and 'diagnostic classifiers' reveal how recurrent and recursive neural networks process hierarchical structure. J. Artif. Intell. Res. **61**, 907–926 (2018)
10. Kim, J., Ohta, T., Tateisi, Y., Tsujii, J.: GENIA corpus - a semantically annotated corpus for bio-textmining. In: Proceedings of the Eleventh International Conference on Intelligent Systems for Molecular Biology, pp. 180–182 (2003)
11. Krakovna, V., Doshi-Velez, F.: Increasing the interpretability of recurrent neural networks using hidden markov models. arXiv preprint arXiv:1606.05320 (2016)
12. Li, J., Sun, A., Han, J., Li, C.: A survey on deep learning for named entity recognition. IEEE Trans. Knowl. Data Eng. **34**(1), 50–70 (2022)
13. McMillan, K.L.: Symbolic model checking. In: Symbolic Model Checking, pp. 25–60. Springer (1993)
14. Müller-Olm, M., Schmidt, D., Steffen, B.: Model-Checking. In: Cortesi, A., Filé, G. (eds.) SAS 1999. LNCS, vol. 1694, pp. 330–354. Springer, Heidelberg (1999). https://doi.org/10.1007/3-540-48294-6_22
15. Nadeau, D., Sekine, S.: A survey of named entity recognition and classification. Lingvisticae Investigationes **30**(1), 3–26 (2007)
16. Pedreschi, D., Giannotti, F., Guidotti, R., Monreale, A., Turini, F.: Meaningful explanations of black box AI decision systems. Proc. AAAI Conf. Artif. Intell. **33**, 9780–9784 (2019)
17. Perera, N., Dehmer, M., Emmert-Streib, F.: Named entity recognition and relation detection for biomedical information extraction. Front. Cell Dev. Biol. **8**, 673 (2020)
18. Saad, F.: Named entity recognition for biomedical patent text using bi-lstm variants. In: Proceedings of the 21st International Conference on Information Integration and Web-based Applications & Services, iiWAS, pp. 617–621. ACM (2019)
19. Vasileiou, S.L., Yeoh, W., Son, T.C., Kumar, A., Cashmore, M., Magazzeni, D.: A logic-based explanation generation framework for classical and hybrid planning problems. J. Artif. Intell. Res. **73**, 1473–1534 (2022)
20. Wisdom, S., Powers, T., Pitton, J., Atlas, L.: Interpretable recurrent neural networks using sequential sparse recovery. arXiv preprint arXiv:1611.07252 (2016)
21. Yao, L., Liu, H., Liu, Y., Li, X., Anwar, M.W.: Biomedical named entity recognition based on deep neutral network. Int. J. Hybrid Inf. Technol. **8**(8), 279–288 (2015)
22. Yuan, B., Chen, Y., Tan, Z., Jinyan, W., Liu, H., Zhang, Y.: Label distribution learning-enhanced dual-knn for text classification. In: Proceedings of the 2024 SIAM International Conference on Data Mining (SDM), pp. 400–408. SIAM (2024)
23. Yuan, B., Chen, Y., Zhang, Y., Jiang, W.: Hide and seek in noise labels: Noise-robust collaborative active learning with llms-powered assistance. In: Proceedings of the 62nd Annual Meeting of the Association for Computational Linguistics (Volume 1: Long Papers), pp. 10977–11011 (2024)

Each of Those Eight Coalition Logics is Also Determined by Four Other Kinds of Models

Zixuan Chen and Fengkui Ju(✉)

School of Philosophy, Beijing Normal University, Beijing, China
fengkui.ju@bnu.edu.cn

Abstract. Coalition Logic is an important logic in logical research on strategic reasoning. In two recent papers, Li and Ju argued that generally, concurrent game models, models of Coalition Logic, have three too strong assumptions: seriality, independence of agents, and determinism. They presented eight coalition logics based on eight classes of general concurrent game models, determined by which of the three assumptions are met. In this paper, we show that each of the eight logics is also determined by four other kinds of models, with respective properties, that is, single-coalition-first action models, single-coalition-first neighborhood models, tree-like grand-coalition-first action models, and tree-like single-coalition-first neighborhood models.

Keywords: coalition logics · action models · neighborhood models · seriality · independence of agents · determinism

1 Introduction

1.1 Eight Coalition Logics Determined by Eight Classes of General Concurrent Game Models

Coalition Logic CL, proposed by Pauly [10,11], is an important logic in logical research on strategic reasoning.

The language of CL is a modal language with the featured operator $\langle C \rangle \phi$, indicating *some available joint action of the coalition* C *ensures* ϕ.

CL has two kinds of models.

The first kind is *concurrent game models*. Roughly, in a concurrent game model: there are some states; there are some agents, who can form coalitions; for every coalition, there is an availability function, specifying available joint actions of the coalition at states; for every coalition, there is an outcome function, specifying possible outcome states of joint actions of the coalition. The formula $\langle C \rangle \phi$ is true at a state in a concurrent game model if C has an available joint action such that ϕ is true at every possible outcome state of the action.

The second kind is alpha neighborhood models. Alpha neighborhood models do not have actions. Consequently, they do not have availability functions and outcome functions. Instead, for every coalition, there is a neighborhood function that specifies the alpha powers of the coalition. An alpha power is a set of states into which the coalition can force the next moment to fall. The formula $\langle\!\langle C \rangle\!\rangle \phi$ is true at a state in an alpha neighborhood model if C has an alpha power such that ϕ is true at every state of the power.

Li and Ju [9] argued that concurrent game models have three too strong assumptions: *seriality, the independence of agents,* and *determinism.* Based on *general concurrent game models,* which do not have the three assumptions, they proposed a Minimal Coalition Logic MCL. Although the three assumptions are generally too strong, we might want to keep some of them when constructing logics for strategic reasoning in some kinds of situations. Considering which of the three properties we want to keep, there are eight coalition logics in total. Li and Ju [8] showed the completeness of the eight logics in a uniform way.

1.2 Our Work

In this paper, we call general concurrent game models *grand-coalition-first action models*. In this work, we show that each of the eight coalition logics is also determined by four other kinds of models, with respective properties.

The first kind is *single-coalition-first action models*. In this kind of models, the outcome functions for single coalitions determine the outcome functions for other coalitions. This kind of models makes good sense for situations where every agent can change a component of the state, and different components of the state that can be changed by different agents are independent of each other.

The second kind is *single-coalition-first neighborhood models*. In this kind of models, the neighborhood function for a coalition specifies the *actual powers* of the coalition. An actual power is a *minimal scope* into which the coalition can force the next moment to fall. In this kind of models, the neighborhood functions for single coalitions determine the neighborhood functions for other coalitions.

The third kind is *tree-like grand-coalition-first action models*. In this kind of models, every state has a determined history.

The fourth kind is *tree-like single-coalition-first neighborhood models*. In this kind of models, every state has a determined history, too.

The rest of the paper is structured as follows. In Sect. 2, we present some general settings of coalition logics, including their language, their action semantics and neighborhood semantics, and the transformation from action semantics to neighborhood semantics. In Sect. 3, we introduce the eight coalition logics determined by eight classes of grand-coalition-first action models. In Sect. 4, we define single-coalition-first action models and show that they are grand-coalition-first action models; we define single-coalition-first neighborhood models and show that they can *represent* single-coalition-first action models. In Sect. 5, we define tree-like grand-coalition-first action models and show that they are single-coalition-first action models; we define tree-like single-coalition-first neighborhood models and show that they can represent tree-like grand-coalition-first action models. In Sect. 6, we show that each of the eight coalition logics is determined by the four kinds of models with respective properties. We conclude in Sect. 7.

Due to the limitation of space, we omit proofs for some results and some examples, which can be found in [3].

2 General Settings of Coalition Logics

2.1 Language

Let AP be a countable set of atomic propositions, and AG be a finite *nonempty* set of agents. The subsets of AG are called **coalitions**, and AG is called the **grand coalition**. In the sequel, when no confusion arises, we often write a instead of $\{a\}$, where $a \in$ AG.

Definition 1 (The language Φ). *The language Φ is defined as follows, where p ranges over AP and $C \subseteq$ AG:*

$$\phi ::= \top \mid p \mid \neg\phi \mid (\phi \wedge \phi) \mid \langle\!\lfloor C \rfloor\!\rangle \phi$$

The formula $\langle\!\lfloor C \rfloor\!\rangle \phi$ indicates *some available joint action of C ensures ϕ*. The propositional connectives $\bot, \vee, \rightarrow$ and $\leftrightarrow$ are defined as usual.

2.2 Action Semantics

Let AC be a *nonempty* set of actions. For every $C \subseteq$ AG, we define $\text{JA}_C = \{\sigma_C \mid \sigma_C : C \rightarrow \text{AC}\}$, which is a set of **joint actions** of C. Joint actions of the grand coalition are called **action profiles**. In the sequel, we sometimes use sequences of actions to represent joint actions of coalitions, where an order among agents is implicitly presupposed. We define $\text{JA} = \bigcup \{\text{JA}_C \mid C \subseteq \text{AG}\}$.

Definition 2 (Action models). *An **action model** is a tuple* $\text{AM} = (\text{ST}, \text{AC}, \{\text{av}_C \mid C \subseteq \text{AG}\}, \{\text{out}_C \mid C \subseteq \text{AG}\}, \text{label})$, *where:*

- *ST is a nonempty set of states.*
- *AC is a nonempty set of actions.*
  Here, AC is dependent on specific models.
- *for every $C \subseteq$ AG, $\text{av}_C : \text{ST} \rightarrow \mathcal{P}(\text{JA}_C)$ is an **availability function** for C.*
- *for every $C \subseteq$ AG, $\text{out}_C : \text{ST} \times \text{JA}_C \rightarrow \mathcal{P}(\text{ST})$ is an **outcome function** for C.*
- *label : $\text{ST} \rightarrow \mathcal{P}(\text{AP})$ is a **labeling function**.*

Different coalition logics might put different constraints on action models.

Definition 3 (Action semantics).

$$
\begin{aligned}
&\text{AM}, s \Vdash \top \\
&\text{AM}, s \Vdash p &&\Leftrightarrow p \in \text{label}(s) \\
&\text{AM}, s \Vdash \neg\phi &&\Leftrightarrow \text{not AM}, s \Vdash \phi \\
&\text{AM}, s \Vdash \phi \wedge \psi &&\Leftrightarrow \text{AM}, s \Vdash \phi \text{ and AM}, s \Vdash \psi \\
&\text{AM}, s \Vdash \langle\!\lfloor C \rfloor\!\rangle \phi &&\Leftrightarrow \text{there is } \sigma_C \in \text{av}_C(s) \text{ such that for all } t \in \text{out}_C(s, \sigma_C), \\
&&&\quad \text{AM}, t \Vdash \phi
\end{aligned}
$$

2.3 Neighborhood Semantics

Definition 4 (Neighborhood models and alpha neighborhood models).
*A **neighborhood model** is a tuple* $\mathsf{NM} = (\mathsf{ST}, \{\mathsf{nei}_C \mid C \subseteq \mathsf{AG}\}, \mathsf{label})$, *where:*

- ST *is a nonempty set of states.*
- *for every* $C \subseteq \mathsf{AG}$, $\mathsf{nei}_C : \mathsf{ST} \to \mathcal{P}(\mathcal{P}(\mathsf{ST}))$ *is a **neighborhood function** for* C.
- $\mathsf{label} : \mathsf{ST} \to \mathcal{P}(\mathsf{AP})$ *is a labeling function.*

A neighborhood model $\mathsf{NM}^\alpha = (\mathsf{ST}, \{\mathsf{nei}_C^\alpha \mid C \subseteq \mathsf{AG}\}, \mathsf{label})$ *is an **alpha neighborhood model** if for every* $C \subseteq \mathsf{AG}$ *and* $s \in \mathsf{ST}$, $\mathsf{nei}_C^\alpha(s)$ *is closed under supersets.*

Different coalition logics might put different constraints on neighborhood models.

Definition 5 (Neighborhood semantics).
$\mathsf{NM}, s \Vdash \top$
$\mathsf{NM}, s \Vdash p \quad \Leftrightarrow p \in \mathsf{label}(s)$
$\mathsf{NM}, s \Vdash \neg \phi \quad \Leftrightarrow \mathrm{not}\ \mathsf{NM}, s \Vdash \phi$
$\mathsf{NM}, s \Vdash \phi \wedge \psi \Leftrightarrow \mathsf{NM}, s \Vdash \phi\ \mathrm{and}\ \mathsf{NM}, s \Vdash \psi$
$\mathsf{NM}, s \Vdash \langle\!\langle C \rangle\!\rangle \phi \Leftrightarrow \mathrm{there\ is}\ Y \in \mathsf{nei}_C(s)\ \mathrm{such\ that\ for\ all}\ t \in Y, \mathsf{NM}, t \Vdash \phi$

The following fact, which is easy to verify, indicates that we can transform a pointed neighborhood model to a pointed alpha neighborhood model without changing the set of formulas it satisfies.

Lemma 1. *Let* $\mathsf{NM} = (\mathsf{ST}, \{\mathsf{nei}_C \mid C \subseteq \mathsf{AG}\}, \mathsf{label})$ *be a neighborhood model and* $\mathsf{NM}^\alpha = (\mathsf{ST}, \{\mathsf{nei}_C^\alpha \mid C \subseteq \mathsf{AG}\}, \mathsf{label})$ *be an alpha neighborhood model such that for all* $C \subseteq \mathsf{AG}$ *and* $s \in \mathsf{ST}$, $\mathsf{nei}_C^\alpha(s)$ *is the closure of* $\mathsf{nei}_C(s)$ *under supersets. Then, for every* $s \in \mathsf{ST}$ *and* $\phi \in \Phi$, $\mathsf{NM}, s \Vdash \phi$ *if and only if* $\mathsf{NM}^\alpha, s \Vdash \phi$.

2.4 Transformation of Action Semantics to Neighborhood Semantics

Definition 6 (Actual effectivity functions and alpha effectivity functions of action models). *Let* $\mathsf{AM} = (\mathsf{ST}, \mathsf{AC}, \{\mathsf{av}_C \mid C \subseteq \mathsf{AG}\}, \{\mathsf{out}_C \mid C \subseteq \mathsf{AG}\}, \mathsf{label})$ *be an action model.*

For every $C \subseteq \mathsf{AG}$, *the function* AE_C *defined as follows is called the **actual effectivity function** for* C *in* AM: *for every* $s \in \mathsf{ST}$,

$$\mathsf{AE}_C(s) = \{\mathsf{out}_C(s, \sigma_C) \mid \sigma_C \in \mathsf{av}_C(s)\}.$$

For every $C \subseteq \mathsf{AG}$, *the function* LE_C *defined as follows is called the **alpha effectivity function** for* C *in* AM: *for every* $s \in \mathsf{ST}$,

$$\mathsf{LE}_C(s) = \{Y \subseteq \mathsf{ST} \mid \mathsf{out}_C(s, \sigma_C) \subseteq Y\ \mathrm{for\ some}\ \sigma_C \in \mathsf{av}_C(s)\}.$$

Actual effectivity functions are more transparent in the following sense: each element of $\mathtt{AE}_C(s)$ can be understood as a class of equivalent actions.

Definition 7 (Action models z-representable by neighborhood models and α-representable by alpha neighborhood models).
An action model $\mathtt{AM} = (\mathtt{ST}, \mathtt{AC}, \{\mathtt{av}_C \mid C \subseteq \mathtt{AG}\}, \{\mathtt{out}_C \mid C \subseteq \mathtt{AG}\}, \mathsf{label})$ is z-*representable* by a neighborhood model $\mathtt{NM} = (\mathtt{ST}, \{\mathtt{nei}_C \mid C \subseteq \mathtt{AG}\}, \mathsf{label})$ if for every $C \subseteq \mathtt{AG}$, $\mathtt{AE}_C = \mathtt{nei}_C$.

A class of action models $\mathbf{AM}$ is z-*representable* by a class of neighborhood models $\mathbf{NM}$ if (1) every action model in $\mathbf{AM}$ is z-representable by a neighborhood mode in $\mathbf{NM}$, and (2) every neighborhood model in $\mathbf{NM}$ z-represents an action mode in $\mathbf{AM}$.

An action model $\mathtt{AM}$ is α-*representable* by an alpha neighborhood model $\mathtt{NM}^\alpha = (\mathtt{ST}, \{\mathtt{nei}_C^\alpha \mid C \subseteq \mathtt{AG}\}, \mathsf{label})$ if for every $C \subseteq \mathtt{AG}$, $\mathtt{LE}_C = \mathtt{nei}_C^\alpha$.

A class of action models $\mathbf{AM}$ is α-*representable* by a class of alpha neighborhood models $\mathbf{NM}^\alpha$ if (1) every action model in $\mathbf{AM}$ is α-representable by an alpha neighborhood model in $\mathbf{NM}^\alpha$, and (2) every alpha neighborhood model in $\mathbf{NM}^\alpha$ α-represents an action mode in $\mathbf{AM}$.

Intuitively, a neighborhood model $\mathtt{NM}$ represents an action model $\mathtt{AM}$ means that $\mathtt{NM}$ contains all the information of $\mathtt{AM}$ to evaluate formulas of Φ.

The following result can be easily shown:

Theorem 1 (Representability implies equivalence).

(1) For every action model $\mathtt{AM}$ and neighborhood model $\mathtt{NM}$, if $\mathtt{AM}$ is z-representable by $\mathtt{NM}$, then for every state s of $\mathtt{AM}$ and formula ϕ in Φ, $\mathtt{AM}, s \Vdash \phi$ if and only if $\mathtt{NM}, s \Vdash \phi$.
Consequently, for every class of action models $\mathbf{AM}$ and class of neighborhood models $\mathbf{NM}$, if $\mathbf{AM}$ is z-representable by $\mathbf{NM}$, then for every formula ϕ in Φ, ϕ is valid with respect to $\mathbf{AM}$ if and only if ϕ is valid with respect to $\mathbf{NM}$.
(2) For every action model $\mathtt{AM}$ and alpha neighborhood model $\mathtt{NM}^\alpha$, if $\mathtt{AM}$ is α-representable by $\mathtt{NM}^\alpha$, then for every state s of $\mathtt{AM}$ and formula ϕ in Φ, $\mathtt{AM}, s \Vdash \phi$ if and only if $\mathtt{NM}^\alpha, s \Vdash \phi$.
Consequently, for every class of action models $\mathbf{AM}$ and class of alpha neighborhood model $\mathbf{NM}^\alpha$, if $\mathbf{AM}$ is α-representable by $\mathbf{NM}^\alpha$, then for every formula ϕ in Φ, ϕ is valid with respect to $\mathbf{AM}$ if and only if ϕ is valid with respect to $\mathbf{NM}^\alpha$.

3 Eight Coalition Logics Determined by Eight Classes of Grand-Coalition-First Action Models

3.1 Eight Classes of Grand-Coalition-First Action Models

Definition 8 (Grand-coalition-first action models). *A **grand-coalition-first action model** is a tuple $\mathtt{G\text{-}AM} = (\mathtt{ST}, \mathtt{AC}, \mathtt{out}_{\mathtt{AG}}, \mathsf{label})$, where:*

- ST *is a nonempty set of states.*
- AC *is a nonempty set of actions.*
- $\mathsf{out}_{\mathsf{AG}} : \mathsf{ST} \times \mathsf{JA}_{\mathsf{AG}} \to \mathcal{P}(\mathsf{ST})$ *is an outcome function for* AG.
- label $: \mathsf{ST} \to \mathcal{P}(\mathsf{AP})$ *is a labeling function.*

Definition 9 (Outcome functions and availability functions of grand-coalition-first action models). *Let* G-AM $= (\mathsf{ST}, \mathsf{AC}, \mathsf{out}_{\mathsf{AG}}, \mathsf{label})$ *be a grand-coalition-first action model.*

For every $C \subseteq \mathsf{AG}$, *define the outcome function* out_C *for* C *as follows: for all* $s \in \mathsf{ST}$ *and* $\sigma_C \in \mathsf{JA}_C$,

$$\mathsf{out}_C(s, \sigma_C) = \bigcup \{\mathsf{out}_{\mathsf{AG}}(s, \sigma_{\mathsf{AG}}) \mid \sigma_{\mathsf{AG}} \in \mathsf{JA}_{\mathsf{AG}} \text{ and } \sigma_C \subseteq \sigma_{\mathsf{AG}}\}.$$

For every $C \subseteq \mathsf{AG}$, *define the availability function* av_C *for* C *as follows: for all* $s \in \mathsf{ST}$,

$$\mathsf{av}_C(s) = \{\sigma_C \in \mathsf{JA}_C \mid \mathsf{out}(s, \sigma_C) \neq \emptyset\}.$$

Definition 10 (Successor functions of grand-coalition-first action models). *Let* G-AM $= (\mathsf{ST}, \mathsf{AC}, \mathsf{out}_{\mathsf{AG}}, \mathsf{label})$ *be a grand-coalition-first action model.*
*Define the **successor function** suc of* G-AM *as follows: for all* $s \in \mathsf{ST}$,

$$\mathsf{suc}(s) = \bigcup \{\mathsf{out}_{\mathsf{AG}}(s, \sigma_{\mathsf{AG}}) \mid \sigma_{\mathsf{AG}} \in \mathsf{JA}_{\mathsf{AG}}\}.$$

For every set X of states, we say $\Delta \subseteq \mathcal{P}(X)$ is a **general cover** of X if $\bigcup \Delta = X$. A general cover Δ is a **cover** if $\emptyset \notin \Delta$. It is easy to verify the following fact:

Lemma 2. *Let* G-AM $= (\mathsf{ST}, \mathsf{AC}, \mathsf{out}_{\mathsf{AG}}, \mathsf{label})$ *be a grand-coalition-first action model.*
Then, for every $C \subseteq \mathsf{AG}$ *and* $s \in \mathsf{ST}$, $\{\mathsf{out}_C(s, \sigma_C) \mid \sigma_C \in \mathsf{JA}_C\}$ *is a general cover of* $\mathsf{suc}(s)$.

Lemma 3. *Let* G-AM $= (\mathsf{ST}, \mathsf{AC}, \mathsf{out}_{\mathsf{AG}}, \mathsf{label})$ *be a grand-coalition-first action model,* $\{\mathsf{av}_C \mid C \subseteq \mathsf{AG}\}$ *be the set of availability functions of* G-AM, *and* $\{\mathsf{out}_C \mid C \subseteq \mathsf{AG}\}$ *be the set of outcome functions of* G-AM.
Then:

(1) for all $s \in \mathsf{ST}, C, D \subseteq \mathsf{AG}$ *such that* $C \cap D = \emptyset$, $\sigma_C \in \mathsf{JA}_C(s)$, *and* $\sigma_D \in \mathsf{JA}_D(s)$,
$\mathsf{out}_{C \cup D}(s, \sigma_C \cup \sigma_D) \subseteq \mathsf{out}_C(s, \sigma_C) \cap \mathsf{out}_D(s, \sigma_D)$;
(2) for all $s \in \mathsf{ST}, C \subseteq \mathsf{AG}$, *where* $C = \{a_1, \ldots, a_n\}$, *and* $\sigma_C \in \mathsf{JA}_C(s)$, *where* $\sigma_C = \sigma_{a_1} \cup \cdots \cup \sigma_{a_n}$, $\mathsf{out}_C(s, \sigma_C) \subseteq \mathsf{out}_{a_1}(s, \sigma_{a_1}) \cap \cdots \cap \mathsf{out}_{a_1}(s, \sigma_{a_1})$.

Note that neither of the converses of the two statements holds. Figure 1 indicates a counterexample for them.

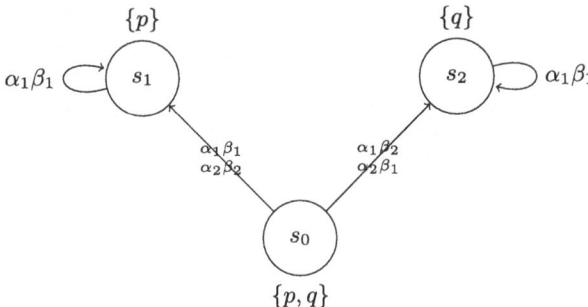

Fig. 1. This figure is used to show that in grand-coalition-first action models, the set of outcome states of a joint action might not contain the intersection of the sets of outcome states of the joint action's parts. A grand-coalition-first action model is indicated in the figure, where we suppose $\mathsf{AG} = \{a,b\}$. It can be seen: (1) $\mathsf{out}_a(s_0, \alpha_1)$, the set of outcome states of a performing α_1 at s_0, equals to $\{s_1, s_2\}$, (2) $\mathsf{out}_a(s_0, \beta_1)$, the set of outcome states of b performing β_1 at s_0, equals to $\{s_1, s_2\}$, but (3) $\mathsf{out}_{\mathsf{AG}}(s_0, \alpha_1\beta_1)$, the set of outcome states of a and b respectively performing α_1 and β_1 at s_0, does not contain the intersection of $\mathsf{out}_a(s_0, \alpha_1)$ and $\mathsf{out}_b(s_0, \beta_1)$.

Definition 11 (Seriality, independence, and determinism of grand-coalition-first action models). *Let* $\mathsf{G\text{-}AM} = (\mathsf{ST}, \mathsf{AC}, \mathsf{out}_{\mathsf{AG}}, \mathsf{label})$ *be a grand-coalition-first action model.*

We say:

- $\mathsf{G\text{-}AM}$ *is* **serial** *if for all* $\mathsf{C} \subseteq \mathsf{AG}$ *and* $s \in \mathsf{ST}$, $\mathsf{av}_\mathsf{C}(s) \neq \emptyset$;
- $\mathsf{G\text{-}AM}$ *is* **independent** *if for all* $s \in \mathsf{ST}$, $\mathsf{C}, \mathsf{D} \subseteq \mathsf{AG}$ *such that* $\mathsf{C} \cap \mathsf{D} = \emptyset$, $\sigma_\mathsf{C} \in \mathsf{av}_\mathsf{C}(s)$, *and* $\sigma_\mathsf{D} \in \mathsf{av}_\mathsf{D}(s)$, $\sigma_\mathsf{C} \cup \sigma_\mathsf{D} \in \mathsf{av}_{\mathsf{C} \cup \mathsf{D}}(s)$;
- $\mathsf{G\text{-}AM}$ *is* **deterministic** *if for all* $s \in \mathsf{ST}$ *and* $\sigma_\mathsf{AG} \in \mathsf{av}_\mathsf{AG}(s)$, $\mathsf{out}_{\mathsf{AG}}(s, \sigma_\mathsf{AG})$ *is a singleton.*

We let the three symbols S, I and D correspond to the three properties, respectively, and let the eight strings ϵ, S, I, D, SI, SD, ID, and SID correspond to the eight combinations of the three properties, respectively. We use ES to indicate the set of the eight strings.

For every $\mathsf{X} \in \mathsf{ES}$ and grand-coalition-first action model G-AM, we say G-AM is an **X-model** if G-AM has the properties corresponding to X.

For every $\mathsf{X} \in \mathsf{ES}$, we use MCL + X to refer to the coalition logic determined by the class of grand-coalition-first action X-models.

3.2 Eight Axiomatic Systems
Definition 12 (An axiomatic system for MCL).
Axioms:

*Tautologies (*A-Tau*): all propositional tautologies*

*No absurd available actions (*A-NAAA*):* $\neg\langle\!\langle C \rangle\!\rangle \bot$

*Monotonicity of goals (*A-MG*):* $\langle\!\langle \emptyset \rangle\!\rangle(\phi \to \psi) \to (\langle\!\langle C \rangle\!\rangle \phi \to \langle\!\langle C \rangle\!\rangle \psi)$

*Monotonicity of coalitions (*A-MC*):* $\langle\!\langle C \rangle\!\rangle \phi \to \langle\!\langle D \rangle\!\rangle \phi$, *where* $C \subseteq D$

Inference rules:

*Modus ponens (*MP*):* $\dfrac{\phi, \phi \to \psi}{\psi}$

*Conditional necessitation (*CN*):* $\dfrac{\phi}{\langle\!\langle C \rangle\!\rangle \psi \to \langle\!\langle \emptyset \rangle\!\rangle \phi}$

We let the following formulas respectively correspond to S, I and D.

*Seriality (*A-Ser*):* $\langle\!\langle C \rangle\!\rangle \top$

*Independence of agents (*A-IA*):* $(\langle\!\langle C \rangle\!\rangle \phi \wedge \langle\!\langle D \rangle\!\rangle \psi) \to \langle\!\langle C \cup D \rangle\!\rangle (\phi \wedge \psi)$
where $C \cap D = \emptyset$

*Determinism (*A-Det*):* $\langle\!\langle C \rangle\!\rangle (\phi \vee \psi) \to (\langle\!\langle C \rangle\!\rangle \phi \vee \langle\!\langle AG \rangle\!\rangle \psi)$

Definition 13 (Axiomatic systems for MCL + X**).** *For every* X *in* ES, *the axiomatic system for* MCL + X *consists of the axioms and inference rules of* MCL, *and the axioms corresponding to the elements of* X.

Theorem 2 Soundness and completeness of MCL + X **[8]).** *For every* X *in* ES, *the axiomatic system for* MCL + X *given in Definition 13 is sound and complete with respect to the set of valid formulas of* MCL + X.

Remarks. The class of grand-coalition-first SID-models is α-representable [5,11], and the class of grand-coalition-first SD-models is α-representable [13]. Are the other six classes of grand-coalition-first action models α-representable? Are the eight classes of grand-coalition-first action models z-representable? All this is yet unknown.

4 Single-Coalition-First Action Models and Single-Coalition First Neighborhood Models

4.1 Single-Coalition-First Action Models

Definition 14 (Single-coalition-first action models). *A single-coalition-first action model is a tuple* S-AM = (ST, AC, suc, {out$_a$ | $a \in$ AG}, label), *where:*

- ST *is a nonempty set of states.*
- AC *is a nonempty set of actions.*
- suc : ST $\to \mathcal{P}$(ST) *is a successor function.*
- *for all* $a \in$ AG, out$_a$: ST $\times$ JA$_a \to \mathcal{P}$(ST) *is an outcome function for a such that for all* $s \in$ ST, {out$_a(s, \sigma_a)$ | $\sigma_a \in$ JA$_a$} *is a general cover of* suc(s).
- label : ST $\to \mathcal{P}$(AP) *is a labeling function.*

Definition 15 (Outcome functions and availability functions of single-coalition-first action models). *Let* S-AM $=$ (ST, AC, suc, $\{\text{out}_a \mid a \in \text{AG}\}$, label) *be a single-coalition-first action model.*

For every $C \subseteq \text{AG}$, *define the outcome function* out_C *for* C *as follows: for all* $s \in \text{ST}$ *and* $\sigma_C \in \text{JA}_C$,

$$\text{out}_C(s, \sigma_C) = \begin{cases} \text{suc}(s) & \text{if } C = \emptyset \\ \bigcap\{\text{out}_a(s, \sigma_a) \mid a \in C, \sigma_a \in \text{JA}_a, \text{ and } \sigma_a \subseteq \sigma_C\} & \text{if } C \neq \emptyset \end{cases}$$

For every $C \subseteq \text{AG}$, *define the availability function* av_C *for* C *as follows: for all* $s \in \text{ST}$,

$$\text{av}_C(s) = \{\sigma_C \in \text{JA}_C \mid \text{out}(s, \sigma_C) \neq \emptyset\}$$

For all $\sigma_C, \sigma'_C, \sigma''_C \in \text{JA}_C$, we say that σ''_C is a **fusion** of σ_C and σ'_C, if for all $a \in C$, $\sigma''_C|_a$ equals to $\sigma_C|_a$ or $\sigma'_C|_a$.

The following result offers two alternative definitions of sing-coalition-first action models.

Theorem 3. *Let* AM $=$ (ST, AC, $\{\text{av}_C \mid C \subseteq \text{AG}\}$, $\{\text{out}_C \mid C \subseteq \text{AG}\}$, label) *be an action model and* $s \in \text{ST}$.

The following three sets of conditions are equivalent:

(1) (a) *for all* $a \in \text{AG}$, $\{\text{out}_a(s, \sigma_a) \mid \sigma_a \in \text{JA}_a\}$ *is a general cover of* $\text{out}_\emptyset(s, \emptyset)$;
(b) *for all nonempty* $C \subseteq \text{AG}$ *and* $\sigma_C \in \text{JA}_C$, $\text{out}_C(s, \sigma_C) = \bigcap\{\text{out}_a(s, \sigma_a) \mid a \in C, \sigma_a \in \text{JA}_a, \text{ and } \sigma_a \subseteq \sigma_C\}$.
It is easy to check this set of conditions is equivalent to the set of constraints on single-coalition-first action models.

(2) (a) *for all* $a \in \text{AG}$, $\{\text{out}_a(s, \sigma_a) \mid \sigma_a \in \text{JA}_a\}$ *is a general cover of* $\text{out}_\emptyset(s, \emptyset)$;
(b) *for all* C, D $\subseteq$ AG *such that* $C \cap D = \emptyset$, $\sigma_C \in \text{JA}_C$, *and* $\sigma_D \in \text{JA}_D$, $\text{out}_{C \cup D}(s, \sigma_C \cup \sigma_D) = \text{out}_C(s, \sigma_C) \cap \text{out}_D(s, \sigma_D)$.

(3) (a) *for all* $C \subseteq \text{AG}$ *and* $\sigma_C \in \text{JA}_C$, $\text{out}_C(s, \sigma_C) = \bigcup\{\text{out}_{\text{AG}}(s, \sigma_{\text{AG}}) \mid \sigma_{\text{AG}} \in \text{JA}_{\text{AG}} \text{ and } \sigma_C \subseteq \sigma_{\text{AG}}\}$;
(b) *for all* $C \subseteq \text{AG}$ *and* $\sigma_C, \sigma'_C, \sigma''_C \in \text{JA}_C$, *if* σ''_C *is a fusion of* σ_C *and* σ'_C, *then* $\text{out}_C(s, \sigma_C) \cap \text{out}_C(s, \sigma'_C) \subseteq \text{out}_C(s, \sigma''_C)$.

The proof for this result can be found in [3].

Theorem 4. *Every single-coalition-first action model is a grand-coalition-first action model, but not vice versa.*

The first part of this result follows from the previous theorem. For the second part, the grand-coalition-first action model indicated in Fig. 1 is a counterexample.

Remarks. We say outcome functions of a class of action models are **compositional** if there is a way such that for every action model in the class, the outcome function of a coalition is determined by the outcome functions of its members in this way.

It is to show that outcome functions in grand-coalition-first action models are not compositional.

In fact, there are many situations where every agent can change a component of the state, and different components of the state that can be changed by different agents are independent of each other. In these situations, the set of outcomes of a joint action is the intersection of the sets of outcomes of individual actions of the joint action. Consequently, outcome functions are compositional in these situations.

In addition, we want to mention that some literature, such as [6,7], deals with agency by *propositional control*: there are some agents; every atomic proposition is controlled by at most one agent. In these settings, outcome functions are compositional.

Clearly, outcome functions of single-coalition-first action models are compositional.

Goranko and Jamroga [4] discussed *convex concurrent game models*, which are closely related to *rectangular game forms* in game theory [1]. It can be verified convex concurrent game models are single-coalition-first action SID-models.

4.2 Single-Coalition-First Neighborhood Models

Let ST be a nonempty set of states and $\Delta_1, \Delta_2 \subseteq \mathcal{P}(\text{ST}) - \{\emptyset\}$. Define $\Delta_1 \odot \Delta_2 = \{Y_1 \cap Y_2 \mid Y_1 \in \Delta_1, Y_2 \in \Delta_2, \text{and } Y_1 \cap Y_2 \neq \emptyset\}$. Let I be a nonempty set of indices. Define $\odot\{\Delta_i \mid i \in I \text{ and } \Delta_i \subseteq \mathcal{P}(\text{ST}) - \{\emptyset\}\}$ as expected. Note $\odot\{\Delta\} = \Delta$.

Definition 16 (Single-coalition-first neighborhood models). *A single-coalition-first neighborhood model is a tuple* S-NM $= (\text{ST}, \text{suc}, \{\text{nei}_a \mid a \in \text{AG}\}, \text{label})$, *where:*

- ST *is a nonempty set of states.*
- suc $: \text{ST} \to \mathcal{P}(\text{ST})$ *is a successor function.*
- *for all* $a \in \text{AG}$, $\text{nei}_a : \text{ST} \to \mathcal{P}(\mathcal{P}(\text{ST}))$ *is a neighborhood function for a such that for all* $s \in \text{ST}$, $\text{nei}_a(s)$ *is a cover of* $\text{suc}(s)$.
- label $: \text{ST} \to \mathcal{P}(\text{AP})$ *is a labeling function.*

Definition 17 (Neighborhood functions of single-coalition-first neighborhood models). *Let* S-NM $= (\text{ST}, \text{suc}, \{\text{nei}_a \mid a \in \text{AG}\}, \text{label})$ *be a single-coalition-first neighborhood model.*

For every $C \subseteq \text{AG}$, *define the neighborhood function* nei_C *for C as follows: for all* $s \in \text{ST}$,

$$\text{nei}_C(s) = \begin{cases} \emptyset & \text{if } \text{suc}(s) = \emptyset \\ \{\text{suc}(s)\} & \text{if } \text{suc}(s) \neq \emptyset \text{ and } C = \emptyset \\ \odot\{\text{nei}_a(s) \mid a \in C\} & \text{if } \text{suc}(s) \neq \emptyset \text{ and } C \neq \emptyset \end{cases}$$

Lemma 4. *Let* S-NM $= (\mathsf{ST}, \mathsf{suc}, \{\mathsf{nei}_a \mid a \in \mathsf{AG}\}, \mathsf{label})$ *be a single-coalition-first neighborhood model, and* $\{\mathsf{nei}_C \mid C \subseteq \mathsf{AG}\}$ *be the class of neighborhood functions of* S-NM.
Then, for all $C \subseteq \mathsf{AG}$ *and* $s \in \mathsf{ST}$, $\mathsf{nei}_C(s)$ *is a cover of* $\mathsf{suc}(s)$.

The proof for this result can be found in [3].

Definition 18 (Seriality, independence, and determinism of single-coalition-first neighborhood models). *Let* S-NM $= (\mathsf{ST}, \mathsf{suc}, \{\mathsf{nei}_a \mid a \in \mathsf{AG}\}, \mathsf{label})$ *be a single-coalition-first neighborhood model.*
 We say:

- S-NM *is* **serial** *if for all* $s \in \mathsf{ST}$ *and* $C \subseteq \mathsf{AG}$, $\mathsf{nei}_C(s) \neq \emptyset$.
- S-NM *is* **independent** *if for all* $s \in \mathsf{ST}$, $C, D \subseteq \mathsf{AG}$ *such that* $C \cap D = \emptyset$, $Y_1 \in \mathsf{nei}_C(s)$ *and* $Y_2 \in \mathsf{nei}_D(s)$, $Y_1 \cap Y_2 \neq \emptyset$.
- S-NM *is* **deterministic** *if for all* $s \in \mathsf{ST}$ *and* $Y \in \mathsf{nei}_\mathsf{AG}(s)$, Y *is a singleton.*

As above, we let the eight strings ϵ, S, I, D, SI, SD, ID, and SID in the set ES correspond to the eight combinations of the three properties, respectively.

For any $X \in \mathsf{ES}$ and single-coalition-first neighborhood model S-NM, we say S-NM is an **X-model** if it has the properties corresponding to X.

Remarks. Alurz, Henzinger, and Kupferman [2] proposed a semantics for ATL, where models are based on *alternating transition systems*. Goranko and Jamroga [4] discussed *tight* alternating transition systems, which we can verify are single-coalition-first neighborhood SID-models.

4.3 Representation of Single-Coalition-First Action Models by Single-Coalition-First Neighborhood Models

Theorem 5. *Every single-coalition-first action model is z-representable by a single-coalition-first neighborhood model.*

This result is easy to show, and we skip its proof.

Theorem 6. *Every single-coalition-first neighborhood model z-represents a single-coalition-first action model.*

Proof. Let S-NM $= (\mathsf{ST}, \mathsf{suc}, \{\mathsf{nei}_a \mid a \in \mathsf{AG}\}, \mathsf{label})$ be a single-coalition-first neighborhood model, and $\{\mathsf{nei}_C \mid C \subseteq \mathsf{AG}\}$ be the set of neighborhood functions of S-NM.

Define a single-coalition-first action model S-AM $= (\mathsf{ST}, \mathsf{AC}, \mathsf{suc}, \{\mathsf{out}_a \mid a \in \mathsf{AG}\}, \mathsf{label})$ as follows:

- $\mathsf{AC} = \{\alpha_{a-s-X} \mid a \in \mathsf{AG}, s \in \mathsf{ST}, \text{and } X \in \mathsf{nei}_a(s)\}$.
- for every $a \in \mathsf{AG}$, $s \in \mathsf{ST}$ and $\alpha_{x-u-X} \in \mathsf{AC}$,

$$\mathsf{out}_a(s, \alpha_{x-u-X}) = \begin{cases} X & \text{if } x = a \text{ and } u = s \\ \emptyset & \text{otherwise} \end{cases}$$

Let $\{\text{out}_C \mid C \subseteq \text{AG}\}$ be the class of outcome functions of S-AM.

We claim that S-AM is z-representable by S-NM.

Let $\{\text{AE}_C \mid C \subseteq \text{AG}\}$ be the class of actual effectivity functions of S-AM. Let $C \subseteq \text{AG}$ and $s \in \text{ST}$. It suffices to show $\text{AE}_C(s) = \text{nei}_C(s)$. Note $\text{AE}_C(s) = \{\text{out}_C(s, \sigma_C) \mid \sigma_C \in \text{JA}_C \text{ and } \text{out}_C(s, \sigma_C)\}$.

Assume $\text{suc}(s) = \emptyset$. Note $\text{AE}_C(s) = \emptyset$ and $\text{nei}_C(s) = \emptyset$. Then, $\text{AE}_C(s) = \text{nei}_C(s)$.

Assume $\text{suc}(s) \neq \emptyset$ and $C = \emptyset$. Note $\text{AE}_C(s) = \{\text{suc}(s)\}$ and $\text{nei}_C(s) = \{\text{suc}(s)\}$. Then, $\text{AE}_C(s) = \text{nei}_C(s)$.

Assume $\text{suc}(s) \neq \emptyset$ and $C \neq \emptyset$. Let $C = \{a_1, \ldots, a_n\}$. Note $\text{nei}_C(s) = \odot\{\text{nei}_a(s) \mid a \in C\}$.

Let $X \in \text{AE}_C(s)$. Then, there is $\sigma_C \in \text{av}_C(s)$ such that $X = \text{out}_C(s, \sigma_C)$. Let $\sigma_C = \sigma_{a_1} \cup \cdots \cup \sigma_{a_n}$. Note that $\text{out}_C(s, \sigma_C) = \text{out}_{a_1}(s, \sigma_{a_1}) \cap \cdots \cap \text{out}_{a_1}(s, \sigma_{a_n})$ and $X \neq \emptyset$. Then, $\text{out}_{a_1}(s, \sigma_{a_1}) \neq \emptyset$, $\ldots$, $\text{out}_{a_n}(s, \sigma_{a_n}) \neq \emptyset$. Let i be such that $1 \leq i \leq n$ and $\sigma_{a_i} = \alpha_{x-u-X_i}$. By the definition of $\text{out}_{a_i}(s, \sigma_{a_i})$, $\text{out}_{a_i}(s, \sigma_{a_i}) = X_i$, $x = a_i$, and $u = s$. Then $\sigma_{a_i} = \alpha_{a_i-s-X_i}$ and $X_i \in \text{nei}_{a_i}(s)$. Then, $X = X_1 \cap \cdots \cap X_n$. Then, $X \in \text{nei}_C(s, C)$.

Let $X \in \text{nei}_C(s, C)$. Then, $X = X_1 \cap \cdots \cap X_n$ for some $X_1 \in \text{nei}_{a_1}(s), \ldots, X_n \in \text{nei}_{a_n}(s)$. Then, $\alpha_{a_1-s-X_1}, \ldots, \alpha_{a_n-s-X_n} \in \text{AC}$. Note $\text{out}_{a_1}(s, \alpha_{a_1-s-X_1}) = X_1, \ldots, \text{out}_{a_n}(s, \alpha_{a_n-s-X_n}) = X_n$. Let $\sigma_C = \alpha_{a_1-s-X_1} \cup \cdots \cup \alpha_{a_n-s-X_n}$. Then, $\text{out}_C(s, \sigma_C) = \text{out}_{a_1}(s, \alpha_{a_1-s-X_1}) \cap \cdots \cap \text{out}_{a_n}(s, \alpha_{a_n-s-X_n}) = X_1 \cap \cdots \cap X_n = X$. Note X is not empty. Then, $X \in \text{AE}_C(s)$.

Theorem 7. *For every single-coalition-first action model S-AM and single-coalition-first neighborhood model S-NM, if S-AM is z-representable by S-NM, then for every $X \in \text{ES}$, S-AM is an X-model if and only if S-NM is an X-model.*

Proof. Let S-AM $= (\text{ST}, \text{AC}, \text{suc}, \{\text{out}_a \mid a \in \text{AG}\}, \text{label})$ be a single-coalition-first action model, $\{\text{av}_C \mid C \subseteq \text{AG}\}$ be the class of availability functions of S-AM, $\{\text{out}_C \mid C \subseteq \text{AG}\}$ be the class of outcome functions of S-AM, and $\{\text{AE}_C \mid C \subseteq \text{AG}\}$ be the class of actual effectivity functions of S-AM. Let S-NM $= (\text{ST}, \text{suc}, \{\text{nei}_a \mid a \in \text{AG}\}, \text{label})$ be a single-coalition-first neighborhood model, and $\{\text{nei}_C \mid C \subseteq \text{AG}\}$ be the set of neighborhood functions of S-NM. Assume S-AM is z-representable by S-NM. Then, for all $C \subseteq \text{AG}$, $\text{AE}_C = \text{nei}_C$.

Let $X \in \text{ES}$. It is easy to see that the following three groups of statements are equivalent, respectively.

(1) – S-AM is serial;
   – for all $s \in \text{ST}$ and $C \subseteq \text{AG}$, $\text{av}_C(s) \neq \emptyset$;
   – for all $s \in \text{ST}$ and $C \subseteq \text{AG}$, $\text{AE}_C(s) \neq \emptyset$;
   – for all $s \in \text{ST}$ and $C \subseteq \text{AG}$, $\text{nei}_C(s) \neq \emptyset$;
   – S-NM is serial.
(2) – S-AM is independent;
   – for all $s \in \text{ST}, C, D \subseteq \text{AG}$ such that $C \cap D = \emptyset, \sigma_C \in \text{JA}_C$, and $\sigma_D \in \text{JA}_D$, if $\sigma_C \in \text{av}_C(s)$ and $\sigma_D \in \text{av}_D(s)$, then $\sigma_C \cup \sigma_D \in \text{av}_{C \cup D}(s)$;
   – for all $s \in \text{ST}, C, D \subseteq \text{AG}$ such that $C \cap D = \emptyset$, and $Y_1, Y_2 \subseteq \text{ST}$, if $Y_1 \in \text{AE}_C(s)$ and $Y_2 \in \text{AE}_D(s)$, then $Y_1 \cap Y_2 \neq \emptyset$;

- for all $s \in \text{ST}, \text{C}, \text{D} \subseteq \text{AG}$ such that $\text{C} \cap \text{D} = \emptyset$, and $Y_1, Y_2 \subseteq \text{ST}$, if $Y_1 \in \text{nei}_\text{C}(s)$ and $Y_2 \in \text{nei}_\text{D}(s)$, then $Y_1 \cap Y_2 \neq \emptyset$;
- S-NM is independent.

(3)
- S-AM is deterministic;
- for all $s \in \text{ST}$ and $\sigma_\text{AG} \in \text{av}_\text{AG}(s)$, $\text{out}_\text{AG}(s, \sigma_\text{AG})$ is a singleton;
- for all $s \in \text{ST}$ and $Y \in \text{AE}_\text{AG}(s)$, Y is a singleton;
- for all $s \in \text{ST}$ and $Y \in \text{nei}_\text{AG}(s)$, Y is a singleton;
- S-NM is deterministic.

It follows that S-AM is an X-model if and only if S-NM is an X-model.

The following result follows from Theorems 5, 6, and 7.

Theorem 8. (Representation of the class of single-coalition-first action X-models by the class of single-coalition-first neighborhood X-models). *For every* $X \in \text{ES}$, *the class of single-coalition-first action X-models is z-representable by the class of single-coalition-first neighborhood X-models.*

5 Tree-Like Grand-Coalition-First Action Models and Tree-Like Single-Coalition-First Neighborhood Models

5.1 Tree-Like Grand-Coalition-First Action Models

Definition 19 (Histories in grand-coalition-first action models).
  Let G-AM = $(\text{ST}, \text{AC}, \text{out}_\text{AG}, \text{label})$ be a grand-coalition-first action model, $\{\text{av}_\text{C} \mid \text{C} \subseteq \text{AG}\}$ be the set of availability functions of G-AM, and $\{\text{out}_\text{C} \mid \text{C} \subseteq \text{AG}\}$ be the set of outcome functions of G-AM.
  For every $\text{C} \subseteq \text{AG}$, a finite sequence $\theta_\text{C} = (s_0, \sigma_\text{C}^1, s_1, \ldots, \sigma_\text{C}^n, s_n)$, where every s_i is a state and every σ_C^i is a joint action of C, is called a C-*history* from s_0 to s_n if for every i such that $0 \leq i < n$, $\sigma_\text{C}^{i+1} \in \text{av}_\text{C}(s_i)$ and $s_{i+1} \in \text{out}_\text{C}(s_i, \sigma_\text{C}^{i+1})$.
  Specially, for every $\text{C} \subseteq \text{AG}$ and $s \in \text{ST}$, s is called a C-*history* from s to s.

Definition 20 (Tree-like grand-coalition-first action models). *Let* G-AM $= (\text{ST}, \text{AC}, \text{out}_\text{AG}, \text{label})$ *be a grand-coalition-first action model.*
  We say G-AM *is a* **tree-like model** *if there is a state* r, *called a* **root**, *such that for every state* s, *there is a unique* AG-*history from* r *to* s.

Note every tree-like model has a unique root.

The following result gives two alternative definitions of tree-like grand-coalition-first action models.

Theorem 9. *Let* G-AM $= (\text{ST}, \text{AC}, \text{out}_\text{AG}, \text{label})$ *be a grand-coalition-first action model,* $\{\text{av}_\text{C} \mid \text{C} \subseteq \text{AG}\}$ *be the set of availability functions of* G-AM, *and* $\{\text{out}_\text{C} \mid \text{C} \subseteq \text{AG}\}$ *be the set of outcome functions of* G-AM.
  The following three conditions are equivalent:

(1) there is a state r of G-AM such that for every $a \in$ AG and $s \in$ ST, there is an unique a-history from r to s;
(2) there is a state r of G-AM such that for every $C \subseteq$ AG and $s \in$ ST, there is an unique C-history from r to s;
(3) there is a state r of G-AM such that for every $s \in$ ST, there is an unique AG-history from r to s.

The proof for this result can be found in [3].

Theorem 10. *Every tree-like grand-coalition-first action model is a single-coalition-first action model, but not vice versa.*

The proof for this result can be found in [3].

Remarks Ågotnes, Goranko, and Jamroga [12] defined *tree-like concurrent game models*, which are different from tree-like grand-coalition-first action SID-models defined here. For the former, it is only required that for every state, there is a unique *computation*, which is a sequence of states, from the root to the state.

5.2 Tree-Like Single-Coalition-First Neighborhood Models

Definition 21 (Histories in single-coalition-first neighborhood models). *Let* S-NM $= ($ ST, suc, $\{\text{nei}_a \mid a \in$ AG$\},$ label$)$ *be a single-coalition-first neighborhood model, and $\{\text{nei}_C \mid C \subseteq$ AG$\}$ be the set of neighborhood functions of* S-NM.

*For every $C \subseteq$ AG, a finite sequence $\theta_C = (s_0, Y_1, s_1, \ldots, Y_n, s_n)$, where every s_i is a state and every Y_i is a set of states, is called a C-**history** from s_0 to s_n if for every i such that $0 \le i < n$, $Y_{i+1} \in \text{nei}_C(s_i)$ and $s_{i+1} \in Y_{i+1}$.*

*Specially, for evey $C \subseteq$ AG and $s \in$ ST, s is called a C-**history** from s to s.*

Definition 22 (Tree-like single-coalition-first neighborhood models). *Let* S-NM $= ($ ST, suc, $\{\text{nei}_a \mid a \in$ AG$\},$ label$)$ *be a single-coalition-first neighborhood model.*

We say S-NM *is a **tree-like model** if there is a state r of* S-NM *such that for every $a \in$ AG and $s \in$ ST, there is a unique a-history from r to s.*

The following result offers an alternative definition of tree-like single-coalition-first neighborhood models.

Theorem 11. *Let* S-NM $= ($ ST, suc, $\{\text{nei}_a \mid a \in$ AG$\},$ label$)$ *be a single-coalition-first neighborhood model, and $\{\text{nei}_C \mid C \subseteq$ AG$\}$ be the class of neighborhood functions of* S-NM.

The following two conditions are equivalent:

(1) there is a state r of S-NM *such that for every $a \in$ AG and $s \in$ ST, there is an unique a-history from r to s;*

(2) there is a state r of S-NM such that for every $C \subseteq$ AG and $s \in$ ST, there is an unique C-history from r to s.

The proof for this result can be found in [3].

By Theorem 9, tree-like grand-coalition-first action models can be equivalently defined in three different ways, which are respectively concerned with all agents, all coalitions, and the grand coalition. It would be expected that the following condition is equivalent to the two conditions in Theorem 11: *there is a state r of S-NM such that for every state $s \in$ ST, there is a unique AG-history from r to s.* In fact, this is not the case. We refer to [3] for a counterexample.

5.3 Representation of Tree-Like Grand-Coalition-First Action Models by Tee-Like Single-Coalition-First Neighborhood Models

Theorem 12. *Every tree-like grand-coalition-first action model is z-representable by a tree-like single-coalition-first neighborhood model.*

Proof. Let G-AM be a tree-like grand-coalition-first action model. By Theorem 10, G-AM is a tree-like single-coalition-first action model. Then, it is easy to show that G-AM is z-representable by a tree-like single-coalition-first neighborhood model.

Theorem 13. *Every tree-like single-coalition-first neighborhood model z-represents a tree-like grand-coalition-first action model.*

Proof. Let S-NM $=$ (ST, suc, $\{\text{nei}_a \mid a \in \text{AG}\}$, label) be a tree-like single-coalition-first neighborhood model. Define a single-coalition-first action model S-AM $=$ (ST, AC, suc, $\{\text{out}_a \mid a \in \text{AG}\}$, label) as in the proof for Theorem 6. As shown there, S-NM z-represents S-AM. It is easy to check that S-AM is tree-like. By Theorem 4, S-AM is a grand-coalition-first action model.

The following result follows from Theorems 12, 13, and 7.

Theorem 14. (Representation of the class of tree-like grand-coalition-first action X-models by the class of tree-like single-coalition-first neighborhood X-models). *For every $X \in$ ES, the class of tree-like grand-coalition-first action X-models is z-representable by the class of tree-like single-coalition-first neighborhood X-models.*

6 Each of Those Eight Coalition Logics is Determined by These Four Kinds of Models, Too

Theorem 15. *Let $X \in$ ES and (G-AM, s) be a pointed grand-coalition-first action X-model.*
There is a pointed tree-like grand-coalition-first action X-model (G-AM$'$, s') such that for all $\phi \in \Phi$, G-AM, $s \Vdash \phi$ if and only if G-AM$'$, $s' \Vdash \phi$.

The proof for this result can be found in [3].

Theorem 16. *For every* X ∈ ES *and* $\phi \in \Phi$, *the following statements are equivalent:*

*(1) ϕ is valid with respect to the class of **grand-coalition-first action** X-models;*

*(2) ϕ is valid with respect to the class of **single-coalition-first action** X-models;*

*(3) ϕ is valid with respect to the class of **single-coalition-first neighborhood** X-models;*

*(4) ϕ is valid with respect to the class of **tree-like grand-coalition-first action** X-models;*

*(5) ϕ is valid with respect to the class of **tree-like single-coalition-first neighborhood** X-models.*

Proof. By Theorem 8 and Theorem 1, (2) and (3) are equivalent. By Theorem 14 and Theorem 1, (4) and (5) are equivalent. It suffices to show that (1), (2), and (4) are equivalent. By Theorem 4, (1) implies (2). By Theorem 10, (2) implies (4). By Theorem 15, (4) implies (1). Therefore, (1), (2), and (4) are equivalent.

7 Conclusion

Li and Ju [8,9] proposed eight coalition logics based on grand-coalition-first action models. In this work, we show that each of them is determined by four other kinds of models, that is, single-coalition-first action models, single-coalition-first neighborhood models, tree-like grand-coalition-first action models, and tree-like single-coalition-first neighborhood models. The four kinds of models make good sense for representing coalitional powers. One type of further work worth doing is to describe these models using different languages than the language of coalition logic.

Acknowledgments. Thanks go to Thomas Ågotnes, Valentin Goranko, and the audience of a logic seminar at Beijing Normal University.

Disclosure of Interests. The authors have no competing interests to declare that are relevant to the content of this article.

References

1. Abdou, J.: Rectangularity and tightness: a normal form characterization of perfect information extensive game forms. Math. Oper. Res. **23**(3), 553–567 (1998)
2. Alur, R., Henzinger, T.A., Kupferman, O.: Alternating-time temporal logic. In: Lecture Notes in Computer Science, vol. 1536, pp. 23–60. Springer-Verlag (1998)
3. Chen, Z., Ju, F.: Each of those eight coalition logics is also determined by six other kinds of models (2025). https://arxiv.org/abs/2501.05466

4. Goranko, V., Jamroga, W.: Comparing semantics of logics for multi-agent systems. Synthese **139**(2), 241–280 (2004)
5. Goranko, V., Jamroga, W., Turrini, P.: Strategic games and truly playable effectivity functions. J. Autonomous Agents Multi-Agent Syst. **26**(2), 288–314 (2013)
6. Harrenstein, P., van der Hoek, W., Meyer, J.J., Witteveen, C.: Boolean games. In: Benthem, J.V. (ed.) Proceedings of the 8th Conference on Theoretical Aspects of Rationality and Knowledge, pp. 287–298. Morgan Kaufmann Publishers Inc. (2001)
7. Hoek, W.v.d., Wooldridge, M.: On the logic of cooperation and propositional control. Artif. Intell. **164**(1), 81–119 (2005)
8. Li, Y., Ju, F.: Completeness of coalition logics with seriality, independence of agents, or determinism (2024). https://arxiv.org/abs/2409.14635
9. Li, Y., Ju, F.: A minimal coalition logic (2024). https://arxiv.org/abs/2403.14704
10. Pauly, M.: Logic for social software (2001), PhD thesis, University of Amsterdam
11. Pauly, M.: A modal logic for coalitional power in games. J. Log. Comput. **12**(1), 149–166 (2002)
12. Ågotnes, T., Goranko, V., Jamroga, W.: Alternating-time temporal logics with irrevocable strategies. In: Samet, D. (ed.) Proceedings of the 11th International Conference on Theoretical Aspects of Rationality and Knowledge (TARK XI), pp. 15–24. Presses Universitaires de Louvain (2007)
13. Shi, C., Wang, W.: Representation theorem for coalition logic without superadditivity (2024), manuscript

Incomplete Higher-Order Abstract Argumentation Frameworks

Sylvie Doutre[1], Marie-Christine Lagasquie-Schiex[2](✉),
Jean-Guy Mailly[1], and Antonio Yuste-Ginel[3]

[1] IRIT, Université Toulouse Capitole, CNRS, Toulouse INP, UTC, Toulouse, France
{doutre,mailly}@irit.fr
[2] IRIT, Université de Toulouse, CNRS, Toulouse INP, UT, Toulouse, France
lagasq@irit.fr
[3] Complutense University of Madrid (UCM), Madrid, Spain
antoyust@ucm.es

Abstract. We propose the combination of two known extensions of Dung's abstract Argumentation Frameworks (AFs): Incomplete Argumentation Frameworks (IAFs), where the existence of arguments and attacks may be uncertain, and Higher-Order Argumentation Frameworks (HOAFs), where attacks can be directed not only towards arguments but also towards attacks. As a result, we obtain Incomplete Higher-Order Argumentation Frameworks (IHOAFs), where attacks on attacks can also be uncertain. We take some important initial steps in the formal understanding of this novel framework by providing: (i) the definition of a conservative notion of completion, the hypothetical removal of uncertainty used to reason about argument acceptability in other formalisms for incomplete argumentation; (ii) complexity results for argument acceptability problems; (iii) an analysis of the previous two points in a well-behaved variant of dynamic logic.

Keywords: Abstract Argumentation · Higher-Order Attacks · Incompleteness

1 Introduction

Formal argumentation is a well-established, interdisciplinary field of research at the intersection of computer sciences, mathematics, linguistics and philosophy. The mathematical modelling of argumentative phenomena developed in this field is deeply influenced by Dung's Abstract Frameworks (AFs) [18]: These are directed graphs where nodes stand for arguments and edges stand for an attack relation among them. This way of approaching argumentation is *abstract*, as one ignores the nature, internal structure and origin of arguments and their interactions in order to focus on more general, dialectical aspects. In this vein, different semantics are used for selecting *extensions* from a given AF, i.e. sets of arguments considered jointly acceptable because they satisfy some intuitive requirements.

One of the reasons for the extreme popularity of Dung's framework is probably its simplicity. However, this feature also renders the approach unsuitable for dealing with more refined argumentative notions that, beyond attacks and together with them, have a crucial impact on arguments' acceptability. This is why, after Dung's work, the research community developed a well-nourished bunch of extensions of his model. Such extensions can be organised into, at least, two big categories. The first one concerns *the addition of new kinds of interactions between arguments*: for instance, *support relations* (representing a "positive" interaction between arguments; [10,31,33]), *higher-order frameworks* (the targets of the interactions can be other interactions, and not only arguments; [5,7,11]), or *collective interactions* (the source of the interactions can be a set of arguments and not only a single one; [29]). The second category consists in *the addition of uncertainty to the model*, either by the use of *weights and preferences over arguments and interactions* [2,6,35], or by considering the uncertainty about the *presence of the different elements* (both in a qualitative [9,27] and in a probabilistic fashion [22]). Argumentation frameworks with qualitative uncertainty are particularly useful in applications where they "may arise as intermediate states in an elicitation process, or when merging different beliefs about an argumentation framework's state, or in cases where complete information cannot be obtained" [9].

The intense interest that these extensions of AFs have awakened among formal argumentation practitioners is witnessed by the independent and synchronous study of the combination of two of these models, taking into account both support relations and qualitative uncertainty, leading to the so-called *Incomplete Bipolar Argumentation Frameworks* (IBAFs) [20,24]. In this paper, we pursue a different extension of AFs, suitable for the simultaneous modelling of higher-order attacks (attacks on attacks) and qualitative uncertainty, resulting in *Incomplete Higher-Order Argumentation Frameworks* (IHOAFs). Our medium-term objective is to extend IHOAFs by incorporating bipolarity, possibly followed by collective interactions, to develop a general argumentation framework that addresses qualitative uncertainty. This contribution represents a first step toward that goal.

Let us start with illustrating the kind of situation that motivates the development and study of IHOAFs through the following simple example:

Example 1. A discussion takes place between friends to decide what to do during the day:

a : "We should go to the beach this afternoon because it is sunny."
b : "Sam told me that it will rain later." (b attacks a)
c : "Yes, but it will not last according to yesterday's weather forecast." (c attacks the attack from b to a)

Argument c attacks neither a nor b, but the fact that b attacks a: This is an attack on an attack. An extension of Dung's framework with *higher-order attacks* (HOAF) is required to model such an example. Moreover, given how imprecise the weather forecast can be (even more when it is yesterday's forecast), argument

c may be uncertain and disregarded. In addition, even short, rain may prevent any outing to the beach, so the attack from c to the attack from b to a may be disregarded. Such a situation regarding argument c and the attack it is at the source of requires the addition of *uncertainty* regarding the presence of elements in the model, that is, an IHOAF. □

Following the presentation of the background (see Sect. 2), this paper provides the first study of IHOAFs through several contributions: (i) in Sect. 3, we formally define IHOAFs and introduce a notion of completion (the hypothetical removal of uncertainty in incomplete frameworks to facilitate reasoning about argument or interaction acceptability); (ii) also in Sect. 3, we analyze the computational complexity of reasoning about arguments and attacks acceptability problems in IHOAFs; (iii) in Sect. 4, we encode these problems using the Dynamic Logic of Propositional Assignments (DL-PA), a well-behaved variant of propositional dynamic logic that has recently proven effective for reasoning about argumentation. Finally, Sect. 5 provides a discussion and conclusion, outlining future perspectives.

2 Background

2.1 Abstract Argumentation Frameworks Without Uncertainty

Let $\mathbf{A}$ be an infinite countable set of arguments. The main definition of an *Abstract Argumentation Framework* has been proposed by Dung in [18]:

Definition 1 (Basic Abstract Argumentation Framework - AF). *An Abstract Argumentation Framework (AF) is a pair $\mathcal{F} = (\mathcal{A}, \mathcal{R})$ with $\mathcal{A} \subseteq \mathbf{A}$ the finite set of arguments and $\mathcal{R} \subseteq \mathcal{A} \times \mathcal{A}$ the set of attacks. For $a, b \in \mathcal{A}$, we say that a attacks b if $(a, b) \in \mathcal{R}$ (and we sometimes use the infix notation $a\mathcal{R}b$). If $(a, b) \in \mathcal{R}$ and b attacks some $c \in \mathcal{A}$, then a defends c against b. Similarly, a set $S \subseteq \mathcal{A}$ attacks (resp. defends) an argument b if there is some $a \in S$ that attacks b (resp. if, for any $a\mathcal{R}b$, there is $c \in S$ that defends b against a).*

Let us consider Example 1 without taking into account argument c: arguments b and a and their relationship can be represented by the following directed graph (the arguments are given in round nodes and the simple plain arrow represents the attack from b to a):

$$b \longrightarrow a$$

We classically use the concept of *extensions*, proposed by Dung [18], for evaluating the acceptability of arguments, i.e. sets of collectively acceptable arguments. The usual semantics are based on two main principles: conflict-freeness and admissibility.

Definition 2 (Conflict-Freeness and Admissibility in AFs). *Given $\mathcal{F} = (\mathcal{A}, \mathcal{R})$ an AF, the set $E \subseteq \mathcal{A}$ is conflict-free iff $\forall a, b \in E$, $(a, b) \notin \mathcal{R}$; $a \in \mathcal{A}$ is acceptable w.r.t. E iff E defends a; E is admissible iff it is conflict-free and $\forall a \in E$, E defends a.*

Four main semantics are proposed by Dung (see more details in [4,18]):

Definition 3 (Extensions for an AF). *Given $\mathcal{F} = (\mathcal{A}, \mathcal{R})$ an AF. Let $E \subseteq \mathcal{A}$ be an admissible set of $\mathcal{F}$. E is:*

- *a complete extension for $\mathcal{F}$ iff E contains all the arguments that it defends;*
- *a preferred extension for $\mathcal{F}$ iff E is a $\subseteq$-maximal admissible set;*
- *a grounded extension for $\mathcal{F}$ iff E is a $\subseteq$-minimal complete extension;*
- *and a stable extension for $\mathcal{F}$ iff $\forall a \in \mathcal{A} \setminus E$, E attacks a.*

We use $\mathsf{co}(\mathcal{F})$, $\mathsf{pr}(\mathcal{F})$, $\mathsf{gr}(\mathcal{F})$ and $\mathsf{st}(\mathcal{F})$ for the sets of (resp.) complete, preferred, grounded and stable extensions of $\mathcal{F}$.

Let $x \in \mathcal{A}$ and $\sigma \in \{\mathsf{co}, \mathsf{pr}, \mathsf{gr}, \mathsf{st}\}$ be a semantics. We say that x is credulously (resp. skeptically) accepted by σ if and only if $\exists E \in \sigma(\mathcal{F})$ such that (resp. $\forall E \in \sigma(\mathcal{F})$) $x \in E$.

2.2 Incomplete Argumentation Frameworks

Incomplete AFs are AFs with qualitative uncertainty about the presence of some arguments or attacks [8,9,13,27]. Formally:

Definition 4 (Incomplete Argumentation Framework - IAF). *An Incomplete Argumentation Framework (IAF) is a tuple $\mathcal{I} = (\mathcal{A}, \mathcal{A}^?, \mathcal{R}, \mathcal{R}^?)$ where:*

- *$\mathcal{A} \subseteq \mathbf{A}$ is the finite set of certain arguments;*
- *$\mathcal{A}^? \subseteq \mathbf{A}$ is the finite set of uncertain arguments;*
- *$\mathcal{R} \subseteq (\mathcal{A} \cup \mathcal{A}^?) \times (\mathcal{A} \cup \mathcal{A}^?)$ is the set of certain attacks;*
- *and $\mathcal{R}^? \subseteq (\mathcal{A} \cup \mathcal{A}^?) \times (\mathcal{A} \cup \mathcal{A}^?)$ is the set of uncertain attacks.*

$\mathcal{A}$ and $\mathcal{A}^?$ are disjoint sets of arguments, and $\mathcal{R}$, $\mathcal{R}^?$ are disjoint sets of attacks.

Intuitively, $\mathcal{A}$ and $\mathcal{R}$ correspond, respectively, to arguments and attacks that certainly exist, while $\mathcal{A}^?$ and $\mathcal{R}^?$ are those that may (or may not) exist. In a multi-agent, adversarial perspective, $\mathcal{A}$ and $\mathcal{R}$ can be understood as the arguments and attacks that an agent knows her opponent is aware of; while $\mathcal{A}^?$ and $\mathcal{R}^?$ are the arguments and attacks such that the agent does not know whether her opponent entertains. This way of modelling uncertainty has a tight connection to some simple epistemic logics of knowing whether (see [21]). Note that a certain attack can exist between two uncertain arguments (these are sometimes called *conditionally certain* attacks); that means that, if the agent is *aware of these arguments*, then the attack is certain. Reasoning about IAFs is usually made through the notion of completion, i.e. a classical AF that represents a "possible world" w.r.t. the uncertain information encoded in the IAF. Formally:

Definition 5 (Completion for an IAF). *Given $\mathcal{I} = (\mathcal{A}, \mathcal{A}^?, \mathcal{R}, \mathcal{R}^?)$ an IAF, a completion of $\mathcal{I}$ is an AF $(\mathcal{A}_c, \mathcal{R}_c)$ such that $\mathcal{A} \subseteq \mathcal{A}_c \subseteq \mathcal{A} \cup \mathcal{A}^?$ and $\mathcal{R} \cap (\mathcal{A}_c \times \mathcal{A}_c) \subseteq \mathcal{R}_c \subseteq (\mathcal{R} \cup \mathcal{R}^?) \cap (\mathcal{A}_c \times \mathcal{A}_c)$.*

Example 2. Consider $\mathcal{I} = (\mathcal{A}, \mathcal{A}^?, \mathcal{R}, \mathcal{R}^?)$ depicted in column 1 of the figure below, where $\mathcal{A} = \{a, b\}$ (plain nodes), $\mathcal{A}^? = \{c\}$ (dashed node), $\mathcal{R} = \{(c, b)\}$ (plain edge) and $\mathcal{R}^? = \{(b, a)\}$ (dashed edge). It means that the arguments a and b certainly exist, and there is uncertainty regarding the existence of the attack (b, a). Moreover, the argument c is uncertain, but if it exists then the attack (c, b) also exists.

Figures in columns 2 to 5 depict the completions of $\mathcal{I}$.

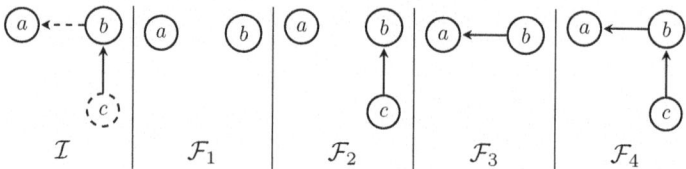

$\mathcal{F}_1$ shows the situation where no uncertain elements actually exist, while $\mathcal{F}_4$ shows the opposite situation (all the uncertain elements appear). $\mathcal{F}_2$ and $\mathcal{F}_3$ show the intermediate situations, where only one uncertain element (either the argument c, or the attack (b, a)) exists. □

Reasoning tasks like credulous (or skeptical) acceptance or verification are thus redefined over completions [8,9,27]. Hence, each classical task has two variants: the possible view (the property holds in some completion) and the necessary view (the property holds in each completion). These reasoning tasks are, in most cases, computationally harder than their counterpart for standard AFs (under the usual assumption that the polynomial hierarchy does not collapse) [8,9]. This can be explained by the exponential number of completions. For instance, the acceptance problems for the grounded semantics are NP or coNP-complete in the case of IAFs whereas it is P-complete for AFs (see [8,27] for more details).

2.3 Higher-Order Argumentation Frameworks

Higher-Order Argumentation Frameworks introduced by Barringer et al. [7] are argumentation frameworks in which attacks can target other attacks. To define such a framework, we need to consider that **A** corresponds to an infinite countable set of *argument names*, whose elements are denoted using small-case Latin letters; and to suppose the existence of an infinite countable set of *attack names* **R**, disjoint with **A**, whose elements are denoted using small-case Greek letters.

Note that, since attacks are now identified from names, we must determine their source and their target and we also must establish the relation between an attack and the couple of its source and target using the following notation:

Notation 1. *Let $\mathcal{R} \subseteq \mathbf{R}$. Let $\alpha \in \mathcal{R}$. $\mathbf{v}(\alpha)$ denotes the pair giving the source and the target of α. For $X \subseteq \mathcal{R}$, $\mathbf{v}(X) = \{\mathbf{v}(\alpha) | \alpha \in X\}$.*

Then the basic definition for Higher-Order Argumentation Frameworks is the following:

Definition 6 (Higher-Order Argumentation Framework - HOAF). *A Higher-Order Abstract Argumentation Framework (HOAF) is a tuple $\mathcal{H} = (\mathcal{A}, \mathcal{R}, \mathbf{src}, \mathbf{trg})$ such that:*

- $\mathcal{A}$ is a finite set of argument names $(\mathcal{A} \subseteq \mathbf{A})$.
- $\mathcal{R}$ is a finite set of attack names $(\mathcal{R} \subseteq \mathbf{R})$.[1]
- **src** : $\mathcal{R} \to \mathcal{A}$ is the function that assigns a source to each attack name.
- **trg** : $\mathcal{R} \to \mathcal{A} \cup \mathcal{R}$ is the function that assigns a target to each attack name.[2]

Moreover, $\forall \alpha, \beta \in \mathcal{R}$, $\alpha \neq \beta$ implies $\mathbf{v}(\alpha) \neq \mathbf{v}(\beta)$.[3,4]

Example 3. To illustrate the previous definition, let us consider the following HOAF (argument names are given in round nodes whereas attack names are the labels on the corresponding arrows) which corresponds to the framework of Example 1 given in the introduction (the discussion about what to do today), without the uncertainty about the presence of elements:

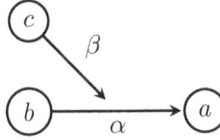

Here we have three arguments (a, b and c) and two attacks (α and β). α is a first-order attack (it targets the argument a) whereas β is a second-order attack (it targets α).

□

This kind of framework has been studied from different angles: Extended Argumentation Frameworks (EAF) by Modgil [28]; Argumentation Frameworks with Recursive Attacks (AFRA) by Baroni et al. [5]; and Recursive Argumentation Frameworks (RAF) by Cayrol et al. [12]. Each approach has produced appropriate but different semantics. In this paper, we only consider the RAF case, leaving the other cases for future work.

Within the RAF approach, semantics are based on the notion of *structure*, which replaces the extensions of [18], and extended versions of acceptability and conflict-freeness (see [12]).

Definition 7 (Acceptability and Conflict-Freeness in RAF). *Let $\mathcal{H} = (\mathcal{A}, \mathcal{R}, \mathbf{src}, \mathbf{trg})$ be an HOAF. Let $x \in \mathcal{A} \cup \mathcal{R}$, $S \subseteq \mathcal{A}$ and $\Gamma \subseteq \mathcal{R}$. Let $U = (S, \Gamma)$. U is called a structure of $\mathcal{H}$ and:*

- *U defeats x iff $\exists \alpha \in \Gamma$ such that $\mathbf{src}(\alpha) \in S$ and $\mathbf{trg}(\alpha) = x$.*
- *x is acceptable w.r.t. U iff $\forall \alpha \in \mathcal{R}$, if $\mathbf{trg}(\alpha) = x$, then $\exists \beta \in \Gamma$ such that $\mathbf{src}(\beta) \in S$ and either $\mathbf{trg}(\beta) = \alpha$ or $\mathbf{trg}(\beta) = \mathbf{src}(\alpha)$. $\mathrm{Acc}(U)$ is the set of acceptable elements w.r.t. U.*
- *U is conflict-free iff $\nexists \alpha \in \Gamma$ such that $\mathbf{src}(\alpha) \in S$ and $\mathbf{trg}(\alpha) \in S \cup \Gamma$.*

Structure-based semantics are defined as shown below (see [12]).

---

[1] Since $\mathbf{A}$ and $\mathbf{R}$ are disjoint, we also have $\mathcal{A} \cap \mathcal{R} = \varnothing$.
[2] Note that this definition allows self-attacking attacks (*i.e.* attacks α such that $\mathbf{trg}(\alpha) = \alpha$) even if the intuition behind this case is not clear.
[3] Note that, following the previous definition and the notation of $\mathbf{v}$, we have: $\forall \alpha \in \mathcal{R}$, $\mathbf{v}(\alpha) = (\mathbf{src}(\alpha), \mathbf{trg}(\alpha))$.
[4] This constraint avoids the fact that two attacks with different names could have the same source and the same target. This has been evoked in [12] as the possibility of having similar attacks in different contexts. Here we do not consider this possibility.

Definition 8 (Semantics for RAF). *Let* $\mathcal{H} = (\mathcal{A}, \mathcal{R}, \text{src}, \text{trg})$, $U = (S, \Gamma)$ *be a structure of* $\mathcal{H}$.

- U *is* complete *iff U is conflict-free and* $\text{Acc}(U) = S \cup \Gamma$.
- U *is* preferred *iff U is a $\subseteq$-maximal conflict-free structure such that* $S \cup \Gamma \subseteq \text{Acc}(U)$.
- U *is* grounded *iff U is the $\subseteq$-minimal complete structure.*
- U *is* stable *iff U is conflict-free and defeats any element* $x \in (\mathcal{A} \cup \mathcal{R}) \setminus (S \cup \Gamma)$.

Let $\sigma \in \{\text{co}, \text{pr}, \text{gr}, \text{st}\}$ be a semantics, $\sigma(\mathcal{H})$ denotes the set of structures of $\mathcal{H}$.

Note that the following proposition holds:

Proposition 1. *Let $\mathcal{H}$ be an HOAF. The preferred structures of $\mathcal{H}$ are its $\subseteq$-maximal complete structures, and the grounded structure is unique.*

Example 4. In the framework of Example 3, $(\{a, b, c\}, \{\beta\})$ is the unique complete, preferred, grounded and stable structure. Note that, even if a is attacked by b, a and b can be accepted together since this attack is invalidated by β. □

3 Incomplete HOAFs: Definitions and Complexity

A first step for defining incompleteness for enriched AFs has been done by [20,24] considering only the addition of a support relation whose elements might be uncertain. Here, we want to take into account qualitative uncertainty together with another kind of enrichment: higher-order attacks.

Definition 9 (Incomplete HOAF - IHOAF). *An* Incomplete Higher-Order Argumentation Framework (IHOAF) *is a tuple* $\mathcal{IH} = (\mathcal{A}, \mathcal{A}^?, \mathcal{R}, \mathcal{R}^?, \textbf{src}, \textbf{trg})$ *where:*

- $\mathcal{A}$ *is the finite set of* certain argument names *($\mathcal{A} \subseteq \mathbf{A}$).*
- $\mathcal{A}^?$ *is the finite set of* uncertain argument names *($\mathcal{A}^? \subseteq \mathbf{A}$).*
- $\mathcal{R}$ *is the finite set of* certain attack names *($\mathcal{R} \subseteq \mathbf{R}$).*
- $\mathcal{R}^?$ *is the finite set of* uncertain attack names *($\mathcal{R}^? \subseteq \mathbf{R}$).*
- $\textbf{src} : (\mathcal{R} \cup \mathcal{R}^?) \to (\mathcal{A} \cup \mathcal{A}^?)$ *is the* source function.
- $\textbf{trg} : (\mathcal{R} \cup \mathcal{R}^?) \to (\mathcal{A} \cup \mathcal{A}^? \cup \mathcal{R} \cup \mathcal{R}^?)$ *is the* target function.

We also assume that $X \cap X^? = \emptyset$, for $X \in \{\mathcal{A}, \mathcal{R}\}$; and that for every $\alpha, \beta \in (\mathcal{R} \cup \mathcal{R}^?)$, $\alpha \neq \beta$ implies $\mathbf{v}(\alpha) \neq \mathbf{v}(\beta)$.

The previous definition is a neat combination of Definition 4 and Definition 6. It is conservative w.r.t. both definitions in the following sense. If $\textbf{trg} : (\mathcal{R} \cup \mathcal{R}^?) \to (\mathcal{A} \cup \mathcal{A}^?)$, then $\mathcal{IH}$ is reduced to an IAF (only first-order attacks). Analogously, if $\mathcal{A}^? = \mathcal{R}^? = \emptyset$, then we obtain an HOAF (without uncertainty).

Table 1 provides a recap of the types of (enriched) abstract argumentation frameworks which are covered by the IHOAF.

We are aware that one could also consider **src** and/or **trg** to be (partly) uncertain, but this option faces at least two problems. Technically, there is no simple way of adapting the forthcoming notion of completion to uncertain source and target functions. Conceptually, it seems way less common/natural than our current choice. Consequently, this case is left for potential future work.

Table 1. The frameworks which are covered by an IHOAF $\mathcal{IH} = (\mathcal{A}, \mathcal{A}^?, \mathcal{R}, \mathcal{R}^?, \textbf{src}, \textbf{trg})$. For each framework, the sets which are not mentioned are empty.

Name	Definition	Sets	**src** :	**trg** :
AF	1	$\mathcal{A}, \mathcal{R}$	$\mathcal{R} \to \mathcal{A}$	$\mathcal{R} \to \mathcal{A}$
HOAF	6	$\mathcal{A}, \mathcal{R}$	$\mathcal{R} \to \mathcal{A}$	$\mathcal{R} \to (\mathcal{A} \cup \mathcal{R})$
IAF	4	$\mathcal{A}, \mathcal{A}^?, \mathcal{R}, \mathcal{R}^?$	$(\mathcal{R} \cup \mathcal{R}^?) \to (\mathcal{A} \cup \mathcal{A}^?)$	$(\mathcal{R} \cup \mathcal{R}^?) \to (\mathcal{A} \cup \mathcal{A}^?)$
IHOAF	9	$\mathcal{A}, \mathcal{A}^?, \mathcal{R}, \mathcal{R}^?$	$(\mathcal{R} \cup \mathcal{R}^?) \to (\mathcal{A} \cup \mathcal{A}^?)$	$(\mathcal{R} \cup \mathcal{R}^?) \to (\mathcal{A} \cup \mathcal{A}^? \cup \mathcal{R} \cup \mathcal{R}^?)$

The next step is the definition of the notion of completion. But before giving a precise definition, we must analyse the impact of higher-order attacks on the notion of completion. Thus, let us revisit the HOAF used in Example 3 and imagine what should intuitively be the possible completions if each one of the elements is uncertain. Notice that the arguments of $\mathcal{A}$ (resp. $\mathcal{A}^?$) are represented with plain (resp. dashed) nodes, the attacks of $\mathcal{R}$ (resp. $\mathcal{R}^?$) with plain (resp. dashed) edges with the attack name as a label on the arrow.

1. Either c is uncertain (all the other elements being certain):

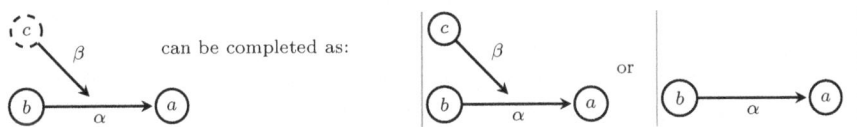

2. Or β is uncertain (all the other elements being certain):

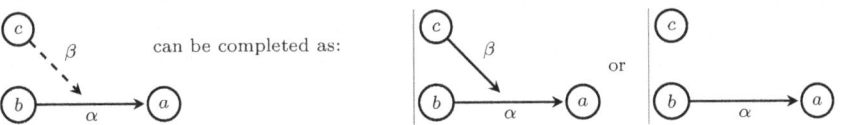

3. Or α is uncertain (all the other elements being certain):

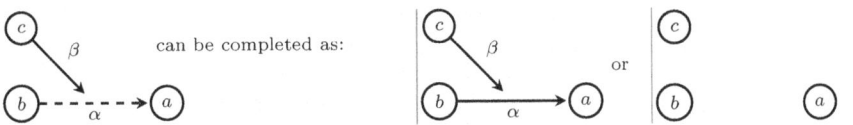

4. Or a is uncertain (all the other elements being certain):

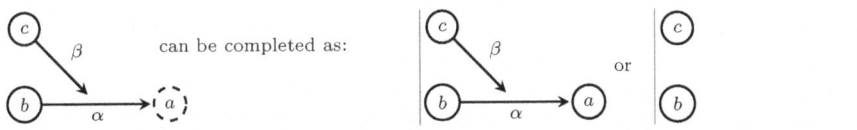

5. Or b is uncertain (all the other elements being certain):

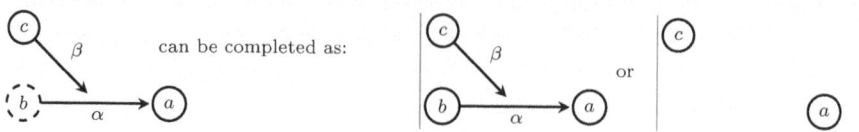

The first interesting point is that, in the last two cases, we have a kind of "removal in cascade": the removal of a (or b) implies the removal of the attack α from b to a and so the removal of the attack β targeting α. Hence, the following question emerges: how to propagate the removal through the graph when computing the completions since, potentially, a given completion could be obtained by several chains of removal?

Another remark is that, here, only one kind of completion seems useful, because there is no semantic notion that should intuitively interact with the removal of uncertainty; unlike what happens with incomplete bipolar AFs [24].[5]

Back to Example 1, where c and β are both uncertain, it can be noticed that the three possible completions are the ones given in case 1 and case 2.

Following the previous discussion, the definition for completions is:

Definition 10 (IHOAF Completions). *Let* $\mathcal{IH} = (\mathcal{A}, \mathcal{A}^?, \mathcal{R}, \mathcal{R}^?, \mathbf{src}, \mathbf{trg})$ *be an IHOAF. A completion of* $\mathcal{IH}$ *is any HOAF* $\mathcal{H} = (\mathcal{A}_c, \mathcal{R}_c, \mathbf{src}_c, \mathbf{trg}_c)$ *with:*

- $\mathcal{A} \subseteq \mathcal{A}_c \subseteq (\mathcal{A} \cup \mathcal{A}^?)$ *and* $\mathcal{R}_c \subseteq (\mathcal{R} \cup \mathcal{R}^?)$.
- $\mathbf{v}(\mathcal{R}) \cap (\mathcal{A}_c \times (\mathcal{A}_c \cup \mathcal{R}_c)) \subseteq \mathbf{v}(\mathcal{R}_c) \subseteq (\mathbf{v}(\mathcal{R} \cup \mathcal{R}^?)) \cap (\mathcal{A}_c \times (\mathcal{A}_c \cup \mathcal{R}_c))$.
- $\mathbf{src}_c = \mathbf{src} \cap (\mathcal{R}_c \times \mathcal{A}_c)$.
- $\mathbf{trg}_c = \mathbf{trg} \cap (\mathcal{R}_c \times (\mathcal{A}_c \cup \mathcal{R}_c))$.

We denote as completions($\mathcal{IH}$) *the set of all completions of* $\mathcal{IH}$.

Note that the second constraint in Definition 10 can be equivalently replaced by:

1. $\forall \alpha \in \mathcal{R}$, $\alpha \in \mathcal{R}_c$ iff $\mathbf{src}(\alpha) \in \mathcal{A}_c$ and $\mathbf{trg}(\alpha) \in \mathcal{A}_c \cup \mathcal{R}_c$, and
2. $\forall \alpha \in \mathcal{R}^?$, $\alpha \in \mathcal{R}_c$ implies that $\mathbf{src}(\alpha) \in \mathcal{A}_c$ and $\mathbf{trg}(\alpha) \in \mathcal{A}_c \cup \mathcal{R}_c$.

The following proposition holds trivially, showing that our notion of completion is conservative w.r.t. the standard one (Definition 5):

Proposition 2. *Let* $\mathcal{IH} = (\mathcal{A}, \mathcal{A}^?, \mathcal{R}, \mathcal{R}^?, \mathbf{src}, \mathbf{trg})$ *be an IHOAF, if* $\mathbf{trg} : \mathcal{R} \cup \mathcal{R}^? \to \mathcal{A} \cup \mathcal{A}^?$, *then* completions($\mathcal{IH}$) = completions($\mathcal{A}, \mathcal{A}^?, \mathbf{v}(\mathcal{R}), \mathbf{v}(\mathcal{R}^?)$).

Using these completions, we can define semantics for IHOAFs:

Definition 11 (IHOAF structures). *Let* $\mathcal{IH} = (\mathcal{A}, \mathcal{A}^?, \mathcal{R}, \mathcal{R}^?, \mathbf{src}, \mathbf{trg})$ *be an IHOAF. We denote as* $\sigma(\mathcal{IH})$ *the set of all σ-structures of* $\mathcal{IH}$ *under the semantics σ ($\sigma \in \{\mathsf{pr}, \mathsf{gr}, \mathsf{co}, \mathsf{st}\}$), and define it as* $\sigma(\mathcal{IH}) = \{(S, \Gamma) \in 2^{(\mathcal{A} \cup \mathcal{A}^?)} \times 2^{(\mathcal{R} \cup \mathcal{R}^?)} | \exists \mathcal{H} \in$ completions($\mathcal{IH}$) *and* $(S, \Gamma) \in \sigma(\mathcal{H})\}$.

---

[5] In the case of IBAFs, three types of completion can be defined (see [24]).

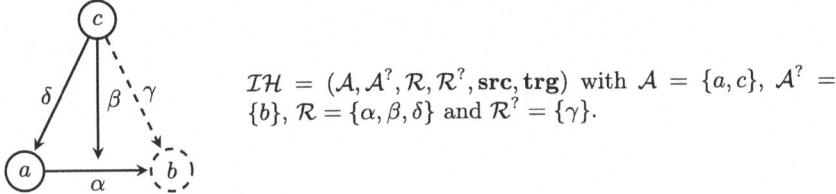

$\mathcal{IH} = (\mathcal{A}, \mathcal{A}^?, \mathcal{R}, \mathcal{R}^?, \text{src}, \text{trg})$ with $\mathcal{A} = \{a, c\}$, $\mathcal{A}^? = \{b\}$, $\mathcal{R} = \{\alpha, \beta, \delta\}$ and $\mathcal{R}^? = \{\gamma\}$.

Fig. 1. An Example of a IHOAF $\mathcal{IH}$

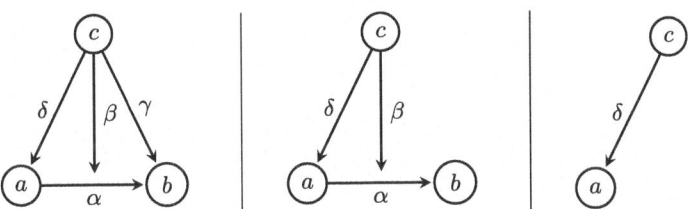

Fig. 2. Three completions for the IHOAF $\mathcal{IH}$

Example 5. In the framework of Example 1 where both c and β are uncertain, each of the 3 possible completions has a unique preferred, grounded, stable and complete structure; thus, given $\sigma \in \{\text{co}, \text{pr}, \text{gr}, \text{st}\}$, $\sigma(\mathcal{IH}) = \{(\{a,b,c\}, \{\beta\}), (\{b\}, \{\alpha\}), (\{b,c\}, \{\alpha\})\}$. □

The following example illustrates the adequacy of the constraints assumed in the definition of completion.

Example 6. Let us consider the IHOAF $\mathcal{IH}$ depicted in Fig. 1 in which the arguments a and c certainly exist, whereas the existence of the argument b is uncertain. Concerning the attacks, they are all certain except γ.

Nevertheless, since the target of α is uncertain, α will exist only if its target also exists. Moreover, since α is the target of β the uncertainty of b also impacts the existence of β whereas it and its source and target are certain. So there are three possible completions given in Fig. 2 and in one of them, β is missing because b is missing. This does not happen to δ, because a and c are not impacted by the uncertainty of b. □

Some classical decision problems can be defined for IHOAF, i.e. possible credulous acceptability (**PCA**), necessary credulous acceptability (**NCA**) and their counterparts for skeptical acceptability (**PSA** and **NSA**):

Definition 12. *Let $\mathcal{IH} = (\mathcal{A}, \mathcal{A}^?, \mathcal{R}, \mathcal{R}^?, \text{src}, \text{trg})$, $x \in (\mathcal{A} \cup \mathcal{R})$ and $\sigma \in \{\text{co}, \text{gr}, \text{pr}, \text{st}\}$. Four decision problems about the acceptability status of x can be defined:*

- *σ-PCA: $\exists \mathcal{H} \in \text{completions}(\mathcal{IH})$, $\exists U = (S, \Gamma) \in \sigma(\mathcal{H})$ such that $x \in S \cup \Gamma$?*
- *σ-NCA: $\forall \mathcal{H} \in \text{completions}(\mathcal{IH})$, $\exists U = (S, \Gamma) \in \sigma(\mathcal{H})$ such that $x \in S \cup \Gamma$?*

- σ-PSA: $\exists \mathcal{H} \in$ completions$(\mathcal{IH})$, $\forall U = (S, \Gamma) \in \sigma(\mathcal{H})$, $x \in S \cup \Gamma$?
- σ-NSA: $\forall \mathcal{H} \in$ completions$(\mathcal{IH})$, $\forall U = (S, \Gamma) \in \sigma(\mathcal{H})$, $x \in S \cup \Gamma$?

Note that, in the definition of these problems, we only consider certain elements similarly to their initial formulation for IAFs [8]. Indeed, if the target element (argument or attack) is uncertain ($x \in \mathcal{A}^? \cup \mathcal{R}^?$), then the necessary variants of the decision problems are trivial (the answer is always "NO" since these elements are absent from some completions). Regarding the possible variants, it can be easily shown that x is possibly (credulously or skeptically) accepted in $\mathcal{IH}$ if and only if it is also the case in $\mathcal{IH}'$, a modified version of $\mathcal{IH}$ where x has been made certain. This is why formal definitions and computational studies of these problems are always limited to certain elements.

Example 7. In the framework of Example 1 where both c and β are uncertain, a, c, α and β, which belong to every structure in some completions according to $\sigma \in \{\text{co}, \text{pr}, \text{gr}, \text{st}\}$, are thus σ-PSA (and σ-PCA), and b, which belongs to every structure in every completion, is σ-NSA (and σ-NCA). This argument b ("Sam told me that it will rain later") is thus the only element accepted whatever be the interpretation of the framework; we may say that this is the only conclusion which can be firmly drawn from the discussion regarding the program of the day.

Notice however that if in the framework of Example 1, it is b which is considered as uncertain (if Sam is known not to be reliable for instance) and c and β as certain, then the 2 possible completions, in this case, have a unique preferred, grounded, stable and complete structure: $\sigma(\mathcal{IH}) = \{(\{a, b, c\}, \{\beta\}), (\{a, c\}, \varnothing)\}$. Arguments a and c are then σ-NSA: going to the beach in the afternoon (argument a) can be concluded from the discussion. □

Complexity of Reasoning with IHOAFs. We recall that RAFs can be polynomially transformed into AFs while preserving the semantics, for classical semantics $\sigma \in \{\text{co}, \text{pr}, \text{st}, \text{gr}\}$ [23, Proposition 32]. This implies that, under these semantics, all standard decision problems have the same complexity for HOAFs as for Dung's AFs [19].

Let us investigate the complexity of reasoning with IHOAFs. We focus on the four acceptability problems given in Definition 12. An IHOAF without higher-order attacks (*i.e.* such that all attacks target an argument) is simply an IAF. This means that the complexity of reasoning with IAFs [8,27] provides a lower bound to the complexity of reasoning with IHOAFs. Then we show that these lower bounds can be transformed into completeness results for each problem.

Proposition 3. *The complexity in the worst case for the acceptability problems defined in Definition 12 is given in the following table (the columns entitled "Cred. Acc" and "Skep. Acc" are only given for comparing with the RAF case, see [23]):*

σ	Cred. Acc (RAF)	σ-PCA	σ-NCA	Skep. Acc. (RAF)	σ-PSA	σ-NSA
gr	P	NP-c	coNP-c	P	NP-c	coNP-c
co	NP-c	NP-c	Π_2^P-c	P	NP-c	coNP-c
st	NP-c	NP-c	Π_2^P-c	coNP-c	Σ_2^P-c	coNP-c
pr	NP-c	NP-c	Π_2^P-c	Π_2^P-c	Σ_3^P-c	Π_2^P-c

Note that the existence of uncertainty significantly increases the complexity of the acceptability problems in the case of the grounded semantics (the credulous and skeptical acceptability problems for RAF are polynomial, see [23]) but the impact is less important for the other semantics (even if the complexity increases also for these semantics in the case of NCA and PSA because exponentially many completions may exist). The difference of complexity is the same between HOAFs and IHOAFs than between AFs and IAFs.

4 Logical Encoding of IHOAFs

We translate IHOAFs argument acceptability problems to the Dynamic Logic of Propositional Assignments (DL-PA) [3], a well-behaved variant of Propositional Dynamic Logic. This encoding extends previous works [16,24,36], and it inherits their benefits over the use of equally expressive and succinct logical languages, such as Quantified Boolean Formulas. Summing up, (i) dynamic logic is much closer to direct argumentation algorithms than QBF; and (ii) it allows a natural extension to argumentation dynamics. In this section, **A** and **R** are assumed to be finite (infinitary formulas being out of the scope of standard DL-PA).

Propositional Variables. Let Prp be a denumerable set of propositional variables Prp = $\{p_1, p_2, \ldots\}$. We suppose that Prp contains several kinds of distinguished variables capturing the statuses of arguments and relations between them.

- **argument variables**, $\mathsf{ARG}_\mathcal{A} = \{\mathtt{arg}_x \mid x \in \mathcal{A}\}$ for any $\mathcal{A} \subseteq \mathbf{A}$.
- **attack variables**, $\mathsf{ATT}_\mathcal{R} = \{\mathtt{r}_\alpha \mid \alpha \in \mathcal{R}\}$ for any $\mathcal{R} \subseteq \mathbf{R}$.
- **source variables**, $\mathsf{SRC}_X = \{\mathtt{src}_{\alpha,y} \mid (\alpha, y) \in X\}$ for any $X \subseteq (\mathbf{R} \times \mathbf{A})$.
- **target variables**, $\mathsf{TRG}_X = \{\mathtt{trg}_{\alpha,y} \mid (\alpha, y) \in X\}$ for any $X \subseteq (\mathbf{R} \times (\mathbf{A} \cup \mathbf{R}))$.
- **structure variables**, $\mathsf{IN}_X = \{\mathtt{in}_\alpha \mid \alpha \in X\}$ for any $X \subseteq (\mathbf{A} \cup \mathbf{R})$.

Let $\mathsf{Prp}_{\mathbf{A} \cup \mathbf{R}} = \mathsf{ARG}_\mathbf{A} \cup \mathsf{IN}_{\mathbf{A} \cup \mathbf{R}} \cup \mathsf{ATT}_\mathbf{R} \cup \mathsf{SRC}_{\mathbf{R} \times \mathbf{A}} \cup \mathsf{TRG}_{\mathbf{R} \times (\mathbf{A} \cup \mathbf{R})}$. We assume that $\mathsf{Prp} \subseteq \mathsf{Prp}_{\mathbf{A} \cup \mathbf{R}}$.

DL-PA Grammar. The DL-PA language contains both formulas and programs, defined as follows:

For formulas: $\varphi ::= p \mid \neg \varphi \mid (\varphi \wedge \varphi) \mid [\pi]\varphi \quad (p \in \mathsf{Prp})$
For programs: $\pi ::= +p \mid -p \mid \varphi? \mid (\pi; \pi) \mid (\pi \cup \pi) \mid \pi^* \quad (p \in \mathsf{Prp})$

The intended meaning of formulas is as usual for atoms and the Boolean connectors. As for modal formulas, $[\pi]\varphi$ reads "φ is true after every possible execution of π", so that the dual $\langle\pi\rangle\varphi$, defined as $\neg[\pi]\neg\varphi$, reads "there is a possible execution of π that makes φ true". As for programs, their intended meaning is as follows: $+p$ (resp. $-p$) is the atomic program that makes p true (resp. false). $\varphi?$ is the program that tests whether φ is true. $(\pi; \pi')$ is the sequential composition of π and π' ("first execute π and then π'"). $(\pi \cup \pi')$ is the non-deterministic choice ("choose non-deterministically between π or π' and execute one of them"). Finally, π^* is the unbounded iteration of π ("execute π a finite number of times").

Semantics of DL-PA. Given a propositional valuation $v \subseteq \mathtt{Prp}$ (so v is the set of the true variables), **truth for formulas** φ and the **meaning of programs** $||\pi||$ is given by mutual recursion:

$$\begin{aligned} v &\models p & &\text{iff } p \in v \\ v &\models [\pi]\varphi & &\text{iff } (v, v') \in ||\pi|| \text{ implies } v' \models \varphi \end{aligned}$$

and as usual for the Boolean connectives; moreover, considering that, given a binary relation R, R^* denotes the reflexive and transitive closure of R, the interpretation of programs is:

$$\begin{aligned} ||+p|| &= \{(v,v') \mid v' = v \cup \{p\}\} & ||-p|| &= \{(v,v') \mid v' = v \setminus \{p\}\} \\ ||\varphi?|| &= \{(v,v) \mid v \models \varphi\} & ||\pi;\pi'|| &= ||\pi|| \circ ||\pi'|| \\ ||\pi \cup \pi'|| &= ||\pi|| \cup ||\pi'|| & ||\pi^*|| &= ||\pi||^* \end{aligned}$$

Some useful DL-PA programs. Here are some useful abbreviations in our object language (where $\mathsf{P} = \{p_1, ..., p_n\}$ is a finite subset of $\mathtt{Prp}$):

$$\begin{aligned} \mathsf{skip} &= \top? \\ \mathsf{mkTrueOne}(\mathsf{P}) &= \bigcup_{p \in \mathsf{P}}(\neg p?; +p) = (\neg p_1?; +p_1) \cup \ldots \cup (\neg p_n?; +p_n) \\ \mathsf{mkFalseOne}(\mathsf{P}) &= \bigcup_{p \in \mathsf{P}}(p?; -p) = (p_1?; -p_1) \cup \ldots \cup (p_n?; -p_n) \\ \mathsf{mkTrueSome}(\mathsf{P}) &= ;_{p \in \mathsf{P}}(+p \cup \mathsf{skip}) = (+p_1 \cup \mathsf{skip}); \ldots; (+p_n \cup \mathsf{skip}) \\ \mathsf{mkFalseAll}(\mathsf{P}) &= ;_{p \in \mathsf{P}}(-p) = -p_1; \ldots; -p_n \\ \mathsf{vary}(\mathsf{P}) &= ;_{p \in \mathsf{P}}(+p \cup -p) = (+p_1 \cup -p_1); \ldots; (+p_n \cup -p_n) \\ \text{if } \varphi \text{ then } \pi \text{ else } \pi' &= (\varphi?; \pi) \cup (\neg\varphi?; \pi') \\ \text{if } \varphi \text{ then } \pi &= \text{if } \varphi \text{ then } \pi \text{ else } \mathsf{skip} \\ \text{while } \varphi \text{ do } \pi &= (\varphi?; \pi)^*; \neg\varphi? \end{aligned}$$

HOAFs and Structures as Propositional Valuations. From our hypothesis that $\mathtt{Prp}$ contains $\mathtt{Prp}_{\mathsf{A} \cup \mathsf{R}}$, we can encode each HOAF $\mathcal{H} = (\mathcal{A}, \mathcal{R}, \mathsf{src}, \mathsf{trg})$ by its **associated propositional valuation** $v_{\mathcal{H}} = \mathsf{ARG}_{\mathcal{A}} \cup \mathsf{ATT}_{\mathcal{R}} \cup \mathsf{SRC}_{\mathsf{src}} \cup \mathsf{TRG}_{\mathsf{trg}}$. Conversely, given $v \subseteq \mathtt{Prp}_{\mathsf{A} \cup \mathsf{R}}$, we define the **quasi-HOAF associated to** v as $\mathcal{H}_v = (\mathcal{A}_v, \mathcal{R}_v, \mathsf{src}_v, \mathsf{trg}_v)$ where:

$$\begin{aligned} \mathcal{A}_v &= \{x \mid \mathsf{arg}_x \in v\}. \\ \mathcal{R}_v &= \{\alpha \mid \mathsf{r}_\alpha \in v\}. \\ \mathsf{src}_v &= \{(\alpha, x) \mid \mathsf{src}_{\alpha,x} \in v\} \cap (\mathcal{R}_v \times \mathcal{A}_v). \\ \mathsf{trg}_v &= \{(\alpha, x) \mid \mathsf{trg}_{\alpha,x} \in v\} \cap (\mathcal{R}_v \times (\mathcal{A}_v \cup \mathcal{R}_v)). \end{aligned}$$

There are some valuations whose associated quasi-HOAFs are indeed HOAFs. These valuations could be identified syntactically by providing a formula that is true exactly at them. However, this is not needed since our reduction will depart from a given, arbitrary HOAF. This nuance was irrelevant in previous DL-PA encodings of argumentative structures [17,24,36], as one could easily force the associated quasi-AF to be an AF by definition (by restricting the set of interactions). However, the more complex interactions in HOAFs make this strategy less appealing.

Given $v \subseteq \mathtt{Prp}_{\mathsf{A} \cup \mathsf{R}}$, the **quasi-structure associated to** v is defined as $\mathcal{U}_v = (S_v, \Gamma_v)$ where $S_v = \{x \in \mathbf{A} \mid \mathsf{in}_x \in v\}$ and $\Gamma_v = \{\alpha \in \mathbf{R} \mid \mathsf{in}_\alpha \in v\}$. We can easily capture in our syntax that U_v is indeed a structure, and this will be useful later on: Structure $= \bigwedge_{x \in \mathbf{A}}(\mathsf{in}_x \to \mathsf{arg}_x) \wedge \bigwedge_{\alpha \in \mathbf{R}}(\mathsf{in}_\alpha \to \mathsf{r}_\alpha)$.

Computing Extensions of HOAFs in DL-PA. Let $x \in \mathbf{A} \cup \mathbf{R}$, and define

$$\begin{aligned}
\mathsf{ConflictFree} &= \mathsf{Structure} \wedge \neg \bigvee_{\alpha \in \mathbf{R}} \Big((\mathsf{in}_\alpha \wedge \bigvee_{x \in \mathbf{A}}(\mathsf{src}_{\alpha,x} \wedge \mathsf{in}_x) \\
&\qquad\qquad\qquad \wedge \bigvee_{y \in \mathbf{A} \cup \mathbf{R}}(\mathsf{trg}_{\alpha,y} \wedge \mathsf{in}_y) \Big) \\
\mathsf{Acc}_x &= (\mathsf{arg}_x \vee \mathsf{r}_x) \wedge \bigwedge_{\alpha \in \mathbf{R}} \Big((\mathsf{r}_\alpha \wedge \mathsf{trg}_{\alpha,x}) \to \\
&\qquad \bigvee_{\beta \in \mathbf{R}} \big(\mathsf{in}_\beta \wedge \bigvee_{y \in \mathbf{A}}(\mathsf{src}_{\beta,y} \wedge \mathsf{in}_y) \\
&\qquad\qquad \wedge (\mathsf{trg}_{\beta,\alpha} \vee \bigvee_{z \in \mathbf{A}}(\mathsf{src}_{\alpha,z} \wedge \mathsf{trg}_{\beta,\alpha})) \big) \Big) \\
\mathsf{Complete} &= \mathsf{ConflictFree} \wedge \bigwedge_{x \in \mathbf{A} \cup \mathbf{R}}(\mathsf{in}_x \leftrightarrow \mathsf{Acc}_x) \\
\mathsf{Preferred} &= \mathsf{Complete} \\
&\quad \wedge \big[\mathsf{mkTrueOne}(\mathsf{IN}_{\mathbf{A} \cup \mathbf{R}}); \mathsf{mkTrueSome}(\mathsf{IN}_{\mathbf{A} \cup \mathbf{R}})\big] \neg \mathsf{Complete} \\
\mathsf{Grounded} &= \mathsf{Complete} \\
&\quad \wedge \big[\mathsf{mkFalseOne}(\mathsf{IN}_{\mathbf{A} \cup \mathbf{R}}); \mathsf{mkFalseSome}(\mathsf{IN}_{\mathbf{A} \cup \mathbf{R}})\big] \neg \mathsf{Complete} \\
\mathsf{Defeated}_x &= \bigvee_{\alpha \in \mathbf{R}} \big(\mathsf{in}_\alpha \wedge \bigvee_{y \in \mathbf{A}}(\mathsf{src}_{\alpha,y} \wedge \mathsf{in}_y \wedge \mathsf{trg}_{\alpha,x}) \big) \\
\mathsf{Stable} &= \mathsf{ConflictFree} \wedge \bigwedge_{x \in \mathbf{A} \cup \mathbf{R}} \big(((\mathsf{arg}_x \vee \mathsf{r}_x) \wedge \neg \mathsf{in}_x) \to \mathsf{Defeated}_x \big)
\end{aligned}$$

For $\sigma \in \{\mathsf{co}, \mathsf{pr}, \mathsf{st}, \mathsf{gr}\}$, we let φ_σ denote the corresponding formula in the previous list. For example, $\varphi_{\mathsf{st}} = \mathsf{Stable}$. Moreover, we define a guess-and-test simple DL-PA program to capture the computation of σ-structures:
$$\mathsf{mkStru}^\sigma = \mathsf{vary}(\mathsf{IN}_{\mathbf{A} \cup \mathbf{R}}); \varphi_\sigma?.$$

Proposition 4. *Let $\mathcal{H}$ be an HOAF, let $\sigma \in \{\mathsf{co}, \mathsf{pr}, \mathsf{gr}, \mathsf{st}\}$, let $v_1 \subseteq \mathsf{Prp}_{\mathbf{A} \cup \mathbf{R}} \setminus \mathsf{IN}_{\mathbf{A}}$ such that $\mathcal{H}_{v_1} = \mathcal{H}$ then $\sigma(\mathcal{H}) = \{U_v \mid (v_1, v) \in \|\mathsf{mkStru}^\sigma\|\}$.*

Example 8. Recall the HOAF of Example 3, let us call it $\mathcal{H}_1$. We have that $v_{\mathcal{H}_1} = \{\mathsf{arg}_a, \mathsf{arg}_b, \mathsf{arg}_c, \mathsf{r}_\alpha, \mathsf{r}_\beta, \mathsf{src}_{\alpha,b}, \mathsf{src}_{\beta,c}, \mathsf{trg}_{\alpha,a}, \mathsf{trg}_{\beta,\alpha}\}$. Let us describe the execution of $\mathsf{mkStru}^{\mathsf{co}}$ at $v_{\mathcal{H}_1}$. First, we have that executing $\mathsf{vary}(\mathsf{IN}_{\mathbf{A} \cup \mathbf{R}})$ at $v_{\mathcal{H}_1}$ leads us to all valuations of the form $v_{\mathcal{H}_1} \cup X$ where $X \subseteq \mathsf{IN}_{\mathbf{A} \cup \mathbf{R}}$ (32 different valuations!). However, from all these valuations, $v_2 = v_{\mathcal{H}_1} \cup \{\mathsf{in}_a, \mathsf{in}_b, \mathsf{in}_c, \mathsf{in}_\beta\}$ is the only one that "survives" to the test $\mathsf{Complete}?$, hence, according to Prop. 4, $U_{v_1} = (\{a, b, c\}, \{\beta\})$ is the only complete structure of $\mathcal{H}_1$. $\square$

Computing Completions of IHOAFs in DL-PA. Programs used for previous encodings of incomplete argumentation frameworks [24,36] do not straightforwardly work here. We need to be sure that the resulting valuation encodes a completion (see Definition 10 and the remark following it):

$$\begin{aligned}
\mathsf{Constraint}_1 &= \bigwedge_{\alpha \in \mathcal{R}} \Big(\mathsf{r}_\alpha \leftrightarrow \big(\bigvee_{x \in \mathbf{A}}(\mathsf{src}_{\alpha,x} \wedge \mathsf{arg}_x) \wedge \bigvee_{y \in \mathbf{A} \cup \mathbf{R}}(\mathsf{trg}_{\alpha,y} \wedge (\mathsf{arg}_y \vee \mathsf{r}_y))\big) \Big) \\
\mathsf{Constraint}_2 &= \bigwedge_{\alpha \in \mathcal{R}^?} \Big(\mathsf{r}_\alpha \to \big(\bigvee_{x \in \mathbf{A}}(\mathsf{src}_{\alpha,x} \wedge \mathsf{arg}_x) \wedge \bigvee_{y \in \mathbf{A} \cup \mathbf{R}}(\mathsf{trg}_{\alpha,y} \wedge (\mathsf{arg}_y \vee \mathsf{r}_y))\big) \Big) \\
\mathsf{Constraint} &= \mathsf{Constraint}_1 \wedge \mathsf{Constraint}_2
\end{aligned}$$

Let us define the **valuation associated to** $\mathcal{IH} = (\mathcal{A}, \mathcal{A}^?, \mathcal{R}, \mathcal{R}^?, \mathbf{src}, \mathbf{trg})$ as $v_{\mathcal{IH}} = \mathsf{ARG}_\mathcal{A} \cup \mathsf{SRC}_{\mathbf{src}} \cup \mathsf{TRG}_{\mathbf{trg}}$. Completions of $\mathcal{IH}$ are computed by executing the following program from $v_{\mathcal{IH}}$:

$$\mathsf{mkComp}(\mathcal{IH}) = \mathsf{mkTrueSome}(\mathsf{ARG}_{\mathcal{A}^?}); \mathsf{vary}(\mathsf{ATT}_{\mathcal{R} \cup \mathcal{R}^?}); \mathsf{Constraint?}$$

Proposition 5. *Let* $\mathcal{IH} = (\mathcal{A}, \mathcal{A}^?, \mathcal{R}, \mathcal{R}^?, \mathbf{src}, \mathbf{trg})$. *Then:*

- *If* $(v_{\mathcal{IH}}, v) \in ||\mathsf{mkComp}(\mathcal{IH})||$, *then* $(\mathcal{A}_v, \mathcal{R}_v, \mathbf{src}_v, \mathbf{trg}_v) \in \mathsf{completions}(\mathcal{IH})$.
- *If* $(\mathcal{A}_c, \mathcal{R}_c, \mathbf{src}_c, \mathbf{trg}_c) \in \mathsf{completions}(\mathcal{IH})$, *then there is a* $v \subseteq \mathsf{Prp}_{\mathbf{A} \cup \mathbf{R}}$ *such that* $\mathcal{H}_v = (\mathcal{A}_c, \mathcal{R}_c, \mathbf{src}_c, \mathbf{trg}_c)$ *and* $(v_{\mathcal{IH}}, v) \in ||\mathsf{mkComp}(\mathcal{IH})||$.

Example 9. Recall the IHOAF of Example 6, $\mathcal{IH}$. We have that $v_{\mathcal{IH}} = \{\mathsf{arg}_a, \mathsf{arg}_c, \mathsf{src}_{\alpha,a}, \mathsf{src}_{\beta,c}, \mathsf{src}_{\gamma,c}, \mathsf{src}_{\delta,c}, \mathsf{trg}_{\alpha,b}, \mathsf{trg}_{\beta,a}, \mathsf{trg}_{\gamma,b}, \mathsf{trg}_{\delta,a}\}$. The figure below represents the execution of $\mathsf{mkComp}(\mathcal{IH})$, where $\pi_1 = \mathsf{mkTrueSome}(\mathsf{ARG}_{\mathcal{A}^?})$, $\pi_2 = \mathsf{vary}(\mathsf{ATT}_{\mathcal{R} \cup \mathcal{R}^?})$, and $\pi_3 = \mathsf{Constraint?}$. Note that many valuations related to $v_{\mathcal{IH}}$ and $v_{\mathcal{IH}} \cup \{\mathsf{arg}_b\}$ through π_2 have been omitted for representational purposes since they do not pass the test performed by π_3.

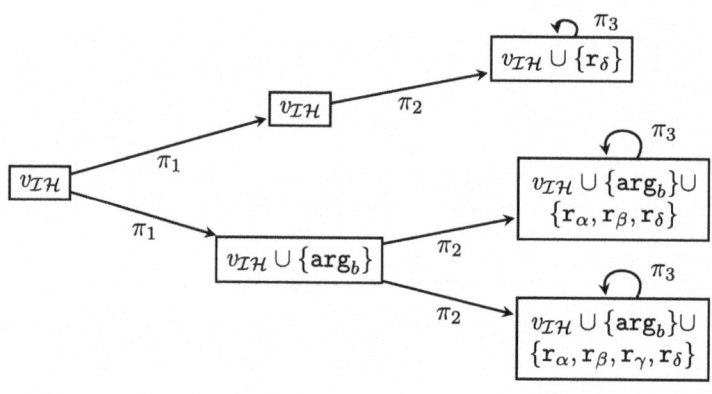

□

Argument Acceptance in DL-PA. We can finally formulate the desired reduction:

Proposition 6. *Given a* $\mathcal{IH} = (\mathcal{A}, \mathcal{A}^?, \mathcal{R}, \mathcal{R}^?, \mathbf{src}, \mathbf{trg})$ *and* $x \in \mathcal{A} \cup \mathcal{R}$, *then:*

- *the answer to* σ-*PCA is YES iff* $v_{\mathcal{IH}} \models \langle \mathsf{mkComp}(\mathcal{IH}); \mathsf{mkStru}^\sigma \rangle \mathsf{in}_x$.
- *the answer to* σ-*NCA is YES iff* $v_{\mathcal{IH}} \models [\mathsf{mkComp}(\mathcal{IH})] \langle \mathsf{mkStru}^\sigma \rangle \mathsf{in}_x$.
- *the answer to* σ-*PSA is YES iff* $v_{\mathcal{IH}} \models \langle \mathsf{mkComp}(\mathcal{IH}) \rangle [\mathsf{mkStru}^\sigma] \mathsf{in}_x$.
- *the answer to* σ-*NSA is YES iff* $v_{\mathcal{IH}} \models [\mathsf{mkComp}(\mathcal{IH}); \mathsf{mkStru}^\sigma] \mathsf{in}_x$.

5 Discussion and Conclusions

This paper is devoted to the study of IHOAFs: enriched frameworks for abstract argumentation taking into account higher-order attacks and considering at the same time that the elements (arguments or attacks) of this framework can be uncertain. Reasoning about IHOAFs is done through the notion of completion: any uncertain element can be considered present or absent, and so several "variants" of the IHOAF may be built. Each variant is called a *completion* and corresponds to a classical HOAF without uncertainty. Then, the semantics of IHOAFs are defined by the application of the corresponding semantics on these completions. Complexity results are given for the possible/necessary credulous/skeptical acceptance problems under several semantics in IHOAFs. Finally, DL-PA programs for computing completions and extensions of IHOAFs are presented, and argument acceptance problems for IHOAFs are shown to be reducible to DL-PA model checking.

This work paves the way for a more general framework that would embed a higher-order support relation in addition to the higher-order attack relation: ongoing work on the combination of IBAFs [20,24] and IHOAFs to obtain IHOBAFs (Incomplete Higher-Order Bipolar Argumentation Frameworks) is being conducted. Besides, since the HOAF semantics can be defined in several ways, it could be interesting to study the impact of the chosen definitions (for instance, RAF approach versus AFRA approach) from a more general point of view.

In terms of additional future works, several directions can be explored. Regarding the framework, a first idea would be to focus on the uncertainty aspect of IHOAFs by, e.g., considering a recursive form of uncertainty [34], or proposing a direct approach (i.e. without using completions) to define extension-based semantics in the style of [26]. Another idea could be the study of instantiations of IHOAFs into structured frameworks (see for instance [32,37] for recent instantiations of IAFs). Dropping the uniqueness of the attack relation may also be investigated: there actually exist approaches such as [12], which considers that if the framework contains arguments and relations coming from different contexts or sources, then several attacks between the same two elements may occur. The consequences of these non-unique attacks on the definition of the completions, semantics and encoding may be studied.

Regarding computational aspects, an interesting point would be to implement the computation of semantics of the incomplete frameworks via the development of a DL-PA solver and to make some experiments for evaluating our encoding and comparing it with other approaches (for instance with a more direct computation of semantics, without using logics).

Two final research avenues can be mentioned: first, the question of explainability for IHOAFs, notably to explain the possible/necessary credulous/skeptical acceptance of an element of the framework. A possible way to address this issue might be to start from the explainability approach of [1] for IAFs, and to extend it to IHOAFs. Another way would be to adapt explanations for AFs [14], in particular, visual approaches such as [15], to IHOAFs.

Second, the question of enforcement in IHOAFs may be addressed: how to make an element possibly/necessarily credulously/skeptically accepted by (minimally) changing the framework. In a situation such as the one of the running example Example 1, if one wishes that argument a be necessarily and not just possibly accepted, then changes on the certainty of arguments and attacks as indicated in Example 7 may be done. Enforcement in IHOAFs may be studied starting from the dynamic approaches for Control Argumentation Frameworks [25,30] and IAFs [36].

To go even further, some approaches to explainability use enforcement results (they explain why an element is not acceptable by presenting the elements of the framework to be changed for it to be [14]): the last two research avenues may be combined in this sense.

Acknowledgments. Jean-Guy Mailly benefited from the support of the projects AGGREEY ANR-22-CE23-0005 and AIDAL ANR-22-CPJ1-0061-01 of the French National Research Agency (ANR). Antonio Yuste-Ginel benefited from the support of the project PHIDELO PID2022-142378NB-I00 funded by the Spanish Ministry of Science MICIU/AEI and by the European Union.

References

1. Alfano, G., Calautti, M., Greco, S., Parisi, F., Trubitsyna, I.: Explainable acceptance in probabilistic and incomplete abstract argumentation frameworks. Artif. Intell. **323**, 103967 (2023)
2. Amgoud, L., Cayrol, C.: A reasoning model based on the production of acceptable arguments. Ann. Math. Artif. Intell. **34**(1–3), 197–215 (2002)
3. Balbiani, P., Herzig, A., Troquard, N.: Dynamic logic of propositional assignments: a well-behaved variant of PDL. In: Proceeding of LICS 2013, pp. 143–152 (2013)
4. Baroni, P., Caminada, M., Giacomin, M.: Abstract argumentation frameworks and their semantics. In: Baroni, P., Gabbay, D., Giacomin, M., van der Torre, L. (eds.), Handbook of Formal Argumentation, pp. 159–236. College Publications (2018)
5. Baroni, P., Cerutti, F., Giacomin, M., Guida, G.: AFRA: argumentation framework with recursive attacks. Int. J. Approximate Reasoning **52**(1), 19–37 (2011)
6. Baroni, P., Giacomin, M., Guida, G.: Extending abstract argumentation systems theory. Artif. Intell. **120**(2), 251–270 (2000)
7. Barringer, H., Gabbay, D., Woods, J.: Temporal dynamics of support and attack networks : from argumentation to zoology. In: Hutter, D., Stephan, W. (eds.), Mechanizing Mathematical Reasoning, Essays in Honor of Jörg H. Siekmann. LNAI 2605, pp. 59–98. Springer (2005)
8. Baumeister, D., Järvisalo, M., Neugebauer, D., Niskanen, A., Rothe, J.: Acceptance in incomplete argumentation frameworks. Artif. Intell. **295**, 103470 (2021)
9. Baumeister, D., Neugebauer, D., Rothe, J., Schadrack, H.: Verification in incomplete argumentation frameworks. Artif. Intell. **264**, 1–26 (2018)
10. Boella, G., Gabbay, D.M., van der Torre, L., Villata, S.: Support in abstract argumentation. In: Baroni, P., Cerutti, F., Giacomin, M., Simari, G.R. (eds.) Proceeding of COMMA 2010, pp. 111–122 (2010)

11. Cayrol, C., Cohen, A., Lagasquie Schiex, M.C.: Higher-order interactions (bipolar or not) in abstract argumentation: a state of the art. In: Gabbay, D., Giacomin, M., Simari, G., Thimm, M. (eds.), Handbook of Formal Argumentation, vol. 2, pp. 3–118. College Publications (2021)
12. Cayrol, C., Fandinno, J., Farinas del Cerro, L., Lagasquie-Schiex, M.-C.: Valid attacks in argumentation frameworks with recursive attacks. Ann. Math. Artif. Intell. (Special Issue: Commonsense 2017) (2020)
13. Coste-Marquis, S., Devred, C., Konieczny, S., Lagasquie-Schiex, M.-C., Marquis, P.: On the merging of Dung's argumentation systems. Artif. Intell. **171**(10–15), 730–753 (2007)
14. Cyras, K., Rago, A., Albini, E., Baroni, P., Toni, F.: Argumentative XAI: a survey. In: Zhou, Z.-H. (ed.), IJCAI vol. 2021, pp. 4392–4399 (2021)
15. Doutre, S., Duchatelle, T., Lagasquie-Schiex, M.-C.: Visual explanations for defence in abstract argumentation. In: Agmon, N., An, B., Ricci, A., Yeoh, W. (eds.), AAMAS, vol. 2023, pp. 2346–2348 (2023)
16. Doutre, S., Herzig, A., Perrussel, L.: A dynamic logic framework for abstract argumentation. In: Baral, C., De Giacomo, G., Eiter, T. (eds.), Proceeding of KR 2014 (2014)
17. Doutre, S., Herzig, A., Perrussel, L.: Abstract argumentation in dynamic logic: representation, reasoning and change. In: Liao, B., Ågotnes, T., Wáng, Y.N. (eds.), Proceeding of CLAR 2018, pp. 153–185 (2018)
18. Dung, P.M.: On the acceptability of arguments and its fundamental role in non-monotonic reasoning, logic programming and n-person games. Artif. Intell. **77**(2), 321–358 (1995)
19. Dvorák, W., Dunne, P.E.: Computational problems in formal argumentation and their complexity. In: Baroni, P., Gabbay, D., Giacomin, M., van der Torre, L. (eds.), Handbook of Formal Argumentation, pp. 631–688. College Publications (2018)
20. Fazzinga, B., Flesca, S., Furfaro, F.: Incomplete bipolar argumentation frameworks. In: Gal, K. et al. (ed.), Proceeding of ECAI 2023, pp. 684–691. IOS Press (2023)
21. Herzig, A., Yuste-Ginel, A.: On the Epistemic logic of incomplete argumentation Frameworks. In: Bienvenu, M., Lakemeyer, G., Erdem, E. (eds.), Proceedings of the 18th International Conference on Principles of Knowledge Representation and Reasoning, pp. 681–685, November 2021
22. Hunter, A., Polberg, S., Potyka, N., Rienstra, T., Thimm, M.: Probabilistic argumentation: a survey. In: Gabbay, D., Giacomin, M., Simari, G., Thimm, M. (eds.), Handbook of Formal Argumentation, vol. 2, pp. 397–441. College Publications (2021)
23. Lafages, M.: Algorithms for Enriched Abstract Argumentation Frameworks for Large-scale Cases. (Algorithmique des systèmes d'argumentation abstraits enrichis, en vue du passage à l'échelle). PhD thesis, Paul Sabatier University, Toulouse, France (2021)
24. Lagasquie-Schiex, M.C., Mailly, J.G., Yuste-Ginel, A.: How to manage supports in incomplete argumentation frameworks. In: Proceeding of FOIKS (2024)
25. Mailly, J.-G.: Possible controllability of control argumentation frameworks. In: 8th International Conference on Computational Models of Argument (COMMA 2020), pp. 283–294 (2020)
26. Mailly, J.-G.: Extension-based semantics for incomplete argumentation frameworks. In: Baroni, P., Benzmüller, C., Wáng, Y.N. (eds.), Proceeding of CLAR 2021, pp. 322–341 (2021)

27. Mailly, J.-G.: Yes, no, maybe, I don't know: complexity and application of abstract argumentation with incomplete knowledge. Argument Comput. **13**(3), 291–324 (2022)
28. Modgil, S.: Reasoning about preferences in argumentation frameworks. Artif. Intell. **173**(9–10), 901–934 (2009)
29. Nielsen, S.H. and Parsons, S.: A generalization of Dung's abstract framework for argumentation: arguing with sets of attacking arguments. In: Maudet, N., Parsons, S., Rahwan, I. (eds.), Argumentation in Multi-Agent Systems - Third International Workshop (ArgMAS 2006), volume 4766 of LNAI, pp. 54–73, Hakodate, Japan, Springer, May 2006
30. Niskanen, A., Neugebauer, D., Järvisalo, M.: Controllability of control argumentation frameworks. In: Proceedings of the Twenty-Ninth International Joint Conference on Artificial Intelligence, IJCAI, vol. 2020, pp. 1855–1861 (2020)
31. Nouioua, F., Risch, V.: Argumentation frameworks with necessities. In: Benferhat, S., Grant, J. (eds.) SUM 2011. LNCS (LNAI), vol. 6929, pp. 163–176. Springer, Heidelberg (2011). https://doi.org/10.1007/978-3-642-23963-2_14
32. Odekerken, D., Lehtonen, T., Borg, A., Wallner, J.P., Järvisalo, M.: Argumentative reasoning in ASPIC+ under incomplete information. In: Marquis, P., Son, T.C., Gabriele, K.-I., (eds.), Proceeding of KR 2023, pp. 531–541 (2023)
33. Oren, N., Norman, T.J.: Semantics for evidence-based argumentation. In: Besnard, P., Doutre, S., Hunter, A. (eds.), Proceeding of COMMA 2008, vol. 172, pp. 276–284. IOS Press (2008)
34. Rienstra, T., Thimm, M., Oren, N.: Opponent models with uncertainty for strategic argumentation. In: Rossi, F. (ed.), Proceeding of IJCAI 2013 (2013)
35. Rossit, J., Mailly, J.-G., Dimopoulos, Y., Moraitis, P.: United we stand: accruals in strength-based argumentation. Argument Comput. **12**(1), 87–113 (2021)
36. Yuste-Ginel, A., Herzig, A.: Qualitative uncertainty and dynamics of argumentation through dynamic logic. J. Log. Comput. (2023)
37. Yuste-Ginel, A., Proietti, C.: On the instantiation of argument-incomplete argumentation frameworks. In: Alfano, G., Ferilli, S., (eds.), 7th Workshop on Advances in Argumentation in Artificial Intelligence. CEUR (2022)

Modal Equivalence, n-Bisimulation and Model Comparison Game for Basic Neighbourhood Logic

Xiaoxuan Fu[1] and Zhiguang Zhao[2]($\boxtimes$)

[1] China University of Political Science and Law, Beijing, People's Republic of China
[2] Taishan University, Tai'an, People's Republic of China
zhaozhiguang23@gmail.com

Abstract. Basic neighbourhood logic is the modal logic in neighbourhood semantics where the neighbourhood functions are not necessarily upward-closed, therefore the modal operator is not necessarily monotonic. In this paper, we study a model comparison game for basic neighbourhood logic, in which there are two players, one of which claims that two pointed models are similar, and the other claims the opposite. The winning strategy of the first player is used to characterize the similarity between two pointed models. We give a definition of n-bisimulation, which characterizes n-modal equivalence and provides the ingredient for the model comparison game for basic neighbourhood logic.

Keywords: Model comparison game · basic neighbourhood logic · bisimulation

1 Introduction

Neighbourhood Semantics. Relational semantics is the most common semantics for modal logic. However, when it comes to non-normal modal logics where the modality does not satisfy at least one of $\Box\top$, $\Box(\varphi \land \psi) \leftrightarrow (\Box\varphi \land \Box\psi)$ and $\Box\varphi \to \Box(\varphi \lor \psi)$, relational semantics is not appropriate. The standard tool to study non-normal modal logics is neighbourhood semantics [3,6–9], in which each world s is associated with a collection $N(s) \subseteq \mathsf{P}(W)$ of subsets of the domain W, whose members are called the neighbourhoods of s. A formula $\Box\varphi$ is true at s iff the truth set of φ is a neighbourhood of s.

Basic Neighbourhood Logic. Basic neighbourhood logic is the modal logic in neighbourhood semantics where the neighbourhood functions are not necessarily upward-closed, i.e. it does not satisfy $(\forall X, Y \subseteq W)(X \in N(s)\ \&\ X \subseteq Y \Rightarrow Y \in N(s))$. Therefore the modal operator is not necessarily monotonic, thus the axiom $\Box\varphi \to \Box(\varphi \lor \psi)$ is not necessarily valid.

Model Similarity Concepts for Basic Neighbourhood Logic. The lack of monotonicity complicates the study of model similarity concepts of basic neighbourhood logic (see [4] for more details). As is mentioned in [4], it is difficult to give a back-and-forth style characterization of behavioural equivalence. Indeed, in [4], the authors give three different equivalence notions: 2^2-bisimulations, behavioural equivalences and precocongruences, which are different on neighbourhood models. They also show that even when two finite pointed neighbourhood models are not bisimilar or linked by precocongruences, they could still be modally equivalent. Therefore, it is still open how to characterize modal equivalence via some model equivalence notions for arbitrary neighbourhood models.

Game Semantics. Game semantics [5,10,11] provides a different perspective in the understanding of logical concepts like truth, model similarity (e.g. bisimulation) and consistency, alternative to model-theoretic semantics. In particular, the model comparison game is designed to characterize the similarity of two given models. This game has two players: one claims that the two models are similar, and the other player claims the opposite. The winning strategy of the first player is used to characterize the similarity between two models.

Our Strategy. In the present paper, we consider modal equivalence and give a new model similarity concept called n-bisimulation, which characterizes n-modal equivalence (i.e. modal equivalence for formulas of depth $\leq n$). We give a model comparison game corresponding to n-bisimulation, in which the winning strategy of the first player is used to characterize n-bisimulation between two pointed neighbourhood models.

Structure of the Paper. Section 2 gives the preliminaries on basic neighbourhood logic. Section 3 defines n-bisimulation for basic neighbourhood logic. Section 4 gives the model comparison game for basic neighbourhood logic. Section 5 gives some discussions on model similarity concepts.

2 Preliminaries

In this section, we give preliminaries on basic neighbourhood logic. For more details, see [4].

2.1 Syntax

Definition 1. *Fix a* **finite** *set* Prop *of propositional variables, we define the syntax of basic neighbourhood logic (BNL) as follows:*

$$\varphi ::= p \mid \top \mid \bot \mid \neg\varphi \mid \varphi \vee \varphi \mid \varphi \wedge \varphi \mid \Box\varphi$$

where $p \in$ Prop. The connectives $\rightarrow, \leftrightarrow, \Diamond$ are defined as usual.

For BNL-formulas, we define their modal depths as the measures of complexity:

Definition 2. *The modal depth $d(\varphi)$ of a* BNL*-formula φ is defined as follows:*

- $d(p) = d(\top) = d(\bot) = 0$.
- $d(\neg \varphi) = d(\varphi)$.
- $d(\varphi \wedge \psi) = d(\varphi \vee \psi) = max\{d(\varphi), d(\psi)\}$.
- $d(\Box \varphi) = d(\varphi) + 1$.

2.2 Semantics

The semantics of BNL is given as follows:

Definition 3 (Frames, Models and Pointed Models).

- A (neighbourhood) frame is a pair $\mathbb{F} = (W, N)$ where $W \neq \varnothing$ is the domain and $N : W \to \mathsf{P}(\mathsf{P}(W))$ is the neighbourhood function.
- $\mathbb{F} = (W, N)$ is finite if W is finite.
- Given a frame $\mathbb{F} = (W, N)$ and a valuation $V : \mathsf{Prop} \to \mathsf{P}(W)$, a (neighbourhood) model is $\mathbb{M} = (\mathbb{F}, V)$. Typically, when we write $\mathbb{M}$ (resp. $\mathbb{M}'$), we denote its domain as W (resp. W'), neighbourhood function as N (resp. N'), and valuation as V (resp. V').
- Given a model $\mathbb{M} = (W, N, V)$ and a point $s \in W$, a pointed (neighbourhood) model is $(\mathbb{M}, s)$.

Definition 4 (Satisfaction Relation). *The satisfaction relation $\mathbb{M}, s \Vdash \varphi$ is defined in a recursive way where the atomic and Boolean cases are defined as usual. We use $[\![\varphi]\!]^{\mathbb{M}} := \{s \in W \mid \mathbb{M}, s \Vdash \varphi\}$ to denote the truth set of φ in $\mathbb{M}$.*

$$\mathbb{M}, s \Vdash \Box \varphi \text{ iff } [\![\varphi]\!]^{\mathbb{M}} \in N(s).$$

The next proposition is useful in the proof of Proposition 2:

Proposition 1. *When* Prop *is finite, there are finitely many* BNL*-formulas of modal depth $\leq n$ modulo semantic equivalence.*

Proof. We prove it by induction on n. When $n = 0$, it follows from the fact that Prop is finite. When $n = k+1$, suppose that there are finitely many BNL-formulas of modal depth $\leq k$ modulo semantic equivalence, then each BNL-formulas of modal depth $k + 1$ can be written as a Boolean combination of propositional variables $p \in$ Prop and formulas of the form $\Box \varphi$ where φ is of modal depth $\leq k$. Since there are finitely many possibilities of $p \in$ Prop and $\Box \varphi$ modulo semantic equivalence, we have that there are finitely many BNL-formulas of modal depth $\leq k + 1$ modulo semantic equivalence.

3 n-Bisimulation

We define n-bisimulation to characterize modal equivalence up to depth n in the language BNL. This definition is inspired by [4, Proposition 3.15], but it is slightly different. We will discuss the difference in the last section.

First of all, we give some auxiliary definitions:

Definition 5. *Given pointed models* $(\mathbb{M}, s)$, $(\mathbb{M}', s')$, $Z \subseteq W \times W'$, $X \subseteq W$ *and* $X' \subseteq W'$,

- $Z[X] := \{x' \in W' \mid \text{for some } x \in X, (x, x') \in Z\}$.
- $Z^{-1}[X'] := \{x \in W \mid \text{for some } x' \in X', (x, x') \in Z\}$.

Definition 6. *Given any pointed model* $(\mathbb{M}, s)$, $Z \subseteq W \times W$ *and* $X \subseteq W$, *we say that X is Z-closed, if for any $s, t \in W$, we have that $s \in X$ and sZt implies $t \in X$.*

Definition 7 (Coherence). *Given two frames* $\mathbb{F} = (W, N)$ *and* $\mathbb{F}' = (W', N')$ *and* $X \subseteq W$, $X' \subseteq W'$, $Z \subseteq W \times W'$, *we say that (X, X') is Z-coherent, if $Z[X] \subseteq X'$ and $Z^{-1}[X'] \subseteq X$.*

Definition 8 (n-equivalence). *Two pointed models $(\mathbb{M}, s)$ and $(\mathbb{M}', s')$ are n-equivalent (notation: $(\mathbb{M}, s) \rightsquigarrow_n (\mathbb{M}', s')$), if $\mathbb{M}, s \Vdash \varphi \Leftrightarrow \mathbb{M}', s' \Vdash \varphi$ for all BNL-formulas φ with $d(\varphi) \leq n$.*

Now we are ready to define n-bisimulation. Notice that in the definition of n-bisimulations, we need a sequence of relations rather than a single relation, as is the case for n-bisimulation of modal logic in Kripke semantics, see e.g. [2, Definition 2.30].

Definition 9 (n-bisimulation). *Given two pointed models $(\mathbb{M}, s)$ and $(\mathbb{M}', s')$, we say that $Z_n \subseteq Z_{n-1} \subseteq \ldots \subseteq Z_0 \subseteq W \times W'$ is an n-bisimulation between $(\mathbb{M}, s)$ and $(\mathbb{M}', s')$, if for all $0 \leq i \leq n-1$, the following holds:*

1. $sZ_n s'$.
2. *For any $v \in W$, $v' \in W'$, if $vZ_0 v'$ then v and v' agree on all propositional variables.*
3. *For any $X_1, X_2 \subseteq W$ which are Z-closed under all i-bisimulations $Z \subseteq Z'_{i-1} \subseteq \ldots \subseteq Z'_0 \subseteq W \times W$, any $t \in Z_{i+1}^{-1}[W']$, if $Z_i^{-1}[W'] \cap X_1 = Z_i^{-1}[W'] \cap X_2$, then $X_1 \in N(t)$ iff $X_2 \in N(t)$.*
4. *For any $X'_1, X'_2 \subseteq W'$ which are Z'-closed under all i-bisimulations $Z' \subseteq Z''_{i-1} \subseteq \ldots \subseteq Z''_0 \subseteq W' \times W'$, any $t' \in Z_{i+1}[W]$, if $Z_i[W] \cap X'_1 = Z_i[W] \cap X'_2$, then $X'_1 \in N'(t')$ iff $X'_2 \in N'(t')$.*
5. *For any $X \subseteq W$ which is Z-closed under all i-bisimulations $Z \subseteq Z'_{i-1} \subseteq \ldots \subseteq Z'_0 \subseteq W \times W$, any $X' \subseteq W'$ which is Z'-closed under all i-bisimulations $Z' \subseteq Z''_{i-1} \subseteq \ldots \subseteq Z''_0 \subseteq W' \times W'$, any $t \in W, t' \in W'$, if $tZ_{i+1}t'$ and (X, X') is Z_i-coherent, then $X \in N(t)$ iff $X' \in N'(t')$.*

Modal Equivalence, n-Bisimulation and Model Comparison Game for BNL   57

We also say that Z_n is an n-bisimulation between $(\mathbb{M}, s)$ and $(\mathbb{M}', s')$ when it is not necessary to mention $Z_{n-1}, \ldots, Z_0$ explicitly.

We use $(\mathbb{M}, s) \underline{\leftrightarrow}_n (\mathbb{M}', s')$ to indicate that $(\mathbb{M}, s)$ and $(\mathbb{M}', s')$ are n-bisimilar, if there is an n-bisimulation between them.

Remark 1. In Definition 9, the most significant feature is that we require that only the subsets closed under all i-bisimulations (i.e. the ones that are definable by formulas of modal depth $\leq i$) are taken into account. This is important in our definition and the main improvement from previous definitions in order to give a concept exactly capturing modal equivalence. This is due to the fact that we only want subsets on both models that are definable to have the properties like $X \in N(t)$ iff $X' \in N'(t')$, since we want our definition to capture modal equivalence, and definable subsets (i.e. the ones that are closed under all i-bisimulations for some $i \leq n-1$) are exactly the ones that we need for the induction step.

Another thing that one might consider is whether this definition is well-defined, or whether it is circular. Indeed, it is not a circular definition because when we define n-bisimulation, we appeal to all i-bisimulations where $i \leq n-1$, so we are essentially defining it inductively on n. However, if we want to define a proper bisimulation concept without using the n-parameters, then we face a problem since we have to appeal to all bisimulations before defining bisimulation.

The next proposition shows the equivalence between n-bisimulation and n-equivalence.

Proposition 2. *For any pointed neighbourhood models $(\mathbb{M}, s)$ and $(\mathbb{M}', s')$, we have that $(\mathbb{M}, s) \underline{\leftrightarrow}_n (\mathbb{M}', s')$ iff $(\mathbb{M}, s) \rightsquigarrow_n (\mathbb{M}', s')$.*

Proof. We prove by induction on n. The case $n = 0$ is trivial. For the case $n = m + 1$,
$\Rightarrow$: Assume $(\mathbb{M}, s) \underline{\leftrightarrow}_{m+1} (\mathbb{M}', s')$, then there is an $m+1$-bisimulation $Z_{m+1} \subseteq Z_m \subseteq \ldots \subseteq Z_0 \subseteq W \times W'$ between $(\mathbb{M}, s)$ and $(\mathbb{M}', s')$. Suppose $\mathbb{M}, s \Vdash \varphi$ where $d(\varphi) \leq m + 1$.

- If $d(\varphi) \leq m$, then $Z_m \subseteq \ldots \subseteq Z_0 \subseteq W \times W'$ is an m-bisimulation between $(\mathbb{M}, s)$ and $(\mathbb{M}', s')$, by IH, $(\mathbb{M}, s) \rightsquigarrow_m (\mathbb{M}', s')$. Therefore, $\mathbb{M}', s' \Vdash \varphi$.
- If $d(\varphi) = m + 1$, it suffices to consider the case where $\varphi = \Box \psi$. Since $\mathbb{M}, s \Vdash \Box \psi$, we have $[\![\psi]\!]^{\mathbb{M}} \in N(s)$. It suffices to show that $[\![\psi]\!]^{\mathbb{M}'} \in N'(s')$.
  - We first show that $[\![\psi]\!]^{\mathbb{M}}$ is Z-closed under all m-bisimulations $Z \subseteq W \times W$: Suppose otherwise, there is an m-bisimulation $Z \subseteq W \times W$ such that $[\![\psi]\!]^{\mathbb{M}}$ is not Z-closed, i.e. there are $t, u \in W$ such that tZu, $t \in [\![\psi]\!]^{\mathbb{M}}$ and $u \notin [\![\psi]\!]^{\mathbb{M}}$, but by IH and $(\mathbb{M}, t) \underline{\leftrightarrow}_m (\mathbb{M}, u)$ we have that $(\mathbb{M}, t) \rightsquigarrow_m (\mathbb{M}, u)$, a contradiction to $t \in [\![\psi]\!]^{\mathbb{M}}$, $u \notin [\![\psi]\!]^{\mathbb{M}}$ and $d(\psi) \leq m$.
  - Similarly, $[\![\psi]\!]^{\mathbb{M}'}$ is Z'-closed under all m-bisimulations $Z' \subseteq W' \times W'$.
  - We can also show that $([\![\psi]\!]^{\mathbb{M}}, [\![\psi]\!]^{\mathbb{M}'})$ is Z_m-coherent. Suppose otherwise, there are $t \in W, t' \in W'$ with $tZ_m t'$ and "$t \in [\![\psi]\!]^{\mathbb{M}}$ iff $t' \in [\![\psi]\!]^{\mathbb{M}'}$" does not hold. Then by IH, from $tZ_m t'$ we have $(\mathbb{M}, t) \rightsquigarrow_m (\mathbb{M}', t')$, so "$t \in [\![\psi]\!]^{\mathbb{M}}$ iff $t' \in [\![\psi]\!]^{\mathbb{M}'}$" holds, a contradiction.

Therefore, $[\![\psi]\!]^{\mathrm{M}} \in N(s)$ iff $[\![\psi]\!]^{\mathrm{M}'} \in N'(s')$, so from $[\![\psi]\!]^{\mathrm{M}} \in N(s)$ we get $[\![\psi]\!]^{\mathrm{M}'} \in N'(s')$, i.e. $\mathrm{M}', s' \Vdash \Box \psi$.

Therefore, $(\mathrm{M}, s) \underline{\leftrightarrow}_{m+1} (\mathrm{M}', s') \Rightarrow (\mathrm{M}, s) \rightsquigarrow_{m+1} (\mathrm{M}', s')$.

$\Leftarrow$: Suppose $(\mathrm{M}, s) \rightsquigarrow_n (\mathrm{M}', s')$. Define $Z_i := \{(t, t') \mid (\mathrm{M}, t) \rightsquigarrow_i (\mathrm{M}', t')\} \subseteq W \times W'$ for $0 \leq i \leq n$. We show that $Z_n \subseteq Z_{n-1} \subseteq \ldots \subseteq Z_0 \subseteq W \times W'$ satisfy the five conditions for n-bisimulation:

1. By the definition of Z_n, $(\mathrm{M}, s) \rightsquigarrow_n (\mathrm{M}', s') \Rightarrow sZ_n s'$.
2. $tZ_0 t' \Rightarrow t$ and t' satisfy the same modality-free formulas, therefore the same propositional variables.
3. Suppose $0 \leq i \leq n-1$, $Z_i^{-1}[W'] \cap X_1 = Z_i^{-1}[W'] \cap X_2$, $t \in Z_{i+1}^{-1}[W']$, $X_1, X_2 \subseteq W$ are Z-closed under all i-bisimulations $Z \subseteq W \times W$, we will show that $X_1 \in N(t)$ iff $X_2 \in N(t)$.
    - We first show that X_1, X_2 are definable by BNL-formulas φ_1, φ_2 respectively where $d(\varphi_1), d(\varphi_2) \leq i$:
      Consider $\Theta_u := \{\theta \mid \mathrm{M}, u \Vdash \theta \text{ and } d(\theta) \leq i\}$ where $u \in W$, then by Proposition 1, Θ_u contains finitely many non-equivalent representatives. Define θ_u to be the conjunction of these finitely many non-equivalent representatives, then θ_u is a BNL-formula with $d(\theta_u) \leq i$. Now define $\Delta_{X_1} := \{\theta_u \mid u \in X_1\}$, then by Proposition 1, Δ_{X_1} contains finitely many non-equivalent representatives. Now define φ_1 to be the disjunction of these finitely many non-equivalent representatives, then we can show that $X_1 = [\![\varphi_1]\!]^{\mathrm{M}}$:
      Since $\mathrm{M}, u \Vdash \theta_u$ for all $u \in W$, we have that $\mathrm{M}, u \Vdash \varphi_1$ for all $u \in X_1$, so $X_1 \subseteq [\![\varphi_1]\!]^{\mathrm{M}}$. For the other direction, suppose that $\mathrm{M}, u \Vdash \varphi_1$, then $\mathrm{M}, u \Vdash \theta_v$ for some $v \in X_1$, so $(\mathrm{M}, u) \rightsquigarrow_i (\mathrm{M}, v)$, by IH, $(\mathrm{M}, u) \underline{\leftrightarrow}_i (\mathrm{M}, v)$. Since X_1 is Z-closed under all i-bisimulations $Z \subseteq W \times W$ and $v \in X_1$, we have that $u \in X_1$. Therefore $[\![\varphi_1]\!]^{\mathrm{M}} \subseteq X_1$.
      Similarly, we can show that X_2 is definable by a BNL-formula φ_2 where $d(\varphi_2) \leq i$.
    - We first show that $Z_i^{-1}[W']$ is definable by a BNL-formula ψ of depth $\leq i$:
      Consider any $w \in W - Z_i^{-1}[W']$, since there is no $w' \in W'$ with $(\mathrm{M}, w) \rightsquigarrow_i (\mathrm{M}', w')$, so for any $w' \in W'$, there is a BNL-formula $\varphi_{w,w'}$ with $d(\varphi_{w,w'}) \leq i$ such that $\mathrm{M}, w \not\Vdash \varphi_{w,w'}$ and $\mathrm{M}', w' \Vdash \varphi_{w,w'}$. Therefore, $\bigvee_{w' \in W'} \varphi_{w,w'}$ is globally true in M', and false at $w \in W$. By Proposition 1, among $\{\varphi_{w,w'} \mid w' \in W'\}$, there are finitely many non-equivalent representatives such that their finite disjunction $\varphi_{w,W'}$ is a BNL-formula and is semantically equivalent to $\bigvee_{w' \in W'} \varphi_{w,w'}$ (i.e. they are satisfied on the same pointed models). Now consider $\varphi := \bigwedge_{w \in W - Z_i^{-1}[W']} \varphi_{w,W'}$, then again by Proposition 1, there is a BNL-formula ψ semantically equivalent to φ such that $d(\psi) \leq i$. Then $[\![\psi]\!]^{\mathrm{M}'} = W'$ and $[\![\psi]\!]^{\mathrm{M}} = Z_i^{-1}[W']$.
    - Since $X_1 = [\![\varphi_1]\!]^{\mathrm{M}}$, $X_2 = [\![\varphi_2]\!]^{\mathrm{M}}$, $Z_i^{-1}[W'] = [\![\psi]\!]^{\mathrm{M}}$, $W' = [\![\psi]\!]^{\mathrm{M}'}$ and $Z_i^{-1}[W'] \cap X_1 = Z_i^{-1}[W'] \cap X_2$, we have that $[\![\varphi_1 \wedge \psi]\!]^{\mathrm{M}} = [\![\varphi_2 \wedge \psi]\!]^{\mathrm{M}}$. Since $t \in Z_{i+1}^{-1}[W']$, there is a $t' \in W'$ such that $tZ_{i+1}t'$. Therefore $X_1 \in N(t)$ iff $[\![\varphi_1]\!]^{\mathrm{M}} \in N(t)$

iff $\mathbb{M}, t \Vdash \Box\varphi_1$
iff $\mathbb{M}', t' \Vdash \Box\varphi_1$
iff $[\![\varphi_1]\!]^{\mathbb{M}'} \in N'(t')$
iff $[\![\varphi_1 \wedge \psi]\!]^{\mathbb{M}'} = [\![\varphi_1]\!]^{\mathbb{M}'} \cap [\![\psi]\!]^{\mathbb{M}'} = [\![\varphi_1]\!]^{\mathbb{M}'} \cap W' = [\![\varphi_1]\!]^{\mathbb{M}'} \in N'(t')$
iff $\mathbb{M}', t' \Vdash \Box(\varphi_1 \wedge \psi)$
iff $\mathbb{M}, t \Vdash \Box(\varphi_1 \wedge \psi)$
iff $[\![\varphi_1 \wedge \psi]\!]^{\mathbb{M}} \in N(t)$.
Similarly, $X_2 \in N(t)$ iff $[\![\varphi_2 \wedge \psi]\!]^{\mathbb{M}} \in N(t)$. Since $[\![\varphi_1 \wedge \psi]\!]^{\mathbb{M}} = [\![\varphi_2 \wedge \psi]\!]^{\mathbb{M}}$, we have $X_1 \in N(t)$ iff $X_2 \in N(t)$.

4. Similar to item 3.
5. Suppose $tZ_{i+1}t'$, $X \subseteq W$ is Z-closed under all i-bisimulations $Z \subseteq W \times W$, $X' \subseteq W'$ is Z'-closed under all i-bisimulations $Z' \subseteq W' \times W'$, and (X, X') is Z_i-coherent.
   - Similar to item 3, we have that $X \subseteq W$ and $X' \subseteq W'$ are definable by BNL-formulas φ_1, φ_2 respectively where $d(\varphi_1), d(\varphi_2) \leq i$.
   - By items 3 and 4, we have $X \in N(t)$ iff $X \cap Z_i^{-1}[W'] \in N(t)$ and $X' \in N'(t')$ iff $X' \cap Z_i[W] \in N'(t')$.
   - It is also easy to see that $X \cap Z_i^{-1}[W']$ and $X' \cap Z_i[W]$ are definable by BNL-formulas $\varphi_1 \wedge \psi, \varphi_2 \wedge \psi$ (ψ is as defined in the proof of item 3) respectively where $d(\varphi_1 \wedge \psi), d(\varphi_2 \wedge \psi) \leq i$.
   - We can also show that $X \cap Z_i^{-1}[W']$ is Z-closed under all i-bisimulations $Z \subseteq W \times W$:
     Suppose otherwise, $X \cap Z_i^{-1}[W'] = [\![\varphi_1 \wedge \psi]\!]^{\mathbb{M}}$ is not Z-closed for some i-bisimulation $Z \subseteq W \times W$, then there are $u, v \in W$ such that uZv, $u \in [\![\varphi_1 \wedge \psi]\!]^{\mathbb{M}}$ and $v \notin [\![\varphi_1 \wedge \psi]\!]^{\mathbb{M}}$. By IH, $(\mathbb{M}, u) \leftrightsquigarrow_i (\mathbb{M}, v)$, which contradicts $d(\varphi_1 \wedge \psi) \leq i$.
   - Similarly, $X' \cap Z_i[W]$ is Z'-closed under all i-bisimulations $Z' \subseteq W' \times W'$.
   - We can also show that $(X \cap Z_i^{-1}[W'], X' \cap Z_i[W])$ is also Z_i-coherent: $Z_i[X \cap Z_i^{-1}[W']] \subseteq Z_i[X] \subseteq X'$ and $Z_i[X \cap Z_i^{-1}[W']] \subseteq Z_i[W]$, and the other direction is similar.
   - Therefore, it suffices to consider the special case where $X \subseteq Z_i^{-1}[W']$ and $X' \subseteq Z_i[W]$.
   - By the proof of item 3, $Z_i^{-1}[W']$ is definable by a BNL-formula ψ of depth $\leq i$, and $W' = [\![\psi]\!]^{\mathbb{M}'}$. Therefore $[\![\varphi_1]\!]^{\mathbb{M}} = X \subseteq Z_i^{-1}[W'] = [\![\psi]\!]^{\mathbb{M}}$.
   - We claim that $[\![\varphi_1]\!]^{\mathbb{M}} = [\![\varphi_2]\!]^{\mathbb{M}} \cap [\![\psi]\!]^{\mathbb{M}}$:
     • Take any $u \in [\![\varphi_1]\!]^{\mathbb{M}} = X$. By the Z_i-coherence of (X, X') and $X \subseteq Z_i^{-1}[W']$, there is a $u' \in X'$ such that $uZ_i u'$, therefore from $u' \in X' = [\![\varphi_2]\!]^{\mathbb{M}'}$ we have $\mathbb{M}', u' \Vdash \varphi_2$, and from $uZ_i u'$ and $d(\varphi_2) \leq i$ we have $\mathbb{M}, u \Vdash \varphi_2$. Therefore, $[\![\varphi_1]\!]^{\mathbb{M}} \subseteq [\![\varphi_2]\!]^{\mathbb{M}}$.
     • Next we show that $[\![\varphi_2]\!]^{\mathbb{M}} \cap [\![\psi]\!]^{\mathbb{M}} \subseteq [\![\varphi_1]\!]^{\mathbb{M}}$. Take any $u \in [\![\varphi_2]\!]^{\mathbb{M}} \cap [\![\psi]\!]^{\mathbb{M}} \subseteq Z_i^{-1}[W']$, then there is a $u' \in W'$ such that $uZ_i u'$, therefore from $d(\varphi_2) \leq i$ we have $\mathbb{M}', u' \Vdash \varphi_2$, so $u' \in X'$. By the Z_i-coherence of (X, X') and $X' \subseteq Z_i[W]$, for any $u \in W$ such that $uZ_i u'$, we have $u \in X$. Therefore $u \in [\![\varphi_1]\!]^{\mathbb{M}}$.

- Now we have $X \in N(t)$
  iff $[\![\varphi_1]\!]^{\mathbb{M}} \in N(t)$
  iff $[\![\varphi_2]\!]^{\mathbb{M}} \cap [\![\psi]\!]^{\mathbb{M}} \in N(t)$
  iff $\mathbb{M}, t \Vdash \Box(\varphi_2 \wedge \psi)$
  iff $\mathbb{M}', t' \Vdash \Box(\varphi_2 \wedge \psi)$
  iff $[\![\varphi_2]\!]^{\mathbb{M}'} \cap [\![\psi]\!]^{\mathbb{M}'} \in N'(t')$
  iff $[\![\varphi_2]\!]^{\mathbb{M}'} \cap W' \in N'(t')$
  iff $[\![\varphi_2]\!]^{\mathbb{M}'} \in N'(t')$
  iff $X' \in N'(t')$.

Proposition 3. *For any n and pointed models $(\mathbb{M}, s), (\mathbb{M}', s')$, if $(\mathbb{M}, s) \underline{\leftrightarrow}_n (\mathbb{M}', s')$, then there is a largest n-bisimulation $Z_n \subseteq Z_{n-1} \subseteq \ldots \subseteq Z_0 \subseteq W \times W'$ in the sense of set-theoretic inclusion, i.e. for any n-bisimulation $Z'_n \subseteq Z'_{n-1} \subseteq \ldots \subseteq Z'_0 \subseteq W \times W'$, we have $Z'_i \subseteq Z_i$ for $i = 0, \ldots, n$.*

Proof. Take $Z_m := \{(t, t') \mid (\mathbb{M}, t) \rightsquigarrow_m (\mathbb{M}', t')\} \subseteq W \times W'$ for $0 \leq m \leq n$, then $Z_n \subseteq Z_{n-1} \subseteq \ldots \subseteq Z_0 \subseteq W \times W'$ is the largest n-bisimulation between $(\mathbb{M}, s)$ and $(\mathbb{M}', s')$.

4 Model Comparison Game

We now introduce the n-round model comparison game. In what follows, we use A_1 and A_2 to denote the two players in the game, and use $\overline{A_i}$ to denote the opponent player of A_i, where $i \in \{1, 2\}$. Given two pointed models $(\mathbb{M}, s), (\mathbb{M}', s')$, player A_1 (resp. A_2) claims they are different (resp. similar) in terms of modal equivalence and bisimulation. The game starts with $(A_1, (\mathbb{M}, s), (\mathbb{M}', s'), n)$, where the first component A_1 means that A_1 is the player trying to show that the two pointed models are different, and the opponent is trying to show that they are similar. The game is inspired from our definition of n-bisimulation.

Definition 10 (n-Round Model Comparison Game). *The n-round model comparison game starts with $(A_1, (\mathbb{M}, s), (\mathbb{M}', s'), n)$ and proceeds as follows:*

At $(A_i, (\mathbb{M}, s), (\mathbb{M}', s'), 0)$, if s, s' agree on all propositional variables, then $\overline{A_i}$ wins.

During the game, at any position $(A_i, (\mathbb{M}, s), (\mathbb{M}', s'), m)$, if s, s' disagree on some propositional variables, then A_i wins.

At any position $(A_i, (\mathbb{M}, s), (\mathbb{M}', s'), m)$ when $m > 0$ and s, s' agree on all propositional variables, player A_i has the following choices:

1. A_i *chooses* $X_1 \in N(s)$ *and* $X_2 \notin N(s)$, *and* $\overline{A_i}$ *has the following choices:*
   (a) $\overline{A_i}$ *picks* $t_1 \in X_1$ *and* $t_2 \in W - X_1$ *and the game continues at* $(A_i, (\mathbb{M}, t_1), (\mathbb{M}, t_2), m-1)$.
   (b) $\overline{A_i}$ *picks* $t_1 \in X_2$ *and* $t_2 \in W - X_2$ *and the game continues at* $(A_i, (\mathbb{M}, t_1), (\mathbb{M}, t_2), m-1)$.

(c) $\overline{A_i}$ picks $t \in (X_1 - X_2) \cup (X_2 - X_1)$ and $t' \in W'$, and the game continues at $(A_i, (\mathbb{M}, t), (\mathbb{M}', t'), m - 1)$.

2. A_i chooses $X_1' \in N'(s')$ and $X_2' \notin N'(s')$, and $\overline{A_i}$ has the following choices:
   (a) $\overline{A_i}$ picks $t_1' \in X_1'$ and $t_2' \in W' - X_1'$ and the game continues at $(A_i, (\mathbb{M}', t_1'), (\mathbb{M}', t_2'), m - 1)$.
   (b) $\overline{A_i}$ picks $t_1' \in X_2'$ and $t_2' \in W' - X_2'$ and the game continues at $(A_i, (\mathbb{M}', t_1'), (\mathbb{M}', t_2'), m - 1)$.
   (c) $\overline{A_i}$ picks $t' \in (X_1' - X_2') \cup (X_2' - X_1')$ and $t \in W$, and the game continues at $(A_i, (\mathbb{M}, t), (\mathbb{M}', t'), m - 1)$.

3. A_i chooses $X \in N(s)$ and $X' \notin N'(s')$, and $\overline{A_i}$ has the following choices:
   (a) $\overline{A_i}$ picks $t_1 \in X$ and $t_2 \in W - X$ and the game continues at $(A_i, (\mathbb{M}, t_1), (\mathbb{M}, t_2), m - 1)$.
   (b) $\overline{A_i}$ picks $t_1' \in X'$ and $t_2' \in W' - X'$ and the game continues at $(A_i, (\mathbb{M}', t_1'), (\mathbb{M}', t_2'), m - 1)$.
   (c) $\overline{A_i}$ picks $t \in X$ and $t' \notin X'$, and the game continues at $(A_i, (\mathbb{M}, t), (\mathbb{M}', t'), m - 1)$.
   (d) $\overline{A_i}$ picks $t \notin X$ and $t' \in X'$, and the game continues at $(A_i, (\mathbb{M}, t), (\mathbb{M}', t'), m - 1)$.

4. A_i chooses $X' \in N'(s')$ and $X \notin N(s)$, and $\overline{A_i}$ has the following choices:
   (a) $\overline{A_i}$ picks $t_1' \in X'$ and $t_2' \in W' - X'$ and the game continues at $(A_i, (\mathbb{M}', t_1'), (\mathbb{M}', t_2'), m - 1)$.
   (b) $\overline{A_i}$ picks $t_1 \in X$ and $t_2 \in W - X$ and the game continues at $(A_i, (\mathbb{M}, t_1), (\mathbb{M}, t_2), m - 1)$.
   (c) $\overline{A_i}$ picks $t \notin X$ and $t' \in X'$, and the game continues at $(A_i, (\mathbb{M}, t), (\mathbb{M}', t'), m - 1)$.
   (d) $\overline{A_i}$ picks $t \in X$ and $t' \notin X'$, and the game continues at $(A_i, (\mathbb{M}, t), (\mathbb{M}', t'), m - 1)$.

Remark 2. The choices of A_i essentially reflect the definition of n-bisimulation:

– For case 1, it corresponds to the attack of item 3 in the definition of n-bisimulation. The responds of $\overline{A_i}$ can be explained as follows: cases (a) and (b) are the attacks of the i-bisimulation closure of X_1 and X_2, respectively, and case (c) is the attack of $Z_i^{-1}[W'] \cap X_1 = Z_i^{-1}[W'] \cap X_2$.
– For case 2, it corresponds to the attack of item 4 in the definition of n-bisimulation, which is symmetric to case 1.
– For cases 3 and 4, they correspond to the attack of item 5 in the definition of n-bisimulation. For the responds of $\overline{A_i}$, cases (a) and (b) are the attacks of the i-bisimulation closure of X and X', respectively, and cases (c) and (d) are the attacks of the coherence.

By a winning strategy of player A_i, we mean that in any execution of the game, no matter how the opponent plays in the game, A_i has a strategy to play in the game such that A_i wins every game that she follows her strategy. The next lemma is obvious to see:

Lemma 1. *If $\overline{A_i}$ has a winning strategy at $(A_i, (\mathbb{M}, s), (\mathbb{M}', s'), n)$, then $\overline{A_i}$ has a winning strategy at $(A_i, (\mathbb{M}, s), (\mathbb{M}', s'), m)$ for all $0 \leq m \leq n$.*

The next theorem shows that the model comparison game characterizes n-bisimulation as well as n-equivalence.

Theorem 1 (Adequacy Theorem). *The followings are equivalent:*

1. $\overline{A_i}$ *has a winning strategy at* $(A_i, (\mathbb{M}, s), (\mathbb{M}', s'), n)$.
2. $(\mathbb{M}, s) \underline{\leftrightarrow}_n (\mathbb{M}', s')$.
3. $(\mathbb{M}, s) \rightsquigarrow_n (\mathbb{M}', s')$.

Proof. $2 \Leftrightarrow 3$ is shown in Proposition 2. We prove $1 \Leftrightarrow 2,3$ by induction on n.

- For $n = 0$, trivial.
- For $n = k+1$, suppose $1 \Leftrightarrow 2,3$ for all $n \leq k$, and the largest n-bisimulation is $Z_n \subseteq Z_{n-1} \subseteq \ldots \subseteq Z_0 \subseteq W \times W'$ where $Z_i := \{(t, t') \mid (\mathbb{M}, t) \rightsquigarrow_i (\mathbb{M}', t')\} \subseteq W \times W'$ for $0 \leq i \leq n$.

$2, 3 \Rightarrow 1$: Suppose $(\mathbb{M}, s) \rightsquigarrow_{k+1} (\mathbb{M}', s')$, and we show that $\overline{A_i}$ has a winning strategy at $(A_i, (\mathbb{M}, s), (\mathbb{M}', s'), k+1)$. Consider the game $(A_i, (\mathbb{M}, s), (\mathbb{M}', s'), k+1)$:

- If A_i chooses $X_1 \in N(s)$ and $X_2 \notin N(s)$, then there are the following possibilities:
  * If X_1 is not Z-closed under some k-bisimulation $Z \subseteq W \times W$, then there are $t_1 \in X_1$ and $t_2 \in W - X_1$ such that $(\mathbb{M}, t_1) \underline{\leftrightarrow}_k (\mathbb{M}, t_2)$. Therefore by IH, $\overline{A_i}$ has a winning strategy at $(A_i, (\mathbb{M}, t_1), (\mathbb{M}, t_2), k)$. Therefore, by picking $t_1 \in X_1$ and $t_2 \in W - X_1$, $\overline{A_i}$ has a winning strategy at this response of A_i.
  * If X_2 is not Z-closed under some k-bisimulation $Z \subseteq W \times W$, the situation is similar.
  * If both X_1 and X_2 are Z-closed under all k-bisimulations $Z \subseteq W \times W$, since $(\mathbb{M}, s) \rightsquigarrow_{k+1} (\mathbb{M}', s')$ and therefore $s \in Z_{k+1}^{-1}[W']$, by the definition of n-bisimulation, $Z_k^{-1}[W'] \cap X_1 \neq Z_k^{-1}[W'] \cap X_2$. Then there is a $t \in Z_k^{-1}[W'] \cap X_1$ such that $t \notin Z_k^{-1}[W'] \cap X_2$, or there is a $t \in Z_k^{-1}[W'] \cap X_2$ s.t. $t \notin Z_k^{-1}[W'] \cap X_1$. Without loss of generality suppose that $t \in Z_k^{-1}[W'] \cap X_1$ and $t \notin Z_k^{-1}[W'] \cap X_2$, then $t \in (X_1 - X_2) \cup (X_2 - X_1)$ and $t \in Z_k^{-1}[W']$. Let $\overline{A_i}$ pick this $t \in (X_1 - X_2) \cup (X_2 - X_1) \subseteq W$ and a $t' \in W'$ such that $t Z_k t'$ (by $t \in Z_k^{-1}[W']$, such t' exists), then by IH, $\overline{A_i}$ has a winning strategy at the game $(A_i, (\mathbb{M}, t), (\mathbb{M}', t'), k)$. Therefore, $\overline{A_i}$ has a winning strategy at this response of A_i.
- If A_i chooses $X_1' \in N'(s')$ and $X_2' \notin N'(s')$, the situation is similar to the previous case.
- If A_i chooses $X \in N(s)$ and $X' \notin N'(s')$, then
  * If X is not Z-closed under some k-bisimulation $Z \subseteq W \times W$, the situation is similar to the first subcase of the first case.
  * If X' is not Z'-closed under some k-bisimulation $Z' \subseteq W' \times W'$, the situation is again similar.

* If X is Z-closed under all k-bisimulations $Z \subseteq W \times W$ and X' is Z'-closed under all k-bisimulations $Z' \subseteq W' \times W'$, then by the definition of n-bisimulation, (X, X') is not Z_k-coherent, so either $Z_k[X] \not\subseteq X'$ or $Z_k^{-1}[X'] \not\subseteq X$.
    · If $Z_k[X] \not\subseteq X'$, then there exist $t \in X, t' \notin X'$ such that $tZ_k t'$ holds. Then let $\overline{A_i}$ pick these $t \in X$ and $t' \notin X'$, then by IH, $\overline{A_i}$ has a winning strategy at the game $(A_i, (\mathbb{M}, t), (\mathbb{M}', t'), k)$. Therefore, $\overline{A_i}$ has a winning strategy at this response of A_i.
    · If $Z_k^{-1}[X'] \not\subseteq X$, the situation is symmetric to the previous subcase.

- If A_i chooses $X' \in N'(s')$ and $X \notin N(s)$, the situation is similar to the previous case.

To summarize, $\overline{A_i}$ has a winning strategy at $(A_i, (\mathbb{M}, s), (\mathbb{M}', s'), k+1)$.

$1 \Rightarrow 2, 3$: Suppose $\overline{A_i}$ has a winning strategy at $(A_i, (\mathbb{M}, s), (\mathbb{M}', s'), k+1)$. We show $d(\varphi) \leq k+1 \Rightarrow (\mathbb{M}, s \Vdash \varphi$ iff $\mathbb{M}', s' \Vdash \varphi)$ by induction on φ.

- For atoms, since $\overline{A_i}$ has a winning strategy at $(A_i, (\mathbb{M}, s), (\mathbb{M}', s'), k+1)$, by Lemma 1, $\overline{A_i}$ has a winning strategy at $(A_i, (\mathbb{M}, s), (\mathbb{M}', s'), 0)$. Therefore $\mathbb{M}, s \Vdash \varphi$ iff $\mathbb{M}', s' \Vdash \varphi$ for any $\varphi \in \mathsf{Prop}$.
- The Boolean cases are easy.
- For $\varphi = \Box \psi$, if $d(\varphi) \leq k$, then since $\overline{A_i}$ has a winning strategy at $(A_i, (\mathbb{M}, s), (\mathbb{M}', s'), k+1)$, by Lemma 1, $\overline{A_i}$ has a winning strategy at $(A_i, (\mathbb{M}, s), (\mathbb{M}', s'), k)$. By IH, $\mathbb{M}, s \Vdash \varphi$ iff $\mathbb{M}', s' \Vdash \varphi$.
  If $d(\varphi) = k+1$, suppose exactly one of $\mathbb{M}, s \Vdash \Box\psi$ and $\mathbb{M}', s' \Vdash \Box\psi$ holds (without loss of generality the former one holds), then $[\![\psi]\!]^{\mathbb{M}} \in N(s)$ and $[\![\psi]\!]^{\mathbb{M}'} \notin N'(s')$. Then, at the game $(A_i, (\mathbb{M}, s), (\mathbb{M}', s'), k+1)$, we let A_i pick $[\![\psi]\!]^{\mathbb{M}} \in N(s)$ and $[\![\psi]\!]^{\mathbb{M}'} \notin N'(s')$, then we consider the winning strategy of $\overline{A_i}$:
    * If $\overline{A_i}$ picks $t_1 \in [\![\psi]\!]^{\mathbb{M}}$ and $t_2 \in W - [\![\psi]\!]^{\mathbb{M}}$ as the winning strategy and the game continues at $(A_i, (\mathbb{M}, t_1), (\mathbb{M}, t_2), k)$, then by IH, $(\mathbb{M}, t_1) \leftrightsquigarrow_k (\mathbb{M}, t_2)$, a contradiction to $t_1 \in [\![\psi]\!]^{\mathbb{M}}$ and $t_2 \in W - [\![\psi]\!]^{\mathbb{M}}$.
    * If $\overline{A_i}$ picks $t_1' \in [\![\psi]\!]^{\mathbb{M}'}$ and $t_2' \in W' - [\![\psi]\!]^{\mathbb{M}'}$, the situation is similar.
    * If $\overline{A_i}$ picks $t \in [\![\psi]\!]^{\mathbb{M}}$ and $t' \notin [\![\psi]\!]^{\mathbb{M}'}$, then $\overline{A_i}$ has a winning strategy at the game $(A_i, (\mathbb{M}, t), (\mathbb{M}', t'), k)$, which by IH implies that $\mathbb{M}, t \Vdash \psi$ iff $\mathbb{M}', t' \Vdash \psi$, a contradiction.
    * If $\overline{A_i}$ picks $t \notin [\![\psi]\!]^{\mathbb{M}}$ and $t' \in [\![\psi]\!]^{\mathbb{M}'}$, the situation is similar.
  Therefore, $\mathbb{M}, s \Vdash \Box\psi$ iff $\mathbb{M}', s' \Vdash \Box\psi$.

Therefore, if $\overline{A_i}$ has a winning strategy at $(A_i, (\mathbb{M}, s), (\mathbb{M}', s'), k+1)$, then $(\mathbb{M}, s) \leftrightsquigarrow_{k+1} (\mathbb{M}', s')$.

5 Discussions on Model Similarity Concepts

In [4], the authors give three different notions of model similarity between neighbourhood structures. The one most similar to us is the notion of 2^2-bisimulation.

Here we use the equivalent formulation as given in [4, Proposition 3.15], modulo adaptations to the pointed neighbourhood model (rather than frame) setting:

Definition 11 (2^2-bisimulation). *Given two pointed models $(\mathbb{M}, s)$ and $(\mathbb{M}', s')$, we say that $Z \subseteq W \times W'$ is a 2^2-bisimulation between $(\mathbb{M}, s)$ and $(\mathbb{M}', s')$, if sZs' and for any tZt', the following holds:*

1. *t and t' agree on all propositional variables.*
2. *For any $X_1, X_2 \subseteq W$, if $Z^{-1}[W'] \cap X_1 = Z^{-1}[W'] \cap X_2$, then $X_1 \in N(t)$ iff $X_2 \in N(t)$.*
3. *For any $X_1', X_2' \subseteq W'$, if $Z[W] \cap X_1' = Z[W] \cap X_2'$, then $X_1' \in N'(t')$ iff $X_2' \in N'(t')$.*
4. *For any $X \subseteq W$, $X' \subseteq W'$, if (X, X') is Z-coherent, then $X \in N(t)$ iff $X' \in N'(t')$.*

As is shown in [4, Example 3.18], behavioural equivalence and 2^2-bisimulation are different. Therefore, we can expect that the notion of 2^2-bisimulation cannot capture modal equivalence. The gap here is exactly the requirement that X, X_1, X_2 and X', X_1', X_2' are closed under respective Z-type i-bisimulation relations. As can be seen from the proofs in the present paper, these closure conditions corresponds to the definability of these subsets by formulas of depth $\leq i$. Therefore, the definability conditions are exactly what we need for the characterization of n-equivalence via n-bisimulation.

A natural question would be how to define a bisimulation concept which removes the n-parameters. The major difficulty is that in Definition 9, in items 3–5, we make use of the closure under all i-bisimulations. When we define n-bisimulation inductively by depth, we use all i-bisimulations for the depth $i+1$ case, but if we need to define bisimulation directly, we need to first have already defined all bisimulations in order to define bisimulation.

Another possibility is to replace the closure-under-bisimulation-condition by some definability-by-formula condition. However, as discussed in [1], a good definition of bisimulation should be structural, i.e. without using logical formulas in the definition.

Acknowledgement. The research of Xiaoxuan Fu is supported by the Young Teacher Support Program of China University of Political Science and Law (project number: CU202044). The research of Zhiguang Zhao is supported by Shandong Provincial Natural Science Foundation, China (project number: ZR2023QF021) and Taishan Young Scholars Program of the Government of Shandong Province, China (No.tsqn201909151). The authors would like to thank Johan van Benthem for his suggestions and comments.

References

1. Baltag, A., Ciná, G.: Bisimulation for conditional modalities. Stud. Logica. **106**, 1–33 (2018)

2. Blackburn, P., de Rijke, M., Venema, Y.: Modal logic, vol. 53 of Cambridge Tracts in Theoretical Computer Science. Cambridge University Press (2001)
3. Chellas, B.F.: Modal Logic: an Introduction. Cambridge University Press (1980)
4. Hansen, H.H., Kupke, C., Pacuit, E.: Neighbourhood structures: bisimilarity and basic model theory. Logical Methods Comput. Sci. **5** (2009)
5. Hodges, W.: Building Models by Games. London Mathematical Society Student Texts, Cambridge University Press (1985)
6. Montague, R.: Universal grammar. Theoria **36**(3), 373–398 (1970)
7. Pacuit, E.: Neighborhood semantics for modal logic. Springer (2017)
8. Scott, D.: Advice on modal logic. In: Philosophical Problems in Logic: Some Recent Developments, pp. 143–173. Springer (1970)
9. Segerberg, K.: An essay in classical modal logic. Number 13 in Filosofiska Studier. Uppsala Universitet (1971)
10. Väänänen, J.: Models and Games. Cambridge Studies in Advanced Mathematics. Cambridge University Press (2011)
11. van Benthem, J.: Logic in Games. The MIT Press, MIT Press (2014)

Preference-Based Extension Enforcement in Argumentation

Nguyen Duy Hung[1](✉) and Van-Nam Huynh[2]

[1] Sirindhorn International Institute of Technology, Thammasat University, Pathum Thani, Thailand
hung@siit.tu.ac.th,hung.nd.siit@gmail.com
[2] Japan Advanced Institute of Science and Technology, Nomi, Japan

Abstract. Abstract Argumentation frameworks (AAFs) unify many approaches to computational argumentation. The dynamics of AAFs has been recently recognized as a potential power of AAFs to cope with dynamic settings such as argumentative dialogues. In this paper, we focus on an arguably understudied form of argumentation dynamics, referred to as *preference-based extension enforcement*, which constrains the commonly studied extension enforcement form by considering only attack removals that can be rationalized by some argument preference relation. In particular, we formalize preference-based extension enforcement and study its relationships with agent's behaviourally revealed preferences. Finally, leveraging a computational framework for *revealed preference argumentation* in our earlier work, we develop sound and complete algorithms for many instances of preference-based extension enforcement.

1 Introduction

Much of the recent development in computational argumentation centers around the abstract argumentation framework (AAF) of [9] defined simply by a pair $\mathcal{F} = (\mathcal{A}rg, \mathcal{A}tt)$ with a set $\mathcal{A}rg$ of arguments and a binary attack relation/graph $\mathcal{A}tt$ between arguments. An argumentation semantics σ identifies a set $\sigma(\mathcal{F}) \subseteq 2^{\mathcal{A}rg}$ of extensions, each of which is a subset of arguments that can be acceptable together[1]. Though simple AAF turns out very powerful, with connections to a range of fields, from knowledge representation and reasoning to philosophy and social sciences, as well as applications in various domains. Recently the field of dynamics of argumentation received much attention [8,19,21] (see [4] for a review) as it shines important aspects of AAFs in dynamic settings such as argumentative dialogues. A common form of argumentation dynamics is the so-called *extension enforcement* where the goal is to modify a given AAF $\mathcal{F}$ so that a given set $\mathcal{E}$ of arguments becomes an extension [3]. In [6], the arguments are fixed but and the attack graph may be subject to any change. Formally argument-fixed sub-extension/full-extension/single-extension enforcement is to compute a set of modified attack graphs defined respectively as follows.

---
[1] Formal definitions are given in Sect. 2.

$\mathtt{ExtEnf}_\sigma^{sb}(\mathcal{F},\mathcal{E}) \triangleq \{\mathcal{A}tt' \mid \mathcal{E} \subseteq E \text{ for some } E \in \sigma(\mathcal{F}') \text{ where } \mathcal{F}' = (\mathcal{A}rg, \mathcal{A}tt')\}$
$\mathtt{ExtEnf}_\sigma^{fl}(\mathcal{F},\mathcal{E}) \triangleq \{\mathcal{A}tt' \mid \mathcal{E} \in \sigma(\mathcal{F}') \text{ where } \mathcal{F}' = (\mathcal{A}rg, \mathcal{A}tt')\}$
$\mathtt{ExtEnf}_\sigma^{sl}(\mathcal{F},\mathcal{E}) \triangleq \{\mathcal{A}tt' \mid \sigma(\mathcal{F}') = \{\mathcal{E}\} \text{ where } \mathcal{F}' = (\mathcal{A}rg, \mathcal{A}tt')\}$

Since these sets can be exponentially big (wrt the number of arguments), many authors restrict themselves to some possibly more interesting solutions, for example the modified attack graph with a minimal distance to the original graph (e.g. when the Hamming distance is used, this is the modified graph with the minimal number of attack removals or additions). In this paper, we restrict ourselves to modified attack graphs that can be "rationalized" by overlaying the original graph $\mathcal{A}tt$ with a pre-order $P \subseteq \mathcal{A}rg \times \mathcal{A}rg$ representing preferences over arguments[2]. As elaborated later, a graph rationalized by P, denoted $\mathcal{A}tt \oplus P$, removes an attack (A, B) of the original graph only if this attack is labelled "preference-dependent" and $B > A \in P$. The resulted problem is hence called *preference-based extension enforcement* which relates to argument-fixed extension enforcement $\mathtt{ExtEnf}_\sigma^x(\mathcal{F},\mathcal{E})$, $x \in \{sb, fl, sl\}$ in the following way:

$$\mathtt{PrefExtEnf}_\sigma^x(\mathcal{F},\mathcal{E}) = \{P \mid \mathcal{A}tt \oplus P \in \mathtt{ExtEnf}_\sigma^x(\mathcal{F},\mathcal{E})\}$$

The following example demonstrates why one may be more interested in preference-based extension enforcement than argument-fixed extension enforcement.

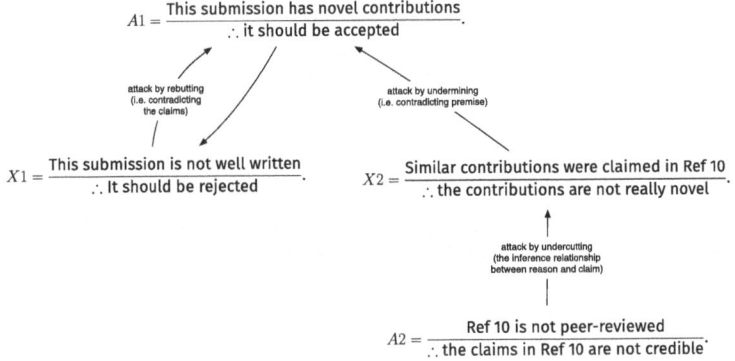

Fig. 1. A sample AAF $\mathcal{F}$

Example 1. Consider AAF $\mathcal{F}$ shown in Fig. 1 which summarizes a review process. Arguments $A1, A2$ are presented by author A, while arguments $X1, X2$ by Reviewer X. $\{A2\}$ is the grounded extension but A wants $\mathcal{E} = \{A1, A2\}$ instead.

---
[2] $(A, B) \in P$ says that A is at least as preferred as B. For convenience, $A > B \in P$ stands for $(A, B) \in P \wedge (B, A) \notin P$, i.e. A is strictly preferred to B.

- If framing the response to reviewer as an instance of argument-fixed enforcement, the author computes $\text{ExtEnf}_{gr}^{sl}(\mathcal{F},\mathcal{E}) = \{\mathcal{A}tt_1, \mathcal{A}tt_2, \mathcal{A}tt_3\}$ where $\mathcal{A}tt_1 = \mathcal{A}tt \setminus \{(X1,A1)\}$, $\mathcal{A}tt_2 = \mathcal{A}tt \setminus \{(X1,A1),(X2,A1)\}$ and $\mathcal{A}tt_3 = \mathcal{A}tt \setminus \{(X1,A1),(X2,A1),(A2,X2)\}$ (For the grounded acceptance of $A1$, the attack $(X1,A1)$ must be removed. The attack $(X2,A1)$ may or may not be removed, and if it is removed, then $(A2,X2)$ can be removed as well).
- If framing the response to reviewer as an instance of preference-based enforcement where only the attacks between $A1, X1$ are preference-dependent, the author computes $\text{PrefExtEnf}_{gr}^{sl}(\mathcal{F},\mathcal{E}) = \{P \mid A1 > X1 \in P\}$.

Note that $\mathcal{A}tt \oplus P = \mathcal{A}tt_1$ but we can say that the removal of attack $(X1,A1)$ in this preference-based enforcement is rationalized by the strict preference of $A1$ over $X1$. In contrast no rationale is given in argument-fixed enforcement. Additionally, preference-based enforcement can prevent the removals of $(X2,A1)$ and $(A2,X1)$ when these attacks are labelled as preference-independent. In this particular case, indeed $(X2,A1)$ and $(A2,X1)$ should be preference-independent because they are an undermining attack and undercutting attack respectively[3].

Hence, if seeing the response to reviewers as argument-fixed enforcement, the author may try to persuade the editor to remove $(X2,A1)$ or $(A2,X2)$ - which is doomed to failure. However if seeing the response as preference-based enforcement, the author shall focus on persuading the editor that $A1 > X1$ (specifically: novelty is more important than presentation).

To sum up, the contribution of this paper is twofold.

1. Define preference-based enforcement problem and characterize its relationships with existing forms of argumentation dynamics, in particular argument-fixed extension enforcement and revealed preference argumentation (RPA).
2. Basing on a computational framework for RPA developed in our earlier work [13,14], we develop sound and complete algorithms for many instances of preference-based extension enforcement.

The rest of this paper is structured as follows. Section 2 recalls the background on AAF and RPA. Section 3 focuses on the relationships between preference-based extension enforcement and revealed preference. In Sect. 4 we adapt the computational framework for RPA [13,14]. In Sect. 5, we develop sound and complete algorithms for preference-based extension enforcement. For the lack of space, we omit the proofs of the presented lemmas and theorems.

2 Background

2.1 Argumentation

An **abstract argumentation** framework AAF is a pair $\mathcal{F} = (\mathcal{A}rg, \mathcal{A}tt)$ of a set $\mathcal{A}rg$ of arguments and an attack relation $\mathcal{A}tt \subseteq \mathcal{A}rg \times \mathcal{A}rg$, where $(A,B) \in \mathcal{A}tt$

---

[3] It has become a consensus in argumentation community that undermining attacks and undercutting attacks should be preference-independent, see e.g. [12,15].

means A *attacks* B. $S \subseteq \mathcal{A}rg$ attacks (or is attacked by) an argument $A \in \mathcal{A}rg$ (or a set of arguments S') if some argument in S attacks (or is attacked by) A (or some argument in S'). $S \subseteq \mathcal{A}rg$ is *conflict-free* if it does not attack itself. S *defends* an argument $A \in \mathcal{A}rg$ if S attacks each argument attacking A. An argumentation semantics σ identifies a set $\sigma(\mathcal{F}) \subseteq 2^{\mathcal{A}rg}$ where each $S \in \sigma(\mathcal{F})$ is called a σ extension. Notably an *admissible extension* of the admissible semantics is such a conflict-free set S that defends each argument in it. A *complete extension* (of the complete semantics) is an admissible extension that contains all arguments it defends. A *preferred extension* is a maximal complete extension; while *the grounded extension* is the least complete extension. The grounded semantics is hence a single-extension semantics, while the other semantics in the above can have multiple extensions. For an argument X, we write $\mathcal{F} \vdash_\sigma X$ if $X \in S$ for some σ extension S.

Abstract argumentation framework has been extended in several directions, one of which is to consider other relations between arguments besides the attack relation. In this paper we are interested in the **preference-based abstract argumentation** (PAF) framework $\mathcal{P} = (\mathcal{A}rg, \mathcal{A}tt, \mathcal{A}tt_{pd}, \mathcal{A}tt_d, Sub, P)$ where $P \subseteq \mathcal{A}rg \times \mathcal{A}rg$ is a pre-order[4] representing whether one argument is preferred to another argument; $Sub \subseteq \mathcal{A}rg \times \mathcal{A}rg$ is a reflexive, anti-symmetric and transitive relation representing the sub-argument relationships between arguments. Further $\mathcal{A}tt$ contains two (not necessarily disjoint) subsets: $\mathcal{A}tt_{pd}$ consisting of so-called *preference-dependent* attacks (elements of $\mathcal{A}tt \setminus \mathcal{A}tt_{pd}$ are called preference-independent attacks), and $\mathcal{A}tt_d$ consisting of so-called *direct* attacks (elements of $\mathcal{A}tt \setminus \mathcal{A}tt_d$ are called *indirect* attacks), where A attacks B iff A *directly* attacks some sub-argument B' of B (i.e. $\forall (A,B) \in \mathcal{A}tt : \exists (B', B) \in Sub$ s.t. $(A, B') \in \mathcal{A}tt_d$). As an indirect attack (A, B) is seen as the accumulation of all direct attacks (A, B') where B' is a sub-argument of B, it is assumed that if for some sub-argument B', (A, B') is a preference-independent attack, then (A, B) is also preference-independent. We say that an attack $(A, B) \in \mathcal{A}tt_{pd}$ is *ineffective due to P* if and only if for any sub-argument B' of B such that $(A, B') \in \mathcal{A}tt_d$, $B' > A \in P$. In this paper, we define the semantics of PAF $\mathcal{P}$ as the semantics of an AAF $\mathcal{P}_\downarrow = (\mathcal{A}rg, \mathcal{A}tt \oplus P)$[5], where $\mathcal{A}tt \oplus P$ is obtained from $\mathcal{A}tt$ by removing preference-dependent attacks that are ineffective due to P.

Example 2. Consider a PAF obtained from the AAF $\mathcal{F} = (\mathcal{A}rg, \mathcal{A}tt)$ in Ex. 1 ($\mathcal{A}rg = \{A1, A2, X1, X2\}$, $\mathcal{A}tt = \{(A1, X1), (X1, A1), (X2, A1), (A2, X2)\}$) by adding $Sub = \{(X, X) \mid X \in \mathcal{A}rg\}$, $\mathcal{A}tt_d = \mathcal{A}tt$, $\mathcal{A}tt_{pd} = \{(A1, X1), (X1, A1)\}$, and $P = \{(A1, X1), (X2, A2)\}$. We have $\mathcal{A}tt \oplus P = \mathcal{A}tt \setminus \{(X1, A1)\}$. Note that the preference-independent attack $(A2, X2)$ cannot be removed by $X2 > A2$.

Note that this semantics of PAF is different from the original one by Amgoud and Cayrol [2] whereby any attack $(A, B) \in \mathcal{A}tt$ is ineffective if $B > A \in P$. We do not use Amgoud and Cayrol's semantics as it fails to capture structured argumentation. Concretely recent accounts of structured argumentation with

---

[4] A reflexive and transitive relation.
[5] That is, $\sigma(\mathcal{P}) = \sigma(\mathcal{P}_\downarrow)$, and for any argument X, $\mathcal{P} \vdash_\sigma X$ iff $\mathcal{P}_\downarrow \vdash_\sigma X$.

preferences [10,11,15,16] all demand that preference-independent attacks succeed irrespective of preferences. More seriously as shown in [15,16], disregarding an attack, say (A, B), simply on the ground that $B > A \in P$ as in [2] may lead to violations of rationality postulates for complete extensions, for example the postulate of sub-argument closure[6] [1,15] and the postulate of consistency[7] [5]. To avoid these problems, the authors of [10,11,15,16] universally prescribe that an attack (A, B) is disregarded only if it is preference-dependent, and for every sub-argument B' of B that A attacks directly, $B' > A$. The modified attack relation $\mathcal{A}tt \oplus P$ defined in the above simply follows this finer application of preference on attack removals. It is easy to see that this PAF semantics is equivalent to the original semantics of Amgoud and Cayrol [2] if we are restricted to the subclass of PAF frameworks that Amgoud and Cayrol assumes implicitly: (a) $Sub = \{(X, X) \mid X \in \mathcal{A}rg\}$; (b) $\mathcal{A}tt_{pd} = \mathcal{A}tt$; and (c) $\mathcal{A}tt_d = \mathcal{A}tt$.

From on now, we shall specify a PAF by a triple $(\mathcal{A}rg, \mathcal{A}tt, P)$ or just a pair $(\mathcal{F}, P)$ where AAF $\mathcal{F} = (\mathcal{A}rg, \mathcal{A}tt)$, assuming that the omitted components $\mathcal{A}tt_{pd}, \mathcal{A}tt_d, Sub$ are implicit.

2.2 Revealed Preference Argumentation

Preference is not quite a settled concept, as there are at least opposing views about preference [7]. Mentalism is the view that preference captures real phenomena of people's mental states that shape people's behaviours, while behaviourism is the view that preference is merely a mathematical construct used to describe regularities of human behaviours. Simply put, according to strict behaviourists *it is not what one says but it is what one does that tells what one prefers.* Behaviourism is very influential in behavioural economics, especially in the form of *Revealed Preference Theory* (RPT [17,18], which is also known as the consumer theory). Intuitively if a collection of goods b could have been bought by a consumer A within her budget but A in fact was observed to buy another collection of goods a, RPT hypothesizes that A has revealed a preference for a over b. As purchasing decision is just a kind of human reasoning, we might wonder how RPT and behaviourism can be generalized with respect to various models of human reasoning in symbolic AI such as argumentation. In a previous work, we propose the so-called *Revealed Preference Argumentation* (RPA [13,14]) framework which extends AAF to deal with an agent's behaviourally revealed preference. Simply put, if a rational agent whose knowledge is bounded by an AA framework $(\mathcal{A}rg, \mathcal{A}tt)$ and the agent is observed to accept (resp. reject) a set $Acc \subseteq \mathcal{A}rg$ (resp. $Rej \subseteq \mathcal{A}rg$) of arguments, then such an observation can be rationalized by any argument preference relation P that ensures the acceptance (resp. rejection) of each and every argument in Acc (resp. Rej) under an argumentation semantics σ that represents the reasoning attitude of the agent.

---

[6] Any complete extension contains all sub-arguments of its arguments (A complete extension is an admissible extension that contains all arguments it defends).

[7] The set of conclusions of arguments in a complete extension is consistent.

Definition 1. *Given $\mathcal{F} = (\mathcal{A}rg, \mathcal{A}tt)$ (with preference-dependent attacks) and two disjoint sets $Acc, Rej \subseteq \mathcal{A}rg^8$, $\texttt{RevealedPref}_\sigma(\mathcal{F}, Acc, Rej)$ denotes the set of preference relations P s.t. for any argument $X \in Acc : PAF(\mathcal{F}, P) \vdash_\sigma X$ and for any $Y \in Rej : (\mathcal{F}, P) \not\vdash_\sigma Y$.*

The disjunction of relations in $\texttt{RevealedPref}_\sigma(\mathcal{F}, Acc, Rej)$ can be deemed as the agent's (behaviourally) revealed preference in this particular observation. The bulk of RPA is then mainly about aggregating the agent's revealed preferences across multiple observations; then rationality check (whether the set of revealed preference relations is not empty); and predicting what the agent will accept given her revealed preferences). However for the current paper, the above definition of $\texttt{RevealedPref}_\sigma(\mathcal{F}, Acc, Rej)$ suffices.

3 The Relationships Between Preference-Based Extension Enforcement and Other Forms of Dynamics

It follows directly from the definition $\texttt{PrefExtEnf}_\sigma^x(\mathcal{F}, \mathcal{E}) = \{P \mid \mathcal{A}tt \oplus P \in \texttt{ExtEnf}_\sigma^x(\mathcal{F}, \mathcal{E})\}$ (in the Introduction) that any preference relation P that is a solution of preference-based enforcement problem instance $\texttt{PrefExtEnf}_\sigma^x(\mathcal{F}, \mathcal{E})$ defines a revised attack graph $\mathcal{A}tt \oplus P$ that is a solution of argument-fixed extension enforcement problem instance $\texttt{ExtEnf}_\sigma^x(\mathcal{F}, \mathcal{E})^9$. Formally

Lemma 1. $\{\mathcal{A}tt \oplus P \mid P \in \texttt{PrefExtEnf}_\sigma^x(\mathcal{F}, \mathcal{E})\} \subseteq \texttt{ExtEnf}_\sigma^x(\mathcal{F}, \mathcal{E})$ *(where $\mathcal{A}tt$ is the attack relation of AAF $\mathcal{F}$).*

Note that $\{\mathcal{A}tt \oplus P \mid P \in \texttt{PrefExtEnf}_\sigma^x(\mathcal{F}, \mathcal{E})\} \subsetneq \texttt{ExtEnf}_\sigma^x(\mathcal{F}, \mathcal{E})$ if $\texttt{ExtEnf}_\sigma^x(\mathcal{F}, \mathcal{E})$ contains a revised graph that cannot be rationalized by any preference relation. For example, if $\mathcal{F} = (\{A, B\}, \{(A, B), (B, A)\})$ with both attacks are preference-dependent, then $\texttt{ExtEnf}_{\text{pr}}^x(\mathcal{F}, \{\texttt{A}, \texttt{B}\})$ contains a revised graph where both attacks are removed. No preference relations can rationalize this revised graph.

The remainder of this section devotes to the relationships between preference-based extension enforcement and revealed preference. These relationships lead to a preliminary version of algorithms for preference-based enforcement, whose weaknesses will be addressed by their final version presented in Sect. 5. It turns out that to prove these relationships, all we need to know about the parameter σ is whether it is a single-extension or a multi-extension semantics.

---

[8] It is not necessary that $Acc \cup Rej = \mathcal{A}rg$.
[9] Note that the notation $\texttt{PrefExtEnf}_\sigma^x(\mathcal{F}, \mathcal{E})$ has two meanings and the context will tell which: 1) a preference-based extension enforcement problem instance with parameters $\sigma, x, \mathcal{F}, \mathcal{E}$; and 2) the set of all solutions of this problem instance (Analogously for two notions $\texttt{RevealedPref}_\sigma(\mathcal{F}, Acc, Rej)$ and $\texttt{ExtEnf}_\sigma^x(\mathcal{F}, \mathcal{E})$).

3.1 Single-Extension Semantics

The two lemmas below say that if σ is a single-extension semantics, then for any instance of preference-based extension enforcement, there exists an instance of revealed preference problem with the same solution set.

Lemma 2. *If σ is a single-extension semantics and $x \in \{fl, sl\}$, then*
$$\mathtt{PrefExtEnf}_\sigma^x(\mathcal{F}, \mathcal{E}) = \mathtt{RevealedPref}_\sigma(\mathcal{F}, \mathcal{E}, \mathcal{A}rg \setminus \mathcal{E}).$$

Lemma 3. *If σ is a single-extension semantics, then*
$$\mathtt{PrefExtEnf}_\sigma^{sb}(\mathcal{F}, \mathcal{E}) = \mathtt{RevealedPref}_\sigma(\mathcal{F}, \mathcal{E}, \emptyset).$$

3.2 Multi-extension Semantics

Lemmas 2, 3 do not hold for multi-extension semantics. Instead we have:

Lemma 4. *If σ is a multi-extension semantics, then for any $x \in \{sb, fl, sl\}$, $\mathtt{PrefExtEnf}_\sigma^x(\mathcal{F}, \mathcal{E}) \subseteq \mathtt{RevealedPref}_\sigma(\mathcal{F}, \mathcal{E}, \emptyset)$.*

Here is an example showing that $\mathtt{PrefExtEnf}_\sigma^x(\mathcal{F}, \mathcal{E})$ may be a proper subset of $\mathtt{RevealedPref}_\sigma(\mathcal{F}, \mathcal{E}, \emptyset)$. Consider AAF $\mathcal{F} = (\{A, B\}, \{(A, B), (B, A)\})$. Clearly $P = \{(A, A), (B, B)\}$ is a solution of $\mathtt{RevealedPref}_{pr}(\mathcal{F}, \{A, B\}, \emptyset)$. However $\mathtt{PrefExtEnf}_{pr}^x(\mathcal{F}, \{A, B\})$ has no solutions.

Note that $\mathtt{RevealedPref}_\sigma(\mathcal{F}, \mathcal{E}, \mathcal{A}rg \setminus \mathcal{E}) \subseteq \mathtt{RevealedPref}_\sigma(\mathcal{F}, \mathcal{E}, \emptyset)$, Lemma 5 below presents a bit stronger assertion than that in Lemma 4 for $x = sl$.

Lemma 5. *Let σ be a multi-extension semantics. Then $\mathtt{PrefExtEnf}_\sigma^{sl}(\mathcal{F}, \mathcal{E}) \subseteq \mathtt{RevealedPref}_\sigma(\mathcal{F}, \mathcal{E}, \mathcal{A}rg \setminus \mathcal{E})$.*

The above two lemmas imply that given an instance of a preference-based extension enforcement under a multi-extension semantics, one may not be able to construct an instance of revealed preference problem that has the same solution set. Hence one cannot solve $\mathtt{PrefExtEnf}_\sigma^x(\mathcal{F}, \mathcal{E})$ by just calling some algorithm for computing revealed preference and return the result as it is. Instead, one needs an extra "verification" step to verify whether a preference relation returned by computing revealed preference is really a solution of $\mathtt{PrefExtEnf}_\sigma^x(\mathcal{F}, \mathcal{E})$. Hence a two-step method for computing $\mathtt{PrefExtEnf}_\sigma^x(\mathcal{F}, \mathcal{E})$ proceeds as follows.

1. Generate a set $\Pi \supseteq \mathtt{PrefExtEnf}_\sigma^x(\mathcal{F}, \mathcal{E})$ by computing $\mathtt{RevealedPref}_\sigma(\mathcal{F}, \mathcal{E}, \emptyset)$ (if $x = \{sb, fl\}$); or $\mathtt{RevealedPref}_\sigma(\mathcal{F}, \mathcal{E}, \mathcal{A}rg \setminus \mathcal{E})$ (if $x = sl$).
2. Verify, for each preference relation $P \in \Pi$, if $\mathcal{E}$ is a sub-extension (for $x = sb$), or a full extension ($s = fl$), or the only extension ($x = sl$) of PAF $(\mathcal{F}, P)$.

Illustratively, algorithm $\mathtt{PrefExtEnfAlgNaive}_\sigma^x(\mathcal{F}, \mathcal{E})$ below assumes an algorithm $\mathtt{IsSolOfExtEnf}_\sigma^x(\mathcal{F}, \mathcal{E}, P)$ for performing the test in the verification step. We shall not discuss possible implementations of $\mathtt{IsSolOfExtEnf}_\sigma^x(\mathcal{F}, \mathcal{E}, P)$ since in the next two sections we shall refine the above generation-verification method and this testing algorithm will not be needed.

Algorithm 1. PrefExtEnfAlgNaive$_\sigma^x(\mathcal{F}, \mathcal{E})$

Require: RevealedPrefAlg$_\sigma(\mathcal{F}, Acc, Rej)$ computes RevealedPref$_\sigma(\mathcal{F}, Acc, Rej)$; IsSolOfExtEnf$_\sigma^x(\mathcal{F}, \mathcal{E}, P)$ verifies if $P \in$ PrefExtEnf$_\sigma^x(\mathcal{F}, \mathcal{E})$.
Ensure: returns all solutions of PrefExtEnf$_\sigma^x(\mathcal{F}, \mathcal{E})$ problem given AAF $\mathcal{F} = (\mathcal{A}rg, \mathcal{A}tt)$ and $\mathcal{E} \subseteq \mathcal{A}rg$.
$Acc \leftarrow \mathcal{E}$
$Rej \leftarrow \emptyset$ ▷ Or $Rej \leftarrow \mathcal{A}rg \setminus \mathcal{E}$ if $x = sl$
$ExtEnfSolutionSet \leftarrow \emptyset$
$\Pi \leftarrow$ RevealedPrefAlg$_\sigma(\mathcal{F}, Acc, Rej)$
for each $P \in \Pi$ **do**
 if IsSolOfExtEnf$_\sigma^x(\mathcal{F}, \mathcal{E}, P)$ **then**
  $ExtEnfSolutionSet \leftarrow ExtEnfSolutionSet \cup \{P\}$
 end if
end for
return $ExtEnfSolutionSet$

3.3 The Relationships Among Different Instances of Preference-Based Extension Enforcement Problem

Given that PrefExtEnf$_\sigma^{sb}(\mathcal{F}, \mathcal{E}) \supseteq$ PrefExtEnf$_\sigma^{sl}(\mathcal{F}, \mathcal{E})$, we want to develop some criterion that a preference relation $P \in$ PrefExtEnf$_\sigma^{sb}(\mathcal{F}, \mathcal{E})$ needs to satisfy in order to be a member of PrefExtEnf$_\sigma^{sl}(\mathcal{F}, \mathcal{E})$. Lemma 6 says that P needs to be a solution of RevealedPref$_\sigma(\mathcal{F}, \emptyset, \mathcal{A}rg \setminus \mathcal{E})$.

Lemma 6. *For any semantics σ,* PrefExtEnf$_\sigma^{sl}(\mathcal{F}, \mathcal{E}) =$ PrefExtEnf$_\sigma^{sb}(\mathcal{F}, \mathcal{E}) \cap$ RevealedPref$_\sigma(\mathcal{F}, \emptyset, Rej)$, *where* $Rej = \mathcal{A}rg \setminus \mathcal{E}$.

4 A Computational Framework for Preference-Based Extension Enforcement

So an instance PrefExtEnf$_\sigma^x(\mathcal{F}, \mathcal{E})$ of preference-based extension enforcement with σ being a single-extension semantics can always be translated into an instance of revealed preference problem. However if σ is a multi-extension semantics, the translation technique no longer works and hence this case is our aim from now on[10]. For readability, this section devotes to the computational framework shared by all developed algorithms, while the next section actually presents these algorithms including their pseudo codes. Let's revisit Lemmas 5 and 6. They suggest that to compute PrefExtEnf$_\sigma^x(\mathcal{F}, \mathcal{E})$, one can first generate a superset $\Pi \supseteq$ PrefExtEnf$_\sigma^x(\mathcal{F}, \mathcal{E})$ and then filter out every element of Π that is proven not a solution of the problem instance, as demonstrated by the preliminary algorithm PrefExtEnfAlgNaive$_\sigma^x(\mathcal{F}, \mathcal{E})$. We shall refine this generation-verification method, so our final algorithms improving on the preliminary algorithm in two important aspects:

---
[10] Note that there are many multi-extension semantics but arguably the *preferred* semantics is one of the most important, and is hence the target of the current paper.

1. Both generation and verification steps of the final algorithms rely on the same computational framework of revealed preference argumentation (RPA [13, 14]), in particular the notion of *preference derivations* (Definition 8), which in turn adapt the notion of *preference-based dispute derivations* for computing PAF semantics (Definition 2).
2. Our final algorithms operate on a compact representation of solution sets, called *preference states*, which shall be presented in Sect. 4.2. As will be seen (in Sect. 5.3), the verification step will be broken down into two sub-steps: refinement and simplification, both of which operate on preference states rather than individual preference relations.

4.1 Preference-Based Dispute Derivations

Preference-based dispute derivations [14] aim at checking whether PAF $(\mathcal{F}, P) \vdash_{pr} X$. In short, preference-based dispute derivations are a slightly modified version of *dispute derivations* presented in [20] for checking whether $\mathcal{F} \vdash_{pr} X$ given an AAF $\mathcal{F} = (\mathcal{A}rg, \mathcal{A}tt)$ and some $X \in \mathcal{A}rg$. A dispute derivation of [20] is defined as a sequence of tuples $\langle P_0, O_0, SP_0, SO_0 \rangle, \ldots, \langle P_i, O_i, SP_i, SO_i \rangle, \ldots$ modelling a dispute between two antagonistic parties called Proponent and Opponent, where Proponent starts by putting forwards X then two parties alternate in attacking each other's previous arguments until Proponent wins. Tuple $\langle P_i, O_i, SP_i, SO_i \rangle$ describes the *dispute state* at step i where: $P_i \subseteq \mathcal{A}rg$ contains arguments presented by Proponent but not yet attacked by Opponent; $O_i \subseteq \mathcal{A}rg$ contains arguments presented by Opponent but not yet counter-attacked by Proponent ($P_0 = \{X\}$ and $O_0 = \emptyset$); SP_i is the set of all arguments presented by Proponent up to step i (so $P_i \subseteq SP_i$); while SO_i is the set of all arguments presented by Opponent and already counter-attacked by Proponent. To simulate a move by Opponent (resp. Proponent) in this dispute, an argument, say A, is selected from P_i (resp. O_i) and some argument B attacking A is considered to extend $\langle P_i, O_i, SP_i, SO_i \rangle$ to obtain the next tuple $\langle P_{i+1}, O_{i+1}, SP_{i+1}, SO_{i+1} \rangle$ of the dispute derivation. A dispute derivation ending with a tuple of the form $\langle \emptyset, \emptyset, SP_n, SO_n \rangle$ means that Proponent wins the dispute[11] and hence represents a proof for $\mathcal{F} \vdash_{pr} X$. To ensure that this is not only a correct proof but also efficient, concrete rules or filtering mechanisms governing the extension of one tuple of an admissible dispute derivation to the next are introduced. For example Proponent is not required to defend the same argument twice, and hence if an argument Y is moved by Proponent at step i and $Y \in SP_i$ then Y should not be added into P_{i+1} (Readers are referred to [20] for further details).

Now to check whether PAF $\mathcal{P} = (\mathcal{F}, P) \vdash_{pr} A$, a *preference-based*[12] *dispute derivation* is defined as a sequence of tuples of the form $\langle P_i, O_i, SP_i, SO_i \rangle$ with:

---

[11] Here $P_n = \emptyset$ says that there are no more arguments presented by Proponent that are unchallenged by Opponent; and $O_n = \emptyset$ says that all counter-arguments by Opponent have been attacked by Proponent.

[12] or preference-fixed because the preferences over arguments are fixed by P.

$P_i \subseteq \mathcal{A}rg$ contains arguments presented by Proponent but not yet attacked by Opponent; SP_i is the set of arguments presented by Proponent up to step i (so $P_i \subseteq SP_i$); $O_i \subseteq \mathcal{A}tt$ now contains attacks presented by Opponent but not yet counter-attacked by Proponent, while SO_i is the set of attacks presented by Opponent and already counter-attacked by Proponent (so $O_i \cup SO_i$ is the set of all attacks used by Opponent up to step i). This justifies item 1 of Definition 2 below. Item 2 of the definition describes the relationship between two consecutive tuples at steps i and $i+1$ according to three cases a, b.i. and b.ii.

Definition 2. *(Wrt a PAF framework $\mathcal{P} = (\mathcal{F}, P)$ with $\mathcal{F} = (\mathcal{A}rt, \mathcal{A}tt)$) Given a selection function sl, a **preference-based dispute derivation** is a sequence $\langle P_0, O_0, SP_0, SO_0 \rangle \ldots \langle P_i, O_i, SP_i, SO_i \rangle \ldots$, where*

1. $P_i, SP_i \subseteq \mathcal{A}rg; O_i, SO_i \subseteq \mathcal{A}tt.$
2. *At each step i, sl selects some element X from P_i or O_i.*
   (a) *If X is an argument selected from P_i, then:*
   $P_{i+1} = P_i \setminus \{X\}; O_{i+1} = O_i \cup \{(Y, X) \mid (Y, X) \in \mathcal{A}tt\};$
   $SP_{i+1} = SP_i; SO_{i+1} = SO_i.$
   (b) *If X is an attack (B, A) selected from O_i, then:*
      i. *If (B, A) is an ineffective preference-dependent attack, then:*
      $P_{i+1} = P_i; O_{i+1} = O_i \setminus \{X\};$
      $SP_{i+1} = SP_i; SO_{i+1} = SO_i.$
      ii. *Otherwise, $B \notin SP_i$ and there exists some preference-independent or effective preference-dependent attack $(C, B) \in \mathcal{A}tt \setminus (SO_i \cup O_i)$ and:*
      $P_{i+1} = P_i \cup \{C\}$ *if* $C \notin SP_i$, *otherwise* $P_{i+1} = P_i$
      $O_{i+1} = O_i \setminus \{X\}; SP_{i+1} = SP_i \cup \{C\};$
      $SO_{i+1} = SO_i \cup \{X\}.$

A preference-based dispute derivation is said to be **successful** if it ends with a dispute state of the form $\langle \emptyset, \emptyset, SP_n, SO_n \rangle$ (indicating that Proponent won the dispute). As proven in [14], for any argument A, if there is a successful preference-based dispute derivation starting with a dispute state $\langle \{A\}, \emptyset, \{A\}, \emptyset \rangle$, then PAF $\mathcal{P} \vdash_{pr} A$ and vice versa. More generally, for any $\mathcal{E} \subseteq \mathcal{A}rg$, there is a successful preference-based dispute derivation starting with a dispute state $\langle \mathcal{E}, \emptyset, \mathcal{E}, \emptyset \rangle$ iff $\mathcal{E}$ is a subset of some preferred extension of the given PAF $\mathcal{P}$.

4.2 Preference States: a Compact Representation of Solution Sets

Basically, preference states allow us to tackle the space complexity of solution sets. Recall that a solution P of a preference-based extension enforcement is just a binary relation over the set of arguments $\mathcal{A}rg$, and hence roughly speaking the size of a solution set can be on par with the power set $2^{\mathcal{A}rg \times \mathcal{A}rg}$. Hence a direct representation of a solution set may lead to an exponential blow-up.

Definition 3. *(Recalled from [14]) Given a universe of arguments:*

1. *A **preference statement** is of the positive form $A > B$ (saying that argument A is strictly preferred to argument B) or the negative form $A \not> B$ (alternatively $\neg (A > B)$).*
2. *A **preference state** $Q = Q^+ \cup Q^-$ contains a set Q^+ (resp. Q^-) of positive (resp. negative) preference statements, such that Q^+ is asymmetric and does not contradict with Q^- (if $A > B \in Q^+$ then $A \not> B \notin Q^-$).*

We say that Q is **regular** if Q^+ is transitive. From now on, we restrict ourselves to the set of regular preference states, denoted $\mathcal{Q}_{reg}$.

A preference state Q represents a set of preference relations $\mathcal{M}(Q)$ as follows.

Definition 4. 1. *We say that a preference relation P **satisfies** a preference statement $A > B$ (resp. $A \not> B$) if and only if $(A, B) \in P$ and $(B, A) \notin P$ (resp. either $(A, B) \notin P$ or $(B, A) \in P$).*
2. *A preference relation P **satisfies** a preference state Q if P satisfies each and every preference statement of Q. The set of all preference relations satisfying Q is denoted by $\mathcal{M}(Q)$.*

For example, $\mathcal{M}(\emptyset)$ is the set of all preference relations.

Note that since each preference relation $P \in \mathcal{M}(Q)$ when overlaid with the original attack graph $\mathcal{A}tt$ yields a revised attack graph $\mathcal{A}tt \oplus P$, $\mathcal{M}(Q)$ can be viewed as a compact representation of a set of revised attack graphs that can be obtained from the original graph $\mathcal{A}tt$ by removing all preference-dependent attacks (A, B) if $B > A \in Q$; but if $B \not> A \in Q$ then (A, B) must be kept. If neither $B > A$ nor $B \not> A$ are in Q, then the attack (A, B) may or may not be removed depending on the specific preference relation $P \in \mathcal{M}(Q)$.

For convenience, a set $\mathcal{Q} = \{Q_1, Q_2, \ldots, Q_n\}$ of preference states is interpreted as the disjunction thereof, i.e. $\mathcal{M}(\mathcal{Q}) = \bigcup_{i=1}^{n} \mathcal{M}(Q_i)$. It is easy to see that for two sets $\mathcal{Q}_1, \mathcal{Q}_2$ of preference states, the union $\mathcal{Q}_1 \cup \mathcal{Q}_2$ is also a set of preference states and $\mathcal{M}(\mathcal{Q}_1 \cup \mathcal{Q}_2) = \mathcal{M}(\mathcal{Q}_1) \cup \mathcal{M}(\mathcal{Q}_2)$. In other words, $\mathcal{Q}_1 \cup \mathcal{Q}_2$ compactly represents the union of two sets of preference states: $\mathcal{M}(\mathcal{Q}_1)$ and $\mathcal{M}(\mathcal{Q}_2)$. The intersection of $\mathcal{M}(\mathcal{Q}_1)$ and $\mathcal{M}(\mathcal{Q}_2)$ is compactly represented by a set of preference states $\mathcal{Q}_1 \otimes \mathcal{Q}_2$ using the operator $\otimes$ defined as follows.

Definition 5. 1. *Given two preference states $Q_1, Q_2 \in \mathcal{Q}_{reg}$, $Q_1 \otimes Q_2$ refers to the unique (if existent) preference state $Q \in \mathcal{Q}_{reg}$ such that $Q^- = Q_1^- \cup Q_2^-$ and Q^+ coincides with the transitive closure of $Q_1^+ \cup Q_2^+$. If this Q does not exist, then we write $Q_1 \otimes Q_2 = null$.*
2. *For two sets of preference states $\mathcal{Q}_1, \mathcal{Q}_2 \subseteq \mathcal{Q}_{reg}$, define $\mathcal{Q}_1 \otimes \mathcal{Q}_2 = \{Q_1 \otimes Q_2 \mid Q_1 \in \mathcal{Q}_1, Q_2 \in \mathcal{Q}_2\} \setminus \{null\}$.*

It is easy to see that $\mathcal{M}(Q_1 \otimes Q_2) = \mathcal{M}(Q_1) \cap \mathcal{M}(Q_2)$; and $\mathcal{M}(\mathcal{Q}_1 \otimes \mathcal{Q}_2) = \mathcal{M}(\mathcal{Q}_1) \cap \mathcal{M}(\mathcal{Q}_2)$.

Our developed algorithms for preference-based extension enforcement shall return sets of preference states. Hence soundness and completeness properties of these algorithms should be understood as follows.

Definition 6. *Suppose* $\texttt{PrefExtEnfAlg}_\sigma^x(\mathcal{F}, \mathcal{E})$ *returns a set* $\mathcal{Q}$ *of preference states. We say that* $\texttt{PrefExtEnfAlg}_\sigma^x(\mathcal{F}, \mathcal{E})$ *is a **sound** (resp. **complete**) algorithm for* $\texttt{PrefExtEnf}_\sigma^x(\mathcal{F}, \mathcal{E})$ *if* $\mathcal{M}(\mathcal{Q}) \subseteq \texttt{PrefExtEnf}_\sigma^x(\mathcal{F}, \mathcal{E})$ *(resp.* $\mathcal{M}(\mathcal{Q}) \supseteq \texttt{PrefExtEnf}_\sigma^x(\mathcal{F}, \mathcal{E})$*).*

5 Algorithms for Preference-Based Extension Enforcement

In this section we develop algorithms for computing $\texttt{PrefExtEnf}_\sigma^x(\mathcal{F}, \mathcal{E})$ for any case of $x \in \{sb, fl, sl\}$ (sub-extension, full-extension or single-extension) but σ is the preferred semantics.

5.1 Preference Derivations

Recall that preference-based derivations can check whether PAF $(\mathcal{F}, P) \vdash_{pr} X$. Now given an AAF framework $\mathcal{F} = (\mathcal{A}rg, \mathcal{A}tt)$ and an argument $X \in \mathcal{A}rg$ (more generally a set $\mathcal{E} \subseteq \mathcal{A}rg$), preference derivations compute possible preferences over $\mathcal{A}rg$ that can ensure the acceptance of X (resp. the acceptance of every argument in $\mathcal{E}$).

Intuitively, a preference derivation simulates a dispute in which Proponent defends the initially given argument X from attacks by Opponent. Like in a preference-based dispute derivation, Opponent can keep bringing up all possible counter-arguments to whatever presented by Proponent. However while in a preference-based dispute derivation, Proponent's moves are constrained by the fixed preferences specified in a given PAF via the stated preference relation, *in a preference derivation Proponent's moves reveal some preference of the Proponent, and are constrained by the revealed preference so far*. Suppose that at some step i of a preference derivation, Proponent needs to counter an attack (B, A) by Opponent (so A is an argument presented previously by Proponent), while *the revealed preference so far is represented by a preference state Q_i*. There are several avenues for Proponent to proceed, as captured by the cases of Definition 7 shortly below.

- Case 2.a: If (B, A) is a preference-independent attack, then Proponent needs to select an argument C to attack B, such that (C, B) is not used by Opponent before, i.e. $(C, B) \in \mathcal{A}tt \setminus (SO_i \cup O_i)$. And then depending on whether (C, B) is preference-independent or preference-dependent:
  - Case 2.a.i: If (C, B) is preference-independent, then $Q_{i+1} = Q_i$ because the selection of (C, B) does not reveal any preferences of Proponent.

- Case 2.a.ii: If (C, B) is preference-dependent, then it must be effective and therefore Q_{i+1} must contain a preference statement $B' \not> C$ for some sub-argument B' of B that C attacks directly.
- Case 2.b: If (B, A) is a preference-dependent attack, then:
  - Case 2.b.i: If (B, A) has been made ineffective by the current preference statements in Q_i, then this attack is simply ignored.
  - Case 2.b.ii: Otherwise, Proponent has two options:
    * Case 2.b.ii.A: Proponent can reveal new preference statements to make (B, A) an ineffective attack. Hence $Q_{i+1} = Q_i \otimes \{(A' > B) \mid A'$ is a sub-argument of A that B attacks directly$\}$.
    * Case 2.b.ii.B: Proponent selects some argument C to attack B, and hence this case proceeds just like Case 2.a.

Definition 7. *(Wrt an AAF $\mathcal{F} = \langle Arg, Att \rangle$ with a set Att_{pd} of preference-dependent attacks) Given a tuple $T_i = \langle P_i, O_i, SP_i, SO_i \rangle$ and a selection function sl that selects an element X from either: (1) P_i component of T_i, or (2) O_i component of T_i; $\texttt{Follow}(T_i, Q_i, sl)$ is defined respectively as follows.*

1. *If X is an argument selected from P_i, then $\texttt{Follow}(T_i, Q_i, sl)$ consists of only one pair (T_{i+1}, Q_{i+1}) where $T_{i+1} = \langle P_{i+1}, O_{i+1}, SP_{i+1}, SO_{i+1} \rangle$ is obtained from T_i as in step 2.a of Definition 2, and $Q_{i+1} = Q_i$.*
2. *If X is an attack (B, A) selected from O_i, then there are two cases.*
   (a) *If (B, A) is preference-independent, then $\texttt{Follow}(T_i, Q_i, sl)$ consists of such pairs (T_{i+1}, Q_{i+1}) with $Q_{i+1} \neq$ null that the following condition hold: There exists $(C, B) \in Att \setminus (SO_i \cup O_i)$ such that $B \notin SP_i$; T_{i+1} is obtained from T_i as in step 2.b.ii of Definition 2; and*
       i. $Q_{i+1} = Q_i$ *if (C, B) is preference-independent,*
       ii. *otherwise $Q_{i+1} = Q_i \otimes \{(B' \not> C)\}$ for some sub-argument B' of B s.t. $(C, B') \in Att_d$.*
   (b) *Otherwise (i.e. (B, A) is preference-dependent), then there are two cases:*
       i. *If $(A > B) \in Q_i$, then $\texttt{Follow}(T_i, Q_i, sl)$ consists of only one pair (T_{i+1}, Q_{i+1}) where $T_{i+1} = \langle P_i, O_i \setminus \{X\}, SP_i, SO_i \rangle$ and $Q_{i+1} = Q_i$.*
       ii. *Otherwise $\texttt{Follow}(T_i, Q_i, sl)$ consists of such pairs (T_{i+1}, Q_{i+1}) with $Q_{i+1} \neq$ null that satisfy either conditions below.*
           A. $Q_{i+1} = Q_i \otimes \{(A' > B) \mid A'$ *is a sub-argument of A s.t. $(B, A') \in Att_d\}$, and $T_{i+1} = \langle P_i, O_i \setminus \{X\}, SP_i, SO_i \rangle$.*
           B. (T_{i+1}, Q_{i+1}) *satisfies condition 2(a) for some attack $(C, B) \in Att \setminus (SO_i \cup O_i)$ such that $B \notin SP_i$.*

Definition 8. *(Wrt an AAF $\mathcal{F} = (\mathcal{A}rg, \mathcal{A}tt)$ with a set $\mathcal{A}tt_{pd}$ of preference-dependent attacks)* A **preference derivation** *using a selection function sl is a sequence of pairs $(T_0, Q_0), \ldots, (T_i, Q_i), (T_{i+1}, Q_{i+1}), \ldots$ where for each $i \geq 0$, two conditions hold: 1) T_i is a tuple of the form $\langle P_i, O_i, SP_i, SO_i \rangle$ as defined in Definition 2 and Q_i is a preference state; and 2) $(T_{i+1}, Q_{i+1}) \in$ Follow(T_i, Q_i, sl).*

A preference derivation is said to be **successful** if it is finite and its last pair has the form $(\langle \emptyset, \emptyset, \_, \_ \rangle, Q_n)$ (representing a dispute won by Proponent with revealed preferences Q_n). The following function ConstructSuccessfulPrefDers$(\mathcal{T})$ constructs all successful preference derivations starting with some pair $(T, Q) \in \mathcal{T}$. The function returns the set of all preference states that occur in the last pairs of these successful derivations.

Algorithm 2. ConstructSuccessfulPrefDers$(\mathcal{T})$

1: **Input**: a set $\mathcal{T}$ of pairs (T, Q) with T a dispute state and Q a preference state.
2: **Output**: a set $\mathcal{Q}$ consisting of such a preference state Q_n that there exists a successful preference derivation starting with some $T \in \mathcal{T}$ and ending with a pair of the form $(\langle \emptyset, \emptyset, \_, \_ \rangle, Q_n)$.
3: $\mathcal{Q} \leftarrow \emptyset$
4: **let** sl be a selection function
5: **while** $\mathcal{T} \neq \emptyset$ **do**
6:    **select** a pair (T, Q) **from** $\mathcal{T}$ **using** sl
7:    **let** $T = \langle P, O, SP, SO \rangle$
8:    **if** $P = O = \emptyset$ **then**
9:       $\mathcal{Q} \leftarrow \mathcal{Q} \cup \{Q\}$
10:   **else**
11:       $\mathcal{T} \leftarrow (\mathcal{T} \cup Follow(T, Q, sl)) \setminus \{(T, Q)\}$
12:   **end if**
13: **end while**
14: **return** $\mathcal{Q}$

5.2 Computing PrefExtEnf$_{pr}^{sb}(\mathcal{F}, \mathcal{E})$

We now show that preference derivations provide a vehicle for computing preference-based extension enforcement.

Definition 9. *(Wrt AAF $\mathcal{F} = (\mathcal{A}rg, \mathcal{A}tt)$)* **A preference derivation for a sub-extension** $\mathcal{E} \subseteq \mathcal{A}rg$ *is a successfully preference derivation starting with an initial pair $(T_0, Q_0) = (\langle \mathcal{E}, \emptyset, \mathcal{E}, \emptyset \rangle, \emptyset)$.*

The algorithm PrefExtEnfAlg$_{pr}^{sb}(\mathcal{F}, \mathcal{E})$ (**Algorithm 3**) computes the set of all preference states Q_n that occur in the last tuple $(\langle \emptyset, \emptyset, \_, \_ \rangle, Q_n)$ of some preference derivation for $\mathcal{E}$. It turns out that PrefExtEnfAlg$_{pr}^{sb}(\mathcal{F}, \mathcal{E})$ is a sound and complete algorithm for PrefExtEnfAlg$_{pr}^{sb}(\mathcal{F}, \mathcal{E})$ as asserted by Theorem 1.

Algorithm 3. $\texttt{PrefExtEnfAlg}_{\text{pr}}^{\text{sb}}(\mathcal{F}, \mathcal{E})$

1: **Input**: an AA framework $\mathcal{F}$; a set of arguments $\mathcal{E}$.
2: **Output**: a set $\mathcal{Q}$ consisting of such a preference state Q_n that there exists a preference derivation for sub-extension $\mathcal{E}$ ending with a pair of the form $(\langle \emptyset, \emptyset, \_, \_\rangle, Q_n)$.
3: $\mathcal{T} \leftarrow \{(\langle \mathcal{E}, \emptyset, \mathcal{E}, \emptyset\rangle, \emptyset)\}$
4: **return** $\texttt{ConstructSuccessfulPrefDers}(\mathcal{T})$

Theorem 1. *If* $\texttt{PrefExtEnfAlg}_{\text{pr}}^{\text{sb}}(\mathcal{F}, \mathcal{E})$ *returns a set* $\mathcal{Q}$ *of preference states, then* $\mathcal{M}(\mathcal{Q}) = \texttt{PrefExtEnf}_{\text{pr}}^{\text{sb}}(\mathcal{F}, \mathcal{E})$.

5.3 Computing $\texttt{PrefExtEnf}_{\text{pr}}^{\text{sl}}(\mathcal{F}, \mathcal{E})$

From $\texttt{PrefExtEnf}_{\sigma}^{\text{sl}}(\mathcal{F}, \mathcal{E}) = \texttt{PrefExtEnf}_{\sigma}^{\text{sb}}(\mathcal{F}, \mathcal{E}) \cap \texttt{RevealedPref}_{\sigma}(\mathcal{F}, \emptyset, \mathcal{A}rg \setminus \mathcal{E})$ (asserted by Lemma 6), we can compute $\texttt{PrefExtEnf}_{\sigma}^{\text{sl}}(\mathcal{F}, \mathcal{E})$ (for any semantics σ) by four steps:

1. **Generation**: Compute $\texttt{PrefExtEnf}_{\sigma}^{\text{sb}}(\mathcal{F}, \mathcal{E})$, obtaining a set of preference states $\mathcal{Q} = \{Q_1, \ldots, Q_m\}$. So we know that $\bigcup_{i=1}^{m} \mathcal{M}(Q_i) \supseteq \texttt{PrefExtEnf}_{\sigma}^{\text{sl}}(\mathcal{F}, \mathcal{E})$ since $\texttt{PrefExtEnf}_{\sigma}^{\text{sb}}(\mathcal{F}, \mathcal{E}) \supseteq \texttt{PrefExtEnf}_{\sigma}^{\text{sl}}(\mathcal{F}, \mathcal{E})$.

2. **Refinement**: But from Lemma 6, we have

$$\texttt{PrefExtEnf}_{\sigma}^{\text{sl}}(\mathcal{F}, \mathcal{E}) = \bigcup_{i=1}^{m}(\mathcal{M}(Q_i) \cap \texttt{RevealedPref}_{\sigma}(\mathcal{F}, \emptyset, \mathcal{A}rg \setminus \mathcal{E}))$$

So for each preference state $Q_i \in \mathcal{Q}$, we compute a set of preference states $\overline{\mathcal{Q}}_i$ such that $\mathcal{M}(\overline{\mathcal{Q}}_i) = \{P \in \mathcal{M}(Q_i) \mid PAF(\mathcal{F}, P) \vdash_{\sigma} X \text{ for some } X \in \mathcal{A}rg \setminus \mathcal{E}\}$. As proven by Theorem 2 below, this relationship between Q_i and $\overline{\mathcal{Q}}_i$ implies that $\mathcal{M}(Q_i) \cap \texttt{RevealedPref}_{\sigma}(\mathcal{F}, \emptyset, \mathcal{A}rg \setminus \mathcal{E}) = \mathcal{M}(Q_i) \setminus \mathcal{M}(\overline{\mathcal{Q}}_i)$ and hence $\texttt{PrefExtEnf}_{\sigma}^{\text{sl}}(\mathcal{F}, \mathcal{E}) = \bigcup_{i=1}^{m}(\mathcal{M}(Q_i) \setminus \mathcal{M}(\overline{\mathcal{Q}}_i))$.

3. **Simplification**: We do not want to return a still complex result $\bigcup_{i=1}^{m}(\mathcal{M}(Q_i) \setminus \mathcal{M}(\overline{\mathcal{Q}}_i))$, and hence for each $i \in \{1, \ldots, m\}$, we shall compute a set $\mathcal{Q}_i^*$ of preference states such that $\mathcal{M}(\mathcal{Q}_i^*) = (\mathcal{M}(Q_i) \setminus \mathcal{M}(\overline{\mathcal{Q}}_i))$. Hence $\texttt{PrefExtEnf}_{\sigma}^{\text{sl}}(\mathcal{F}, \mathcal{E}) = \bigcup_{i=1}^{m} \mathcal{M}(\mathcal{Q}_i^*)$, which is equal $\mathcal{M}(\bigcup_{i=1}^{m} \mathcal{Q}_i^*)$.

4. **Return**: Compute $\mathcal{Q}^* = \bigcup_{i=1}^{m} \mathcal{Q}_i^*$ by taking set union every $\mathcal{Q}_i^*$, for $i = \{1, \ldots, m\}$ and return $\mathcal{Q}^*$.

Theorem 2. If $\texttt{PrefExtEnf}^{\texttt{sb}}_{\sigma}(\mathcal{F},\mathcal{E}) = \mathcal{M}(\mathcal{Q})$ with $\mathcal{Q} = \{Q_1,\ldots,Q_m\}$ such that for each $Q_i \in \mathcal{Q}$, $\{P \in \mathcal{M}(Q_i) \mid \exists X \in \mathcal{A}rg \setminus \mathcal{E} : PAF(\mathcal{F},P) \vdash_\sigma X\} = \mathcal{M}(Q_i)$ for a set of preference states $\mathcal{Q}_i$, then $\texttt{PrefExtEnf}^{\texttt{sl}}_{\sigma}(\mathcal{F},\mathcal{E}) = \bigcup_{i=1}^{m} (\mathcal{M}(Q_i) \setminus \mathcal{M}(\mathcal{Q}_i))$.

Now we focus on the case $\sigma = pr$. Since we can compute $\texttt{PrefExtEnf}^{\texttt{sb}}_{\texttt{pr}}(\mathcal{F},\mathcal{E})$ by **Algorithm 3**, it remains to develop two algorithms:

– An algorithm for the refinement step: Given a preference state Q, compute a set $\mathcal{Q}$ of preference states extending Q, so that $\mathcal{M}(\mathcal{Q}) = \{P \in \mathcal{M}(Q) \mid \exists X \in \mathcal{A}rg \setminus \mathcal{E} : PAF(\mathcal{F},P) \vdash_{pr} X\}$. As asserted by Lemma 7, **Algorithm 4** below serves this purpose.
– An algorithm for the simplification step: Given a preference state R and a set $\mathcal{R} = \{R_1,\ldots,R_j,\ldots R_k\}$ of preference states where each $R_j \supseteq R$, compute a set $\mathcal{R}^*$ of preference states so that $\mathcal{M}(\mathcal{R}^*) = \mathcal{M}(R) \setminus \mathcal{M}(\mathcal{R})$. As asserted by Lemma 8, **Algorithm 5** below serves this purpose.

Lemma 7. If $\texttt{RefinementAlg}_{\texttt{pr}}(\mathcal{F},Q,\mathcal{E})$ returns a set of preference states $\mathcal{Q}$ then $\mathcal{M}(\mathcal{Q}) = \{P \in \mathcal{M}(Q) \mid \exists X \in \mathcal{A}rg \setminus \mathcal{E} : PAF(\mathcal{F},P) \vdash_{pr} X\}$.

Lemma 8. $\texttt{Transform}(R,\mathcal{R})$ always returns a set of preference states $\mathcal{R}^*$ such that $\mathcal{M}(\mathcal{R}^*) = \mathcal{M}(R) \setminus \mathcal{M}(\mathcal{R})$.

Finally, our algorithm for computing $\texttt{PrefExtEnf}^{\texttt{sl}}_{\texttt{pr}}(\mathcal{F},\mathcal{E})$ is presented in **Algorithm 6**. Theorem 3 below says that indeed $\texttt{PrefExtEnfAlg}^{\texttt{sl}}_{\texttt{pr}}(\mathcal{F},\mathcal{E})$ is a sound and complete algorithm for computing $\texttt{PrefExtEnf}^{\texttt{sl}}_{\texttt{pr}}(\mathcal{F},\mathcal{E})$.

Algorithm 4. $\texttt{RefinementAlg}_{\texttt{pr}}(\mathcal{F},Q,\mathcal{E})$

1: **Input**: an AAF $\mathcal{F}$; an initial preference state Q; and a set of arguments $\mathcal{E}$.
2: **Output**: a set $\mathcal{Q}$ consisting of such a preference state Q_n that there exists a preference derivation starting with $(\langle\{X\},\emptyset,\{X\},\emptyset\rangle,Q)$ for some $X \in \mathcal{A}rg \setminus \mathcal{E}$ and ending with a pair of the form $(\langle\emptyset,\emptyset,\_,\_\rangle,Q_n)$.
3: $\mathcal{T} \leftarrow \{(\langle\{X\},\emptyset,\{X\},\emptyset\rangle,Q) \mid X \in \mathcal{A}rg \setminus \mathcal{E}\}$
4: **return** $\texttt{ConstructSuccessfulPrefDers}(\mathcal{T})$

Algorithm 5. $\texttt{Transform}(R,\mathcal{R})$

1: **Input**: A preference state R and a set $\mathcal{R} = \{R_1,\ldots,R_j,\ldots,R_k\}$ of preference where every $R_j \supseteq R$.
2: **Output**: A set $\mathcal{R}^*$ of preference states so that $\mathcal{M}(\mathcal{R}^*) = \mathcal{M}(R) \setminus \mathcal{M}(\mathcal{R})$.
3: $\Pi \leftarrow \{\{\overline{s_1},\ldots,\overline{s_j},\ldots,\overline{s_k}\} \mid s_1 \in R_1,\ldots,s_j \in R_j,\ldots,s_k \in R_k\}$ ▷ Note that $\overline{s}$ refers to the negation of preference statement s.
4: $\mathcal{R}^* \leftarrow \{R \otimes S \mid S \in \Pi\} \setminus \{null\}$; **return** $\mathcal{R}^*$

Theorem 3. *If* $\text{PrefExtEnfAlg}_{\text{pr}}^{\text{sl}}(\mathcal{F}, \mathcal{E})$ *returns a set* $\mathcal{Q}^*$ *of preference states, then* $\text{PrefExtEnf}_{\text{pr}}^{\text{sl}}(\mathcal{F}, \mathcal{E}) = \mathcal{M}(\mathcal{Q}^*)$.

Algorithm 6. $\text{PrefExtEnfAlg}_{\text{pr}}^{\text{sl}}(\mathcal{F}, \mathcal{E})$

1: **Input**: an AA framework $\mathcal{F}$; a set of arguments $\mathcal{E}$.
2: **Output**: a set $\mathcal{Q}^*$ of preference states so that $\mathcal{M}(\mathcal{Q}^*) = \text{PrefExtEnf}_{\text{pr}}^{\text{sl}}(\mathcal{F}, \mathcal{E})$.
3: $\mathcal{Q} \leftarrow \text{PrefExtEnfAlg}_{\text{pr}}^{\text{sb}}(\mathcal{F}, \mathcal{E})$
4: let $\mathcal{Q} = \{Q_1, \ldots, Q_m\}$
5: **for each** $i \in \{1, \ldots, m\}$ **do**
6: $\quad Q_i \leftarrow \text{RefinementAlg}_{\text{pr}}(\mathcal{F}, Q_i, \mathcal{E})$
7: $\quad Q_i^* \leftarrow \text{Transform}(Q_i, \mathcal{Q}_i)$
8: **end for**
9: $\mathcal{Q}^* \leftarrow \bigcup_{i=1}^{m} \mathcal{Q}_i^*$
10: **return** $\mathcal{Q}^*$

---

6 Conclusion

The field of dynamics of argumentation received much attention recently [4,8,19,21] as it shines important aspects of AAFs in dynamic settings. In this paper we focus on an understudied form of argumentation dynamics, referred to as *preference-based enforcement*, which constrains the well-known argument-fixed extension enforcement by considering only attack removals that can be rationalized by some argument preference relation. In particular, we formalize preference-based extension enforcement and study its relationships with agent's behaviourally revealed preferences. Harnessing a computational framework for revealed preference argumentation, we develop sound and complete algorithms for many instances of preference-based extension enforcement. We leave several important issues for future work, however, notably complexity analysis, implementations and practical applications of the presented algorithms. Computing optimal solutions of preference-based enforcement is also an interesting topic.

Acknowledgement. Nguyen Duy Hung is supported by Thailand Science Research and Innovation (TSRI) Fundamental Fund, fiscal year 2025. Van-Nam Huynh is supported by the Office of Naval Research (ONR) and the Office of Naval Research Global (ONRG) under grant number N62909-23-1-2058.

References

1. Amgoud, L.: Postulates for logic-based argumentation systems. Int. J. Approximate Reasoning **55**(9), 2028–2048 (2014)

2. Amgoud, L., Cayrol, C.: A reasoning model based on the production of acceptable arguments. Ann. Math. AI **34**(1–3), 197–215 (2002)
3. Baumann, R., Brewka, G.: Expanding argumentation frameworks: Enforcing and monotonicity results. In: COMMA 2010, volume 216 of Frontiers in Artificial Intelligence and Applications, pp. 75–86. IOS Press (2010)
4. Baumann, R., Doutre, S., Mailly, J.-G., Wallner, J.P.: Handbook of Formal Argumentation, Volume 2, Chapter Enforement in Formal Argumentation. College Publications (2021)
5. Caminada, M., Amgoud, L.: On the evaluation of argumentation formalisms. Artif. Intell. **171**(5–6), 286–310 (2007)
6. Coste-Marquis, S., Konieczny, S., Mailly, J.G., Marquis, P.: Extension enforcement in abstract argumentation as an optimization problem. In: Proceedings of the 24th International Conference on Artificial Intelligence, IJCAI 2015, pp. 2876–2882. AAAI Press (2015)
7. Dietrich, F., List, C.: Mentalism versus behaviourism in economics: a philosophy-of-science perspective. Econ. Philos. **32**(2), 249–281 (2016)
8. Diller, M., Haret, A., Linsbichler, T., Rümmele, S., Woltran, S.: An extension-based approach to belief revision in abstract argumentation. Int. J. Approximate Reasoning **93**, 395–423 (2018)
9. Phan Minh Dung: On the acceptability of arguments and its fundamental role in nonmonotonic reasoning, logic programming and n-person games. Artif. Intell. **77**(2), 321–357 (1995)
10. Phan Minh Dung: An axiomatic analysis of structured argumentation with priorities. Artif. Intell. **231**, 107–150 (2016)
11. Phan Minh Dung and Phan Minh Thang: Fundamental properties of attack relations in structured argumentation with priorities. Artif. Intell. **255**, 1–42 (2018)
12. Dung, P.M., Thang, P.M., Son, T.C.: On structured argumentation with conditional preferences. In: Proceedings of the AAAI Conference on Artificial Intelligence, vol. 33, pp. 2792–2800 (2019)
13. Nguyen Duy Hung and Van-Nam Huynh: Revealed preference in argumentation: algorithms and applications. Int. J. Approximate Reasoning **131**, 214–251 (2021)
14. Hung, N.D., Huynh, V.-N.: Integrated preference argumentation and applications in consumer behaviour analyses. Int. J. Approximate Reasoning **159**, 108938 (2023)
15. Modgil, S., Prakken, H.: A general account of argumentation with preferences. Artif. Intell. **195**, 361–397 (2013)
16. Modgil, S., Prakken, H.: The aspic+ framework for structured argumentation: a tutorial. Argument Comput. **5**(1), 31–62 (2014)
17. Samuelson, P.A.: A note on the pure theory of consumer's behaviour. Economica **5**(17), 61–71 (1938)
18. Samuelson, P.A.: Consumption theory in terms of revealed preference. Economica **15**(60), 243–253 (1948)
19. Snaith, M., Reed, C.: Argument revision. J. Logic Comput. **27**(7), 2089–2134 (2016)
20. Thang, P.M., Dung, P.M. and Hung, N.D.: Towards a common framework for dialectical proof procedures in abstract argumentation. J. Logic Comput. **19**(6) (2009)
21. Wallner, J.P., Niskanen, A., Järvisalo, M.: Complexity results and algorithms for extension enforcement in abstract argumentation. In: Proceedings of the Thirtieth AAAI Conference on Artificial Intelligence, pp. 1088–1094. AAAI Press (2016)

Argumentation Framework with Attitude Classification: A New Approach to Handle Controversial Arguments, Defeat Cycles and Self-defeating Arguments

Lehuai Jiang(✉) and Wei Chen

Department of Philosophy, Fudan University, Shanghai 200433, China
lhjiang23@m.fudan.edu.cn, weichen@fudan.edu.cn

Abstract. Dung's theory has become the de facto standard in the field of argumentation-based inference. However, it has been noted that his semantics may yield results that go against our expectations when dealing with controversial arguments. A pair of controversial arguments may belong to the same extension under his semantics, meaning that they can be accepted simultaneously. Several semantics have been proposed to address this issue, including prudent semantics, careful semantics and solid semantics. The common feature of these approaches is that they all refuse to allow a pair of controversial arguments to appear in the same extension. However, in this paper, we argue that the contexts in which controversial arguments arise are highly complex, and therefore we need a new method to handle controversial arguments more flexibly. We propose a new class of argumentation frameworks called "argumentation framework with attitude classification" (ACAF) and show that through this new framework, we can handle controversial arguments appropriately in different contexts. We also find that our new framework provides a new method for handling "defeat cycles" and "self-defeating arguments".

Keywords: Abstract argumentation framework · Controversial argument · Defeat cycle · Self-defeating argument

1 Introduction

Argumentation, as a distinct research field, mainly focuses on the study of how to model arguments and their relationships, and how to resolve conflicts in the presence of divergent opinions. Over the past few decades, it has become a major focus in AI, and has already had a significant impact on many other subfields of AI, such as knowledge representation and nonmonotonic reasoning [8]. There are two main research lines in the study of argumentation: the "logic-based" approach and the "abstract" approach. The logic-based approach emphasizes the logical structure within an argument, while the abstract approach treats arguments as atomic items. The abstract approach assumes that arguments and their relationships have already been defined by background knowledge, evaluates the resulting argumentation system as a whole, and ultimately determines which sets of arguments are acceptable given the complex relationships between the arguments [8,27].

In the abstract approach, the most influential work comes from a seminal paper by Dung [15]. He develops a theory for evaluating arguments using just two simple concepts, argument and attack, which has now become the de facto standard in the field of argumentation-based inference [25]. A Dung-style argumentation framework is a pair $\langle \mathcal{A}, \mathcal{R} \rangle$, where $\mathcal{A} \neq \emptyset$ is the set of arguments and $\mathcal{R} \subseteq \mathcal{A} \times \mathcal{A}$ denotes the (direct) attack relation between arguments [15]. Every argumentation framework can naturally be represented by a directed graph, where $\mathcal{A}$ is the set of vertices and $\mathcal{R}$ is the set of edges of the directed graph. In his seminal paper, Dung also proposes four different semantics. Formally, an extension-based semantics σ is a function such that for any argumentation framework $AF = \langle \mathcal{A}, \mathcal{R} \rangle$, $\sigma(AF) \in 2^{2^{\mathcal{A}}}$, i.e., $\sigma(AF)$ is a collection of subsets of $\mathcal{A}$ [29]. Elements of $\sigma(AF)$ are called extensions, and each extension represents a set of arguments that can be accepted simultaneously under σ. The justification state of an argument $a \in \mathcal{A}$ under a semantics σ is then determined by the membership of a to the extensions.

Although in most frameworks the justification state of the arguments under Dung's semantics aligns with our expectations, it has been noted that some particular frameworks do not behave this way. For example, the unique extension of the framework AF_1 (see Fig. 1) obtained under Dung's semantics is $\{i, n, a\}$, which indicates that a is skeptically justified and that a and i can be accepted simultaneously. The reason why a can appears in the unique extension is that b, which attacks a, is attacked by i. However, since i both indirectly attacks and indirectly defends a, i is controversial w.r.t. a. Coste-Marquis et al. argue that inferring a in this case would be incautious [13].

Definition 1 (Dung's semantics). *Given an argumentation framework $AF = \langle \mathcal{A}, \mathcal{R} \rangle$ and $S \subseteq \mathcal{A}$. S is conflict-free if there are no arguments $a, b \in S$ such that $a\mathcal{R}b$. $a \in \mathcal{A}$ is acceptable w.r.t. S if for every $b \in \mathcal{A}$, $b\mathcal{R}a \Rightarrow S\mathcal{R}b$ (we write $S\mathcal{R}b$ if there exists an argument $c \in S$ such that $c\mathcal{R}b$). S is admissible if S is conflict-free and every argument in S is acceptable w.r.t. S itself. S is a preferred extension of AF if S is a maximal (w.r.t. $\subseteq$) admissible set of AF. S is a stable extension of AF if S is conflict-free and for every $a \in \mathcal{A}\setminus S$, $S\mathcal{R}a$. S is a complete extension of AF if S is admissible and for every $a \in \mathcal{A}$, if a is acceptable w.r.t. S then $a \in S$. S is the grounded extension of AF if S is the least (w.r.t. $\subseteq$) complete extension.*

Definition 2 (controversial argument). *Given an argumentation framework $AF = \langle \mathcal{A}, \mathcal{R} \rangle$. $a \in \mathcal{A}$ indirectly attacks $b \in \mathcal{A}$ if there is an odd-length path from a to b. $a \in \mathcal{A}$ indirectly defends $b \in \mathcal{A}$ if there is an even-length path from a to b. $a \in \mathcal{A}$ is controversial w.r.t. $b \in \mathcal{A}$ if a both indirectly attacks and indirectly defends b. An argument $a \in \mathcal{A}$ is controversial if it is controversial w.r.t. some argument $b \in \mathcal{A}$.*

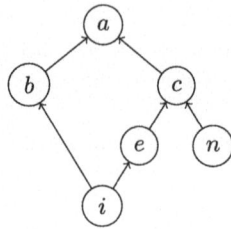

Fig. 1. The directed graph of argumentation framework $AF_1 = \langle\{a,b,c,e,n,i\}, \{(i,e), (e,c), (i,b), (n,c), (c,a), (b,a)\}\rangle$, where i is controversial w.r.t. a. AF_1 is also taken from a paper by Coste-Marquis et al. [13]

Coste-Marquis et al. argue that it is not prudent to infer two indirectly conflicting arguments at the same time (two arguments conflict indirectly if one indirectly attacks the other) and with this idea, they develop prudent semantics. They define the concept of p(rudent)-admissible sets, which do not allow indirect conflicts. All p-extensions are p-admissible sets, so that a pair of controversial arguments cannot belong to the same p-extension. As a result, the unique preferred (grounded, complete) p-extension of framework AF_1 is $\{i, n\}$, and a is not justified. Coste-Marquis et al. claim that prudent semantics handles controversial arguments better than Dung's semantics [13].

Other approaches for handling controversial arguments include careful semantics proposed by Coste-Marquis et al. [12,14] and solid semantics proposed by Liu et al. [19]. In the case of careful semantics, all c(areful)-extensions are c-admissible sets, which cannot contain argument pairs a and b such that a indirectly attacks an argument while b indirectly defends it at the same time. When $a = b$, a is a controversial argument. Therefore, c-extensions cannot contain any controversial arguments, and thus cannot contain any pair of controversial arguments. For solid semantics, Liu et al. prove that if an argument a is controversial w.r.t. another argument b, then b cannot belong to any s(olid)-admissible extension. Consequently, no s-extension can contain a pair of controversial arguments.

These existing approaches share the common feature that once an argument is controversial w.r.t. another, they cannot belong to the same extension. Our question, however, is whether such an absolute rejection is really appropriate. If an argument both indirectly attacks and indirectly defends another, should we place so much emphasis on their conflict that we conclude they cannot be accepted simultaneously? Are there situations in which a pair of controversial arguments do not actually conflict severely and can therefore be accepted simultaneously? If so, these approaches may potentially lead to results that contradict our intuition.

In this paper, we argue that the contexts in which controversial arguments arise are highly complex. Actually, in some cases, a pair of controversial arguments may not conflict at all, and therefore existing approaches wrongly prevent them from being accepted simultaneously. Although the existing approaches treat controversial arguments more cautiously than Dung's semantics, they overemphasize the conflict between a pair of controversial arguments and neglect the possible other relationships between them. We propose a new class of argumentation frameworks called "argumentation frameworks with attitude classification" (ACAF) to capture the complex relationships between arguments. We show that, compared to Dung's semantics and the existing approaches, our new framework can handle controversial arguments more flexibly and appropriately in different contexts. We also find that our new framework provides a new method for handling "defeat cycles" and "self-defeating arguments".

The rest of this paper is organized as follows. In Sect. 2, we give some concrete examples to illustrate the complexity of the contexts in which controversial arguments arise. In Sect. 3, we define our new framework, define semantics for the new framework, and demonstrate the relationships between the semantics by proving some theorems. In Sect. 4, using the examples from Sect. 2, we show that the new framework can handle controversial arguments more flexibly and appropriately in different contexts. In Sect. 5, we conclude this paper, discuss some related work and provide an outlook for future work, including a brief description of handling "defeat cycles".

2 Different Contexts in Which Controversial Arguments Arise

In this section, we give four concrete examples to illustrate the complexity of the contexts in which controversial arguments arise. All the examples we provide correspond to the original framework AF_1, but the results we aim to obtain are different. Therefore, we need a new method to handle controversial arguments more flexibly. Suppose Jack and Kevin are discussing whether they should choose to drive or fly to their destination for a long-distance trip now.

Example 1 (travel mode choice).
J(a): "We should drive to the destination because it allows us to enjoy the scenic views along the way."

K(b): "Based on my experience driving last year, there aren't any noteworthy scenic views on the road from here to our destination."

K(c): "In any case, the distance from here to the destination is too far, and driving would be too tiring, so we shouldn't drive."

J(i): "I've learned that a new highway has been constructed this year from here to our destination, passing through many forest parks. We could take that highway, and it will certainly offer beautiful views."

J(n): "Compared to the need to arrive at the airport a few hours early, with the risk of delays, driving there doesn't seem so tiring."

Finally, Kevin agrees with Jack and after some reflection, presents argument e.

K(e): "You're right. Although there won't be many scenic views during the trip, since we can at least stop and stretch anytime, driving is indeed less tiring in comparison."

In Example 1, Kevin initially disagrees with Jack's viewpoint and presents b and c to attack a. Then, in response to Kevin, Jack presents arguments i and n, where i attacks b and n attacks c. Kevin finally agrees with Jack's position and after reflecting, presents e to counter his own argument c. However, Kevin still does not believe that there will be good scenery on the driving route, which leads to Jack's argument i also attacking argument e. Ultimately, the framework corresponding to Example 1 is AF_1, in which i is controversial w.r.t. a.

We consider how to handle i and a now. First look at how the existing methods handle this case. Under prudent semantics, careful semantics or solid semantics, neither i nor a can belong to the same extension, meaning that i and a cannot be accepted simultaneously. However, the question is whether this treatment is truly satisfactory. We believe the answer is negative, for two main reasons. First, both a and i are put forward by Jack, and i is introduced specifically to defend a. Second, in terms of content, a states, "We should drive to the destination because it allows us to enjoy the scenic views along the way", while i states "I've learned that a new highway has been constructed this year from here to our destination, passing through many forest parks. We could take that highway, and it will certainly offer beautiful views". There is no conflict in content between these two arguments.

Example 1 indicates that the existing methods for handling controversial arguments fail to produce the expected results in certain situations. It is worth noting that Example 1 is not overly specific or atypical. The key point is that even if argument i is originally introduced to defend a, there is always a way to make i controversial w.r.t. a by constructing an indirect attack of i on a. The indirect attack of i on a in Example 1 is caused by Kevin's argument e. However, we can imagine a scenario where someone who disagrees with Jack deliberately introduces e to create an indirect attack of i on a.

On the other hand, under Dung's semantics, the only extension obtained for AF_1 is $\{i, n, a\}$. Arguments a and i can be accepted simultaneously. Does this mean that Dung's semantics offers a better handling of controversial arguments? We consider another example. Suppose Jack, Kevin, and Smith are discussing whether it is a good time to buy a house in the city center in this case.

Example 2 (House-buying problem 1).

J(a): "Now is the best time to buy a house. Based on the recent trends in housing prices, there is a high probability that prices will continue to rise in the near future, and buying later will be more expensive."

K(b): "The current economic situation is unstable, and we should keep cash on hand. Therefore, now is not the right time to buy a house."

K(c): "From what I know, the government is about to implement a policy restricting purchases, which should cause housing prices in the city center to drop, not rise."

J(e): "Given the current unstable economic situation, rising inflation, and increasing currency devaluation, housing prices are of course going to rise."

J(n): "In the past, the government also implemented a restriction policy, but it did not lead to a drop in housing prices in the city center; on the contrary, prices continued to rise."

Then, Smith disagrees with Jack and presents argument i to counter e.

S(i): "Over the past year, our GDP has been growing rapidly, which indicates that the economic situation is very stable."

In Example 2, Kevin disagrees with Jack and presents arguments b and c to attack a. Then, in response to Kevin, Jack presents arguments e and n to attack c. After that, Smith disagrees with Jack and presents i to counter e. Coincidentally, since the conclusion of i also contradicts the premise of b, i also attacks Kevin's argument b. The framework corresponding to Example 2 is also AF_1.

Under Dung's semantics, both i and a can still be accepted simultaneously. However, unlike in Example 1, accepting both i and a in Example 2 seems less satisfactory. We also have two reasons for this. First, the reason why a can belong to the unique extension is that b, which attacks a, is attacked by Smith's argument i. However, attacking b is not Smith's original intention for presenting argument i and the attack occurs by chance. Second, Smith presents i to attack Jack's argument e and e is introduced to defend a. Argument i indirectly attacks a and Dung himself believes that while indirect attacks are not direct attacks, they can still play a decisive role in defeating the attacked argument [15]. Therefore, the potential role of i in defeating a should not be overlooked according to Dung's own view.

At this point, prudent semantics, careful semantics and solid semantics seem to provide more satisfactory result. Together, Examples 1 and 2 demonstrate that in some cases, a pair of controversial arguments should be accepted simultaneously, while in others, this is not the case. When one argument both indirectly attacks and indirectly defends another, it becomes challenging to determine whether they should be accepted simultaneously. Thus we need a new method to handle controversial arguments more flexibly. To further illustrate the complexity of the contexts in which controversial arguments arise, we make a simple modification to Example 2, resulting in Examples 3 and 4.

Example 3 (House-buying problem 2).

We make a simple modification to Example 2. The presentation of arguments a, b, c, e, and n remains unchanged, and the content of i is also unchanged. However, at this point, although i is still presented by Smith, he agrees with Jack's viewpoint on the appropriateness of buying a house now and presents i to attack Kevin's argument b.

How should we handle i and a in Example 3? Considering that Smith presents i to attack b in defense of a, and that Jack could attack c with n even without argument e, it is best to accept both i and a simultaneously. Note that simply modifying Smith's intention in presenting argument i results in a completely different outcome, even though the framework remains unchanged. This suggests that to handle controversial arguments effectively, we need to consider factors beyond the framework. We modify Example 2 again as follows.

Example 4 (House-buying problem 3).

We make a simple modification to Example 2. The process of presenting arguments a, b, c, e, and n remains unchanged, and the content of i also remains the same. However, at this point, Smith presents argument i solely to refute the shared premise "the current economic situation is unstable" in b and e, without caring whether argument a is defended or defeated.

At this point, although i is controversial w.r.t. a, in terms of the intention behind presenting the argument, i neither seeks to defend a nor to attack a. Given that Smith is completely uninterested in whether argument a is defended and only aims to refute the common premise of Jack's argument b and Kevin's argument e, a fair approach would be to neither consider Smith as defending a for Jack nor as helping Kevin defeat a. Therefore, a cannot be exempt from the attack by b on it, and should not belong to any extension.

In Example 4, we also only modified Smith's intention behind presenting argument i, without changing the framework. Although we expect the same result for Examples 4 and 2, the reason why argument i and a cannot belong to the same extension is not exactly the same. This once again suggests that to properly handle controversial arguments in different contexts, we need to consider additional factors beyond the framework. We discuss what the factor is in the next section.

3 Argumentation Framework with Attitude Classification

In this section, we introduce a new class of argumentation frameworks called "argumentation framework with attitude classification" (ACAF) and define semantics for it. Before that, it is necessary to briefly discuss the additional factor required for handling controversial arguments, which is related to the contexts in which controversial arguments arise.

We note that, in Example 1, the defense role of argument i for a seems stronger than its attack on a, whereas in Example 2, the attack of argument i on a seems stronger than its defense of a. Therefore, a natural idea is to assign weights to indirect attack and indirect defense, and decide whether a pair of controversial arguments should be accepted simultaneously based on their relative magnitudes: when i is controversial w.r.t. a, if the weight of i's indirect attack on a is smaller than the weight of its indirect defense, they can appear in the same extension and be accepted simultaneously; otherwise, they should not be accepted simultaneously. Unfortunately, no work has discussed this approach thus far. However, there have been studies that assign weights to direct attacks to represent the varying strengths of them. Dunne et al. extend Dung's original framework by introducing a function that assigns positive real values to direct attacks (weighted argumentation framework, abbreviated as WAF) [16,17], and

Martınez et al. directly assign different types to direct attacks (argumentation framework with varied strength attacks, abbreviated as AFV) [20,21].

The current question is whether we can adopt a similar approach to represent the strength of indirect attacks and indirect defenses. Dunne et al. provide some methods for determining the weight of direct attacks [16], however, we find that assigning weights to indirect attacks and indirect defenses is much more complex. First, direct attacks and indirect attacks are fundamentally different. Direct attacks can be distinguished into three different forms, including "undermine", "undercut" and "rebut" [18,22], and if there is a direct conflict between two arguments, it is easy to detect. Indirect attacks, on the other hand, arise from alternating direct attacks and are difficult to distinguish at the argument structure level. Even if there is an indirect conflict between two arguments, we may not realize it because we may overlook the arguments involved in the indirect attack path. Second, in an odd (even) length defeat cycle, one argument indirectly attacks (defends) another argument every two rounds (one round). When an argument indirectly attacks (indirectly defends) another argument through multiple overlapping paths, how should we handle the relationships between the weights of these indirect attacks (indirect defenses)? More importantly, as seen in Example 3, simply modifying Smith's intention in presenting argument i leads to a completely different outcome than what we expect in Example 2. Assigning weights to indirect attacks and indirect defenses cannot explain the emergence of such changes. Therefore, we argue that the weights of indirect attacks and indirect defenses are not the factor required for handling controversial arguments.

Another idea is to introduce preferences over arguments to handle controversial arguments. Some influential works, including "preference-based argumentation framework" (PAF) [1] and "value-based argumentation framework" (VAF) [5,6], extend Dung's original framework by introducing preferences over arguments (values). Preference-based argumentation frameworks add a preorder over the set of arguments to represent preferences over them, with the basic idea being that when an argument a is strictly less preferred than an argument b, the attack of a on b is ignored. Value-based argumentation frameworks (VAF) posit that different arguments advocate different values, and the preferences over arguments sometimes depend on the preferences over the values they advocate. Unfortunately, we find that this approach is also not applicable. Indeed, we can make argument i in Example 3 strictly less preferred than argument e, thereby blocking the indirect attack of i on a by ignoring i's direct attack on e, and avoiding the controversy between i and a. However, on one hand, we cannot explain why we should treat it this way. On the other hand, we cannot explain why the same approach is not taken in Example 2. Therefore, we believe that using preferences over arguments to handle controversial arguments actually avoids the real issue.

The existing modifications to Dung's original framework can be roughly divided into two categories. On one hand, some approaches do not add new concepts, but simply extend some of the concepts in the original framework's definition. On the other hand, some works enrich the original framework by adding new concepts [2]. We have already pointed out that handling controversial arguments requires considering certain factors beyond the original framework. Therefore, we follow the second research line in this paper. In addition to the previously mentioned WAF, AFV, PAF and VAF, we have also carefully examined other works that enrich the original framework with additional concepts. Unfortunately, we find that none of them are suitable for handling controversial arguments. Hence, we propose a new class of frameworks called "argumentation framework with attitude classification" (ACAF) in this paper.

Our basic idea is that when an argument a is controversial w.r.t. another argument b, whether they can be accepted simultaneously depends on the intention behind the presentation of a, in other words, depends on a's attitude towards b. Actually, in the four examples we provide, the attitude of argument i towards argument a is the key reason for the differing outcomes in how they are handled: In Example 1, the reason why we accept both a and i simultaneously is that i is presented to defend a. In Example 2, the reason why we are not willing to accept both a and i simultaneously is that i is presented to attack e in order to refute a. In Example 3, the reason why we accept both a and i is that i is presented to defend a. And in Example 4, the reason why a cannot be exempt from the attack by b is that i's attitude towards a is not defensive.

We observe that an argument may have three possible attitudes towards other arguments, namely "defensive", "attacking" and "neutral". For instance, in Example 2, the attitude of i towards a and e is attacking, the attitude of i towards c is defensive, and since the presentation of i has no relation to n, the attitude of i towards n is neutral. However, what should be the attitude of i towards b in Example 2? We argue that, although both Smith and Kevin oppose Jack's argument a, and Smith's argument i's attack on b is formed accidentally, since the attack of i on b is direct, the attitude of i towards b should be considered as attacking. We argue that direct attacks have a stronger determinacy than indirect ones (the length of the attack path > 1) : as long as one argument directly attacks another, its attitude towards the latter should be considered as attacking. In any case, it would be quite odd to consider the attitude of an argument towards another as neutral or defensive when it directly attacks the latter.

Then, when an argument a does not directly attack another argument b, we need to consider whether a has an indirect attack on b (the length of the attack path > 1) and whether there is an indirect defense of b. In this case, we argue that if a does not indirectly attack b, then the attitude of a towards b can only be "neutral" or "defensive"; if a does not indirectly defend b, then the attitude of a towards b can only be "neutral" or "attacking". This is because if an argument has no conflict (defense) with another argument, its attacking (defensive) attitude towards the latter (if any) cannot be verified within the framework and should not play any role. As a corollary, if in this case a neither indirectly attacks b nor indirectly defends b, then the attitude of a towards b can only be "neutral". This approach ensures that no argument holds an attacking attitude towards an unattacked argument. Specifically, an unattacked argument will not hold an attacking attitude towards another unattacked argument. An argument that neither directly nor indirectly attacks itself will not have an attacking attitude towards itself.

We do not require that when an argument does not directly attack another argument but only indirectly attacks (the length of the attack path > 1) it, its attitude towards the latter must be attacking. As we have seen in Examples 1, 3 and 4, even though i indirectly attacks a, i's attitude towards a could still be neutral or even defensive. We argue that indirect attacks do not have the decisive power to determine the attitude between arguments.

Now, we define the so-called "argumentation framework with attitude classification" (ACAF). We add an attitude function u to the original framework, where "1" represents the defensive attitude, "-1" represents the attacking attitude, and "0" represents the neutral attitude. $u(a,b) = 1$, $u(a,b) = 0$, and $u(a,b) = -1$ intuitively represent that the attitude of a towards b is defensive, neutral and attacking respectively. And u needs to satisfy the two conditions we mentioned.

Definition 3 (argumentation framework with attitude classification). *An argumentation framework with attitude classification (ACAF) is a triple $ACAF = \langle \mathcal{A}, \mathcal{R}, u \rangle$, where $\langle \mathcal{A}, \mathcal{R} \rangle$ is the original framework, and $u : A \times A \to \{-1, 0, 1\}$ is an attitude function that satisfies the following two conditions: (1) If $(a,b) \in \mathcal{R}$, then $u(a,b) = -1$; (2) Suppose that $a \in \mathcal{A}$ does not directly attack $b \in \mathcal{A}$. If a does not indirectly attack (the length of the attack path > 1) b, then $u(a,b) = 0$ or $u(a,b) = 1$; if a does not indirectly defend b, then $u(a,b) = 0$ or $u(a,b) = -1$.*

We define the concept of "attitude conflict-free" (denoted as **acf**). We don't allow an **acf** set to contain two arguments such that one argument has an attacking attitude towards the other. Since the attitude function u of an ACAF satisfies condition (1), every **acf** set of an ACAF is always a conflict-free set in the original framework.

Definition 4 (attitude conflict-free set). *Given an argumentation framework with attitude classification $ACAF = \langle \mathcal{A}, \mathcal{R}, u \rangle$ and $S \subseteq \mathcal{A}$, S is an **acf** set if there do not exist arguments $a, b \in S$ such that $u(a, b) = -1$.*

We then define the concept of "attitude admissible" (denoted as **aad**).

Definition 5 (attitude admissible set). *Given an argumentation framework with attitude classification $ACAF = \langle \mathcal{A}, \mathcal{R}, u \rangle$, $a \in \mathcal{A}$ is a(ttitude)-acceptable w.r.t. $S \subseteq \mathcal{A}$ if for any $b \in \mathcal{A}$, if $u(b, a) = -1$, then there exists $c \in S$ such that $u(c, a) = 1$ and $c\mathcal{R}b$. $S \subseteq \mathcal{A}$ is an **aad** set if S is an **acf** set and all arguments in S are a-acceptable w.r.t. to S.*

For a set of arguments S defending a, our definition requires that S not only attacks all arguments that have an attacking attitude towards a, but also that the attacks on those arguments are indeed made with the purpose of defending a. Under this definition, in Example 2, since i has an attacking attitude towards a, a will not be defended by $\{i, n\}$. At first glance, the requirement that S must attack an argument whenever it has an attacking attitude towards a seems too demanding. However, since the attitude function satisfies condition (2), our definition does not require S to attack arguments that neither directly nor indirectly attack a. We actually strengthen Dung's definition of admissible sets: for any $a \in \mathcal{A}$ and $S \subseteq \mathcal{A}$, if a is a-acceptable w.r.t. to S, then a is acceptable w.r.t. S; if S is an **aad** set, then S is also an admissible set; $\emptyset$ is always an **aad** set. Moreover, we have the following theorem regarding **aad** sets.

Theorem 1. *Given an argumentation framework with attitude classification $ACAF = \langle \mathcal{A}, \mathcal{R}, u \rangle$, an **aad** set $S \subseteq \mathcal{A}$ and $a \in \mathcal{A}$, if there exists $b \in \mathcal{A}$ such that*

(1) $u(b, a) = -1$ and
(2) there does not exist $c \in \mathcal{A}$ such that $u(c, a) = 1$ and $c\mathcal{R}b$, then $a \notin S$.

Proof. Obvious.

By Theorem 1, for any $a \in \mathcal{A}$, if there exists an unattacked argument $b \in \mathcal{A}$ such that $u(b, a) = -1$, then a will not belong to any **aad** set, and thus will not belong to any extension that we define next. This reflects another fundamental idea we have, which is "We can only claim to have fully defended an argument after addressing all arguments that have an attacking attitude towards it".

We define semantics for our framework, including a(ttitude)-preferred semantics, a(ttitude)-stable semantics, a(ttitude)-complete semantics and a(ttitude)-grounded semantics.

Definition 6 (a-preffered semantics, a-stable semantics, a-complete semantics). *Given an argumentation framework with attitude classification $ACAF = \langle \mathcal{A}, \mathcal{R}, u \rangle$ and $S \subseteq \mathcal{A}$. S is an a-preferred extension of $ACAF$ if S is a maximal (w.r.t. $\subseteq$) **aad** set of $ACAF$. S is an a-stable extension of $ACAF$ if S is an **aad** set and for every $a \in \mathcal{A} \setminus S$, there exists $b \in S$ such that $b\mathcal{R}a$. S is an a-complete extension of $ACAF$ if S is an **aad** set and for every $a \in \mathcal{A}$, if a is a-acceptable w.r.t. S, then $a \in S$.*

Our definition of a-stable semantics appears to differ from Dung's stable semantics. This is because, in the definition of stable semantics, the conditions "S is conflict-free" and "S attacks all arguments that are not in it" imply that "S is an admissible set". However, the conditions "S is an **acf** set" and "S attacks all arguments that are not in it" can not guarantee that "S is an **aad** set". Actually, for any $a \in S$ and $b \in \mathcal{A} \setminus S$ such that $u(b, a) = -1$, these two conditions can not ensure that the argument in S attacking b has a defensive attitude towards a. Therefore, we need to explicitly state in the definition that a-stable extensions are always **aad** sets.

Definition 7 (a-characteristic function). *Given an argumentation framework with attitude classification $ACAF = \langle \mathcal{A}, \mathcal{R}, u \rangle$, we define its a-characteristic function F_{ACAF} as follows:*

$$F_{ACAF} : 2^{\mathcal{A}} \to 2^{\mathcal{A}}$$
$$F_{ACAF}(S) = \{a : a \text{ is a-acceptable w.r.t. } S\}$$

We prove that F_{ACAF} is monotonic w.r.t. $\subseteq$.

Theorem 2. *F_{ACAF} is monotonic w.r.t. $\subseteq$.*

Proof. Assume $S \subseteq S'$. We prove that $F_{ACAF}(S) \subseteq F_{ACAF}(S')$. For any $a \in F_{ACAF}(S)$, by the definition of F_{ACAF}, a is a-acceptable w.r.t. S. By Definition 5, for any $b \in \mathcal{A}$ such that $u(b,a) = -1$, there exists $c \in S$ such that $u(c,a) = 1$ and $c\mathcal{R}b$. Since $S \subseteq S'$, for any $b \in \mathcal{A}$ such that $u(b,a) = -1$, there exists $c \in S'$ such that $u(c,a) = 1$ and $c\mathcal{R}b$. By Definition 5, a is a-acceptable w.r.t. S', so $a \in F_{ACAF}(S')$.

Definition 8 (a-grounded semantics). *Given an argumentation framework with attitude classification $ACAF = \langle \mathcal{A}, \mathcal{R}, u \rangle$, by Theorem 2 and the fixpoint theorem [28], we define the unique a-grounded extension of ACAF as the minimal fixed point of F_{ACAF}.*

In the remaining part of this section, we prove some additional theorems. Through these theorems, we will see that the relationships between the four newly defined semantics are similar to those between the four semantics defined by Dung.

Theorem 3. *Given an argumentation framework with attitude classification $ACAF = \langle \mathcal{A}, \mathcal{R}, u \rangle$ and an **aad** set $S \subseteq \mathcal{A}$, if a and b are both a-acceptable w.r.t. S, then*

*(1) $S' = S \cup \{a\}$ is an **aad** set;*
(2) b is a-acceptable w.r.t. S'.

Proof. (1) First, we prove that S' is **acf**. Assume the contrary, that there exists $c \in S$ such that $u(c,a) = -1$ or $u(a,c) = -1$. If $u(c,a) = -1$, since a is a-acceptable w.r.t. S, there exists $d \in S$ such that $u(d,a) = 1$ and $d\mathcal{R}c$. Therefore, $u(d,c) = -1$, which contradicts that S is **acf**. On the other hand, if $u(a,c) = -1$, since c is a-acceptable w.r.t. S, there exists $d \in S$ such that $u(d,c) = 1$ and $d\mathcal{R}a$. Thus, $u(d,a) = -1$. Furthermore, since a is a-acceptable w.r.t. S, there exists $e \in S$ such that $u(e,a) = 1$ and $e\mathcal{R}d$, which implies $u(e,d) = -1$, contradicting that S is **acf**.
Then, we prove that every argument in S' is a-acceptable w.r.t. itself. Let $c \in S' = S \cup \{a\}$. Since c is a-acceptable w.r.t. S, by Theorem 2, c is a-acceptable w.r.t. S'.
(2) This follows directly from Theorem 2.

Theorem 4. *Given an argumentation framework with attitude classification $ACAF = \langle \mathcal{A}, \mathcal{R}, u \rangle$, the following propositions hold:*

(1) For any **aad** set $S \subseteq \mathcal{A}$, there exists an a-preferred extension $E \subseteq \mathcal{A}$ such that $S \subseteq E$;
(2) $ACAF$ has at least one a-preferred extension;
(3) All a-stable extensions of $ACAF$ are a-preferred extensions, but the converse does not necessarily hold;
(4) All a-preferred extensions of $ACAF$ are a-complete extensions, but the converse does not necessarily hold.

Proof. (1) If S is a maximal **aad** set, then S itself is an a-preferred extension. If S is not a maximal **aad** set, then $S^* = \{S' \subseteq \mathcal{A} : S' \supset S$ and S' is an **aad** set $\} \neq \emptyset$. Assume $S_0 \subseteq S_1 \subseteq S_2 \subseteq \cdots$ is a chain in S^*, we prove that $\bigcup_{i \in \mathbb{N}} S_i \in S^*$. In fact, we only need to prove that $\bigcup_{i \in \mathbb{N}} S_i$ is an **aad** set. On one hand, $\bigcup_{i \in \mathbb{N}} S_i$ is **acf**. Otherwise, there exist some S_j in the chain and $a, b \in S_j$ such that $u(a, b) = -1$, which contradicts the assumption that S_j is **aad**. On the other hand, for any $a \in \bigcup_{i \in \mathbb{N}} S_i$, there exists some S_j in the chain such that $a \in S_j$. Since S_j is **aad**, a is a-acceptable w.r.t. S_j. By Theorem 2, a is a-acceptable w.r.t. $\bigcup_{i \in \mathbb{N}} S_i$. Thus, $\bigcup_{i \in \mathbb{N}} S_i$ is an **aad** set. Therefore, any chain $S_0 \subseteq S_1 \subseteq S_2 \subseteq \cdots$ in S^* has an upper bound $\bigcup_{i \in \mathbb{N}} S_i$. By Zorn's Lemma, S^* contains at least one maximal element. These maximal elements are a-preferred extensions that contain S.
(2) This follows directly from (1) and the fact that $\emptyset$ is an **aad** set of $ACAF$.
(3) Assume $S \subseteq \mathcal{A}$ is an a-stable extension of $ACAF$, we prove that S is a maximal **aad** set. Suppose otherwise, i.e., there exists an **aad** set $S' \supset S$. We take $a \in S' \setminus S$. Since S is an a-stable extension, there exists $b \in S$ such that $b\mathcal{R}a$. By condition (1), $u(b, a) = -1$. Hence, there exist $a, b \in S'$ such that $u(b, a) = -1$, which contradicts the assumption that S' is **acf**. Conversely, a-preferred extensions are not necessarily a-stable extensions. For example, for a defeat cycle of length 3, $AF_2 = \langle \{a, b, c\}, \{(a, b), (b, c), (c, a)\}\rangle$, if we add an attitude function u that satisfies $u(a, b) = u(b, a) = u(b, c) = u(c, b) = u(c, a) = u(a, c) = -1$ (that is to say, the attitude of any argument towards other arguments is attacking), then $\langle AF_2, u\rangle$ will have no a-stable extension, and the unique a-preferred extension of $\langle AF_2, u\rangle$ is the empty set.
(4) Assume $S \subseteq \mathcal{A}$ is an a-preferred extension of $ACAF$, we prove that S is also an a-complete extension. Suppose otherwise, i.e., there exists $a \in \mathcal{A}$, a is a-acceptable w.r.t. S, but $a \notin S$. Since S is an **aad** set and by Theorem 3, $S' = S \cup \{a\} \supset S$ is an **aad** set, which contradicts the assumption that S is a maximal **aad** set. Conversely, a-complete extensions are not necessarily a-preferred extensions. For instance, for the argumentation framework $AF_3 = \langle\{a, b, c\}, \{(a, b), (b, a)\}\rangle$, when we add an attitude function u which satisfies $u(a, b) = u(b, a) = -1$ and $u(a, a) = u(b, b) = 1$, then $\langle AF_3, u\rangle$ will possess three a-complete extensions, namely $\{c\}, \{a, c\}, \{b, c\}$, and two a-preferred extensions, that is, $\{a, c\}, \{b, c\}$.

Theorem 5. *Given an argumentation framework with attitude classification $ACAF = \langle \mathcal{A}, \mathcal{R}, u\rangle$, the following propositions hold:*

(1) For any $S \subseteq \mathcal{A}$, S is **add** iff S is **acf** and $S \subseteq F_{ACAF}(S)$;
(2) For any $S \subseteq \mathcal{A}$, S is an a-complete extension of $ACAF$ iff S is **acf** and S is a fixed point of F_{ACAF};
(3) The unique a-grounded extension of $ACAF$ is the least a-complete extension w.r.t. $\subseteq$.

Proof. (1) Obvious.
(2) Assume S is an a-complete extension of $ACAF$. Then S is an **aad** set. By (1), S is **acf** and $S \subseteq F_{ACAF}(S)$. For any $a \in F_{ACAF}(S)$, by Definition 7, a is a-acceptable w.r.t. S. Since S is an a-complete extension of $ACAF$, it follows that $a \in S$. Therefore, $F_{ACAF}(S) \subseteq S$, and S is a fixed point of F_{ACAF}.
Conversely, assume S is **acf** and $F_{ACAF}(S) = S$. Then, by (1), S is an **aad** set. For any $a \in \mathcal{A}$, if a is a-acceptable w.r.t. S, then $a \in F_{ACAF}(S) = S$. Therefore, S is an a-complete extension of $ACAF$.
(3) By (2) and Definition 8, if $S \subseteq \mathcal{A}$ is the unique a-grounded extension, S is included in all a-complete extensions. We only need to show that S is an a-complete extension. By (2) again, it suffices to show that S is **acf**. By Theorems 4, $ACAF$ has at least one a-complete extension S'. Since S' is **acf**, $S \subseteq S'$ is also **acf**.

4 Handling Controversial Arguments Within ACAF

In this section, we show how argumentation frameworks with attitude classification can handle controversial arguments appropriately in different contexts. We review the examples introduced in Sect. 2 and for different examples, we add different attitude functions to the original framework. For convenience, we denote a-preferred semantics, a-stable semantics, a-complete semantics and a-grounded semantics as $\mathcal{APR}$, $\mathcal{AST}$, $\mathcal{ACO}$ and $\mathcal{AGR}$ respectively.

In Example 1, since Jack's intention in presenting i is to defend his own argument a, we have $u_1(i, a) = 1$. Additionally, we have $u_1(e, a) = u_1(n, a) = 1$, and $u_1(i, e) = u_1(i, b) = u_1(b, a) = u_1(e, c) = u_1(c, a) = u_1(n, c) = -1$ according to condition (1). i's attitude towards c is somewhat ambiguous. According to condition (2), since i neither directly attacks nor indirectly attacks c, its attitude towards c can only be neutral or defensive. Given that Jack disagrees with c, and that i's proposal is unrelated to c, we let $u_1(i, c) = 0$. All other argument pairs are assigned values of 0 by u_1 according to condition (2). We get an argumentation framework with attitude classification $ACAF_1 = \langle AF_1, u_1 \rangle$. At this point, for any a-semantics $\sigma \in \{\mathcal{APR}, \mathcal{AST}, \mathcal{ACO}, \mathcal{AGR}\}$, we have $\sigma(AF_1, u_1) = \{\{a, i, n\}\}$. The reason a belongs to the unique extension is that it is defended by i and n, which respectively attack b and c and both hold a defensive attitude towards a. This result aligns with our expectations.

In Example 2, since Smith's intention in presenting i is to attack Jack's argument e, we have $u_2(i, a) = -1$. Additionally, we have $u_2(i, c) = u_2(n, a) = u_2(e, a) = 1$ and $u_2(i, e) = u_2(i, b) = u_2(b, a) = u_2(e, c) = u_2(c, a) = u_2(n, c) =$

-1 according to condition (1). According to condition (2), all remaining argument pairs can only be assigned values of 0 by u_2. We get an argumentation framework with attitude classification $ACAF_2 = \langle AF_1, u_2 \rangle$. At this point, for any a-semantics $\sigma \in \{\mathcal{APR}, \mathcal{ACO}, \mathcal{AGR}\}$, we have $\sigma(AF_1, u_2) = \{\{i, n\}\}$. And $ACAF_2$ has no a-stable extension. a cannot belong to the extension $\{i, n\}$, partly because i holds an attacking attitude towards a, and we cannot find an argument that attacks b and hold an defensive attitude towards a. On the other hand, since i holds an attacking attitude towards a and is an unattacked argument, we cannot find an argument that defends a to attack i. This result also aligns with our expectations.

In Example 3, since Smith supports Jack's argument a and the intention of presenting i is to attack Kevin's argument b, we have $u_3(i, a) = 1$. Additionally, we have $u_3(n, a) = u_3(e, a) = 1$ and $u_3(i, e) = u_3(i, b) = u_3(b, a) = u_3(e, c) = u_3(c, a) = u_3(n, c) = -1$ according to condition (1). i's attitude towards c is somewhat ambiguous. According to condition (2), since i neither directly attacks nor indirectly attacks c, its attitude towards c can only be neutral or defensive. Considering that Smith supports Jack and that i's proposal is unrelated to c, we set $u_3(i, c) = 0$. All other argument pairs are assigned values of 0 by u_3 according to condition (2). We get an argumentation framework with attitude classification $ACAF_3 = \langle AF_1, u_3 \rangle$. At this point, for any a-semantics $\sigma \in \{\mathcal{APR}, \mathcal{AST}, \mathcal{ACO}, \mathcal{AGR}\}$, we have $\sigma(AF_1, u_3) = \{\{a, i, n\}\}$. a belongs to the extension because b and c are attacked by i and n, which hold a defensive attitude towards a. This aligns with our expectations.

In Example 4, since Smith's intention in presenting i is to simultaneously refute both Jack's argument b and Kevin's argument e's premise, without caring whether argument a is justified, we have $u_4(i, a) = u_4(i, c) = 0$. Additionally, we have $u_4(n, a) = u_4(e, a) = 1$, and $u_4(i, e) = u_4(i, b) = u_4(b, a) = u_4(e, c) = u_4(c, a) = u_4(n, c) = -1$ according to condition (1). All other argument pairs are assigned values of 0 by u_4 according to condition (2). We get an argumentation framework with attitude classification $ACAF_4 = \langle AF_1, u_4 \rangle$. At this point, for any a-semantics $\sigma \in \{\mathcal{APR}, \mathcal{ACO}, \mathcal{AGR}\}$, we have $\sigma(AF_1, u_4) = \{\{i, n\}\}$. And $ACAF_4$ has no a-stable extension. a cannot belong to the extension $\{i, n\}$ because i holds a neutral attitude towards a, and we cannot find an argument that hold a defensive attitude towards a and attacks b. This result aligns with our expectation that Smith remains neutral in this case.

Through the above analysis, we have shown that our new framework can handle controversial arguments appropriately in different contexts. Although all the examples we provide correspond to the original framework AF_1, controversial arguments in other frameworks can also be handled by considering attitudes between arguments. We show the general handling of controversial arguments by $ACAF$ as well as the relationship between a-semantics and Dung's semantics through the following theorems.

Theorem 6. *Given an argumentation framework with attitude classification $ACAF = \langle \mathcal{A}, \mathcal{R}, u \rangle$, the following proposition holds: For any arguments $a, b \in \mathcal{A}$,* where a is controversial w.r.t. b, if $u(a,b) = -1$ or $u(b,a) = -1$, then a and b can not belong to any a-extension simultaneously.

Proof. Obvious. This proposition is similar to a proposition in prudent semantics, that is, if there is an indirect conflict between two arguments a and b, then they cannot belong to any p-extension simultaneously. On the other hand, if there is no attitudinal conflict between a and b, then it is possible for them to belong to the same a-extension.

Theorem 7. *Given an argumentation framework with attitude classification $ACAF = \langle \mathcal{A}, \mathcal{R}, u \rangle$, if the attitude function u also satisfies the following two conditions (3) and (4):*

(3) there do not exist $a, b \in \mathcal{A}$ such that a does not directly attack but only indirectly attacks b (the length of the attack path > 1) and $u(a,b) = -1$,
(4) for any $a, b \in \mathcal{A}$, if a indirectly defends b, then $u(a,b) = 1$,

*then the set of **aad** sets is identical to the set of admissible sets. Therefore, the set of a-preferred extensions (a-stable extensions, a-complete extensions, a-grounded extensions) of $ACAF$ is identical to the set of preferred extensions (stable extensions, complete extensions, grounded extension) of $\langle \mathcal{A}, \mathcal{R} \rangle$.*

Proof. We only need to prove that any admissible set $S \subseteq \mathcal{A}$ is an **aad** set. First, we prove that S is an **acf** set. Suppose this is not the case, that is, there exist $a, b \in S$ such that $u(a, b) = -1$. Then, according to conditions (1) and (2), either a directly attacks b or a does not directly attack b but only indirectly attacks b (the length of the attack path > 1). If a directly attacks b, then it contradicts the fact that S is a conflict-free set. If a does not directly attack b but only indirectly attacks b, then it contradicts the fact that u satisfies condition (3). Therefore, S is **acf**.

Then we prove that any argument $a \in S$ is a-acceptable w.r.t. S. For any $b \in \mathcal{A}$ such that $u(b, a) = -1$, according to conditions (1) and (2), either b directly attacks a or b does not directly attack a but only indirectly attacks a (the length of the attack path > 1). The case where b does not directly attack a but only indirectly attacks a contradicts condition (3), so b directly attacks a. Then, since a is acceptable w.r.t. S, there exists $c \in S$ such that $c\mathcal{R}b$. By condition (4), $u(c, a) = 1$. Therefore, $a \in S$ is a-acceptable w.r.t. S.

The above two theorems indicate that our new framework can indeed handle controversial arguments more comprehensively than Dung's semantics and the existing methods. When argument a is controversial w.r.t. argument b, if we want to strictly reject their appearance in the same extension, just as the existing methods such as prudent semantics do, then we only need to set $u(a,b) = -1$ to achieve this goal. On the other hand, if we want to obtain results consistent with Dung's semantics, we just need to ensure that the attitude function u satisfies conditions (3) and (4). Based on this, we claim that our new approach does handle controversial arguments better.

Finally, it is worth pointing out that, as we have already seen, it is not difficult to determine the attitude of one argument towards another. After all, an argument is always presented for a specific reason.

5 Conclusion and Future Work

In this paper, our main contribution is the proposal of a new class of argumentation frameworks and the definition of four semantics based on them. We show that compared to Dung's semantics and the existing methods, our new framework has the advantage of handling controversial arguments more flexibly and appropriately in different contexts, yielding results that align with our expectations.

Although in this paper we mainly focus on how to deal with controversial arguments, we also find that our new framework provides a new method for handling other important issues, such as "defeat cycles" and "self-defeating arguments". There is still no established consensus on how to deal with odd length cycles and even length cycles. On one hand, scholars including Pollock and Baroni believe that there are problems with treating odd-length cycles and even-length cycles differently. Pollock states that the differences in the ways of determining the justification status of arguments within odd length cycles and even length cycles are "puzzling" [23]; Baroni et al. argue that in some situations, we lack sufficient grounds to handle these two types of cycles differently and the ability of odd length defeat cycles to defeat external arguments can even vary with changes in the framework structure [3,4]. On the other hand, some scholars accept the possibility of treating the two types of cycles differently. Prakken et al. point out that a alternative perspective is that odd length cycles are essentially different from even length cycles [26]; Bench-Capon states that even length cycles should be treated as dilemmas, while odd length cycles should be treated as paradoxes [7].

In this paper, a-semantics defined on the new framework deals with odd length cycles and even length cycles differently, which is in line with the second type of viewpoint. Specifically, a-preferred semantics handles odd length cycles in the same way as Dung's preferred semantics, however, it offers a flexible approach to dealing with even length cycles. For example, for a defeat cycle of length 4, $AF_4 = \langle\{a,b,c,d\},\{(a,b),(b,c),(c,d),(d,a)\}\rangle$, if we add an attitude function u satisfying $u(a,c) = u(c,a) = u(b,d) = u(d,b) = u(a,a) = u(b,b) = u(c,c) = u(d,d) = 1$ (i.e., the attitudes of a towards c, c towards a, b towards d, d towards b, and their attitudes towards themselves are all defensive), then $\sigma_{\mathcal{APR}}\langle AF_4, u\rangle = \{\{d,b\},\{a,c\}\}$, which means that the extensions obtained under a-preferred semantics are the same as the extensions obtained under Dung's preferred semantics. However, if $u(a,c) = 0$, i.e., a attacks b but has no defensive attitude towards c, then according to Theorem 1, c cannot belong to any **aad** set, and thus cannot belong to any a-extension. In the extreme case where $u(a,c) = u(c,a) = u(b,d) = u(d,b) = 0$ (i.e., the attitudes of a towards c, c towards a, b towards d, and d towards b are all non-defensive), we even have $\sigma_{\mathcal{APR}}\langle AF_4, u\rangle = \{\emptyset\}$. Then all arguments in AF_4 are not justified, just like the arguments in odd length cycles. Due to space limitations, we only provide a brief description here, and the remaining work will be carried out in the future.

A recent related work is "argumentation frameworks with attack classification" proposed by Vassiliades et al. [30] They argue that direct attacks within a framework can serve two potential roles. On the one hand, direct attacks may generate conflicts; on the other hand, direct attacks may defend other arguments and shield them from attacks. Although Vassiliades et al. also add a classification to the original framework, their approach differs from ours in that they classify attacks within the framework, whereas we focus on classifying attitudes between arguments. And we additionally consider a type, namely the neutral attitude. Moreover, unlike them, we argue that an argument's defensive attitude towards another is the fundamental reason why direct attacks can play a defensive role: if argument c can defend argument a which is attacked by argument b through an attack on b, this is not because c's attack on b inherently possesses a "defending" property, but because c's attitude towards a happens to be defensive. From this perspective, our approach seems more intuitive. Furthermore, as Vassiliades et al. themselves have noted, one potential theoretical extension of their work is to "make the 'defending' property attack-specific". After all, one might argue that "a defending attack from argument a to argument b may be defending some (but not all) of the conflict-generating attacks originating from b" [30]. Our new framework, by taking into account the attitude between every pair of arguments within the framework, has effectively addressed this issue.

Although we have to provide some specific examples to illustrate the complexity of the contexts in which controversial arguments arise, the framework we define remains abstract and independent of the specific content of arguments. In fact, our new framework can be regarded as a tool that allows attitude functions to be freely defined, provided the two requirements for attitude functions are satisfied. In ASPIC project, excellent work has already been done to connect the structure of arguments with abstract argumentation frameworks [9,22,24]. It is exciting to see whether our work can benefit from them in the future.

Finally, Cayrol et al. consider a different kind of interaction between arguments, namely support relation, in "bipolar argumentation frameworks" [10,11]. In this paper, the concept of defense we discuss refers to indirect defense arising from the alternation of direct attacks, which differs from support relations. We also look forward to integrating our framework with bipolar argumentation frameworks in the future.

References

1. Amgoud, L., Cayrol, C.: A reasoning model based on the production of acceptable arguments. Ann. Math. Artif. Intell. **34**, 197–215 (2002)
2. Baroni, P., Cerutti, F., Giacomin, M., Guida, G.: Afra: argumentation framework with recursive attacks. Int. J. Approximate Reasoning **52**(1), 19–37 (2011)
3. Baroni, P., Giacomin, M.: Solving semantic problems with odd-length cycles in argumentation. In: European Conference on Symbolic and Quantitative Approaches to Reasoning and Uncertainty, pp. 440–451. Springer (2003)
4. Baroni, P., Giacomin, M., Guida, G.: Scc-recursiveness: a general schema for argumentation semantics. Artif. Intell. **168**(1–2), 162–210 (2005)
5. Bench-Capon, T., Atkinson, K.: Abstract argumentation and values. Argumentation Artif. Intell. 45–64 (2009)

6. Bench-Capon, T.J.: Persuasion in practical argument using value-based argumentation frameworks. J. Log. Comput. **13**(3), 429–448 (2003)
7. Bench-Capon, T.J.: Dilemmas and paradoxes: cycles in argumentation frameworks. J. Log. Comput. **26**(4), 1055–1064 (2014)
8. Brewka, G., Polberg, S., Woltran, S.: Generalizations of dung frameworks and their role in formal argumentation. IEEE Intell. Syst. **29**(1), 30–38 (2013)
9. Caminada, M., Amgoud, L.: On the evaluation of argumentation formalisms. Artif. Intell. **171**(5–6), 286–310 (2007)
10. Cayrol, C., Lagasquie-Schiex, M.C.: On the acceptability of arguments in bipolar argumentation frameworks. In: European Conference on Symbolic and Quantitative Approaches to Reasoning and Uncertainty, pp. 378–389. Springer (2005)
11. Cayrol, C., Lagasquie-Schiex, M.C.: Bipolar abstract argumentation systems. In: Argumentation in Artificial Intelligence, pp. 65–84. Springer (2009)
12. Coste-Marquis, S., Devred, C., Marquis, P.: Inference from controversial arguments. In: International Conference on Logic for Programming Artificial Intelligence and Reasoning, pp. 606–620. Springer (2005)
13. Coste-Marquis, S., Devred, C., Marquis, P.: Prudent semantics for argumentation frameworks. In: 17th IEEE International Conference on Tools with Artificial Intelligence (ICTAI'05), pp. 5–pp. IEEE (2005)
14. Coste-Marquis, S., Devred, C., Marquis, P.: Handling controversial arguments. J. Appl. Non-Classical Logics **19**(3), 311–369 (2009)
15. Dung, P.M.: On the acceptability of arguments and its fundamental role in nonmonotonic reasoning, logic programming and n-person games. Artif. Intell. **77**(2), 321–357 (1995)
16. Dunne, P.E., Hunter, A., McBurney, P., Parsons, S., Wooldridge, M.: Weighted argument systems: basic definitions, algorithms, and complexity results. Artif. Intell. **175**(2), 457–486 (2011)
17. Dunne, P.E., Hunter, A., McBurney, P., Parsons, S., Wooldridge, M.J.: Inconsistency tolerance in weighted argument systems. In: AAMAS (2), pp. 851–858 (2009)
18. van Eemeren, F.H., Garssen, B., Krabbe, E.C.W., Henkemans, A.F.S., Verheij, B., Wagemans, J.H.: Handbook of argumentation theory (2014)
19. Liu, X., Chen, W.: Solid semantics for abstract argumentation frameworks and the preservation of solid semantic properties. In: Rosenfeld, A., Talmon, N. (eds.) EUMAS 2021. LNCS (LNAI), vol. 12802, pp. 178–193. Springer, Cham (2021). https://doi.org/10.1007/978-3-030-82254-5_11
20. Martınez, D.C., Garcıa, A.J., Simari, G.R.: An abstract argumentation framework with varied-strength attacks. In: Proceedings of the Eleventh International Conference on Principles of Knowledge Representation and Reasoning (KR 2008), pp. 135–144 (2008)
21. Martínez, D.C., García, A.J., Simari, G.R.: Operations on admissible attack scenarios. In: XV Congreso Argentino de Ciencias de la Computación (2009)
22. Modgil, S., Prakken, H.: The aspic+ framework for structured argumentation: a tutorial. Argum. Comput. **5**(1), 31–62 (2014)
23. Pollock, J.L.: Defeasible reasoning with variable degrees of justification. Artif. Intell. **133**(1–2), 233–282 (2001)
24. Prakken, H.: An abstract framework for argumentation with structured arguments. Argum. Comput. **1**(2), 93–124 (2010)
25. Prakken, H.: Historical overview of formal argumentation. In: Handbook of Formal Argumentation, pp. 73–141. College Publications (2018)
26. Prakken, H., Vreeswijk, G.: Logics for defeasible argumentation. In: Handbook of Philosophical Logic, pp. 219–318 (2002)

27. Sadiq, A.T., Abdulah, H.S., Kareem, A.T.: Argumentation frameworks-a brief review. Int. J. Online Biomed. Eng. **18**(2) (2022)
28. Tarski, A.: A lattice-theoretical fixpoint theorem and its applications. (1955)
29. van der Torre, L., Vesic, S.: The principle-based approach to abstract argumentation semantics. IfCoLog J. Logics Their Appl. (2017)
30. Vassiliades, A., Flouris, G., Patkos, T., Bikakis, A., Bassiliades, N., Plexousakis, D.: Argumentation frameworks with attack classification. J. Log. Comput. **33**(2), 192–229 (2023)

Ontology of Autonomous Driving as a Tool for Argumentation on Responsibility

Piotr Kulicki[1](✉) and Robert Trypuz[2]

[1] The John Paul II Catholic University of Lublin, 20950 Lublin, Poland
kulicki@kul.pl
[2] Lublin, Poland
robert@trypuz.pl

Abstract. The increasing deployment of autonomous vehicles (AVs) necessitates a clearer understanding of responsibility distribution in accidents involving these technologies. This paper examines the fatal Uber AV accident in Tempe, Arizona, through the lens of the SAE-J3016 standard and the Ontology of Autonomous Driving. Using formal knowledge representation, we analyze the roles of key actors to assess liability in this case. Our findings reveal that the Uber AV failed to detect and appropriately react to a pedestrian crossing the road, while the human operator was assigned a role that did not align with their actual capabilities within the system's operational constraints. Despite broader systemic failures, only the operator faced criminal charges, which created a discrepancy between legal interpretations and technical reality. By leveraging the ontology, we demonstrate how structured conceptual frameworks can clarify liability in AV incidents. Our analysis underscores the importance of integrating ontological tools into argumentation in legal contexts and regulatory frameworks to ensure a more precise and just assessment of responsibility.

Keywords: Autonomous driving · responsibility · ontology based argumentation · formal knowledge representation

1 Introduction

A whole chapter of a recent book on ethical aspects of AI development *Moral AI: and how to get there* by Jana Scheich Borg, Vincent Conitzer, and Walter Sinnott-Armstrong [3] concerning responsibility for AI fault behavior is built around the case of a fatal accident that took place during the test drive of an autonomous vehicle. This fact underscores the importance of thoroughly understanding such events, particularly when considering the proper implementation of this technology. Although the technology is designed to reduce accidents caused by human factors, its use inherently carries the risk of accidents. By comprehensively analyzing such events from both technical and legal perspectives, we can establish regulations that define the responsibilities of the involved parties. This, in turn, will shape the development of new technological solutions and influence their implementation to ensure both safety and user-friendliness.

A reliable and detailed account of the accident is given in the report of the National Transportation Safety Board (NTSB) [1] published a year and a half after the accident. Three years later Lauren Smiley in an article in Wired [17] reconstructs the actual events and tells the story behind that accident. The community confirms the quality of her journalistic work, cf. [16]. Therefore, we will use the reconstruction provided in the report and the article as the primary sources for analyzing the event and the argumentation employed in the surrounding discussion.

Unsurprisingly, the accident immediately garnered attention from researchers interested in autonomous vehicles. An initial analysis of Patric Lin [10] appeared just after the accident (the authors of [3] go along similar lines). Below is a summary of the five points that define the potential culpability in the accident involving Elaine Herzberg and the autonomous Uber vehicle.

1. The Victim (Elaine Herzberg): The victim's status (e.g., being homeless or potentially impaired) is irrelevant in determining responsibility. Regardless of the victim's behavior, the Uber vehicle still must avoid collisions, especially in unavoidable situations. The vehicle should have been driven cautiously to prevent accidents, even if it had the right of way.
2. Uber: While Tempe's police chief suggested that Uber might not be at fault regarding traffic laws, the company's responsibility extends beyond that. If Uber failed to account for the limitations of its technology, such as detecting pedestrians hidden behind obstacles or recognizing bicycles, the company could share the liability. Uber's marketing of its autonomous vehicle capabilities may also have been misleading, overselling its readiness for public streets.
3. Volvo: Although Uber modified the original vehicle software, the company could be criticized for collaborating with a company known for its controversial reputation and for allowing modifications to its products. Volvo may not be directly responsible but could be considered guilty by association.
4. Uber's Driver/Operator (Rafaela Vasquez): the Uber employee in the vehicle could be blamed for being inattentive while monitoring the vehicle's operation. Uber may also share responsibility for not correctly vetting or training employees, leading to a false sense of confidence about the vehicle's capabilities.
5. Society or No One: Broader societal factors, such as government and city planning, may bear some responsibility for the accident. Arizona, with a high rate of pedestrian deaths, may have failed to address issues related to public safety, allowing the test driving of autonomous vehicles on public roads without procedures sufficient to take care of safety. The federal government also shares the blame for rolling back safety guidelines for autonomous vehicles. Ultimately, societal structures prioritizing cars over pedestrians could

have contributed, or it could be argued that no one is directly responsible, as accidents are an inherent risk in the imperfect world of transportation.

Several years after the accident, we can see that opinions on the distribution of liability between Uber and the operator expressed in both the NTSB report [1] and some legal scholars [5, 18] diverge from actual legal settlements. In fact, contrary to those opinions, only Vasquez has been held criminally liable, with no charges brought against anyone else at Uber.

Introducing self-driving cars and other autonomous systems has disrupted the ontology underlying existing legal frameworks, introducing inconsistencies and gaps that have been recognized in the legal argumentation community (see, e.g., [12]). In this paper, we contribute to developing a new ontology better suited to emerging technologies. We analyze the accident within the conceptual framework established by the *Taxonomy and definitions for terms related to driving automation systems for on-road motor vehicle* [14,15], an industrial standard provided by SAE International, and further supported by an autonomous driving ontology based on this standard [20]. We believe that the rigorous conceptual framework, grounded in technical knowledge and supported by formal tools, accurately defines the situation and the roles of its participants and enables a proper assessment of the weight of the arguments presented in the discourse. In particular, we focus on the role of *vehicle operator*, which appears to be critical in understanding the distribution of responsibility.

The paper is organized as follows. Section 2 presents the facts surrounding the accident and some of the arguments discussed in the debate. Section 3 establishes the ontological background by introducing the SAE-J3016 standard and the Ontology of Autonomous Driving. In Sect. 4, we analyze the Arizona accident within this conceptual framework and discuss its implications for the distribution of responsibility. The paper concludes with a summary and an outline of directions for further work.

2 The Accident

2.1 Basic Facts About the Accident

As stated in the NTSB report [1, p. 1], "[o]n Sunday, March 18, 2018, at 9:58 p.m. mountain standard time, an automated test vehicle, based on a modified 2017 Volvo XC90 sport utility vehicle (SUV), struck a pedestrian walking midblock across the northbound lanes of N. Mill Avenue in Tempe, Arizona. The SUV was operated by the Advanced Technologies Group (ATG) of Uber Technologies, Inc., which had modified the vehicle by installing a proprietary developmental automated driving system (ADS). The ADS was active at the time of the crash." The SUV was occupied by an ATG employee, Rafaela Vasquez, whose position was called *vehicle operator* (after the accident, Uber used the name *mission specialist* [1, p. 31] instead; other names sometimes used for that role are *safety driver* and *human backup operator*). The car was equipped with two cameras: one monitoring the road ahead and the other recording the operator's behavior so the course of the accident is well documented.

Let us revoke a reconstruction of the very moment of the accidents presented by Smiley [17]:

The Uber driving system—which had been in full control of the car for 19 minutes at that point—registered a vehicle ahead that was 5.6 seconds away, but it delivered no alert to Vasquez. Then, the computer nixed its initial assessment; it didn't know what the object was. Then it switched the classification back to a vehicle, then waffled between vehicle and "other." At 2.6 seconds from the object, the system identified it as a "bicycle." At 1.5 seconds, it switched back to considering it "other." Then back to "bicycle" again. The system generated a plan to try to steer around whatever it was but decided it couldn't. Then, at 0.2 seconds to impact, the car let out a sound to alert Vasquez that the vehicle was going to slow down. At two-hundredths of a second before impact, traveling at 39 mph, Vasquez grabbed the steering wheel, which wrested the car out of autonomy and into manual mode. It was too late. The smashed bike scraped a 25-foot wake on the pavement. A person lay crumpled in the road.

As a result of the collision, a female pedestrian, Eleine Herzberg, who was walking across the street while pushing a bicycle on her left side was fatally injured and died of her injuries later that evening.

2.2 The Conduct of People Involved in the Accident and the Functionalities and Settings of Uber's ADS

The Pedestrian. Herzberg was jaywalking on a two-lane road with a speed limit of 45 miles per hour. Signs near the crash site clearly warned against jaywalking, directing pedestrians to a crosswalk located 380 feet away. This indicates her clear responsibility for creating the hazardous circumstances that made the accident possible.

Additionally, Herzberg was intoxicated at the time of the accident. Toxicology reports revealed the presence of methamphetamine in her bloodstream at the time of her death, which is significant as it suggests that her reactions could be impaired.

The Operator. A video recording of Vasquez in the driver's seat reveals that, throughout the journey leading up to the accident, she is observed gazing downward toward her right knee. On average, her downward glances lasted 2.56 s. However, during the initial loop, in the same place where later the accident took place, her turn down lasted more than 26 s. The investigators interpreted her facial expressions as a smirk. Vasquez's gaze remained directed downward for approximately five seconds in the critical moments preceding the collision with Herzberg. Just before the crash, she looked up and gasped.

Vasques had two active cell phones in the car, one for work purposes and the other for personal use. No calls or texts were sent directly before the accident. The phones have also been checked for other activities through service providers, including YouTube, Netflix, and Hulu. While YouTube and Netflix services were not in use, Hulu was streaming the talent show The Voice between 9:16 and 9:59 p.m. (the crash occurred at 9:58) on Vasques's personal phone.

There are inconsistent records regarding where the two phones were located in the crucial period before the accident. According to the NTSB's records, Vasques told them that her personal phone was in her purse behind her, and her work phone was on the passenger seat. Later, she testified that her personal phone was placed on the passenger seat and that she had her work phone on her knee. The latter statement appears to be true. It is supported by video evidence, as the dashcam shows Vasques reaching over to the passenger side and grabbing a phone from the passenger's side to call emergency services. It was her personal phone that was used for the call.

The placement of the phones in the car is significant because the talent show is being streamed on one of them. If, as the operator later asserts, the phone was on the passenger seat, it would imply that she was not watching the show, which would have been prohibited. However, if she only listened, as allowed during the test drive, this would not violate the conditions.

There was one additional device in the car: the Uber tablet mounted on the center console used as human-machine interface (HMI) and the tool of communication between operators and the office of Advanced Technology Group. Vasquez informed NTSB officers that she had been monitoring this device just before she observed Herzberg with her bike. Uber representatives, however, informed that there was no new messages on the device at that time.

The police analysis concluded that had Vasquez been paying attention to the road, she could have stopped more than 42 feet before reaching Herzberg. They classified the crash as "entirely avoidable." However, after the accident, Sylvia Moir, the police chief of Tempe at the time, told the San Francisco Chronicle, "It's very clear it would have been difficult to avoid this collision in any mode (autonomous or driven) based on how she came out of the shadows and into the roadway." Moir added that Uber "would likely not be at fault," although she did not rule out charges for the human operator. (cf. [17]).

According to Uber representatives, though their ADS recognized Herzberg and did not react to avoid hitting her, the failure was on the operator's side. That was her job to take control of the vehicle and stop on time.

Overall, it appears that Vasquez's attention throughout her entire trip that day, and especially in the moments leading up to the accident, fell below expectations. However, it remains debatable whether she was solely to blame, or even the most responsible among those who should have contributed to preventing the crash.

Michael Piccarreta, a defense attorney in Arizona, investigated the case at Smiley's request. In his opinion, the outcome of a potential trial would depend on whether the operator *grossly deviated* from the standard defined by a *reasonable person* in her place. Here, the main issue is to clarify what actually was *her place*. The standard for a driver may, of course, differ from the standard of an operator. Piccarreta noticed that persecution through the whole legal procedure treated Vasques as a driver, which is not accurate. He said that to prove that Vasquez was guilty it has to be shown that she was *grossly* negligent. "If she's just negligent, she's not guilty." (cf. [17])

It is worth mentioning that, in general, Vasquez had a good reputation within the Advanced Technologies Group and took her job very seriously. Jonatan Barentine, a former group employee who trained the *human backup operators*, endorsed Vasques for her commitment during the training: "She really cared about making sure that she could do her job." She remained active during her time as an operator as well. A supervisor noted that Vasquez would approach her manager's desk to share new information about the cars or offer suggestions. Her performance was recognized with a bonus in late 2017. (cf. [17])

Additional information, which could influence social perception and the court's judgment but does not appear to be directly relevant to the case, was made public shortly after the accident as reporters began uncovering personal details. It was revealed that Vasquez had two felony convictions—one for making false statements to obtain unemployment benefits and another for attempted armed robbery. At the time she was 18, went by the name Rafael, and was identified as male. The exact time of her transition to female is not publicly known. Smiley casts doubt on the conviction for robbery, which led to Vasquez's four-year imprisonment, showing that the situation was far from being clear. Anyway, madia media turned against Vasques. The following *Daily Mail* headline is symptomatic: "Convicted Felon Behind the Wheel of Uber Self-Driving Car Was Streaming The Voice on Her Phone and Laughing Before Crash Which Killed a Pedestrian in Arizona." (cf. [17]).

Settings and Actions of Uber's Automated Driving System. It is clear that Uber's ADS failed to recognize a bicycle crossing the road, and it neither stopped nor slowed down when approaching an unidentified obstacle in its path. If it had been a fully autonomous trip, this should be regarded as a system failure. Volvo's original automatic braking system was deactivated, as it interfered with Uber's ADS.

In general, the ADS was calibrated to minimize braking in potential emergency situations to reduce false positives, shifting the responsibility for action to the vehicle operator, who must assume control to prevent accidents.

Uber had programmed the car to delay hard braking for one second to allow the system to verify the emergency—and avoid false alarms—and for the human to take over. The system would brake hard only if it could entirely avoid the crash, otherwise it would slow down gradually and warn the operator. In other words, by the time it deemed it couldn't entirely avoid Herzberg that night, the car didn't slam on the brakes, which might have made the impact less severe. (cf. [17])

These settings for the test drives reflect the preferences of Uber's engineers, prioritizing mobility over safety in autonomous driving mode. At the same time, there was a lack of automated support for operators from the ADS. The ADS not only failed to respond to obstacles in a timely manner but also did not send any alert to the operator in the vehicle.

Volvo. Lin in his early opinion on the accident mentioned Volvo as potentially associated with the case. After the crash, Volvo ran their simulation tests and reported them to NTSB. They found that their automatic braking system inactivated in Uber test car would have prevented the crash in 17 out of 20 scenarios. In the remaining three, one would have reduced the speed and avoided death [1, pp. 21-22].

2.3 Uber Advanced Technologies Group Policies

Arizona became the principal site for the Uber Advanced Technology Group test in 2017. Their objective was to maximize the overall length of the test drives: *crash miles* as they called it. At the end of the year they achieved the level of 84,000 miles a week. Initially, they were two people working together in each car. The person in the driver's seat would call out obstacles and traffic signs, while the person in the passenger seat confirmed detection by the system on a laptop. If any issues arose, the one on the driver's side could take control and the other one would document the problem. At the end of 2017 the policy was changed to a single-operator one. (cf. [17])

NTSB identified that ATG at the time made operators responsible for the following tasks:

- Monitoring the driving environment and the operation of the ADS.
- Hovering with their hands above the steering wheel and their foot above the brake pedal for fast takeover of vehicle control.
- Detecting unusual events in the driving environment or in ADS performance and noting them through interaction with the HMI.
- Taking control of the vehicle and intervening in emergency situations to avoid a collision. [1, p. 42]

Just five days before the Tempe accident, Robbie Miller, the manager of the self-driving truck division, sent an email to the executives suggesting the reinstatement of a second operator and a reduction in the fleet size. He expressed concerns about vehicles being involved in accidents nearly every other day. However, the proposed changes were not implemented. (cf. [17])

In an NTSB board meeting its chair Robert Sumwalt summarized Uber's role in the accident: "The collision was the last link of a long chain of actions and decisions made by an organization that unfortunately did not make safety the top priority." Perhaps the company's attitude shifted after the accident, as NTSB investigator David Pereira praised the post-crash safety modifications aimed at preventing further incidents. (cf. [17])

Stamp [18, p. 72] cites a particularly significant excerpt from an email sent by Uber's CEO to the C-suite the day after the fatal accident: "We can afford to make mistakes. We can't afford to slow down." That seems to be a good summary of Uber's corporate culture, which is strongly influencing its safety policies.

2.4 Consequences of the Accident

Rafaela Vasques pleaded guilty to endangerment in the pedestrian death case and was sentenced to three years probation in 2023 [2].

Ten days after the accident, Uber agreed to a settlement with Elaine Herzberg's husband and daughter, Christine Wood. Wood stated that the amount was in the low millions. Several months later, Uber also reached a settlement with Herzberg's parents and son. (cf. [17])

One year after the crash, an Arizona prosecutor announced that the state would not pursue criminal charges against Uber in connection with the fatality. The following month, the Advanced Technologies Group secured a $1 billion investment from SoftBank, Denso, and Toyota, which valued the division at $7.25 billion, just three weeks before Uber's initial public offering (IPO). Despite the incident and the ensuing challenges, no leaders within the Advanced Technologies Group were dismissed as a result of Herzberg's death.

Ultimately, in 2020, Uber discontinued its autonomous taxi trials and sold its autonomous vehicle operations to Aurora. While Aurora has made significant progress in developing autonomous vehicle technology, commercial autonomous vehicle services have yet to be made available. Since then, Uber has continued to advance its autonomous technologies but still relies on human drivers to operate its transportation services.

Arizona was one of the first states where Waymo initiated its commercial self-driving taxi services [9]. In 2020, Waymo launched its Waymo One service in Phoenix, providing autonomous rides within designated areas of the city. Unlike other companies, Waymo operates vehicles with no driver present, meaning passengers are transported by fully autonomous vehicles. The service is available in Phoenix and parts of the Valley of the Sun, with passengers able to request rides via a mobile app.

3 Ontological Background

3.1 SAE-J3016 Standard and Ontology of Autonomous Driving Based on It

The *Taxonomy and Definitions for Terms Related to Driving Automation Systems for On-Road Motor Vehicles* [14,15] is an industrial standard that presents a comprehensive glossary of terms specific to the field of driving automation, including definitions of key concepts central to the domain. Despite a criticism of some authors who claim that it should be reviewed in some places [8,19], SAE-J3016 is widely recognized as the industry's most influential reference for automated vehicles [6,11]. All other relevant documents, such as those issued by the BASt or NHSTA, accept its main principles [6]. The standard contains numerous annotations that enhance it with insights into various aspects of autonomous driving, making it a unique source of expertise.

The standard was used as a foundation for an ontology named the Ontology of Autonomous Driving [20]. Ontology is understood as a formal, structured framework that defines the types, properties, and relationships of entities within a specific domain of knowledge. It provides a shared vocabulary and a set of concepts that allow for consistent understanding, communication, and reasoning about the domain.

The ontology is intended to be a further step toward clarifying the nomenclature related to autonomous driving, autonomous vehicles, different levels of autonomy, and other concepts beyond the SAE-J3016 standard. This is especially important given the increasing public interest in autonomous vehicles and the need to shape the future of the automotive industry. In addition, it can serve as a tool in discussions about the responsibility of various parties involved in autonomous driving in the event of an accident.

The value added by the ontology, as compared to the standard, primarily stems from its integration of a more advanced conceptual framework sourced from outside the automotive sector. This framework includes important distinctions between roles and the agents who occupy them, as well as differentiations between functions, capabilities, and the processes that realize these functions. It also draws a clear distinction between systems and their characteristics. By explicitly introducing these distinctions, the ontology offers formal definitions for the terms used in the standard, thus ensuring their precise and consistent interpretation.

In addition, the ontology serves as a machine-readable version of the standard, which can be seamlessly incorporated into information systems. The OWL counterpart of the formalization is available in the GitHub repository[1]. However, this particular aspect is not relevant to the present paper.

3.2 SAE-J3016 Conceptual Framework

In Sect. 4, we will demonstrate how the ontology interprets the facts surrounding the Uber accident. In the meantime, we will provide an overview of some basic classifications derived from SAE-J3016 to give the reader a sense of the ontology's structure, with more detailed discussions available in the paper [20], where the ontology is fully presented.

Types of Motor Vehicles. Contemporary motor vehicles are equipped with numerous electronic systems. Some of these systems are designed to support drivers, while the most advanced ones are designed to transform a vehicle into an autonomous agent. The latter systems are referred to as automated driving systems (ADS). According to [15], the ontology [20] classifies motor vehicles based on how they implement ADSs. The four vehicle types are conventional, ADS-equipped, ADS-dedicated, and ADS-equipped dual-mode (see Fig. 1).

Note that an ADS-equipped vehicle can still be a conventional vehicle if "an in-vehicle driver is required for at least part of every trip" ADS dedicated vehicle is an ADS-equipped vehicle designed for driverless operation under routine/normal operating conditions during all trips within its given operational

---

[1] https://github.com/kul-ai/ontology-autonomous-driving.

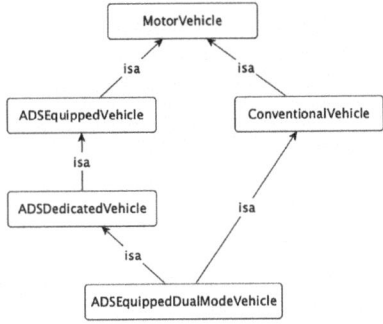

Fig. 1. Types of motor vehicles [20, p. 1844]

design domain (ODD), if ODD is specified. ADS-equipped dual-mode vehicle allows the user to chose between conventional and autonomous driving. (cf. [p. 23] [15])

Types of Processes and the Levels of Automation. The best known part of SAE-J3016 standard is its definition of 6 levels of automation:

- Level 0: no automation,
- Level 1: driver assistance,
- Level 2: partial driving automation,
- Level 3: conditional driving automation,
- Level 4: high driving automation,
- Level 5: full driving automation.

It is important to emphasize that the levels refer to specific parts of a trip (i.e. certain processes), not the vehicles themselves. As a result, the same vehicle can operate at different levels of autonomy even within a single trip (see Fig. 2).

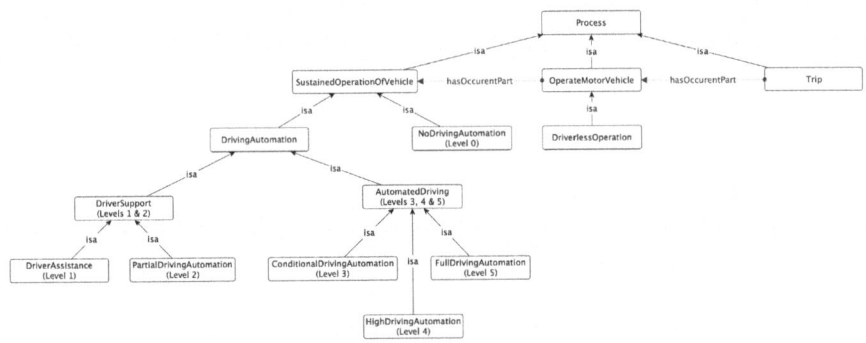

Fig. 2. Types of processes [20, p. 1856]

Types of Human Users. Human users can play various roles during vehicle operation. It is important to distinguish between a role and a person itself, as the role of a person can change during the trip, in particular, when a level of autonomy of driving changes. When a vehicle is operating in full driving automation mode (SAE Level 5) every person in the vehicle is in a passenger role. However, when circumstances (or preferences in an ADS-equipped dual-mode vehicle) change, one of the passengers may take the role of driver. Thus, human users are classified by the role they play in a current phase of a trip. From all user types presented in Fig. 3 the following three are relevant to the subject of the present paper:

- in vehicle driver,
- in vehicle DDT fallback ready user,
- passenger.

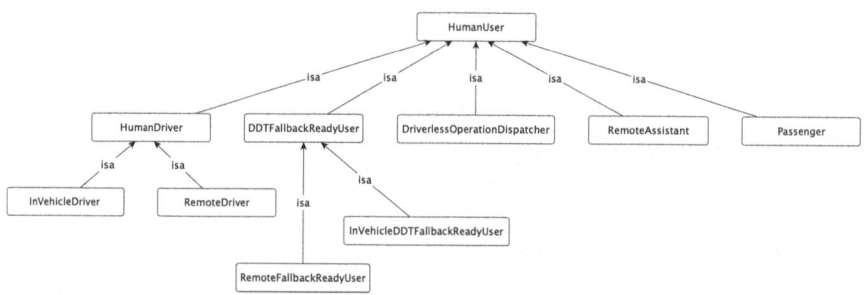

Fig. 3. Types of human users [20, p. 1850]

In Sect. 4 we analyze Tempe accident using these categories. From that point of view it is crucial to understand the role of fallback ready users and to distinguish it from the role of (in vehicle) driver.

In vehicle driver is defined as a "driver who manually exercises in-vehicle braking, accelerating, steering, and transmission gear selection input devices in order to operate a vehicle." *Driver* itself is a "user who performs in real time part or all of the DDT and/or DDT fallback for a particular vehicle." DDT fallback is a part of a trip after an ADS failure or request to intervene. (cf. [15, p. 20-21])

[DDT] fallback-ready user is defined as the "user of a vehicle equipped with an engaged Level 3 ADS feature who is properly qualified and able to operate the vehicle and is receptive to ADS-issued requests to intervene and to evident DDT performance-relevant system failures in the vehicle compelling him or her to perform the DDT fallback." (cf. [15, p. 22])

What is important for our further analysis is that there is no role for a person in a car other than as the driver of the vehicle, the DDT fallback ready user of the vehicle or the passenger. Moreover, the roles are mutually exclusive, in the sense that any person in a car, Uber's operator in particular, had to play only one of those roles at the same time.

4 Uber Accident in the SAE's Autonomous Driving Ontology

4.1 Ontological Analysis of the Accident

In this section, we model the Uber accident using the conceptual framework provided by the SAE's autonomous driving ontology. We present the logical description of the relevant ontological axioms and reasoning steps in natural language, noting that the entire process can be automated if desired.

Figures 4 and 5 will help us understand the components of the model and how they interact. Rectangles and arrows depict components of the SAE's Autonomous Driving Ontology, classes and properties, respectively. Each resource is uniquely identified by a URI with the prefix https://onto.kul.pl/av/ (e.g., https://onto.kul.pl/av/AutomatedDrivingSystem). Meanwhile, small circles denote individuals that are properly classified and linked via the ontology's properties.

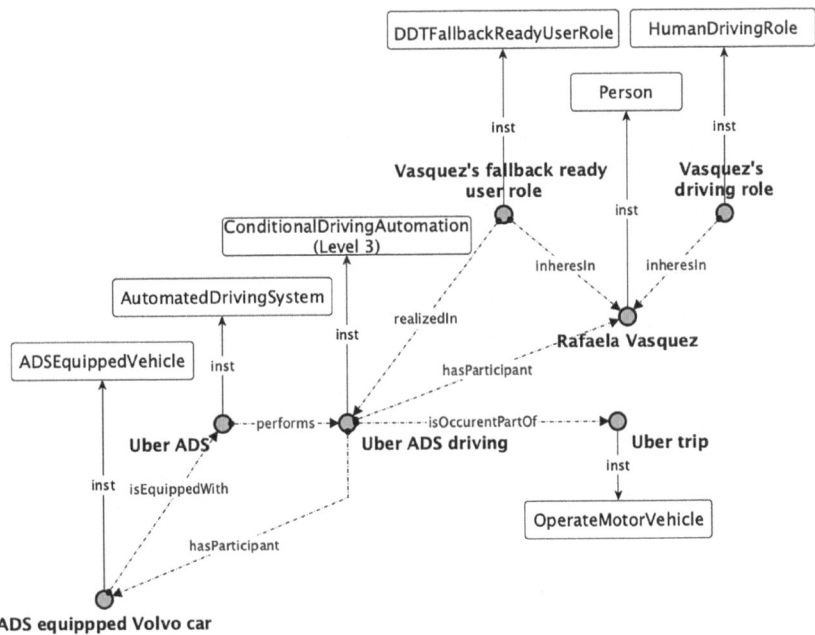

Fig. 4. The Volvo vehicle is classified as an ADS-equipped vehicle, with its ADS operating at Level 3 conditional automated driving. Rafaela Vasquez is realizing the in-vehicle fallback-ready role. Since the ADS is nominally controlling the vehicle, her human driver role remains unexercised.

The Volvo car involved in the accident is classified as an "ADS-equipped vehicle", a motor vehicle equipped with an automated driving system (ADS). According to SAE, an ADS is a vehicle system capable of performing the dynamic driving task (DDT), i.e., "all of the real-time operational and tactical functions required to operate a vehicle in on-road traffic." When the car executes the DDT, it is considered on a "trip" (or operating phase). Each phase of a trip can be associated with a particular level of driving automation. We will revisit this point later.

Rafaela Vasquez was seated in the driver's seat and was attached to two roles: an in-vehicle fallback-ready role and an in-vehicle human driver role. She started her trip with the in-vehicle fallback-ready role and was supposed to switch to the in-vehicle human driver role, when needed. She gained both roles at the trip's start; however, merely having a role is not the same as realizing it. From the beginning of the trip until 0.2 s before the accident—for approximately 19 min—Vasquez was realizing the in-vehicle fallback-ready role. Realizing this role requires staying receptive to ADS-issued requests to intervene as well as any DDT performance-relevant system failures (ADS failures and malfunctions, in particular) that would necessitate performing the DDT fallback. In other words, she needed to be always prepared to switch to the human driving role and manually operate the vehicle. The presence of a DDT fallback-ready user indicates that this was a Level 3 (i.e., "conditional driving automation") trip, as Level 3 is the only level that mandates a fallback-ready user.

In this context, being receptive is a normative relation requiring the user to reliably and appropriately focus their attention in response to a stimulus. The stimulus could be a malfunction of the ADS that prevents it from reliably performing the DDT on a sustained basis or a request to intervene—an alert from a Level 3 ADS that instructs the fallback-ready user to perform the DDT fallback promptly. This fallback may involve resuming manual operation (i.e., realizing the human driver role) or achieving a minimal risk condition if the vehicle is no longer operable.

In principle, Vasquez could have noticed the obstacle ahead, namely Eleine Herzberg with her bike, at about the same time the ADS did—roughly 5.6 s before impact when the object was around 100 m away—and observed that the ADS was not braking or steering away. At that point, she might have decided to take control sooner. Had she done so, she would have realized the human driving role and potentially performed a DDT fallback that could have achieved minimal risk conditions before the collision.

Although Vasquez could see that the vehicle was not slowing down, she had no specific indication that the ADS was struggling to classify the object as it switched between "bicycle" and "other." Without a timely alert or consistent reaction from the ADS, it was tough for her to recognize that the system was failing and to assume control in time.

At the very last moment—only 0.2 s before impact—the Uber's ADS finally recognized its failure and issued a request to intervene. Unfortunately, this alert arrived far too late for any effective action. At that instant, the car was traveling at 39 mph. Although Vasquez grabbed the steering wheel—thereby switching the vehicle from Level 3 (autonomous) mode to nonautomated driving mode—there was no longer sufficient time to prevent the collision. The delayed response of

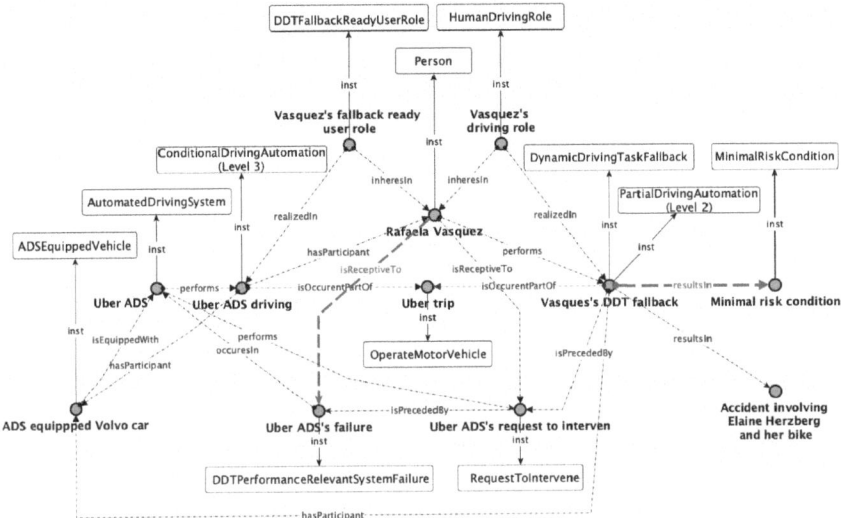

Fig. 5. The figure illustrates that the ADS's inability to reliably classify the object and decelerate constitutes the ADS's failure. The bold dashed line labeled "isReceptiveTo" represents the hypothetical scenario in which Vasquez is attentive to the ADS's improper behavior, allowing her to react more quickly and achieve a minimal risk condition (as indicated by the second bold dashed line labeled "resultsIn"). In reality, however, this scenario did not occur; the ADS, not Vasquez, detected its failure and issued a request to intervene far too late for effective action.

the ADS, along with its failure to communicate the classification issue earlier or take corrective action, left Vasquez with no realistic opportunity to intervene successfully.

4.2 Complacency

SAE-3016 assumes that "an ADS is capable of continuing to perform the DDT for at least several seconds after providing the fallback-ready user with a request to intervene. The DDT fallback-ready user is then expected to resume manual vehicle operation, or to achieve a minimal risk condition if s/he determines it to be necessary." [15, p. 11]

This constraint reflects automation complacency, a well-documented phenomenon in human-automation interaction [7, p. iii]. Research shows that when automated systems perform reliably most of the time, human operators tend to pay less attention to monitoring them, assuming the system will function correctly [13]. This complacency leads to reduced vigilance and slower reaction times when failures occur.

The complacency effect was introduced to the considerations on Vasquez case by NTSB. They claim that Vasques' prolonged visual distraction is a direct result of automation complacency and prevented her from detecting the pedestrian in time. Although she was supposed to be ready to take control of the car at any moment, she consciously or subconsciously expected the ADS not to fail and the ADS did not indicate that it was struggling with object classification. When the system finally issued an alert, there was simply no time left to react meaningfully.

4.3 Implications of Our Ontological Analysis

The consequent application of the SAE-J3016 standard supported by the use of the Ontology of Autonomous Driving formalizing it enables us to recognize the true role of *operator*. That is crucial in order to understand the accident that took place in Arizona. We claim that operator is nothing else than dynamic driving task fallback ready user defined in Ontology of Autonomous Driving after SAE-J3016.

On that basis, we can assert that the Uber's operator simply could not do what she was expected to do from the company. That fact should be taken into consideration when responsibility is distributed. Moreover, the management of Uber's Advanced Technologies Group should be aware of risks. Public authorities responsible for investigation on that case and persecution of Vasques also should take that knowledge into account.

SAE levels of autonomy are present in the NTSB report and in articles discussing the case, including [18]. However, the authors seem not to recognize the role of person in the car as an in vehicle fallback ready user. In the report, the car is claimed to be at Level 4 [1, p. 49], and [18, footnote 4. p. 4] follows this interpretation. We believe that recognizing the actual level of autonomy and the role of the operator makes argumentation clearer.

5 Conclusions and Further Works

This paper presented an ontological framework for understanding the Uber autonomous driving accident, utilizing the SAE-J3016 standard and the Ontology of Autonomous Driving. By introducing these concepts into the debate, we provided a clearer understanding of the roles involved in autonomous driving, particularly the operator's role, and analyzed its implications for the distribution of responsibility in the event of an accident.

We argued that the Uber operator, Rafaela Vasquez, while performing her duties within the boundaries of the technology's design, faced a failure of the system that could not be fully mitigated by her intervention. This highlights the complexities inherent in the human-machine interaction within autonomous systems, where the responsibilities of the vehicle's operator and the system itself are often blurred.

The case of the Uber accident underscores the importance of developing precise definitions, those concerning roles in particular, in the ontology of autonomous driving. These definitions can not only enrich legal and regulatory frameworks, but also aid in the design and implementation of safer, more effective autonomous driving technologies.

Therefore, we postulate that standards reflecting state-of-the-art expertise should be taken seriously by policymakers and actors in the justice system. Ontology offers means to make them even more precise and easier to use. We thus join the voice of Selmer Bringsjord and Atriya Sen, who call for the inclusion of logicians in the work on the design of autonomous vehicles in their article *On Creative Self-Driving Cars: Hire the Computational Logicians, Fast* [4] and we extend their request to the process of legal assessment of the performance of AVs.

For future work, we plan to analyze other accidents that occurred during autonomous driving, their causes and legal consequences. In particular, we are interested in a Los Angeles accident in which Tesla, running on her autopilot left a highway and hit another car passing the red light at a crossroads. A person in the car will pay more than $23,000 in restitution for the deaths of two people killed in this accident. Apparently, the court did not correctly recognize the roles of him.

Several additional directions for future work, which we consider worth pursuing, were suggested by anonymous reviewers during the CLAR 2025 review process. These include linking our ontology of automated driving with existing legal ontologies, providing a more formal exposition of the case study that combines established formal and logical tools for representing and reasoning about arguments with the ontological representation of facts and background knowledge, and exploring the automation of ontology extraction from industrial standards.

Acknowledgements. We would like to thank Selmer Bringsjord for encouraging discussions on the use of logic and ontology in the context of autonomous vehicles, as well as for referring us to Lauren Smiley's article [17]. We are also grateful to the anonymous reviewers for their insightful and inspiring comments.

Disclosure of Interests. The authors have no competing interests to declare that are relevant to the content of this article.

References

1. Collision Between Vehicle Controlled by Developmental Automated Driving System and Pedestrian, Tempe, Arizona, March 18, 2018. Highway Accident Report NTSB/HAR-19/03. Technical report, National Transportation Safety Board (2019). https://www.ntsb.gov/investigations/accidentreports/reports/har1903.pdf
2. Rafaela vasques plea agreement (2023). https://www.maricopacountyattorney.org/DocumentCenter/View/2780/Rafaela-Vasquez-Plea-Agreement
3. Borg, J., Sinnott-Armstrong, W., Conitzer, V.: Moral AI: And How We Get There. Pelican Books, Penguin Books (2024). https://books.google.pl/books?id=wH7wzwEACAAJ
4. Bringsjord, S., Sen, A.: On creative self-driving cars: hire the computational logicians, fast. Appl. Artif. Intell. **30**(8), 758–786 (2016). https://doi.org/10.1080/08839514.2016.1229906

5. DeArman, A.: The wild, wild west: a case study of self-driving vehicle testing in Arizona. Arizona Law Rev. **61**(4), 983 (2019). https://arizonalawreview.org/the-wild-wild-west-a-case-study-of-self-driving-vehicle-testing-in-arizona/
6. Hopkins, D., Schwanen, T.: Talking about automated vehicles: what do levels of automation do? Technol. Soc. **64**, 101488 (2021). https://doi.org/10.1016/j.techsoc.2020.101488
7. Prinzel III, L.J.: The relationship of self-efficacy and complacency in pilot-automation interaction. Technical report NASA/TM-2002-211925, National Aeronautics and Space Administration, Hampton, Virginia (2002)
8. Inagaki, T., Sheridan, T.B.: A critique of the SAE conditional driving automation definition, and analyses of options for improvement. Cogn. Technol. Work **21**(4), 569–578 (2018). https://doi.org/10.1007/s10111-018-0471-5
9. Krafcik, J.: Waymo is opening its fully driverless service to the general public in phoenix (2020). https://waymo.com/blog/2020/10/waymo-is-opening-its-fully-driverless-service-in-phoenix
10. Lin, P.: Who's at fault in uber's fatal collision? (2018). https://spectrum.ieee.org/reflecting-on-ubers-fatal-crash
11. Lipson, H., Kurman, M.: Driverless: Intelligent Cars and the Road Ahead. The MIT Press (2017)
12. Lu, Y., Yu, Z., Lin, Y., Schafer, B., Ireland, A., Urquhart, L.: An argumentation and ontology based legal support system for AI vehicle design. In: Francesconi, E., Borges, G., Sorge, C. (eds.) Legal Knowledge and Information Systems - JURIX 2022: The Thirty-Fifth Annual Conference, Saarbrücken, Germany, 14–16 December 2022. Frontiers in Artificial Intelligence and Applications, vol. 362, pp. 213–218. IOS Press (2022). https://doi.org/10.3233/FAIA220469
13. Parasuraman, R., Manzey, D.H.: Complacency and bias in human use of automation: an attentional integration. Hum. Factors **52**(3), 381–410 (2010). https://doi.org/10.1177/0018720810376055
14. SAE-J3016: Taxonomy and definitions for terms related to driving automation systems for on-road motor vehicles. Technical report, SAE International (2018)
15. SAE-J3016: Taxonomy and definitions for terms related to driving automation systems for on-road motor vehicles. Technical report, SAE International (2021)
16. Scanlan, C.: Reconstructing a murky maze of blame (2023). https://niemanstoryboard.org/2023/06/01/investigative-journalism-public-records-narrative-structure-uber-fatal-crash/
17. Smiley, L.: 'I'm the Operator': The Aftermath of a Self-Driving Tragedy (2022). https://www.wired.com/story/uber-self-driving-car-fatal-crash/
18. Stamp, H.: Innovative technologies and the deepening regulatory capture of law enforcement agencies: the Uber Herzberg case study. Notre Dame J. Emerg. Tech. **5**(1), 70–113 (2023)
19. Stayton, E., Stilgoe, J.: It's time to rethink levels of automation for self-driving vehicles [opinion]. IEEE Technol. Soc. Mag. **39**(3), 13–19 (2020). https://doi.org/10.1109/MTS.2020.3012315
20. Trypuz, R., Kulicki, P., Sopek, M.: Ontology of autonomous driving based on the SAE J3016 standard. Semant. Web **15**(5), 1837–1862 (2024). https://doi.org/10.3233/SW-243578

A Proposal for the Reconstruction and Evaluation of Multimodal Argumentation in Print Advertisements

Ting Lan and Jianying Cui(✉)

Institute of Logic and Cognition, Department of Philosophy, Sun Yat-sen University, Guangzhou, China
lant27@mail2.sysu.edu.cn, cuijiany@mail.sysu.edu.cn

Abstract. With the rapid growth of digitization and multimedia, multimodal argumentation in advertisements has become a key focus in pragmatics and argumentation theory. Print advertisements, with their concise and elliptical communication, often rely on images to build logical coherence and practical effectiveness, presenting a unique challenge for multimodal argumentation research. In response, this paper combines a pragmatic perspective with argumentation theory to analyze the visual and linguistic elements as well as argumentation schemes in advertisements. It proposes a method for analyzing and evaluating multimodal arguments, particularly double-mode arguments in advertisements. This method consists of three steps: (1) the pragmatic interpretation of visual and verbal information in advertisements, (2) the reconstruction of argumentation structures including the typical argumentation schemes and their connections in print advertisements, and (3) the evaluation of reconstructed arguments based on argumentation scheme theory. By applying this method to the case study of the well-known commercial advertisement for the Sauce-flavored Latte, it offers an analytical framework for the systematic analysis and evaluation of double-mode argumentation in advertisements, thereby providing theoretical support and practical guidance for optimizing advertising design, fostering critical thinking in consumers, and identifying false advertisements.

Keywords: Advertisements · Argumentation schemes · Multimodal argumentation · Speech acts

1 Introduction

In the contemporary communication environment, the expression of meaning through images and multimedia formats has become increasingly significant, making multimodal argumentation a crucial topic of discussion [2,16]. Multimodal argumentation involves the construction of meaning through multiple semiotic systems, such as visuals and language, and can be understood as a specific form of visual argument [4,18]. In "double code" communication such as print advertising, the interaction between text and images creates layered meanings, offering fresh perspectives on how meaning is constructed and interpreted in multimodal communication [19,20]. As a specific form of discourse, the persuasive nature of print advertising implies that the analysis and evaluation of such multimodal arguments are essentially the analysis and evaluation of the arguments they express. Naturally, this involves identifying and reconstructing the arguments they convey. Recent research has highlighted the importance of combining pragmatic interpretation with argument analysis, providing insights into how advertisements function as sophisticated acts of persuasion [26].

This paper also argues that analyzing and evaluating multimodal arguments in advertising requires an integrated approach that combines pragmatics and argumentation theory, and that pragmatic interpretation serves as the foundation for the reconstruction and evaluation of arguments in advertisements. The framework developed in this paper for analyzing and evaluating multimodal argumentation in advertisements includes several key components. First, a comprehensive pragmatic interpretation is essential to facilitate the understanding of the semantic representations of verbal and visual elements in advertisements. This involves examining the social and cultural context, specifications of explicature, analyzing polyphonic structures, dialogical functions, and commitments. Second, building on this pragmatic analysis, the study retrieves logical forms and reconstructs the argumentation structures within advertisements, identifying the inference relations between different argument types. Meanwhile, the paper explores the most typical argumentation schemes used in multimodal arguments within print advertisements. Finally, it proposes to evaluate the reconstructed arguments by addressing critical questions, considering the perspectives of various agents and voices. To illustrate the practical application of this integrated approach, the paper uses a case study of the "sauce-flavored latte" advertisement from the Chinese coffee brand Luckin Coffee. The analysis demonstrates how combining pragmatic perspectives with argumentation scheme theory can provide a comprehensive and effective method for reconstructing and evaluating multimodal arguments in advertisements.

2 Previous Research on Multimodal Argumentation

Visual arguments can be rational, as non-verbal signs can also convey meaning and thus express propositions that are suitable for argumentative communication [13,14,17]. i.e., visual elements can contribute to argumentative communication by conveying meaning and supporting propositional content, which also serves as the basis for the subsequent analysis of multimodal arguments in this paper. Scholars of argumentation theory and rhetoric who advocate this view have studied a wide variety of multimodal discourses.

Early studies list advertisements, political cartoons, and scientific communication as three widely researched genres, and apply the Toulmin argument structure to analyze multimodal argumentation in advertisements [17,18]. Over the past two decades, studies primarily concentrated on advertising as a promotional genre, including both commercial and political advertisements, whether in print or television formats [23,24,30]. Among the various semiotic modes, the combination of verbal and visual modes has been the main focus of research. Some studies have also explored audio mode, bodily posture and gestures in rhetoric and argumentation research [11,12]. Several critical issues of the reconstruction of multimodal argumentation have been investigated in depth, such as the unique roles of different semiotic modes (language, images, sound) in communicating arguments and rhetorical effects [17,28]. Analyzing the hierarchical structure and interaction of these modes reveals the complex construction of argumentation, particularly how visual elements work with language to form persuasive arguments [22].

A key challenge in the theory and analysis of multimodal argumentation is establishing appropriate criteria for evaluating multimodal arguments. The question of whether existing evaluation norms need to be revised is still under discussion. Some scholars believe that current theories and standards are sufficiently effective [1,15], while others suggest developing specific argumentation schemes and critical questions for visual arguments [9]. Evaluation can be conducted by distinguishing between general normative standards and mode-specific criteria. When it comes to theoretical tools for studying multimodal argumentation, the Pragma-Dialectical approach has introduced a strategy for reconstructing multimodal arguments [10]. Similarly, the argumentation scheme method, as proposed by [21], can also be employed to reconstruct multimodal arguments.

While scholars have explored multimodal argumentation through various approaches, there is still significant potential in combining pragmatic analysis with argumentation scheme theory for reconstructing and evaluating multimodal arguments. Especially, it becomes increasingly evident that a comprehensive and systematic framework for both reconstructing and evaluating multimodal argumentation in advertisements is required.

3 Pragmatic Interpretation

Analyzing multimodal argumentation requires an initial pragmatic interpretation to extract and decode the visual and textual elements, which can then be expanded into propositional structures as a foundation for further argumentation analysis [21]. The following sections highlight key aspects of the pragmatic interpretation of argumentation in print advertising, including its social and cultural background, the specification of explicature, polyphonic structure, and the dialogical function and commitment structure.

Social and Cultural Background. The construction of arguments is a social and discursive activity deeply intertwined with the contextual practices in which it occurs. The production and interpretation of texts depend on internalized text models (genres) and are adjusted to fit specific contexts. Consequently, analyzing such texts requires consideration of the social practices they are embedded in [29] and a top-down approach that begins with the social background before examining how information is expressed and conveyed [6]. Building on this, evaluating multimodal arguments requires attention not only to the symbolic resources used to convey arguments but also to the contexts in which they are created and interpreted [27]. It is asserted by [3] that any account of visual argument must include understanding the contexts in which images are interpreted. Clearly, this holistic perspective emphasizes the interaction between text elements and their context, while also providing us with a comprehensive framework for analyzing multimodal parameters.

Specification of Explicature. As the advertisement's messages are quite elliptical and require supplementary information from the visual context, the need for explicature specification becomes evident. To ensure accurate transmission and understanding of information in linguistic communication especially those through advertisements, it is necessary to clarify the ambiguous parts caused by the inherent vagueness, ellipsis, and other forms of implicit meaning in advertising texts through pragmatic operations, with the specification of explicature being an important component.

To reconstruct the arguments in an advertisement, it is essential to enrich the "logical form" of the linguistic information. Grice distinguished between two aspects of a linguistic communicative act: (a) what is said by the sentence, and (b) what is merely implied. However, this dichotomy is insufficient, as relying solely on lexical content and syntactic structure can result in an incomplete logical (propositional) form [21]. According to Borg, a linguistic communicative act can be understood from three perspectives: (a) the standing meaning of the sentence; (b) the propositional content, derived from the standing meaning through various pragmatic processes; and (c) the implicatures, or indirect meanings conveyed by the speaker [5]. The set of pragmatic operations including disambiguation and reference assignment give rise to explicatures, which are defined as pragmatically inferred developments of logical form or explicitly communicated propositions [7].

The enrichment of an incomplete logical form can be broadly categorized into two main operations: disambiguation and specification [21]. Several operations are involved in this specification process, including indexical resolution, reference identification, the identification of unarticulated constituents, ellipsis unpacking, generality narrowing (or modulation), and bridging inferences [5]. Through these specification operations, we can clearly articulate the visual and textual information in the discourse, thus providing a solid foundation for the subsequent reconstruction of multimodal arguments.

Polyphonic Structure. All natural utterances inherently involve a plurality of points of view, as they reflect the interaction of different voices. This plurality is a fundamental characteristic of communication, especially in advertising argumentation, which often incorporates a variety of voices, reflecting the complex interplay of visual, verbal, and contextual elements that shape meaning. We adopt the method of classifying voices as proposed in [8] which distinguishes between three types of "voices" that can be detected in an utterance. First, the speaking subject refers to the physical person who produces the utterance. Second,

the locutor (locuteur) is the person responsible for the act of enunciation, often referred to as "I" in the discourse. Finally, the enunciator(s) (énonciateurs) are the discourse entities responsible for the various viewpoints that are manifested within the utterance [6]. Each of them contributes to the formation of meaning and perspective in distinct ways. Understanding this polyphonic nature is crucial when evaluating arguments based on the theory of argumentation schemes. The critical questions associated with different argumentation schemes serve as key evaluative tools [31]. Given that the reconstructed advertising arguments are composed structures of multiple argumentation schemes, and that the top-level argument types usually fall under value-based practical reasoning, it is crucial to clarify the polyphonic nature of advertisements. Additionally, identifying the subjective value perspectives embedded within the different voices is essential for a comprehensive and reasoned evaluation of the reconstructed advertising arguments.

Dialogical Function and Commitment Structure. The final dimension of the reconstruction process of advertising argumentation involves determining the dialogical function and commitment structure of an utterance. Verbal and visual communication in advertisements is not merely an exchange of information; it also constitutes the performance of a speech act. To fully understand an utterance as a speech act, it is essential to identify both its informative content and its pragmatic goal, as these elements help explain its overall function. This process contributes to the pragmatic development of the logical form of the discourse.

The persuasive nature of advertising is central to its genre: its primary aim is to convince a specific audience to act in a particular way or achieve a certain goal. Advertisements are designed to persuade consumers to purchase a product, adopt an idea, or embrace a particular concept. Thus, advertising is not simply about transmitting information; it functions as a promotion or call to action, intending to prompt the audience to take specific actions or make decisions [22]. In this context, extracting the commitment structure is crucial, as it reveals the promises and guarantees that fuel the advertisement's persuasive power. These commitments influence consumer trust and expectations, guiding their decision-making process. Analyzing them helps identify key persuasive mechanisms and illustrates how different voices – those of the advertiser, the product, and the consumer – interact to form a coherent narrative that drives the audience toward the intended action.

4 Reconstruction of the Argumentation Structure

Advertising argumentation is not merely a way of conveying information; it also involves the complex use of various argumentation schemes that collectively form a coherent and unified overarching argument. There is a significant difference in the top-level argumentation (i.e., the core claim and objective of the advertisement) within different activity types [25]. For example, Business advertisements, particularly print ads, belong to the activity type of promotion, aiming to persuade potential consumers that the advertised product is worth purchasing. In contrast, public service ads serve as a call to action. They focus on informing, educating, or encouraging positive social behaviors, aiming to raise awareness of issues like health, safety, and environmental protection.

Distinct advertising argumentation often involves different use of argumentative strategies, which can be represented and analyzed using the tools of argumentation schemes. Previous research suggests this difference. In business advertisements, the argumentative strategy frequently takes the form of practical reasoning [32] because their primary goal is to persuade consumers that purchasing a product is the best way to achieve their desires or needs [17,22,32]. In this structure, the potential consumer has a goal, and buying product X is a means to achieve that goal, so they should buy X. In public service advertisements, the argumentation tends to take the form of argumentation from consequences, which is a subtype of causal argumentation, as it highlights potential negative consequences of certain actions, thereby discouraging them. It often uses a structure like "If action X leads to a negative result such as Y it should not be carried out" [27].

In reconstructing advertising argumentation, the first step is recognizing its hierarchical structure. Advertising argumentation often involves multiple layers, typically comprising top-level and bottom-level arguments. The top-level argument presents the core claim, such as a value proposition in commercial ads or a call to action in public service ads, while the bottom-level argument supports this claim with evidence and facts to enhance its persuasiveness. Then, identifying the type of advertisement is key to distinguishing between the top-level and bottom-level arguments, based on the ad's objectives and target audience. In commercial advertisements, the top-level argument typically uses value-based practical reasoning, supported by bottom-level evidence such as product functionality, pricing advantages, or consumer reviews. In addition, we can apply critical questions to evaluate the strength and coherence of the argument. For example, in commercial ads, we might ask the critical questions corresponding to practical reasoning: "What other goals might conflict with this one?" or "What evidence supports the feasibility of achieving this goal?" [31]. Through the step-by-step reconstruction of advertising argumentation, we can better understand how ads flexibly adjust their argumentation schemes based on their target audience and the advertiser's goals. Such reconstruction provides a clearer logical framework for the identification of argumentation schemes in print advertisements.

In the process of reconstructing advertising argumentation, accurately identifying different argumentation schemes not only helps argument analysts better understand how to connect one argument with other related arguments, but also contributes to the evaluation of the rationality of multimodal argumentation. This is because the specific critical questions corresponding to each argumentation scheme are crucial for the correct assessment of the overall argument. As mentioned earlier, identifying the top-level argumentation schemes in multimodal advertisements primarily involves analyzing the discourse goals of different advertisement types. In contrast, identifying the bottom-level argumentation schemes places more emphasis on analyzing the inference structure. Bottom-level argumentation schemes support the top-level argument or arguments from the previous layer. Therefore, when identifying bottom-level argumentation schemes, it is important to focus on the topics involved in the premises of the previous layer's arguments. These premises often form the foundation of the argumentation chain in the advertisement, supporting the core claims of the top-level argument. Based on this, further exploration of the reasoning structure in that layer helps us identify the argumentation schemes present. For example, by analyzing how the premises of top-level arguments are further supported by other evidence and facts in the multimodal elements in advertisements, we can identify the typical argumentation schemes in advertising, thereby more clearly mapping out the hierarchical relationships in advertising argumentation. By identifying these argumentation schemes and their connections, we can gain a deeper understanding of how the argumentative process unfolds in advertisements, as well as how various elements collaborate to persuade the audience and shape decision-making.

5 Evaluation of Multimodal Arguments

Traditional methods of evaluating arguments primarily focus on assessments based on argumentation schemes. By answering critical questions related to these schemes, analysts can gain insights into whether the argument is correctly structured and whether the use of the scheme effectively transfers the acceptability of the premises to the conclusion. However, some scholars argue that relying solely on critical questions is insufficient for assessing the overall quality of an argument. It is contended by [27] that traditional scheme-based evaluations fail to fully address the complexities involved in evaluating multimodal arguments, believing that evaluating multimodal argumentation requires a more nuanced evaluation process, which needs to takes into account its design complexity and the context in which it is situated. This paper argues that when evaluating multimodal argumentation in print advertisements, it is necessary to consider the perspectives of different agents (that is, agent-oriented) to examine whether an argument can respond to the critical questions related to the relevant argumentation schemes.

First, based on the analytical framework previously proposed, we must retrieve the corresponding critical questions for each scheme. Next, we need to consider the polyphonic structure of the advertisement, distinguishing and evaluating the perspectives of different agents. Advertisements often feature multiple voices or agents, such as brands, consumers, experts, and ordinary people. Each agent may represent different viewpoints, needs, or values, making it crucial to account for the positions and voices of these various participants when assessing the arguments in advertisements. Given that consumer data and public opinion are the most direct and effective indicators reflecting the effectiveness of advertisements, we therefore advocate taking the two aspects as effective indicators for detecting the rationality of the evaluation results of arguments in advertisements. On the one hand, consumer data directly reflects the impact of the advertisement on the market, such as changes in sales or increased conversion rates. On the other hand, public opinion reflects the broader societal response to the advertisement, including whether it has sparked positive social discussions and acceptance, as well as the overall attitudes and feedback from consumers. Consumer data and public opinions can be enriched by the reconstructed advertising arguments, and can also be utilized to test the soundness of the evaluation results of the latter.

In conclusion, the evaluation of multimodal argumentation in advertisements requires not only attention to the logical soundness of the different argumentation schemes but also consideration of the polyphonic structure. Ultimately, the soundness of the evaluation of arguments in advertisements needs to be verified through consumer data and public opinion feedback. Thus, the comprehensive assessment of these dimensions helps to fully understand the impact of multimodal argumentation in print advertisements.

6 A Case Study of Luckin Coffee

Based on the analysis through pragmatics and argumentation theory above, we have proposed a methodological framework for analyzing and evaluating multimodal argumentation, particularly in print advertisements. This framework follows a step-by-step process: (1)Pragmatic interpretation of dual code information in advertisements; (2) Reconstruction of the arguments including identification of argumentation schemes and their relations in advertisements; (3) Evaluation of the reconstructed arguments. In the following, we will illustrate how this framework can be practically applied through a case study of an advertisement that has achieved notable success in the Chinese market.[1]

Fig. 1. Advertisement from Luckin coffee-2023

---

[1] Figure 1 is taken from a corpus of corporate communication documents of both commercial and non-governmental organizations.

Luckin Coffee, founded in 2017, is a fast-growing Chinese coffee chain headquartered in China. Today, Luckin Coffee has over 11,000 stores nationwide, far surpassing Starbucks in China. The Kweichow Moutai Latte (sauce-flavored latte), launched in 2023 through a collaboration between Luckin Coffee and Kweichow Moutai, is an innovative beverage that achieved annual sales exceeding 900 million yuan, marking a tremendous success.

6.1 Pragmatic Interpretation

When interpreting the multimodal argumentation in the Sauce-flavored Latte advertisement, it is essential to begin with a pragmatic analysis. This should encompass several key aspects: the sociocultural context, the identification of the polyphonic structure, the specification operations, as well as an exploration of the dialogical functions and commitment structures. These elements provide the foundation for the subsequent argumentation analysis.

Contextual and Textual Analysis. From a social and cultural perspective, Moutai, as a symbol of traditional Chinese high-end liquor, embodies status, tradition, and quality. Moutai's deep historical and cultural significance has long made it a luxury item associated with exclusivity, accessible primarily to high-consuming groups due to its high price and rarity. However, by launching the Sauce-flavored Latte, Luckin Coffee offers a unique opportunity for consumers with more limited financial means to taste Moutai. Through this product, they can enjoy a taste of the Moutai liquor at the affordable price of 38 yuan ($5.20).

The multimodal argumentation in this advertisement combines visual and verbal elements to convey a strong brand message. The image shows two main products: a bottle of Moutai liquor and a cup of Luckin Coffee. Combining these two items creates a unique blend, mixing the high-end image of Moutai with the modern feel of Luckin Coffee. The following utterances can be read (translated from the Chinese) from the Luckin Coffee advertisement:

1. Brand Collaboration Logo: Luckin Coffee × Moutai.
2. Product Name: The Kweichow Moutai Latte (Sauce-Flavored Latte).
3. Slogan: Moutai Liquor and Coffee, This is the Cup I Love.
4. Product Feature: Every cup contains Kweichow Moutai.
5. Product Ingredient: Sauce-Flavored Latte is made with baijiu-flavored thick milk (contains 53% vol Kweichow Moutai).
6. Health Warning: Not recommended for minors, pregnant women, drivers, and those allergic to alcohol (It has an alcohol content of less than 0.5%vol).

Polyphonic Structure. To analyze the polyphonic structure of this advertisement, we begin by identifying the viewpoints and the dialogical entities represented in the various elements. The brand collaboration logo represents the combined viewpoint of the two brands. The slogan introduces a personal viewpoint, likely representing the consumer's perspective or emotional response to the product. The phrase "This is the Cup I Love" suggests a consumer's preference, which positions the individual as a participant in the dialogue, expressing affection for the product. In summary, the polyphonic structure of the advertisement reflects the interplay of multiple voices: the corporate voices of Luckin Coffee and Moutai, the consumer's voice expressing preference. The enunciators in this case are the brands and the consumer, while the locutor is primarily represented by the brands speaking directly to the consumer. For example, the polyphony of the statements (3) and (4) can be represented as follows:

(3) Slogan: [I, Luckin Coffee × Moutai] Moutai Liquor and Coffee, [I, consumer] This is the Cup I Love.
(4) Product feature: [I, Luckin Coffee × Moutai] Every cup contains Kweichow Moutai.

Specifications of Explicature. As previously stated, the advertisement's messages are quite elliptical and enriching its logical form requires pragmatic operations such as specification. Specifically, the utterances read from the Luckin advertisement can be specified by incorporating information that facilitate the formation of a full proposition form. For example, the utterances 3–4 could be enriched as follows through specifications. (3) Slogan: [Kweichow] Moutai Liquor and [Luckin] Coffee, [I, consumer] [claimed that] This [the sauce-flavored latte] is the Cup I Love. (4) Product Feature: Every cup [of Luckin's sauce-flavored latte] contains Kweichow Moutai.

In the provided examples, the slogan and product feature both involve explicatures that directly convey the key aspects of the product. In the slogan, the explicature explicitly asserts that the consumer loves the sauce-flavored latte. It makes the information more direct and clear, explicitly conveying that the combination of Moutai and Luckin Coffee creates a unique flavor that resonates with consumers. In the product feature, the explicature directly informs consumers about the key ingredient in the latte, establishing its uniqueness.

Dialogical Function and Commitment Structure. The final step in reconstructing the message and arguments in advertisements is to interpret their dialogical function and commitment structures. In this case, the dialogical function of the advertisement is clearly persuasive, aiming to convince consumers to purchase the unique sauce-flavored latte. The slogan functions primarily as an expressive speech act, conveying the psychological attitude or state of the speaker. Additionally, the phrase "Each cup contains Moutai liquor" serves as a commissive speech act, making a commitment that guarantees the authenticity of the product.

The core commitment of the advertisement is that by purchasing the Sauce-flavored Latte, consumers can indulge in a unique experience that fuses traditional Chinese liquor culture with modern coffee flavors. The main commitment structures in this advertisement can be analyzed from the following aspects:

(1) [Luckin Coffee and Moutai]: By purchasing the Sauce-flavored Latte, you are guaranteed that each cup contains authentic Kweichow Moutai liquor.

(2) [Luckin Coffee and Moutai]: By choosing the Sauce-flavored Latte, you can indulge in a high-end, innovative beverage.
(3) [Consumer]: By purchasing the Sauce-flavored Latte, I enjoy the fusion of fine liquor and coffee, and what I love most is the fresh and delicious experience this cup brings me.

6.2 Reconstruction of Argumentative Inferences

Reconstructing the argumentation in this advertisement can help extract further inferences derived from its integration with the context. Araucaria is a software tool for analyzing and diagramming arguments, which can be used for working with argumentation schemes. The following diagram[2] created using Araucaria centers on the main claim "You should choose Sauce-flavored Latte", and constructs a comprehensive support structure through five main types of argumentation schemes: value-based practical reasoning, argument from commitment, position-to-know ad populum argument, argument from composition and argument from positive consequences (Fig. 2).

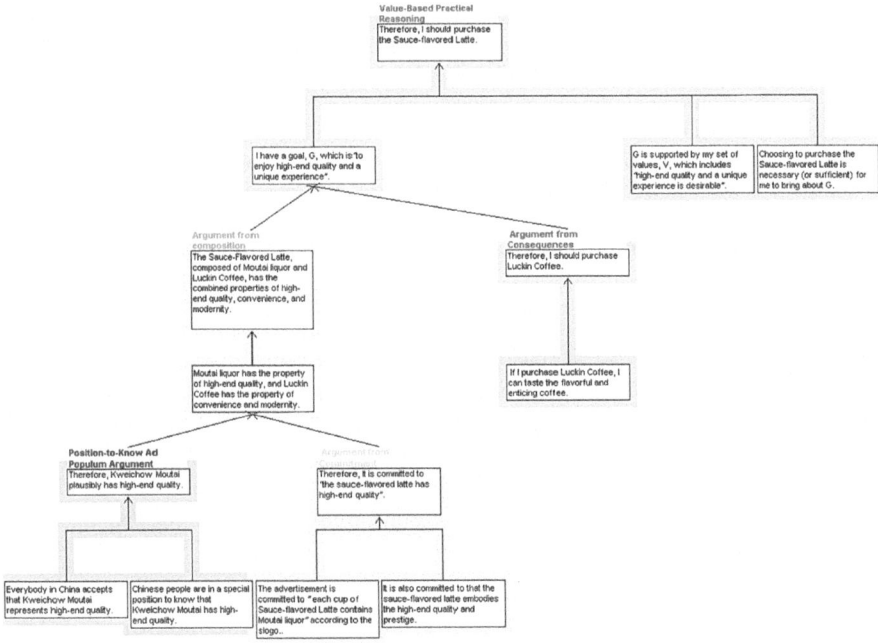

Fig. 2. Argumentative structures in the case study through Araucaria

The argumentation for purchasing the Sauce-flavored Latte is multifaceted, beginning with value-based practical reasoning (it is also the top-level argument

---
[2] Due to space limitations, clearer images are available upon request via email to the authors.

of the entire argumentation) that emphasizes an individual's aspiration for high-end quality and a unique experience, underpinned by their values. This is complemented by the argument from composition, which highlights the Sauce-flavored Latte as a synergistic blend of Moutai liquor's high-end quality and Luckin Coffee's attributes of convenience and modernity. The argument from consequences further strengthens the case with the added benefit of a rich and flavorful coffee experience. Lastly, the position-to-know ad populum argument leverages the cultural recognition of Kweichow Moutai. Additionally, the argument from commitment is based on the commitment that each cup of the Sauce-flavored Latte contains Moutai liquor. Ultimately, the advertisement integrates those argumentation schemes into a complex argumentative structure that persuades the target audience to try this specific product.

Argumentation Scheme: Value-Based Practical Reasoning. The first type of argumentation is the value-based practical reasoning. The structure of this argument is represented in ([31], p. 324). Using the value-based practical reasoning structure, we can analyze the advertisement as follows:

> **Premise 1**: I have a goal, G, which is "to enjoy high-end quality and a unique experience".
> **Premise 2**: G is supported by my set of values, V, which includes "high-end quality and a unique experience are desirable".
> **Premise 3**: Choosing to purchase the Sauce-flavored Latte (Action A) is necessary (or sufficient) for me to bring about G because it combines the premium qualities of Moutai and Luckin Coffee, delivering the promised high-end experience.
> **Conclusion**: Therefore, I should (practically ought to) purchase the Sauce-flavored Latte.

The Luckin Coffee advertisement strategically employs various elements to support the value-based practical reasoning argument structure. First, it establishes the goal of enjoying high-end quality and a unique experience through the slogan. The collaborative branding further reinforces the product's luxurious appeal, combining the tradition and prestige of Moutai with the modern and innovative image of Luckin Coffee. Together, these elements appeal to the consumer's values, particularly the desirability of high-end quality and unique experience.

Argumentation Scheme: Argument from Commitment. The second key type of reasoning in this advertisement is argument from commitment represented in ([31], p. 335), which can be analyzed as follows:

> **Commitment Evidence Premise:** The advertisement is committed to proposition A that each cup of Sauce-flavored Latte contains Moutai liquor according to the evidence of the slogo.
> **Linkage of Commitments Premise**: Generally, when the advertisement is committed to proposition A, it can be inferred that he is also committed to proposition B that the sauce-flavored latte embodies the high-end quality and prestige associated with Moutai liquor.

Conclusion: Therefore, in this case, the advertisement is committed to proposition that the sauce-flavored latte has high-end quality.

In this structure, the direct claim "Every cup contains Kweichow Moutai" reinforces the commitment evidence premise by emphasizing the product's inclusion of Moutai liquor. This commitment is further solidified by the visual pairing of the Moutai bottle and the latte cup, which visually conveys the premium nature of the product. The linkage between these commitments is established through Moutai's well-recognized status as a high-end brand. By associating the latte with Moutai, the advertisement signals that the sauce-flavored latte inherits the prestige and premium quality of its key ingredient.

Argumentation Scheme: Position-to-Know Ad Populum Argument. The third type of argumentation is the position-to-know ad populum argument represented in ([31], p. 311).

Premise 1: Every adult with Chinese nationality (Group G consists of Chinese people) accepts that Kweichow Moutai represents high-end quality (A).
Premise 2: Chinese people are in a special position to know that Kweichow Moutai has high-end quality because Moutai liquor is China's national liquor and has been receiving strong support and promotion from the government.
Conclusion: Therefore, Kweichow Moutai plausibly has high-end quality.

The advertisement employs this argumentation by leveraging the widely accepted perception of Kweichow Moutai as a symbol of premium quality. The product is strategically linked to Moutai's well-established reputation. By doing so, the ad suggests that the "Sauce-Flavored Latte" inherits Moutai's prestigious and high-end attributes, thus reinforcing the product's perceived value and credibility among consumers.

Argumentation Scheme: Argument from Composition. The Luckin Coffee advertisement also employs generic composition, a subtype of argument from composition to persuade consumers ([31], p.316).

Premise: Moutai liquor has the property of high-end quality, and Luckin Coffee has the property of convenience and modernity.
Conclusion: The Sauce-Flavored Latte, composed of Moutai liquor and Luckin Coffee, has the combined properties of high-end quality, convenience, and modernity.

The iconic image of the Moutai bottle alongside the latte cup emphasizes the integration of two distinct and well-known brands. By visually and conceptually merging these two brands, the advertisement conveys that the Sauce-Flavored Latte inherits the desirable qualities of both, offering consumers a unique product that combines luxury with accessibility. The message implies that the latte's quality derives directly from its two components, each of which has already earned consumer trust and recognition.

Argumentation Scheme: Argument from Positive Consequences. The fifth type of argumentation is the argument from positive consequences represented in ([31], p.332).

> **Premise**: If I purchase Luckin Coffee, I can taste the flavorful and enticing coffee.
> **Conclusion**: Therefore, I should purchase Luckin Coffee.

The advertisement highlights the desirable consequences of purchasing the Sauce-Flavored Latte by emphasizing the sensory experience it promises. Through visuals such as the creamy layers of the latte infused with Moutai liquor, the ad creates the expectation of a unique, indulgent, and satisfying flavor profile. By suggesting that the act of purchasing the latte will lead to a pleasurable drinking experience, the argument appeals to consumers' values, encouraging them to act in pursuit of these positive outcomes.

6.3 Evaluation of Multimodal Arguments

As analyzed above, the multimodal argumentation in this advertisement encompasses five distinct types of argumentation schemes. Each of them represents a form of argument (structure of inference) and requires corresponding critical questions for evaluating the argument. Therefore, we can begin by addressing the critical questions and determining whether they have been appropriately answered, thereby assessing the cogency of these arguments.[3] At the same time, we must also consider whether the responses to these questions are consistent across different agents and whether the needs of the various agents have been met. As the analysis of the polyphonic structure above, three core agents are involved: Luckin coffee, Moutai, and consumers. In this case, the consumers include the following groups: Consumers who enjoy both coffee and Moutai; Consumers who wish to experience Moutai at a lower cost; Consumers who are loyal to Luckin Coffee.

First, the value-based practical reasoning in this advertisement effectively addresses the corresponding critical questions, especially regarding the targeting of the consumer group. From the consumer's perspective, this approach aligns with their values, making the advertisement resonate with the audience and reinforcing the argument's persuasive power. Among the seven critical questions, CQ1 and CQ7 focus on potential conflicts and risks, CQ2 and CQ5 concern the consistency of values and action choices, CQ3 and CQ4 assess alternative actions and their efficiency, and CQ6 focuses on the feasibility of the action ([31], p.324). For CQ1 and CQ7, the advertisement's positioning aligns perfectly with the needs of this target group, avoiding conflicts with other potential goals. For CQ3 and CQ4, currently, there are no alternative products on the market that combine Moutai with coffee, making the Sauce-flavored Latte the only option

---

[3] Due to page limitations, the following critical questions corresponding to different types of argumentation schemes abbreviated as CQs can be referred in [31] for more details.

for achieving G. For CQ2 and CQ5, the Sauce-flavored Latte is the ideal choice for consumers who value innovation and are eager to try new things. For CQ6, this advertisement responds to it by demonstrating the feasibility of purchasing the Sauce-flavored Latte.

As for the argument from commitment used in this advertisement, this advertisement clearly commits to certain propositions and links these commitments to the product's high-end attributes. Within this scheme, the CQ1 evaluates evidence supporting a commitment claim and considers contrary evidence, while CQ2 questions if an exception exists to the rule linking commitment to A with commitment to B ([31], p. 335). Regarding CQ1, the Luckin coffee brand directly commits to proposition that every Sauce-flavored Latte includes Moutai liquor. For CQ2, the ad associates Moutai with the Sauce-flavored Latte to conclude that "this Sauce-flavored Latte has high-end quality". This advertisement responds to CQ2 by clearly linking the commitment to Moutai liquor (A) with the commitment to high-end quality (B).

The Luckin Coffee advertisement also employs the position-to-know ad populum argument. The main voice here pertains to the general public, specifically the shared consensus among Chinese consumers. Regarding the two critical questions, the advertisement responds to CQ1 by using the widespread reputation of Moutai as supporting evidence, appealing to the cultural and societal recognition of the Moutai brand. As a symbol of high-end Chinese liquor, Moutai's status is widely accepted, and it has formed a general consensus of "luxury quality" in the minds of consumers. For CQ2, the Luckin Coffee advertisement responds to it by reinforcing the general acceptance of Moutai's high-end quality through its strong cultural and national associations, leaving little room for doubt.

In the case of argument from composition, the main voices involved are those of the two brands: Moutai primarily expresses the high-end nature and quality of its product, while Luckin emphasizes the deliciousness and convenience of its offerings. In response to CQ1 of this scheme, the advertisement effectively conveys the combination of Moutai's high-end quality and Luckin Coffee's convenience and modernity to the Sauce-flavored Latte through brand associations. By merging the image of the Moutai bottle with the coffee cup, the ad reinforces this perception. Furthermore, the ad integrates the tradition of Moutai with the innovation of Luckin, creating a fusion experience that enhances consumer acceptance of this compositional reasoning.

As for the argument from consequences in this advertisement, CQ1, CQ2, and CQ3 all focus on evaluating the likelihood and evidence of consequences ([31], p.332). CQ1 looks at how likely the consequences are, CQ2 examines if there is enough supporting evidence, and CQ3 considers whether opposing consequences should be considered. The advertisement responds to the three critical questions by strengthening the likelihood of positive outcomes (CQ1) through the emphasis on the indulgent sensory experience of the latte. It supports this claim with visual evidence, such as the creamy layers and Moutai infusion, which suggest a pleasurable taste (CQ2). Finally, it does not address any potential negative consequences, focusing solely on the positive outcomes (CQ3).

Based on the above analysis, the argumentation in the Luckin Coffee advertisement addresses most of the critical questions and fully takes into account the pursuits and values of different voices, aiming to align with the values of the different agents, thus enhancing the persuasive power of the argument. Therefore, it can be considered a successful case in terms of multimodal argumentation. This demonstrates that the method of evaluating the effectiveness of multimodal argumentation using critical questions, while considering the role of polyphonic structures in responding to these questions, is effective. Additionally, this approach can be further validated by consumer data and public opinion feedback.

In terms of consumer data, the Sauce-flavored Latte achieved impressive sales figures, with over 5.42 million cups sold and a revenue surpassing 100 million yuan on its first day. This not only demonstrates the ad's powerful short-term sales conversion ability but also indicates that the multimodal argumentation in the ad effectively guided consumers' purchasing decisions. At the same time, the ad has shown remarkable social influence in the realm of public opinion. Following its release, the advertisement sparked widespread discussion and buzz on social media, with the term "Sauce-flavored Latte" frequently trending on Weibo. Thus, the success of the Luckin Coffee advertisement in terms of consumer data and social influence validates the effectiveness of its argumentative strategy, and indirectly demonstrates the soundness of the argument evaluation of this advertisement based on the multimodal argument evaluation framework proposed in the paper.

7 Conclusion

This paper constructs an integrated framework to illustrate how to integrate pragmatic interpretation and argumentation scheme theory, so as to reconstruct and evaluate multimodal arguments in print advertisements.

Firstly, a pragmatic interpretation of the visual and linguistic information in advertisements is required, which covers the analysis of cultural and social contexts, the examination of polyphonic structures, specification of explicatures, and the analysis of the dialogical functions and commitments. Secondly, this framework needs to reconstruct multimodal arguments and outline their inferential relations, and then identify various argumentation schemes in print advertisements. Finally, a multi-perspective evaluation method is proposed to assess the multimodal argumentation in advertisements by correlating critical questions with the agents in polyphonic analysis.

This analytical framework not only strengthens the advantages of the analytical framework mentioned in Macagno and Pinto's work [21], but also retains the ability to conduct a systematic analysis of the interpretive activities involved in multimodal arguments (or at least those expressed through a double-mode). Meanwhile, it provides a method for evaluating multimodal arguments (or at least double-mode arguments) based on argumentation theory, and offers a structured approach for understanding how visual and linguistic elements work together to persuade consumers. Additionally, further exploration is needed on how to assess the correctness of these identifications, especially in cases where multiple modes may convey subtle, implicit messages that require more nuanced interpretations. These issues warrant further investigation to refine the framework and ensure its robustness in practical applications.

Acknowledgments. The paper is supported by Major Project of the National Social Science Fundation of China (No. 19ZDA042) and Philosophy and Social Science Planning Projects of Guangdong Province (No. GD24CZX02).

References

1. Blair, A.J.: Probative norms for multimodal visual arguments. Argumentation **29**(2), 217–233 (2015). https://doi.org/10.1007/S10503-014-9333-3
2. Blair, A.: The possibility and actuality of visual argument. Argumentation Advocacy **33**(1), 23–39 (1996)
3. Birdsell, D., Groarke, L.: Toward a theory of visual argument. Argumentation Advocacy **33**(1), 1–10 (1996)
4. Birdsell, D., Groarke, L.: Outlines of a theory of visual argument. Argumentation Advocacy **43**(3–4), 103–113 (2007)
5. Borg, E.: Exploding explicatures. Mind Lang. **31**(3), 335–355 (2016)
6. Bronckart, J.-P.: Activité de langage, textes et discours. Pour un interactionisme socio-discursive. Delachaux et Niestlé, Lausanne and Paris (1996)
7. Carston, R.: Linguistic meaning, communicated meaning, and cognitive pragmatics. Mind Lang. **17**(1–2), 127–148 (2002)
8. Ducrot, O.: Le dire et le dit. Minuit, Paris, France (1984)
9. Dove, I.J.: Visual scheming: assessing visual arguments. Argumentation Advocacy **52**(4), 254–264 (2016)
10. Feteris, E.T., Groarke, L., Plug, H.J.: Strategic manoeuvring with visual arguments in political cartoons: a pragma-dialectical analysis of the use of topoi based on common cultural heritage. In: Feteris, E.T., Garssen, B., Snoeck Henkemans, A.F. (eds.) Keeping in touch with PragmaDialectics: In honor of Frans H. van Eemeren, pp. 59–74. John Benjamins, Amsterdam (2011)
11. Gelang, M., Kjeldsen, J.: Nonverbal communication as argumentation. In: van Eemeren, F.H., Garssen, B., Godden, D., Mitchell, G. (eds.) Proceedings of the 7th International Conference of the International Society for the Study of Argumentation, pp. 567–576. SicSat, Amsterdam (2011)
12. Groarke, L.: Are musical arguments possible? In: van Eemeren, F.H., Blair, A.J., Willard, C.A., Snoeck Elenkemans, A.F. (eds.) Proceedings of the 5th Conference of the International Society for the Study of Argumentation, pp. 419–422. SicSat, Amsterdam (2002)
13. Groarke, L.: Going multimodal: what is a mode of arguing and why does it matter? Argumentation **29**(2), 133–155 (2015). https://doi.org/10.1007/s10503-014-9336-0
14. Gronbeck, B.E.: Unstated propositions: relations among verbal, visual, and acoustic languages. In: Jackson, S. (ed.) Proceedings of the 9th SCA/AFA Conference on Argumentation, pp. 539–542. SCA, Annandale, VA (1995)
15. Godden, D.: On the norms of visual argument: a case for normative non-revisionism. Argumentation **31**(2), 395–431 (2017). https://doi.org/10.1007/S10503-016-9411-9

16. Hyland, K.: Teaching and Researching Writing. Pearson, Harlow (2009)
17. Kjeldsen, J.: Pictorial argumentation in advertising: Visual tropes and figures as a way of creating visual argumentation. In: van Eemeren, F.H., Garssen, B. (eds.) Topical Themes in Argumentation Theory, pp. 239–255. Springer, Amsterdam (2012)
18. Kjeldsen, J.: The study of visual and multimodal argumentation. Argumentation **29**(2), 115–132 (2015)
19. Kress, G., Van Leeuwen, T.: Multimodal Discourse: The Modes of Media of Contemporary Communication. Arnold, London (2001)
20. Kress, G., Van Leeuwen, T.: Reading Images: The Grammar of Visual Design. Routledge, London; New York (2006)
21. Macagno, F., Botelho Wakim Souza Pinto, R.: Reconstructing multimodal arguments in advertisements: combining pragmatics and argumentation theory. Argumentation **35**(1), 141–176 (2021)
22. Pollaroli, C.: T(r)opical patterns in advertising. In: Mohammed, D., Lewiński, M. (eds.) Virtues of Argumentation: Proceedings of the 10th International Conference of the Ontario Society of the Study of Argumentation (OSSA), pp. 1–12. OSSA, Windsor, ON (2013)
23. Pollaroli, C., Rocci, A.: The argumentative relevance of pictorial and multimodal metaphor in advertising. J. Argumentation Context **4**(2), 158–199 (2015). https://doi.org/10.1075/jaic.4.2.02pol
24. Ripley, L.M.: Argumentation theorists argue that an ad is an argument. Argumentation **22**(4), 507–519 (2008)
25. Rigotti, E., Rocci, A.: Towards a definition of communication context. Foundations of an interdisciplinary approach to communication. Stud. Commun. Sci. **6**(2), 155–180 (2006)
26. Tseronis, A., Pollaroli, C.: Introduction. Pragmatic insights for multimodal argumentation. Int. Rev. Pragmatics **10**(2), 147–157 (2018)
27. Tseronis, A., Younis, R., Üzelgün, M.A.: A proposal for the evaluation of multimodal argumentation: assessing reasonableness and effectiveness in environmental campaign posters. J. Argumentation Context **13**(2), 292–317 (2024). https://doi.org/10.1075/jaic.00028.tse
28. van Eemeren, F.H., Houtlosser, R., Snoeck Henkemans, A.F.: Argumentative indicators in discourse. A pragma-dialectical study. Springer, Dordrecht (2007). https://doi.org/10.1007/978-1-4020-6244-5
29. van Eemeren, F.H.: In context: giving contextualization its rightful place in the study of argumentation. Argumentation **25**(2), 141–161 (2011)
30. Van den Hoven, P.: Getting your ad banned to bring the message home? A rhetorical analysis of an ad on the US national debt. Informal Logic **32**(3), 381–402 (2012)
31. Walton, D., Reed, C., Macagno, F.: Argumentation Schemes. Cambridge University Press, New York (2008)
32. Walton, D.: Enthymemes and argumentation schemes in health product ads. In: Proceedings of the Workshop W5: Computational Models of Natural Argument, Twenty-First International Joint Conference on Artificial Intelligence, pp. 49–56. Pasadena (2009)

Validity of Attacks Related to Argument Set in Higher-Order Argumentation Frameworks

Hengfei Li[1] and Jiachao Wu[2](✉)

[1] School of Computer Science and Technology, Shandong Jianzhu University, Jinan 250101, China
`lihengfei@sdjzu.edu.cn`
[2] School of Mathematics and Statistics, Shandong Normal University, Jinan 250358, China
`wujiachao@sdnu.edu.cn`

Abstract. In the study of higher-order argumentation frameworks (HO-AFs), the validity of attacks plays a particular role. In this paper, we further study HO-AF theory by focusing on this validity of attacks w.r.t. a set of arguments. Given a set of arguments, the attacks whose sources are in this set are classified into seven types, and the attacks whose sources are out of this set are classified into five types. This classification provides a theoretical foundation for the further study of HO-AF semantics.

Keywords: Higher-order argumentation frameworks · Validity of attacks · Higher order attacks · Credulous attitude · Sceptical attitude

1 Introduction

Argumentation frameworks (AF) [2,15] have been widely applied in artificial intelligence [20,26,28], such as multi-agent systems, decision making, non-monotonic reasoning, etc. Dung's original framework has been extended in various forms, such as bipolar AFs [7,9,11–13], weighted AFs [1,16,25], probabilistic AFs [21,23,27], fuzzy AFs [19,30–32], and so on. In particular, *higher-order argumentation frameworks (HO-AFs)* [10] extend Dung's AFs by allowing attacks on attacks.

HO-AFs have been proven to be a useful reasoning model adopted in many fields. For example, in [4], the notion of higher-order attacks is first introduced to demonstrate the strength of attacks and temporal dynamics. In [24], preference-based AFs are studied by *Modgil's extended AFs (M-EAF)*, where the preference relation is transferred into attacks on attacks. In [5,6], coalitions are discussed based on HO-AFs.

In the literature, semantics of HO-AFs are generally in two forms. In [3,14,17], extensions generated by the semantics include both arguments and attacks. In [18,22,24], extensions of the semantics only contain sets of arguments. In each of these two ways, a key task is to identify which attacks are valid.

The validity of attacks is first explicitly put forward in [8], where the validity of attacks depends on the semantics. It can be seen as a further development of the acceptability of attacks in [3,17], where the validity is used implicitly. In [18,22,24], the validity of attacks depending on a set of arguments is applied implicitly. In [18], the concept of inductive defence is introduced: Given an argument set S, a set of attacks is *inductively defended (i-defended)* by the set S. The i-semantics is then built based on inductive defence. In [24], the attacks, which have reinstatement sets, are applied to define acceptability. In [22,29], recursive defence of attacks w.r.t. an argument set S is represented by the introduced renovation sets. However, to the authors' knowledge, there has been no study focused on the validity of attacks with respect to a set of arguments. This paper provides an exploration of this field. The goal is to offer a foundation for the research of HO-AF semantics whose extensions contain no attack.

In this paper, we first introduce a reduction process to give a first step division of attacks. Then, based on this division, for a given argument set S, the attacks whose sources in S are divided into seven types, and the attacks whose sources are not in S are divided into five types. This division provides a theoretical foundation for the further study of HO-AFs semantics in the form of argument sets.

The contents are organised as follows. The next section presents some basic terminologies in HO-AFs. Section 3 investigates the validity of attacks w.r.t. a set of arguments. Section 4 discusses related works and Sect. 5 concludes.

2 Terminologies

In previous works, several types of HO-AFs have been introduced. In this paper, we focus on finite HO-AFs.

Definition 1. *[HO-AF] A higher-order argumentation framework (HO-AF) is a pair $(Ar, \mathcal{R})$, where Ar is a finite set of arguments and $\mathcal{R} = \cup_{k=0}^{n} \mathcal{R}_k$, for some $n \in \mathbb{N}$, recursively defines the attacks:*

$\mathcal{R}_0 \subseteq Ar \times Ar$,
$\mathcal{R}_{k+1} \subseteq Ar \times \mathcal{R}_k$, *for all $0 \leq k < n$.*

Obviously, for any finite HO-AF, the number of attacks is finite, i.e., the cardinal $|\mathcal{R}|$ of $\mathcal{R}$ is a finite number in $\mathbb{N}$.

In [17], an HO-AF in this definition is called a level $(0,n)$ HO-AF, and an attack α in $\mathcal{R}_k, k \leq n$, is called a level $(0,k)$ attack. In this paper, for convenience, $\alpha \in \mathcal{R}_k$ is called a *level k attack*, denoted by $level(\alpha) = k$.

For an attack $\alpha \in \mathcal{R}$, $trg(\alpha)$ stands for the target element of α, while $src(\alpha)$ is its source argument. Obviously, $src(\alpha) \in Ar$, but $trg(\alpha) \in Ar \cup \mathcal{R}$.

An attack α *directly* attacks an element $\chi \in Ar \cup \mathcal{R}$, iff $\chi = trg(\alpha)$. α *indirectly* attacks an attack β, iff $trg(\alpha) = src(\beta)$. Moreover, $\alpha \to_\mathcal{R} \chi$ means that α *directly or indirectly* attacks χ [3].

We define two symbols S^+ and S^-. Given a set $S \subseteq Ar \cup \mathcal{R}$, $S^+ = \{\alpha \in \mathcal{R} : src(\alpha) \in S\}$ and $S^- = \{\alpha \in \mathcal{R} : trg(\alpha) \in S\}$[1]. Particularly, for an element

---
[1] Note that in this paper S^+ and S^- are sets of attacks, unlike other literature where these two symbols normally denote sets of arguments.

$\chi \in Ar \cup \mathcal{R}$, $\chi^- = \{\alpha \in \mathcal{R}: trg(\alpha) = \chi\}$. Obviously, $\forall \alpha, \beta \in \mathcal{R}$, $\beta \in \alpha^-$ iff $trg(\beta) = \alpha$.

The HO-AF semantics are built similarly to Dung's semantics in [15]. The semantics are based on two key notions: acceptability and conflict-freeness. For example, admissible extensions are self-defended conflict-free sets and preferred extensions are maximal admissible extensions. Complete extensions are fixed points of the characteristic function. The difference is that in different papers, the acceptability and conflict-freeness are defined in different ways.

Definition 2 (Renovation sets). *In an HO-AF $(Ar, \mathcal{R})$, let $S \subseteq Ar$ be a set of arguments. A set $R_S \subseteq S^+$ is called a renovation set (abbreviated as R-set) w.r.t. S, iff $\forall \beta \in R_S^- \; \exists \gamma \in R_S$ s.t. $\gamma \to_R \beta$.*

Particularly, when an attack $\alpha \in R_S$ is attracted special attention, R_S is called an R-set of α w.r.t. S, denoted by R_S^α.

3 Validity of Attacks w.r.t. a Set of Arguments

In this section, we will discuss the validity of the attacks w.r.t. a set of arguments. In general, the validity of an attack has two requirements: First, it should be recursively defended. Second, it can output defence for other arguments and/or attacks. In most existing works about HO-AFs, when discussing an argument set S, if an attack acts as a defender, its source argument is in S. Therefore, in this section, the attacks in S^+ and out of S^+ are discussed separately. Before the discussion, we introduce a reduction process of the attacks w.r.t. an argument set S.

3.1 A Reduction of the Attacks

Suppose $S \subseteq Ar$ is a set of arguments. Then $S^+ \subseteq \mathcal{R}$ is a subset of the attacks. We introduce a reduction of the attack set $\mathcal{R}$ according to the set S.

A reduction process:
Step 1: Define 0 layer acceptable attacks as $R_{a0} = \{\alpha \in S^+ : \alpha \text{ is not attacked}\}$. Define 0 layer unacceptable attacks as $R_{r0} = \{\alpha \in \mathcal{R}: \exists \beta \in R_{a0} \text{ such that } trg(\beta) = \alpha\}$. By omitting the attacks in R_{r0} out of $\mathcal{R}$, we obtain an attack set $\mathcal{R} \setminus R_{r0}$.
Step 2: Define the set of first layer acceptable attacks as $R_{a1} = \{\alpha \in S^+ : \alpha \text{ is not attacked by } \mathcal{R} \setminus R_{r0}\}$. Define the set of first layer unacceptable attacks as $R_{r1} = \{\alpha \in \mathcal{R}: \exists \beta \in R_{a1} \text{ such that } trg(\beta) = \alpha\}$. By omitting the attacks in R_{r1}, we obtain an attack set $\mathcal{R} \setminus \cup_{i=0}^{1} R_{ri}$.
... ...
Step k: Define the set of k-layer acceptable attacks as $R_{ak} = \{\alpha \in S^+ : \alpha \text{ is not attacked by } \mathcal{R} \setminus \cup_{i=0}^{k-1} R_{ri}\}$. Define the set of k-layer unacceptable attacks as $R_{rk} = \{\alpha \in \mathcal{R}: \exists \beta \in R_{ak} \text{ such that } trg(\beta) = \alpha\}$. By omitting the attacks in R_{rk}, we obtain an attack set $\mathcal{R} \setminus \cup_{i=0}^{k} R_{ri}$.

For this process, we have the following conclusions.

Lemma 1. *Given a set $S \subseteq Ar$ in an HO-AF, for any $k \leq k' \in \mathbb{N}$, we have $R_{ak} \subseteq R_{ak'}$ and $R_{rk} \subseteq R_{rk'}$.*

Proof. It is obvious from the fact that $\mathcal{R} \setminus \cup_{i=0}^{k-1} R_{ri} \supseteq \mathcal{R} \setminus \cup_{i=0}^{k'-1} R_{ri}$.

Proposition 1. *For any $S \subseteq Ar$ in a finite HO-AF, there is some $N_S \in \mathbb{N}$ such that $R_{aN_S} = R_{a(N_S+1)}$. Hence, $\forall k \geq N_S$, $R_{ak} = R_{a(k+1)}$ and $R_{rk} = R_{r(k+1)}$.*

Proof. If not, $\forall k \in \mathbb{N}$, $R_{ak} \subsetneq R_{a(k+1)}$. Hence, for any $k \in \mathbb{N}$, there exists $A_k \in R_{a(k+1)} \setminus R_{ak}$. From Lemma 1, for any $k' < k$, it follows that $A_{k'} \in R_{a(k'+1)} \subseteq R_{ak}$. Because $A_k \notin R_{ak}$, we have $A_k \neq A_{k'}$. Therefore, the set $\{A_k : k \in \mathbb{N}\} \subseteq \mathcal{R}$ is infinite. It contradicts the fact that $\mathcal{R}$ is finite.

Following from this proposition, it can be seen that the reduction process terminates in finite steps. For each set $S \subseteq Ar$, the number of steps is N_S, and the terminal condition is $R_{ak} = R_{a(k+1)}$. In order to use these fixed points, we introduce two symbols: $R_a = \cup_{i=1}^{\infty} R_{ai}$ and $R_r = \cup_{i=1}^{\infty} R_{ri}$. Obviously, these two are the limit of R_{ak} and R_{rk}, correspondingly, for $k \in \mathbb{N}$. When one wishes to strengthen the relation to the argument set S, these sets can be represented as R_{ak}^S, R_{rk}^S, R_a^S and R_r^S, correspondingly.

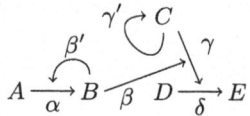

Fig. 1. A simple HO-AF

Example 1. *Consider the HO-AF $(Ar, \mathcal{R})$ in Fig. 1, where $Ar = \{A, B, C, D, E\}$ and $\mathcal{R} = \{\alpha = (A, B), \beta = (B, \gamma), \beta' = (B, \alpha), \delta = (D, E), \gamma = (C, \delta), \gamma' = (C, C)\}$. Suppose $S = \{A, B, D\}$.*

Obviously, $R_{a0} = \{\beta, \beta'\}$ and $R_{r0} = \{\alpha, \gamma\}$. Consequently, $R_{a1} = \{\beta, \beta', \delta\}$ and $R_{r1} = \{\alpha, \gamma\}$. As a result,

$$R_a^{\{A,B,D\}} = \{\beta, \beta', \delta\} \text{ and } R_r^{\{A,B,D\}} = \{\alpha, \gamma\}.$$

3.2 Validity of Attacks in S^+

Given a set $S \subseteq Ar$, we discuss different levels of the validity of the attacks in S^+ in this subsection.

First, a rational agent will accept the attacks in S^+ that are not attacked, i.e., the attacks in R_{a0}^S.

Second, an attack in R_a^S in general can also be accepted by sceptical reasoners. Therefore, the attacks in R_r^S will be rejected by sceptical reasoners.

In order to discuss the validity of attacks in more detail, we introduce the following definition of defence.

Definition 3. *Suppose $\Gamma \subseteq \mathcal{R}$ is a set of attacks and $\alpha \in \mathcal{R}$ is an attack in an HO-AF $(Ar, \mathcal{R})$. α is called to be defended by Γ, if for any $\beta \in \alpha^-$, there is some $\alpha' \in \Gamma$ such that $\alpha' \to_R \beta$.*

We then introduce a function $F \colon 2^\mathcal{R} \to 2^\mathcal{R}$ defined as follows: For any set $\Gamma \subseteq \mathcal{R}$, $F(\Gamma) = \{\alpha \in \mathcal{R} \colon \alpha \text{ is defended by } \Gamma\}$.

Third, we can accept attacks that are *eventually defended* by R_a^S. This type of accepted attacks can be formally represented as follows:

Denote $R_{3a}^{S0} = R_a^S$, and $\forall k \in \mathbb{N}$, $R_{3a}^{Sk+1} = F(R_{3a}^{Sk})$. Let $R_{3a}^S = (\cup_{k=0}^\infty R_{3a}^{Sk}) \setminus R_a^S$. We then say that each attack $\alpha \in R_{3a}^{Sk}$ is eventually defended by R_a^S within k steps. And the attacks in R_{3a}^S are the third type of accepted attacks.

Obviously, the attacks in $R_a^S \cup R_{3a}^S$ are the i-defended attacks in [18]. These attacks can be accepted by sceptical reasoners, and hence they are called *sceptically accepted attacks* [18]. The set of all the sceptically accepted attacks w.r.t. S is denoted by R_{sa}^S, i.e., $R_{sa}^S = R_a^S \cup R_{3a}^S$.

Fourth, for an attack in $S^+ \setminus (R_a \cup R_{3a} \cup R_r)$, if it is recursively defended, then it can also be seen as accepted. This type of accepted attacks is denoted by R_{4a}^S. Borrowing the notion of renovation sets from [22,29], this type of attacks can be formally defined as follows:

An attack α is in R_{4a}^S, iff there is an R-set $R_S \subseteq S^+ \setminus (R_a \cup R_{3a} \cup R_r)$ such that $\alpha \in R_S$.

Attacks in R_{4a}^S are not *sceptically* accepted. But they can be accepted by some credulous reasoners. Therefore, all these four types of attacks are collectively called *credulously accepted attacks*. The set of all the credulously accepted attacks w.r.t. S is denoted by R_{ca}^S, i.e., $R_{ca}^S = R_{sa}^S \cup R_{4a}^S$.

For an attack in S^+, if it is attacked by some sceptically accepted attacks, then it can be seen as *sceptically rejected*. And if it is attacked by some credulously accepted attacks, then it is called *credulously rejected*. Denote the set of all the sceptically rejected attacks by R_{sr}^S and the set of all the credulously rejected attacks by R_{cr}^S. Then, we have the following classification for the attacks in S^+.

Definition 4. *Suppose $S \subseteq Ar$ is a set of arguments in an HO-AF $(Ar, \mathcal{R})$. Then, an attack in S^+ is called*

a first kind accepted attack *if it is in R_{a0}^S;*
a second kind accepted attack *if it is in $R_a^S \setminus R_{a0}^S$;*
a third kind accepted attack *if it is in R_{3a}^S;*
sceptically accepted *if it is in $R_a^S \cup R_{3a}^S$;*

a fourth kind accepted attack *if it is in* R_{4a}^S;
sceptically rejected *if it is in* R_{sr}^S;
credulously rejected *if it is in* R_{cr}^S;
undecided *if it is none of the above.*

Example 2 *[Continues Example 1]. Consider the classification w.r.t. three sets:* $S = \{A, B, D\}$, $S_1 = \{A, D\}$ and $S_2 = \{A, C, D\}$.

Case 1: $S = \{A, B, D\}$. As discussed in Example 1, $R_{a0}^{\{A,B,D\}} = \{\beta, \beta'\}$ and $R_a^{\{A,B,D\}} = \{\beta, \beta', \delta\}$. Obviously, $R_{3a}^{\{A,B,D\}} = \emptyset$. Hence, $R_{sr}^{\{A,B,D\}} = \{\alpha, \gamma\} \cap S^+ = \{\alpha\}$.

Though α recursively defends itself, it cannot belong to R_{4a}^S because it is in S_r. As a result, $R_{4a}^S = \emptyset$ and $R_{ca}^S = R_{sa}^S = \{\beta, \beta', \delta\}$. Therefore, $R_{cr}^S = R_{sr}^S = \{\alpha\}$ and there are no undecided attacks in S^+.

Case 2: $S_1 = \{A, D\}$. $R_{a0}^{S_1} = R_{sa}^{S_1} = \emptyset$. Hence, $R_{sr}^{S_1} = \emptyset$.

It is not difficult to check that $\{\alpha\}$ is an R-set w.r.t. S_1. Hence, $\alpha \in R_{4a}$. δ is neither defended nor attacked by α. Hence, it is not in $R_{ca}^{S_1}$ or $R_{cr}^{S_1}$. Therefore, $R_{ca}^{S_1} = \{\alpha\}$, $R_{cr}^{S_1} = \emptyset$ and $\delta \in R_{un}^{S_1}$.

Case 3: $S_2 = \{A, C, D\}$. $R_{a0}^{S_2} = R_a^{S_2} = \{\gamma'\}$ and $R_{3a}^{S_2} = \{\delta\}$. Hence, $R_{sa}^{S_2} = \{\gamma', \delta\}$ and $R_{sr}^{S_2} = \emptyset$.

Since $\{\alpha, \gamma\}$ is an R-set w.r.t. S_2, we have $R_{4a}^{S_2} = \{\alpha, \gamma\}$. Consequently, $R_{ca}^{S_2} = \{\alpha, \gamma, \gamma', \delta\}$ and $R_{cr}^{S_2} = \{\delta\}$. Finally, we have $R_{un}^{S_2} = \emptyset$.

Note 1: For the first case in this example, the attack α is not credulously accepted, though it recursively defends itself. The reason is that in the definition of R_{4a}^S, the R-set R_S is not permitted to include attacks in R_r. This is also the reason why we introduce the reduction process in the first subsection.

Note 2: In Case 3 in this example, the attack δ belongs to both $R_{ca}^{S_2}$ and $R_{cr}^{S_2}$. Therefore, in general, $R_{ca}^{S_2} \cap R_{cr}^{S_2} \neq \emptyset$. In fact, the set $R_{sa}^{S_2} \cap R_{sr}^{S_2}$ can also be non-empty.

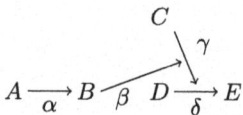

Fig. 2. An HO-AF for Example 3

Example 3. *Consider the HO-AF in Fig. 2, which is the HO-AF in Example 1 omitting* β' *and* γ'. *Let us consider* R_{sa}^S *and* R_{sr}^S *w.r.t.* $S = Ar = \{A, B, C, D, E\}$.

Obviously, $R_{a0} = \{\alpha, \beta\}$ and $R_{r0} = \{\gamma\}$. Consequently, $R_a = \{\alpha, \beta, \delta\}$ and $R_r = \{\gamma\}$. At the same time, α defends γ by attacking the source of β. Therefore, $R_{3a}^S = \{\gamma\}$.

As a result, $R_{sa}^S = R_{3a}^S \cup R_a^S = \{\alpha, \beta, \gamma, \delta\}$ and $R_{sr}^S = \{\gamma, \delta\}$. Particularly, $R_{sa}^S \cap R_{sr}^S = \{\gamma, \delta\} \neq \emptyset$.

The fact that $R_{ca}^{S_2} \cap R_{cr}^{S_2} \neq \emptyset$ and $R_{sa}^{S_2} \cap R_{sr}^{S_2} \neq \emptyset$ comes from the conflict of S. In fact, from Lemma A.1 in [18], if S is i-conflict-free, then $R_{sa}^{S_2} \cap R_{sr}^{S_2} = \emptyset$. Similarly, we have the next results.

Definition 5. *Suppose $S \subseteq Ar$ is a set of arguments in an HO-AF. If $\forall A, B \in S$, (A, B) is not a credulously accepted attack w.r.t. S, then S is conflict-free.*

Since $R_{sa}^S \subseteq R_{ca}^S$, we have that if S is conflict-free then S is i-conflict-free.

Proposition 2. *In an HO-AF, if a set $S \subseteq Ar$ is conflict-free, then for any $\alpha, \beta \in R_{ca}^S$, $trg(\alpha) \neq \beta$.*

Proof (Reduction to absurdity). Assume there exist some $\alpha, \beta \in R_{ca}^S$ such that $trg(\alpha) = \beta$.

Since $\beta \in R_{ca}^S$, there is some $\beta_1 \in R_{ca}^S$ such that $trg(\beta_1) = \alpha$ or $trg(\beta_1) = src(\alpha)$. Because S is conflict-free, $trg(\beta_1) \neq src(\alpha)$. Hence, $trg(\beta_1) = \alpha$.

Similarly, since $\alpha \in R_{ca}^S$, there exists some $\alpha_1 \in R_{ca}^S$ such that $trg(\alpha_1) = \beta_1$. This process continues, and we get two series of attacks α_i and β_i, $i = 1, 2, \ldots$ satisfying that $trg(\alpha_i) = \beta_i$ and $trg(\beta_{i+1}) = \alpha_i$.

Obviously, for any $i > 0$, $level(\alpha_i) = level(\beta_i) + 1$ and $level(\beta_{i+1}) = level(\alpha_i) + 1$. This means that $\alpha_i \neq \alpha_j$ and $\alpha_i \neq \beta_j$, $\forall i, j > 0$. Therefore, the number of α_i is infinite. It contradicts the fact that $\mathcal{R}$ is finite.

From this proposition, when S is conflict-free, the sets R_{ca}^S and R_{cr}^S have no common element. In this case, the classification of the attacks in S^+ is more meaningful.

3.3 Validity of Attacks in $\mathcal{R} \setminus S^+$

The attacks in $\mathcal{R} \setminus S^+$ can be classified into seven types according to the attacks defined in Definition 4. From Proposition 2, the classification according to the sceptical attitude of reasoners is more meaningful. Hence, we only classify the attacks out of S^+ into five types in this paper.

Definition 6. *Suppose $S \subseteq Ar$ is a set of arguments in an HO-AF $(Ar, \mathcal{R})$. Then, an attack out of S^+ is called*

sceptically accepted *if it is defended by R_{sa}^S;*
sceptically rejected *if it is attacked by R_{sa}^S;*
credulously accepted *if it is defended by R_{ca}^S;*
credulously rejected *if it is attacked by R_{ca}^S;*
undecided *if it does not belong any of the above kinds.*

For convenience, we introduce the following symbols.

$^1R_{sa}^S$: The set of sceptically accepted attacks in S^+.
$^2R_{sa}^S$: The set of sceptically accepted attacks out of S^+.
$^1R_{sr}^S$: The set of sceptically rejected attacks in S^+.

$^2R^S_{sr}$: The set of sceptically rejected attacks out of S^+.
$^1R^S_{ca}$: The set of credulously accepted attacks in S^+.
$^2R^S_{ca}$: The set of credulously accepted attacks out of S^+.
$^1R^S_{cr}$: The set of credulously rejected attacks in S^+.
$^2R^S_{cr}$: The set of credulously rejected attacks out of S^+.
$^1R^S_{un}$: The set of undecided attacks in S^+.
$^2R^S_{un}$: The set of undecided attacks out of S^+.

Example 4 (Continues Example 2). *The validity of the attacks in the HO-AF w.r.t. the three sets are listed in Table 1.*

Table 1. Validity of attacks

S	$\{A,B,D\}$	$\{A,D\}$	$\{A,C,D\}$
$^1R^S_{sa}$	$\{\beta,\beta',\delta\}$	$\emptyset$	$\{\gamma',\delta\}$
$^1R^S_{ca}$	$\{\beta,\beta',\delta\}$	$\emptyset$	$\{\alpha,\gamma,\gamma',\delta\}$
$^1R^S_{un}$	$\emptyset$	$\{\delta\}$	$\emptyset$
$^1R^S_{cr}$	$\{\alpha\}$	$\emptyset$	$\{\delta\}$
$^1R^S_{sr}$	$\{\alpha\}$	$\emptyset$	$\emptyset$
$^2R^S_{sa}$	$\emptyset$	$\{\beta,\beta',\gamma'\}$	$\{\beta,\beta'\}$
$^2R^S_{ca}$	$\emptyset$	$\{\gamma\}$	$\emptyset$
$^2R^S_{un}$	$\{\gamma'\}$	$\emptyset$	$\emptyset$
$^2R^S_{cr}$	$\emptyset$	$\emptyset$	$\emptyset$
$^2R^S_{sr}$	$\{\gamma\}$	$\emptyset$	$\emptyset$

4 Discussion

In the literature, HO-AFs have been studied in many papers. In this subsection, we focus on the validity of attacks w.r.t. a set S of arguments. For the attacks in S^+, the attacks are divided into 7 types. For the attacks out of S^+, they are divided into 5 types.

To the authors' knowledge, a special discussion on the validity of attacks is first given in [8]. Unlike our paper, the validity of the attacks in [8] is with respect to a set including both arguments and attacks.

In [18], the sceptically accepted attacks are the i-defended attacks. Here, in our paper, we also introduce the concept of sceptically accepted attacks. There is a little difference between these two.

Example 5. *Consider the HO-AF in Fig. 2, which is the HO-AF in Example 1 omitting β' and γ'. We discuss the validity of the attacks w.r.t. $S = Ar = \{A,B,C,D,E\}$.*

Obviously, $R_{a0} = \{\alpha,\beta\}$ and $R_{r0} = \{\gamma\}$. Consequently, $R_a = \{\alpha,\beta,\delta\}$ and $R_r = \{\gamma\}$. Therefore, in our theory, γ is sceptically rejected, and not sceptically accepted.

For the attack γ, it is not difficult to check that it is defended by α, which is not attacked. Hence, γ is i-defended within 1 step. As a result, γ is sceptically accepted w.r.t. S in the theory of Hanh et al.[2]

In [22,29], the validity of attacks w.r.t. an argument set S is discussed by introducing the concept of R-sets. R-sets represent the recursive defence of the attacks well. But that paper does not identify the first three types of accepted attacks.

In [24], a special kind of HO-AFs, named *EAF*, is discussed. In each EAF, the attacks are in $\mathcal{R}_0$ or $\mathcal{R}_1$. Given an argument set S, the attacks in $\mathcal{R}_0$ are refined by $S^+ \cap \mathcal{R}_1$. The directly attacked attacks are omitted, and the remaining attacks are denoted as $defeat_S$. The set of all defeats are denoted by $Defeat^S$. Obviously, the omitted attacks form the set of R_r^S and $\mathcal{R}_1 \cap S^+$ is a subset of R_{a0}^S. The attacks in $Defeat^S \cap S^+$ are further discussed by introducing the concept of reinstatement sets, which is used to represent the recursive defence of the attacks. The attacks, which have reinstatement sets, can be used to define acceptability. These attacks can be read as valid. They can be divided into two types: The non-attacked ones form the set $R_{a0}^S \setminus (\mathcal{R}_1 \cap S^+)$. Those attacked form the set $R_{3a}^S \cup R_{4a}^S$.

In other literature on HO-AFs, e.g., [3,17], the accepted attacks are the attacks in the extensions of the semantics. In fact, the complete sets in [3] only accept attacks in $^1R_{sa}^S \cup {}^1 R_{ca}^S$, and the complete sets in [17] also accept attacks in $^2R_{sa}^S \cup {}^2 R_{ca}^S$.

Similarly to the four types of accepted attacks, the rejected attacks, both in S^+ and out of S^+, can be more elaborately classified. But we have not seen any work using these rejected attacks. Hence we only classify these attacks into two types. In the future, if necessary, a more elaborative classification can be defined.

At the same time, there is no semantics established. In fact, we can build a semantics similar to those in the works [18,24]. We do not do this duplication of the previous works.

5 Conclusion

In this paper, we discuss the validity of attacks w.r.t. a set S of arguments. The attacks in S^+ are classified into seven types, and the attacks out of S^+ are classified into five types. Particular, when S is conflict-free, there is no attack that is both credulously accepted and credulously rejected.

This classification is a development of HO-AFs. It provides a theoretical foundation for the further study of HO-AF semantics, especially in the form of argument sets.

In the future, we will explore meaningful semantics based on this classification. If necessary, more types of valid attacks can be identified.

---

[2] If S is i-conflict-free, at least one of γ and δ will not be accepted.

Acknowledgement. This work is supported by the National Natural Science Foundation of China (11601288), the Natural Science Foundation of Shandong (ZR2016AQ21).

References

1. Amgoud, L., Doder, D., Vesic, S.: Evaluation of argument strength in attack graphs: foundations and semantics. Artif. Intell. **302**, 103607 (2022). https://doi.org/10.1016/j.artint.2021.103607. https://www.sciencedirect.com/science/article/pii/S0004370221001582
2. Baroni, P., Caminada, M., Giacomin, M.: An introduction to argumentation semantics. Knowl. Eng. Rev. **26**(04), 365–410 (2011)
3. Baroni, P., Cerutti, F., Giacomin, M., Guida, G.: AFRA: argumentation framework with recursive attacks. Int. J. Approximate Reasoning **52**(1), 19–37 (2011)
4. Barringer, H., Gabbay, D., Woods, J.: Temporal dynamics of support and attack networks: from argumentation to zoology. Mechanizing Mathematical Reasoning: Essays in Honor of Jörg H. Siekmann on the Occasion of His 60th Birthday, pp. 59–98 (2005)
5. Boella, G., van der Torre, L., Villata, S.: Attack relations among dynamic coalitions. In: Twenty Belgian-Netherlands Conference on Artificial Intelligence, pp. 25–32 (2008)
6. Boella, G., Van Der Torre, L., Villata, S.: Social viewpoints for arguing about coalitions. In: Pacific Rim International Conference on Multi-Agents, pp. 66–77. Springer (2008)
7. Budán, M., Cobo, M., Martinez, D., Simari, G.: Proximity semantics for topic-based abstract argumentation. Inf. Sci. **508**, 135–153 (2020). https://doi.org/10.1016/j.ins.2019.08.037. https://www.sciencedirect.com/science/article/pii/S0020025519307777
8. Cayrol, C., Fandinno, J., Fariñas del Cerro, L., Lagasquie-Schiex, M.C.: Valid attacks in argumentation frameworks with recursive attacks. Ann. Math. Artif. Intell. **89**(1), 53–101 (2021)
9. Cayrol, C., Lagasquie-Schiex, M.C.: Logical encoding of argumentation frameworks with higher-order attacks and evidential supports. Int. J. Artif. Intell. Tools **29**, 2060003 (2020). https://hal.archives-ouvertes.fr/hal-03265608
10. Cayrol, C., Cohen, A., Lagasquie-Schiex, M.: Higher-order interactions (bipolar or not) in abstract argumentation: a state of the art. In: Handbook of Formal Argumentation, vol. 2, pp. 3–18. College Publications (2021)
11. Cayrol, C., Lagasquie-Schiex, M.C.: Bipolarity in argumentation graphs: towards a better understanding. Int. J. Approximate Reasoning **54**(7), 876–899 (2013)
12. Cohen, A., Parsons, S., Sklar, E., Mcburney, P.: A characterization of types of support between structured arguments and their relationship with support in abstract argumentation. Int. J. Approximate Reasoning **94**, 76–104 (2018). https://doi.org/10.1016/j.ijar.2017.12.008
13. Cohen, A., Gottifredi, S., García, A.J., Simari, G.R.: A survey of different approaches to support in argumentation systems. Knowl. Eng. Rev. **29**(5), 513–550 (2014)
14. Doutre, S., Lagasquie-Schiex, M.: Computing the labellings of higher-order abstract argumentation frameworks. In: 4th International Workshop on Systems and Algorithms for Formal Argumentation, vol. 3236, pp. 45–58. CEUR-WS. org (2022)

15. Dung, P.: On the acceptability of arguments and its fundamental role in non-monotonic reasoning, logic programming and n-person games. Artif. Intell. **77**(2), 321–357 (1995)
16. Dunne, P., Hunter, A., McBurney, P., Parsons, S., Wooldridge, M.: Weighted argument systems: basic definitions, algorithms, and complexity results. Artif. Intell. **175**(2), 457–486 (2011)
17. Gabbay, D.: Semantics for higher level attacks in extended argumentation frames part 1: overview. Stud. Logica. **93**(2–3), 357–381 (2009)
18. Hanh, D., Dung, P., Hung, N., Thang, P.: Inductive defense for sceptical semantics of extended argumentation. J. Log. Comput. **21**(2), 307–349 (2010)
19. Janssen, J., Cock, M.D., Vermeir, D.: Fuzzy argumentation frameworks. In: Information Processing and Management of Uncertainty in Knowledge-Based Systems, pp. 513–520 (2008)
20. Kökciyan, N., Sassoon, I., Sklar, E., Modgil, S., Parsons, S.: Applying metalevel argumentation frameworks to support medical decision making. IEEE Intell. Syst. **36**(2), 64–71 (2021). https://doi.org/10.1109/MIS.2021.3051420
21. Li, H., Oren, N., Norman, T.: Probabilistic argumentation frameworks. In: International Workshop on Theorie and Applications of Formal Argumentation, pp. 1–16. Springer (2011)
22. Li, H., Wu, J.: Semantics of extended argumentation frameworks defined by renovation sets. In: International Conference on Principles and Practice of Multi-Agent Systems, pp. 532–540. Springer (2019)
23. Mantadelis, T., Bistarelli, S.: Probabilistic abstract argumentation frameworks, a possible world view. Int. J. Approximate Reasoning **119**, 204–219 (2020). https://doi.org/10.1016/j.ijar.2019.12.006. https://www.sciencedirect.com/science/article/pii/S0888613X19301550
24. Modgil, S.: Reasoning about preferences in argumentation frameworks. Artif. Intell. **173**(9–10), 901–934 (2009)
25. Pigozzi, G., Vesic, S.: United we stand: accruals in strength-based argumentation. Argument Comput. **12**(1), 87–113 (2021)
26. Prakken, H., Sartor, G.: Law and logic: a review from an argumentation perspective. Artif. Intell. **227**, 214–245 (2015)
27. Riveret, R., Oren, N., Sartor, G.: A probabilistic deontic argumentation framework. Int. J. Approximate Reasoning **126**, 249–271 (2020). https://doi.org/10.1016/j.ijar.2020.08.012. https://www.sciencedirect.com/science/article/pii/S0888613X20302188
28. Timotheus, K., Carlos, N.J.: Abstract argumentation and the rational man. J. Log. Comput. **31**(2), 654–699 (2021)
29. Wu, J., Li, H.: Renovation sets and their applications in higher-order argumentation frameworks. J. Logic Comput. **exad067** (2023)
30. Wu, J., Li, H., Oren, N., Norman, T.: Gödel fuzzy argumentation frameworks. In: Computational Models of Argument, vol. 287, pp. 447–458. IOS Press (2016)
31. Wu, J., Li, L., Sun, W.: Gödel semantics of fuzzy argumentation frameworks with consistency degrees. AIMS Math. **5**(4), 4045–4064 (2020)
32. Zhao, S., Wu, J.: An efficient algorithm of fuzzy reinstatement labelling. AIMS Math. **7**(6), 11165–11187 (2022)

Deontic Sufficiency in Dyadic Deontic Logic

Xu Li

University of Luxembourg, Esch-sur-Alzette, Luxembourg
xu.li@uni.lu

Abstract. In this paper, we introduce and study the logics for conditionals of the form "Given φ, it suffices to do ψ", which are known as "deontic sufficiency" in the deontic logic literature and are useful in the decision and game theory contexts. We completely axiomatize the logics under different assumptions about the properties of the preference relations and establish decidability results for each logic.

Keywords: Deontic sufficiency · Dyadic deontic logic · Reasoning about preference

1 Introduction

Deontic logic is an area of logic that studies normative concepts such as obligation and permission [6]. Among the different approaches to deontic logic, the modal logic approach investigates deontic logic as a branch of modal logic. This is based on an analogy between the deontic modality "It is obligatory that" and the alethic modality "It is necessary that", since the obligatory is "what is necessary for a good person to do", as suggested by Leibniz [11]. As such, the most discussed deontic logic system, standard deontic logic (SDL), is just modal logic of type **KD**. The necessity modality $\Box \varphi$ (or, following the convention in deontic logic, $O\varphi$) in SDL is interpreted as "It is obligatory that φ" and the possibility modality $\Diamond \varphi$ ($P\varphi$) "It is permitted that φ".

Given that obligation can be interpreted as (deontic) necessity, one may wonder whether other modal notions can be applied in deontic logic, e.g. sufficiency. In his paper [20], von Wright noticed the connection between deontic sufficiency and the notion of strong permission, which is deemed different from the notion of weak permission as characterized in SDL. Strong permission is argued to satisfy the free choice principle $P(p \vee q) \leftrightarrow (Pp \wedge Pq)$ (for example, "You may have cake or coffee" implies both "You may have cake" and "You may have coffee"). However, it is not part of SDL (as the $\Diamond$-operator does not distribute over disjunction). Von Wright suggested that interpreting strong permission as deontic sufficiency validates this principle. Van Benthem [2] pursued this idea formally in modal logic. The deontic sufficiency operator $S\varphi$ is interpreted on a Kripke model $M = (W, R, V)$ as follows:

$$M, w \models S\varphi \text{ iff } wRv \text{ for all } v \in W \text{ such that } M, v \models \varphi$$

© The Author(s), under exclusive license to Springer Nature Singapore Pte Ltd. 2025
T. Ågotnes and D. Doder (Eds.): CLAR 2025, LNAI 15712, pp. 150–167, 2025.
https://doi.org/10.1007/978-981-96-7956-0_10

Since wRv represents that "v is an ideal situation relative to w", the operator $S\varphi$ states that φ is a sufficient condition to achieve ideality.[1] In the deontic logic literature, the deontic sufficiency operator has received far less attention than deontic necessity. However, it has recently regained interest, see [17,19].

This paper follows the above research line. We aim to study a conditional variant of the deontic sufficiency operator, analogous to how monadic obligation in SDL is generalized to conditional obligation in dyadic deontic logic (DDL) [9,18]. In DDL, a new dyadic operator $O(\psi/\varphi)$ is introduced to express the condition obligation that "Given φ, it is obligatory that ψ", which is not representable in SDL when contrary-to-duty scenarios like Chisholm's are considered [5]. This dyadic operator is interpreted on the so-called "preference models", where possible worlds are ranked according to their comparative goodness (instead of divided into either ideal or non-ideal ones), such that $O(\psi/\varphi)$ is true iff all the best φ-worlds are also ψ-worlds.

In this paper, inspired by the semantics of the dyadic obligation in DDL, we introduce and study a dyadic operator $S(\psi/\varphi)$ which is to be understood as "Given φ, ψ is a sufficient condition for achieving ideality". Semantically, this operator states that all $\varphi \wedge \psi$-worlds are best φ-worlds in a preference model.

We could regard $S(\psi/\varphi)$ as a conditional version of strong permission. However, the use of the deontic sufficiency operator in the decision and game theory contexts has already been noted by a series of authors, e.g., [1,4,17]. We illustrate this by the following example:

Example 1 (The umbrella). A professor wakes up in the morning and recalls that there is an important exam today. She must bring the test papers to the classroom. However, she is unsure whether it will rain today. She needs to bring an umbrella to protect the test papers if it rains. Otherwise, there is no need. As a cautious person, the professor decides to bring an umbrella regardless of whether it rains.

The point of the above example is that we cannot explain the professor's decision if we interpreted it as the *necessary* conditions for achieving her goal, i.e., bringing the test papers to the classroom without wetting them. This is because carrying an umbrella is not necessary in case it does not rain. As will be seen, the professor's decision can be explained only if it is interpreted as the *sufficient* conditions for achieving the goal. Our paper presents a series of logic systems to reason about them.

This paper is structured as follows. Following the convention in the modal logic research, we start by introducing the formal language and semantics of our logical systems in Sect. 2. In Sect. 3, we analyze the impacts of different properties of the preference relations on the resulting logics. Based on this analysis, three Hilbert-style axiom systems are proposed in Sect. 4 and the completeness results are established in the next two sections: Sects. 5 and 6. Finally, in Sect. 7, we conclude with some discussions.

---

[1] In [2], the notation $P\varphi$ is used. But the semantic definition is the same. $S\varphi$ is also known as the "window" modality in the modal logic literature [3].

2 Syntax and Semantics

We start by presenting the basics of our logical systems, including the formal language and semantics.

Let $Prop$ be a countable infinite set of propositional variables or atoms. In addition to Boolean connectives, there are two modalities $\Box \varphi$ and $S(\psi/\varphi)$ in our language. $\Box \varphi$ is the alethic necessity modality, which can be read as "φ is necessarily true". The dyadic modality $S(\psi/\varphi)$ is read as "Given φ, it suffices to do ψ".

Definition 1 (Language). *The language $\mathcal{L}$ is given by the following BNF grammar:*
$$\varphi ::= p \mid \neg \varphi \mid (\varphi \wedge \varphi) \mid \Box \varphi \mid S(\varphi/\varphi)$$
where $p \in Prop$. Other Boolean connectives are defined as usual.

The formulas are interpreted on preference models from DDL. In a preference model, possible worlds are ordered according to their comparative goodness.

Definition 2 (Preference model). *A preference model $M = (W, \succeq, V)$ is a tuple where:*

1. *W is a non-empty set of possible worlds (states);*
2. *$\succeq$ is binary relation over W ($s \succeq y$ means that "s is at least as good as y");*
3. *$V : Prop \to \wp(W)$ is a valuation.*

As an example of the preference models, consider the umbrella example in the Introduction. For simplicity, we assume that there are only two atoms r and u in the language: r stands for "It rains" and u for "The professor brings an umbrella". As illustrated in Fig. 1, the most preferred worlds (s_1, s_2, and s_3) are those in which the professor can bring the test papers to the classroom without wetting them, i.e., either it does not rain or she brings an umbrella. The worst is where the professor does not bring an umbrella while it rains.

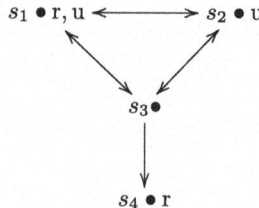

Fig. 1. A preference model M, where $s \to t$ means $s \succeq t$. The reflexive and transitive arrows are omitted.

Next, we present the semantics. Recall that the operator $S(\psi/\varphi)$ is intended to express that ψ is a sufficient condition for achieving ideality in the context of φ. In a preference model, it means that all ψ-worlds (in the context of φ) are the best φ-worlds. This gives rise to the following semantic definition:

Definition 3 (Satisfaction). *Given a preference model $M = (W, \succeq, V)$, for all $w \in W$ and formulas φ, the satisfaction relation $M, s \models \varphi$ is inductively defined as follows (where the clauses for atoms and Boolean connectives are as usual and thus omitted):*

- $M, s \models \Box \varphi$ *iff, for all $t \in W$, $M, t \models \varphi$*
- $M, s \models S(\psi/\varphi)$ *iff* $[\![\psi \wedge \varphi]\!]_M \subseteq opt_\succeq([\![\varphi]\!]_M)$

where $[\![\varphi]\!]_M = \{s \in W \mid M, s \models \varphi\}$ is the truth set of φ (and same for $[\![\psi \wedge \varphi]\!]_M$), and $opt_\succeq([\![\varphi]\!]_M) = \{s \in [\![\varphi]\!]_M \mid s \succeq t$ for all $t \in [\![\varphi]\!]_M\}$. The notion of validity is defined as usual.

Remark 1. In DDL [18], the truth definition for conditional obligation $O(\psi/\varphi)$ is given by the expression "$opt_\succeq([\![\varphi]\!]_M) \subseteq [\![\psi]\!]_M$". Thus, the truth definition for $S(\psi/\varphi)$ is roughly the inverted version of that for $O(\psi/\varphi)$. Note also that, like in DDL, the truth of $\Box \varphi$ and $S(\psi/\varphi)$ does not depend on the evaluating states.

Remark 2. In the truth definition for $S(\psi/\varphi)$, $opt_\succeq([\![\varphi]\!]_M)$ could have been replaced by the set of all $\succeq$-maximal φ-worlds. The choice between optimality and maximality is a long-known problem in the DDL literature, see [13,15]. Here we follow [16] and [18]. We plan to study the maximality version in the future.

Consider again the umbrella example. In the preference model M depicted in Fig. 1, $M, s_1 \models S(\text{u}/\top)$, which means that bringing an umbrella is sufficient to achieve the goal. In contrast, given that it will not rain, whether or not bringing an umbrella will suffice ($M, s_1 \models S(\text{u}/\neg\text{r}) \wedge S(\neg\text{u}/\neg\text{r})$). Note that in both contexts of $\top$ and $\neg\text{r}$, bringing an umbrella is not necessary (to achieve the goal): $M, s_1 \not\models O(\text{u}/\top)$ and $M, s_1 \not\models O(\text{u}/\neg\text{r})$.

A key feature of the operator $S(\psi/\varphi)$ is that it satisfies the principle of strengthening the antecedent, which distinguishes it from the conditional obligation $O(\psi/\varphi)$ in DDL. The operator $S(\psi/\varphi)$ also validates the principle of strengthening the consequent: $S(\psi/\varphi) \rightarrow S(\psi \wedge \chi/\varphi)$.[2] Moreover, $S(\psi/\varphi)$ validates a conditional version of the free choice principle:

Proposition 1. *The following hold for all formulas φ, ψ, χ:*

(1) $\models S(\psi/\varphi) \rightarrow S(\psi/\varphi \wedge \chi)$.
(2) $\models S(\psi/\varphi) \rightarrow S(\psi \wedge \chi/\varphi)$.
(3) $\models S(\psi \vee \chi/\varphi) \leftrightarrow S(\psi/\varphi) \wedge S(\chi/\varphi)$.

3 Properties of Preference Relations

In this section, we examine the impacts of different properties of preference relations on the resulting logics. We will consider four familiar properties in the DDL literature [18]. Other interesting properties (such as antisymmetry) are left for future investigation.

---

[2] We thank an anonymous referee for pointing out this. The validity of strengthening the consequent is considered to be problematic if we interpret $S(\psi/\varphi)$ as (conditional) permission, see [10].

Definition 4. *A preference model* $M = (W, \succeq, V)$ *is*

- reflexive *if, for all* $s \in W$, $s \succeq s$;
- total *(or* connected*) if, for all* $s, t \in W$, $s \succeq t$ *or* $t \succeq s$;
- transitive *if, for all* $s, t, w \in W$, $s \succeq t$ *and* $t \succeq w$ *implies* $s \succeq w$;
- limited *if, for all formulas* φ, $\llbracket \varphi \rrbracket_M \neq \varnothing$ *implies* $\mathrm{opt}_{\succeq}(\llbracket \varphi \rrbracket_M) \neq \varnothing$.

The class of all reflexive (total, transitive, limited, respectively) preference models is denoted by $\mathbb{R}$ *(*$\mathbb{C}$, $\mathbb{T}$, $\mathbb{L}$, *respectively). A nonempty subset of* $\{\mathbb{R}, \mathbb{C}, \mathbb{T}, \mathbb{L}\}$ *will denote the intersection of all its members, e.g.,* $\mathbb{RTL}$ *denotes the class of all reflexive, transitive, and limited preference models. For each nonempty subset* $X \subseteq \{\mathbb{R}, \mathbb{C}, \mathbb{T}, \mathbb{L}\}$, L_X *is the set of all validities on the model class* X. *Finally,* L *is the set of validities on the class of all models.*

We completely studied the logics generated by the 16 (possibly equivalent) classes of models. The results are summarized in Fig. 2. The main observation is that, unlike transitivity, imposing only totalness or limitedness on models has no import to the logic. Only when totalness and limitedness are combined with transitivity can we obtain stronger logics.

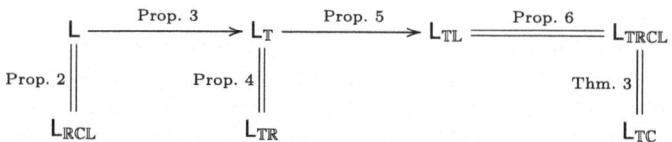

Fig. 2. The logics generated by different model classes, where $\mathsf{L}_X = \mathsf{L}_Y$ means that the two logics are the same and $\mathsf{L}_X \longrightarrow \mathsf{L}_Y$ means that L_X is a proper subset of L_Y.

The first proposition in the section shows that the assumptions of reflexivity, totalness, and limitedness have no import to the logic.[3]

Proposition 2. *For every preference model* $M = (W, \succeq, V)$ *and* $s \in W$, *there is a reflexive, total, and limited preference model* $M' = (W', \succeq', V')$ *and* $s' \in W'$ *such that for all formulas* φ, $M, s \models \varphi$ *iff* $M', s' \models \varphi$.

Proof. We construct $M' = (W', \succeq', V')$ as follows:

- $W' = \{(a, n) \mid a \in W, n \in \{0, 1\}\}$
- $(a, n) \succeq' (b, m)$ iff $a \succeq b$ or $n \geq m$
- $V'(p) = \{(a, n) \mid a \in V(p)\}$

Let $s' = (s, 0)$. We first show that

$$\text{for all } a \in W \text{ and } n \in \{0, 1\}, a \models \varphi \text{ iff } (a, n) \models \varphi \qquad (*)$$

---

[3] This result is similar to [14, Theorem 3.3], but, of course, we work on different formal languages. We thank an anonymous referee for pointing out this.

We show only the case for $S(\psi/\varphi)$. *From left to right.* Suppose $a \models S(\psi/\varphi)$. Let $(b,m) \models \psi \wedge \varphi$. To show that $(b,m) \in opt_{\succeq'}(\llbracket\varphi\rrbracket_{M'})$, let $(c,l) \models \varphi$ be arbitrary. If $(b,m) \not\succeq' (c,l)$, then $b \not\succeq c$. Note that $b \models \psi \wedge \varphi$ and $c \models \varphi$ by IH. Thus, $\llbracket\psi \wedge \varphi\rrbracket_M \not\subseteq opt_{\succeq}(\llbracket\varphi\rrbracket_M)$, contradicting the assumption. Hence, $(b,m) \succeq' (c,l)$. Thus, $(b,m) \in opt_{\succeq'}(\llbracket\varphi\rrbracket_{M'})$. Therefore, $(a,n) \models S(\psi/\varphi)$. *From right to left.* Suppose $(a,n) \models S(\psi/\varphi)$. Let $b \models \psi \wedge \varphi$. To show that $b \in opt_{\succeq}(\llbracket\varphi\rrbracket_M)$, let $c \models \varphi$ be arbitrary. Suppose, toward a contradiction, that $b \not\succeq c$. Then $(b,0) \not\succeq' (c,1)$. Note that, by IH, $(b,0) \models \psi \wedge \varphi$ and $(c,1) \models \varphi$. Hence, $\llbracket\psi\wedge\varphi\rrbracket_{M'} \not\subseteq opt_{\succeq'}(\llbracket\varphi\rrbracket_{M'})$, contradicting the assumption. Hence, $b \succeq c$ and thus $b \in opt_{\succeq}(\llbracket\varphi\rrbracket_M)$. Therefore, $a \models S(\psi/\varphi)$.

It remains to show that M' satisfies the required properties. Clearly, M' is total (and therefore reflexive). For all formulas φ with $\llbracket\varphi\rrbracket_{M'} \neq \varnothing$, it follows from (*) that $\llbracket\varphi\rrbracket_{M'} \cap (W \times \{1\}) \neq \varnothing$ (since $(s,0) \models \varphi$ iff $(s,1) \models \varphi$ for all $s \in W$). Let $(s,1) \models \varphi$. It is easy to see that $(s,1) \in opt_{\succeq'}(\llbracket\varphi\rrbracket_{M'})$. Therefore, $opt_{\succeq}(\llbracket\varphi\rrbracket_M) \neq \varnothing$. Thus, M' is limited.

The next proposition shows that, by imposing only transitivity on the models, we obtain a stronger logic. Let (Tran) be the following formula:

$$S(\varphi/\varphi \vee \psi) \wedge S(\psi/\psi \vee \chi) \wedge \Diamond \psi \to S(\varphi/\varphi \vee \chi) \tag{Tran}$$

Proposition 3. *The following hold:*

(1) (Tran) is valid on the class of all transitive preference models.
(2) (Tran) is invalid on the class of all preference models.

Proof. (1) Let $M = (W, \succeq, V)$ be a transitive preference model. Suppose:

(i) $M, s \models \Diamond \psi$,
(ii) $M, s \models S(\varphi/\varphi \vee \psi)$,
(iii) $M, s \models S(\psi/\psi \vee \chi)$,

Let $t_1 \models \varphi \wedge (\varphi \vee \chi)$ (i.e., $t_1 \models \varphi$) and $t_2 \models \varphi \vee \chi$. To show $M, s \models S(\varphi/\varphi \vee \chi)$, it suffices to show that $t_1 \succeq t_2$. If $t_2 \models \varphi$, since $s \models S(\varphi/\varphi \vee \psi)$, $t_1 \succeq t_2$ by semantics. Otherwise, $t_2 \models \chi$, from (i) and (iii) it follows that there must be $t_3 \models \psi$ such that $t_3 \succeq t_2$. Note that $t_1 \succeq t_3$ by (ii). Thus, by transitivity, $t_1 \succeq t_2$.
(2) A counter model is provided in Fig. 3 where $s_1 \not\models S(p/p \vee q) \wedge S(q/q \vee r) \wedge \Diamond q \to S(p/p \vee r)$.

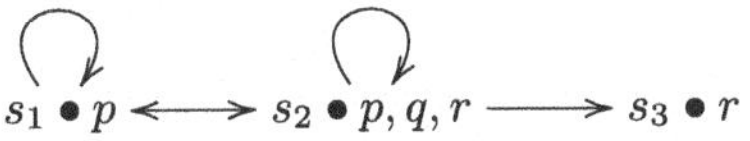

$$s_1 \bullet p \longleftrightarrow s_2 \bullet p, q, r \longrightarrow s_3 \bullet r$$

Fig. 3. A preference model M.

Proposition 4. *For every transitive preference model $M = (W, \succeq, V)$ and $s \in W$, there is a reflexive and transitive preference model $M' = (W', \succeq', V')$ and $s' \in W'$ such that, for all formulas φ, $M, s \models \varphi$ iff $M', s' \models \varphi$.*

Proof. We construct M' as follows:

- $W' = W \times \{0, 1\}$ (the elements of W are denoted by $s_0, s_1, t_0, t_1, \dots$)
- $\succeq' = \{(s_i, t_j) \mid s \succeq t\} \cup \{(s_i, s_i) \mid s_i \in W'\}$
- $s_i \in V'(p)$ iff $s \in V(p)$

Obviously, $\succeq'$ is reflexive and transitive. It can be verified that, for all $s \in W$ and $i \in \{0, 1\}$, $M, s \models \varphi$ iff $M', s_i \models \varphi$ for all formulas φ. Here we show only the case for $S(\psi/\varphi)$. The direction from left to right is trivial. From right to left. Suppose $M', s_i \models S(\psi/\varphi)$. Let $M, u \models \psi \wedge \varphi$ and $M, t \models \varphi$. Then, by IH, $M', u_0 \models \psi \wedge \varphi$ and $M', t_1 \models \varphi$. Since $M', s_i \models S(\psi/\varphi)$, $u_0 \succeq' t_1$. By the definition of $\succeq'$, it must be $u \succeq t$. Hence, $M, s \models S(\psi/\varphi)$.

Next we show that, given transitivity, the addition of either limitedness or totalness changes the logic. For this, we need the following lemma.[4]

Lemma 1. *The following holds for every preference model $M = (W, \succeq, V)$ that is either transitive and limited or transitive and total: for all $X, Y \subseteq W$, if $X \subseteq opt_\succeq(\llbracket \psi \rrbracket)$ and $Y \subseteq opt_\succeq(\llbracket \theta \rrbracket)$, then $X \subseteq opt_\succeq(\llbracket \psi \vee \theta \rrbracket)$ or $Y \subseteq opt_\succeq(\llbracket \psi \vee \theta \rrbracket)$.*

Proof. Suppose M is transitive and limited. We consider two cases: (1) $X = \varnothing$ or $Y = \varnothing$. Then $X \subseteq opt_\succeq(\llbracket \varphi \vee \psi \rrbracket)$ or $Y \subseteq opt_\succeq(\llbracket \varphi \vee \psi \rrbracket)$. (2) $X \neq \varnothing$ and $Y \neq \varnothing$. Then $\llbracket \psi \vee \theta \rrbracket \neq \varnothing$. By limitedness, $opt_\succeq(\llbracket \psi \vee \theta \rrbracket) \neq \varnothing$. Let $s \in opt_\succeq(\llbracket \psi \vee \theta \rrbracket)$. Then $s \in \llbracket \psi \vee \theta \rrbracket$. Without loss of generality, we assume $s \in \llbracket \psi \rrbracket$. For every $t \in X$, $t \in opt_\succeq(\llbracket \psi \rrbracket)$. Thus, $t \succeq s$. By transitivity, $t \in opt_\succeq(\llbracket \psi \vee \theta \rrbracket)$. Hence, $X \subseteq opt_\succeq(\llbracket \psi \vee \theta \rrbracket)$.

The case where M is transitive and total remains to be considered. We split into the same two subcases as above. We consider only the subcase where both X and Y are nonempty. Let $x \in X$ and $y \in Y$. Since M is total, $x \succeq y$ or $y \succeq x$. (a) If $x \succeq y$, let $x' \in X$ be arbitrary. For all $z \in \llbracket \psi \vee \theta \rrbracket$, $z \in \llbracket \psi \rrbracket$ or $z \in \llbracket \theta \rrbracket$. If $z \in \llbracket \psi \rrbracket$, then $x' \succeq z$ since $X \subseteq opt_\succeq(\llbracket \psi \rrbracket)$. If $z \in \llbracket \theta \rrbracket$, then $y \succeq z$ as $Y \subseteq opt_\succeq(\llbracket \theta \rrbracket)$. Since $x' \succeq x$, $x \succeq y$ and $y \succeq z$, $x' \succeq z$ by transitivity. Therefore, $x' \in opt_\succeq(\llbracket \psi \vee \theta \rrbracket)$, i.e., $X \subseteq opt_\succeq(\llbracket \psi \vee \theta \rrbracket)$. (b) Otherwise, $y \succeq x$. Similarly, we can show that $Y \subseteq opt_\succeq(\llbracket \psi \vee \theta \rrbracket)$.

In what follows, let (Lim) be the formula below:

$$S(\varphi/\psi) \wedge S(\chi/\theta) \to (S(\varphi \wedge \psi/\psi \vee \theta) \vee S(\chi \wedge \theta/\psi \vee \theta)) \qquad \text{(Lim)}$$

Proposition 5. *The following hold:*

(1) (Lim) is valid on the class of all transitive and limited preference models.
(2) (Lim) is valid on the class of all transitive and total preference models.
(3) (Lim) is invalid on the class of all transitive models.

Proof. (1) and (2) follow immediately from Lemma 1. For (3), a counter-model is provided in Fig. 4 where $s \not\models S(p/p) \wedge S(\neg p/\neg p) \to (S(p/p \vee \neg p) \vee S(\neg p/p \vee \neg p))$.

Fig. 4. A counter model M.

The last proposition in the section shows that, given transitivity and limitedness, totalness has no import to the logic. In the proof, we use the same model construction method as in the proof of [13, Prop. 13]:

Proposition 6. *For all transitive and limited preference models $M = (W, \succeq, V)$ and $s \in W$, there is a reflexive, total, transitive, and limited preference model $M' = (W', \succeq', V')$ and $s' \in W'$ such that for all formulas φ, $M, s \models \varphi$ iff $M', s' \models \varphi$.*

Proof. Let $U = \{x \in W \mid$ there is a formula φ such that $x \in opt_{\succeq}(\llbracket\varphi\rrbracket_M)\}$. We construct M' as follows:

- $W' = W$ and $V' = V$,
- For all $x, y \in W$:
  - If $x, y \in U$, then $x \succeq' y$ iff $x \succeq y$;
  - If $x \in U$ and $y \notin U$, then $x \succeq' y$;
  - If $x \notin U$ and $y \notin U$, then $x \succeq' y$ and $y \succeq' x$.

We first show that

$$\text{for all } x \in W \text{ and formulas } \varphi, M, x \models \varphi \text{ iff } M', x \models \varphi. \qquad (*)$$

We show only the case $S(\psi/\chi)$. *From left to right.* Suppose $M, x \models S(\psi/\chi)$. Then $\llbracket\psi \wedge \chi\rrbracket_M \subseteq opt_{\succeq}(\llbracket\chi\rrbracket_M)$. Let $y \in \llbracket\psi \wedge \chi\rrbracket_{M'}$. Then, by IH, $y \in \llbracket\psi \wedge \chi\rrbracket_M \subseteq opt_{\succeq}(\llbracket\chi\rrbracket_M)$. For every $z \in \llbracket\chi\rrbracket_{M'}$, by IH we have $z \in \llbracket\chi\rrbracket_M$. Thus, $y \succeq z$. If $z \in U$, then $y \succeq' z$ by the definition of $\succeq'$ (note that $y \in U$). Otherwise, $z \notin U$, we also have $y \succeq' z$ by the definition of $\succeq'$. Hence, $y \in opt_{\succeq'}(\llbracket\chi\rrbracket_{M'})$. Therefore, $\llbracket\psi \wedge \chi\rrbracket_{M'} \subseteq opt_{\succeq'}(\llbracket\chi\rrbracket_{M'})$ and thus $M', x \models S(\psi/\chi)$. *From right to left.* Suppose $M', x \models S(\psi/\chi)$. Then $\llbracket\psi \wedge \chi\rrbracket_{M'} \subseteq opt_{\succeq'}(\llbracket\chi\rrbracket_{M'})$. If $\llbracket\chi\rrbracket_M = \varnothing$, then it holds trivially that $M, x \models S(\psi/\chi)$. Otherwise, $\llbracket\chi\rrbracket_M \neq \varnothing$, by the limitedness of $\succeq$ it follows that $opt_{\succeq}(\llbracket\chi\rrbracket_M) \neq \varnothing$. Let $t \in opt_{\succeq}(\llbracket\chi\rrbracket_M)$. Thus, $t \in U$. For each $y \in \llbracket\psi \wedge \chi\rrbracket_M = \llbracket\psi \wedge \chi\rrbracket_{M'}$, since $t \in \llbracket\chi\rrbracket_M = \llbracket\chi\rrbracket_{M'}$, we have $y \succeq' t$ by our assumption that $M', x \models S(\psi/\chi)$. Since $t \in U$, it follows from the definition of $\succeq'$ that $y \succeq t$. As $t \in opt_{\succeq}(\llbracket\chi\rrbracket_M)$, by the transitivity of $\succeq$ we have $y \in opt_{\succeq}(\llbracket\chi\rrbracket_M)$. Therefore, $M, x \models S(\psi/\chi)$.

It remains to show that M' satisfies the required properties. *Transitivity*: Suppose, toward a contradiction, that there are x, y, z such that $x \succeq' y$, $y \succeq' z$, and $x \not\succeq' z$. Since $x \not\succeq' z$, by the definition of $\succeq'$, it can only be the following two cases: (1) $x, z \in U$ and $x \not\succeq z$. Since $x \succeq' y$ and $y \succeq' z$, it must be that $y \in U$, $x \succeq y$, and $y \succeq z$ by the definition of $\succeq'$. Thus, by the transitivity of $\succeq$,

---

[4] This is a generalization of [13, Lemma 8]. We thank an anonymous referee for pointing out this.

$x \succeq z$ and thus $x \succeq' z$. Contradiction! (2) $x \notin U$ and $z \in U$. Since $x \succeq y$, $y \notin U$. However, it implies that $y \not\succeq z$. Contradiction!

The *limitedness* of M' follows directly from that of M and (*). To show that $\succeq'$ is *total*, let $x, y \in W$. The only non-trivial case is when $x, y \in U$. By the definition of U, $x \in opt_{\succeq}(\llbracket \psi \rrbracket)$ and $y \in opt_{\succeq}(\llbracket \theta \rrbracket)$. By Lemma 1, $x \in opt_{\succeq}(\llbracket \psi \vee \theta \rrbracket)$ or $y \in opt_{\succeq}(\llbracket \psi \vee \theta \rrbracket)$. In either case, $x \succeq y$ or $y \succeq x$. Hence, $x \succeq' y$ or $y \succeq' x$. Thus, $\succeq'$ is total and thus reflexive.

4 Axiomatizations

In this section, we present three Hilbert-style axiom systems for our language $\mathcal{L}$.

Definition 5 (Axiomatizations). *The axiomatization* $\mathbf{DLDS}_0$ *consists of the axioms and rules listed below. The axiomatization* $\mathbf{DLDS}_1$ *is obtained by supplementing* $\mathbf{DLDS}_0$ *with the axiom* (Tran). *The axiomatization* $\mathbf{DLDS}_2$ *is obtained by supplementing* $\mathbf{DLDS}_1$ *with the axiom* (Lim). *For each* $x \in \{0, 1, 2\}$, *let the set of* $\mathbf{DLDS}_x$-*theorems be the least set of formulas that contains all instances of the axiom schemas and is closed under the inference rules in* $\mathbf{DLDS}_x$. *If a formula* φ *is a* $\mathbf{DLDS}_x$-*theorem, we write* $\vdash_{\mathbf{DLDS}_x} \varphi$.

> PL All instances of propositional tautologies
> $\Box$-K $\Box(\varphi \to \psi) \to (\Box\varphi \to \Box\psi)$
> $\Box$-T $\Box\varphi \to \varphi$
> $\Box$-5 $\neg\Box\varphi \to \Box\neg\Box\varphi$
> $A1$ $S(\psi/\varphi) \to \Box S(\psi/\varphi)$
> $A2$ $S(\psi/\varphi) \wedge S(\chi/\varphi) \to S(\psi \vee \chi/\varphi)$
> $A3$ $S(\varphi/\varphi \vee \psi) \to (S(\varphi/\varphi \vee \chi) \to S(\varphi/\varphi \vee \psi \vee \chi))$
> $A4$ $\Box(\psi \to \chi) \to (S(\chi/\varphi) \to S(\psi/\varphi))$
> $A5$ $\Box(\psi \to \varphi) \to (S(\chi/\varphi) \to S(\chi/\psi))$
> $A6$ $\Box\neg(\psi \wedge \varphi) \to S(\psi/\varphi)$
> MP From φ and $\varphi \to \psi$, infer ψ
> Nec From φ, infer $\Box\varphi$

The following result on $\mathbf{DLDS}_2$ will be used in the completeness proof.

Proposition 7. *The following holds for all integers* $n \geq 1$:

$$\vdash_{\mathbf{DLDS}_2} \left(\bigwedge_{1 \leq i \leq n} \Box(\varphi_i \to \psi_i) \wedge S(\varphi_i/\psi_i) \right) \to \bigvee_{1 \leq i \leq n} S(\varphi_i / \bigvee_{1 \leq i \leq n} \psi_i).$$

Proof. Induction on n. The axiom (Lim) is used in the inductive step.

It is not hard to verify that all the axioms and rules in $\mathbf{DLDS}_0$ are valid or preserve validity on the class of all preference models. Therefore,

Proposition 8. *The axiomatization* $\mathbf{DLDS}_0$ *is sound with respect to the class of all preference models.*

5 Canonical Model

In this and the next sections, we establish the completeness results for $\mathbf{DLDS_0}$–$\mathbf{DLDS_2}$ with respect to the intended model classes. We will focus on the *weak* completeness of the three systems. Following the classical canonical model method, we construct the canonical model using maximal consistent sets (MCS). However, since we aim only to prove weak completeness, we assume a finite number of propositional variables in the language. The main novelty of our proof lies in using a propositional formula as the "name" of each MCS t, which we denote by $Nom(t)$. This allows us to reduce the truth of formulas $S(\psi/\varphi)$ to that of formulas like $S(Nom(t)/\varphi)$ (the latter can be semantically regarded as a monadic modality).

Throughout this section, let $A \subset Prop$ be a finite nonempty set of atoms and $\mathcal{L}_A$ be the sublanguage of $\mathcal{L}$ restricted to atoms in A. Let Λ range over $\{\mathbf{DLDS_0}, \mathbf{DLDS_1}, \mathbf{DLDS_2}\}$. A set Γ of formulas in $\mathcal{L}_A$ is said to be Λ-*consistent* if there are no $\varphi_1, \ldots, \varphi_n \in \Gamma$ such that $\vdash_\Lambda \varphi_1 \wedge \cdots \wedge \varphi_n \to \bot$. Γ is *maximal Λ-consistent* if Γ is Λ-consistent, and any set of formulas in $\mathcal{L}_A$ properly containing Γ is Λ-inconsistent. The standard properties of maximal consistent sets are taken as granted, i.e., for all Λ-maximal consistent sets Γ and formulas $\varphi, \psi \in \mathcal{L}_A$:

- $\neg\varphi \in \Gamma$ iff $\varphi \notin \Gamma$, and
- $\varphi \wedge \psi \in \Gamma$ iff $\varphi \in \Gamma$ and $\psi \in \Gamma$.

The Lindenbaum lemma also holds, which claims that every Λ-consistent set of formulas in $\mathcal{L}_A$ can be extended to a maximal Λ-consistent one. The set of all Λ-maximal consistent sets in $\mathcal{L}_A$ will be denoted by MCS_Λ.

In what follows, we fix a $w \in MCS_\Lambda$ and let $\Box w = \{\varphi \in \mathcal{L}_A \mid \Box\varphi \in w\}$. For each $s \in MCS_\Lambda$, let $Nom(s)$ be the formula $\bigwedge_{p \in s} p \wedge \bigwedge_{p \in A \setminus s} \neg p$. Note that $Nom(s) \in \mathcal{L}_A$ and $Nom(s) \in s$ (by the properties of maximal consistent sets).

Lemma 2. *For all $s, t \in MCS_\Lambda$, if $Nom(t) \in s$ then $Nom(s) = Nom(t)$.*

Proof. It suffices to show that for all $p \in A$, $p \in s$ iff $p \in t$. For all $p \in A$, if $p \in t$ then $Nom(t) \to p$ is a propositional tautology. Since $Nom(t) \in s$, $p \in s$. Conversely, if $p \notin t$ then $Nom(t) \to \neg p$ is a propositional tautology. Since $Nom(t) \in s$, $\neg p \in s$. Thus, $p \notin s$.

Now we are ready to define the canonical model.

Definition 6 (Canonical model). *The canonical model for $w \in MCS_\Lambda$ is a structure $M(w) = (W, \succeq, V)$ such that*

- $W = \{s \in MCS_\Lambda \mid \Box w \subseteq s\}$.
- $s \succeq t$ *iff there is* $\varphi \in \mathcal{L}_A$ *such that* $\varphi \in t \cap s$ *and* $S(Nom(s)/\varphi) \in w$.
- *For all* $p \in Prop$, $s \in V(p)$ *iff* $p \in s$.

It is clear that $M(w)$ is a preference model and $w \in W$. For each formula $\psi \in \mathcal{L}_A$, let $\|\psi\| = \{s \in W \mid \psi \in s\}$ and $[\![\psi]\!] = [\![\psi]\!]_{M(w)}$.

Lemma 3. *The following holds for all $s \in W$:*

(1) for all formulas $\Box\varphi \in \mathcal{L}_A$, $\Box\varphi \in s$ iff $\Box\varphi \in w$;
(2) for all formulas $S(\psi/\varphi) \in \mathcal{L}_A$, $S(\psi/\varphi) \in s$ iff $S(\psi/\varphi) \in w$.

Proof. Since $\Box\varphi$ is an $S5$-modality, (1) follows from the standard argument.

(2): The direction from right to left follows directly from the axiom A1 and the definition of W. For the converse, if $S(\psi/\varphi) \in s$ then $\Box S(\psi/\varphi) \in s$ by A1. From (1) it follows that $\Box S(\psi/\varphi) \in w$. Hence, $S(\psi/\varphi) \in w$ by $\Box$-T.

Lemma 4. *For all $s, t \in W$, if $Nom(s) = Nom(t)$ then $s = t$. Thus, by Lemma 2, if $Nom(t) \in s$ then $s = t$.*

Proof. Suppose $Nom(s) = Nom(t)$. We show that for all formulas $\varphi \in \mathcal{L}_A$, $\varphi \in s$ iff $\varphi \in t$. The cases for atoms and Boolean connectives are trivial. The cases $\Box\varphi$ and $S(\psi/\varphi)$ follow directly from Lemma 3.

Note that Lemma 4 implies that W is finite. The next lemma is standard.

Lemma 5. *The following hold:*

(1) for all propositional formulas $\pi \in \mathcal{L}_A$ and $s \in W$, $\pi \in s$ iff $M(w), s \models \pi$;
(2) for all formulas $\Box\varphi \in \mathcal{L}_A$, $\Box\varphi \in w$ iff $\varphi \in t$ for all $t \in W$.

Lemma 6. *For all formulas $\psi \in \mathcal{L}_A$, $\Box(\psi \leftrightarrow \bigvee_{t \in \|\psi\|} Nom(t)) \in w$.*

Proof. By Lemma 5(2), it suffices to show that $\psi \leftrightarrow \bigvee_{t \in \|\psi\|} Nom(t) \in s$ for all $s \in W$. That is, $\psi \in s$ iff $\bigvee_{t \in \|\psi\|} Nom(t) \in s$. The direction from left to right is straightforward (as $Nom(s) \in s$). For the converse, let $s \in W$ be such that $\bigvee_{t \in \|\psi\|} Nom(t) \in s$. Then there must be $t \in \|\psi\|$ such that $Nom(t) \in s$. Thus, by Lemma 4, $s = t \in \|\psi\|$.

Lemma 7. *For all formulas $S(\psi/\varphi) \in \mathcal{L}_A$, $S(\psi/\varphi) \in w$ iff for all $t \in \|\psi\|$, $S(Nom(t)/\varphi) \in w$.*

Proof. From left to right. Let $t \in \|\psi\|$. By Lemma 6, $\Box(Nom(t) \to \psi) \in w$. Since $S(\psi/\varphi) \in w$, $S(Nom(t)/\varphi) \in w$ by A4. From right to left. Suppose that for all $t \in \|\psi\|$, $S(Nom(t)/\varphi) \in w$. Then, by A2 and A6, $S(\bigvee_{t \in \|\psi\|} Nom(t)/\varphi) \in w$. Since $\Box(\psi \to \bigvee_{t \in \|\psi\|} Nom(t)) \in w$ by Lemma 6, $S(\psi/\varphi) \in w$ by A4.

Lemma 8. *For all formulas $S(\psi/\varphi) \in \mathcal{L}_A$, $w \models S(\psi/\varphi)$ iff for all $t \in [\psi]$, $w \models S(Nom(t)/\varphi)$.*

Proof. From left to right. Suppose $w \models S(\psi/\varphi)$. Let $t \in \llbracket \psi \rrbracket$ and $s \models Nom(t) \wedge \varphi$. Since $s \models Nom(t)$, $Nom(t) \in s$ by Lemma 5(1). Therefore, $s = t$ by Lemma 4. Since $w \models S(\psi/\varphi)$ and $s \models \psi \wedge \varphi$, $s \in opt_\succeq(\llbracket \varphi \rrbracket)$. Thus, $w \models S(Nom(t)/\varphi)$. From right to left. Suppose that for all $t \in \llbracket \psi \rrbracket$, $w \models S(Nom(t)/\varphi)$. Let $s \in \llbracket \psi \wedge \varphi \rrbracket$. Since $w \models S(Nom(s)/\varphi)$ and $s \models Nom(s) \wedge \varphi$, $s \in opt_\succeq(\llbracket \varphi \rrbracket)$. Therefore, $w \models S(\psi/\varphi)$.

Lemma 9 (Truth). *For all $s \in W$ and $\alpha \in \mathcal{L}_A$, $\alpha \in s$ iff $M(w), s \models \alpha$.*

Proof. Induction on the structure of α. We show only the case for $S(\psi/\varphi)$. We first show the following claim:

Claim. For all $s \in W$ and $\varphi \in \mathcal{L}_A$, $S(Nom(s)/\varphi) \in w$ iff $M(w), w \models S(Nom(s)/\varphi)$.

Proof. From left to right. Suppose $S(Nom(s)/\varphi) \in w$. Let $t \models Nom(s) \wedge \varphi$. By Lemma 5(1), $Nom(s) \in t$. Thus, by Lemma 4, $t = s$. It then suffices to show that $s \succeq s'$ for all $s' \models \varphi$. Since $s' \models \varphi$ and $s \models \varphi$, $\varphi \in s \cap s'$ by IH. As we assume $S(Nom(s)/\varphi) \in w$, $s \succeq s'$ by the construction of $\succeq$.

From right to left. Suppose $S(Nom(s)/\varphi) \notin w$. We need to show that there is $s' \in W$ such that $s' \models Nom(s) \wedge \varphi$ and $s' \notin opt_\succeq(\llbracket \varphi \rrbracket)$. Since $s \models Nom(s)$, it suffices to show that $s \models \varphi$ and $s \notin opt_\succeq(\llbracket \varphi \rrbracket) = opt_\succeq(\|\varphi\|)$. Since $S(Nom(s)/\varphi) \notin w$, by A6, $\Box \neg(Nom(s) \wedge \varphi) \notin w$. Thus, by Lemma 5(2), there must be $t \in W$ with $Nom(s) \wedge \varphi \in t$. Thus, $s = t$ (by Lemma 4). Since $\varphi \in t = s$, $s \models \varphi$ by IH.

It remains to show that $s \notin opt_\succeq(\|\varphi\|)$, i.e., there is $t \in W$ such that $\varphi \in t$ and $s \not\succeq t$. We consider two cases:
(1) For all $S(Nom(s)/\psi) \in w$, $\psi \notin s$. Then $s \not\succeq s$ by the construction of $\succeq$.
(2) Otherwise, by the Lindenbaum lemma and the construction of $\succeq$, it suffices to show that the following set of formulas is consistent:

$$\Gamma = \Box w \cup \{\varphi\} \cup \{\neg \psi \mid S(Nom(s)/\psi) \in w \ \& \ \psi \in s\}$$

Suppose, toward a contradiction, that Γ is inconsistent. Then there must be $\Box \chi_1, \ldots, \Box \chi_m \in w$ and $S(Nom(s)/\psi_1), \ldots, S(Nom(s)/\psi_n) \in w$ (with $n \geq 1$ and each $\psi_i \in s$) such that

$$\vdash_\Lambda \chi_1 \wedge \cdots \wedge \chi_m \to (\varphi \to (\psi_1 \vee \cdots \vee \psi_n))$$

Since $\Box$ is a normal modality, $\Box(\varphi \to \psi_1 \vee \cdots \vee \psi_n) \in w$ (*). For each ψ_i, since $s \in \|\psi_i\|$, it follows from Lemma 6 that $\Box(Nom(s) \to \psi_i) \in w$. Thus, $\Box(Nom(s) \vee \psi_i \to \psi_i) \in w$. Since $S(Nom(s)/\psi_i) \in w$, by A5 we have $S(Nom(s)/Nom(s) \vee \psi_i) \in w$ for all $1 \leq i \leq n$. Using A3, we derive that $S(Nom(s)/Nom(s) \vee \psi_1 \vee \cdots \vee \psi_n) \in w$. From (*) and A5, it follows that $S(Nom(s)/\varphi) \in w$, contradicting our assumption.

Given the above claim, we are ready to show the inductive case $S(\psi/\varphi)$:

$S(\psi/\varphi) \in s$
iff $S(\psi/\varphi) \in w$ (Lemma 3)
iff for all $t \in \|\psi\|$, $S(Nom(t)/\varphi) \in w$ (Lemma 7)
iff for all $t \in [\![\psi]\!]$, $w \models S(Nom(t)/\varphi)$ (IH and the above claim)
iff $w \models S(\psi/\varphi)$ (Lemma 8)
iff $s \models S(\psi/\varphi)$ (by semantics)

6 Completeness

Given the canonical model and the truth lemma in the previous section, we are ready to present our completeness results for the three systems $\mathbf{DLDS_0}$, $\mathbf{DLDS_1}$, and $\mathbf{DLDS_2}$.

6.1 $\mathbf{DLDS_0}$

The completeness of $\mathbf{DLDS_0}$ with respect to the class of all preference models follows from the routine argument (the soundness has been established in Proposition 8). Together with Proposition 2, it implies that $\mathbf{DLDS_0}$ is also sound and complete with respect to the model class $\mathbb{RCT}$.

Theorem 1 (Completeness of $\mathbf{DLDS_0}$). *The axiomatization $\mathbf{DLDS_0}$ is sound and weakly complete with respect to the class of all preference models and the class of all reflexive, total, and limited preference models.*

Since the canonical model is finite, the decidability of $\mathbf{DLDS_0}$ is straightforward:

Proposition 9. *The theoremhood problem in $\mathbf{DLDS_0}$ is decidable.*

6.2 $\mathbf{DLDS_1}$

To establish the completeness of $\mathbf{DLDS_1}$ with respect to the class of all transitive preference models, we need the following lemma (which is called the canonicity lemma in the literature):

Lemma 10. *If $w \in MCS_{\mathbf{DLDS_1}}$, then $M(w)$ is a transitive preference model.*

Proof. Suppose $w \in MCS_{\mathbf{DLDS_1}}$. Suppose $s \succeq t$ and $t \succeq u$. Then there must be $\varphi, \psi \in \mathcal{L}_A$ such that $\varphi \in s \cap t$, $S(Nom(s)/\varphi) \in w$, $\psi \in t \cap u$, and $S(Nom(t)/\psi) \in w$. We need to show that $s \succeq u$.

Since $s, t \in \|\varphi\|$, it follows from Lemma 6 that $\Box(Nom(s) \vee Nom(t) \to \varphi) \in w$. Since $S(Nom(s)/\varphi) \in w$, by A5, $S(Nom(s)/Nom(s) \vee Nom(t)) \in w$ (∗). On the other hand, since $t \in \|\psi\|$, $\Box(Nom(t) \to \psi) \in w$ and thus $\Box(Nom(t) \vee \psi \to \psi) \in w$. As $S(Nom(t)/\psi) \in w$, $S(Nom(t)/Nom(t) \vee \psi) \in w$ by A5 (∗∗). Note that since $Nom(t) \in t$, $\Diamond Nom(t) \in w$ by Lemma 5(2). By (∗) and (∗∗), it follows from (Tran) that $S(Nom(s)/Nom(s) \vee \psi) \in w$. Since $Nom(s) \vee \psi \in s \cap u$, by the definition of $\succeq$ it follows that $s \succeq u$.

Theorem 2. *The axiomatization* **DLDS**$_1$ *is sound and weakly complete with respect to the class of all transitive preference models and the class of all reflexive and transitive preference models.*

Proof. The soundness of **DLDS**$_1$ with respect to the class of all transitive preference models follows from Proposition 8 and Proposition 3(1). For completeness, let $\varphi \in \mathcal{L}$ be a **DLDS**$_1$-consistent formula, and let A be the set of atoms occurred in φ. By the Lindenbaum lemma, there is $w \in MCS_{\mathbf{DLDS}_1}$ such that $\varphi \in w$. By the truth lemma, $M(w), w \models \varphi$. Note that $M(w)$ is transitive by Lemma 10. Hence, φ is satisfiable on the class of all transitive preference models.

The soundness and completeness of **DLDS**$_1$ with respect to the class of all reflexive and transitive models follows from the above and Proposition 4.

Proposition 10. *The theoremhood problem in* **DLDS**$_1$ *is decidable.*

6.3 DLDS$_2$

The completeness of **DLDS**$_2$ is more involved. We aim to show that **DLDS**$_2$ is complete with respect to the class of all transitive and limited preference models. However, there is no guarantee that the canonical model for **DLDS**$_2$ is limited. Fortunately, we can transform the canonical model for **DLDS**$_2$ into an equivalent limited preference model. In the following, we describe the transformation.

Definition 7. *Given a preference model* $M = (W, \succeq, V)$, *the transformed model of* M, *notation* $\tau(M)$, *is a preference model* $\tau(M) = (W', \succeq', V')$ *where:*

(1) $W' = W \times \{0, 1\}$ *(the elements of* W' *are denoted by* $s_0, s_1, t_0, t_1, \dots$*);*
(2) $\succeq' = \{(s_i, t_j) \mid s \succeq t\} \cup \{(s_1, t_0), (s_1, t_1) \mid \text{for all } u \in W, u \succeq s \text{ implies } u \succeq t\}$;
(3) $s_i \in V'(p)$ *iff* $s \in V(p)$.

It is essential that the above transformation preserves the truth of formulas:

Proposition 11. *For every preference model* $M = (W, \succeq, V)$ *and its transformed model* $\tau(M) = (W', \succeq', V')$, *it holds that, for all* $s \in W$, $i \in \{0, 1\}$, *and formulas* φ, $M, s \models \varphi$ *iff* $\tau(M), s_i \models \varphi$.

Proof. Induction on the structure of φ. We consider only the inductive case $S(\psi/\varphi)$. From left to right. Suppose $M, s \models S(\psi/\varphi)$. Let $x_i \in \llbracket \psi \wedge \varphi \rrbracket_{\tau(M)}$ and $y_j \in \llbracket \varphi \rrbracket_{\tau(M)}$. By IH, $x \in \llbracket \psi \wedge \varphi \rrbracket_M$ and $y \in \llbracket \varphi \rrbracket_M$. Since $M, s \models S(\psi/\varphi)$, $x \succeq y$. Thus, $x_i \succeq' y_j$. Therefore, $\tau(M), s_i \models S(\psi/\varphi)$. From right to left. Suppose $M, s \not\models S(\psi/\varphi)$. Then there must be $x \in \llbracket \psi \wedge \varphi \rrbracket_M$ and $y \in \llbracket \varphi \rrbracket_M$ such that $x \not\succeq y$. By the definition of $\succeq'$, $x_0 \not\succeq' y_1$. Note that $\tau(M), x_0 \models \psi \wedge \varphi$ and $\tau(M), y_1 \models \varphi$ by IH. Hence, $\tau(M), s_i \not\models S(\psi/\varphi)$.

For the transformed model to be limited, the original model needs to satisfy a property. We call a preference model $M = (W, \succeq, V)$ *almost-limited* if, for all formulas φ, $\llbracket \varphi \rrbracket_M \neq \varnothing$ implies that there is $s \in \llbracket \varphi \rrbracket_M$ such that, for all $t \in W$, if $t \succeq s$ then $t \succeq u$ for all $u \in \llbracket \varphi \rrbracket_M$.

Proposition 12. *Given a transitive and almost-limited preference model $M = (W, \succeq, V)$, the transformed model of M is a transitive and limited preference model.*

Proof. We first show that $\succeq'$ is transitive. Let $s_i \succeq' t_j$ and $t_j \succeq' u_k$. We consider the following cases:

(1) $s \succeq t$ and $t \succeq u$. Then $s \succeq u$ by the transitivity of $\succeq$. Hence, $s_i \succeq' u_k$.
(2) $s \not\succeq t$ and $t \succeq u$. Then $i = 1$. To see $s_1 \succeq' u_k$, it suffices to show that $v \succeq s$ implies $v \succeq u$ for all $v \in W$. Let $v \succeq s$. Since $s_1 \succeq' t_j$ and $s \not\succeq t$, by the definition of $\succeq'$, $v \succeq t$. Thus, $v \succeq u$ by the transitivity of $\succeq$.
(3) $s \succeq t$ and $t \not\succeq u$. Since $t_j \succeq' u_k$ and $t \not\succeq u$, by definition it follows that $s \succeq t$ implies $s \succeq u$. Thus, $s \succeq u$. Thus, $s_i \succeq u_k$.
(4) $s \not\succeq t$ and $t \not\succeq u$. Then $i = j = 1$. To see $s_1 \succeq' u_k$, it suffices to show that $v \succeq s$ implies $v \succeq u$ for all $v \in W$. Suppose $v \succeq s$. Since $s_1 \succeq' t_1$ and $s \not\succeq t$, $v \succeq t$. Since $t_1 \succeq u_k$ and $t \not\succeq u$, $v \succeq u$.

It remains to show that $\tau(M)$ is limited. Let $\llbracket \varphi \rrbracket_{\tau(M)} \neq \varnothing$. By Proposition 11, $\llbracket \varphi \rrbracket_{\tau(M)} = \llbracket \varphi \rrbracket_M \times \{0, 1\}$. Thus, $\llbracket \varphi \rrbracket_M \neq \varnothing$. Since M is almost-limited, there is $s \in \llbracket \varphi \rrbracket_M$ such that, for all $t \in W$, if $t \succeq s$ then $t \succeq u$ for all $u \in \llbracket \varphi \rrbracket_M$. Thus, by the definition of $\succeq'$, $s_1 \succeq' u_0$ and $s_1 \succeq' u_1$ for all $u \in \llbracket \varphi \rrbracket_M$. Since $\llbracket \varphi \rrbracket_{\tau(M)} = \llbracket \varphi \rrbracket_M \times \{0, 1\}$, we conclude that $s_1 \in opt_{\succeq'}(\llbracket \varphi \rrbracket_{\tau(M)})$.

Now we are ready to show the completeness of **DLDS**$_2$. Given the previous two propositions, it suffices to show that the canonical model for **DLDS**$_2$ is transitive and almost-limited.

Lemma 11. *If w is a **DLDS**$_2$-maximal consistent set, then the canonical model for w, $M(w) = (W, \succeq, V)$, is transitive and almost-limited.*

Proof. The transitivity follows from Proposition 10. To show that $M(w)$ is almost-limited, it suffices to show that, for all $\varnothing \neq U \subseteq W$, there is $s \in U$ such that, for all $t \in W$, if $t \succeq s$ then $t \succeq u$ for all $u \in U$. Suppose, toward a contradiction, that for all $s \in U$, there are $s^* \in W$ and $s^\dagger \in U$ such that $s^* \succeq s$ and $s^* \not\succeq s^\dagger$. We are going to show that for some $t \in U$, $t^* \succeq y$ for all $y \in U$ (which contradicts that $t^* \not\succeq t^\dagger$).

For each $s \in U$, since $s^* \succeq s$, by the definition of the canonical model, there is $\varphi_s \in s^* \cap s$ such that $S(Nom(s^*)/\varphi_s) \in w$. Note also that, since $\varphi_s \in s^*$, $\Box(Nom(s^*) \to \varphi_s) \in w$ by Lemma 6. Thus, it follows from Proposition 7 that

$$\bigwedge_{s \in U} S(Nom(s^*)/\varphi_s) \to \bigvee_{t \in U} S\left(Nom(t^*)/\bigvee_{s \in U} \varphi_s\right) \in w$$

Thus, $\bigvee_{t \in U} S\left(Nom(t^*)/\bigvee_{s \in U} \varphi_s\right) \in w$. This implies that there is $t \in U$ such that $S(Nom(t^*)/\bigvee_{s \in U} \varphi_s) \in w$. For each $y \in U$, since $\bigvee_{s \in U} \varphi_s \in t^* \cap y$, $t^* \succeq y$ by the definition of the canonical model. This contradicts the fact that $t^* \not\succeq t^\dagger$.

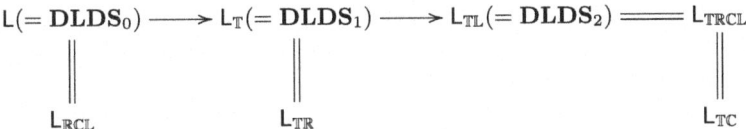

Fig. 5. Summary of the soundness and completeness results, where the same convention is adopted as in Fig. 2.

Theorem 3. $\mathbf{DLDS}_2$ *is sound and weakly complete with respect to*

(1) the class of all transitive and limited preference models;
(2) the class of all transitive, limited, and total (thus reflexive) preference models;
(3) the class of all transitive and total preference models.

Proof. (1) Straightforward. (2) follows from (1) and Proposition 6.

(3) The soundness follows from Propositions 8, 3(1), and 5(2). For completeness, note that $\mathsf{L}_{\mathrm{TC}} \subseteq \mathsf{L}_{\mathrm{TRCL}}$. Thus, the completeness of $\mathbf{DLDS}_2$ with respect to the class of all transitive and total preference models follows from (2).

Proposition 13. *The theoremhood problem in $\mathbf{DLDS}_2$ is decidable.*

7 Discussion and Conclusion

In this paper, following the previous work on deontic sufficiency in deontic logic, we introduced and studied the logics of conditionals $S(\psi/\varphi)$ which state that ψ is a sufficient condition for achieving ideality in the context of φ. For the semantics of the operator $S(\psi/\varphi)$, we adopted the preference semantics used in DDL. Like in DDL, preference relations may exhibit different properties. In this paper, we considered four such properties, i.e., reflexivity, totalness, transitivity, and limitedness, and we comprehensively analyzed the logics generated by different combinations of the four properties. Our results are summarized in Fig. 5. In general, we obtained three logics $\mathbf{DLDS}_0$ – $\mathbf{DLDS}_2$ with increasing deductive power, which is analogous to the situation in DDL (where we also have three systems [18]: **E**, **F**, and **G**). However, the main difference is that the operator $S(\psi/\varphi)$ is monotonic, which may make it less interesting than the conditional obligation operator $O(\psi/\varphi)$ as the latter can be used for nonmonotonic reasoning. Another difference is that our language $\mathcal{L}$ does not distinguish between the class of all preference models and the class of limited preference models. Thus, in a certain sense, our language $\mathcal{L}$ can be said to be "weaker" than the language of DDL.

The method used in our completeness proof is, to the best of our knowledge, new in the DDL literature. The general idea is to reduce the truth of the dyadic operator $S(\psi/\varphi)$ to that of a set of monadic operators. Our method has some advantages. First, the construction of the canonical model is relatively straightforward. Second, it allows us to obtain completeness results for different model classes in a modular way. Last, since the canonical model is finite, we automatically derive the decidability of our logics. However, this method seems to be hard to be adapted to obtain strong completeness results. For this, we may need more involved constructions of the canonical model, as we have seen in the literature [7,8,12,13].

For future work, one direction is to incorporate the conditional obligation in the language, which will enable us to reason about both deontic sufficiency and deontic necessity. One can also explore different truth definitions for the operator $S(\psi/\varphi)$, e.g., employing the maximality condition instead of optimality.

Acknowledgments. We thank three anonymous referees for their detailed comments. This work was supported by the Fonds National de la Recherche Luxembourg through the project Deontic Logic for Epistemic Rights (OPEN O20/14776480).

References

1. Apostel, L.: Game theory and the interpretation of deontic logic. Logique et Analyse **3**(10), 70–90 (1960). http://www.jstor.org/stable/44083424
2. van Benthem, J.: Minimal deontic logics. Bull. Sect. Logic **8**(1), 36–42 (1979)
3. Blackburn, P., de Rijke, M., Venema, Y.: Modal Logic, Cambridge Tracts in Theoretical Computer Science, vol. 53. Cambridge University Press (2001)
4. Boutilier, C.: Toward a logic for qualitative decision theory. In: Doyle, J., Sandewall, E., Torasso, P. (eds.) Principles of Knowledge Representation and Reasoning, pp. 75–86. The Morgan Kaufmann Series in Representation and Reasoning, Morgan Kaufmann (1994). https://doi.org/10.1016/B978-1-4832-1452-8.50104-4. https://www.sciencedirect.com/science/article/pii/B9781483214528501044
5. Chisholm, R.M.: Contrary-to-duty imperatives and deontic logic. Analysis **24**(2), 33–36 (1963). http://www.jstor.org/stable/3327064
6. Gabbay, D., Horty, J., Parent, X., van der Meyden, R., van der Torre, L. (eds.): Handbook of Deontic Logic and Normative Systems. College Publications (2013)
7. Goble, L.: Axioms for hansson's dyadic deontic logics. Filosofiska Notiser **6**(1), 13–61 (2019)
8. Grossi, D., van der Hoek, W., Kuijer, L.B.: Reasoning about general preference relations. Artif. Intell. **313**, 103793 (2022). https://doi.org/10.1016/j.artint.2022.103793. https://www.sciencedirect.com/science/article/pii/S0004370222001333
9. Hansson, B.: An analysis of some deontic logics. In: Hilpinen, R. (ed.) Deontic Logic: Introductory and Systematic Readings, pp. 121–147. Springer, Dordrecht (1971). https://doi.org/10.1007/978-94-010-3146-2_5
10. Hilpinen, R.: Disjunctive permissions and conditionals with disjunctive antecedents. Acta Philosophica Fennica **35** (1982)
11. Hilpinen, R., McNamara, P.: Deontic logic: a historical survey and introduction. In: Gabbay, D., Horty, J., Parent, X., van der Meyden, R., van der Torre, L. (eds.) Handbook of Deontic Logic and Normative Systems, pp. 3–136. College Publications (2013)

12. Parent, X.: On the strong completeness of Åqvist's dyadic deontic logic G. In: van der Meyden, R., van der Torre, L. (eds.) Deontic Logic in Computer Science, pp. 189–202. Springer, Heidelberg (2008)
13. Parent, X.: Maximality vs. optimality in dyadic deontic logic. J. Philos. Logic **43**(6), 1101–1128 (2014). https://doi.org/10.1007/s10992-013-9308-0
14. Parent, X.: Completeness of Åqvist's systems E and F. Rev. Symb. Logic **8**(1), 164–177 (2015). https://doi.org/10.1017/S1755020314000367
15. Parent, X.: Preference semantics for hansson-type dyadic deontic logic: a survey of results. In: Handbook of Deontic Logic and Normative Systems, vol. 2, pp. 7–70. College Publications (2021)
16. Åqvist, L.: An Introduction to Deontic Logic and the Theory of Normative Systems. Humanities Press (1988)
17. Roy, O.: Deontic logic and game theory. In: Handbook of Deontic Logic and Normative Systems, vol. 2, pp. 765 – 782. College Publications (2021)
18. van der Torre, L., Parent, X.: Introduction to Deontic Logic and Normative Systems. College Publications (2018)
19. Van De Putte, F.: "That will do": logics of deontic necessity and sufficiency. Erkenntnis **82**(3), 473–511 (2017). https://doi.org/10.1007/s10670-016-9829-3
20. Von Wright, G.H.: Deontic logic and the theory of conditions. In: Deontic logic: Introductory and systematic readings, pp. 159–177. Springer (1971)

Reasoning in Coalition Planning

Yanjun Li[✉]

Nankai University, Tianjin, China
lyjlogic@nankai.edu.cn

Abstract. Coalition planning is the planning based on synchronous concurrent models. This paper presents a logic for reasoning about the coalition and knowledge in coalition planning, and also proposes a proof system and shows its completeness. It is shown that the plan-existence problem of coalition planning based on this logic framework is in PTIME.

Keywords: Multi-agent planning · Coalition logic · Epistemic logic

1 Introduction

Automated planning is a branch of artificial intelligence concerned with computing plans leading to some desired goal [11]. In classical planning, the planning domain is a labeled transition system, and the labels are actions available to the agent. The planning task is to find a plan such that if the agent executes the plan in the initial state then it will be guaranteed to terminate in the goal states. In classical planning, only one agent is involved.

Multi-agent planning is the enrichment of classical planning where multiple agents are involved. The planning domain of multi-agent planning has at least two types: planning domain based on asynchronous models and planning domain based on synchronous models. In synchronous models, agents act concurrently, whereas in asynchronous models, agents do not act concurrently (see [15]). Epistemic planning (see [3,7,13,16]), a popular multi-agent planning approach, is based on asynchronous models. In this paper, we will focus on multi-agent planning based on synchronous models.

In multi-agent planning, cooperation and collaboration among group members play an important role. Depending on the type of the planning domain, cooperation and collaboration are implemented in different ways. In the asynchronous planning domain, by collaboration among group members, the group as a whole can do more actions than each single group member. For example, if the agent i can do only the action a and the agent j can do only the action b, then the group composed of i and j can do both a and b. In the synchronous planning domain, cooperation means that the group works collectively as a coalition.

In literature, there are several logics for reasoning about coalition and knowledge. Coalition logic [17] is a modal logic that is concerned with reasoning about the effects of collective actions in a multi-agent system. It uses the formula $S_C\varphi$

© The Author(s), under exclusive license to Springer Nature Singapore Pte Ltd. 2025
T. Ågotnes and D. Doder (Eds.): CLAR 2025, LNAI 15712, pp. 168–184, 2025.
https://doi.org/10.1007/978-981-96-7956-0_11

to express that "there is a strategy of coalition C that guarantees φ". In [20], coalition logic is extended with epistemic logic operators to reason about both the effects of collective actions and knowledge. In [14], they propose a logic for describing an interplay between one-step coalition strategies and distributed knowledge. Alternating-time temporal logic ATL [1] is designed to reason about coalition and strategies in synchronous multi-agent systems. Alternating-time temporal epistemic logic ATEL [19] extends ATL with epistemic operators from epistemic logic. Different from this paper, in these logics the coalition actions are only *implicitly* referred to by their syntax.

Walther, van der Hoek, and Wooldridge extended ATL with explicit strategies and gave its complete axiomatization [18]. In this logic, it is possible to express properties of computation paths, but knowledge modality is missing. Decidability and model checking problems for ATL-like systems have also been widely studied [2,4,5]. Deuser and Naumov [9] proposed a trimodal logical system that can express the strategic ability of coalitions to learn from their experience. It uses the formula $[s]\varphi$ to mean that "φ will be true after the strategy s is executed". The strategy s in their paper is a one-step strategy, and in this paper, we call it a joint coalition action. They also have a modality to refer to the past, while the system in the current paper cannot. The interplay between coalition action and coalition distributed knowledge, such as the property of perfect recall, is not discussed in [9], which is present in the logic in this paper. Perfect recall, which is also called *no forgetting* in temporal logic literature, is an important property in reasoning about planning under uncertainty (see [12]). Moreover, by being restricted within finite agents and finite actions, this paper gives an axiomatic system that is strongly complete, while in [9], it is shown that their system is not strongly complete to models that have actions explicitly mentioned in the language.

This paper presents a logic framework for reasoning in coalition planning. By coalition planning, we mean multi-agent planning based on synchronous models. The rest of this article is structured as follows. The next section introduces the syntax and the formal semantics of the logical system. Section 3 proposes a deductive system and shows that the system is sound and strongly complete. Section 4 defines the coalition planning problem in this logic framework and shows that the plan-existence problem of coalition planning is in PTIME. Section 5 concludes with some remarks.

2 Language and Semantics

Let **P** be a non-empty set of propositional letters, let **I** be a finite set of agents, and let **A** be a finite set of actions. A subset G of **I** is called a coalition.

Definition 1. *Given a coalition $G \subseteq \mathbf{I}$, each function $\sigma \in \mathbf{A}^G$ is called a* joint G-action *(or simply joint action). A joint **I**-action is also called a* full joint action.

Let σ be a joint action. We use $dom(\sigma)$ to denote the domain of the function σ. Let G be a coalition. We use $\overline{G}$ to denote the agent set $\mathbf{I} \setminus G$. Hence, $\mathbf{A}^{\overline{G}}$ is the set of joint $\overline{G}$-actions.

Definition 2. *The language $\mathcal{L}$ is defined by the following BNF rules:*

$$\varphi ::= p \mid \neg\varphi \mid (\varphi \wedge \varphi) \mid \mathcal{K}_G\varphi \mid [\sigma]\varphi$$

where $p \in \mathbf{P}$, $\sigma \in \mathbf{A}^G$ and $\emptyset \neq G \subseteq \mathbf{I}$.

The auxiliary boolean connectives $\rightarrow, \vee$ are defined as abbreviations as usual. The modality $\langle \cdot \rangle$ is defined as $\neg[\cdot]\neg$.

The epistemic formula $\mathcal{K}_G\varphi$ is the distributed-knowledge formula in epistemic logic, which reads that the coalition G together knows that φ holds. The action formula $[\sigma]\varphi$ reads that the joint coalition action σ will make sure that φ holds.

Definition 3. *A model $\mathcal{M}$, also called an epistemic transition system, is a tuple $(W, \{\sim_i \mid i \in \mathbf{I}\}, R, V)$ where*

- *W is a non-empty set of states;*
- *$\sim_i$ is an equivalence relation on W for each $i \in \mathbf{I}$;*
- *$R \subseteq W \times \mathbf{A}^\mathbf{I} \times W$ is a transition relation where for each $w \in W$ and each $\delta \in \mathbf{A}^\mathbf{I}$, there is a state $w' \in W$ such that $(w, \delta, w') \in R$;*
- *$V : \mathbf{P} \rightarrow \mathcal{P}(W)$ is a valuation function.*

For each $w \in W$, the pair $(\mathcal{M}, w)$ is a pointed model.

Let G be a coalition. We use $\sim_G$ to denote the equivalence relation $\bigcap_{i \in G} \sim_i$.

The following definition extends the transition relation R from the set of joint $\mathbf{I}$-actions to the set of all joint G-actions, where $G \subseteq \mathbf{I}$.

Definition 4. *Let Σ be the set of all joint actions, that is, $\Sigma = \bigcup_{G \subseteq \mathbf{I}} \mathbf{A}^G$. Given a model $\mathcal{M} = (W, \{\sim_i \mid i \in \mathbf{I}\}, R, V)$, the transition relation R in $\mathcal{M}$ can be extended to be a relation on $W \times \Sigma \times W$ by the following way:*

$$(w, \sigma, w') \in R \iff \text{there exists } \delta \in \mathbf{A}^\mathbf{I} : \sigma \subseteq \delta \text{ and } (w, \delta, w') \in R.$$

We also use $w \xrightarrow{\sigma} w'$ to denote $(w, \sigma, w') \in R$.

Proposition 1. *Let σ be a joint G-action and τ be a joint G'-action. If $\sigma \cup \tau$ is a function, then in any model $\mathcal{M}$ we have that $\xrightarrow{\sigma \cup \tau} \subseteq (\xrightarrow{\sigma} \cap \xrightarrow{\tau})$.*

Proof. Given two states $w, w' \in W$ with $w \xrightarrow{\sigma \cup \tau} w'$, we will show that $w \xrightarrow{\sigma} w'$ and $w \xrightarrow{\tau} w'$. Because of $w \xrightarrow{\sigma \cup \tau} w'$, it follows that there exists $\delta \in \mathbf{A}^\mathbf{I}$ such that $(\sigma \cup \tau) \subseteq \delta$ and $w \xrightarrow{\delta} w'$. Due to $(\sigma \cup \tau) \subseteq \delta$, it follows that $\sigma \subseteq \delta$ and $\tau \subseteq \delta$. Hence, we have that $w \xrightarrow{\sigma} w'$ and $w \xrightarrow{\tau} w'$.

Please note that the other direction of Proposition 1 is not true. That is $(\xrightarrow{\sigma} \cap \xrightarrow{\tau}) \not\subseteq \xrightarrow{\sigma \cup \tau}$. Consider the following example:

Example 1. Let the model $\mathcal{M}$ be depicted as Fig. 1. The sequence '01' in the picture represents the joint action: the first agent chooses to do the action '0' and the second agent chooses to do the action '1'. Let σ be the function that the first agent chooses to do the action '0', and let τ be the function that the second agent also chooses to do the action '0'. Then, $\sigma \cup \tau$ is the joint action '00'. It can be seen from the figure that $w \xrightarrow{\sigma} w'$ and $w \xrightarrow{\tau} w'$, but $w \xcancel{\xrightarrow{\sigma \cup \tau}} w'$.

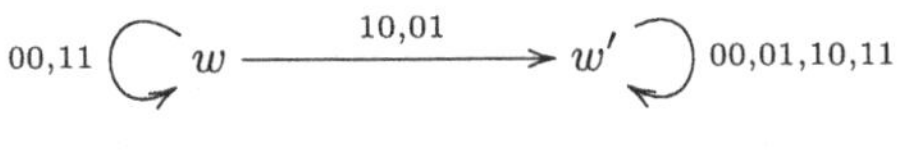

$$00,11 \circlearrowleft w \xrightarrow{10,01} w' \circlearrowright 00,01,10,11$$

Fig. 1. $\mathcal{M}$

Perfect recall is a natural property that involves the interaction between the epistemic relation and the transition relation. Intuitively, it means that if the coalition cannot distinguish two states after doing the joint action σ then it could not distinguish them before. In this paper, we will restrict ourselves to models with perfect recall.

Definition 5. *Given a model $\mathcal{M}$, we say that coalitions in $\mathcal{M}$ have* perfect recall*, iff the following statement holds: for each coalition G and each joint G-action σ, if $w \xrightarrow{\sigma} v$ and $v \sim_G v'$ then there exists a state $w' \in W$ such that $w \sim_G w'$ and $w' \xrightarrow{\sigma} v'$.*

Definition 6. *For any state $w \in W$ of a model $\mathcal{M} = (W, \{\sim_i | i \in \mathbf{I}\}, R, V)$ and any formula $\varphi \in \mathcal{L}$, the satisfaction relation $\mathcal{M}, w \vDash \varphi$ is defined as follows:*

- $\mathcal{M}, w \vDash p$ *iff* $w \in V(p)$;
- $\mathcal{M}, w \vDash \neg \varphi$ *iff* $\mathcal{M}, w \nvDash \varphi$;
- $\mathcal{M}, w \vDash \varphi \wedge \psi$ *iff* $\mathcal{M}, w \vDash \varphi$ *and* $\mathcal{M}, w \vDash \psi$;
- $\mathcal{M}, w \vDash K_G \varphi$ *iff for each state $w' \in W$, if $w \sim_G w'$ then $\mathcal{M}, w' \vDash \varphi$;*
- $\mathcal{M}, w \vDash [\sigma]\varphi$ *iff for each state $w' \in W$, if $w \xrightarrow{\sigma} w'$ then $\mathcal{M}, w' \vDash \varphi$.*

The remaining part of this section will show some valid formulas, which reflect the features of reasoning in coalition planning.

The following formula states that if the joint action σ can ensure φ and the joint action τ can ensure ψ and $\sigma \cup \tau$ is a well-defined joint action, then $\sigma \cup \tau$ can ensure $\varphi \wedge \psi$.

Proposition 2. $\vDash [\sigma]\varphi \wedge [\tau]\psi \rightarrow [\sigma \cup \tau](\varphi \wedge \psi)$ *where $\sigma \cup \tau$ is a function.*

Proof. Let $\mathcal{M}, w \vDash [\sigma]\varphi \wedge [\tau]\psi$ and $\sigma \cup \tau$ be a function, which means that $\sigma \cup \tau$ is also a joint action. We will show that $\mathcal{M}, w \vDash [\sigma \cup \tau](\varphi \wedge \psi)$. Assume that $\mathcal{M}, w \nvDash [\sigma \cup \tau](\varphi \wedge \psi)$. By the semantics, it follows that there exists a state w' such that $w \xrightarrow{\sigma \cup \tau} w'$ and $\mathcal{M}, w' \nvDash \varphi \wedge \psi$.

By Proposition 1, we know that $\xrightarrow{\sigma \cup \tau} \subseteq (\xrightarrow{\sigma} \cap \xrightarrow{\tau})$. Because of $w \xrightarrow{\sigma \cup \tau} w'$, it follows that $w \xrightarrow{\sigma} w'$ and $w \xrightarrow{\tau} w'$. Since $\mathcal{M}, w \models [\sigma]\varphi$ and $w \xrightarrow{\sigma} w'$, it follows that $\mathcal{M}, w' \models \varphi$.

Moreover, since $\mathcal{M}, w \models [\tau]\psi$ and $w \xrightarrow{\tau} w'$, it follows that $\mathcal{M}, w' \models \psi$. Hence, we have that $\mathcal{M}, w' \models \varphi \wedge \psi$. Contradiction! Thus, $\mathcal{M}, w \models [\sigma \cup \tau](\varphi \wedge \psi)$.

The following formula states that if a small joint action σ can ensure φ then each of its extensions τ can also ensure φ.

Proposition 3. $\models [\sigma]\varphi \to [\tau]\varphi$ where $\sigma \subseteq \tau$.

Proof. Let $\mathcal{M}, w \models [\sigma]\varphi$, then we will show that $\mathcal{M}, w \models [\tau]\varphi$. Assume that $\mathcal{M}, w \not\models [\tau]\varphi$. By the semantics, it follows that there exists a state w' such that $w \xrightarrow{\tau} w'$ and $\mathcal{M}, w' \not\models \varphi$.

Moreover, because of $\sigma \subseteq \tau$, we then have that $w \xrightarrow{\sigma} w'$. Due to $\mathcal{M}, w' \not\models \varphi$, it follows by the semantics that $\mathcal{M}, w \not\models [\sigma]\varphi$. Contradiction! Hence, we have that $\mathcal{M}, w \models [\tau]\varphi$.

Let σ be a joint G-action. The following formula states that if for each $\tau \in \mathbf{A}^{\overline{G}}$, the full joint action $\sigma \cup \tau$ can ensure a formula φ_τ then the joint G-action σ can ensure the disjunction of all such φ_τ.

Proposition 4. $\models \bigwedge_{\tau \in \mathbf{A}^{\overline{G}}} [\sigma \cup \tau] p_\tau \to [\sigma] \bigvee_{\tau \in \mathbf{A}^{\overline{G}}} p_\tau$ where σ is a joint G-action.

Proof. Let $\mathcal{M}, w \models \bigwedge_{\tau \in \mathbf{A}^{\overline{G}}} [\sigma \cup \tau] p_\tau$. We are going to show that $\mathcal{M}, w \models [\sigma] \bigvee_{\tau \in \mathbf{A}^{\overline{G}}} p_\tau$.

Suppose that $\mathcal{M}, w \not\models [\sigma] \bigvee_{\tau \in \mathbf{A}^{\overline{G}}} p_\tau$. It follows that there is a state v such that $w \xrightarrow{\sigma} v$ and $\mathcal{M}, v \not\models \bigvee_{\tau \in \mathbf{A}^{\overline{G}}} p_\tau$.

Due to $w \xrightarrow{\sigma} v$, by Definition 4, it follows that there exists $\tau' \in \mathbf{A}^{\overline{G}}$ such that $w \xrightarrow{\sigma \cup \tau'} v$.

Moreover, due to $\mathcal{M}, w \models \bigwedge_{\tau \in \mathbf{A}^{\overline{G}}} [\sigma \cup \tau] p_\tau$, we then have that $\mathcal{M}, w \models [\sigma \cup \tau'] p_{\tau'}$, and then $\mathcal{M}, v \models p_{\tau'}$.

However, because of $\mathcal{M}, v \not\models \bigvee_{\tau \in \mathbf{A}^{\overline{G}}} p_\tau$, it follows that $\mathcal{M}, v \not\models p_{\tau'}$. Contradiction!

The other direction of Proposition 4 does not hold. For example, it might be the case that $\mathcal{M}, w \models [\sigma](p_1 \vee p_2)$, but for each $\tau \in \mathbf{A}^{\overline{G}}$, $\mathcal{M}, w \not\models [\sigma \cup \tau] p_1$ and $\mathcal{M}, w \not\models [\sigma \cup \tau] p_2$.

The following formula states the property of perfect recall.

Proposition 5. $\models \mathcal{K}_G[\sigma]\varphi \to [\sigma]\mathcal{K}_G\varphi$ where σ be a joint G-action.

Proof. Let $\mathcal{M}, w \models \mathcal{K}_G[\sigma]\varphi$, then we will show that $\mathcal{M}, w \models [\sigma]\mathcal{K}_G\varphi$. Assume that $\mathcal{M}, w \not\models [\sigma]\mathcal{K}_G\varphi$. By the semantics, it follows that there are states v and v' such that $w \xrightarrow{\sigma} v$, $v \sim_G v'$ and $\mathcal{M}, v' \models \neg\varphi$.

By the property of perfect recall, we then have that there exists a state w' such that $w \sim_G w'$ and $w' \xrightarrow{\sigma} v'$. Moreover, due to $\mathcal{M}, v' \models \neg\varphi$, by the semantics, we then have that $\mathcal{M}, w \not\models \mathcal{K}_G[\sigma]\varphi$. Contradiction! Hence, we have that $\mathcal{M}, w \models [\sigma]\mathcal{K}_G\varphi$.

3 Proof System

This section proposes a deductive system and shows its completeness.

Definition 7. *The* deductive system $\mathbb{S}$ *consists of axioms and rules in Table 1.*

Proposition 6 (A3'). $\vdash \langle\sigma\rangle p \to \bigvee_{\tau \in \mathbf{A}^{\overline{G}}} \langle\sigma \cup \tau\rangle p$ *where* $dom(\sigma) = G$.

Table 1. The deductive system $\mathbb{S}$

Axioms

TAUT	all tautologies of propositional logic
DIST$_\mathcal{K}$	$\mathcal{K}_G(p \to q) \to (\mathcal{K}_G p \to \mathcal{K}_G q)$
DIST$_\sigma$	$[\sigma](p \to q) \to ([\sigma]p \to [\sigma]q)$
T	$\mathcal{K}_G p \to p$
4	$\mathcal{K}_G p \to \mathcal{K}_G \mathcal{K}_G p$
5	$\neg \mathcal{K}_G p \to \mathcal{K}_G \neg \mathcal{K}_G p$
A1	$\mathcal{K}_G \varphi \to \mathcal{K}_{G'} \varphi$ where $G \subseteq G'$
A2	$[\sigma]p \to [\tau]p$ where $\sigma \subseteq \tau$
A3	$\bigwedge_{\tau \in \mathbf{A}^{\overline{G}}}[\sigma \cup \tau]p_\tau \to [\sigma]\bigvee_{\tau \in \mathbf{A}^{\overline{G}}} p_\tau$ where $dom(\sigma) = G$
PR	$\mathcal{K}_G[\sigma]p \to [\sigma]\mathcal{K}_G p$ where $dom(\sigma) = G$

Rules

MP	$\dfrac{\varphi, \varphi \to \psi}{\psi}$	SUB	$\dfrac{\varphi}{\varphi[\psi/p]}$
NEC$_\mathcal{K}$	$\dfrac{\varphi}{\mathcal{K}_G \varphi}$	NEC$_\sigma$	$\dfrac{\varphi}{[\sigma]\varphi}$

Proof By substituting all the propositional letters p_τ in the axiom A3 with p, we get $\vdash \bigwedge_{\tau \in \mathbf{A}^{\overline{G}}}[\sigma \cup \tau]p \to [\sigma]p$. Then, by using rules in propositional logic, we can have that $\vdash \langle\sigma\rangle p \to \bigvee_{\tau \in \mathbf{A}^{\overline{G}}} \langle\sigma \cup \tau\rangle p$ where $dom(\sigma) = G$.

From the proof above, it can be seen that the formula $\langle\sigma\rangle p \to \bigvee_{\tau \in \mathbf{A}^{\overline{G}}} \langle\sigma \cup \tau\rangle p$ is a special case of the axiom A3. We will use A3' to denote this formula.

Proposition 7. $\vdash [\sigma]p \wedge [\tau]q \to [\sigma \cup \tau](p \wedge q)$ *where* $\sigma \cup \tau$ *is a function.*

Proof.

(1) $\vdash [\sigma]p \to [\sigma \cup \tau]p$,   A2
(2) $\vdash [\tau]q \to [\sigma \cup \tau]q$,   A2
(3) $\vdash [\sigma]p \wedge [\tau]q \to [\sigma \cup \tau]p \wedge [\sigma \cup \tau]q$,   due to (1), (2)
(4) $\vdash [\sigma \cup \tau]p \wedge [\sigma \cup \tau]q \to [\sigma \cup \tau](p \wedge q)$,   due to DIST$_\sigma$, NEC$_\sigma$
(5) $\vdash [\sigma]p \wedge [\tau]q \to [\sigma \cup \tau](p \wedge q)$,   due to (3), (4)

The remaining part of this section will show that the deductive system is complete for models with perfect recall. To do this, we will build a canonical model and show the truth lemma, as in [6].

Since the epistemic formula of distributed knowledge is included in our framework, we will build the canonical model based on epistemic paths of maximal consistent sets (see [10]).

Definition 8. *An* epistemic path *is a mixed sequence of maximal $\mathbb{S}$-consistent sets and subsets of* **I**, *which is defined as follows:*

- *For each maximal $\mathbb{S}$-consistent set X, X is an epistemic path;*
- *Let $X_0 \ldots X_n$ be an epistemic path, Y be a maximal consistent set, and G be a subset of* **I**. *If $\varphi \in Y$ for all $\mathcal{K}_G \varphi \in X_n$, then $X_0 \ldots X_n GY$ is also an epistemic path.*

It is obvious that each epistemic path is a finite sequence. Let s be an epistemic path. We use $fnl(s)$ to denote the final element in the sequence s, which is always a maximal consistent set.

Definition 9. *For each agent $i \in$* **I**, *the* indistinguishability relation $\sim_i^G$ *is a binary relation on the set of epistemic paths, which is defined as follows: for any epistemic paths $s = X_0, G_1, X_1, G_2, \ldots, G_n, X_n$ and $s' = X_0, G_1', X_1', G_2', \ldots, G_m', X_m'$, $s \sim_i^c s'$ iff there is an integer k such that*

- $0 \leq k \leq \min\{n, m\}$,
- $X_l = X_l'$ *for each l such that $0 \leq l \leq k$,*
- $G_l = G_l'$ *for each l such that $0 \leq l \leq k$,*
- $i \in G_l$ *for each l such that $k < l \leq n$,*
- $i \in G_l'$ *for each l such that $k < l \leq m$.*

It is easy to check that $\sim_i^G$ is an equivalence relation.

Definition 10. *The* canonical model $\mathcal{M}^c = (W^c, \{\sim_i^c | \ i \in$ **I**$\}, R^c, V^c)$ *is defined as follows:*

- *W is the set of all epistemic paths;*
- *for each $i \in$* **I**, *the equivalence relation $\sim_i^c$ is defined in Definition 9;*
- *for each full joint action $\delta \in$* **A**$^{\mathbf{I}}$, $(s, \delta, s') \in R^c$ *iff $\varphi \in fnl(s')$ for all $[\delta]\varphi \in fnl(s)$;*
- *for each $p \in$* **P**, $s \in V^c(p)$ *iff $p \in fnl(s)$.*

The following proposition and lemma can be proved in the same way as in [6,10].

Proposition 8. *If $\mathcal{K}_G \varphi \in fnl(s)$, then $\varphi \in fnl(s')$ for each s' with $s \sim_G^c s'$.*

Lemma 1 (Existence lemma for $\mathcal{K}$). *If $\neg \mathcal{K}_G \varphi \in fnl(s)$, then there is an epistemic path s' such that $s \sim_G^c s'$ and $\neg \varphi \in fnl(s')$.*

Next, we will show the existence lemma for $[\cdot]$-formulas.

Lemma 2 (Existence lemma for $[\cdot]$). *If $\langle\sigma\rangle\varphi \in fnl(s)$, then there is an epistemic path s' such that $s \xrightarrow{\sigma} s'$ and $\varphi \in fnl(s')$.*

Proof. Because of $\langle\sigma\rangle\varphi \in fnl(s)$, by the theorem A3', it follows that there exists a full joint action $\delta \in \mathbf{A}^\mathbf{I}$ such that $\sigma \subseteq \delta$ and $\langle\delta\rangle\varphi \in fnl(s)$.

Let Δ be the following set:
$$\Delta = \Delta' \cup \{\varphi\} \text{ where } \Delta' = \{\psi \mid [\delta]\psi \in fnl(s)\}.$$

Suppose that Δ is not consistent. It follows that there are finitely many formulas $\psi_1, \ldots, \psi_n \in \Delta'$ such that
$$\vdash \psi_1 \wedge \cdots \wedge \psi_n \to \neg\varphi.$$

By the rule NEC_δ, we then have that
$$\vdash [\delta](\psi_1 \wedge \cdots \wedge \psi_n \to \neg\varphi).$$

By the axiom DIST_δ and the rules SUB and MP, it follows that
$$\vdash [\delta](\psi_1 \wedge \cdots \wedge \psi_n) \to [\delta]\neg\varphi. \tag{1}$$

Due to the axiom DIST_δ and the rule NEC_δ, we know that the modality $[\cdot]$ is a normal modality. Hence, we have that
$$\vdash [\delta](\psi_1 \wedge \cdots \wedge \psi_n) \leftrightarrow [\delta]\psi_1 \wedge \cdots \wedge [\delta]\psi_n. \tag{2}$$

From (1) and (2), it can be derived that
$$\vdash [\delta]\psi_1 \wedge \cdots \wedge [\delta]\psi_n \to [\delta]\neg\varphi.$$

Since $\psi_1, \ldots, \psi_n \in \Delta'$, it follows that $fnl(s) \vdash [\delta]\psi_1 \wedge \cdots \wedge [\delta]\psi_n$. We then have that
$$fnl(s) \vdash [\delta]\neg\varphi.$$

This contradicts the fact that $\langle\delta\rangle\varphi \in fnl(s)$ and $fnl(s)$ is consistent. Thus, we have shown that Δ is consistent.

By Lindenbaum's lemma, it follows that there is a maximal consistent set X such that $\Delta \subseteq X$. It follows that $\varphi \in X$. Moreover, X is an epistemic path, and $s \xrightarrow{\delta} X$. Because of $\sigma \subseteq \delta$, it follows that $s \xrightarrow{\sigma} X$.

Proposition 9. *Let σ be a joint G-action and s be an epistemic path. If $[\sigma]\varphi \in fnl(s)$, then for each s' with $s \xrightarrow{\sigma} s'$ we have that $\varphi \in fnl(s')$.*

Proof. Given $[\sigma]\varphi \in fnl(s)$ and $s \xrightarrow{\sigma} s'$, we will show that $\varphi \in fnl(s')$.

Due to $s \xrightarrow{\sigma} s'$, it follows that there exists a full joint action $\delta \in \mathbf{A}^\mathbf{I}$ such that $s \xrightarrow{\delta} s'$ and $\sigma \subseteq \delta$.

Because of $\sigma \subseteq \delta$ and $[\sigma]\varphi \in fnl(s)$, it follows by the axiom A2 that $[\delta]\varphi \in fnl(s)$.

Moreover, due to $[\delta]\varphi \in fnl(s)$ and $s \xrightarrow{\delta} s'$, by the definition of the canonical model $\mathcal{M}^c$, it follows $\varphi \in fnl(s')$.

Lemma 3 (Truth lemma). $\mathcal{M}^c, s \vDash \varphi$ iff $\varphi \in fnl(s)$.

Proof. We prove it by induction on φ. We will only focus on the cases of modal formulas; the other cases are straightforward.

Case of $\mathcal{K}_G\varphi$:

Left-to-Right: Given $\mathcal{M}^c, s \vDash \mathcal{K}_G\varphi$, we will show that $\mathcal{K}_G\varphi \in fnl(s)$. Assume that $\mathcal{K}_G\varphi \notin fnl(s)$. Since $fnl(s)$ is a maximal consistent set, it follows that $\neg\mathcal{K}_G\varphi \in fnl(s)$.

By Lemma 1, we then have that there exists an epistemic path s' such that $s \sim_G^c s'$ and $\neg\varphi \in fnl(s')$. By IH, it follows that $\mathcal{M}^c, s' \nvDash \varphi$. This contradicts the fact that $\mathcal{M}^c, s \vDash \mathcal{K}_G\varphi$ and $s \sim_G^c s'$. Hence, we have shown that $\mathcal{K}_G\varphi \in fnl(s)$.

Right-to-Left: Given $\mathcal{K}_G\varphi \in fnl(s)$, we will show that $\mathcal{M}^c, s \vDash \mathcal{K}_G\varphi$. Assume that $\mathcal{M}^c, s \nvDash \mathcal{K}_G\varphi$. It follows that there exists an epistemic path s' such that $s \sim_G^c s'$ and $\mathcal{M}^c, s' \nvDash \varphi$.

Because of $s \sim_G^c s'$ and $\mathcal{K}_G\varphi \in fnl(s)$, by Proposition 8, it follows that $\varphi \in fnl(s')$. Due to $\mathcal{M}^c, s' \nvDash \varphi$, by IH, it then follows that $\varphi \notin fnl(s')$. Contradiction! Hence, we have that $\mathcal{M}^c, s \vDash \mathcal{K}_G\varphi$.

Case of $[\sigma]\varphi$:

Left-to-Right: Given $\mathcal{M}^c, s \vDash [\sigma]\varphi$, we will show that $[\sigma]\varphi \in fnl(s)$. Assume that $[\sigma]\varphi \notin fnl(s)$. It follows that $\neg[\sigma]\varphi \in fnl(s)$, namely $\langle\sigma\rangle\neg\varphi \in fnl(s)$.

By Lemma 2, it then follows that there exists an epistemic path s' such that $s \xrightarrow{\sigma} s'$ and $\neg\varphi \in fnl(s')$. Since $fnl(s')$ is maximal consistent, it follows that $\varphi \notin fnl(s')$.

By IH, we then have that $\mathcal{M}^c, s' \nvDash \varphi$. Due to $s \xrightarrow{\sigma} s'$, this means that $\mathcal{M}^c, s \nvDash [\sigma]\varphi$. This contradicts the fact that $\mathcal{M}^c, s \vDash [\sigma]\varphi$. Hence, $[\sigma]\varphi \in fnl(s)$.

Right-to-Left: Given $[\sigma]\varphi \in fnl(s)$, we will show that $\mathcal{M}^c, s \vDash [\sigma]\varphi$. Assume that $\mathcal{M}^c, s \nvDash [\sigma]\varphi$. It follows that there exists an epistemic path such that $s \xrightarrow{\sigma} s'$ and $\mathcal{M}^c, s' \nvDash \varphi$.

Due to $s \xrightarrow{\sigma} s'$ and $[\sigma]\varphi \in fnl(s)$, by Proposition 9, it follows that $\varphi \in fnl(s')$. Moreover, due to $\mathcal{M}^c, s' \nvDash \varphi$, by IH, we then have that $\varphi \notin fnl(s')$. Contradiction! Hence, we have that $\mathcal{M}^c, s \vDash [\sigma]\varphi$.

To show the completeness, we still need to show that the canonical model has the property of perfect recall. Before that, we first show two auxiliary propositions.

Proposition 10. *Let X, Y be maximal consistent sets and σ be a joint G-action. We have that $\{\varphi \mid [\sigma]\varphi \in X\} \subseteq Y$ iff $\{\langle\sigma\rangle\varphi \mid \varphi \in Y\} \subseteq X$.*

Proof. $\Rightarrow$: If $\langle\sigma\rangle\varphi \notin X$ for some $\varphi \in Y$, then we have $[\sigma]\neg\varphi \in X$. It follows that $\neg\varphi \in Y$. Contradiction!

$\Leftarrow$: If $\varphi \notin Y$ for some $[\sigma]\varphi \in X$, then we have $\neg\varphi \in Y$. It follows that $\langle\sigma\rangle\neg\varphi \in X$, and then $\neg[\sigma]\varphi \in X$. Contradiction!

Proposition 11. *Let X, Y be maximal consistent sets and σ be a joint G-action. If $\{\langle\sigma\rangle\varphi \mid \varphi \in Y\} \subseteq X$, then there is a full joint $\delta \in \mathbf{A}^I$ such that $\sigma \subseteq \delta$ and $\{\langle\delta\rangle\varphi \mid \varphi \in Y\} \subseteq X$.*

Proof. Suppose not. It follows that for each $\delta \in \mathbf{A}^\mathbf{I}$, if $\sigma \subseteq \delta$, then there exists $\varphi \in Y$ such that $\langle \delta \rangle \varphi \notin X$.

Note that σ is a joint G-action. Let $\{\tau_1, \ldots, \tau_n\}$ be the set $\mathbf{A}^{\overline{G}}$ of all joint $\overline{G}$-actions. We then have that for each $\tau_i \in \mathbf{A}^{\overline{G}}$, there exists a formula $\varphi_i \in Y$ such that $\langle \sigma \cup \tau_i \rangle \varphi_i \notin X$, and then $[\sigma \cup \tau_i] \neg \varphi_i \in X$.

Hence, for each $\tau_i \in \mathbf{A}^{\overline{G}}$, we have that $[\sigma \cup \tau_i] \neg \varphi_i \in X$. By the axiom A3, we have that $[\sigma](\neg \varphi_1 \vee \cdots \vee \neg \varphi_n) \in X$.

Moreover, due to $\{\langle \sigma \rangle \varphi \mid \varphi \in Y\} \subseteq X$, by Proposition 10, it follows that $\{\varphi \mid [\sigma]\varphi \in X\} \subseteq Y$. Thus, we have that $(\neg \varphi_1 \vee \cdots \vee \neg \varphi_n) \in Y$. This contradicts the fact that $\varphi_1, \ldots, \varphi_n \in Y$.

Thus, we have shown that there exists some $\tau_i \in \mathbf{A}^{\overline{G}}$ such that $\{\langle \sigma \cup \tau_i \rangle \varphi \mid \varphi \in Y\} \subseteq X$.

Proposition 12. *Coalitions in $\mathcal{M}^c$ have perfect recall.*

Proof. Let σ be a joint G-action σ. Given $s \xrightarrow{\sigma} t$ and $t \sim_G^c t'$, we will show that there exists a state $s' \in W$ such that $s \sim_G^c s'$ and $s' \xrightarrow{\sigma} t'$.

Let Δ be the following set:

$$\Delta = \Delta_1 \cup \Delta_2$$
$$\Delta_1 = \{\varphi \mid \mathcal{K}_G \varphi \in fnl(s)\}$$
$$\Delta_2 = \{\langle \sigma \rangle \psi \mid \psi \in fnl(t')\}.$$

Suppose that Δ is not consistent. It follows that there are $\varphi_1, \ldots, \varphi_n \in \Delta_1$ and $\langle \sigma \rangle \psi_1, \ldots, \langle \sigma \rangle \psi_m \in \Delta_2$ such that

$$\vdash \varphi_1 \wedge \cdots \wedge \varphi_n \rightarrow [\sigma]\neg\psi_1 \vee \cdots \vee [\sigma]\neg\psi_m. \tag{3}$$

Due to the axiom DIST_σ and the rule NEC_σ, we know that the modality $[\cdot]$ is a normal modality. Hence, we have that

$$\vdash [\sigma]\neg\psi_1 \vee \cdots \vee [\sigma]\neg\psi_m \rightarrow [\sigma](\neg\psi_1 \vee \cdots \vee \neg\psi_m). \tag{4}$$

By (3) and (4), we have

$$\vdash \varphi_1 \wedge \cdots \wedge \varphi_n \rightarrow [\sigma](\neg\psi_1 \vee \cdots \vee \neg\psi_m).$$

By the rules $\text{NEC}_\mathcal{K}$ and MP and the axiom $\text{DIST}_\mathcal{K}$, we have

$$\vdash \mathcal{K}_G(\varphi_1 \wedge \cdots \wedge \varphi_n) \rightarrow \mathcal{K}_G[\sigma](\neg\psi_1 \vee \cdots \vee \neg\psi_m). \tag{5}$$

Due to the axiom $\text{DIST}_\mathcal{K}$ and the rule $\text{NEC}_\mathcal{K}$, we know that the modality $\mathcal{K}_G$ is a normal modality. Thus, by (5), it follows that

$$\vdash \mathcal{K}_G\varphi_1 \wedge \cdots \wedge \mathcal{K}_G\varphi_n \rightarrow \mathcal{K}_G[\sigma](\neg\psi_1 \vee \cdots \vee \neg\psi_m). \tag{6}$$

Moreover, by the axiom PR, we have that

$$\vdash \mathcal{K}_G[\sigma](\neg\psi_1 \vee \cdots \vee \neg\psi_M) \rightarrow [\sigma]\mathcal{K}_G(\neg\psi_1 \vee \cdots \vee \neg\psi_m). \tag{7}$$

By (6) and (7), it follows that

$$\vdash \mathcal{K}_G\varphi_1 \wedge \cdots \wedge \mathcal{K}_G\varphi_n \to [\sigma]\mathcal{K}_G(\neg\psi_1 \vee \cdots \vee \neg\psi_m).$$

By the definition of Δ_1, we know that $\mathcal{K}_G\varphi_1, \ldots, \mathcal{K}_G\varphi_n \in fnl(s)$. It follows that $[\sigma]\mathcal{K}_G(\neg\psi_1 \vee \cdots \vee \neg\psi_m) \in fnl(s)$. Due to $s \xrightarrow{\sigma} t$, by Proposition 9, it follows that $\mathcal{K}_G(\neg\psi_1 \vee \cdots \vee \neg\psi_m) \in fnl(t)$. Furthermore, due to $t \sim_G^c t'$, by Proposition 8, it follows that $(\neg\psi_1 \vee \cdots \vee \neg\psi_m) \in fnl(t')$. However, by the definition of Δ_2, we know that $\psi_1, \ldots, \psi_m \in fnl(t')$. Contradiction! Hence, we have shown that Δ is consistent.

Since Δ is consistent, by Lindenbaum's lemma, there is a maximal consistent set X such that $\Delta \subseteq X$. By Definition 8, we know that sGX is an epistemic path. Moreover, by Definition 9, we know that $s \sim_G^c sGX$.

To show the perfect-recall property, we still need to show that $sGX \xrightarrow{\sigma} t'$. Due to $\Delta_2 \subseteq \Delta$ and $\Delta \subseteq X$, we already know that $\{\langle\sigma\rangle\psi \mid \psi \in fnl(t')\} \subseteq X$. By Proposition 11, it follows that there exists a full joint action $\delta \in \mathbf{A}^\mathbf{I}$ such that $\sigma \subseteq \delta$ and $\{\langle\delta\rangle\psi \mid \psi \in fnl(t')\} \subseteq X$. By Proposition 10, we then have that $\{\psi \mid [\delta]\psi \in X\} \subseteq fnl(t')$. Then, by Definition 10, we know that $sGX \xrightarrow{\delta} t'$. Due to $\sigma \subseteq \delta$, it follows that $sGX \xrightarrow{\sigma} t'$.

Theorem 1 (Soundness and strong completeness). $\Gamma \vdash \varphi$ iff $\Gamma \vDash \varphi$.

Proof. Soundness: Propositions 3, 4, and 5 show that the axioms A2, A3, and PR are valid, respectively. It also can be checked that the other axioms are valid and that the rules preserve validity. Hence, the proof system is sound to models with perfect recall, that is, if $\Gamma \vdash \varphi$ then $\Gamma \vDash \varphi$.

Completeness: The key is to show that each maximal consistent set is satisfiable. Lemma 3 shows that each maximal consistent set is satisfiable on $\mathcal{M}^c$. Moreover, Proposition 12 shows that coalitions in $\mathcal{M}^c$ have perfect recall. Hence, the proof system is complete to models with perfect recall, that is, if $\Gamma \vDash \varphi$ then $\Gamma \vdash \varphi$.

4 Coalition Planning

This section defines coalition planning problems and shows that the plan-existence problem is in PTIME.

Given a model $\mathcal{M}$, a belief state of a group G in $\mathcal{M}$ is a set of states closed over the epistemic relation $\sim_G$.

Definition 11. *A coalition planning problem P is a tuple $\langle \mathcal{M}, G, |s_0|_G, \varphi_g \rangle$ where*

- $\mathcal{M} = (W, \{\sim_i \mid i \in \mathbf{I}\}, R, V)$ *is a finite model, which is also called a planning domain;*
- $G \subseteq \mathbf{I}$ *is a coalition;*
- $|s_0|_G$ *is the initial belief state of the coalition G;*
- $\varphi_g \in \mathcal{L}$ *is the goal formula.*

Before we define the notion of planning solution—strong solutions, we first introduce the following two auxiliary notions.

Definition 12. *Given a planning domain $\mathcal{M}$ and a coalition G, a* uniform policy *of G for $\mathcal{M}$ is a partial function from W into $\mathbf{A}^G$ such that if $s \sim_G t$ then $f(s) = f(t)$.*

A policy is a partial function rather than a total function because its execution cannot continue indefinitely and must terminate after a finite number of steps.

Definition 13. *Given a planning domain $\mathcal{M}$, a coalition G and a uniform policy f of G for $\mathcal{M}$, an* execution path *induced by f from a state $s \in W$ is a possibly infinite sequence $s = s_0, s_1, s_2, \ldots$ of states such that, for all s_i in the sequence:*

- *either s_i is the last element of the sequence,*
- *or $s_i \xrightarrow{f(s_i)} s_{i+1}$.*

We also refer to execution paths induced by f as f-paths for short. If $s_0 \ldots s_n$ is an f-path and s_n is not in the domain of f, then s_n is called a *terminal state* of f-paths from s_0. Let $\texttt{TerStas}(f, S)$ be the set of all terminal states of f-paths from states in S.

Definition 14. *A* strong solution *(or simply, solution) to a planning problem $P = \langle \mathcal{M}, |s_0|_G, G, \varphi_g \rangle$ is a uniform policy f of G for $\mathcal{M}$ such that*

- *all f-paths from states in $|s_0|_G$ are finite;*
- *$\mathcal{M}, t \vDash \varphi_g$ for all $t \in \texttt{TerStas}(f, |s_0|_G)$.*

The remaining part of this section will show that the plan-existence problem of coalition planning is in PTIME. The strategy is reducing plan-existence problem of coalition planning to plan-existence problem of single-agent conditional planning. It is already proved that plan-existence problem of single-agent conditional planning is in PTIME (see [8]).

Definition 15. *A* Single-Agent Conditional Planning *(SACP) planning problem is a tuple $\mathcal{P} = \langle \mathcal{T}, \mathcal{I}, \mathcal{G} \rangle$ where*

- *$\mathcal{T} = \langle \mathcal{S}, \mathcal{A}, \mathcal{R} \rangle$ is a transition system where*
  - *$\mathcal{S}$ is a finite set of states;*
  - *$\mathcal{A}$ is a finite set of actions;*
  - *$\mathcal{R} \subseteq \mathcal{S} \times \mathcal{A} \times \mathcal{S}$ is a transition relation;*
- *$\mathcal{I} \subseteq \mathcal{S}$ is the set of initial states;*
- *$\mathcal{G} \subseteq \mathcal{S}$ is the set of goal states.*

Definition 16. *Let* $\mathcal{T} = \langle \mathcal{S}, \mathcal{A}, \mathcal{R} \rangle$ *be an SACP planning domain.*

An SACP *policy* $\mathfrak{f}$ *of* $\mathcal{T}$ *is a partial function from* $\mathcal{S}$ *into* $\mathcal{A}$.

An SACP *execution path induced by* $\mathfrak{f}$ *from* w *is a possibly infinite sequence* $w = w_0, w_1, w_2, \ldots$ *of states such that, for all w_i in the sequence: either w_i is the last state of the sequence, or* $(w_i, \mathfrak{f}(w_i), w_{i+1}) \in \mathcal{R}$.

Definition 17. *An* SACP *solution to an SACP planning problem* $\mathcal{P} = \langle \mathcal{T}, w_0, \mathcal{G} \rangle$ *is an SACP policy* $\mathfrak{f}$ *such that*

- *all* $\mathfrak{f}$-*paths from w_0 are finite;*
- *all terminal states of* $\mathfrak{f}$-*path from states in I are in $\mathcal{G}$.*

In Definition 19 below, we will build a SACP planning problem from a given coalition planning problem. To do that, we first build a transition system from a given model and a given coalition.

Given a model $\mathcal{M}$, $s \in W$ and a coalition $G \subseteq \mathbf{I}$, we use $|s|_G$ to denote the equivalence class of s in W, namely, the set $\{t \in W \mid s \sim_G t\}$. $W/\!\sim_G$ is the set of all equivalence classes, that is, $W/\!\sim_G = \{|s|_G \mid s \in W\}$.

Definition 18. *Given a model* $\mathcal{M} = (W, \{\sim_i \mid i \in \mathbf{I}\}, R, V)$ *and a coalition* $G \subseteq \mathbf{I}$, *the transition system based on $\mathcal{M}$ and G is the tuple* $\mathcal{T}_{\mathcal{M}}^G = \langle W/\!\sim_G, \mathbf{A}^G, \mathcal{R} \rangle$ *where* $\mathcal{R} \subseteq |W|_G \times \mathbf{A}^G \times |W|_G$ *is defined as follows:*

$$(|s|_G, \sigma, |t|_G) \in \mathcal{R} \iff \text{there exist } s' \in |s|_G, t' \in |t|_G : s' \xrightarrow{\sigma} t'.$$

We also write $|s|_G \xrightarrow{\sigma} |t|_G$ for $(|s|_G, \sigma, |t|_G) \in \mathcal{R}$.

Definition 19. *Given a coalition planning problem* $P = \langle \mathcal{M}, G, |s_0|_G, \varphi_g \rangle$, *the SACP planning problem based on P is the SACP planning problem* $P^* = \langle \mathcal{T}_{\mathcal{M}}^G, \{|s_0|_G\}, \mathcal{G} \rangle$ *where* $\mathcal{G} = \{|t|_G \in W/\!\sim_G \mid \mathcal{M}, t \vDash \varphi_g\}$.

Next, we need to show that P has a solution iff P^* has a solution (namely Lemma 4 below). Before that, we first show the following two auxiliary propositions.

Let $\mathfrak{f}$ be an SACP policy on $P^* = \langle \mathcal{T}_{\mathcal{M}}^G, \{|s_0|_G\}, \mathcal{G} \rangle$. Then, each execution path induced by $\mathfrak{f}$ is a sequence of equivalence classes in $W/\!\sim_G$. We use $\texttt{TerEC}(\mathfrak{f}, |s|_G)$ to denote the set of all terminal equivalence classes of $\mathfrak{f}$-paths from $|s|_G$.

Proposition 13. *Let* $P = (\mathcal{M}, G, |s_0|_G, \varphi_g)$ *be a coalition planning problem, and P^* is the SACP planning problem based on P. Let f be a uniform policy on P and $\mathfrak{f}$ be a SACP policy on P^*. If $f(s) = \mathfrak{f}(|s|_G)$ for each $s \in W$, then the following statements hold:*

1. *all f-paths from states in $|s_0|_G$ are finite, iff, all $\mathfrak{f}$-paths from $|s_0|_G$ are finite;*
2. $t \in \texttt{TerStas}(f, |s_0|_G)$ *iff* $|t|_G \in \texttt{TerEC}(\mathfrak{f}, |s_0|_G)$.

Proof. For (i), if there is an infinite f-path, by Definition 18, then there is an infinite $\mathfrak{f}$-path. Thus, we only need to show that if $|s_0|_G|s_1|_G\ldots$ is an infinite $\mathfrak{f}$-path, then there is an infinite f-path.

Since the planning domain $\mathcal{M}$ is finite, while $|s_0|_G|s_1|_G\ldots$ is infinite, it follows that there exist two equivalence classes $|s_i|_G$ and $|s_{i+n}|_G$ (where $n > 0$) in the infinite $\mathfrak{f}$-path such that they are the same, namely $|s_i|_G = |s_{i+n}|_G$.

Let $\mathfrak{f}(|s_j|_G) = \sigma_j$ for each $i \leq j < n$. It follows that

$$|s_i|_G \xrightarrow{\sigma_i} \cdots |s_{i+n}|_G.$$

Let $t_{i+n} \in |s_{i+n}|_G$. Due to the property of perfect recall, there are $t_j \in |s_j|_G$ for all $i \leq j < i+n$ such that

$$t_i \xrightarrow{\sigma_i} \cdots t_{i+n}.$$

Moreover, due to $t_i \in |s_i|_G$ and $|s_i|_G = |s_{i+n}|_G$, it follows that $t_i \in |s_{i+n}|_G$. Then the process above can be repeated. That is, due to the property of perfect recall, then there are $v_j \in |s_j|_G$ for all $i \leq j < i+n$ such that

$$v_i \xrightarrow{\sigma_i} \cdots t_i \xrightarrow{\sigma_i} \cdots t_{i+n}.$$

Again, because of $v_i \in |s_i|_G$ and $|s_i|_G = |s_{i+n}|_G$, then the process can be repeated once more time. This means that the process can be repeated forever. However, since $|s_i|_G$ is finite, this means there is a cyclic f-path from some state in $|s_i|_G$.

Due to the property of perfect recall, for each state x in $|s_i|_G$, there is an f-path from some state in $|s_0|_G$ to the state x.

Since we have shown that there is a cyclic f-path from some state in $|s_i|_G$, it follows that there is an infinite f-path from some state in $|s_0|_G$.

For (ii), if $t \in \texttt{TerStas}(f, |s_0|_G)$, then there are $s_1, \ldots, s_n$ such that

$$s_0 \xrightarrow{f(s_0)} s_1 \xrightarrow{f(s_1)} \cdots s_n \xrightarrow{f(s_n)} t.$$

By Definition 18, it follows that

$$|s_0|_G \xrightarrow{f(s_0)} |s_1|_G \xrightarrow{f(s_1)} \cdots |s_n|_G \xrightarrow{f(s_n)} |t|_G.$$

Due to $f(x) = \mathfrak{f}(|x|_G)$, we have that $|t|_G \in \texttt{TerEC}(\mathfrak{f}, |s_0|_G)$.

Thus, we have shown that if we have $t \in \texttt{TerStas}(f, |s_0|_G)$ then we have $|t|_G \in \texttt{TerEC}(\mathfrak{f}, |s_0|_G)$. Next, we are going to show that if $|t|_G \in \texttt{TerEC}(\mathfrak{f}, |s_0|_G)$ then $t \in \texttt{TerStas}(f, |s_0|_G)$.

If $|t|_G \in \texttt{TerEC}(\mathfrak{f}, |s_0|_G)$, then there are $|s_0|_G, \ldots, |s_n|_G$ such that

$$|s_0|_G \xrightarrow{\mathfrak{f}(|s_0|_G)} |s_1|_G \xrightarrow{\mathfrak{f}(|s_1|_G)} \cdots |s_n|_G \xrightarrow{\mathfrak{f}(|s_n|_G)} |t|_G.$$

Because of $t \in |t|_G$, by the property of perfect recall, it follows that there are $t_0 \in |s_0|_G, t_1 \in |s_1|_G, \ldots, t_n \in |s_n|_G$ such that

$$t_0 \xrightarrow{\mathfrak{f}(|s_0|_G)} s_1 \xrightarrow{\mathfrak{f}(|s_1|_G)} \cdots t_n \xrightarrow{\mathfrak{f}(|s_n|_G)} t.$$

Since $f(x) = \mathfrak{f}(|x|_G)$ and f is a uniform policy, then we have that $t \in$ TerStas$(f, |s_0|_G)$.

Lemma 4. *Let $P = \langle \mathcal{M}, G, |s_0|_G, \varphi_g \rangle$ be a coalition planning problem, and let P^* be the SACP planning problem based on P. The following statements are equivalent:*

1. *there is a strong solution to the coalition problem P;*
2. *there is an SACP solution to the SACP planning problem P^*.*

Proof. (i)⇒(ii): Let f be a strong solution to P. We define the SACP policy f^* to the SACP planning problem P^* as follows: for each $|s|_G \in W/\sim_G$, $f^*(|s|_G) = f(s)$.

By Proposition 13(i), all f^*-path from $|s_0|_G$ are finite. Thus, to show that f^* is an SACP solution to P^*, we only need to show that if $|t|_G \in$ TerEC$(f^*, |s_0|_G)$ then $\mathcal{M}, t \vDash \varphi_g$.

From $|t|_G \in$ TerEC$(f^*, |s_0|_G)$, by Proposition 13(ii), we know that $t \in$ TerStas$(f, |s_0|_G)$. Moreover, since f is a strong solution to P, it follows that $\mathcal{M}, t \vDash \varphi_g$.

(ii)⇒(i): Let $\mathfrak{f}$ be an SACP solution to the SACP planning problem P^*. We define the function $\mathfrak{f}^\bullet$ as follows: for each s, $\mathfrak{f}^\bullet(s) = \mathfrak{f}(|s|_G)$. It is obvious that $\mathfrak{f}$ is a uniform policy on the coalition planning problem P.

By Proposition 13(i), all $\mathfrak{f}^\bullet$-path from $|s_0|_G$ are finite. Thus, to show that $\mathfrak{f}^\bullet$ is a strong solution to P, we only need to show that if $t \in$ TerStas$(\mathfrak{f}^\bullet, |s_0|_G)$, then $\mathcal{M}, t \vDash \varphi_g$.

From $t \in$ TerStas$(\mathfrak{f}^\bullet, |s_0|_G)$, by Proposition 13(ii), we know that $|t|_G \in$ TerEC$(\mathfrak{f}, |s_0|_G)$. Since $\mathfrak{f}$ is a solution to P^*, it follows that $\mathcal{M}, t \vDash \varphi_g$.

Theorem 2. *The plan-existence problem of coalition planning is in PTIME in the size of the planning domain.*

Proof. Given a coalition planning problem P, let n be the size of the planning domain. Lemma 4 shows that P can be reduced to the SACP planning problem P^*. By Definition 19, we know that the size of the transition system of P^* is at most n. Moreover, the reduction can be done in PTIME, since the model checking of the logic can be done in PTIME. In [8], it is shown that the plan-existence problem of SACP planning is in PTIME in the size of the transition system. Thus, the plan-existence problem of P is in PTIME.

5 Conclusion

This paper presents a logical framework for reasoning in coalition planning. As shown in [9], if the logical language permits infinitely many agents and actions, the system fails to be strongly complete. By restricting the framework to finite agents and actions, we establish a strongly complete proof system. This paper also defines coalition planning based on the logical framework of this current paper and shows that the plan-existence problem is in PTIME.

Acknowledgement. The author is grateful to the three anonymous reviewers, whose detailed comments helped to improve the presentation of the paper. This study was funded by the Fundamental Research Funds for the Central Universities (No. 63243020).

References

1. Alur, R., Henzinger, T.A., Kupferman, O.: Alternating-time temporal logic. In: de Roever, W.P., Langmaack, H., Pnueli, A. (eds.) COMPOS. LNCS, vol. 1536, pp. 23–60. Springer (1997)
2. Aminof, B., Murano, A., Rubin, S., Zuleger, F.: Prompt alternating-time epistemic logics. In: Proceedings of the Fifteenth International Conference on Principles of Knowledge Representation and Reasoning, KR 2016, pp. 258-267. AAAI Press (2016)
3. Aucher, G.: DEL-sequents for regression and epistemic planning. J. Appl. Non-Classical Logics **22**(4), 337–367 (2012)
4. Berthon, R., Maubert, B., Murano, A.: Decidability results for ATL* with imperfect information and perfect recall. In: Proceedings of the 16th Conference on Autonomous Agents and MultiAgent Systems (Richland, SC, 2017), AAMAS 2017, International Foundation for Autonomous Agents and Multiagent Systems, pp. 1250–1258 (2017)
5. Berthon, R., Maubert, B., Murano, A., Rubin, S., Vardi, M.Y.: Strategy logic with imperfect information. ACM Trans. Comput. Logic **22**(1) (2021)
6. Blackburn, P., de Rijke, M., Venema, Y.: Modal Logic. Cambridge University Press (2002)
7. Bolander, T., Andersen, M.B.: Epistemic planning for single and multi-agent systems. J. Appl. Non-Classical Logics **21**(1), 9–34 (2011)
8. Cimatti, A., Pistore, M., Roveri, M., Traverso, P.: Weak, strong, and strong cyclic planning via symbolic model checking. Artif. Intell. **147**(1–2), 35–84 (2003)
9. Deuser, K., Naumov, P.: Strategic knowledge acquisition 17:1–17:18 (2021)
10. Fagin, R., Halpern, J., Moses, Y., Vardi, M.: Reasoning About Knowledge. MIT Press, Cambridge (1995)
11. Ghallab, M., Nau, D., Traverso, P.: Automated Planning: Theory and Practice. Morgan Kaufmann (2004)
12. Li, Y., Yu, Q., Wang, Y.: More for free: a dynamic epistemic framework for conformant planning over transition systems. J. Logic Comput. **27**(8), 2383–2410 (2017)
13. Löwe, B., Pacuit, E., Witzel, A.: DEL planning and some tractable cases. In: van Ditmarsch, H., Lang, J., Ju, S. (eds.) Logic, Rationality, and Interaction, pp. 179–192. Springer, Heidelberg (2011)
14. Naumov, P., Tao, J.: Coalition power in epistemic transition systems. In: Larson, K., Winikoff, M., Das, S., Durfee, E.H. (eds.) AAMAS, pp. 723–731. ACM (2017)
15. Osborne, M.J., Rubinstein, A.: A course in game theory. The MIT Press, Cambridge (1994). Electronic edition
16. Pardo, P., Sadrzadeh, M.: Planning in the logics of communication and change. In: van der Hoek, W., Padgham, L., Conitzer, V., Winikoff, M. (eds.) AAMAS, pp. 1231–1232. IFAAMAS (2012)
17. Pauly, M.: A modal logic for coalitional power in games. J. Log. Comput. **12**(1), 149–166 (2002)

18. Walther, D., van der Hoek, W., Wooldridge, M.: Alternating-time temporal logic with explicit strategies. In: Proceedings of the 11th Conference on Theoretical Aspects of Rationality and Knowledge, TARK 2007, pp. 269–278. Association for Computing Machinery (2007)
19. Wooldridge, M.J., van der Hoek, W.: Time, knowledge, and cooperation: alternating-time temporal epistemic logic and its applications. In: Arbab, F., Talcott, C.L. (eds.) COORDINATION. Lecture Notes in Computer Science, vol. 2315, p. 4. Springer (2002)
20. Ågotnes, T., Alechina, N.: Coalition logic with individual, distributed and common knowledge. J. Log. Comput. **29**(7), 1041–1069 (2019)

The Surprise Exam in Full Modal Fixed-Point Logic

Yanjun Li[1], Jie Ren[1], and Thomas Ågotnes[2,3](✉)

[1] Nankai University, Tianjin, China
lyjlogic@gmail.com, 2120222184@mail.nankai.edu.cn
[2] University of Bergen, Bergen, Norway
thomas.agotnes@uib.no
[3] Shanxi University, Taiyuan, China

Abstract. The modal μ-calculus significantly extends the expressive power of basic modal logic, by adding fixed-point operators. In this paper, we study the extension of public announcement logic with such fixed-point operators. Besides the general increased expressive power, this will in particular allow us to reason about self-referential announcements, as in "after this very announcement, φ will be true". Such self-referential announcements have been of recent interest in the study of the so-called surprise exam paradox. However, a straightforward combination of the two logics would rule out formulas expressing such self-referential announcements due to the restriction of variables in fixed-point operators to be positive, which ensures that the corresponding function is monotonic which again ensures that it has a greatest fixed-point. We argue, however, that first, even without the positivity requirement the function might still be monotonic in a given model, and, second, that greatest fixed-points might exist even if the corresponding function is not monotonic. We propose an extension of public announcement logic with generalised fixed-point operators, without restricting variables to be positive, and take some first steps in analysing it. We show that the logic can be reduced to the logic without public announcement operators: to what we call "full" modal fixed-point logic. We also show that the logic is strictly more expressive than the standard modal fixed-point logic. The logic offers a simpler way of modeling self-referential announcements in the surprise exam paradox, than existing approaches.

1 Introduction

Public announcement logic (PAL) [15] extends epistemic logic, the logic of knowledge, with public announcement operators: $[\varphi]\psi$ means that if φ is true, then after φ is publicly announced ψ will be true. Using the dual ("diamond") form $\langle\varphi\rangle = \neg[\varphi]\neg\psi$ we can write $\langle\varphi\rangle\psi$ to express that φ is true and after it is announced, ψ will be true.

The modal μ-calculus [5] significantly extends the expressive power of modal logic, by adding fixed-point operators. Roughly speaking, the expression $\mu x.\varphi(x)$

($\nu x.\varphi(x)$), where φ is a formula with a free occurrence of x, is true in the set of states in a model $\mathcal{M}$ that is the least (greatest) fixed-point of the function $F_\varphi^\mathcal{M}$ that maps a set of states S to the set of states where $\varphi(x)$ is true if x is true exactly in S. There is a syntactic restriction on formulas: the occurrences of x in $\varphi(x)$ must be *positive* (occur in the scope of an even number of negations) – this ensures monotonicity of $F_\varphi^\mathcal{M}$ and hence the existence of least and greatest fixed-points.

In this paper, we are interested in extending PAL with fixed-point operators. We have one particular application in mind: reasoning about self-referential announcements, which, e.g., have been of recent interest in the analysis of the surprise exam paradox [2]. Consider the straightforward combination of the two languages. That is indeed what is done, e.g., in [17]. To ensure monotonicity, in [17] occurrences of x in $\varphi(x)$ are said to be required to be positive "in an obvious sense" without a formal definition being given. Consider now an expression of the form

$$\nu x.\langle x \rangle \psi \tag{1}$$

where x does not occur in ψ. Intuitively, the formula expresses the self-referential sentence "after *this* very announcement, ψ will be true". Is the (single) occurrence of x in $\langle x \rangle \psi$ here negative or positive? The answer is at least less obvious than for standard modal fixed-point logic, for one thing because the fact that we have formulas "inside" modalities potentially makes the definition sensitive to whether or not we take modal "diamonds" or "boxes" as primitive (unlike in standard modal fixed-point logic). Let's consider both possibilities. It could be considered to be negative, e.g., if "boxes" $[\cdot]$ are taken as primary modalities in the definition of positivity and thus letting $\varphi(x)$ here be $\neg[x]\neg\psi$. But then (1) is not actually a well-formed formula since the occurrence of x is in the scope of a negative number of negations. It could be considered positive, e.g., by taking "diamonds" $\langle \cdot \rangle$ as primary modalities in the definition of positivity. But then that notion of positivity does not "work" – as we shall see, it does not ensure monotonicity nor the existence of a greatest fixed point and the semantics of (1) would thus not be well defined[1].

---

[1] There are alternative definitions of positivity that perhaps are less "obvious". One would be to treat public announcement operators as basic modalities and not look inside them when evaluating the positivity requirement. In that case, as we will see, positivity again does not ensure a monotonic function nor the existence of least/greatest fixed-points. Another alternative would be to avoid public announcement operators altogether in the definition of positivity, and require that the *translation* of $\varphi(x)$ to a formula without public announcement operators is positive in the standard sense. Indeed, while the formula (here, $\mathcal{K}_i \varphi$ means that i knows φ, see Sect. 2) $[x]\mathcal{K}_i p$ is negative in the sense above, its translation $x \wedge \neg \mathcal{K}_i \neg(x \wedge \neg p)$ is positive – and thus least/greatest fixed-points exists. Leaving aside the issue that this would not be a *syntactic* restriction, and the question of *which* translation (there are many logically equivalent reduction axioms), as we will see that definition still rules out many of the interesting self-referential sentences we are interested in and which actually have greatest fixed-points in certain situations.

However, as we will show, first, even without the positivity requirement, $F_\varphi^\mathcal{M}$ might still be monotonic in a given model (and thus least/greatest fixed-points exist), and, second, least/greatest fixed-points might exist even if the corresponding function is not monotonic.

In this paper, we propose an extension of PAL with *generalised* fixed-point operators, that do not have the positivity requirement, and that capture fixed-points whenever they exist, whether the corresponding function is monotonic or not. A strong motivation is to capture self-referential sentences such as (1), but as we shall see these operators extend the expressive power beyond that.

The remainder of the paper is organised as follows. In the next section, we give a quick recap of PAL and modal fixed-point logic. In Sect. 3 we present the language and semantics of our generalised logic, as well as some examples, before we model the surprise exam paradox in Sect. 4. In Sect. 5 we look at the expressive power of the language, before we conclude in Sect. 6.

2 Preliminaries

2.1 Public Announcement Logic (PAL)

We very briefly recall the main concepts in Public Announcement Logic (PAL) [15], and refer the reader to [8] for details.

Let **P** be a set of propositional letters and **I** be a finite set of agents.

Definition 1 (Language of $\mathcal{L}'$). *The language $\mathcal{L}'$ is defined by the following BNF rules (where $p \in \mathbf{P}$ and $i \in \mathbf{I}$):*

$$\varphi := p \mid \neg\varphi \mid (\varphi \wedge \varphi) \mid \mathcal{K}_i\varphi \mid \langle\varphi\rangle\varphi.$$

The connectives $\vee, \rightarrow, \leftrightarrow$ are defined using the standard abbreviations. The formula $[\varphi]\psi$ is defined as $\neg\langle\varphi\rangle\neg\psi$. Intuitively, the formula $\mathcal{K}_i\varphi$ expresses that "the agent i knows that φ", and the formula $\langle\varphi\rangle\psi$ expresses that "φ holds, and after φ is announced, ψ holds".

The semantics of this language is defined as follows.

Definition 2 (Model). *A model $\mathcal{M}$ is a tuple $\langle W, \{\sim_i \mid i \in \mathbf{I}\}, V\rangle$ where*

- *W is a non-empty set of states;*
- *for each $i \in \mathbf{I}$, $\sim_i$ is an equivalence relation on W;*
- *$V : \mathbf{P} \rightarrow \mathcal{P}(W)$ is a valuation function.*

Definition 3 (Update). *Given model $\mathcal{M} = \langle W, \{\sim_i \mid i \in \mathbf{I}\}, V\rangle$ and a subset $S \subseteq W$, the model $\mathcal{M}|_S$ is the tuple $= \langle W', \{\sim_i' \mid i \in \mathbf{I}\}, V'\rangle$ where*

- *$W' = S$;*
- *for each $i \in \mathbf{I}$, $\sim_i' = \sim_i \cap (W' \times W')$;*
- *$V'(p) = V(p) \cap W'$.*

Definition 4 (Semantics of $\mathcal{L}'$). *Given an epistemic model $\mathcal{M} = \langle W, \{\sim_i | i \in \mathbf{I}\}, V \rangle$ and a formula φ, the satisfaction relation between states and formulas, denoted by $\vDash$, is defined as follows:*

$$\mathcal{M}, w \vDash p \iff w \in V(p);$$
$$\mathcal{M}, w \vDash \neg \varphi \iff \mathcal{M}, w \nvDash \varphi;$$
$$\mathcal{M}, w \vDash \varphi \wedge \psi \iff \mathcal{M}, w \vDash \varphi \text{ and } \mathcal{M}, w \vDash \psi;$$
$$\mathcal{M}, w \vDash \mathcal{K}_i \varphi \iff \text{for all } v \in W, w \sim_i v \text{ implies } \mathcal{M}, v \vDash \varphi;$$
$$\mathcal{M}, w \vDash \langle \varphi \rangle \psi \iff \mathcal{M}, w \vDash \varphi \text{ and } \mathcal{M}|_{[\![\varphi]\!]^\mathcal{M}}, w \vDash \psi;$$

where $[\![\varphi]\!]^\mathcal{M} = \{w \in W \mid \mathcal{M}, w \vDash \varphi\}$. $\mathcal{M}|_{[\![\varphi]\!]^\mathcal{M}}$ is also abbreviated $\mathcal{M}|_\varphi$.

2.2 Modal Fixed-Point Logic

We briefly recall the main concepts of the standard modal fixed-point logic (the modal μ-calculus) and refer the reader to, e.g., [19] for details.

Definition 5 (Language of $\mathcal{L}^{MFPL}$). *The language $\mathcal{L}^{MFPL}$ is defined by the following BNF rules (where $p, x \in \mathbf{P}$ and $i \in \mathbf{I}$):*

$$\varphi := p \mid \neg \varphi \mid (\varphi \wedge \varphi) \mid \mathcal{K}_i \varphi \mid \nu x. \varphi$$

where, for $\nu x. \varphi$, all free occurrences of x in φ are positive (see below).

It is worth noting here that both x and p are ("merely") propositional letters[2] – the definition would have been equivalent if it said $\nu p.\varphi$. However, we will stick to the convention in modal fixed-point logic of using x in such expressions, keeping in mind that we use $p, q, \ldots, x, y, \ldots$ for propositional letters.

The syntactic combination νx is the greatest fixed-point modality. The notation $\varphi(x)$ is used to indicate that x is a free variable of φ.

Definition 6 (Free and positive occurrence). *An occurrence of a propositional letter x in a formula φ is free if this occurrence is not in a subformula of the form $\nu x.\psi$. Otherwise, it is a bound occurrence. An occurrence of a propositional letter x in a formula φ is positive if the maximal number of negations of which it is in the scope is even. Otherwise, this occurrence is negative.*

Given a model $\mathcal{M}$ and a set of states $S \subseteq W$, let $\mathcal{M}[x := S]$ be the model that is the same as $\mathcal{M}$ except that the valuation $V^{\mathcal{M}[x:=S]}(x) = S$.[3]

---

[2] Several equivalent variants of the language are found in the literature. In particular, x is often taken from a set of variables disjoint from the set of propositional letters. The variant we use here, where propositional letters are used for quantification, i.e., where x and p are both propositional letters and there is no separate set of "variables", is also frequently used (e.g., in [3]) and is equivalent [19, Remark 3.25].

[3] Similar "updates" are found naturally in many dynamic logic settings, e.g., in [7,9], in addition to in the standard modal fixed-point logic.

Definition 7 (Induced Function and monotonicity). *Given a formula $\varphi(x)$ and a model $\mathcal{M}$, the function $F_\varphi^\mathcal{M} : \mathcal{P}(W) \to \mathcal{P}(W)$ is defined as follows: for each $S \subseteq W$,*

$$F_\varphi^\mathcal{M}(S) = \{w \in W \mid \mathcal{M}[x := S], w \vDash \varphi\}.$$

A function $F : \mathcal{P}(W) \to \mathcal{P}(W)$ is monotonic if the following condition holds:

$$\text{if } X \subseteq Y \text{ then } F(X) \subseteq F(Y).$$

The positivity requirement on the fixed-point operator ν is a syntactic means of ensuring that $F_\varphi^\mathcal{M}$ always is a monotonic function. By the Knaster-Tarski Theorem, the greatest fixed-point of a monotonic function always exists and equals to the union of all its post-fixed points.

Definition 8 (Semantics of $\mathcal{L}^{\text{MFPL}}$). *The language $\mathcal{L}^{\text{MFPL}}$ is interpreted on the same models as $\mathcal{L}^!$ (Definition 2). The truth of fixed-point formulas is defined as follows, and the other cases are as in Definition 4.*

$$\mathcal{M}, w \vDash \nu x.\varphi \iff w \in \bigcup \{S \subseteq W \mid S \subseteq [\![\varphi]\!]^{\mathcal{M}[x:=S]}\}.$$

3 Language and Semantics of $\mathcal{L}^{!\text{FMFPL}}$

We now introduce the language and the semantics of our logic that extends PAL with fixed-point operators with no syntactic "positivity" restriction.

Definition 9 (Language of $\mathcal{L}^{!\text{FMFPL}}$). *The language $\mathcal{L}^{!\text{FMFPL}}$ is defined by the following BNF rules (where $p, x \in \mathbf{P}$ and $i \in \mathbf{I}$):*

$$\varphi := p \mid \neg\varphi \mid (\varphi \wedge \varphi) \mid \mathcal{K}_i \varphi \mid \nu x.\varphi \mid \langle\varphi\rangle\varphi.$$

The notions of free and bound occurrences of propositional letters are defined exactly as in Definition 6.

Note that, different from $\mathcal{L}^{\text{MFPL}}$, there is no positivity requirement in $\mathcal{L}^{!\text{FMFPL}}$. We use $\mathcal{L}^{\text{FMFPL}}$ to denote the fragment of $\mathcal{L}^{!\text{FMFPL}}$ without announcement modalities $\langle \cdot \rangle$. Since there is also no positivity requirement in $\mathcal{L}^{\text{FMFPL}}$, we call it *full modal fixed-point logic*. Since there is no positivity requirement in $\mathcal{L}^{!\text{FMFPL}}$, the function $F_\varphi^\mathcal{M}$ is not necessarily monotonic. Hence, the truth relation in Definition 8 cannot be used directly for fixed-point formulas in $\mathcal{L}^{!\text{FMFPL}}$ and $\mathcal{L}^{\text{FMFPL}}$.

Definition 10 (Semantics of $\mathcal{L}^{!\text{FMFPL}}$). *The language $\mathcal{L}^{!\text{FMFPL}}$ is interpreted on the same models of Definition 2 as $\mathcal{L}^!$. The truth of fixed-point formula is defined as follows, and the other cases are as in Definition 4.*

$$\mathcal{M}, w \vDash \nu x.\varphi \iff w \in grt\{S \subseteq W \mid S = [\![\varphi]\!]^{\mathcal{M}[x:=S]}\}$$

where the function grt is defined as follows: for each $\Gamma \subseteq \mathcal{P}(W)$,

$$grt(\Gamma) = \begin{cases} X & \text{if } X \in \Gamma \text{ and for all } Y \in \Gamma, Y \subseteq X \\ \emptyset & \text{if there is no such } X. \end{cases}$$

According to this definition, $\nu x.\varphi$: is false if there is no greatest fixed-point, and is true exactly in the greatest fixed-point if it exists. Without the positivity restriction, we don't necessarily have monotonicity, and a greatest fixed-point don't necessarily exist. It might exist in one model, but not in another, for the same formula.

The reader might want to contrast Definitions 8 and 10. In the standard modal fixed-point logic, all occurrences of bound variables are positive. Consequently, in Definition 8, the Knaster-Tarski Theorem ensures that the greatest fixed-point is the union of all its post-fixed points (that is why "$\cup$" and "$\subseteq$" are used). In contrast, our Definition 10 allows for negative occurrences, which means the Knaster-Tarski Theorem no longer applies. Therefore, we define the greatest fixed-point in terms of fixed-points (using "$=$" instead of $\subseteq$) and specifically identify the greatest one using the function grt.

Definition 11 (Modality of self-referential announcement). *Given φ, the self-referential announcement formula $①\varphi$ is defined as follows (where x does not occur in φ):*

$$①\varphi := \nu x.\langle x\rangle\varphi.$$

Intuitively, the formula $①\varphi$ means "It will be the case that φ, after *this* very announcement". It is easy to see that it has the following semantics:

$$\mathcal{M}, w \vDash ①\varphi \iff w \in grt\{S \subseteq W \mid S = [\![\varphi]\!]^{\mathcal{M}|s}.\}$$

Example 1. Let the model $\mathcal{M}_0$ be depicted as follows (where the i-line indicates that $s_0 \sim_i s_1$): $s_0 : p \relbar\!\!\relbar i\!\relbar\!\!\relbar s_1 : \neg p$. We then have the following:

a) $\mathcal{M}_0, s_0 \vDash ①\mathcal{K}_i p$, since $S = \{s_0\}$ is the only non-empty set such that $S = [\![\mathcal{K}_i p]\!]^{\mathcal{M}_0|s}$. In this case, the function $F^{\mathcal{M}_0}_{\langle x\rangle\mathcal{K}_i p}$ is not monotonic, but the greatest fixed-point still exists.

b) $\mathcal{M}_0, s_0 \nvDash ①(\mathcal{K}_i p \vee \mathcal{K}_i \neg p)$. Let $S_0 = \{s_0\}$, $S_1 = \{s_1\}$ and $W = \{s_0, s_1\}$. We then have the following:

$$S_0 = [\![\mathcal{K}_i p \vee \mathcal{K}_i \neg p]\!]^{\mathcal{M}_0|s_0} \quad S_1 = [\![\mathcal{K}_i p \vee \mathcal{K}_i \neg p]\!]^{\mathcal{M}_0|s_1} \quad W \neq [\![\mathcal{K}_i p \vee \mathcal{K}_i \neg p]\!]^{\mathcal{M}_0|w}$$

Although each of S_0 and S_1 is a fixed-point, neither is the greatest. Hence, $grt\{S \mid S = [\![\mathcal{K}_i p]\!]^{\mathcal{M}_0|s}\} = \emptyset$. Here, the function is also not monotonic, but there is no greatest fixed-point.

In this example it might look like a logical paradox that $①\mathcal{K}_i p$ holds but $①(\mathcal{K}_i p \vee \mathcal{K}_i \neg p)$ does not. But even though the operator $①$ is the same in both cases, don't forget that it denotes self-referential announcement: *it is not the same announcement* in the two cases. The example illustrates that the *monotonicity rule* from [2], in our language written as from $\varphi \to \psi$ derive $①\varphi \to ①\psi$, does not hold.

Example 2. Let model $\mathcal{M}_1$ be : $w_0 : \neg p \relbar\!\!\relbar i\!\relbar\!\!\relbar w_1 : p \relbar\!\!\relbar j\!\relbar\!\!\relbar w_2 : \neg p$. Let:

$$\varphi_1 := \neg\mathcal{K}_i p \wedge \neg\mathcal{K}_i \neg p \wedge \mathcal{K}_i(\mathcal{K}_j p \vee \mathcal{K}_j \neg p)$$
$$\varphi_2 := \neg\mathcal{K}_j p \wedge \neg\mathcal{K}_j \neg p \wedge \mathcal{K}_j(\mathcal{K}_i p \vee \mathcal{K}_i \neg p).$$

The formula φ_1 means that the agent i does not know whether p is true, but i knows that j knows whether p is true, and the formula φ_2 means that the agent j does not know whether p is true, but j knows that i knows whether p is true. It can be checked that $\mathcal{M}_1, w_1 \not\models \mathbb{O}(\varphi_1 \vee \varphi_2)$. The reason is that there are two fixed-points: $\{w_0, w_1\}$ and $\{w_1, w_2\}$, but neither is the greatest. Hence, there is no greatest fixed-point.

An interesting property is a truthful announcement *of* the self-referential φ-announcement will always be successful in the sense that it will always achieve φ.

Proposition 1. $\models [\mathbb{O}\varphi]\varphi$.

Proof. For each pointed model $(\mathcal{M}, w)$, we are going to show that if $\mathcal{M}, w \models \mathbb{O}\varphi$ then $\mathcal{M}|_{\mathbb{O}\varphi}, w \models \varphi$. Suppose that $\mathcal{M}, w \models \mathbb{O}\varphi$. It follows that there exists a subset $S \subseteq W$ such that $w \in S$ and S is the greatest set satisfying $S = [\![\varphi]\!]^{\mathcal{M}|_S}$. We then have that $[\![\mathbb{O}\varphi]\!]^{\mathcal{M}} = S$. Due to $w \in S$ and $S = [\![\varphi]\!]^{\mathcal{M}|_S}$, it follows that $w \in [\![\varphi]\!]^{\mathcal{M}|_S}$. Moreover, due to $[\![\mathbb{O}\varphi]\!]^{\mathcal{M}} = S$, we then have that $w \in [\![\varphi]\!]^{\mathcal{M}|_{\mathbb{O}\varphi}}$. Thus, $\mathcal{M}|_{\mathbb{O}\varphi}, w \models \varphi$.

4 The Surprise Exam in $\mathcal{L}^{!\mathrm{FMFPL}}$

The surprise exam puzzle has a long history – we refer to [10,18] for details. The following variant is taken from [10]:

> "In the kind of school where you get exactly one exam every week, a teacher announces to his class: "This week, the exam will be a surprise." It is commonly understood that an exam comes as a surprise if you do not know, the evening before, that it is given the next day. A smart student, called Marilyn, reasons as follows. "Suppose the exam is given on Friday. In that case, come Thursday evening, I will not have gotten an exam yet, and I will know that it must be on Friday, which means that it would not be a surprise. So, it is not on Friday. Suppose that it is on Thursday. Then, on Wednesday evening, I will know that it must be on Friday or on Thursday. I know it is not on Friday, so it must be on Thursday: again, it would not be a surprise. So Thursday is out as well. I can repeat this argument excluding all the other days of the week. So I will not get a surprise exam; in fact, I will not get an exam at all!" The teacher gives the exam on Wednesday, surprising all students in the class. So, the teacher was right after all. What went wrong with Marilyn's reasoning?"

Formal logical analyses of the surprise exam puzzle go back at least to [12]; see [10,13,18]. Gerbrandy [10,11] was the first to propose a formal analysis in the framework of Public Announcement Logic. Here, we first review Gerbrandy's formalisation, which can be considered "non-self-referential" [2], for reference, and then propose a self-referential one, following the motivation in [2], using the operators we introduced above.

4.1 Non-self-referential Version

Gerbrandy's approach [10,11] relies on a non-self-referential version of the paradox, treating the teacher's announcement as a non-self-referential statement. Our formal analysis builds upon Gerbrandy's analysis, which we will briefly reformulate here. See also [18] for a discussion of the history of the paradox and Gerbrandy's analysis.

Since only the students' knowledge is considered in the paradox, in this section, we will restrict the agent set $\mathbf{I}$ to be a singleton and write $\mathcal{K}$ instead of $\mathcal{K}_i$. There are five propositional letters p_1, p_2, p_3, p_4, p_5, and the letter p_i ($1 \leq i \leq 5$) means the exam will be on the ith day. The model $\mathcal{M}_{\text{surprise}} = \langle W, \sim, V \rangle$ is defined as follows:

$$W = \{w_1, w_2, w_3, w_4, w_5\} \quad \sim = W \times W \quad V(p_i) = \{w_i\}, 1 \leq i \leq 5$$

We have that $\mathcal{M}_{\text{surprise}} \vDash \mathcal{K}(\bigvee_{i=1}^{5} p_i)$, which captures the assumption that the students know that there will be an exam one workday of the week.

The teacher's announcement "the exam day will be a surprise" means that even in the evening before the exam, the students will still not know for sure that the exam is tomorrow. If there is no exam on the ith day, what the students learn on the evening of the ith day from that fact is the same as what they can learn from the public announcement "the exam is not on the ith day". Hence, the teacher's announcement can be formalized as follows:

$$(p_1 \to \neg \mathcal{K} p_1) \wedge (p_2 \to [\neg p_1] \neg \mathcal{K} p_2) \wedge \cdots \wedge (p_5 \to [\neg p_1][\neg p_2][\neg p_3][\neg p_4] \neg \mathcal{K} p_5).$$

This formula can be reduced to the following

$$\varphi_{\text{surprise}} := \bigwedge_{i=1}^{5} \varphi_i, \text{ where } \varphi_i = (p_i \to [\bigwedge_{j=1}^{i-1} \neg p_j] \neg \mathcal{K} p_i).$$

It can be checked that $\mathcal{M}_{\text{surprise}} \vDash \varphi_i$ and $\mathcal{M}_{\text{surprise}}, w_i \vDash \varphi_5$ for all $1 \leq i \leq 4$, but $\mathcal{M}_{\text{surprise}}, w_5 \nvDash \varphi_5$. Hence, we have that $[\![\varphi_{\text{surprise}}]\!]^{\mathcal{M}_{\text{surprise}}} = \{w_1, w_2, w_3, w_4\}$. Thus, after the teacher's announcement, the students can conclude that the exam is not on the 5th day. According to Gerbrandy [10], this is the only valid conclusion the students can derive from the teacher's announcement.

4.2 Self-referential Version

Gerbrandy's formalization above of the sentence $\varphi_{\text{surprise}}$ naturally expresses the meaning that the students do not know the exam day before the exam. However, it can be convincingly argued [2] that the teacher's announcement should not be interpreted directly as an epistemic proposition that holds at the point in time it was made, but that it also refers to the future state after the announcement. There is an implicit self-referentiality in the teacher's announcement, a point according to Baltag et al. [2] most commentators agree on.

As pointed out in et al. [2], to make the implicit self-referentiality explicit, the announcement should be read as *it will be the case that you do not know in advance the exam day, after you hear this very announcement*. Baltag et al. [2] presents a topological epistemic logic to formalize this self-referential version of the paradox, and topological notions, like *Cantor derivative* and *perfect core*, play an important role in their analysis. They argue that the teacher's self-referential announcement can be formalized as $\nu x.\langle x \rangle \Diamond \top$ where $\Diamond \top$ in their framework expresses the same as $\varphi_{\mathsf{surprise}}$. They do not have explicit fixed-point modalities in their logical language, but they show that their formula $\odot \top$ is equivalent to $\nu x.\langle x \rangle \Diamond \top$.

We agree with Baltag et al. [2] that the teacher's self-referential announcement can be expressed by using the modal greatest fixed-point modality. However, we think it may not be necessary to use topology to formalize the self-referential announcement. Given that the key to formalizing self-referential announcements lies in using the modal greatest fixed-point modality, a natural extension of Gerbrandy's approach with modal fixed-point logic, namely the framework of $\mathcal{L}^{!\mathsf{FMFPL}}$, would work for the formalization in a natural way.

This section presents a formal analysis of the self-referential version of the paradox within the framework of $\mathcal{L}^{!\mathsf{FMFPL}}$. The teacher's announcement that *it will be the case that the exam day is a surprise after this very announcement* is expressed by the formula

$$\textcircled{!}\varphi_{\mathsf{surprise}} := \nu x.\langle x \rangle \varphi_{\mathsf{surprise}}.$$

By the semantics of $\mathcal{L}^{!\mathsf{FMFPL}}$, it follows that $[\![\textcircled{!}\varphi_{\mathsf{surprise}}]\!]^{\mathcal{M}_{\mathsf{surprise}}}$ is the greatest S such that $S = [\![\varphi_{\mathsf{surprise}}]\!]^{\mathcal{M}_{\mathsf{surprise}}|S}$. We now show that $[\![\textcircled{!}\varphi_{\mathsf{surprise}}]\!]^{\mathcal{M}_{\mathsf{surprise}}} = \emptyset$, by showing that $\emptyset$ is the only solution of $S = [\![\varphi_{\mathsf{surprise}}]\!]^{\mathcal{M}_{\mathsf{surprise}}|S}$.

Suppose that $S \subseteq W$ is not empty. Let k be the greatest number in $\{1,2,3,4,5\}$ such that $w_k \in S$. If S is a singleton, i.e. $S = \{w_k\}$, then $\mathcal{M}_{\mathsf{surprise}}|S, w_k \not\models \varphi_{\mathsf{surprise}}$ due to $\mathcal{M}_{\mathsf{surprise}}|S, w_k \not\models p_k \to [\neg p_1] \ldots [\neg p_{k-1}] \neg \mathcal{K} p_k$. It follows that $[\![\varphi_{\mathsf{surprise}}]\!]^{\mathcal{M}_{\mathsf{surprise}}|S} = \emptyset$. Thus, the singleton set S is not the solution of $S = [\![\varphi_{\mathsf{surprise}}]\!]^{\mathcal{M}_{\mathsf{surprise}}|S}$. In the following, we will continue to show that each subset S with at least 2 states is not the solution of $S = [\![\varphi_{\mathsf{surprise}}]\!]^{\mathcal{M}_{\mathsf{surprise}}|S}$ as well.

Let w_i be an another state in S, say $w_i \in S$ where $i < k$. For each $1 \leq j \leq 5$, there are two cases: $i = j$ or $i \neq j$.

If $i \neq j$, it is obvious that $\mathcal{M}_{\mathsf{surprise}}|S, w_i \models \varphi_j$ due to $\mathcal{M}_{\mathsf{surprise}}|S, w_i \not\models p_j$.

If $i = j$, then $\varphi_j = \varphi_i = p_i \to [\bigwedge_{l=1}^{i-1} \neg p_l] \neg \mathcal{K} p_i$. Since the announcement of $\bigwedge_{l=1}^{i-1} \neg p_l$ will remove only the states w_l where $l < i$, so both w_i and w_k remain in the model $\mathcal{M}_{\mathsf{surprise}}|S|_{\bigwedge_{l=1}^{i-1} \neg p_l}$. It follows that $\mathcal{M}_{\mathsf{surprise}}|S|_{\bigwedge_{l=1}^{i-1} \neg p_l}, w_i \models \neg \mathcal{K} p_i$. Thus, we have $\mathcal{M}_{\mathsf{surprise}}|S, w_i \models \varphi_i$.

Hence, we have shown that for each $1 \leq j \leq 5$, $\mathcal{M}_{\mathsf{surprise}}|S, w_i \models \varphi_j$, and thus $\mathcal{M}_{\mathsf{surprise}}|S, w_i \models \varphi_{\mathsf{surprise}}$.

Next, we will check $\mathcal{M}_{\mathsf{surprise}}|S, w_k \not\models \varphi_k$ where $\varphi_k = p_k \to [\bigwedge_{l=1}^{k-1} \neg p_l] \neg \mathcal{K} p_k$. First, it is obvious that $\mathcal{M}_{\mathsf{surprise}}|S, w_k \models p_k$. Moreover, since the announcement of $\bigwedge_{l=1}^{k-1} \neg p_l$ will remove any state w_j where $j < k$ and w_k is the greatest indexed state, it follows that w_k is the only state that remains in $\mathcal{M}_{\text{surprise}}|S|_{\bigwedge_{l=1}^{k-1} \neg p_l}$. So, we have that $\mathcal{M}_{\text{surprise}}|S|_{\bigwedge_{l=1}^{i-1} \neg p_l}, w_k \not\models \neg \mathcal{K} p_k$. Thus, we have checked that $\mathcal{M}_{\text{surprise}}|S, w_k \not\models \varphi_k$. It follows that $\mathcal{M}_{\text{surprise}}|S, w_k \not\models \varphi_{\text{surprise}}$.

So, if $S \subseteq W$ is not empty and w_k is the greatest indexed state in S, then $[\![\varphi_{\text{surprise}}]\!]^{\mathcal{M}_{\text{surprise}}|S} = (S \setminus \{w_k\})$. It follows that if $S \subseteq W$ is not empty, then $S \neq [\![\varphi_{\text{surprise}}]\!]^{\mathcal{M}_{\text{surprise}}|S}$. In other words, the empty set is the only fixed-point. Thus, we have that

$$[\![\mathbb{D}\varphi_{\text{surprise}}]\!]^{\mathcal{M}_{\text{surprise}}} = \emptyset.$$

Hence, the teacher's self-referential announcement $\mathbb{D}\varphi_{\text{surprise}}$ is false, and cannot be truthfully made. Moreover, in the self-referential version of the paradox, the students' inductive eliminative reasoning is correct, which reflects the process of searching for the greatest fixed-point. The contradiction of the paradox is between the assumption that it is known that the teacher never lies and the fact that the announcement is known to be false.

Furthermore, in our framework, the reason the announcement $\mathbb{D}\varphi_{\text{surprise}}$ is false is not that it is a liar-like sentence, as is also the case for $\odot \top$ in [2]. Although the formula $\mathbb{D}\varphi_{\text{surprise}}$ is not satisfiable on the model $\mathcal{M}_{\text{surprise}}$, it is satisfiable on some other model. Consider the model $\mathcal{M}' = \langle W', \sim', V' \rangle$ where $W' = \{s, t\}$, $\sim' = W' \times W'$, $V'(p_2) = \{s\}$ and $V'(p) = \emptyset$ for all $p \neq p_2$. It is easy to check that $\mathcal{M}', s \models \varphi_2$ where $\varphi_2 = p_2 \rightarrow [\neg p_1] \neg \mathcal{K} p_2$. Moreover, it is obvious that $\mathcal{M}', s \models \bigwedge_{i \in \{1,3,4,5\}} \varphi_i$ and $\mathcal{M}', t \models \bigwedge_{i=1}^{5} \varphi_i$. (Please recall the definitions of φ_i and $\varphi_{\text{surprise}}$ in the above subsection). Hence, $\mathcal{M}', s \models \varphi_{\text{surprise}}$ and $\mathcal{M}', t \models \varphi_{\text{surprise}}$. It follows that $W' = [\![\varphi_{\text{surprise}}]\!]^{\mathcal{M}'}$. So, we have that $[\![\mathbb{D}\varphi_{\text{surprise}}]\!]^{\mathcal{M}'} = W'$. The self-referential formula $\mathbb{D}\varphi_{\text{surprise}}$ is satisfiable.

In summary, our formalization agrees with Baltag *et al.* [2]: The teacher who is known not to lie cannot truthfully make the announcement, and this impossibility is not due to the self-referential character of the announcement. Different from [2], our formalization is built upon the full modal fixed-point language $\mathcal{L}^{!\text{FMFPL}}$ and relational semantics. Our formalization shows that self-referentiality like $\mathbb{D}\varphi$ is safe even when applied to non-monotonic operators.

5 Expressivity of $\mathcal{L}^{!\text{FMFPL}}$, $\mathcal{L}^{\text{FMFPL}}$ and $\mathcal{L}^{\text{MFPL}}$

We now turn to expressive power. We first show that any formula with public announcement operators is equivalent to one without, by exhibiting a reduction axiom in the familiar style of public announcement logic. We then show that full modal fixed-point logic is strictly more expressive than standard modal fixed-point logic (with the positivity restriction).

5.1 Reducing $\mathcal{L}^{!\text{FMFPL}}$ Into $\mathcal{L}^{\text{FMFPL}}$

We will show that any $\mathcal{L}^{!\text{FMFPL}}$ formula φ is logically equivalent to some $\mathcal{L}^{\text{FMFPL}}$ formula φ''. The idea is to first translate φ into a *well-named* formula φ', which can then be reduced to a formula without announcement operators by using reduction axioms.

Definition 12 (Well-named formulas). *A formula φ is well named if no propositional letter occurs both free and bound in φ and each propositional letter is bound at most once. We use WNF($\mathcal{L}$) to denote the fragment of a language $\mathcal{L}$ that consists of all well-named formulas.*

Proposition 2 (Replacement of equivalents). *Given $\varphi, \psi, \psi' \in \mathcal{L}^{!FMFPL}$, if $\vDash \psi \leftrightarrow \psi'$ then $\vDash \varphi \leftrightarrow \varphi(\psi'/\psi)$, where $\varphi(\psi'/\psi)$ is obtained by replacing one or more occurrence ψ in φ with ψ'.*

Proof. The proof is by induction on the length of φ. We only show the case for $\varphi = \nu x.\varphi$, the other cases are straightforward. Suppose that for any $w \in W, \mathcal{M}, w \vDash \varphi \leftrightarrow \varphi(\psi'/\psi)$. According to the semantics, we have $\mathcal{M}, w \vDash \nu x.\varphi$ if and only if $w \in grt\{S \subseteq W \mid S = \llbracket \varphi \rrbracket^{\mathcal{M}[x:=S]}\}$. By the induction hypothesis, $\llbracket \varphi \rrbracket^{\mathcal{M}[x:=S]} = \llbracket \varphi(\psi'/\psi) \rrbracket^{\mathcal{M}[x:=S]}$, therefore $w \in grt\{S \subseteq W \mid S = \llbracket \varphi \rrbracket^{\mathcal{M}[x:=S]}\}$ if and only if $w \in grt\{S \subseteq W \mid S = \llbracket \varphi(\psi'/\psi) \rrbracket^{\mathcal{M}[x:=S]}\}$, which is the semantics of $\mathcal{M}, w \vDash \nu x.\varphi(\psi'/\psi)$.

Proposition 3. *If y does not occur in $\nu x.\varphi$, then $\vDash \nu x.\varphi \leftrightarrow \nu y.\varphi(y/x)$.*

Proof. Consider the semantics of $\nu y.\varphi(y/x)$. $\mathcal{M}, w \vDash \nu y.\varphi(y/x)$ if and only if $w \in grt\{S \subseteq W \mid S = \llbracket \varphi(y/x) \rrbracket^{\mathcal{M}[y:=S]}\}$. As y does not occur in $\nu x.\varphi$, the y in $\varphi(y/x)$ only replaces the x in φ and does not introduce new free variables or binding variable conflicts. Thus, we can get: $\llbracket \varphi \rrbracket^{\mathcal{M}[x:=S]} = \llbracket \varphi(y/x) \rrbracket^{\mathcal{M}[y:=S]}$. That is, for any $S \subseteq W : \{w \in W \mid \mathcal{M}[x := S], w \vDash \varphi\} = \{w \in W \mid \mathcal{M}[y := S], w \vDash \varphi(y/x)\}$. Thus $\{S \subseteq W \mid S = \llbracket \varphi \rrbracket^{\mathcal{M}[x:=S]}\} = \{S \subseteq W \mid S = \llbracket \varphi(y/x) \rrbracket^{\mathcal{M}[y:=S]}\}$. According to the definition of the greatest fixed-point, we have $w \in grt\{S \subseteq W \mid S = \llbracket \varphi \rrbracket^{\mathcal{M}[x:=S]}\}$ if and only if $w \in grt\{S \subseteq W \mid S = \llbracket \varphi(y/x) \rrbracket^{\mathcal{M}[y:=S]}\}$. Therefore, $\mathcal{M}, w \vDash \nu x.\varphi$ if and only if $\mathcal{M}, w \vDash \nu y.\varphi(y/x)$, that is, $\vDash \nu x.\varphi \leftrightarrow \nu y.\varphi(y/x)$.

The following follows immediately from Propositions 2 and 3.

Corollary 1. *Each formula $\varphi \in \mathcal{L}^{!FMFPL}$ is equivalent to a well-named formula in WNF($\mathcal{L}^{!FMFPL}$).*

We now define the mentioned translation.

Definition 13 (Translation). *The translation $t : \mathcal{L}^{!FMFPL} \to \mathcal{L}^{FMFPL}$ is defined as follows:*

$$
\begin{aligned}
t(p) &= p & t(\langle\varphi\rangle p) &= t(\varphi) \wedge p \\
t(\neg\varphi) &= \neg t(\varphi) & t(\langle\varphi\rangle\neg\psi) &= t(\varphi) \wedge \neg t(\langle\varphi\rangle\psi) \\
t(\varphi \wedge \psi) &= t(\varphi) \wedge t(\psi) & t(\langle\varphi\rangle(\psi \wedge \chi)) &= t(\langle\varphi\rangle\psi) \wedge t(\langle\varphi\rangle\chi) \\
t(\mathcal{K}_i\varphi) &= \mathcal{K}_i t(\varphi) & t(\langle\varphi\rangle\mathcal{K}_i\psi) &= t(\varphi) \wedge \mathcal{K}_i(t(\varphi) \to t(\langle\varphi\rangle\psi)) \\
t(\nu x.\varphi) &= \nu x.t(\varphi) & t(\langle\varphi\rangle\nu x.\psi) &= t(\varphi) \wedge \nu x.t(\langle\varphi\rangle\psi) \\
t(\langle\varphi\rangle\langle\psi\rangle\chi) &= t(\langle\langle\varphi\rangle\psi\rangle\chi)
\end{aligned}
$$

The proof of the following is straightforward.

Proposition 4. *For each $\varphi \in \mathcal{L}^{!FMFPL}$, we have that $t(\varphi) \in \mathcal{L}^{FMFPL}$.*

Translation preserves well-namedness; the proof of the following is also straightforward.

Proposition 5. *For each $\varphi \in WNF(\mathcal{L}^{!FMFPL})$, $t(\varphi) \in WNF(\mathcal{L}^{FMFPL})$.*

In [17], it is shown that the following reduction axiom holds for MFPL extended with PAL modalities. We show that it still holds for !FMFPL.

Proposition 6. *If x does not occur in φ, then $\vDash \langle\varphi\rangle\nu x.\psi \leftrightarrow \varphi \wedge \nu x.\langle\varphi\rangle\psi$.*

Proof. For any pointed model $\mathcal{M}, w$, we have the following:

(1). $\mathcal{M}, w \vDash \langle\varphi\rangle\nu x.\psi \iff \mathcal{M}, w \vDash \varphi$ and $\mathcal{M}|_\varphi, w \vDash \nu x.\psi$.
$\iff \mathcal{M}, w \vDash \varphi$ and $w \in grt\{S \mid [\![\psi]\!]^{\mathcal{M}|_\varphi[x:=S]} = S\}$.
(2). $\mathcal{M}, w \vDash \varphi \wedge \nu x.\langle\varphi\rangle\psi \iff \mathcal{M}, w \vDash \varphi$ and $w \in grt\{S \mid [\![\langle\varphi\rangle\psi]\!]^{\mathcal{M}[x:=S]} = S\}$.

Therefore, to show that (1) if and only if (2), we only need to show that

$$[\![\psi]\!]^{\mathcal{M}|_\varphi[x:=S]} = [\![\langle\varphi\rangle\psi]\!]^{\mathcal{M}[x:=S]}.$$

This indeed holds:

$[\![\langle\varphi\rangle\psi]\!]^{\mathcal{M}[x:=S]} = [\![\varphi]\!]^{\mathcal{M}[x:=S]} \cap [\![\psi]\!]^{\mathcal{M}[x:=S]|_\varphi}$,
$= [\![\psi]\!]^{\mathcal{M}[x:=S]|_\varphi}$ (due to $[\![\psi]\!]^{\mathcal{M}[x:=S]|_\varphi} \subseteq [\![\varphi]\!]^{\mathcal{M}[x:=S]}$),
$= [\![\psi]\!]^{\mathcal{M}|_\varphi[x:=S]}$ (due to x not occurring in φ).

We thus get that every formula is equivalent to a formula without public announcement operators:

Proposition 7. *For each $\varphi \in \mathcal{L}^{!FMFPL}$, there is a $\varphi'' \in \mathcal{L}^{FMFPL}$ such that $\vDash \varphi \leftrightarrow \varphi''$.*

Proof. For any $\varphi \in \mathcal{L}^{!FMFPL}$, there is an equivalent well-named formula $\varphi' \in WNF(\mathcal{L}^{!FMFPL})$ by Corollary 1. The reduction axioms of public announcement logic, together with the new reduction axiom given above (Proposition 6), give that φ' is equivalent to $t(\varphi')$. The latter axiom can always be used in the translation of φ', since the translation preserves well-namedness (Proposition 5).

5.2 $\mathcal{L}^{MFPL} \prec \mathcal{L}^{FMFPL}$

In this section, we will show that the expressive power of $\mathcal{L}^{FMFPL}$ is strictly stronger than its fragment $\mathcal{L}^{MFPL}$.

It is known that the language $\mathcal{L}^{MFPL}$ is bisimulation invariant (cf. [5]). The following example will show that the language $\mathcal{L}^{FMFPL}$ can distinguish bisimilar models.

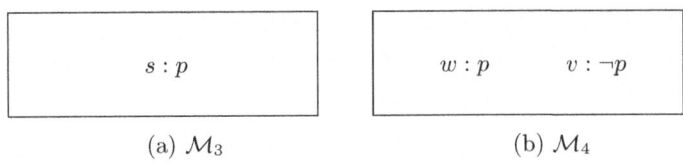

Fig. 1. Models $\mathcal{M}_3$ and $\mathcal{M}_4$.

Example 3. Let models $\mathcal{M}_3$ and $\mathcal{M}_4$ be as in Fig. 1.

It is obvious that $(\mathcal{M}_3, s)$ and $(\mathcal{M}_4, w)$ are bisimilar. However, the formula $\nu x.\neg x \vee p$ can distinguish them:

- $\mathcal{M}_3, s \models \nu x.\neg x \vee p$, since the set $S = \{s\}$ is the greatest fixed-point of the function $F^{\mathcal{M}_3}_{\neg x \vee p}(x)$:
$$F^{\mathcal{M}_3}_{\neg x \vee p}(S) = S.$$

- $\mathcal{M}_4, w \not\models \nu x.\neg x \vee p$, since there is no non-empty fixed-point of the function $F^{\mathcal{M}_4}_{\neg x \vee p}(x)$:
  - if $S = \{w\}$, then $F^{\mathcal{M}_4}_{\neg x \vee p}(S) = \{w, v\}$;
  - if $S = \{v\}$, then $F^{\mathcal{M}_4}_{\neg x \vee p}(S) = \{w\}$;
  - if $S = \{w, v\}$, then $F^{\mathcal{M}_4}_{\neg x \vee p}(S) = \{w\}$;

Thus, $\mathcal{L}^{\text{FMFPL}}$ is strictly more expressive than $\mathcal{L}^{\text{MFPL}}$. Note that in the example above, the single occurrence of x is undoubtedly *negative* – also illustrating the expressive power added by allowing negative occurrences. More generally, we have the following.

Let U be the universal modality, that is:
$$\mathcal{M}, w \models U\varphi \iff \mathcal{M}, t \models \varphi \text{ for all } t \in W.$$

The following proposition shows that the universal modality can be defined in $\mathcal{L}^{\text{FMFPL}}$.

Proposition 8. $\mathcal{M}, w \models \nu x.\neg x \vee \varphi$ iff $\mathcal{M}, w \models U\varphi$, where x does not occur in φ.

Proof. Right-to-Left: Due to $\mathcal{M}, w \models U\varphi$, it follows that $[\![\varphi]\!]^{\mathcal{M}} = W$. Since x does not occur in φ, it follows that, for each $S \subseteq W$: $[\![\varphi]\!]^{\mathcal{M}[x:=S]} = [\![\varphi]\!]^{\mathcal{M}} = W$. We then have the following:

$$\begin{aligned}F^{\mathcal{M}}_{\neg x \vee \varphi}(W) &= [\![\neg x \vee \varphi]\!]^{\mathcal{M}[x:=W]} \\ &= [\![\neg x]\!]^{\mathcal{M}[x:=W]} \cup [\![\varphi]\!]^{\mathcal{M}[x:=W]} \\ &= \emptyset \cup [\![\varphi]\!]^{\mathcal{M}} \\ &= W.\end{aligned}$$

It follows that W is a fixed-point of the function $F^{\mathcal{M}}_{\neg x \vee \varphi}(x)$, and it obviously is the greatest fixed-point. Thus, $\mathcal{M}, w \models \nu x.\neg x \vee \varphi$.

Left-to-Right: Due to $\mathcal{M}, w \vDash \nu x. \neg x \vee \varphi$, it follows that there is some $S \subseteq W$ such that $w \in S$ and $S = [\![\neg x \vee \varphi]\!]^{\mathcal{M}[x:=S]}$. Due to $[\![\varphi]\!]^{\mathcal{M}[x:=S]} = [\![\varphi]\!]^{\mathcal{M}}$ and $[\![\neg x]\!]^{\mathcal{M}[x:=S]} = (W \setminus S)$, it follows that

$$S = (W \setminus S) \cup [\![\varphi]\!]^{\mathcal{M}}.$$

Then, the set $W \setminus S$ must be empty. Otherwise, if it there is some $v \in (W \setminus S)$, it follows that $v \notin S$ and $v \in (W \setminus S) \cup [\![\varphi]\!]^{\mathcal{M}}$. This contradicts $S = (W \setminus S) \cup [\![\varphi]\!]^{\mathcal{M}}$. Thus, $W \setminus S = \emptyset$, and then $S = W$. Hence, $[\![\varphi]\!]^{\mathcal{M}} = W$, and then $\mathcal{M}, w \vDash U\varphi$.

6 Conclusions

Adding fixed-point operators to public announcement logic has been proposed before. In particular, [17] shows that PAL extended with the μx operator with the standard semantics admits reduction axioms. However, the exact definition of the syntactic positivity requirement ("in the scope of an odd number of negations") is not entirely clear and obvious candidates rule out certain interesting formulas expressing properties of self-referential announcements and/or do not actually do the job of guaranteeing that the corresponding function is monotonic. We have seen that even for formulas that can be considered to be negative, the corresponding function might be monotonic (e.g., the self-referential version of surprise exam in the case that boxes are taken as primary modalities), and that greatest fixed-points might still exist even if it is not (e.g., Example 1.a). Furthermore, we have shown that there are formulas that are *obviously* negative, like $\neg x \vee \varphi$ in the expression of the universal modality, which still have greatest fixed-points.

We proposed an extension of PAL with generalised fixed-point operators, which is well-defined in the sense that they capture the greatest fixed-points whenever they exist – also in the case of non-monotonicity. The logic is reducible to the logic without public announcement operators – *full modal fixed-point logic*. We also showed that the logic is strictly more expressive than standard modal fixed-point logic. Taking a cue from [2], where it is convincingly argued that the announcement in the surprise exam paradox should be seen as a *self-referential* announcement, we used the logic to model that scenario. The difference to [2] is that we do that in standard public announcement logic with general fixed-point operators and relational semantics, rather than in a more complex logic with topological semantics and other operators.

While we have focused particularly on self-referential announcements, the extension of PAL with the new fixed-point operators can of course express much more. We gave a small example: the universal modality. An obvious direction for future work is to study the full modal fixed-point logic in detail, in particular axiomatic characterisation and expressive power. Axiomatic completeness might be challenging, as proving completeness for the standard modal μ-calculus [20] has been notoriously difficult. Also, the extended logic probably lacks many of the nice logical properties that the modal μ-calculus has. Studying the logic of the self-referential announcement operator ⓘ is also obvious future work.

Applications to other examples, such as a self-referential variant of Hollis' paradox [1] would be of interest as well. We also leave for future work a comparison with *refinement modal logic (RML)* [4], which has quantifiers over "refinements", which are bisimulations without the "forth" condition, and which has been extended with the modal μ-calculus to RML$^\mu$ (variables are still required to be positive). Finally, it has been shown [6] that extending modal logic with operators for so-called inflationary fixed-points significantly extends the expressive power compared to least/greatest fixed-points. We leave a comparison with our operators for future work. A closely related question is the expression of iterated announcement operators [14], which van Benthem [16] has pointed out do not have a montone functions but do have deflationary fixed-points in the limit.

Acknowledgement. The authors thank the anonymous reviewers for their detailed comments that improved the presentation of the paper. Yanjun Li acknowledges support from the Fundamental Research Funds for the Central Universities (No. 63253022). Thomas Ågotnes acknowledges support by Major Project of National Social Science Foundation of China (Grant No. 24&ZD227).

References

1. Ågotnes, T., Sakama, C.: A formal analysis of hollis' paradox. In: Alechina, N., Herzig, A., Liang, F. (eds.) Logic, Rationality, and Interaction. Lecture Notes in Computer Science, vol. 14329, pp. 306–321. Springer, Cham (2023)
2. Baltag, A., Bezhanishvili, N., Fernández-Duque, D.: The topology of surprise. In: Proceedings of the International Conference on Principles of Knowledge Representation and Reasoning, vol. 19, pp. 33–42 (2022)
3. Baltag, A., Bezhanishvili, N., Fernández-Duque, D.: The topological mu-calculus: completeness and decidability. J. ACM **70**(5), 1–38 (2023)
4. Bozzelli, L., van Ditmarsch, H., French, T., Hales, J., Pinchinat, S.: Refinement modal logic. Inf. Comput. **239**, 303–339 (2014)
5. Bradfield, J., Stirling, C.: Modal μ-calculi. In: Blackburn, P., Van Benthem, J., Wolter, F. (eds.) Handbook of Modal Logic, Studies in Logic and Practical Reasoning, vol. 3, pp. 721–756. Elsevier (2007). https://doi.org/10.1016/S1570-2464(07)80015-2
6. Dawar, A., Grädel, E., Kreutzer, S.: Inflationary fixed points in modal logic. ACM Trans. Comput. Logic (TOCL) **5**(2), 282–315 (2004)
7. van Ditmarsch, H.P., van der Hoek, W., Kooi, B.P.: Dynamic epistemic logic with assignment. In: Proceedings of the Fourth International Joint Conference on Autonomous Agents and Multiagent Systems, pp. 141–148 (2005)
8. van Ditmarsch, H., van der Hoek, W., Kooi, B.: Dynamic Epistemic Logic, Synthese Library, vol. 337. Springer (2007)
9. van Eijck, J., Ju, F.: Modelling legal relations. In: Proceedings of Conference on Logic and the Foundations of Game and Decision Theory (2016)
10. Gerbrandy, J.: The surprise examination in dynamic epistemic logic. Synthese **155**(1), 21–33 (2007). https://doi.org/10.1007/s11229-005-2211-7
11. Gerbrandy, J.: Bisimulations on planet Kripke. University of Amsterdam (1999)

12. Halpern, J.Y., Moses, Y.: Taken by surprise: the paradox of the surprise test revisited. J. Philos. Log. **15**, 281–304 (1986)
13. Marcoci, A.: The surprise examination paradox in dynamic epistemic logic. Master's thesis, Universiteit van Amsterdam (2010)
14. Miller, J.S., Moss, L.S.: The undecidability of iterated modal relativization. Stud. Logica. **79**, 373–407 (2005)
15. Plaza, J.A.: Logics of public communications. In: Proceedings of ISMIS, pp. 201–216 (1989)
16. Van Benthem, J.: Logical Dynamics of Information and Interaction. Cambridge University Press (2011)
17. Van Benthem, J., Ikegami, D.: Modal fixed-point logic and changing models. In: Pillars of Computer Science: Essays Dedicated to Boris (Boaz) Trakhtenbrot on the Occasion of His 85th Birthday, pp. 146–165. Springer (2008)
18. Van Ditmarsch, H., Kooi, B.: The secret of my success. Synthese **151**, 201–232 (2006)
19. Venema, Y.: Lectures on the modal μ-calculus. Tsinghua University (China) (2024)
20. Walukiewicz, I.: Completeness of kozen's axiomatisation of the propositional μ-calculus. Inf. Comput. **157**(1–2), 142–182 (2000)

Which One Takes Priority?—Reflections on the Concept of Argument

Runcheng Liang(✉)

School of Marxism, Guangdong University of Education, Guangzhou 510303, China
liangruncheng@gdei.edu.cn

Abstract. Argument is a foundational concept in argumentation theory. While many scholars have proposed perspectives on this topic, it remains controversial. Recently, Siegel published two papers addressing the concept of argument, distinguishing four senses of argument and asserting that the abstract propositional sense holds priority. Consequently, he argues that epistemic function of argument are also primary. Siegel's understanding of the four senses of argument is insightful, and his argument in support of the priority claim is compelling. However, to justify a priority claim, we need to consider potential alternatives and make comparisons. If there are multiple plausible answers to the question of priority, then we should suspend judgment. In this paper, I present new counterarguments to Siegel's priority claim. I clarify the meaning of conceptual priority, arguing that it has a close relationship with grounding in metaphysics. My counterarguments have two parts. First, I posit that argumentative precedents—instances of the fourth sense of argument in Siegel's theory—are conceptually prior, meaning that the abstract propositional sense of argument is grounded in precedents. Siegel's priority claim represents a specific form of conceptual grounding that concerns thin and thick modes, whereas my claim about priority involves the truth-maker mode and the objective basis mode. Second, I distinguish between the basic function, which is epistemic, and the oriented function, which reflects arguers' goals. These two functions exist at the same conceptual level with abstract propositional sense of argument. Both Siegel's argument and mine are plausible. Therefore, I contend that the problem of priority is inherently complex and underdetermined.

Keywords: argument · priority · abstract propositional sense of argument · precedents · Siegel

1 Introduction

The concept of argument plays a central role in both the descriptive and normative dimensions of argumentation theory. Despite extensive scholarly engagement—from foundational works by O'Keefe [11], Willard [24] and Wenzel [23] to contemporary contributions by Dutilh Novaes [5]—the definition and prioritization of argument remain contested. Recent interventions by Siegel [18, 19] have reinvigorated this debate. Siegel delineates four distinct senses of argument and advocates for the primacy of the abstract propositional sense, while critiquing alternative frameworks such as pragma-dialectics (PD), virtue argumentation theory (VAT), and rhetorical approach (RA). These critiques prompted rebuttals from proponents of PD, VAT, and RA, to which Siegel subsequently responded. The dialectical exchange offers a valuable opportunity to evaluate the theoretical strengths and limitations of these competing frameworks, thereby advancing our understanding of argument.

Siegel distinguishes between 'argument' and 'arguments'. Normally, the former refers to the abstract concept, while the latter refers to specific real-world instances that reflect the concept. In the second part, I summarize Siegel's original arguments on the concept of argument. In the third part, I outline his responses to critics representing other theoretical perspectives. In the fourth part, I provide comments on Siegel's arguments and propose my arguments. The final part presents my conclusions.

2 Siegel's Original Arguments

2.1 Four Senses of Argument

There are four senses of argument that are best distinguished: (a) arguments in the abstract propositional sense, (b) arguments in the complex speech act sense, which may or may not constitute instances of argumentation, (c) arguments as communicative activities that constitute instances of argumentation involving arguments in either or both of the first two senses, and (d) extended episodes of argumentative interaction [18, p. 474]. The first sense of argument refers to structured sets of propositions connected by logical or epistemic relations—also called premise-conclusion complexes—such as a mathematical proof. The speech act sense of argument involves actions (spoken, written, or enacted) that instantiate this first sense; this is often termed arguing. For example, presenting a mathematical proof aloud to others constitutes arguing. Importantly, arguing does not require a dialectical or communicative context, as individuals can argue with themselves. When arguing occurs in a social, dialogical, or communicative context, it becomes argumentation, which represents the third sense of argument (e.g., political debates). The fourth sense of argument will be elaborated in Part Four of this article.

Siegel provides two ways to understand the relationship between the four senses of argument. The first is the traffic metaphor: "arguments are most fundamentally what arguers traffic in when arguing" [18, p. 471]. Siegel uses this metaphor to illustrate the role of argument. The phrase 'traffic in' implies dealing in, exchanging, or circulating something. In the metaphor, he regards the abstract propositional sense of argument as the 'goods' being traded, while arguers are akin to businessmen making deals. Just as businessmen exchange goods, arguers exchange abstract propositional arguments. Regardless of the methods used in arguing, the process must involve the abstract propositional sense of argument; otherwise, it becomes self-contradictory.

The second approach is the comparison between abstract structures and sequences of actions: "Argument is used to refer both to the abstract propositional structure advanced or challenged by arguers in the course of their argumentative activities and to the acts of arguing, usually speech acts, in which arguers engage when arguing" [4, p. 92]. On one side is the abstract propositional sense of argument, which includes premises and conclusions. On the other side is arguing, where people may argue either with themselves, with others who do not respond, in a communicative way without following rules, or in a dialectical way following strict rules.

The abstract propositional sense of argument serves an epistemic role, aiming to advance knowledge or rational understanding. Arguing involves providing reasons to support or challenge beliefs, acceptance, doubt, or other attitudes: "Arguments (in the abstract propositional sense) engage in this epistemic task of advancing/challenging the cases made for and against the standpoints at issue" [18, p. 472]. An argument's quality depends on how well it fulfills this role, determined by the premise-conclusion relationship: "An argument is good, epistemically, to the extent to which its premises/reasons warrant belief in its conclusion/standpoint" [18, p. 472].

2.2 The Critique of Pragma-Dialectics

In PD, dialectical exchanges take priority over abstract propositional argumentation. "Argumentation arises in response to, or in anticipation of, a difference of opinion, and the lines of justification that are chosen are contrived to realize the purpose of resolving this difference of opinion in the case concerned" [6, p. 524]. Resolution occurs through argumentative speech acts, which may sometimes breach reasonableness standards. To ensure normativity, PD employs critical discussion—a four-stage, ten-rule framework assessing reasonableness, where violations lead to fallacies. This forms a problem-valid and convention-valid procedure, ensuring rational resolution and participant acceptance [8, p. 281]. Problem validity ensures that resolution depends on arguers' speech acts, while conventional validity requires participants' acceptance of discussion rules.

Siegel's critique of PD has two dimensions. First, he rejects its descriptive aspect. "As Biro notes, PD takes arguments to be fundamentally dialogical or dialectical exchanges" [18, p. 475]. PD treats argumentation as foundational, with other theoretical constructs built around it. It views the abstract propositional sense of argument as deriving from argumentation, constituted by complex speech acts—a view Siegel opposes. Second, Siegel argues that PD prioritizes evaluating argumentation over epistemic evaluation. "Although it incorporates epistemic evaluative terms like 'validity,' 'rational,' 'fallacy,' and the like, it reconceives these terms so that they apply to dialectical 'moves' that do or do not conform to the theory's rules for conducting critical discussions, rather than to arguments in the abstract propositional sense" [18, p. 475]. This embeds epistemic norms within dialectical rules, creating tension between epistemic goals and PD's framework. Consequently, argumentation may satisfy dialectical norms while failing epistemic standards.

2.3 The Critique of Virtue Argumentation Theory

VAT views argument dialectically. Aberdein asserts that "the dialectical nature of argumentation" is fundamental [1, p. 165], stating, "Argument, unlike knowledge, is intrinsically dialectical" [1, p. 175]. This aligns with PD, which sees arguing as a process where claims are justified, contested, and revised through critique. For Aberdein, argument evolves through dialogue, whereas knowledge can exist independently of interaction.

Unlike PD, which evaluates argumentation by adherence to discussion rules, Aberdein assesses the arguer's character traits (e.g., open-mindedness, intellectual humility) as essential virtues for normative argumentation. Traditional approaches focus on logical structure, evidence, or coherence, whereas VAT evaluates behavior and intent. Proponents argue that "Arguers, rather than (just) arguments" [3, p. 340], emphasize "the importance of agents to the normative evaluation of arguments" [3, p. 339]. Arguers must not only present arguments but also engage constructively. For instance, if one argues for climate action arrogantly, mocking opponents instead of addressing concerns, VAT deems the quality of the argument poor despite its propositional validity.

Siegel's critique of Aberdein has two dimensions. First, he argues that Aberdein diminishes the abstract propositional sense of argument by prioritizing dialectical traits, similar to critiques of PD. He asserts, "it is argumentation, rather than argument, that might be intrinsically dialectical" [18, p. 487]. While argumentation unfolds dialectically, an argument itself is not inherently dialectical but has a propositional structure with premises and conclusions. Second, Siegel argues that an arguer's character is irrelevant to an argument's epistemic strength. A flawed individual can present a strong argument, just as a virtuous one can offer a weak one. The key determinant of argument quality is the support between premises and conclusion, not the arguer's virtues. As Siegel states, "When it comes to argument evaluation as determined by the degree of support offered to a conclusion by its reasons/premises, it is that support (or its absence) that determines an argument's quality. The virtues manifested might reflect that independently established quality, but they do not determine it" [18, p. 492]. Eloquence or good character does not affect logical strength.

2.4 The Critique of Rhetorical Approach

Tindale sees argumentation as "a means of expression and a gathering place of ideas and styles" [21, p. i], with arguments as "expressions of meaningfulness, or simply sources of meaning" [21, p. 165]. Tindale explores diverse cultures to uncover real-life reasoning beyond the abstract propositional sense. Argumentation is a communicative space where viewpoints, rhetorical styles, and cultural influences intersect. Challenging the notion that argument depends on written propositions [21, p. 57], Tindale allows premises to take forms like gestures, images, or sounds, with conclusions often inferred rather than explicitly stated.

Tindale emphasizes the persuasive power of a broader conception of reasons. In various cultures or contexts, elements not traditionally seen as reasons can still influence people's beliefs. For example, "myths have important argumentative force... and serve as sources of reasons in certain circumstances" [21, p. 110]. Myths go beyond stories; they are persuasive tools that convey values, morals, and worldviews, serving as shared premises for reasoning and justification in specific cultural or historical contexts.

Siegel's critique of Tindale has two dimensions. First, he argues that the concept of argument is too broad. If Tindale is right, Siegel claims, argument and argumentation lose meaning, as any communicative act could be considered an argument, diluting the definitions that argumentation theorists seek [18, p. 501]. While Tindale treats the abstract propositional sense of argument as just one possibility, Siegel rejects this broader inclusion. More importantly, he criticizes the lack of emphasis on the privileged status of the abstract propositional sense, arguing that it should take theoretical primacy, much like a skilled manager leading rather than performing frontline tasks. Second, Siegel does not consider persuasive power or influence to be criteria for judging the quality of an argument, as they may overlook the epistemic traits of arguments. An argument that is persuasive may still be epistemically weak. As Siegel states, "Let us grant that myths and narratives can and do have rhetorical force. Does it follow that they also have epistemic, probative, justificatory force? Clearly not" [18, p. 502]. Persuasion differs from justification, and in Siegel's theory, justification takes priority.

3 Critics and Siegel's Responses

3.1 Pragma-Dialectics

Garssen outlines his responses to Siegel as below. "I will focus on what I see as the most important problems in Siegel's argument: 1) the ambiguity of the term 'argument' and the alleged negligence of this ambiguity in pragma-dialectics; 2) the critical rational perspective of the pragma-dialectical account; and 3) the alleged negligence of the 'abstract propositional sense' of argument in pragma-dialectics" [9, p. 528]. The first problem Garssen raises regarding Siegel's arguments is the lack of clarity in Siegel's explanation of argument.

The second and third problems concern PD's defense, particularly its descriptive and normative dimensions. Garssen argues that dialectification, a core principle of PD, evaluates the abstract propositional sense of argument in speech acts by establishing rules for assessing conclusions drawn from premises, ensuring logical and fair reasoning. Thus, PD aligns with Siegel's four senses of argument and provides corresponding evaluative norms, grounded in reasonableness from a critical rational perspective. "Critical rationalists place great emphasis on the consequence of the fact that a statement and its negation cannot both be true at the same time: one of these statements must be withdrawn. They equate a dialectical testing of statements with the detection of contradictions" [7, p. 282]. This is a fundamental rule of classical logic: if one statement is true, its direct opposite (negation) must be false. Differences of opinion may appear as contradictions, and one of them should be retracted. In argumentation, one side proposes claims as hypotheses, and the other side examines them critically. The ultimate goal of these rules is to identify the weaknesses in the hypotheses.

Siegel's responses also focus on these three aspects. In his first response, Siegel clarifies the meaning of abstract propositional sense of argument. "Argument picks out sets of propositions organized in premise-conclusion or reason-conclusion complexes, the members of which are connected by logical/inferential or epistemological relations" [19, p. 510]. In this sense, an argument is a structured set of statements, where some statements (premises) provide support for another statement (conclusion). These statements are connected by logical or epistemological relationships. A logical relationship can lead to epistemic justification if: the premises are true or at least acceptable and the inference is valid or strong (has high inductive strength or plausibility). Arguments are not necessarily justified because the premises can be false, and the support relationship can be weak.

The term 'abstract' denotes that arguments in the propositional sense do not exist physically—they are not material objects (like tables or trees) but rather conceptual constructs. In contrast, a speech act refers to the physical act of speaking—uttering a sentence or articulating words. This is a tangible event because it occurs at a specific time and place (e.g., saying "Hello" in a meeting at 10:00 AM). It involves measurable physical processes, such as sound waves, movements of the jaw and tongue, and airflow.

In his second response, Siegel argues that the critical rationalist perspective in pragma-dialectics cannot justify the epistemic traits of an argument. While critical rationalism focuses on error detection and scrutiny, it does not equate criticism with epistemic justification. Even if a standpoint is refuted, critical rationalism does not justify rejecting it, as "Criticism has no epistemic import if it doesn't offer positive reason to reject its target. According to critical rationalism, it cannot offer any such reason" [19, p. 515]. Epistemic import involves providing positive reasons to justify beliefs, but criticism only highlights failures without offering conclusive reasons to confirm an alternative or reject the theory.

In his third response, Siegel appreciates PD's inclusion of four senses of argument but criticizes the theoretical hierarchy among them, arguing that the abstract propositional sense does not receive adequate attention. He also critiques PD's presupposition that argumentation's sole purpose is to manage disagreement and resolve differences of opinion, calling it too narrow. This focus, Siegel argues, overlooks other legitimate purposes, such as inquiry and discovery, where achieving true beliefs takes priority and the abstract propositional sense deserves more attention [19, p. 512].

3.2 Virtue Argumentation Theory

Aberdein again emphasizes that argument is fundamentally rooted in dialogue and interaction. From this perspective, the essence of argumentation lies in its role as a tool for resolving disputes or engaging in critical discussion. Due to this intrinsic focus on dialogue, Aberdein positions c-arguments (dialectical arguments) as the primary sense of 'argument'. Other interpretations, such as a-arguments (abstract propositions) or b-arguments (persuasive efforts), are viewed as secondary or derivative, dependent on the foundational dialectical function [2, p. 545].

Aberdein divides Siegel's critique into three problems and addresses each individually. First, the Alignment Problem: although virtuous arguers can sometimes produce poor arguments—and vice versa—Aberdein maintains that good arguments are those typically made by virtuous arguers acting virtuously. Second, the Relevance Problem: he introduces virtue-based rules (v-rules) for evaluating arguments, which, while primarily applied to dialectical and rhetorical aspects, can also extend to the logical dimension. Third, the Euthyphro Problem: questioning whether arguments are good because they align with virtues or for independent epistemic reasons, Aberdein distinguishes between practical and normative justification—arguing that arguments are practically good due to their epistemic merits, while their normative justification may stem from virtue-based evaluation methods [2, p. 557].

In the descriptive dimension, Siegel repeats his understanding of relationship between four senses of argument. "This trafficking is a necessary condition of a bit of dialogue's constituting an argument" [19, p. 518]. In this context, 'trafficking' likely refers to the exchange of ideas, reasons, or standpoints between participants in a dialogue. The abstract propositional sense of argument is what is exchanged in dialogue. Without this type of argument, the dialogue cannot be argumentative. We should first understand the dialogue or dialectical process in terms of abstract propositions.

In the normative dimension, an argument's quality depends on how well its premises justify its conclusion, not on the arguer's virtue or adherence to v-rules. While virtues like honesty and fairness may correlate with better arguments, they do not determine epistemic quality. "A further worry concerns the character of the argumentative virtues, namely that they do not have directly epistemic ramifications" [19, p. 520]. For instance, a fair and thorough arguer may still reach a false conclusion if the evidence is deceptive or insufficient. While such virtues enhance discussion structure and mediation, they do not guarantee epistemically sound conclusions.

3.3 Rhetorical Approach

Olmos summarizes Siegel's view as prioritizing an argument's logical structure—its premises, conclusion, and inferential relations—over factors like virtues, context, or rhetorical goals. However, she sees this as an unproven assumption reflecting analytic philosophy's framing rather than a neutral truth: "That is what analytic philosophy has been doing for the past hundred years with (in my opinion) not so wonderful results" [12, p. 565].

In other words, Olmos argues that real-world argumentation extends beyond the abstract propositional sense, aligning with Tindale's broader view. Argumentation is not merely a collection of abstract arguments but a complex, interconnected process: "argumentation is not a collection of arguments (in their abstract propositional sense) but something much more entangled and web-like"

[12, p. 565]. Arguers use rhetorical devices to enhance persuasiveness, while audiences draw inferences and respond, forming an argumentative connection between both parties.

This view of argument shapes its evaluative norms. Olmos, citing Tindale, emphasizes a rhetorical approach where reasonableness arises from collective argumentative practices rather than abstract rules or virtues. Unlike logic-focused or virtue-based approaches, Tindale's view is immanent—standards emerge from arguers' activities: "There is no alternative source for our standard of what is reasonable other than the activities of reasoners themselves" [20, p. 217]. Reasonableness evolves as arguers construct, assess, and refine arguments through practice.

In the descriptive dimension, Siegel reiterates his claim of priority: the speech act and social/dialogical aspects of argumentation depend on the presence of this propositional core. "Still, for it to count as argumentation at all, arguments in the abstract propositional sense must be in play" [19, p. 526]. Although we begin arguing within a practical context, Olmos's arguments do not diminish the value of the abstract propositional sense of argument that Siegel emphasizes. Without the abstract propositional sense of argument, we do not know what arguing or argumentation is.

In the normative dimension, Siegel agrees with Olmos that belief systems are shaped by culture, language, and experience but argues this does not limit argumentative practices. Objective norms can still guide evaluation without falling into relativism, and progress within a framework can be justified: "That argumentative evaluations are conducted from within argumentative practice does not entail... Nor does it mean that such improvements are not 'objective'" [19, p. 530]. While practices vary, Siegel emphasizes that common abstract structures in argumentation provide the necessary evaluative norms.

4 Reflections on Siegel's Arguments

4.1 The Reconstruction of Siegel's Arguments

Siegel summarizes his major argument about priority: "However, although the norms are complementary, they are not of equal priority. On the epistemic view that Biro and I have defended, epistemic norms are of highest priority. This is because arguments are what arguers traffic in when arguing. The other senses of 'argument' are derivative of this one" [18, p. 516]. While multiple types of norms play a role in evaluating arguments, they serve different purposes and are not equally important. According to the 'epistemic view' supported by Siegel, epistemic norms take precedence because they address the primary function of arguments: to present justified reasoning or claims based on truth and evidence. Other norms are secondary and depend on this epistemic foundation. The prioritization of the epistemic function originates from the fact that argumentative speech acts, or argumentation, depend on the abstract propositional content of arguments.

The priority Siegel refers to is a conceptual one rather than a causal one. He explains: "My priority claim is not causal, though. It is rather a claim concerning conceptual priority, based on my claim, argued for throughout, that arguments are most fundamentally abstract propositional structures that make cases for their conclusions. This is why their epistemic evaluation-how strong is the case made?—is the most fundamental sort of argument evaluation" [18, p. 517]. Causal priority represents a sequence in time where one event happens first, causing the subsequent event. The earlier event is the cause, and the latter is the effect. The event in the priority position is the cause. The cause necessarily or to high degree brings about the effect. In contrast, a concept has conceptual priority if it provides the foundational framework for understanding other concepts. In a relationship of conceptual priority, two concepts have special relationship without a temporal sequence, which connect to 'grounding' in metaphysics. Schaffer gives us such description: "Roughly speaking, just as causation links the world across time, grounding links the world across levels. Grounding connects the more fundamental to the less fundamental, and thereby backs a certain form of explanation" [14, p. 122]. Some levels are basic, while other levels depend on them. By appealing to the basic level elements, we can explain the higher-level objects. Grounding do not limit in metaphysics but can apply into other domain of as social objects, properties, and events [16, p. 753]. Metaphysics examines the structure of reality. Argument and argumentation are part of reality. I am sure grounding can also be applied to the analysis of both. We can summarize Siegel's arguments as follows:

1. There are four senses of argument.
2. Among these four senses, the abstract propositional sense of argument holds conceptual priority.
3. Within this abstract propositional framework, premises support conclusions, primarily serving an epistemic function.
4. Therefore, evaluating the epistemic characteristics of argument should also hold conceptual priority.

4.2 The Weakness of Siegel's Arguments

Through this reconstruction, I consider that Siegel's arguments are epistemic strong. The premises are acceptable. The connection between premises and conclusion is good. But can we consider other senses of argument to be conceptually prior? This problem is important for the priority claim. The term 'priority' generally refers to the state of being more important or having a higher rank, status, or urgency compared to something else. Priority inherently carries a value dimension. For instance, Tom considers money his priority, while Mary prioritizes health. There is no objective criterion to determine what should take precedence because this depends on values. To justify something as a priority, what kind of reasoning is required? I argue that this involves a process of weighing and balancing. Every theory has both strengths and weaknesses. For something to attain a position of priority, its value must not only outweigh its drawbacks but also surpass the value of other competing claims. In other words, to justify the priority of a theory, we must consider potential alternatives and make a comparative judgment.

By counterarguments, I mean arguments that offer competing views on the priority claim. We cannot accept Siegel's arguments outright if such counterarguments exist, as they present alternative explanations for the same issue. PD, VAT, and RA all propose counterarguments to Siegel's priority claim. Siegel responds to these arguments, but what he misses are the comparisons. His response seems to assume the priority of the epistemic perspective without considering the reasonableness of other theories' priority claims. If other theories' claims are correct, then we would have different, yet equally good, answers to the same problem. Therefore, we cannot accept the epistemic perspective directly and should suspend judgment about priority claims.

I will not discuss the correctness of the priority claims made by PD, VAT, and RA here. What I want to do here is to propose new counterarguments focusing on Proposition 2 and Proposition 3 in the reconstruction. My counterarguments are similar to the RA approach, but they draw on different theoretical resources. I appeal to the concept of grounding in metaphysics to construct my arguments.

4.3 The Construction of Counterarguments

Precedents normally refers to previous legal case that work as a standard to help judge make decision. Righ here, I want to change its meaning to previous argumentative examples created by real arguers—not abstract constructions, but real events in the world—which may be regarded as instances of the fourth sense of argument (extended episodes of argumentative interaction) in Siegel's paper. Siegel rarely discusses this fourth sense of argument. The phrase 'extended episode' appears only twice, and he provides just one brief example: "Over the past two weeks, my students have had a rip-roaring argument about the mind-body problem" [18, pp. 473–474]. From this, we can infer that the fourth sense of argument does not receive as much attention as the first one. However, from an ontological perspective, the fourth sense of argument-as real argumentative events-is crucial for us to understand argument.

Siegel consider practice of argumentation is causal priority over abstract sense of argument under some conditions. "There is a case to be made that argumentation is causally prior to arguments (in the abstract propositional sense) in the sense that the latter are, as Ralph Johnson puts it, 'the distillate of the practice of argumentation'. I am happy to grant the plausibility of this causal priority claim, although I think it needs qualification in various ways" [18, p. 517]. The practice of argumentation corresponds to the fourth sense of argument in Siegel's theory. The practice of argumentation is different from argumentation: the former refers to real events in the world, while the latter is a conceptual description of a certain kind of action. Siegel cannot directly accept that the practice of argumentation is causally prior to the abstract sense of argument, arguing that more conditions are needed to constrain such a claim.

I agree with Siegel's opinion on this point, arguing that the practice of argumentation is not causally prior to the abstract propositional sense of argument directly. In a causal relationship, there are two events: the prior one is the cause, and the latter is the effect. When the cause occurs, the effect necessarily or highly probably follows. Events are generally understood as occurrences or happenings in time and space, having a temporal location-they begin and end. We can say that the practice of argumentation is a kind of event involving arguers and different kinds of argumentative actions. The abstract propositional sense of argument is a kind of theoretical construction that reflects the necessary conditions of an argument, which do not occur because it is a finished product. We can say that the creation of theoretical construction is an event. However, the practice of argumentation does not have a causal relationship with the creation of theoretical construction. In the practice of argumentation, arguers do not necessarily or with high probability create theoretical construction; rather, they focus on practical issues such as political policies or legal judgments. Only scholars in argumentation theory engage in reflecting on the practice of argumentation. Therefore, it is incorrect to argue that the practice of argumentation has causal priority over the abstract propositional sense of argument.

Rather than causal priority, I argue that the abstract propositional sense of argument is grounded in precedents. To illustrate the concept of grounding, Schaffer presents five paradigm examples. In the first example, he cites Aristotle's work: If a man exists, the statement affirming his existence is true, and vice versa—if the statement is true, a man exists. While the statement does not cause the man's existence, the man's existence determines the statement's truth or falsehood [15, p. 52]. A proposition describes the world, and if the reference of the proposition exists, then the proposition is true. This is similar to the relationship between precedents and the abstract propositional sense of argument. Why does Siegel need to propose the abstract sense of argument that is a mode of propositions? He wants to capture the essential features of arguments in real life. However, such theoretical constructions are not necessarily correct. We need a threshold to judge the truth of these theoretical constructions. Argumentative precedents as objective events provide the truth value for theoretical constructions that aim to describe the essential features of arguments. If the essential feature is correct, we will not find any counterexamples in real life that lack an abstract propositional structure yet are still considered arguments. A theoretical construction cannot determine its correctness by itself but must appeal to a more fundamental level of existence to confirm it. Argumentative precedents serve this purpose by recording the history of argument and argumentation, providing an objective threshold for testing theoretical constructions.

In the second example, Schaffer describes the situation that subjective existences are grounded in objective existences. "Consider the physical state of Socrates and his mental state. For the physicalist, the physical state realizes the mental state" [15, p. 52]. There is a hierarchical relationship between the physical and the mental. In physicalist theories, mental states depend on physical states—not the other way around. This mode of grounding can also be applied to explain the relationship between the abstract sense of argument and the fourth sense of argument. The abstract sense of argument is a kind of subjective construction, whereas the fourth sense of argument refers to objective events. Subjective things depend on objective things—this is a form of constitutive dependence. If a subjective thing exists, there must be an objective basis to support it. Siegel uses the word 'abstract' to modify the first sense of argument, indicating that this sense of argument is a type of abstraction. Abstraction must regard individual objects as targets, aiming to capture the common features they share. In argumentation theory, these objects are real events in the practice of argumentation, providing the foundational material for people to construct theoretical frameworks about arguments.

There is no need to consider the process of creating abstract propositional senses of arguments here; we can assume their existence directly. The key point to focus on is what makes them true and the objective basis that provides the material for their construction. The answer to this question reflects a conceptual level that differentiates various existences. The elements that determine the truth value of a theoretical construction are more fundamental than the thing being tested. The content of abstract constructions relies on the characteristics of real events in the world. These relationships are not affected by time; they are synchronic.

What is the difference between my priority claim and Siegel's claim? In the fourth example, Schaffer distinguishes the qualified thing ('thick particular') from its substratum ('thin particular') and its modes ('such') [15, p. 53]. The abstract propositional sense of argument belongs to the thin particular, which serves as the basis, while other senses of argument are thick particulars that originate from the mode of the thin particular. My claim about priority concerns the truth-makers and objective basis underlying the abstract propositional sense of argument. Siegel's claim and mine both offer plausible understandings of priority, but from different perspectives.

4.4 Addressing Potential Objections

I want to address a potential objection from Lumer. He provides an instrumental argument to justify the epistemic function of arguments. Let us summarize his arguments briefly. In the first part, Lumer reviews the semantic argument presented by Siegel. "In my opinion, the sentence 'arguments are what arguers traffic in when arguing' can also be expressed in this way: In argumentation acts (arguments5), arguments1 are put forward; the former therefore contain arguments1. One can then add: Argumentative discussions (arguments2) in turn consist largely and essentially of argumentation acts (arguments5), that is, they contain them. Arguments5 and arguments2 are thus ontologically and definitionally more complex; arguments1 are ontologically and definitionally, conceptually the simplest and most fundamental of these three types of objects" [10, p. 585]. Lumer captures the main point of Siegel's argument, emphasizing the conceptual analysis of argument and argumentation. In Lumer's framework: Argument1 refers to the abstract propositional sense of argument; Argument2 refers to argumentation; Argument5 refers to argumentative speech acts. According to this analysis, in the conceptual dimension, Argument1 is the most fundamental.

Other types of arguments cannot exist without containing Argument1. Lumer considers this part of Siegel's argument to be convincing. However, Lumer misses the same point as Siegel. Both provide a plausible analysis of arguments and argumentation but fail to consider other plausible explanations for the priority among the four senses of argument. This oversight weakens the overall persuasive power of their arguments.

The second part of Lumer's arguments emphasizes the priority of the epistemic function, and argues that Siegel fails in this regard. He critiques Siegel's stance, stating, "I fear that this argument in favour of the primacy of the epistemic conception of arguments1 is begging the question" [10, p. 587]. To support epistemic priority, he appeals to two factors: the etymology of 'argument', linking it to the pursuit of knowledge, and the practical benefits of Argument1's various functions.

I focus on Lumer's second reason supporting epistemic function: "Rather, importance is a practical question of value, answered by value judgments—primarily prudential and only secondarily moral" [10, p. 589]. 'Importance' is not intrinsic to objects, actions, or goals but depends on societal and individual valuations shaped by context, needs, and circumstances. Prudential judgments assess what benefits an individual's well-being or goals (e.g., job choice based on salary or work-life balance), while moral judgments consider ethical principles and societal norms (e.g., fairness, justice). Lumer argues that prudential value should take precedence over moral value in such assessments.

Lumer justifies prudential value by weighing the pros and cons of different functions. On knowledge, he argues: "To orient ourselves and plan actions successfully, we need substantial, true beliefs that represent the world correctly and provide relevant information" [10, p. 589]. For instance, a farmer optimizing crop yield must understand local climate, soil, and seasonal patterns. True beliefs guide effective action; without them, goals remain unattainable. Lumer contends that other functions, like persuasion or consensus-seeking, are inferior to the epistemic function, as they do not primarily produce true beliefs and may spread falsehoods, hindering real-world success.

Lumer's understanding of argument's function is insightful, as it fills the gap in Siegel's theory. He poses the question: Can we accept an argument that is epistemically weak but achieves another pragmatic goal? Lumer's answer is no—other pragmatic functions should be built on epistemic standards. Similar to Siegel's priority claim, the epistemic function is the thin thing, while other functions are the thick thing. Therefore, the latter is grounded in the former. This argument is strong, but can we consider the priority of an argument's function from another perspective to formulate a complete claim?

The essential function of argument is to justify conclusions, as Lumer suggests. However, argument is not merely an abstract concept; it is used in real life, where it serves additional functions. The work of Perelman [13] and Toulmin [22] supports the claim that argument and argumentation are not a priori things that can exist independently of the real world. Instead, it remains grounded in practical contexts where arguers use it. "Determining which argumentative norms are operative within any given social group and which ought to be normative is not the task of the argumentation theorist alone. It is a collaborative effort among various disciplines and, importantly, social actors themselves" [17, p. 40]. Therefore, argument should serve a function that connects with the goals of people operating within a social context. The role of argument is similar to that of a hammer: while a hammer possesses essential traits, its practical use depends on human goals, such as pulling nails out of a wooden board.

So, I aim to distinguish between the basic epistemic function of argument and the oriented function that reflects the arguer's goal. While arguers' goals may align with achieving true beliefs, this is not always the case. There are numerous precedents where the goals of argumentation include persuasion or the expression of personal or collective desires rather than the pursuit of truth. For example, in political deliberation, arguers seek to determine the correct course of action. However, their fundamental motivations are often shaped by values such as wealth, power, or authority. To achieve success, they must rely on true beliefs about relevant matters, yet true beliefs are not their ultimate goal. In other words, by treating true beliefs as a means, one can achieve various objectives beyond simply seeking the truth. Therefore, it is difficult to convincingly argue that the epistemic function should take precedence over the oriented function, as they are interconnected rather than one being prioritized over the other. Staying on the same conceptual level with the abstract propositional sense of argument, the function of argument is also a kind of abstraction grounded in argumentative precedents.

5 Conclusions

Dutilh Novaes says: "One possible interpretation of my investigation is that it dissolves, rather than solves (in Wittgenstein's terms), the problem of the justification of deduction as traditionally construed by emphasizing the 'human factor' behind the abstract concept" [5, p. 237]. My work is similar to hers, emphasizing the practical dimension contained within the abstract understanding of argument.

The four senses of argument distinguished by Siegel are insightful, and his priority claim is epistemically strong. However, alternative perspectives on the priority claim are possible. In this paper, I propose two priority claims that differ from Siegel's. First, the abstract propositional sense of argument is grounded in argumentative precedents through two distinct modes: truth-making and objective basis. Second, the epistemic function and the oriented function of argument are entangled, existing on the same conceptual level as the abstract propositional sense of argument. On the topic of the meta-consideration of argumentation theory, we arrive at different conclusions. Both Siegel's argument and mine are plausible, suggesting that the problem of priority in argumentation theory remains open—complex and still undetermined.

Acknowledgments. I extend my sincere gratitude to the two anonymous reviewers for their valuable comments, which have significantly improved this paper.

References

1. Aberdein, A.: Virtue in argument. Argumentation **24**, 165–179 (2010)
2. Aberdein, A.: Virtues suffice for argument evaluation. Informal Logic **43**(4), 543–559 (2023)
3. Aberdein, A., Cohen, D.H.: Introduction: virtues and arguments. Topoi **35**, 339–343 (2016)
4. Biro, J., Siegel, H.: In defense of the objective epistemic approach to argumentation. Informal Logic **26**(1), 91–101 (2006)
5. Dutilh Novaes, C.: The Dialogical Roots of Deduction: Historical, Cognitive, and Philosophical Perspectives on Reasoning. Cambridge University Press, Cambridge (2021)
6. van Eemeren, F.H., Garssen, B., van Haaften, T., et al.: Handbook of Argumentation Theory. Springer, Dordrecht (2014)
7. van Eemeren, F.H., Grootendorst, R.: Rationale for a pragma-dialectical perspective. Argumentation **2**(2), 271–291 (1988)
8. van Eemeren, F.H., Grootendorst, R.: A Systematic Theory of Argumentation: The Pragma-Dialectical Approach. Cambridge University Press, Cambridge (2004)
9. Garssen, B.: A reaction to critique from the epistemological sidelines. Informal Logic **43**(4), 527–542 (2023)
10. Lumer, C.: Justifying the epistemological theory of argumentation: on harvey siegel's approach. Informal Logic **43**(4), 574–600 (2023)
11. O'Keefe, D.J.: Two concepts of argument. J. Am. Forensic Assoc. **13**, 121–128 (1977)
12. Olmos, P.: That obscure object of (philosophical) desire. Informal Logic **43**(4), 560–573 (2023)
13. Perelman, C.: Reflections on practical reason. In: The New Rhetoric and the Humanities: Essays on Rhetoric and Its Applications, pp. 124–133. D. Reidel Publishing Company, Dordrecht (1979)
14. Schaffer, J.: Grounding, transitivity, and contrastivity. In: Correia, F., Schnieder, B. (eds.) Metaphysical Grounding: Understanding the Structure of Reality, pp. 122–138. Cambridge University Press, Cambridge (2012)
15. Schaffer, J.: Grounding in the image of causation. Philos. Stud. **173**(1), 49–100 (2016)
16. Schaffer, J.: Anchoring as grounding: on epstein's the ant trap. Philos. Phenomenological Res. **95**(3), 666–672 (2017)
17. Scott, B.D.: What makes an argument strong? Contrastivism in the new rhetoric. Informal Logic **44**(1), 19–43 (2024)
18. Siegel, H.: Arguing with arguments: argument quality, argumentative norms, and the strengths of the epistemic theory. Informal Logic **43**(4), 465–526 (2023)
19. Siegel, H.: Arguing about arguing with arguments: replies to my critics. Informal Logic **44**(4), 509–542 (2024)
20. Tindale, C.W.: The Philosophy of Argument and Audience Reception. Cambridge University Press, Cambridge (2015)
21. Tindale, C.W.: The Anthropology of Argument: Cultural Foundations of Rhetoric and Reason. Routledge, New York (2021)

22. Toulmin, S.E.: The Uses of Argument. Cambridge University Press, New York (2003)
23. Wenzel, J.W.: Three perspectives on argument. In: Trapp, R., Schutz, J. (eds.) Perspectives on Argumentation: Essays in Honour of Wayne Brockriede, pp. 9–16. Waveland Press, Prospect Heights (1990)
24. Willard, C.A.: Argumentation and the Social Grounds of Knowledge. University of Alabama Press, Tuscaloosa (1983)

Argument-Based Belief and the Evidence Topology

John I. Lindqvist[1](✉) and Chenwei Shi[2]

[1] University of Bergen, 5007 Bergen, Norway
john.lindqvist@uib.no
[2] Tsinghua University, Haidian District, Beijing 100084, China

Abstract. This manuscript introduces Argument Belief Models (AB models), a framework for reasoning about belief, knowledge, and evidence, integrating epistemic evidence logic and abstract argumentation. Building on the ideas of Topological Argumentation Models (TA models), that incorporate tools from argumentation theory into topological evidence logic, AB models distinguish between evidence (information states) and arguments (supporting justifications for evidence), thereby allowing for a more nuanced selection of rational beliefs. By defining an attack relation on arguments rather than directly on evidence, AB models clarify how relative argument strength influences belief formation. We formally define AB models, investigate their logical properties, and establish a connection between grounded belief in AB models and TA models. Finally, we show that under certain conditions, AB models align with TA models. This work contributes to a more refined logical understanding of belief formation and opens pathways for further research into structured epistemic reasoning based on argumentation.

Keywords: Epistemic Logic · Topological Argumentation Models · Attack Graphs · Grounded Belief · Argument Belief Models

1 Introduction

Evidence, belief, and knowledge are fundamental to rational thought and human understanding. Evidence serves as the foundation for validating claims, supporting theories, and guiding decisions. Belief refers to the acceptance of ideas, which often shape individual and collective actions, even in the absence of certainty. Knowledge can emerge when evidence and belief converge to form true and justified beliefs, enabling deeper understanding and more informed interactions with the world.

Epistemic logic [8] is a simple and powerful framework for reasoning about knowledge and belief and related notions. In models where information is represented abstractly by ranges of possibilities, epistemic notions find natural interpretations. Several variants and extensions of epistemic logic exist, with some [3,4] specifically focusing on evidence and its relationship to belief and knowledge. These epistemic evidence logics take a semantic approach to the task of providing a tool for reasoning about evidence, defining the logic on evidence models. This approach can be contrasted with more syntactic approaches, such as that in justification logic [1,2]. In evidence models, a piece of evidence is represented by a range of possible worlds (the set of situations compatible with the evidence). The evidence possessed by an agent is modelled as a set of such ranges of possible worlds. Rational (evidence-based) belief is defined so that the agent believes a proposition when (all) the evidence it possesses can be strengthened to support the proposition. While infallible knowledge can be defined as it usually is in epistemic logic (as truth throughout the considered possibilities), a weaker and more general form of knowledge can be defined as correctly justified belief – belief supported by factive evidence. Topological evidence models (TE models) [3] capture the topological structure of evidence, making them a good tool for reasoning about the evidence, belief and knowledge of (idealized) rational agents. An evidence topology begins with basic evidence from external sources. It incorporates reasoning through intersections, which represent combinations of evidence, and unions, which represent its weakening.

However, topological reasoning provides no way to differentiate and select between conflicting evidence. Abstract argumentation theory [5], on the other hand, specifically studies the selection of arguments from a set of conflicting (abstract) arguments. The impetus for the work on topological argumentation models (TA models) in [12–16] is the idea that evidence in TE models can be treated as abstract arguments. Attack graphs from abstract argumentation provide a very general way of representing the differing strength of conflicting arguments. Tools from argumentation theory can then be used to select among the evidence, giving stronger rational beliefs built on both (topo-)logical and argumentation-theoretic reasoning. Making use of this, *grounded belief* is defined using the notion of the grounded extension of a set of arguments, along with notions of grounded knowledge.[1] These capture a notion of rational belief and knowledge based on the 'best' evidence, by incorporating tools from argumentation theory into epistemic logic.

The work on TA models employs tools from abstract argumentation primarily to manage conflicting evidence. In contrast, other proposals aim to integrate abstract argumentation with epistemic logic to enable reasoning about agents' beliefs concerning arguments. For instance, [11] and [9] develop multiagent frameworks that represent agents' debates, their awareness of arguments, and changes in that awareness over time. Similarly, [7] combines abstract argumentation with epistemic logic using product models – structures formed by taking the product of attack graphs and epistemic models. In this setting, both argumentation-theoretic properties and argument endorsement can be represented, allowing justified belief to be defined as belief supported by endorsed arguments with the right properties. In contrast, the logic of belief in TA models does not reason explicitly about arguments. Rather, the structure of attack graphs is used implicitly to guide the selection of evidence. Unlike paraconsistent approaches that handle conflicting evidence by providing non-classical logics for

---

[1] [15] also explores a notion of 'fully' grounded belief, while [13] explores different variants of grounded knowledge.

reasoning directly about contradictions (e.g. [6,10]), the logic of evidence, belief, and knowledge on TA models remains monotonic.

The present manuscript builds on the work on grounded belief and knowledge in TA models by introducing a similar framework for belief, knowledge, and evidence, in which evidence (in the sense above) is distinguished from argument. Throughout the manuscript, 'evidence' will be used in the sense of an information state, a set of possible worlds, that the agent has reason to accept while whatever is giving an agent a reason to accept that information state is referred to as 'argument' – the argument is what supports the evidence. Although the treatment of evidence as arguments makes sense there are also advantages to separating the evidence from the arguments supporting the evidence. It allows distinction between multiple sources supporting the same evidence and separating the evaluation of argument strength from the evidence topology makes it clearer how the relative weight of arguments guides the selection of evidence for further reasoning. We therefore introduce *argument belief models* (AB models), and study the logic of belief, knowledge, and evidence on AB models. In these models a set of abstract arguments are related to sets of possible worlds – to the evidence they support. The attack relation is defined on the arguments, and the basic evidence supported by arguments generates the evidence topology.

The manuscript is organised as follows. Section 2 presents the basics of TE models, TA models, as well as the language of belief, knowledge and evidence on those models, and illustrates the different notions of belief with an example. Section 3 motivates and introduces the new AB models, as well as a lifting of the attack relation to collections (or 'camps') of arguments. This new attack relation is used to relate the arguments to evidence (and propositions) in general. The attack relation is studied and a version of the previous example is used to demonstrate how the models work. Section 4 defines *argument-based belief* and *knowledge*, and studies validity of the language of belief, knowledge and evidence on AB models. In Sect. 5, the relationship between the camps of arguments in AB models and the evidence topology is investigated, and conditions are identified under which AB models and TA models coincide. Finally, Sect. 6 concludes with a discussion of future directions.

2 Background

What follows is the definition of the original TE models of [3], the definition of attack graphs of [5], and the definitions of TA models and the language of grounded belief, knowledge and evidence of [15].

Definition 1. *A* topological evidence frame (TEF) *[3] is a tuple* $(W, \mathcal{E}, \tau_\mathcal{E})$, *in which* $W \neq \varnothing$ *is a set of possible worlds;* $\mathcal{E} \subseteq 2^W$ *is the set of* basic evidence *– a collection of non-empty subsets of* W *(with* $W \in \mathcal{E}$*);* $\tau_\mathcal{E} \subseteq \mathcal{P}(W)$ *is the* evidence topology *generated by* $\mathcal{E}$, *the smallest set such that:* $\mathcal{E} \subseteq \tau_\mathcal{E}$, $\varnothing, W \in \tau_\mathcal{E}$, $\tau_\mathcal{E}$ *is closed under finite intersections and arbitrary unions.*

A topological evidence model *is a tuple* $(W, \mathcal{E}, \tau_\mathcal{E}, v)$, *in which* $(W, \mathcal{E}, \tau_\mathcal{E})$ *is a TEF and* v *is a valuation function.* ◄

Definition 2. *An* attack graph *[5] is a tuple* $(A, \hookleftarrow)$, *where* $A \neq \emptyset$ *is a set of* arguments; $\hookleftarrow \subseteq (A \times A)$ *is the* attack relation; $a \hookleftarrow b$ – *read as* '*b attacks a*'. ◂

Definition 3. *Let* $\mathcal{A} = (A, \hookleftarrow)$ *be an attack graph. A set of arguments* $B \subseteq A$ defends *an argument* $a \in A$ *iff* $\forall b \in A$ *such that* $a \hookleftarrow b$, $\exists c \in B$ *such that* $b \hookleftarrow c$.

The defense function $d_\mathcal{A}$ *of* $\mathcal{A}$ *takes a set of arguments* $B \subseteq A$ *and returns the arguments defended by* B:

$$d_\mathcal{A}(B) := \{c \in A \mid c \text{ is defended by } B\}.$$

The grounded extension[2] $LFP_\mathcal{A}$ *of* $\mathcal{A}$ *is the least fixed point of* $d_\mathcal{A}$: *the smallest set* $B \subseteq A$ *such that* $d_\mathcal{A}(B) = B$. *(When* $\hookleftarrow$ *is understood by context,* d_A *and* LFP_A *are used to refer to* $d_\mathcal{A}$ *and* $LFP_\mathcal{A}$.) ◂

Definition 4. *A* topological argumentation frame *(TAF) [15] is a tuple* $(W, \mathcal{E}, \tau_\mathcal{E}, \hookleftarrow)$ *where* $(W, \mathcal{E}, \tau_\mathcal{E})$ *is a TEF, and* $\hookleftarrow \subseteq \tau_\mathcal{E} \times \tau_\mathcal{E}$ *is an attack relation such that for* $T, T_1, T_2 \in \tau_\mathcal{E}$:

(i) $T_1 \hookleftarrow T_2$ *or* $T_2 \hookleftarrow T_1$ *if and only if* $T_1 \cap T_2 = \emptyset$;
(ii) $\emptyset \hookleftarrow T$ *and* $T \not\hookleftarrow \emptyset$.

A topological argumentation model *(TA model)* $(W, \mathcal{E}, \tau_\mathcal{E}, \hookleftarrow, v)$ *extends a TAF with a valuation function* v. ◂

Abstract argumentation allows evaluation of evidence based not only on what each piece individually states but also on its relationship with other pieces of evidence. This relationship can be specified with the attack relation. The attack relation in TA models is set up to allow a form of priority between conflicting (i.e., mutually inconsistent) pieces of evidence.

This manuscript will be considering formal languages of belief, knowledge and evidence, defined on TE, TA and AB models. $\mathcal{L}$ denotes the basic propositional language, and $\mathcal{L}_{X_1,...,X_n}$ denotes the language that extends $\mathcal{L}$ with the modalities $X_1, ..., X_n$. Formulas are interpreted relative to pointed models $\mathcal{M}, w$ (with $w \in W \in \mathcal{M}$), and truth of a formula φ relative to a pointed model $\mathcal{M}, w$ is denoted $\mathcal{M}, w \vDash \varphi$. $[\![\varphi]\!]_\mathcal{M}$ denotes the set of worlds $w \in W$ in $\mathcal{M}$ such that $\mathcal{M}, w \vDash \varphi$. A formula is valid on a model $\mathcal{M}$ (in symbols, $\mathcal{M} \vDash \varphi$) if $\mathcal{M}, w \vDash \varphi$ for all $w \in W$. It is valid in a class of models if it is valid in each model of that class. What follows are the semantics for belief in TE and TA models.

Definition 5. *Let* $\mathcal{M} = (W, \mathcal{E}, \tau_\mathcal{E}, \hookleftarrow, v)$ *be a TA model and* $w \in W$. *The agent has* topological belief *that* φ *(in symbols:* $B^t \varphi$*) if and only if every piece of evidence in the evidence topology can be strengthened to a piece of evidence that supports* φ *[3].*

The agent has grounded belief *that* φ *(in symbols:* $B^g \varphi$*) if and only if there is an argument in the grounded extension of* $\tau_\mathcal{E}$ *supporting* φ *[15], that is*

---

[2] The *extension* of an attack graph in abstract argumentation is a subset of arguments with some desirable properties. The grounded extension is an example of this, and is the smallest set of arguments that is conflict-free and self-defending.

$$\mathcal{M}, w \vDash B^t\varphi \quad \textit{iff} \quad \forall E \in \tau_\mathcal{E}, \exists E' \in \tau_\mathcal{E} \text{ such that } E' \subseteq E \text{ and } E' \subseteq \llbracket\varphi\rrbracket_\mathcal{M}$$
$$\mathcal{M}, w \vDash B^g\varphi \quad \textit{iff} \quad \exists F \in LFP_{\tau_\mathcal{E}} \text{ such that } F \subseteq \llbracket\varphi\rrbracket_\mathcal{M}.$$

◀

Below is a simple example illustrating the difference between the two notions of belief.

Example 1. *An investigator is trying to figure out the colour of the clothes of the perpetrator of a crime, based on the testimony of three witnesses. One of the witnesses, A, is generally more reliable than the other two, B and C, who in turn seem equally reliable (perhaps B and C were returning home from a social gathering and may have been less observant when they witnessed the crime, while A is sober and seems like an observant person). The testimony that the investigator gets is as follows: A claims that the perpetrator was wearing an orange jacket, while B claims that the perpetrator was wearing a green jacket and C that the perpetrator was wearing a yellow jacket.*

The investigator then ends up considering three possibilities in W, $W = \{o, g, y\}$, such that the jacket in question is orange (O) in o, green (G) in g and yellow (Y) in y, and three pieces of evidence in $\mathcal{E}$, $e_O = \{o\}$, $e_G = \{g\}$ and $e_Y = \{y\}$ (and to get an evidence topology $\tau_\mathcal{E}$, simply add $\varnothing$ and W). The attack relation that captures the difference in reliability of the testimony is then $\hookleftarrow = \{(e_O, e_G), (e_O, e_Y), (e_G, e_Y), (e_Y, e_G)\}$ (omitting the attacks on the empty set for presentation), and we have a TA model $\mathcal{M}$:

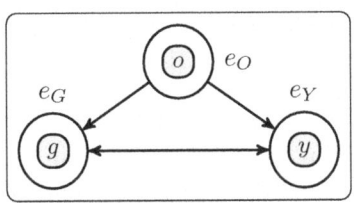

It is easy to see that $LFP_\tau = \{W, e_O\}$. Thus, while $\mathcal{M} \vDash \neg B^t O$ - the investigator does not have topological belief that the perpetrators jacket is orange, $\mathcal{M} \vDash B^g O$ - the investigator has grounded belief that the perpetrators jacket was orange based on the strongest evidence e_O, since its relative strength allows her to discard the weaker conflicting evidence e_G and e_Y.

◀

As well as belief, the languages under consideration have operators for evidence and knowledge. The language $\mathcal{L}_{U,\square,K^g}$ [15] has modal operators for infallible knowledge (U), factive evidence ($\square$) and grounded knowledge (K^g).

Definition 6.
$$\mathcal{M}, w \vDash U\varphi \quad \textit{iff} \quad W \subseteq \llbracket\varphi\rrbracket_\mathcal{M}$$
$$\mathcal{M}, w \vDash \square\varphi \quad \textit{iff} \quad \exists T \in \tau_\mathcal{E} \setminus \varnothing \text{ such that } w \in T \subseteq \llbracket\varphi\rrbracket_\mathcal{M}$$
$$\mathcal{M}, w \vDash K^g\varphi \quad \textit{iff} \quad \exists F \in LFP_{\tau_\mathcal{E}} \text{ such that } w \in F \subseteq \llbracket\varphi\rrbracket_\mathcal{M}$$

◀

Note that the operators for infallible knowledge and factive evidence rely only on the evidence topology, and so are defined for TE models as well as TA models (and as we will see, for AB models). Note also that in $\mathcal{L}_{U,\Box,K^g,B^g}$, K^g and B^g are mutually definable [15].

In [13] additional conditions on the attack relation $\hookleftarrow$ are considered. These conditions concern assumptions about when elements of the evidence topology that represent weakening or strengthening of attacking/attacked evidence should also be attacking/attacked by the same conflicting evidence.

Definition 7. *A TAF++ [13] is a TAF satisfying the following two conditions on $\hookleftarrow$:*

(1) for every $T_1, T_1', T_2 \in \tau_\mathcal{E}$: if $T_1 \hookleftarrow T_2$ and $T_1' \subseteq T_1$, then $T_1' \hookleftarrow T_2$;
(2) for every T_1, T_2, T_2' : if $T_1 \hookleftarrow T_2$, $T_2 \subseteq T_2'$ and $T_1 \cap T_2' = \varnothing$, then $T_1 \hookleftarrow T_2'$.

The additional conditions on a TAF++ can be seen as rationality constraints on the agent whose evidence is modelled. Together, they ensure that the grounded extension of the attack graph in the frame is easy to compute: in a TAF++ $LFP_{\tau_\mathcal{E}} = d_{\tau_\mathcal{E}}(d_{\tau_\mathcal{E}}(\varnothing))$ (Corollary 4.6 in [13]). Meanwhile, the axiomatization for TA models and TAF++ models is the same.

3 Argument Belief Models

This manuscript introduces and analyses a new type of argumentation-based belief models, in which the attack relation is defined on a set of abstract arguments, and the evidence is generated by these arguments.

Separating the evidence from the underlying argument makes conceptual sense, and 'attacks' between arguments may seem more intuitive than 'attacks' between pieces of evidence. It separates the evaluation of argument strength from the evidence topology, eliminating the need to define an attack relation for the entire topology. In contrast to TA models – where topological reasoning occurs before establishing the attack relation and selecting the best evidence – linking the attack relation directly to the arguments clarifies how their relative strengths determine which evidence informs further reasoning. Separating the arguments from the evidence also allows more flexibility when modelling e.g. allowing different arguments (with different strength relative to conflicting arguments) to support the same proposition. For example, the arguments in question could be testimony and multiple sources (with different reliability-related properties) could provide the same testimony.

What follows is the definition of the AB models.

Definition 8. *Argument belief model*

An argument belief frame (ABF) *is a tuple $(W, Arg, f, \hookleftarrow)$ where W is a non-empty set of possible worlds; Arg is a non-empty set of arguments; $f : Arg \to 2^W \setminus \varnothing$ is a function mapping arguments in Arg to sets of possible worlds; and $\hookleftarrow$ is an attack relation such that $(Arg, \hookleftarrow)$ is an attack graph and:*

$$a \hookleftarrow a' \text{ or } a' \hookleftarrow a \text{ if and only if } f(a) \cap f(a') = \varnothing;$$

An argument belief model (AB model) *is a tuple* $(W, Arg, f, \hookleftarrow, v)$ *consisting of an argument belief frame* $(W, Arg, f, \hookleftarrow)$ *and a valuation function* v. *The evidence set* ϵ *is defined:*

$$\epsilon = \{E \subseteq W \mid \exists a \in Arg : f(a) = E\}. \qquad \blacktriangleleft$$

The function f tells us what information is supported by each abstract argument, generating the evidence set ϵ. The role of the attack relation is, like in the original TA models, to capture a situation in which the agent finds the source of some of her information more reliable (or, somehow better) than other sources. To do this, the attack relation is defined to include at least one attack between arguments that support conflicting information (that is, arguments a and a' such that $f(a) \cap f(a') = \varnothing$). Note that it is also assumed that there are no attacks if the supported information is consistent. That is because in such cases, there is no need to consider which source of information is more reliable.[3] If the agent considers both sources of information (arguments) equally reliable, it is captured by attacks in both directions. Otherwise, the more reliable argument attacks the less reliable argument, and not vice versa. Note that unlike a preference ordering on the information, the way that the agent differentiates the strength of the arguments means that when considering several arguments, the difference does not need to be transitive.

In order to define belief, we first lift the attack relation to the groups of arguments in support of a proposition, or the 'camps' of arguments.

Definition 9. *For* $P \subseteq W$ *define* $Arg(P) = \{a \in Arg \mid f(a) \subseteq P\}$, *the set of arguments that support the proposition* P. *(Note that* Arg *is still used for the set of all arguments.) For an argument belief model* $\mathcal{M} = (W, Arg, f, \hookleftarrow, v)$ *the set of camps* $\mathcal{C}$ *is defined:*

$$\mathcal{C} = \{C \in 2^{Arg} \setminus \varnothing \mid \exists P \subseteq W . Arg(P) = C\}.$$

For $C \in \mathcal{C}$, *let* $f(C) = \bigcup_{a \in C} f(a)$. *The 'lifted' attack graph* $(\mathcal{C}, \hookleftarrow)$, *for* $C_1, C_2 \in \mathcal{C}$, *is then defined:*

$C_1 \hookleftarrow C_2$ *iff (1)* $f(C_1) \cap f(C_2) = \varnothing$, *and*

(2) for all $a \in C_1$ *there is some* $b \in C_2$ *such that* $a \hookleftarrow b$. $\qquad \blacktriangleleft$

Note that the attack graph on camps is defined in such a way that similar to the underlying attack graph there will be at least one attack between camps if and only if the propositions they support are inconsistent.

Proposition 1. *Let* $C_1, C_2 \in \mathcal{C}$. *Then*

$$C_1 \hookleftarrow C_2 \text{ or } C_2 \hookleftarrow C_1 \text{ iff } f(C_1) \cap f(C_2) = \varnothing.$$

---

[3] If one wanted to capture situations in which arguments supporting the same propositions attack each other, this condition would have to be weakened.

Proof. The left-to-right direction follows immediately from the definition. For the right-to-left direction, assume $f(C_1) \cap f(C_2) = \emptyset$. Then, for all $a \in C_1$ and $a' \in C_2$, $a \hookleftarrow a'$ or $a' \hookleftarrow a$. Now assume that $C_1 \not\hookleftarrow C_2$. Then, there is some $a \in C_1$ such that for all $a' \in C_2$, $a \not\hookleftarrow a'$. Then, for all $a' \in C_2$, $a' \hookleftarrow a$, and thus $C_2 \hookleftarrow C_1$.

A camp of arguments C_2 (unified by their support of a proposition) attacks another camp C_1 in case the evidence they support conflict and the arguments of C_2 defend themselves against any arguments for C_1. Considering camps rather than individual arguments through this lifting operation allows the attack graph to be directly related to arbitrary propositions. It also allows camps into the grounded extension of camps in situations where no corresponding argument will be included in the grounded extension, thereby allowing 'stronger' beliefs – beliefs in the propositions supported by those camps. To see how this works, consider the following example.

Example 2. *Consider again the investigator trying to figure out the colour of the clothes of a perpetrator. This time there are four witnesses. Two of the witnesses, A_1 and A_2, are generally more reliable than the other two, B and C. The testimony that the investigator gets is as follows: A_1 and A_2 both claim that the perpetrator was wearing an orange jacket, while B claims that the perpetrator was wearing a green jacket and C that the perpetrator was wearing a yellow jacket. Now, while they are generally more reliable, A_1 and A_2 suffer from different kinds of colour blindness: A_1 suffers from protanomaly, and is unable to tell orange from green, while A_2 suffers from deuteranomaly, and is unable to tell orange from yellow. The investigator, taking these factors into account, considers A_1 generally more reliable than C but, in this specific case, views B as more reliable than A_1. Similarly, the investigator considers A_2 more reliable than B but in this particular instance considers C more reliable than A_2. That gives us the attack graph $\hookleftarrow$ on set of arguments $Arg = \{a_{A_1}, a_{A_2}, a_B, a_C\}$:*

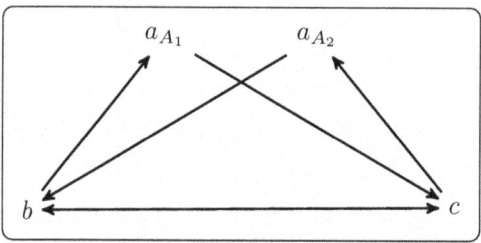

A first thing to note is that a_{A_1} and a_{A_2} do not end up in LFP_{Arg}. Since every argument in Arg is attacked $d_{Arg}(\emptyset) = \emptyset = LFP_{Arg}$. This means that a_{A_1} and a_{A_2} will not be available if we define beliefs on the grounded extension of the attack graph.[4]

---

[4] LFP_{Arg} being empty would cause more trouble for a definition of grounded belief like that in Definition 5. That could however be dealt with, e.g. by assuming an argument always exists for the unit W of possible worlds, in order not to end up

However, the situation is different when we consider attacks among camps.
$\mathcal{M}$ generates the camps $\mathcal{C} = \{C_A = \{a_{A_1}, a_{A_2}\}, C_B = \{a_B\}, C_C = \{a_C\}, C_{AB} = \{a_{A_1}, a_{A_2}, a_B\}, C_{AC} = \{a_{A_1}, a_{A_2}, a_C\}, C_{BC} = \{a_B, a_C\}, C_W = Arg\}$, with the attack graph on camps (C_W omitted as it is not attacking or attacked by any camp):

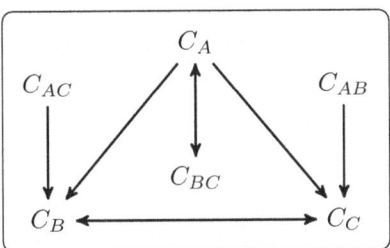

Then, $d_{\mathcal{C}}(\varnothing) = \{C_{AB}, C_{AC}, C_W\}$, and $d_{\mathcal{C}}(\{C_{AB}, C_{AC}, C_W\}) = LFP_{\mathcal{C}}$. Since the camps supporting $O \vee G$ and $O \vee Y$ is in $LFP_{\mathcal{C}}$ ($C_{AB} = Arg(\{o, g\})$, $C_{AC} = Arg(\{o, y\})$), the investigator is able to take this evidence into account. As defined below, this allows the inspector to form the argument-based beliefs otherwise unavailable.

The example shows a situation in which sources of conflicting evidence, if the sources are taken individually, may not yield some strongest evidence (in the sense of a non-empty grounded extension of arguments), while considering camps of arguments together yields a different result, allowing a selection of some strongest evidence.

Because of the way camps of arguments and the lifting of the attack relation from arguments to camps is defined, conditions corresponding to the rationality constraints on a TAF++ will hold of the attack relation on camps in an ABF.

Proposition 2. Let $\mathcal{M}$ be an AB model. Then, the following holds of $(\mathcal{C}, \hookleftarrow)$. For $C_1, C_1', C_2, C_2' \in \mathcal{C}$:

(1) if $C_1 \hookleftarrow C_2$ and $C_1' \subseteq C_1$, then $C_1' \hookleftarrow C_2$,
(2) if $C_1 \hookleftarrow C_2$, $C_2 \subseteq C_2'$ and $f(C_1) \cap f(C_2') = \varnothing$, then $C_1 \hookleftarrow C_2'$.

Proof. (1) Assume that $C_1 \hookleftarrow C_2$ and $C_1' \subseteq C_1$. Then $f(C_1) \cap f(C_2) = \varnothing$, and for all $a \in C_1$ there is some $a' \in C_2$ such that $a \hookleftarrow a'$. Since $C_1' \subseteq C_1$, for all $a \in C_1'$ there is some $a' \in C_2$ such that $a \hookleftarrow a'$. By the definition of $\mathcal{C}$, $f(C_1') \subseteq f(C_1)$, which means that $f(C_1') \cap f(C_2) = \varnothing$. Thus, the (1) and (2) conditions on the lifting are satisfied for $C_1' \hookleftarrow C_2$.
(2) Assume $C_1 \hookleftarrow C_2$, $C_2 \subseteq C_2'$, and $f(C_1) \cap f(C_2') = \varnothing$. Due to the last fact, the condition (1) for $C_1 \hookleftarrow C_2'$ is satisfied. From the assumption that $C_1 \hookleftarrow C_2$ it follows that for every $a \in C_1$, there is some $a' \in C_2$ such that $a \hookleftarrow a'$. Then, since $C_2 \subseteq C_2'$, for every $a \in C_1$, there is some $a' \in C_2'$ such that $a \hookleftarrow a'$ and condition (2) is satisfied. Thus, $C_1 \hookleftarrow C_2'$.

---

quantifying over an empty set. The definition of camps ensures the camp supporting W is always in $LFP_{\mathcal{C}}$.

As beliefs will be defined using the grounded extension of the attack graph on camps, $LFP_\mathcal{C}$, it is worth noting that if the camp supporting a proposition P is in $LFP_\mathcal{C}$ then so are the camps supporting any propositions $P' \supseteq P$.

Proposition 3. *Let $\mathcal{M}$ be an argument belief model and $P \subseteq P' \subseteq W$. Then,*

$$\text{if } Arg(P) \in LFP_\mathcal{C} \text{ then } Arg(P') \in LFP_\mathcal{C}.$$

Proof. Assume that $P \subseteq P' \subseteq W$, and that $Arg(P) \in LFP_\mathcal{C}$. It suffices to show that for any $X \subseteq 2^\mathcal{C}$, if $Arg(P) \in d_\mathcal{C}(X)$ then $Arg(P') \in d_\mathcal{C}(X)$. Assume that $Arg(P) \in d_\mathcal{C}(X)$. Assume further that there is some $C \in \mathcal{C}$ such that $Arg(P') \hookleftarrow C$. By Proposition 2 item **(1)**, $Arg(P) \hookleftarrow C$. Thus, since $Arg(P) \in d_\mathcal{C}(X)$, there is some $C' \in X$ such that $C \hookleftarrow C'$. Since this is true for arbitrary $C \in \mathcal{C}$ such that $Arg(P') \hookleftarrow C$, $Arg(P')$ is defended by X and $Arg(P') \in d_\mathcal{C}(X)$.

It is also worth noting that the camp supporting a proposition is the same camp as that supporting the interior of the proposition (the largest open subset contained within the proposition: $Int(P) = \bigcup\{U \in \tau \mid U \subseteq P\}$).

Proposition 4. *Let $\mathcal{M} = (W, Arg, f, \hookleftarrow, v)$ be an AB model, $P \subseteq W$ and let τ_ϵ be the topology generated by ϵ. Then*

$$Arg(Int(P)) = Arg(P).$$

Proof. For left to right, take arbitrary $T \in \tau_\epsilon$ such that $T \subseteq P$. Since $T \subseteq P$, $Arg(T) \subseteq Arg(P)$. Thus, $Arg(\bigcup\{T \in \tau_\epsilon \mid T \subseteq P\}) \subseteq Arg(P)$. For right to left, simply note that $f(Arg(P)) \subseteq \bigcup\{T \in \tau_\epsilon \mid T \subseteq P\}$ (since $\forall a \in Arg(P)$, $f(a) \in \epsilon$). Thus $Arg(f(Arg(P))) = Arg(P) \subseteq Arg(\{T \in \tau_\epsilon \mid T \subseteq P\})$.

Corollary 1. *Let $\mathcal{M} = (W, Arg, f, \hookleftarrow, v)$ be an AB model and $P \subseteq W$. Then*

$$Arg(Int(P)) \in LFP_\mathcal{C} \quad \text{iff} \quad Arg(P) \in LFP_\mathcal{C}.$$

Then, a proposition P is supported by a camp in $LFP_\mathcal{C}$ if and only if there is some evidence $(Int(P))$ in the topology supported by a camp in $LFP_\mathcal{C}$.

4 Argument-Based Grounded Belief and Knowledge

The attack graph on the camps can be used to pick the strongest evidence support: the evidence supported by some camp in the grounded extension of the set of camps. The supporting arguments can then be used to define *argument-based grounded belief*.

Definition 10. *Let $\mathcal{M} = (W, Arg, f, \hookleftarrow, v)$ be an AB model and $w \in W$. The agent has* argument-based grounded belief *that φ (in symbols: $B^a\varphi$) if and only if the camp of arguments supporting φ is in the grounded extension of $\mathcal{C}$, that is*

$$\mathcal{M}, w \vDash B^a\varphi \quad \text{iff} \quad Arg(\llbracket\varphi\rrbracket_\mathcal{M}) \in LFP_\mathcal{C}. \quad \triangleleft$$

The agent thus believes φ if and only if φ is supported by a camp of arguments that is in LFP_C. In Example 2 above, the inspector is able to form the belief that the perpetrator was wearing orange or green ($B^a O \vee G$), based on the combined evidence provided by A_1 and B, and similarly that the perpetrator was wearing orange or yellow ($B^a O \vee Y$), based on the evidence provided by A_2 and C. Note however that $B_a O$ does not follow from this.

This definition of belief specifies that the camp of arguments supporting the believed formula φ has to be in LFP_C. On the surface, that makes it look different from the definition of grounded belief on TA models, that simply requires that some evidence that is a subset of the extension of φ is in LFP_τ. However, it is easy to see that the following is a corollary of Proposition 3.

Corollary 2. Let $\mathcal{M} = (W, Arg, f, \hookleftarrow, v)$ be an AB model and $w \in W$. Then

$$\exists Arg(P) \in LFP_C \text{ such that } P \subseteq [\![\varphi]\!]_\mathcal{M} \quad \text{iff} \quad Arg([\![\varphi]\!]_\mathcal{M}) \in LFP_C.$$

This means that argument-based grounded belief that φ could equivalently be defined using the existence of some camp supporting some proposition P such that $P \subseteq [\![\varphi]\!]_\mathcal{M}$ (making the similarity to grounded belief more clearly visible).

4.1 Validities on AB Models

Below are some validities and non-validities for the argument-based grounded belief operator, starting with the KD45 axioms typically associated with belief. Like for grounded belief, the K axiom fails for argument-based belief. The D, 4 and 5 axioms are valid, however.

Proposition 5.

(1) $\not\models B^a(\varphi \to \psi) \to (B^a \varphi \to B^a \psi)$
(2) $\models B^a \varphi \to \neg B^a \neg \varphi$
(3) $\models B^a \varphi \to B^a B^a \varphi$
(4) $\models \neg B^a \varphi \to B^a \neg B^a \varphi$

Proof. *(1)* Consider the model $\mathcal{M} = (Arg, \hookleftarrow, W, f, v)$, where

- $W = \{w_1, w_2, w_3\}$,
- $Arg = \{a_1, a_2, a_3\}$,
- $f(a_1) = \{w_1, w_2\}, f(a_2) = \{w_2, w_3\}, f(a_3) = \{w_1, w_3\}$
- $\hookleftarrow = \emptyset$.
- $v(P) = \{w_1, w_2\}, v(Q) = \{w_2\}$.

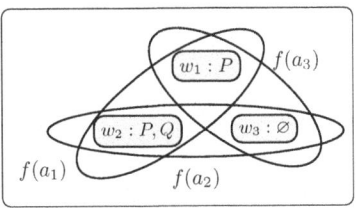

In this model, $LFP_C = \{\{a_1\}, \{a_2\}, \{a_3\}, Arg\}$. Then, $Arg([\![P]\!]_\mathcal{M}) \in LFP_C$ and since $[\![P \to Q]\!]_\mathcal{M} = \{2, 3\}$, $Arg([\![P \to Q]\!]_\mathcal{M}) = \{a_2\} \in LFP_C$, and thus $\mathcal{M}, w_1 \models B^a(P \to Q)$ and $\mathcal{M}, w_1 \models B^a P$. However, $Arg([\![Q]\!]_\mathcal{M}) = \emptyset \notin LFP_C$, and thus $\mathcal{M}, w_1 \not\models B^a Q$.

(2) Assume $\mathcal{M}, w \vDash B^a\varphi$. This means that $Arg([\![\varphi]\!]_\mathcal{M}) \in LFP_\mathcal{C}$. It is easy to see that $f(Arg([\![\varphi]\!]_\mathcal{M})) \cap f(Arg([\![\neg\varphi]\!]_\mathcal{M})) = \varnothing$, and thus (by Proposition 1) $Arg([\![\varphi]\!]_\mathcal{M}) \hookleftarrow Arg([\![\neg\varphi]\!]_\mathcal{M})$ or $Arg([\![\neg\varphi]\!]_\mathcal{M}) \hookleftarrow Arg([\![\varphi]\!]_\mathcal{M})$. But then, since $LFP_\mathcal{C}$ is conflict-free, $Arg([\![\neg\varphi]\!]_\mathcal{M}) \notin LFP_\mathcal{C}$, and $\mathcal{M}, w \vDash \neg B^a \neg\varphi$. Items (3) and (4) are straightforward, as $[\![B^a\varphi]\!]_\mathcal{M} \in \{W, \varnothing\}$.

Argument-based knowledge can be defined similar to grounded knowledge (K^g) on the evidence topology τ_ϵ generated by the AB models:

Definition 11.
$\mathcal{M}, w \vDash K^a\varphi$ iff $\exists T \in \tau_\epsilon$ such that $Arg(T) \in LFP_\mathcal{C}$ and $w \in T \subseteq [\![\varphi]\!]_\mathcal{M}$ ◀

Like for K^g and B^g on TA models, K^a is definable in $\mathcal{L}_{U,\square,B^a}$ and B^a definable in $\mathcal{L}_{U,\square,K^a}$ on AB models.

Proposition 6. Let $\mathcal{M} = (W, Arg, f, \hookleftarrow, v)$ be an AB model and $w \in W$ and $\varphi \in \mathcal{L}_{U,\square,B^a,K^a}$. Then,

$$\mathcal{M}, w \vDash K^a\varphi \quad \text{iff} \quad \mathcal{M}, w \vDash B^a\varphi \wedge \square\varphi$$

Proof. From left to right. Assume $\mathcal{M}, w \vDash K^a\varphi$. Then $\exists T \in \tau_\epsilon$ such that $Arg(T) \in LFP_\mathcal{C}$ and $w \in T \subseteq [\![\varphi]\!]_\mathcal{M}$. $\mathcal{M}, w \vDash \square\varphi$ follows immediately, and $\mathcal{M}, w \vDash B^a\varphi$ follows by Corollary 2.

From right to left. Assume that $\mathcal{M}, w \vDash B^a\varphi \wedge \square\varphi$. Then (i) $Arg([\![\varphi]\!]_\mathcal{M}) \in LFP_\mathcal{C}$ and (ii) $\exists T \in \tau_\epsilon$ such that $w \in T \subseteq [\![\varphi]\!]_\mathcal{M}$. From (i) by Corollary 1 it follows that $Arg(Int([\![\varphi]\!]_\mathcal{M})) \in LFP_\mathcal{C}$. By (ii), there is some $T \in \tau_\epsilon$ such that $w \in T$ and $T \subseteq [\![\varphi]\!]_\mathcal{M}$. This means that $w \in Int([\![\varphi]\!]_\mathcal{M})$, and thus there is some $T' = Int([\![\varphi]\!]_\mathcal{M}) \in \tau_\epsilon$ such that $Arg(T') \in LFP_\mathcal{C}$ and $w \in T' \subseteq [\![\varphi]\!]_\mathcal{M}$, meaning that $\mathcal{M}, w \vDash K^a\varphi$.

Proposition 7. Let $\mathcal{M} = (W, Arg, f, \hookleftarrow, v)$ be an AB model and $w \in W$ and $\varphi \in \mathcal{L}_{U,\square,B^a,K^a}$. Then,

$$\mathcal{M}, w \vDash B^a\varphi \quad \text{iff} \quad \mathcal{M}, w \vDash \widehat{U}K^a\varphi$$

Proof. For left to right, assume $\mathcal{M}, w \vDash B^a\varphi$. This means that $Arg([\![\varphi]\!]_\mathcal{M}) \in LFP_\mathcal{C}$, and by Corollary 1, that $Arg(Int([\![\varphi]\!]_\mathcal{M})) \in LFP_\mathcal{C}$. $Int([\![\varphi]\!]_\mathcal{M}) \neq \varnothing$, thus $\exists w' \in W$ such that $Arg(Int([\![\varphi]\!]_\mathcal{M})) \in LFP_\mathcal{C}$ and $w' \in Int([\![\varphi]\!]_\mathcal{M}) \subseteq [\![\varphi]\!]_\mathcal{M}$. It follows that $\exists w' \in W$ and $\exists T \in \tau_\epsilon$ such that $Arg(T) \in LFP_\mathcal{C}$ and $w' \in T \subseteq [\![\varphi]\!]_\mathcal{M}$. This means that $\exists w' \in W$ such that $\mathcal{M}, w' \vDash K^a\varphi$, and thus $\mathcal{M}, w \vDash \widehat{U}K^a\varphi$.

For right to left, assume $\mathcal{M}, w \vDash \widehat{U}K^a\varphi$. Then $\exists w' \in W$ and $\exists T \in \tau_\epsilon$ such that $Arg(T) \in LFP_\mathcal{C}$ and $w' \in T \subseteq [\![\varphi]\!]_\mathcal{M}$. Since $\exists T \in \tau_\epsilon$ such that $Arg(T) \in LFP_\mathcal{C}$ and $T \subseteq [\![\varphi]\!]_\mathcal{M}$, $Arg([\![\varphi]\!]_\mathcal{M}) \in LFP_\mathcal{C}$ (by Corollary 2), meaning that $\mathcal{M}, w \vDash B^a\varphi$.

Having seen that the relationship between the operators K^g and B^g on TA models hold also between K^a and B^a on AB models, next consider the rules and formulas corresponding to those of the axiom system for $\mathcal{L}_{U,\Box,K^g}$ [12]. First, all the axioms and rules except one are valid in AB models. The proofs of validity and soundness are straightforward.

Proposition 8. *The following formulas and rules are valid in the class of all AB models:*

(1) S5 for U
(2) S4 for $\Box$
(3) from $\vdash \varphi \to \psi$ infer $\vdash K^a\varphi \to K^a\psi$
(4) $\vDash K^a\top$
(5) $\vDash K^a\varphi \to K^aK^a\varphi$
(6) $\vDash K^a\varphi \to \varphi$
(7) $\vDash (K^a\varphi \wedge U\psi) \to K^a(\varphi \wedge U\psi)$
(8) $\vDash K^a\varphi \to \Box\varphi$
(9) $\vDash K^a\varphi \to U(\Box\varphi \to K^a\varphi)$
(10) $\vDash U\Diamond\Box\varphi \to B^a\varphi$

One axiom in the logic of $\mathcal{L}_{U,\Box,K^g}$ is however invalid:

Proposition 9. $\nvDash \left(B^a\varphi \wedge \neg B^a\psi \wedge U((\varphi \wedge \psi) \to \Box(\varphi \wedge \psi))\right) \to \widehat{U}\Box(\varphi \wedge \neg\psi)$

Proof. Consider the model:

- $W = \{w_1, w_2, w_3\}$,
- $Arg = \{a_1, a_3\}$,
- $f(a_1) = \{w_1, w_2\}$,
  $f(a_2) = \{w_1, w_3\}$,
- $\hookleftarrow = \varnothing$.

- $v(P) = \{w_1, w_2\}$, $v(Q) = \{w_1\}$,
- $\tau_\epsilon = \{\varnothing, \{w_1\}, \{w_1, w_2\}, \{w_2, w_3\}, W\}$
- $LFP_C = \{\{a_1\}, \{a_3\}, \{a_1, a_3\}\}$.

In this model $\mathcal{M}, w_1 \vDash B^aP$, as $Arg(\llbracket P \rrbracket_\mathcal{M}) = \{a_1\} \in LFP_C$; $\mathcal{M}, w \vDash \neg B^aQ$, as $Arg(\llbracket Q \rrbracket_\mathcal{M}) = \varnothing \notin LFP_C$; and $\mathcal{M}, w_1 \vDash U\bigl((P \wedge Q) \to \Box(P \wedge Q)\bigr)$, as $\{w_1\} = \llbracket P \wedge Q \rrbracket_\mathcal{M} \in \tau_\epsilon$ and thus $\llbracket \Box(P \wedge Q) \rrbracket_\mathcal{M} = \{w_1\} = \llbracket P \wedge Q \rrbracket_\mathcal{M}$. However, $\mathcal{M}, w \nvDash \widehat{U}\Box(P \wedge \neg Q)$, as $\llbracket P \wedge \neg Q \rrbracket_\mathcal{M} = \{w_2\}$, while $\{w_2\} \notin \tau_\epsilon$.

As one might suspect, the invalidity of the formula is related to the lack of arguments for intersections of elements of the evidence topology. In TA models, any evidence consisting of the intersection of two elements of the topology will either be attacked by some other evidence, or will be in the grounded extension of the defence function (and the proof of the validity in TA models in [12] makes use of this attacking evidence). However, in AB models, there does not need to be any argument supporting the intersection of two pieces of evidence.

When considering the model in the proof of Proposition 9, it seems strange that the agent would not be able combine the two arguments, to for example go from belief that P and belief that $P \to Q$ to belief that Q. Unlike examples where this kind of reasoning fails in TA models, there is no conflict among arguments in the present example. In order to capture combined arguments, we will in the next section consider AB models where we assume that the intersections of evidence generated by arguments in turn have arguments of their own.

5 Argument Belief Models and the Evidence Topology

In TA models attack graphs are defined on the evidence topology generated by the basic evidence $\mathcal{E}$. In this section, AB models and TA models are compared. We start by looking at the relationship between the camps of arguments and the evidence topology in an AB model. That is, the topology τ_ϵ generated by closing under unions and finite intersections the evidence set ϵ. After that, we show that each AB model has a corresponding TAF++ model, provided that the evidence set generated by the arguments in the argument belief model is closed under (finite) intersections, and that each TAF++ model has a corresponding AB model.

As each element E of ϵ corresponds to an argument in Arg, there will be a unique camp of arguments corresponding to every such E. However, when we consider the evidence topology τ_ϵ generated by the basic evidence in ϵ, that is no longer the case.

Proposition 10. *Let* $\forall E, E' \in \epsilon$, *and let* $T, T' \in \tau_\epsilon$. *Then,*

(1) $E \neq E' \Leftrightarrow Arg(E) \neq Arg(E')$.
(2) $T \neq T' \not\Rightarrow Arg(T) \neq Arg(T')$.

Proof. The example from the proof of Proposition 9 demonstrates item (2). In that model, $\varnothing, \{w_1\} \in \tau_\epsilon$, while $Arg(\varnothing) = Arg(\{2\}) = \varnothing$.

However, there is a one-to-one correspondence between the arbitrary unions on the evidence set ϵ and the camps in $\mathcal{C}$.

Proposition 11. *Let* $\cup_\epsilon = \{\bigcup \mathcal{F} \mid \mathcal{F} \subseteq \epsilon\}$ *and* $U_1, U_2 \in \cup_\epsilon$. *Then,*

$$U_1 \neq U_2 \Leftrightarrow Arg(U_1) \neq Arg(U_2).$$

Proof. Right-to-left is immediate as $Arg(\cdot)$ is a function. For the left-to-right direction, Assume $U_1 \neq U_2$. It follows that there is some $E \in \epsilon$ such that either $U_1 \supseteq E \not\subseteq U_2$ or $U_2 \supseteq E \not\subseteq U_1$. Assume, without loss of generality, that $U_1 \supseteq E \not\subseteq U_2$. Then, $f^-(E) \in Arg(U_1)$, while $f^-(E) \notin Arg(U_2)$, and thus $Arg(U_1) \neq Arg(U_2)$.

Corollary 3. *Let* ϵ *be closed under finite intersections and let* $T_1, T_2 \in \tau_\epsilon$. *Then,*

$$T_1 \neq T_2 \Leftrightarrow Arg(T_1) \neq (Arg(T_2)).$$

In order to reason about evidence topologies, one way to proceed is to consider Arg's such that the generated ϵ is closed under intersections. Here it is shown that 'intersection AB models' correspond to TAF++ models. Hence, making the assumption yields the same logic for $\mathcal{L}_{U,\square,K^a}$ as that of $\mathcal{L}_{U,\square,K^g}$ in [15].

Proposition 12. Let $\mathcal{M}^a = (W, Arg, f, \hookleftarrow, v)$ be an argument belief model such that ϵ is a closed under finite intersections, $w \in W$, and $\varphi \in \mathcal{L}_{U,\square,B^g}$. Then there is a TA model $\mathcal{M}^g = (W, \mathcal{E}, \tau_{\mathcal{E}}, \hookleftarrow^g, v)$ such that

$$\mathcal{M}^a, w \vDash \varphi \text{ if and only if } \mathcal{M}^g, w \vDash \varphi[B^a \setminus B^g]$$

Proof. Let $\mathcal{E} = \epsilon$. Then by Corollary 3, for every $T \in \tau_{\mathcal{E}} \setminus \varnothing$, there is some $C \in \mathcal{C}$ such that $C = Arg(T)$ (and vice versa). For $T, T_1, T_2 \in \tau_{\mathcal{E}}$ let:

(i) $T_1 \hookleftarrow^g T_2$ iff $Arg(T_1) \hookleftarrow Arg(T_2)$;
(ii) $\varnothing \hookleftarrow^g T$ and $T \not\hookleftarrow^g \varnothing$.

Note first that by of condition (1) in Definition 9 (and by of condition (ii) in the construction of $\hookleftarrow^g$), the conditions on the attack graphs in TA models are satisfied by $\hookleftarrow^g$, and $\mathcal{M}^g$ is a TA model. Note second that by the construction of $\hookleftarrow^g$, (A) $\exists C \in LFP_{\mathcal{C}}$ if and only if $\exists T \in \tau_{\mathcal{E}}$ such that $C = Arg(T)$ and $T \in LFP_{\tau_{\mathcal{E}}}$. To see this, simply note that every $C \in \mathcal{C}$ corresponds to a $T \in \tau$, and that every $T \in \tau$ that could also be in LFP_{τ} corresponds to a $C \in \mathcal{C}$ (since by item (ii) in the construction of $\hookleftarrow^g$, if $T = \varnothing$ then $T \notin LFP_{\tau}$).

We show by induction on the structure of φ that $\mathcal{M}^a, w \vDash \varphi$ if and only if $\mathcal{M}^g, w \vDash \varphi[B^a \setminus B^g]$. The base case and Boolean cases are straightforward, as are the ones for U and $\square$. We show the case $\varphi = B^a \psi$.

$\mathcal{M}^a, w \vDash B^a \psi \Leftrightarrow Arg(\llbracket \psi \rrbracket_{\mathcal{M}^a}) \in LFP_{\mathcal{C}} \Leftrightarrow$ (by Corollary 2) $\exists C \in LFP_{\mathcal{C}}$ such that $C = Arg(E)$ and $E \subseteq \llbracket \psi \rrbracket_{\mathcal{M}^a} \Leftrightarrow \exists C \in LFP_{\mathcal{C}}$ such that $C = Arg(E)$ and $\mathcal{M}^a, w' \vDash \psi$ for all $w' \in E \Leftrightarrow$ (by inductive hypothesis) $\exists C \in LFP_{\mathcal{C}}$ such that $C = Arg(E)$ and $\mathcal{M}^g, w' \vDash \psi$ for all $w' \in T = E \in \tau \Leftrightarrow$ (by (A)) $\exists T \in LFP_{\tau_{\mathcal{E}}}$ such that $T \subseteq \llbracket \psi \rrbracket_{\mathcal{M}^g} \Leftrightarrow \mathcal{M}^g, w \vDash B^g \psi$, and $\mathcal{M}^g, w \vDash \varphi$.

Since every intersection AB model has a corresponding TA model, it follows that all formulas valid in TA models are valid in intersection AB models.

Corollary 4. Let I be the class of intersection AB models. Then

$$I \vDash \left(B^a \varphi \wedge \neg B^a \psi \wedge U((\varphi \wedge \psi) \rightarrow \square(\varphi \wedge \psi)) \right) \rightarrow \widehat{U}\square(\varphi \wedge \neg \psi)$$

By Proposition 2, it also follows that $\mathcal{M}^g$ is a TAF++ model. Next, it is shown that given a TAF++ model, an equivalent AB model can be defined.

Proposition 13. Let $\mathcal{M}^g = (W, \mathcal{E}, \tau, \hookleftarrow, v)$ be an TAF++ model, $w \in W$ and $\varphi \in \mathcal{L}_{U,\square,B^g}$. Then there is an argument belief model $\mathcal{M}^a = (W, Arg, f, \hookleftarrow^a, v)$ such that

$$\mathcal{M}^g, w \vDash \varphi \text{ if and only if } \mathcal{M}^a, w \vDash \varphi[B^g \setminus B^a]$$

Proof. First define Arg so that for each non-empty $T \in \tau_{\mathcal{E}}$, there is an argument $a_T \in Arg$ ($Arg = \{a_T \mid T \in \tau_{\mathcal{E}} \setminus \varnothing\}$), and define f so that $f(a_T) = T$. Then define $\hookleftarrow^a$, for $T_1, T_2 \in \tau_{\mathcal{E}} \setminus \varnothing$:

$$a_{T_1} \hookleftarrow^a a_{T_2} \text{ iff } T_1 \hookleftarrow T_2.$$

Note that the condition on the attack graph in an argument belief model is satisfied (since the corresponding condition holds of the attack graph on $\tau_{\mathcal{E}}$).

We show that for all $T_1, T_2 \in \tau_{\mathcal{E}}$, $Arg(T_1) \hookleftarrow^a Arg(T_2)$ iff $T_1 \hookleftarrow T_2$. From right to left: assume that $T_1 \hookleftarrow T_2$. Next, assume that $a \in Arg(T_1)$. By definition of $Arg(\cdot)$, $f(a) \subseteq T_1$. Then, by condition (1) on TAF++ models, $f(a) \hookleftarrow T_2$, and by the construction of $\hookleftarrow^a$, $a \hookleftarrow^a a_{T_2}$. Also, since $f(a) \subseteq T_1$ and $T_1 \cap T_2 = \varnothing$, $f(a) \cap T_2 = \varnothing$. Then, for all $a \in Arg(T_1)$, $a \hookleftarrow^a a_{T_2}$, and thus $Arg(T_1) \hookleftarrow^a Arg(T_2)$.

From left to right: assume that $Arg(T_1) \hookleftarrow^a Arg(T_2)$. Then, $T_1 \cap T_2 = \varnothing$ (by condition (1) in Definition 9) and thus $T_1 \hookleftarrow T_2$ or $T_2 \hookleftarrow T_1$ (by condition (i) in Definition 4) and $a_{T_1} \hookleftarrow^a a_{T_2}$ or $a_{T_2} \hookleftarrow^a a_{T_1}$. Because of this, and since $Arg(T_1) \hookleftarrow^a Arg(T_2)$, there is some $a \in Arg(T_2)$ such that $a_{T_1} \hookleftarrow^a a$ (otherwise, a_{T_1} would have to attack a_{T_2}, who would then be undefended). Then, by construction of $\hookleftarrow^a$, there is some $a \in Arg(T_2)$ such that $T_1 \hookleftarrow f(a)$. It then follows, since $T_1 \cap T_2 = \varnothing$ and $f(a) \subseteq T_2$, by condition (2) on TAF++ models that $T_1 \hookleftarrow T_2$.

Then, noting that $Arg(T_1) \hookleftarrow^a Arg(T_2)$ iff $T_1 \hookleftarrow T_2$ and that the camps in $\mathcal{C}$ correspond to elements of $\tau_{\mathcal{E}}$ (minus the attack-wise inert $\varnothing$), it is easy to see that $\exists T \in LFP_{\tau_{\mathcal{E}}}$ if and only if $\exists Arg(E) \in LFP_{\mathcal{C}}$ such that $E = T$ and $Arg(E) \in LFP_{\mathcal{C}}$. Once this is established the proof is similar to that of Proposition 5.

6 Conclusion

This manuscript has introduced and investigated AB models and the logic of belief, knowledge, and evidence on AB models. In AB models, abstract arguments represent the sources of evidence of an agent, and an attack relation on the arguments captures differences in strength in case of conflict between supported evidence. The models give a more granular picture of the relationship between argument, evidence, belief, and knowledge than the TA models, providing for clearer intuitions. The fact that the additional conditions on TAF++ models arise naturally in (intersection) AB models, along with the fact that TAF++ models and intersection AB models have the same logic, provides motivation for assuming the conditions and thereby for the TAF++ topological setting and its logic. Basic properties of the AB models and validities and non-validities of $\mathcal{L}_{U,\square,K^a,B^a}$ were studied in Sects. 3 and 4, and the relationship between arguments and evidence topology in Sect. 5, where it was also shown that $\mathcal{L}_{U,\square,K^a,B^a}$ on intersection AB models is equivalent to $\mathcal{L}_{U,\square,K^g,B^g}$ on TA models. While we thus know how to axiomatize $\mathcal{L}_{U,\square,K^g,B^g}$ on intersection AB models, it is still an open question whether the rules and formulas of Proposition 6 provide the complete axiomatization of the language on arbitrary AB models.

In Sect. 5, we considered the class of intersection AB models. Simply assuming that such arguments are included leaves open the question of how they should relate to their 'parent' arguments leaving it to the modeller to define the attack graph for the intersection arguments. Future work could investigate the possibility of adding intersection arguments to arbitrary ABFs along with new attack relations that let the new arguments inherit the strength from their parent arguments relative to other arguments. Provided that the construction allows the camps supporting the 'intersection evidence' into LFP_C whenever both parent camps are in LFP_C (restoring the K axiom), this could give the agent access to the full topological reasoning on the evidence selected through argumentation-theoretic reasoning.

Disclosure of Interests. The authors have no competing interests to declare that are relevant to the content of this article.

References

1. Artemov, S.: The logic of justification. Rev. Symb. Logic **1**, 477–513 (2008). https://doi.org/10.1017/S1755020308090060
2. Artemov, S., Nogina, E.: Introducing justification into epistemic logic. J. Log. Comput. **15**(6), 1059–1073 (2005). https://doi.org/10.1093/logcom/exi053
3. Baltag, A., Bezhanishvili, N., Özgün, A., Smets, S.: Justified belief and the topology of evidence. In: Väänänen, J., Hirvonen, Å., de Queiroz, R. (eds.) Logic, Language, Information, and Computation, pp. 83–103. Springer, Heidelberg (2016)
4. van Benthem, J., Pacuit, E.: Dynamic logics of evidence-based beliefs. Stud. Logica. **99**(1), 61–92 (2011). https://doi.org/10.1007/s11225-011-9347-x
5. Dung, P.M.: On the acceptability of arguments and its fundamental role in nonmonotonic reasoning, logic programming and n-person games. Artif. Intell. **77**(2), 321–357 (1995). https://doi.org/10.1016/0004-3702(94)00041-X. https://www.sciencedirect.com/science/article/pii/000437029400041X
6. Fitting, M.: Paraconsistent logic, evidence, and justification. Studia Logica **105**(6), 1149–1166 (2017). https://doi.org/10.1007/s11225-017-9714-3
7. Grossi, D., van der Hoek, W.: Justified beliefs by justified arguments. In: Proceedings of the Fourteenth International Conference on Principles of Knowledge Representation and Reasoning, KR 2014, pp. 131–140. AAAI Press (2014)
8. Hintikka, J.: Knowledge and Belief: An Introduction to the Logic of the Two Notions. Cornell University Press, Ithaca (1962)
9. Proietti, C., Yuste-Ginel, A.: Dynamic epistemic logics for abstract argumentation. Synthese **199**(3), 8641–8700 (2021). https://doi.org/10.1007/s11229-021-03178-5
10. Rodrigues, A., Bueno-Soler, J., Carnielli, W.: Measuring evidence: a probabilistic approach to an extension of belnap–dunn logic. Synthese **198**(22), 5451–5480 (2021). https://doi.org/10.1007/s11229-020-02571-w
11. Schwarzentruber, F., Vesic, S., Rienstra, T.: Building an epistemic logic for argumentation. In: del Cerro, L.F., Herzig, A., Mengin, J. (eds.) Logics in Artificial Intelligence, pp. 359–371. Springer, Heidelberg (2012)
12. Shi, C.: Reason to believe. Ph.D. thesis, University of Amsterdam (2018)
13. Shi, C.: No false grounds and topology of argumentation. J. Logic Comput. **31**(4), 1079–1101 (2020). https://doi.org/10.1093/logcom/exaa057
14. Shi, C., Smets, S., Velazquez-Quesada, F.: Argument-based belief in topological structures. Electron. Proc. Theor. Comput. Sci. **251**, 489–503 (2017). https://doi.org/10.4204/EPTCS.251.36

15. Shi, C., Smets, S., Velazquez-Quesada, F.: Logic of justified beliefs based on argumentation. Erkenntnis **88**, 1207–1243 (2021). https://doi.org/10.1007/s10670-021-00399-5
16. Shi, C., Smets, S., Velázquez-Quesada, F.R.: Beliefs based on evidence and argumentation. In: Moss, L.S., de Queiroz, R., Martinez, M. (eds.) Logic, Language, Information, and Computation, pp. 289–306. Springer, Heidelberg (2018)

On Pluralistic Methods for Explaining Argument Acceptance in Abstract Argumentation

Siyi Liu, Ziyi Gao, Beishui Liao, and Chen Chen[✉]

Zhejiang University, Hangzhou, China
12104018@zju.edu.cn

Abstract. Abstract argumentation (AA), a non-monotonic reasoning framework, has attracted growing interest in the AI community. Explaining why an argument is accepted in AA emerges as a promising alternative for advancing explainable artificial intelligence (XAI). Driven by diverse practical needs, the logical structure and attributes of explanations must cater to varying contextual demands. This implies that multiple explanation methods are necessary to accommodate situational needs, with no single approach being absolutely superior or inferior. This paper categorizes the methodology of explanation in AA into five types: strong, presumptive, iterative, tree-like, and root explanation methods. To systematically capture the logical features underlying these explanation methods, we set twelve principles and ten properties, including but not limited to Non-Redundancy, Influence, and Composition. These principles and properties are employed to thoroughly analyze the five explanation methods. The results of this principle-and-property-based analysis highlight the importance of aligning explanation methods with practical requirements and provide valuable insights for future research in formal argumentation for explanation generation.

Keywords: Explaining Argument Acceptance · Abstract Argumentation · Principle-and-Property-Based Analysis · Explainable Artificial Intelligence

1 Introduction

Recently, eXplainable Artificial Intelligence (XAI) has garnered significant attention in the Artificial Intelligence (AI) community. While data-driven models provide impressive predictive power, their opacity complicates traceability, crucial for applications like autonomous systems, medical diagnosis, and judicial defense. Although most XAI research focuses on data-driven approaches, our study diverges by exploring XAI through logical methods. Logical methods offer a structured way to generate explanations, providing the clarity and traceability essential for explainability in high-stakes applications.

As noted in [8,27,29], there is no universally agreed-upon definition of "what constitutes an explanation". However, some characteristics of explanation are widely accepted in the literature: (1) Explanations typically exhibit a contrastive nature, involving counterfactual reasoning that compares actual situations to hypothetical alternatives; (2) Explanations demonstrate selective disclosure, focusing on key causes rather than exhaustive factors; (3) Explanations often occur as dialogic interactions, facilitating knowledge transfer within a conversational context; (4) Explanations are inherently context-sensitive, requiring adaptation to specific situations, audiences, and purposes.

In this context, *computational argumentation* (cf. [11] for an overview) emerges as a promising logical reasoning mechanism for addressing AI explainability. It organizes evidence defending or opposing claims step-by-step and is recognized for its potential in XAI [19,22,28,33,34,37]. Central to it, abstract argumentation (AA) represents and reasons about arguments, instantiating arguments and attacks within the argumentation framework (AF). AA treats these arguments and attacks as abstract entities and uses argumentation semantics to determine the acceptable sets of arguments[1].

In addition to employing semantics to evaluate the acceptability of arguments, one of the primary objectives in AA is to develop alternative explanation methods that address the fundamental question "Why is an argument accepted". These methods, fundamentally distinct from semantics, are supposed to be mathematically rigorous, convey more information, or reflect certain features of explanation.

Moreover, the application of AA in providing explanation for AI systems offers several advantages. AA facilitates agent interactions in Multi-Agent Systems, thereby improving negotiation processes. AA can also simultaneously explain both the acceptability and unacceptability of arguments using a unified method [12,14,24,31,32][2]. Additionally, the abstract nature of AA enables the identification of key decision-making factors, thereby improving the precision and depth of explanation processes.

As previously highlighted, explanations are context-sensitive. The scenarios demanding explanations are diverse, and the nature of these scenarios significantly influences the type and depth of explanations required. For instance, a straightforward cause like a blocked artery for a heart attack might suffice in an emergency room. In contrast, in life-threatening situations, such as dealing with a complex cancer diagnosis, explanations need to be as comprehensive and detailed as possible. Meanwhile, in contexts requiring meticulous root cause analysis, like in industrial accident investigations, explanations must approximate the root causes.

The need for context-sensitive explanations is fundamental, especially in complex and critical decision-making scenarios like medical treatments. The following example illustrates a decision-making scenario in renal cancer diagnosis, which demands comprehensive and detailed explanations that meet rigorous standards.

Example 1 (Decision Making in Cancer Diagnosis). Figure 1 illustrates a scenario in which a man's medical tests indicate a high likelihood of renal cell carcinoma. This diagnosis triggers a complex decision-making process regarding the optimal treatment. The following arguments are considered:

(a_1) Physician *A* suggests a total nephrectomy, to prevent the spread of cell carcinoma.
(a_2) Physician *B* suggests the cancerous tissue is removed, preserving the healthy parts.

---

[1] See [7,36] for an overview of the principle-based analysis of abstract argumentation semantics.
[2] Explanations for the unacceptability of arguments are beyond the scope of this paper.

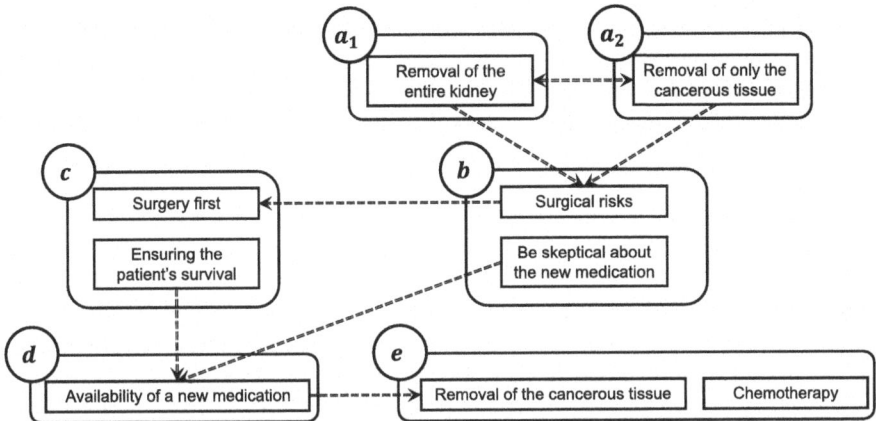

Fig. 1. Constructing AF for Example 1. The boxes labeled with letters represent *arguments*. The arrows between the boxes indicate *attack relations* between the arguments.

(*b*) The family is concerned about the patient's poor health condition which increases surgical risks, while they are also skeptical about the experimental drugs.
(*c*) All agree that the primary focus is ensuring the patient's survival, which may necessitate surgical intervention.
(*d*) A new medication is available, potentially avoiding the risky surgery.
(*e*) The final decision is to have a partial nephrectomy followed by chemotherapy.

The left half of Fig. 2 depicts the abstract argumentation framework of Example 1. Under certain criteria, e.g. complete semantics, there are two acceptable sets, namely $\{a_1,c,e\}$ and $\{a_2,c,e\}$. Both of the sets suggest that the final treatment is "a partial nephrectomy followed by chemotherapy (*e*)". Below, we outline alternative explanations for the explained argument (specifically, *e* in Example 1) from several perspectives:

1. In general, the explanation should be internally consistent. When multiple explanations coexist, the property of non-redundancy is emphasized. Moreover, the explanations are expected to assure the acceptability of the explained argument.
2. As shown in [14,20,23,35], it is expected that the explanations provide more information than what is already obtained from the acceptable sets containing the explained argument. Hence, we aim to explore the relationship between explanation and acceptable sets, such as the set inclusion relation.
3. We would like to clarify the direct causes, root causes, and sufficient causes for the explained argument:
   - **Directed causes** are arguments that directly defend *e*, namely *c* and *b*. They serve as directed causes because they attack "using new medication to avoid surgery (*d*)" which attacks *e*.
   - **Root causes** are those arguments that firstly "protect" themselves and (in)directly defend *e*, namely a_1 and a_2. The reason is that a_1 and a_2 are the

suggestions from two physicians, which are somehow self-attesting and do not need any external defense.
- **Sufficient causes** are identified by the monotonic property, where any superset of the explanation still justify the explained argument. For the subframework of F containing only c and e, it is sufficient to defense e. The only counter to c is "the risk of the surgery (b)", which is also a counterargument to "the availability of the new medicine (d)".
4. Considering the distinction between internal and external explanations [29], we want to determine whether the explanation involves arguments outside the given acceptable set. Specifically, the given acceptable set $\{a_1, c, e\}$ already explains the acceptability of e. However, deleting a_1 would not make e unacceptable, as a_2 which "protects" itself also indirectly defends e. Therefore, only the deletion of both a_1 and a_2 could act as an explanation for the acceptance of e, indicating that two physicians' suggestions are indispensable to justify the final treatment.

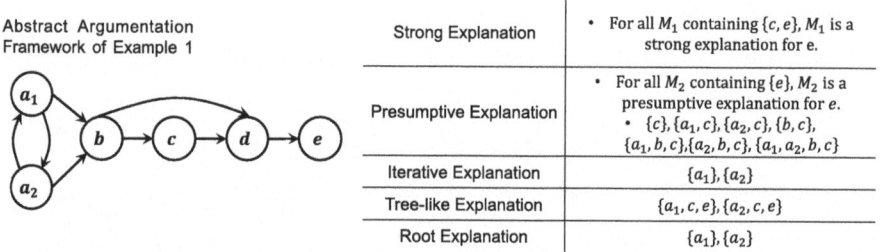

Fig. 2. The Output of Pluralistic Explanation Methods for accepting e.

We categorize the methodology of explanation in AA into five types: strong, presumptive, iterative, tree-like, and root explanation methods. Each of them is grounded in specific intuition and defined by respective literature sources [10, 18, 26, 31, 35]. While principle-based (or axiomatic) analysis has been employed in other logical explanation models, such as classification models [3], no comprehensive study has yet applied this kind of analysis to evaluate diverse explanation methods in AA.

A principle-and-property-based analysis of these explanation methods is essential. These principles and properties should comprehensively address diverse real-world requirements, encompassing root causes, direct causes, and complete reasons, while simultaneously satisfying general expectations like consistency, coherence, and non-redundancy. This analysis will help select suitable methods for complex scenarios, and guide the development of new explanation methods. We conclude that explanation methods in AA are inherently pluralistic, with each method possessing its distinct characteristics. Identifying and understanding these characteristics is a prerequisite and foundation for the appropriate application of these explanation methods in practical scenarios.

The remainder of this paper is organized as follows. Section 2 introduces AA. Section 3 categorizes the methodology of explanations in AA into five argument-based explanation methods. In Sect. 4, we define twelve principles and ten properties that capture the intuition of "what characteristics an explanation should possess to align with practical situations", and apply these principles and properties to analyze the five explanation methods. Section 5 discusses related work and concludes the paper.

2 Abstract Argumentation

An argumentation framework (AF) is a directed graph $F = (A, R)$, where A is a finite set of arguments and $R \subseteq A \times A$ represents attacks [21]. The universe of AF is represented by the set $\mathfrak{UF}$, while the set of arguments that appear within $\mathfrak{UF}$ is denoted as $\mathfrak{UA}$.

Let $F = (A, R)$ be an AF. For $a, b \in A$, we say a attacks b if $(a, b) \in R$. For $a \in A$, we denote $a^+ = \{b \in A \mid a \text{ attacks } b\}$ and $a^- = \{b \in A \mid b \text{ attacks } a\}$. For $a \in A$ and $E \subseteq A$, we say a attacks E if there is an argument in E that is attacked by a, and we say E attacks a if there is an argument in E that attacks a. For $E \subseteq A$, we denote $E^+ = \{a \in A \mid E \text{ attacks } a\}$ and $E^- = \{a \in A \mid a \text{ attacks } E\}$. And the range E is defined as $E^\oplus = E \cup E^+$. Besides, the E-reduct of F is the AF denoted as $F^E = (E^*, R \cap (E^* \times E^*))$ where $E^* = A \setminus E^\oplus$. The notion of subframework of F induced by $E \subseteq A$ is defined by $F \downarrow_E = (E, R \cap (E \times E))$.

The characteristic function of an AF $F = (A, R)$ is a function Γ s.t. for every $E \subseteq A$, we have $\Gamma_F(E) = \{a \in E \mid E \text{ defends } a\}$.

Definition 1. *Let $F = (A, R)$ be an AF. A set $E \subseteq A$ is conflict-free in F, denoted by $E \in cf(F)$, iff for all $a, b \in E$, it holds that $(a, b) \notin R$. A set E defends an argument a iff for all $b \in a^-$, there exists $c \in E$, s.t. $(c, b) \in R$.*

The acceptability of an argument is prescribed by specific argumentation semantics. Given an AF, each semantics returns a set of sets of acceptable arguments called extensions (cf. [6] for a recent overview).

Definition 2. *Let $F = (A, R)$ be an AF. Argumentation semantics σ is a function $\mathfrak{UF} \mapsto 2^{2^{\mathfrak{UA}}}$, associating with each AF F a subset of 2^A, denoted as $\sigma(F)$.*

Classical semantics includes admissible, complete, grounded, preferred, and stable semantics (abbr. *ad*, *co*, *gr*, *pr*, *st*). And we refer to an extension under a semantics $\sigma \in \{ad, co, gr, pr, st\}$ as σ-extension.

Definition 3. *Let $F = (A, R)$ be an AF and $E \in cf(F)$.*

1. *$E \in ad(F)$ iff E defends all its elements;*
2. *$E \in co(F)$ iff $E \in ad(F)$ and any $a \in A$ defended by E is in E;*
3. *$E \in gr(F)$ iff E is $\subseteq$-minimal in $co(F)$;*
4. *$E \in pr(F)$ iff E is $\subseteq$-maximal in $co(F)$;*
5. *$E \in st(F)$ iff E attacks each $a \in A \setminus E$.*

Let $F = (A, R)$ be an AF and σ any semantics, an argument $a \in A$ is *credulously accepted* iff $a \in \bigcup \sigma(F)$, and argument $a \in A$ is *skeptically accepted* iff $a \in \bigcap \sigma(F)$. It holds that if an argument is skeptically accepted in an AF, then it is also credulously accepted.

3 Explanations in Abstract Argumentation

In this section, for the explanatory task of acceptance of an argument, we first introduce the general definition of argument-based explanation method, then define specific explanation methods, including strong ($\mathcal{S}_\sigma$), presumptive ($\mathcal{P}_\sigma$), iterative ($\mathcal{I}_\sigma$), tree-like ($\mathcal{T}_\sigma$) and root ($\mathcal{R}_\sigma$) explanation methods.

Definition 4 (Argument-based Explanation Method). *Let $F = (A, R)$ be an AF and $x \in A$ an argument. An argument-based explanation method $\mathbb{M}$ is a function $\mathfrak{AF} \times \mathfrak{UA} \mapsto 2^{2^{\mathfrak{UA}}}$, associating with each AF $F = (A, R)$ and $x \in A$ a subset of 2^A, denoted as $\mathbb{M}_F(x)$. We call x the topic and each element $M \in \mathbb{M}_F(x)$ an argument-based explanation.*

Let $\Theta \in \{\mathcal{S}, \mathcal{P}, \mathcal{I}, \mathcal{T}, \mathcal{R}\}$ and $\sigma \in \{ad, co, gr, pr, st\}$. Given an AF F and the topic x, we denote Θ_σ-explanation as the instantiation of $\mathbb{M}_F(x)$ using the explanation method Θ under the semantics σ. An illustrative example of Θ_σ-explanation is provided in the right part of Fig. 2.

Recent advances, initially termed strong explanation for strong inconsistency [16, 17], promote the definition of strong explanation in AA. The basic idea of strong explanation can be articulated as follows: a strong explanation is a set of arguments such that the topic x is acceptable in each subframework including the explaining set M [35].

Definition 5 ($\mathcal{S}_\sigma$-Explanation). *Let $F = (A, R)$ be an AF, $x \in A$ the topic and σ any semantics. A set $M \subseteq A$ is a $\mathcal{S}_\sigma$-explanation for x iff for each AF $F' = F \downarrow_{A'}$ with $M \subseteq A' \subseteq A$, there is $E' \in \sigma(F')$ with $x \in E'$.*

In this method, we actually do not distinguish the explanation for semantics $\sigma \in \{ad, co, pr\}$ (Proposition 3.12 in [35]), as stated in Proposition 1. And we also point out two necessary conditions for it in Lemma 1 and Lemma 2 (Proposition 3.13 in [35]).

Proposition 1. *Let $F = (A, R)$ be an AF, $x \in A$ the topic and σ any semantics. A set $M \subseteq A$ is a $\mathcal{S}_{ad}$-explanation for x iff M is a $\mathcal{S}_{co}$-explanation for x iff M is a $\mathcal{S}_{pr}$-explanation for x.*

Lemma 1. *Let $F = (A, R)$ be an AF, $x \in A$ the topic and σ any semantics. If a set $M \subseteq A$ is a $\mathcal{S}_\sigma$-explanation for x, then $x \in M$.*

Lemma 2. *Let $F = (A, R)$ be an AF, $x \in A$ the topic and σ any semantics. If a set $M \subseteq A$ is a $\mathcal{S}_\sigma$-explanation for x, then $x^- \subseteq M^+$.*

Existing works for abduction in AA have focused on presenting a model in which additions (or removals) of arguments act as an explanation for an argument's acceptance or rejection [12,31]. We argue that instead of focusing on the additions (or removals) of AF, abduction can also be approached with the hypothesis that if the explanation did not exist, then the topic x could not be credulously accepted. We call this kind of explanation method the presumptive explanation method, drawing conceptual inspiration from counterfactual reasoning in AA [2].

Definition 6 ($\mathcal{P}_\sigma$-Explanation). *Let $F = (A, R)$ be an AF, $x \in A$ the topic and σ any semantics. A set $M \subseteq A$ is an $\mathcal{P}_\sigma$-explanation for x iff $x \in \bigcup \sigma(F)$ and $x \notin \bigcup \sigma(F')$ with $F' = F \downarrow_{A \setminus M}$.*

The relationship between $\mathcal{P}_\sigma$-explanation and $\mathcal{S}_\sigma$-explanation is stated in Proposition 2. The idea is that any set M containing the topic x is an $\mathcal{P}_\sigma$-explanation for x, therefore any explanation method satisfying the condition that any explanation in this explanation method must contain the topic x is also an $\mathcal{P}_\sigma$-explanation. Also, we point out two sufficient conditions for $\mathcal{P}_\sigma$-explanation in Lemma 3 and Lemma 4.

Proposition 2. *Let $F = (A, R)$ be an AF, $x \in A$ the topic and σ any semantics. If a set $M \subseteq A$ is a $\mathcal{S}_\sigma$-explanation, then M is an $\mathcal{P}_\sigma$-explanation.*

Lemma 3. *Let $F = (A, R)$ be an AF, $M \subseteq A$ a set, $x \in A$ the topic and σ any semantics. If $x \in M$ and $x \in \bigcup \sigma(F)$, then M is an $\mathcal{P}_\sigma$-explanation.*

Lemma 4. *Let $F = (A, R)$ be an AF, $M \subseteq A$ a set, $x \in A$ the topic and σ any semantics. If for all $a \in x^-$, there exists $b \in M$ s.t. $(b, a) \in R$, then M is an $\mathcal{P}_\sigma$-explanation.*

The iterative explanation method revolves around the concept of "choices and their consequences" [10]. There are two primary definitions for this concept: one known as "explanation schemes" and the other being the method we present here. Despite their mathematical differences, they share the same intuition.

Before delving into this explanation method, let's recall that a strongly connected component (SCC) of an AF $F = (A, R)$ is a set $S \subseteq A$, s.t. in the subframework $F \downarrow_S$, for any $a, b \in M$ there is some path from a to b. An SCC S is called initial iff the arguments in S are not attacked by any argument occurring in some other SCCs. The concept of this explanation method for a given topic x involves recursively considering the grounded extensions of the current AF and making specific choices within an initial SCC to continue the iteration [1, 10].

Definition 7 ($\mathcal{I}_\sigma$-Explanation). *Given an AF $F = (A, R)$ and σ any semantics. Let $G \in gr(F)$ and $E \subseteq A$. For $a_1, \cdots, a_n \in A$, a sequence $X = (a_1, \cdots, a_n)$ is an iteration-based extension explanation for E w.r.t. F if either $n = 0$ and $E = G$ or*

- *a_1 belongs to some initial SCCs of F^G;*
- *$(a_2, \cdots, a_n)$ is an explanation for $E \setminus G$ w.r.t. the AF F^G without incoming attacks of a_1, i.e. $(F^G) \downarrow_{A \setminus a_1^-}$.*

Given $x \in A$ the topic, the set $M = \{a_1, \cdots, a_n\}$ is an $\mathcal{I}_\sigma$-explanation for x iff (there is some order s.t.) the sequence $(a_1, \cdots, a_n)$ is an iteration-based extension explanation for some $E \in \sigma(F)$ with $x \in E$.

The relation between iteration-based extension explanation and the σ-extension is stated in Theorem 1 (Proposition 1 in [1]).

Theorem 1. *Given an AF $F = (A, R)$ and any semantics σ. Let $X = \{a_1, \cdots, a_n\}$ be an iteration-based extension explanation for some $E \in \sigma(F)$ w.r.t. F. Then,*

- *there exists a unique $E \in \sigma(F)$ for which X is an iteration-based explanation; and*
- *there exists at least one iteration-based explanation for each $E \in \sigma(F)$.*

Dispute trees are a widely used form of explanation in AA. The core concept is to represent the acceptance of the given topic within a dialogue framework, where both the proponent and the opponent, denoted as P and O, present their arguments. Dispute trees exhibit several desirable properties, including existence, correctness (ensuring the explanation confirms the acceptance of the topic), and relevance (ensuring all arguments in the explanation contribute to the acceptance) [18, 19, 23, 30].

Definition 8 (Dispute Trees). *Let $F = (A, R)$ be an AF, a dispute tree for the topic $x \in A$ is a (possibly infinite) tree $\mathcal{T}$, s.t:*

1. *every node of $\mathcal{T}$ is of the form $[L : x]$, with $L \in \{P, O\}$ and $x \in A$: the node is labelled by argument x and assigned the status of either proponent(P) or opponent(O);*
2. *the root of $\mathcal{T}$ is a P node labelled by A;*
3. *for every P node n labelled by an argument b, and for every argument c that attacks b, these exists a child of n, which is an O node labelled by c;*
4. *for every O node n labelled by an argument b, there exists at most one child of n which is a P node labelled by an argument which attacks b;*
5. *there are no other nodes in $\mathcal{T}$ except those given by (1)–(4).*

The set of all arguments labelling P nodes in $\mathcal{T}$ is called the *defense set* of $\mathcal{T}$, denoted by $\mathcal{D}(\mathcal{T})$. A dispute tree $\mathcal{T}$ is an *admissible dispute tree* iff: 1) every O node in $\mathcal{T}$ has a child, and 2) no argument in $\mathcal{T}$ labels both P and O nodes. Then, the definition of $\mathcal{T}_\sigma$-explanation is defined directly upon the admissible dispute tree.

Definition 9 ($\mathcal{T}_\sigma$-Explanation). *Given an AF $F = (A, R)$, the topic $x \in A$ and any semantics σ. Let $\mathcal{T}$ be a dispute tree for x. If $\mathcal{T}$ is an admissible dispute tree, then $M = \mathcal{D}(\mathcal{T})$ is a $\mathcal{T}_\sigma$-explanation for x.*

There is a relation between the AF F and dispute tree $\mathcal{T}$ for F, as pointed out in Theorem 2: if $\mathcal{T}$ is an admissible dispute tree, then $\mathcal{D}(\mathcal{T})$ is an *ad*-extension in F; if $E \in ad(F)$, then there exists $\mathcal{T}$, s.t. $\mathcal{D}(\mathcal{T}) = E'$ with $E' \subseteq E$ is also an *ad*-extensions (Theorem 1 in [23]).

Theorem 2. *Given an AF $F = (A, R)$, an argument $a \in A$ and the dispute tree $\mathcal{T}$ for a. The relation between the defence set $\mathcal{D}(\mathcal{T})$ and the extension E could be stated as follows:*

- *if $\mathcal{T}$ is an admissible dispute tree, then $\mathcal{D}(\mathcal{T})$ is admissible; and*
- *if $a \in E$ where $E \in ad(F)$, then there exists an admissible dispute tree $\mathcal{T}$ for a with $\mathcal{D}(\mathcal{T}) = E'$, s.t. $E' \subseteq E$ and $E' \in ad(F)$.*

Defense relations can be defined in terms of attack relations. Given an AF $F = (A, R)$ and $a, b \in A$, a defenses b iff there exists $c \in b^-$, s.t. $c \in a^+$. The transitive closure of the defense relation is defined as follows. This method comes from [13, 15, 25, 26].

Definition 10 (Transitive Closure of Defense Relation). *Given an AF $F = (A,R)$, for any $B \subseteq A$, let $\overline{B} = \{(a,b) \mid a,b \in B \text{ and } a \text{ defenses } b\}$. The transitive closure of $\overline{B}$ is denoted as $\overline{B}^+$.*

Let $B \subseteq A$ be a σ-extension, from Definition 10, we know that for any element $(a,b) \in \overline{E}^+$, it holds that the arguments $a,b \in E$.

Lemma 5. *Let $F = (A,R)$ be an AF and $E \in \sigma(F)$ a σ-extension. For $a,b \in A$, if $(a,b) \in \overline{E}^+$, then $a,b \in E$.*

Given an AF $F = (A,R)$, an argument $a \in A$ is a self-defending argument iff $(a,a) \in \overline{A}^+$, and an argument b is an initial argument iff there exists no $c \in A$, s.t. $(c,b) \in R$. We denote the set of self-defending arguments and initial arguments as A_S and A_I respectively. The root causes for the accepted arguments are the arguments belong to initial arguments or self-defending arguments since only these two kinds of arguments could "protect themselves" without the involvement of other arguments [25, 26].

Definition 11 ($\mathcal{R}_\sigma$-Explanation). *Given an AF $F = (A,R)$, the topic $x \in A$ and any semantics σ. Let E be a σ-extension with $x \in E$. A $\mathcal{R}_\sigma$-explanation M for x is defined as:*

$$M = \{a \in A_S \cup A_I \mid (a,x) \in \overline{E}^+ \text{ or } a = x \in A_I\}$$

From Definition 11, it can be seen that self-defending and initial arguments play a crucial role in providing the explanation for the acceptance of the topic.

Proposition 3. *Given an AF $F = (A,R)$, the topic $x \in A$ and any semantics σ. If the set $M \subseteq A$ is a $\mathcal{R}_\sigma$-explanation for x, then $M \neq \emptyset$.*

Example 2. (Continue of Example 1) Various explanation methods under complete semantics for accepting e are shown in Fig. 2. It can be observed that there is an overlap among the five explanation methods. For instance, the $\mathcal{I}_{co}$-explanation and $\mathcal{R}_{co}$-explanation coincide for the acceptance of e. However, differences also exist among these explanation methods.

4 Principle-and-Property-Based Analysis Among Forms of Explanations

In this section, we summarized twelve principles and ten properties for explanation methods, where the principles reflect the fundamental requirements that an explanation method needs to satisfy, while the properties represent some characteristic an explanation method may potentially possess. Following this, we conducted a principle-and-property-based analysis of various explanation methods, as detailed in Table 1.

4.1 Principles for Explanations

The initial three principles pertain to the intrinsic requirements of the explanation methods. Principle 1 stipulates that when the topic x is credulously accepted, the explanation method must provide at least one explanation. Subsequently, Principle 2 and Principle 3 state that a good explanation should be conflict-free and self-defended.

Principle 1 (Existence). *Given an AF $F = (A, R) \in \mathfrak{AF}$ and the topic $x \in A$. If $x \in E$ for some $E \in \sigma(F)$ then $\mathbb{M}_F(x) \neq \emptyset$.*

Principle 2 (Conflict-Freeness). *Given an AF $F = (A, R) \in \mathfrak{AF}$ and the topic $x \in A$. If $M \in \mathbb{M}_F(x)$, then M is a conflict-free set.*

Principle 3 (Self-Defense). *Given an AF $F = (A, R) \in \mathfrak{AF}$ and the topic $x \in A$. If $M \in \mathbb{M}_F(x)$, then M defends all its elements.*

Principle 4 and its weak version Principle 5 extend the requirements for explanation focusing on the notion of assurance. The intuition behind the assurance principle is that: firstly, the reduct F^M can be interpreted as setting the arguments in M to true and inspecting the remaining AF, then an explanation M should again render the topic x to be acceptable [10, 35][3].

Principle 4 (Assurance). *Given an AF $F = (A, R) \in \mathfrak{AF}$ and the topic $x \in A$. $M \in \mathbb{M}_F(x)$ implies $x \in E \cup M$ for some $E \in \sigma(F^M)$.*

Principle 5 (Weak Assurance). *Given an AF $F = (A, R) \in \mathfrak{AF}$ and the topic $x \in A$. For some $M \in \mathbb{M}_F(x)$, there is $x \in E \cup M$ for some $E \in \sigma(F^M)$.*

Principle 6, Principle 7, and Principle 8 are about the structural aspect of explanation methods. Influence states that for every argument within the explanation, it can (in)directly defend the topic x through a series of arguments, thereby providing a directional explanative path to x. Principle 7 is a weak version of Principle 6. Besides, Principle 8 makes sure that any pair of arguments within the explanation is connected, thereby enhancing the structural consistency of the explanation as a cohesive whole.

Principle 6 (Influence). *Given an AF $F = (A, R) \in \mathfrak{AF}$ and the topic $x \in A$. If $M \in \mathbb{M}_F(x)$ is an explanation for x, then for every $a \in M$, there exists a path $P = (a_1, \cdots, a_n)$ in AF, s.t. $a_1 = a$, $a_n = x$ and $(a_i, a_j) \in R$ $(1 \leq i, j \leq n, j = i+1)$[4].*

Principle 7 (Weak Influence). *Given an AF $F = (A, R) \in \mathfrak{AF}$ and the topic $x \in A$. If $M \in \mathbb{M}_F(x)$ is an explanation for x, then there exists $a \in M$, s.t. there exists a path $P = (a_1, \cdots, a_n)$ in AF, s.t. $a_1 = a$, $a_n = x$ and $(a_i, a_j) \in R$ $(1 \leq i, j \leq n, j = i+1)$.*

Principle 8 (Connectivity). *Given an AF $F = (A, R) \in \mathfrak{AF}$ and the topic $x \in A$. If $M \in \mathbb{M}_F(x)$, then for any $a, b \in M$ $(a \neq b)$, there is a path $P = (a_1, \cdots, a_n)$ in AF, s.t. $a_1 = a$, $a_n = b$ (or $a_1 = b, a_n = a$) and $(a_i, a_j) \in R$ $(1 \leq i, j \leq n, j = i+1)$.*

---

[3] Also called σ-basic principle in other literature [10, 35].
[4] $P = (x)$ indicates that $x \in M$.

The following four properties are about the relationship among multiple explanations within an explanation method. Property 1 states that the union of two explanations constitutes another explanation, thereby defending that explanations can be combined to form more comprehensive ones. Property 2 enforces that there is a unique explanation for the given explanation method. Property 3 aims to eliminate superfluous explanations by requiring that the explanations are minimal and do not contain redundant arguments. Property 4 formalizes the idea that whenever the explanation M suffices to explain the topic, then so should every superset of M [10,35].

Property 1 (Composition). *Given an AF $F = (A,R) \in \mathfrak{UF}$ and the topic $x \in A$. For any $M_1, M_2 \in \mathbb{M}_F(x)$, $M_1 \cup M_2$ is also in $\mathbb{M}_F(x)$.*

Specifically, we can generalize the property of composition to show that the union of a finite collection of explanations is still an explanation in the explanation method.

Proposition 4. *Given an AF $F = (A,R) \in \mathfrak{UF}$ and the topic $x \in A$. If $\mathbb{M}_F(x)$ is an explanation method satisfying Composition, then for $M_1, \cdots, M_n \in \mathbb{M}_F(x)$, it holds that $\bigcup_{i \in n} M_n \in \mathbb{M}_F(x)$.*

Property 2 (Uniqueness). *Given an AF $F = (A,R) \in \mathfrak{UF}$ and the topic $x \in A$. For any $M_1, M_2 \in \mathbb{M}_F(x)$, $M_1 = M_2$.*

Property 3 (Non-Redundancy). *Given an AF $F = (A,R) \in \mathfrak{UF}$ and the topic $x \in A$. For any $M_1, M_2 \in \mathbb{M}_F(x)$, it is not the case that $M_1 \subset M_2$.*

Property 4 (Monotonicity). *Given an AF $F = (A,R) \in \mathfrak{UF}$ and the topic $x \in A$. If $M \in \mathbb{M}_F(x)$, then $M' \in \mathbb{M}_F(x)$ for any M' with $M \subseteq M' \subseteq A$.*

As pointed out in [10,35], Monotonicity somewhat contradicts the idea behind the Conflict-Freeness. Given an AF F, if the explanation method satisfies both Principle 2 and Property 4, then F is trivial.

Proposition 5. *Given an AF $F = (A,R) \in \mathfrak{UF}$ and the topic $x \in A$. If $\mathbb{M}_F(x)$ satisfies both Monotonicity and Conflict-Freeness, then $\mathbb{M}_F(x) = \emptyset$ or $R = \emptyset$.*

An explanation method satisfying Monotonicity implies its satisfaction with Composition.

Proposition 6. *Given an AF $F = (A,R) \in \mathfrak{UF}$ and the topic $x \in A$. If $\mathbb{M}_F(x)$ satisfies Monotonicity, then it satisfies Composition.*

Independence requires that an explanation does not rely on any arguments other than itself [10,35].

Property 5 (Independence). *Given an AF $F = (A,R) \in \mathfrak{UF}$ and the topic $x \in A$. If $M \in \mathbb{M}_F(x)$ and $a \notin M \cup \{x\}$, then M is also an explanation for x in $F \downarrow_{A \setminus \{a\}}$.*

The following four properties and principles focus on the relationships between explanations and extensions. Property 6 characterizes the special case where the cardinalities of explanations and extensions coincide. Property 7 states that the set of extensions is entirely contained within the set of explanations. Principle 9 requires every explanation must be a subset of some extensions. Principle 10 is a weak version of Principle 9, requiring that at least one explanation be partially contained in some extensions.

Property 6 (Quantitative Restriction). *Given an AF $F = (A, R) \in \mathfrak{AF}$ and the topic $x \in A$. If $\mathbb{M}_F(x)$ is a Θ_σ-explanation method for x, then let $\mathbb{E} = \{E \subseteq A \mid E \in \sigma(F) \text{ and } x \in E\}$, it holds that $|\mathbb{M}_F(x)| = |\mathbb{E}|$.*

Property 7 (Containing Extensions). *Given an AF $F = (A, R) \in \mathfrak{AF}$ and the topic $x \in A$. If $\mathbb{M}_F(x)$ is an Θ_σ-explanation method for x, then let $\mathbb{E} = \{E \subseteq A \mid E \in \sigma(F) \text{ and } x \in E\}$, it holds that $\mathbb{E} \subseteq \mathbb{M}_F(x)$.*

Principle 9 (Sub-Extension). *Given an AF $F = (A, R) \in \mathfrak{AF}$ and the topic $x \in A$. If $\mathbb{M}_F(x)$ is an Θ_σ-explanation method for x, then for all $M \in \mathbb{M}_F(x)$, $M \subseteq E$ for some $E \in \sigma(F)$ and $x \in E$.*

Principle 10 (Sub-Extension Permission). *Given an AF $F = (A, R) \in \mathfrak{AF}$ and the topic $x \in A$. If $\mathbb{M}_F(x)$ is a Θ_σ-explanation method for x, then there exists $M \in \mathbb{M}_F(x)$, s.t. $M \subseteq E$ for some $E \in \sigma(F)$ and $x \in E$.*

In addition to being a weak version of Principle 9, Principle 10 can also be regarded as a weak variant of Property 7.

Proposition 7. *Given an AF $F = (A, R) \in \mathfrak{AF}$ and the topic $x \in A$. If $\mathbb{M}_F(x)$ satisfies Containing Extensions, then it satisfies Sub-Extension Permission.*

As discussed in [9, 10], for any argument set M that is the subset of the σ-extension, there exists $E \in F^M$ which is also a σ-extension. Therefore, for any explanation M that is the subset of some σ-extension, M could satisfy the requirement that the explained argument $x \in E \cup M$ for some $E \in \sigma(F^M)$.

Lemma 6. *Let $F = (A, R)$ be an AF and let $E' \in \sigma(F)$. For any $M \subseteq E'$, there is a set E satisfying that $M \cup E = E'$ and $E \in \sigma(F^M)$.*

Proposition 8. *Given an AF $F = (A, R) \in \mathfrak{AF}$ and the topic $x \in A$. If $\mathbb{M}_F(x)$ satisfies Containing Extensions, then it satisfies Weak Assurance. If $\mathbb{M}_F(x)$ satisfies Sub-Extension, then it satisfies Assurance.*

The property of external explanation emphasizes the importance of arguments outside the given extension. Property 8 states that there may be some explanation M which is not the subset of the given extension E.

Property 8 (External Explanation). *Given an AF $F = (A, R) \in \mathfrak{AF}$ and the topic $x \in A$. If $\mathbb{M}_F(x)$ is a Θ_σ-explanation method, then there exists $M \in \mathbb{M}_F(x)$, s.t. $M \setminus E \neq \emptyset$ for some $E \in \sigma(F)$ and $x \in E$.*

Principle 11 and Property 9 are about the direct causes and root causes, respectively. Direct Explanation requires the explanations directly defending the topic x. Root Explanation requires the explanation containing arguments that could "protect" themselves or are not attacked by any argument. Principle 12 and Property 10 are the weak versions of Principle 11 and Property 9.

Principle 11 (Direct Explanation). *Given an AF $F = (A, R) \in \mathfrak{AF}$ and the topic $x \in A$. If $M \in \mathbb{M}_F(x)$ is an explanation for x, then M defends x.*

Principle 12 (Weak Direct Explanation). *Given an AF $F = (A, R) \in \mathfrak{AF}$ and the topic $x \in A$. For some $M \in \mathbb{M}_F(x)$ as an explanation for x, M defends x.*

Recall that given an AF $F = (A, R)$, an argument $a \in A$ is a self-defending argument iff $(a, a) \in \overline{A}^+$, and an argument b is an initial argument iff there exists no $c \in A$, s.t. $(c, b) \in R$, denoted as A_S and A_I respectively.

Property 9 (Root Explanation). *Given an AF $F = (A, R) \in \mathfrak{AF}$ and the topic $x \in A$. If $M \in \mathbb{M}_F(x)$, then there exists $a \in M$ where $a \in A_I \cup A_S$.*

Property 10 (Weak Root Explanation). *Given an AF $F = (A, R) \in \mathfrak{AF}$ and the topic $x \in A$. For some $M \in \mathbb{M}_F(x)$, there exists $a \in M$ where $a \in A_I \cup A_S$.*

For σ-extension E that contains the topic x, it is always possible to find the direct explanation and root explanation in E. Therefore, for the explanation method satisfying Property 7, it also satisfies the weak version of the Principle 11 and Property 9.

Proposition 9. *Given an AF $F = (A, R) \in \mathfrak{AF}$ and the topic $x \in A$. If $\mathbb{M}_F(x)$ satisfies Containing Extensions, then it satisfies Weak Direct Explanation and Weak Root Explanation.*

4.2 Principle-and-Property-Based Analysis

The comparison is summarized in Table 1, which provides a clear overview of the satisfaction or dissatisfaction with the twelve principles and ten properties by the five explanation methods. The comparative analysis reveals distinct characteristics and trade-offs:

Table 1. Principle-based Analysis of Five Explanation Methods. Symbols: ✓ = principle satisfied, × = principle not satisfied, {···} = partial satisfaction and − = not yet confirmed. Results marked with asterisks (∗) are taken from the literature [1,10,35].

	$\mathcal{S}_\sigma$	$\mathcal{P}_\sigma$	$\mathcal{I}_\sigma$	$\mathcal{T}_\sigma$	$\mathcal{R}_\sigma$
Existence	✓*	✓	✓*	✓	✓
Conflict-Freeness	×*	×	✓*	✓	✓
Self-Defense	×*	×	{gr}	✓	×
Assurance	✓*	×	✓*	✓	✓
Weak Assurance	✓	✓	✓	✓	✓
Influence	×	×	×	✓	✓
Weak Influence	✓	✓	×	✓	✓
Connectivity	×	×	{gr}	×	×
Composition	✓	×	{gr}	×	{gr}
Uniqueness	×	×	{gr}	×	{gr}
Non-Redundancy	×	×	−	✓	−
Monotonicity	✓*	×	×*	×	×
Independence	✓*	×	×*	×	×
Containing Extensions	✓*	✓	×	×	×
Sub-Extension	×	×	✓*	{ad,co,pr,st}	✓
Sub-Extension Permission	✓	✓	✓	{ad,co,pr,st}	✓
Quantitative Restriction	×	×	{gr}	{ad}	✓
External Explanation	×	×	×	×	×
Direct Explanation	✓*	×	×	✓	×
Weak Direct Explanation	✓	✓	×	✓	×
Root Explanation	×	×	×	✓	✓
Weak Root Explanation	✓	✓	×	✓	✓

– All five methods satisfy two core principles (Existence and Weak Assurance), and Sub-Extension Permission is satisfied by most explanation methods except for $\mathcal{T}_{gr}$-explanation method, which highlights their foundational role in the explanation.
  • Existence ensures a non-empty explanation method when the target argument is credulously accepted, establishing baseline validity across methods.
  • Weak Assurance reveals a unified capability: for any method, at least one explanation maintains the topic's acceptability when accepted the explanation.
  • Sub-Extension Permission emphasizes the efficiency of the explanation method by showing that it can provide an explanation with fewer arguments than those required by semantics, while still achieving equivalent explanatory capacity.
– Some principles or properties are commonly satisfied by three or four methods, e.g. Weak Influence, Weak Direct Explanation, and Weak Root Explanation, which demonstrates both consensus and divergence among explanation methods. What's more, Sub-Extensions is satisfied by $\mathcal{I}_\sigma$ and $\mathcal{R}_\sigma$-explanation methods, as well as

$\mathcal{T}_\sigma$-explanation method except for $\mathcal{T}_{gr}$-explanation method; Quantitative Restriction is satisfied by $\mathcal{R}_\sigma$, $\mathcal{T}_{ad}$, and $\mathcal{T}_{gr}$-explanation methods.
  - The shared satisfaction of Weak Influence and Weak Root Explanation by four methods ($\mathcal{S}_\sigma, \mathcal{P}_\sigma, \mathcal{T}_\sigma, \mathcal{R}_\sigma$) underscores the importance of the explanation providing both defensive influence and root causes justification for the topic. And Weak Direct Explanation is satisfied by three explanation methods ($\mathcal{S}_\sigma, \mathcal{P}_\sigma, \mathcal{T}_\sigma$), highlighting their capacity to directly explain the acceptance of the topic.
  - The satisfaction of Sub-Extension implies that the explanation they provide is included in the corresponding σ-extensions, highlighting their ability to offer a valid explanation with fewer arguments than required by the semantics. Moreover, methods satisfying Sub-Extensions adhere to Conflict-Freeness.
  - For $\mathcal{T}_{gr}$, $\mathcal{T}_{ad}$, and $\mathcal{R}_\sigma$-explanation methods, they all satisfy Quantitative Restriction which indicates that the number of the explanation they provide is equivalent to the number of the corresponding σ-extensions containing the topic.
- Certain principles or properties are frequently violated, e.g. Monotonicity, Independence, Influence, Direct Explanation, and Root Explanation, and External Explanation is not satisfied by any methods, suggesting that they may be too stringent.
  - The exclusive adherence of the $\mathcal{S}_\sigma$-explanation method to Monotonicity and Independence suggests that these two properties may serve as the characterization of the $\mathcal{S}_\sigma$-explanation method.
  - The primary reason for External Explanation's failure with the five methods lies in its requirement that the condition (namely, $M \setminus E \neq \emptyset$ for some $E \in \sigma(F)$ and $x \in E$) is met in every AF $F \in \mathfrak{UF}$. This condition can be satisfied in most AFs, except for the trivial one, for instance, $F = (A, R)$ where $A = \{x\}$ and $R = \emptyset$. Hence, it is worth investigating the topological restriction of External Explanation and defining a weaker version based on it.
  - Direct Explanation and Root Explanation are satisfied by two methods: $\mathcal{S}_\sigma$ and $\mathcal{T}_\sigma$-explanation methods satisfy Direct Explanation; $\mathcal{T}_\sigma$ and $\mathcal{R}_\sigma$-explanation methods satisfy Root Explanation. The reason for $\mathcal{S}_\sigma$-explanation method satisfying Direct Explanation is that M defending x being the sufficient conditions for M to be a $\mathcal{S}_\sigma$-explanation. And the property of Root Explanation can act as the characterization of the $\mathcal{R}_\sigma$-explanation method. The satisfaction of both principles by $\mathcal{T}_\sigma$-explanation method indicates that it provides the direct explanation and the root causes at the same time.
- The analysis also reveals an inherent trade-off between explanatory breadth and structural precision across the explanation methods.
  - Methods prioritizing comprehensive coverage achieve broad explanation coverage: $\mathcal{S}_\sigma$-explanation method adhering to Monotonicity and Composition allows incremental expansion of explanation; while $\mathcal{P}_\sigma$-explanation method satisfying Containing Extensions ensures compatibility with diverse semantic outcomes. However, this breadth comes at the cost of internal consistency, as both methods violate Conflict-Freeness and Self-Defense.
  - Conversely, $\mathcal{T}_\sigma$-explanation method exemplifies precision by generating explanations that are contained in the extensions, which enhances specificity in providing explanation. The more focused explanation methods ($\mathcal{T}_\sigma$ and $\mathcal{R}_\sigma$) satisfy core requirements for semantics, that is Conflict-Freeness and Self-Defense, yet have limitations in compositional flexibility and extensions coverage.

5 Related Work and Conclusion

Numerous studies have employed logic-based models for XAI [3–5], which inspired our work on explainability in AA. In this study, regarding the question of "why accept an argument", we have categorized different explanation methods in the literature into five distinct types: strong ($\mathcal{S}_\sigma$), presumptive ($\mathcal{P}_\sigma$), iterative ($\mathcal{I}_\sigma$), tree-like ($\mathcal{T}_\sigma$), and root ($\mathcal{R}_\sigma$) explanation methods. Integrating these explanation methods into a unified framework enables systematic, principle-and-property-based comparisons.

Strong explanation, first introduced in [35], is primarily designed to guarantee that the explanations satisfy the property of monotonicity. Besides, the authors discussed properties that are essentially consistent with the principles named in this paper: Self-Defense, Assurance, and so on (marked with asterisks ($*$) in column $\mathcal{S}_\sigma$ of Table 1). However, in our discussion, we find that Monotonicity, which is considered crucial in [35], does not apply to the other four explanation methods.

The presumptive explanation method is a novel approach partially inspired by the concept of "abductive reasoning in AA" as discussed in [12,31]. In contrast to prior research, we focus on using additions (or removals) of arguments to serve as an explanation for the argument's acceptance. We adopt a fresh perspective: presumptive explanation can be conceptualized through the premise that the absence of the explanation would preclude the acceptance of the topic.

The iterative ($\mathcal{I}_\sigma$) and tree-like ($\mathcal{T}_\sigma$) explanation methods are respectively adapted from [10] and [23], with certain modifications about the details in order to align with our general definition of explanation method, that is using Θ_σ-explanation as the instantiation of $\mathbb{M}_F(x)$ with $\Theta \in \{\mathcal{S}, \mathcal{P}, \mathcal{I}, \mathcal{T}, \mathcal{R}\}$ and $\sigma \in \{ad, co, pr, gr, st\}$.

The root explanation method proposed in this paper builds upon two key concepts: "self-explanation" from [25] and "root reasons for accepting arguments" from [26]. In [25], the authors developed a new semantics called explainable semantics of AF. It not only identifies acceptable arguments but also provides explanations by tracing through the defense relation beginning with certain arguments. Our definition of the root explanation method extracts and integrates the most essential components from [26] and [25], namely the transitive closure of defense relation, in order to identify the root explanation of the topic, but in contrast to these works, prioritizes conceptual simplicity by abstaining from developing new semantics.

Through an interdisciplinary synthesis of explanatory theories, we identify four fundamental characteristics of effective explanatory methods: Contrastive Nature, Selective Disclosure, Dialogical Interaction, and Context Sensitivity. Operationalizing these characteristics within the explanatory task in AA, we derive twenty-two evaluation principles and properties that systematically assess five prominent explanation methods proposed in the literature. As summarized in Table 1, the principle-and-property-based analysis reveals the strengths and limitations of each explanation method through the lens of these criteria. This principle-and-property-based approach for explanation research in formal argumentation has multiple advances: (1) a transparent assessment methodology, (2) an alignment between explanation methods design and practical requirement, and (3) diagnostic insights for future explanation methods improvement.

Our principle-and-property-based analysis for the explanation methods in AA lays the foundational work for future research of explanation in computational argumentation, with the following potential directions:

- While our current defined principles capture essential explanation dimensions, future work should incorporate additional perspectives. For principles that reflect the relationship between explanations in the explanation method, there is more to discuss. Non-Redundancy, which ensures minimal information overlap, remains formally unproven for $\mathcal{I}_\sigma$ and $\mathcal{R}_\sigma$-explanation methods, though empirical observations suggest its satisfaction under preferred, stable and grounded semantics.
- The principle-and-property-based approach for explanation methods in AA can be extended to structural argumentation, which is another main field in computational argumentation. Many of the explanation methods introduced in Sect. 3 can also be extended into structural argumentation [4,14,15,23]. Also, the principle-and-property-based approach for explanation methods can be applied to extended abstract argumentation, e.g. bipolar AF, probabilistic AF, and so on. For instance, the $\mathcal{I}_\sigma$-explanation method has been introduced into probabilistic AF in [1].
- The axiomatic methodology outlined in this paper holds the potential for advancing formal characterizations of explanation methods through the establishment of such representation theorems, which systematically optimize these explanation methods to meet domain-specific demands. Such developments will necessitate and reinforce the principle-and-property-based analysis as a cornerstone for both theoretical refinement and practical implementation in providing explanation using formal argumentation.

Acknowledgements. The authors would like to thank three anonymous reviewers for their helpful comments. This work is supported by the National Social Science Foundation Major Project of China (20&ZD047).

References

1. Alfano, G., Calautti, M., Greco, S., Parisi, F., Trubitsyna, I.: Explainable acceptance in probabilistic abstract argumentation: complexity and approximation. In: Proceedings of the Seventeenth International Conference on Principles of Knowledge Representation and Reasoning, pp. 33–43 (2020)
2. Alfano, G., Greco, S., Parisi, F., Trubitsyna, I.: Counterfactual and semifactual explanations in abstract argumentation: Formal foundations, complexity and computation. In: Proceedings of the Twenty-First International Conference on Principles of Knowledge Representation and Reasoning, pp. 14–26 (2024)
3. Amgoud, L., Ben-Naim, J.: Axiomatic foundations of explainability. In: Proceedings of the Thirty-First International Joint Conference on Artificial Intelligence, pp. 636–642 (2022)
4. Arieli, O., Borg, A., Hesse, M., Strasser, C.: Explainable logic-based argumentation. In: Computational Models of Argument, pp. 32–43 (2022)
5. Arioua, A., Croitoru, M.: Formalizing explanatory dialogues. In: Scalable Uncertainty Management, pp. 282–297 (2015)

6. Baroni, P., Caminada, M., Giacomin, M.: Abstract argumentation frameworks and their semantics. In: Handbook of Formal Argumentation, 1 edn, vol. 1, pp. 159–236. College Publications, London (2018)
7. Baroni, P., Giacomin, M.: On principle-based evaluation of extension-based argumentation semantics. Artif. Intell. **171**(10), 675–700 (2007)
8. Barredo Arrieta, A., et al.: Explainable artificial intelligence (XAI): concepts, taxonomies, opportunities and challenges toward responsible AI. Inf. Fusion **58**, 82–115 (2020)
9. Baumann, R., Brewka, G., Ulbricht, M.: Comparing weak admissibility semantics to their dung-style counterparts – reduct, modularization, and strong equivalence in abstract argumentation. In: Proceedings of the Seventeenth International Conference on Principles of Knowledge Representation and Reasoning, pp. 79–88 (2020)
10. Baumann, R., Ulbricht, M.: Choices and their consequences - explaining acceptable sets in abstract argumentation frameworks. In: Proceedings of the Eighteenth International Conference on Principles of Knowledge Representation and Reasoning, pp. 110–119 (2021)
11. Bench-Capon, T., Dunne, P.E.: Argumentation in artificial intelligence. Artif. Intell. **171**(10), 619–641 (2007)
12. Booth, R., Gabbay, D., Kaci, S., Rienstra, T., van der Torre, L.: Abduction and dialogical proof in argumentation and logic programming. In: ECAI, vol. 263, pp. 117–122 (2014)
13. Borg, A., Bex, F.: A basic framework for explanations in argumentation. IEEE Intell. Syst. **36**(2), 25–35 (2021)
14. Borg, A.M., Bex, F.: Necessary and sufficient explanations for argumentation-based conclusions. In: Vejnarová, J., Wilson, N. (eds.) ECSQARU 2021. LNCS (LNAI), vol. 12897, pp. 45–58. Springer, Cham (2021). https://doi.org/10.1007/978-3-030-86772-0_4
15. Borg, A., Bex, F.: Minimality, necessity and sufficiency for argumentation and explanation. Int. J. Approximate Reasoning **168**, 109143 (2024)
16. Brewka, G., Thimm, M., Ulbricht, M.: Strong inconsistency in nonmonotonic reasoning. In: Proceedings of the Twenty-Sixth International Joint Conference on Artificial Intelligence, pp. 901–907 (2017)
17. Brewka, G., Ulbricht, M.: Strong explanations for nonmonotonic reasoning. In: Description Logic, Theory Combination, and All That, vol. 11560, pp. 135–146. Springer, Cham (2019)
18. Čyras, K., et al.: Explanations by arbitrated argumentative dispute. Expert Syst. Appl. **127**, 141–156 (2019)
19. Čyras, K., Rago, A., Albini, E., Baroni, P., Toni, F.: Argumentative XAI: a survey. In: Proceedings of the Thirtieth International Joint Conference on Artificial Intelligence, pp. 4392–4399 (2021)
20. Doutre, S., Duchatelle, T., Lagasquie-Schiex, M.C.: Classes of explanations for the verification problem in abstract argumentation. In: Journées d'Intelligence Artificielle Fondamentale, pp. 1–10 (2023)
21. Dung, P.M.: On the acceptability of arguments and its fundamental role in nonmonotonic reasoning, logic programming and n-person games. Artif. Intell. **77**(2), 321–357 (1995)
22. Engelmann, D., Damasio, J., Panisson, A.R., Mascardi, V., Bordini, R.H.: Argumentation as a method for explainable AI: a systematic literature review. In: 2022 17th Iberian Conference on Information Systems and Technologies, pp. 1–6 (2022)
23. Fan, X., Toni, F.: On computing explanations in argumentation. In: Proceedings of the Twenty-Ninth AAAI Conference on Artificial Intelligence, vol. 29, pp. 1496–1502 (2015)
24. Fan, X., Toni, F.: On explanations for non-acceptable arguments. In: Black, E., Modgil, S., Oren, N. (eds.) TAFA 2015. LNCS (LNAI), vol. 9524, pp. 112–127. Springer, Cham (2015). https://doi.org/10.1007/978-3-319-28460-6_7
25. Liao, B., Van Der Torre, L.: Explanation semantics for abstract argumentation. In: Computational Models of Argument, pp. 271–282 (2020)

26. Liao, B., Van Der Torre, L.: Attack-defense semantics of argumentation. In: Computational Models of Argument, pp. 133–144 (2024)
27. Lipton, P.: What good is an explanation? In: Explanation: Theoretical Approaches and Applications, pp. 43–59. Springer, Dordrecht (2001)
28. Mahmood, Y., Hecher, M., Ngomo, A.C.N.: Dung's argumentation framework: unveiling the expressive power with inconsistent databases. arXiv:2412.11617 (2024)
29. Miller, T.: Explanation in artificial intelligence: insights from the social sciences. Artif. Intell. **267**, 1–38 (2019)
30. Modgil, S., Caminada, M.: Proof theories and algorithms for abstract argumentation frameworks. In: Argumentation in Artificial Intelligence, pp. 105–129. Springer, Boston (2009)
31. Sakama, C.: Abduction in argumentation frameworks. J. Appl. Non-Classical Logics **28**(2–3), 218–239 (2018)
32. Saribatur, Z.G., Wallner, J.P., Woltran, S.: Explaining non-acceptability in abstract argumentation. In: European Conference on Artificial Intelligence, pp. 881–888 (2020)
33. Scheffers, R., Bex, F., Borg, A.: Related explanations in formal argumentation, an empirical study. In: Computational Models of Argument, pp. 265–276 (2024)
34. Sklar, E.I., Azhar, M.Q.: Explanation through argumentation. In: Proceedings of the 6th International Conference on Human-Agent Interaction, pp. 277–285 (2018)
35. Ulbricht, M., Wallner, J.P.: Strong explanations in abstract argumentation. In: Proceedings of the Thirty-Fifth AAAI Conference on Artificial Intelligence, vol. 35, pp. 6496–6504 (2021)
36. Van Der Torre, L., Vesic, S.: The principle-based approach to abstract argumentation semantics. J. Logics Appl. **4**(8), 2735–2778 (2017)
37. Vassiliades, A., Bassiliades, N., Patkos, T.: Argumentation and explainable artificial intelligence: a survey. Knowl. Eng. Rev. **36**, e5 (2021)

Proportional Acceptability of Arguments

Xiaolong Liu[1] and Weiwei Chen[2(✉)]

[1] Department of Philosophy, Xiangtan University, Xiangtan, China
liuxiaolong@xtu.edu.cn
[2] Institute of Logic and Cognition and Department of Philosophy,
Sun Yat-sen University, Guangzhou, China
chenweiwei@mail.sysu.edu.cn

Abstract. This paper introduces the concept of proportional acceptability (or defense) as a means to distinguish different levels at which an argument can be accepted or rejected. The key idea of this paper is to evaluate the degree of justification of arguments by taking into account the proportion of attacks that are not counter-attacked. More Specifically, an argument is considered successfully defended by a set of arguments if there is not a significant enough proportion of its attackers such that there is not a significant enough proportion of the counter-attackers in the set. Building on this idea, we develop proportional semantics, which are generalizations Dung's semantics and variants of graded semantics. Furthermore, proportional semantics offer a new perspective on argument rankings, contributing to the topic of ranking-based semantics.

Keywords: proportional acceptability · graded semantics · argument

1 Introduction

Formal argumentation is a research field that focuses on the construction and evaluation of arguments. Its origins can be traced back to the contributions of [18–20]. Dung's abstract argumentation theory [7] is highly influential in this field because it incorporates numerous approaches to nonmonotonic reasoning and logic programming as specific instances. In Dung's work, an argumentation framework (AF) is a directed graph, where nodes represent arguments and edges represent elements of a binary relation. It has been studied widely over the last decades. One of the core notions of argumentation frameworks is *acceptability* (or *defense*). A set of arguments defend an argument if and only if whenever the argument has an attacker, there exists a counter-attacker in the set of arguments.

The topic of distinguishing the statuses or strengths of arguments in abstract argumentation is intriguing, since an argument requires only a single mandatory defender for it to be successfully defended. On one hand, the statuses of arguments can be differentiated by using techniques for value propagation on argumentation framework graphs. Specifically, when initial information about the strength of arguments is given, measures of the strengths of arguments based on the numbers of attackers or defenders are propagated through the graphs. These

Fig. 1. Comparison of A being defended by $\{C_1\}$ in 2023 and 2024

approaches are generally exogenous to Dung's theory, as they typically do not rely on Dung's original notions, e.g., acceptability or extensions under various semantics. In contrast, an endogenous approach proposed in [10] offers a more fine-grained assignment of status to arguments. This approach does not depend on exogenous information (such as preferences or weights); instead, it only considers the absolute numbers of attackers and defenders of arguments in a given argumentation framework. Moreover, it can be formalized as a generalization of Dung's concepts of conflict-freeness and defense.

Inspired by the graded semantics proposed by [10], we also introduce an endogenous approach to distinguishing the statuses of arguments in terms of *proportionality*: an aspect not addressed by the graded semantics. Our key idea is to evaluate the statuses of arguments by taking into account the proportion of attacks that are not counter-attacked, rather than their absolute number. Let us recall from [10] that the graded defense (or graded acceptability), which is the base of the graded semantics, offers an approach to understanding the degrees of justification for arguments by parameterizing the defense of an argument with the absolute numbers of its attackers and their counter-attackers. The graded defense states a set of arguments Δ mn-defends an argument A whenever A has at most $m-1$ attackers that are not counter-attacked by at least n arguments in Δ. However, the graded defense cannot distinguish the statuses of arguments regarding proportionality. We illustrate this issue with the following example.

Example 1. Consider a scenario regarding the state of health of a person, Kais:

A: Kais assumes that he is in good health as he has no symptoms of illness.
B: A new type of blood test t_1 that he undertook in 2023 indicates that he has a rare asymptomatic illness.
C_1: A scientific paper p_1 in 2023 says that the new blood test is unreliable.

We observe that A is attacked by B, which in turn is attacked by C_1. This scenario can be represented with Fig. 1a. It is reasonable to assert that $\{C_1\}$ provides a strong defense for A in the sense that all counter-attackers of A's attacker B belong to this set. One year later, "*another scientific paper p_2 in 2024 also highlights the unreliability of the blood test*" (C_2). Then we have the updated AF in 2024 where C_2 attacks B (see Fig. 1b). Consequently, compared to 2023, the degree to which A is defended by $\{C_1\}$ is intuitively weakened in 2024, given that in 2024 this set contains only half of B's counter-attackers opposing the claim that Kais has a rare asymptomatic illness. However, by the graded defense

[10,11], the strength of A being defended by $\{C_1\}$ is the same in both 2023 and 2024 in the sense that every attacker of A has at least 1 counter-attacker within $\{C_1\}$ (i.e., C_1 11-defends A) in both 2023 and 2024, since the graded semantics consider only absolute number of counter-attackers of A's attacker within $\{C_1\}$.

The problem stems from the fact that the graded acceptability distinguishes argument statuses based on the absolute number of attacks that are not defended, rather than the proportion. Hence, this paper proposes *proportional acceptability* by using the concept of proportionality to quantify the attackers and defenders of arguments, thereby distinguishing the statuses of arguments that are not considered in the graded acceptability. Specifically, an argument A is *proportionally acceptable* w.r.t. a set of arguments Δ (or Δ *proportionally defends* A) if there is not at least a specific proportion of A's attackers that have no at least specific proportion of the counter-attackers in Δ. For example, informally, we can require that Δ proportionally defends A if one hundred percent of A's attackers have more than half of their counter-attackers within Δ. Therefore, according to this standard of defense, in Example 1, $\{C_1\}$ proportionally defends A in Fig. 1a while $\{C_1\}$ fails to proportionally defends A in Fig. 1b. Hence, we can say that A is "better" defended by $\{C_1\}$ in 2023 than in 2024. This example illustrates how the concept of proportionality can be used to distinguish the statuses of arguments by quantifying their defenders. Furthermore, proportionality can also be applied to differentiate argument statuses by quantifying their attackers. Namely, we can allow a proportion of an argument's attackers that lack a sufficient proportion of counter-attackers within a given set of arguments. For instance, we can require that Δ proportionally defends A if there are not at least half of its attackers that do no have at least half counter-attackers in Δ. Generally, given a set of arguments Δ, our approach to differentiating the degrees of justification of arguments is built upon the following two assumptions:

(A1) having a smaller proportion of attackers that are not counter-attacked by enough arguments in Δ is considered "better" than having a larger proportion;

(A2) having a larger proportion of defenders in Δ is considered "better" than having a smaller proportion.

Based on proportional acceptability, we develop *proportional semantics* which generalize Dung's semantics and act as variants of graded semantics. Additionally, proportional semantics offer a new perspective on argument rankings.

Contribution. First, we introduce a novel concept of acceptability, termed *proportional acceptability*, in abstract argumentation. This acceptability enables a nuanced analysis of argument statuses by parameterizing attackers and counter-attackers through proportionality. Second, we define the proportional defense function and the proportional neutrality function to characterize different levels of defense and conflict-freeness, thereby enabling argument rankings. Third, based on the the two functions, we propose proportional semantics, which are generalizations of Dung's semantics [7] and variants of graded semantics [11].

Structure. The rest of this paper is organized as follows. Section 2 provides the necessary background by reviewing basic notions of Dung's semantics, graded semantics concepts, and solid semantics. Section 3 proposes proportional acceptability and conflict-freeness by constructing proportional defense and neutrality functions. Besides, we explore some properties of the functions. At the end of this section, we rank proportional defense functions, and rank arguments with proportional defense functions. Sect. 4 develops proportional semantics by utilizing the two functions. Additionally, we rank arguments with proportional semantics. Sect. 5 introduces the related work of proportional semantics. Section 6 summarizes this paper and points out two potential research avenues.

2 Preliminaries

This section reviews some basic and necessary notions of Dung's semantics, graded semantics, and solid semantics from [7,11,14], respectively.

Definition 1 (Argumentation framework). *An argumentation framework $\mathcal{AF}$ is a pair $\langle Arg, \rightarrowtail \rangle$, where Arg is a finite set of arguments, and $\rightarrowtail$ is a binary relation on Arg.*

Given $\mathcal{AF} = \langle Arg, \rightarrowtail \rangle$. For any $A \in Arg$ and any $B \in Arg$, $A \rightarrowtail B$ denotes that A attacks B. For any $\Delta \subseteq Arg$ and any $A \in Arg$, $\Delta \rightarrowtail A$ denotes that there exists $B \in \Delta$ such that $B \rightarrowtail A$. We say $A \in Arg$ is acceptable w.r.t. $\Delta \subseteq Arg$ (or Δ defends A), if for any $B \in Arg$ such that $B \rightarrowtail A$, there exists $C \in \Delta$ such that $C \rightarrowtail B$. For any $A \in Arg$, $\overline{A} = \{B \in Arg \mid B \rightarrowtail A\}$, namely, $\overline{A}$ denotes the set of the attackers of A.

Definition 2 (Defense function). *Given $\mathcal{AF} = \langle Arg, \rightarrowtail \rangle$. The defense function $d: 2^{Arg} \longrightarrow 2^{Arg}$ for $\mathcal{AF}$ is defined as: $d(\Delta) = \{A \in Arg \mid \forall B \in Arg: \text{if } B \rightarrowtail A \text{ then } \Delta \rightarrowtail B\}$.*

Definition 3 (Neutrality function). *Given $\mathcal{AF} = \langle Arg, \rightarrowtail \rangle$. The neutrality function $n: 2^{Arg} \longrightarrow 2^{Arg}$ for $\mathcal{AF}$ is defined as: $n(\Delta) = \{A \in Arg \mid \text{not } \Delta \rightarrowtail A\}$.*

Given $\mathcal{AF} = \langle Arg, \rightarrowtail \rangle$, $\Delta \subseteq Arg$, and $A \in Arg$. $d(\Delta)$ denotes the set of arguments that are defended against any attacker by Δ. Δ defends A iff $A \in d(\Delta)$. $n(\Delta)$ denotes the set of arguments that have no attackers in Δ. Δ is *conflict-free* iff $\Delta \subseteq n(\Delta)$. The defense and neutrality functions capture Dung's semantics (see [11]). Next, we present the graded semantics in [11], especially, introducing two fundamental functions, i.e., graded defense and graded neutrality functions.

Definition 4 (Graded defense function). *Given $\mathcal{AF} = \langle Arg, \rightarrowtail \rangle$. Let m and n be two positive integers ($m, n > 0$). The graded defense function $d_{\frac{m}{n}}: 2^{Arg} \longrightarrow 2^{Arg}$ of $\mathcal{AF}$ is defined: $d_{\frac{m}{n}}(\Delta) = \{A \in Arg: |\{B \in \overline{A}: |\{C \in \overline{B} \cap \Delta\}| < n\}| < m\}$.*

Definition 5 (Graded neutrality function). *Given $\mathcal{AF} = \langle Arg, \rightarrowtail \rangle$ and a positive integer ℓ. Then the graded neutrality function $n_\ell: 2^{Arg} \longrightarrow 2^{Arg}$ for $\mathcal{AF}$ is defined as follows: $n_\ell(\Delta) = \{A \in Arg : |\overline{A} \cap \Delta| < \ell\}$.*

$d_m(\Delta)$ denotes the set of arguments that have at most $m-1$ attackers that are not counter-attacked by at least n arguments in Δ. An argument A is mn-acceptable w.r.t. a set of arguments Δ iff $A \in \underset{n}{d_m}(\Delta)$. $n_\ell(\Delta)$ denotes the set of arguments that have at most $\ell-1$ attackers in Δ. A set of arguments Δ is ℓ-conflict-free if and only if $\Delta \subseteq n_\ell(\Delta)$. Last, we review *solid defense* [14,15] which states that a set of arguments solidly defends (or s-defends) an argument iff the set can counterattack all the attackers of its elements and contain all the counter-attackers of the attackers. $d_s(\Delta)$ denotes the set of arguments A such that Δ defends (in Dung's sense) A, and Δ contains all the defenders of A.

Definition 6 (Solid defense function). *Given $\mathcal{AF} = \langle Arg, \rightarrowtail \rangle$. The solid defense function $d_s: 2^{Arg} \longrightarrow 2^{Arg}$ for $\mathcal{AF}$ is defined as: $d_s(\Delta) = \{A \in Arg \mid \forall B \in Arg:$ if $B \rightarrowtail A$ then $\Delta \rightarrowtail B$ and $\overline{B} \subseteq \Delta\}$.*

3 Proportional Acceptability and Conflict-Freeness

In this section, we first formally propose *proportional acceptability* and *proportional conflict-freeness*, which generalize Dung's defense and conflict-freeness. The notions are founded on two key functions: *proportional defense function* and *proportional neutrality function*. Second, we investigate the properties of the functions. Third, we rank arguments using proportional defense functions.

3.1 Proportional Defense and Neutrality Functions

We introduce the proportional defense and proportional neutrality functions to define novel concepts of acceptability and conflict-freeness regarding proportionality. The functions are based on the two assumptions mentioned in Sect. 1.

Before defining the two functions, we first need to define a *proportional function*, which maps a set of arguments Δ to a set of its non-empty subsets, each containing at least a certain proportion of the elements in Δ.

Definition 7 (Proportional function). *Given $\mathcal{AF} = \langle Arg, \rightarrowtail \rangle$ and a real number δ such that $0 \leqslant \delta \leqslant 1$. The proportion function $\mathscr{P}_\delta: 2^{Arg} \longrightarrow 2^{2^{Arg}}$ for $\mathcal{AF}$ is defined as: $\mathscr{P}_\delta(\Delta) = \{\Gamma \subseteq \Delta: |\Gamma| \geqslant \delta \cdot |\Delta|$ and $\Gamma \neq \varnothing\}$*

$\mathscr{P}_\delta(\Delta)$ denotes the set of Δ's non-empty subsets Γ such that the proportion of Γ's size to Δ's size is more than or equal to δ. For a set of arguments Δ, we say that

- there exists at least δ proportion of Δ if there exists a set of arguments $\Gamma \in \mathscr{P}_\delta(\Delta)$;
- there exists at least δ proportion of Δ belonging to a set of arguments Σ if there exists a set of arguments Γ such that $\Gamma \in \mathscr{P}_\delta(\Delta)$ and $\Gamma \subseteq \Sigma$.

Example 2. Given a set of arguments $\Delta = \{A, B, C\}$ and $\delta = \frac{1}{2}$. Then $\mathscr{P}_{1/2}(\Delta)$ is the set of Δ's subsets that contain at least half of Δ's elements, namely, $\mathscr{P}_{1/2}(\Delta) = \{\{A,B\}, \{A,C\}, \{B,C\}, \{A,B,C\}\}$.

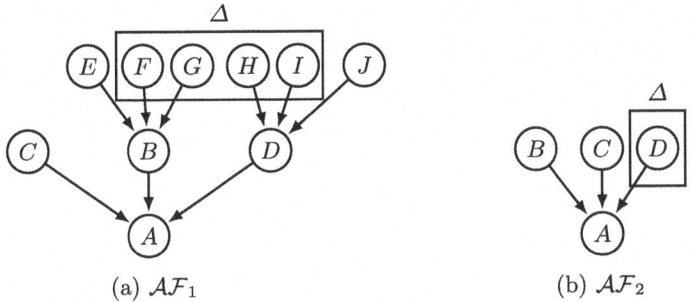

Fig. 2. Illustrations for proportional defense and proportional neutrality

Next, we construct a *proportional defense function* to establish a notion of defense that tolerates a proportion of attackers not having the desired proportion of counter-attackers in a given set of arguments.

Definition 8 (Proportional defense function). *Given $\mathcal{AF} = \langle Arg, \rightarrowtail \rangle$. Let δ and γ be real numbers such that $0 \leqslant \delta, \gamma \leqslant 1$. The proportional defense function $\mathscr{D}_\delta^\gamma : 2^{Arg} \longrightarrow 2^{Arg}$ for $\mathcal{AF}$ is defined as follows. For any $\Delta \subseteq Arg$:*

$$\mathscr{D}_\delta^\gamma(\Delta) = \left\{ A \in Arg \mid \nexists \Gamma \in \mathscr{P}_\delta(\overline{A}) \left[\forall B \in \Gamma \left[\nexists \Sigma \in \mathscr{P}_\gamma(\overline{B}) \left[\Sigma \subseteq \Delta \right] \right] \right] \right\}.$$

$\mathscr{D}_\delta^\gamma(\Delta)$ denotes the set of arguments A such that there does not exist at least δ proportion of the set of A's attackers such that there does not exists at least γ proportion of the set of the counter-attackers belonging to Δ. The specific thresholds (i.e., the proportions) are determined by parameters δ and γ. To illustrate the proportional defense function, consider the following example.

Example 3. In Fig. 2a, $A \in \mathscr{D}_{1/2}^{1/2}(\Delta)$ since there does not exist at least $\frac{1}{2}$ proportion of the set of A's attackers such that there does not exist at least $\frac{1}{2}$ proportion of the set of the counter-attackers belonging to Δ. However, $A \notin \mathscr{D}_{1/3}^{1/2}(\Delta)$ as there exists at least $\frac{1}{3}$ proportion of the set of A's attackers such that there does not exist at least $\frac{1}{2}$ proportion of the set of the counter-attackers belonging to Δ.

The following proposition shows that Dung's defense is a special case of proportional defense.

Proposition 1. *Give $\mathcal{AF} = \langle Arg, \rightarrowtail \rangle$ and $\Delta \subseteq Arg$. Then $\mathscr{D}_0^0(\Delta) = d(\Delta)$ holds.*

Proof. By Definition 8, $\mathscr{D}_0^0(\Delta)$ denotes the set of arguments A such that there does not exist at least 0 proportion of the set of A's attackers such that there does not exist at least 0 proportion of the set of the counter-attackers belonging to Δ. Namely, $\mathscr{D}_0^0(\Delta)$ denotes the set of arguments A that is defended by Δ. Hence, $\mathscr{D}_0^0(\Delta) = d(\Delta)$ by Definition 2. □

Recall that a set of arguments s-defends an argument iff the set can counter-attack all the attackers of its elements and contain all the counter-attackers of the attackers. Hence, the solid defense is a special case of the p-defense.

Proposition 2. *Given $\mathcal{AF} = \langle Arg, \rightarrowtail \rangle$ and $\Delta \subseteq Arg$. Then $\mathcal{D}_0^1(\Delta) = d_s(\Delta)$.*

Proof. $\mathcal{D}_0^1(\Delta)$ denotes the set of arguments A such that there does not exist at least 0 proportion of the set of A's attackers such that there does not exists at least 1 proportion of the set of the counter-attackers belonging to Δ. In other words, $\mathcal{D}_0^1(\Delta)$ denotes the set of arguments A such that A is defended against any attacker by Δ, and all defenders of A are included in Δ. Therefore, $\mathcal{D}_0^1(\Delta) = d_s(\Delta)$ by Definition 6. □

A new concept of acceptability can be defined based on the proportional defense function. We refer to it as *proportional acceptability*.

Definition 9 (Proportional acceptability). *Give $\mathcal{AF} = \langle Arg, \rightarrowtail \rangle$. An argument $A \in Arg$ is p-acceptable at degree $\delta\gamma$ w.r.t. a set of arguments $\Delta \subseteq Arg$ iff $A \in \mathcal{D}_\delta^\gamma(\Delta)$.*

We also say Δ $\delta\gamma$-p-defends A if $A \in \mathcal{D}_\delta^\gamma(\Delta)$. Namely, Δ $\delta\gamma$-p-defends A if there does not exist at least δ proportion of the set of A's attackers, such that there does not exist at least γ proportion of the set of counter-attackers belonging to Δ. To illustrate the proportional acceptability, consider the following example which demonstrates how the proportional acceptability differentiates the statuses of arguments in ways that the graded acceptability cannot.

Example 4. Consider Fig. 3a, we have $A \in \mathcal{D}_0^{2/3}(\Delta)$ while $F \notin \mathcal{D}_0^{2/3}(\Delta)$, namely, Δ can $0\frac{2}{3}$-p-defends A while Δ fails to $0\frac{2}{3}$-p-defend F. Therefore, argument A receives a stronger defense from the set of arguments Δ than F does from the same set, in the sense that two-thirds of the counter-attackers are in Δ when A is attacked, whereas less than two-thirds of the counter-attackers are in Δ when F is attacked. However, according to graded acceptability, in Fig. 3a, the strengths of A and F being defended by Δ cannot be differentiated at grade 12 since $A, F \in d_1^2(\Delta)$. Namely, both A and F satisfy the standard that at most 0 attacker that is not counter-attacked by at least 2 arguments in Δ.

Consider Fig. 3b, we have $A \notin \mathcal{D}_{1/2}^1(\Delta)$ while $E \in \mathcal{D}_{1/2}^1(\Delta)$. In other words, Δ fails to $\frac{1}{2}1$-p-defends A while Δ $\frac{1}{2}1$-p-defends A. Hence, argument A receives a weaker defense from the set of arguments Δ than E does from the same set, in the sense that half of A's attackers are such that not all their counter-attackers are in Δ, while less than half of E's attackers are such that not all their counter-attackers are in Δ. However, in Fig. 3b, by graded acceptability, A and E are not differentiated as $A, E \in d_2^1(\Delta)$, i.e., both A and E satisfy the standard that at most 1 attacker that is not counter-attacked by at least 2 arguments in Δ.

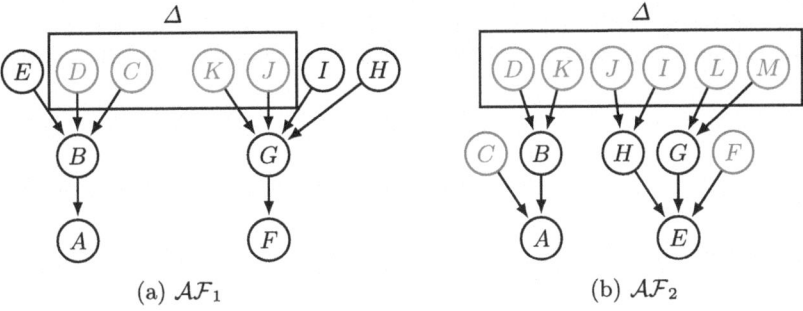

Fig. 3. Illustrations for proportional acceptability

The following proposition follows directly from Definitions 8 and 9.

Proposition 3. *Given $\mathcal{AF} = \langle Arg, \rightharpoonup \rangle$ and a set of arguments $\Delta \subseteq Arg$. The following equation holds: $\mathcal{D}_\delta^\gamma(\Delta) = \{A \in Arg \mid \Delta \ \delta\gamma\text{-p-defends}\ A\}$.*

A set of arguments is *p-self-defending* at a degree if the set p-defends each element of the set at the degree. A set of arguments is *p-reinstating* at a degree if each argument that the set p-defends at the degree is in the set.

Definition 10 (Proportional self-defense). *Given $\mathcal{AF} = \langle Arg, \rightharpoonup \rangle$. A set of arguments $\Delta \subseteq Arg$ is $\delta\gamma$-p-self-defending in $\mathcal{AF}$ iff $\Delta \subseteq \mathcal{D}_\delta^\gamma(\Delta)$.*

Definition 11 (Proportional reinstatement). *Given $\mathcal{AF} = \langle Arg, \rightharpoonup \rangle$. A set of arguments $\Delta \subseteq Arg$ is $\delta\gamma$-p-reinstating in $\mathcal{AF}$ iff $\Delta \supseteq \mathcal{D}_\delta^\gamma(\Delta)$.*

Recall that in Dung's work [7], a set of arguments is conflict-free if and only if the set contains no internal conflict. We now turn to generalize Dung's conflict-freeness by requiring that the internal conflicts of a set of arguments should not exceed a specific proportion. Based on this idea, we define a *proportional neutrality function* as below.

Definition 12 (Proportional neutrality function). *Given $\mathcal{AF} = \langle Arg, \rightharpoonup \rangle$. Let τ be a real number such that $0 \leqslant \tau \leqslant 1$. The proportional neutrality function $\mathcal{N}_\tau : 2^{Arg} \longrightarrow 2^{Arg}$ for $\mathcal{AF}$ is defined as follows. For any $\Delta \subseteq Arg$: $\mathcal{N}_\tau(\Delta) = \{A \in Arg \mid \nexists \Gamma \in \mathcal{P}_\tau(\overline{A})[\Gamma \subseteq \Delta]\}$.*

$\mathcal{N}_\tau(\Delta)$ denotes the set of arguments A such that there does not exist at least τ proportion of the set of A's attackers belonging to Δ. We give an example below to illustrate the proportional neutrality function.

Example 5. In Fig. 2b, $A \in \mathcal{N}_{1/2}(\Delta)$ since A does not have at least half of its attackers in Δ. However, $A \notin \mathcal{N}_{1/3}(\Delta)$ since A has at least one-thirds of its attackers in Δ.

The following proposition shows that Dung's neutrality function n corresponds to the proportional neutrality function $\mathcal{N}_\tau$ where $\tau = 0$.

Proposition 4. *Given* $\mathcal{AF} = \langle Arg, \rightarrowtail \rangle$ *and* $\Delta \subseteq Arg$. *Then* $n(\Delta) = \mathcal{N}_0(\Delta)$.

Proof. According to Definition 12, $\mathcal{N}_0(\Delta)$ denotes the set of arguments A such that there does not exist at least 0 proportion of the set of A's attackers belonging to Δ. In other words, $\mathcal{N}_\tau(\Delta)$ denotes the set of arguments A that has no attacker in Δ. Hence, $\mathcal{N}_0(\Delta) = n(\Delta)$ by Definition 3. □

Using the proportional neutrality function, we define *proportional conflict-freeness*, which tolerates a proportion of internal conflicts in a set of arguments.

Definition 13 (Proportional conflict-freeness). *Given* $\mathcal{AF} = \langle Arg, \rightarrowtail \rangle$ *and* $\Delta \subseteq Arg$. *Let* τ *be a real numbers such that* $0 \leqslant \gamma \leqslant 1$. Δ *is* τ-p-conflict-free *iff* $\Delta \subseteq \mathcal{N}_\tau(\Delta)$.

According to the definition above, a set of arguments Δ is τ-p-conflict-free if and only if for each argument A in Δ, there does not exist at least τ proportion of the set of A's attackers belonging to Δ.

3.2 Properties of Proportional Defense and Neutrality Functions

We next investigate some properties of the proportional defense and proportional neutrality functions. First, we show that the proportional defense function is monotonic while the neutrality function is antitonic. It follows from the monotonicity that if a set of arguments p-defends an argument at some degree, then any superset of the set also p-defends the argument at the same grade. Besides, the antitonicity entails that if a set of arguments is p-conflict-free at some degree, then any subset of the set is also p-conflict-free at the same degree.

Proposition 5. *Given* $\mathcal{AF} = \langle Arg, \rightarrowtail \rangle$ *and* $\Delta \subseteq Arg$. *Let* δ *and* γ *be real numbers such that* $0 \leqslant \delta, \gamma \leqslant 1$. *The following items hold:* (i) *if* $\Delta \subseteq \Gamma$, *then* $\mathcal{D}_\delta^\gamma(\Delta) \subseteq \mathcal{D}_\delta^\gamma(\Gamma)$; (ii) *if* $\Delta \subseteq \Gamma$, *then* $\mathcal{N}_\tau(\Gamma) \subseteq \mathcal{N}_\tau(\Delta)$.

Proof. (i) It follows from Definition 8. (ii) It follows from Definition 12. □

An interesting result below is that the composition of the proportional neutrality function is the proportional defense function.

Theorem 1. *Given* $\mathcal{AF} = \langle Arg, \rightarrowtail \rangle$. *For any* $\Delta \subseteq Arg$, $\mathcal{D}_\delta^\gamma(\Delta) = \mathcal{N}_\delta(\mathcal{N}_\gamma(\Delta))$.

Proof. According to the definitions of the proportional defense function (Definition 8) and the proportional neutrality function (Definition 12), we have:

$$\mathcal{N}_\delta(\mathcal{N}_\gamma(\Delta)) = \{A \in Arg \mid \nexists \Gamma \in \mathscr{P}_\delta(\overline{A})[\Gamma \subseteq \mathcal{N}_\gamma(\Delta)]\} \tag{1a}$$
$$= \{A \in Arg \mid \nexists \Gamma \in \mathscr{P}_\delta(\overline{A})[\forall B \in \Gamma[B \in \mathcal{N}_\gamma(\Delta)]]\} \tag{1b}$$
$$= \{A \in Arg \mid \nexists \Gamma \in \mathscr{P}_\delta(\overline{A})[\forall B \in \Gamma[\nexists \Sigma \in \mathscr{P}_\gamma(\overline{B})[\Sigma \subseteq \Delta]]]\} \tag{1c}$$
$$= \mathcal{D}_\delta^\gamma(\Delta) \tag{1d}$$

We have Eq. (1a) by Definition 12, Eq. (1b) by the definition of a subset, Eq. (1c) by Definition 12, and Eq. (1d) by Definition 8. □

We next demonstrate how varying the parameters of the proportional defense and proportional neutrality functions affects the values of the functions.

Theorem 2. *Given $\mathcal{AF} = \langle Arg, \rightarrowtail \rangle$ and $\Delta \subseteq Arg$. Let τ, δ and γ be real number such that $0 \leqslant \tau, \delta, \gamma \leqslant 1$. The following hold:*

(i) $\mathcal{N}_\tau(\Delta) \subseteq \mathcal{N}_{\tau'}(\Delta)$ for any real number τ' such that $0 \leqslant \tau \leqslant \tau' \leqslant 1$;
(ii) $\mathcal{D}_\delta^\gamma(\Delta) \subseteq \mathcal{D}_{\delta'}^\gamma(\Delta)$ for any real number δ' such that $0 \leqslant \delta \leqslant \delta' \leqslant 1$;
(iii) $\mathcal{D}_\delta^{\gamma'}(\Delta) \subseteq \mathcal{D}_\delta^\gamma(\Delta)$ for any real number γ' such that $0 \leqslant \gamma \leqslant \gamma' \leqslant 1$.

Proof. (i) It follows from Definition 12. (ii) $\mathcal{D}_\delta^\gamma(\Delta) = \mathcal{N}_\delta(\mathcal{N}_\gamma(\Delta)) \subseteq \mathcal{N}_{\delta'}(\mathcal{N}_\gamma(\Delta)) = \mathcal{D}_{\delta'}^\gamma(\Delta)$ by Theorem 1 and the first claim. (iii) $\mathcal{D}_\delta^\gamma(\Delta) = \mathcal{N}_\delta(\mathcal{N}_\gamma(\Delta)) \supseteq \mathcal{N}_\delta(\mathcal{N}_{\gamma'}(\Delta)) = \mathcal{D}_\delta^{\gamma'}(\Delta)$ by Theorem 1, Proposition 5, and the first claim. □

Hence, the parameters of the functions determine various standards for proportional conflict-freeness and proportional acceptability. Intuitively, a higher value of τ allows for the tolerance of more internal conflicts. An increase in δ results in a diminished level of proportional acceptability, while an increase in γ enhances it. Let us consider the following example to illustrate this theorem.

Example 6. In Fig. 2b, $\{A, D\} \subseteq \mathcal{N}_{1/2}(\{A, D\})$ but $\{A, D\} \not\subseteq \mathcal{N}_{1/3}(\{A, D\})$, since $\mathcal{N}_{1/2}$ tolerates more internal conflicts in $\{A, D\}$ than $\mathcal{N}_{1/3}$. In Fig. 2a, $A \in \mathcal{D}_{1/2}^{1/2}(\Delta)$ but $A \notin \mathcal{D}_{1/3}^{1/2}(\Delta)$, since compared with $\mathcal{D}_{1/3}^{1/2}$, $\mathcal{D}_{1/2}^{1/2}$ tolerates a larger proportion of attackers that do not have the desired proportion of counter-attackers in Δ. In Fig. 2a, $A \in \mathcal{D}_{1/2}^{1/2}(\Delta)$ but $A \notin \mathcal{D}_{1/2}^{1}(\Delta)$, as $\mathcal{D}_{1/2}^{1}$ requires a larger proportion of counter-attackers in Δ than $\mathcal{D}_{1/2}^{1/2}$ does.

At last, we show that the proportional function is continuous.

Proposition 6. *The proportional function $\mathcal{D}_\delta^\gamma$ of $\mathcal{AF}$ is ω-continuous.*

Proof. We only show that $\mathcal{D}_\delta^\gamma$ is upward continuous. Let $\Delta_0 \subseteq \cdots \subseteq \cup \Delta_s \cdots$ be an increasing sequence of sets of arguments, and let $\Delta = \Delta_0 \cup \cdots \cup \Delta_s \cup \cdots$. Let an argument $A \in \mathcal{D}_\delta^\gamma(\Delta)$. As there exist only finite arguments in Arg which attacks A, there exists a number t such that $A \in \mathcal{D}_\delta^\gamma(\Delta_t)$. Thus, we have: $\mathcal{D}_\delta^\gamma(\Delta) = \mathcal{D}_\delta^\gamma(\Delta_0) \cup \cdots \cup \mathcal{D}_\delta^\gamma(\Delta_s) \cup \cdots$. □

3.3 Ranking Arguments with Proportional Defense Functions

This part shows how we can rank arguments using proportional defense functions. Recall the two assumptions in Sect. 1, now we can provide a more accurate explanation for the assumptions with proportional defense. Given a set of arguments Δ:

(A1) For a fixed parameter γ regarding counter-attackers, the less proportion of attackers such that there does not exist at least γ proportion of the set of the counter-attackers belonging to Δ, the better. Hence, for $\delta < \delta'$, an argument in $\mathscr{D}_\gamma^\delta(\Delta)$ is "better" than it in $\mathscr{D}_\gamma^{\delta'}(\Delta)$.

(A2) For a fixed parameter δ regarding attackers, the greater proportion of counter-attackers belonging to Δ, the better. Hence, for $\gamma' < \gamma$, an argument in $\mathscr{D}_\gamma^\delta(\Delta)$ is "better" than it in $\mathscr{D}_{\gamma'}^\delta(\Delta)$.

Proportional defense functions can be understood as different standards of defense or acceptability. We can rank these functions with the following relation:

Definition 14 (Ranking proportional defense functions). *Given* $\mathcal{AF} = \langle Arg, \rightarrow \rangle$. *Let* δ, δ', γ *and* γ' *be real numbers such that* $0 \leqslant \delta, \delta', \gamma, \gamma' \leqslant 1$. *Define:*

$$\mathscr{D}_\gamma^\delta \blacktriangleright \mathscr{D}_{\gamma'}^{\delta'} \iff \delta \leqslant \delta' \text{ and } \gamma' \leqslant \gamma.$$

The notation $\mathscr{D}_\gamma^\delta \blacktriangleright \mathscr{D}_{\gamma'}^{\delta'}$ can be interpreted as: "being proportionally defended at the degree $\delta\gamma$ is *preferable* to being proportionally defended at the degree $\delta'\gamma'$"; alternatively, "the proportional defense function at the degree $\delta\gamma$ is *at least as strong* as the proportional defense function at the degree $\delta'\gamma'$." It is easy to see that the relation $\blacktriangleright$ is a partial order, as showed by the following proposition.

Proposition 7. *The relation* $\blacktriangleright$ *is reflexive, antisymmetric and transitive.*

Proof. (i) For any $\delta, \gamma \in [0, 1]$, we have $\mathscr{D}_\gamma^\delta \blacktriangleright \mathscr{D}_\gamma^\delta$ by Definition 14. Therefore, $\blacktriangleright$ is reflexive. (ii) Suppose $\mathscr{D}_\gamma^\delta \blacktriangleright \mathscr{D}_{\gamma'}^{\delta'}$ and $\mathscr{D}_{\gamma'}^{\delta'} \blacktriangleright \mathscr{D}_\gamma^\delta$. Then, according to Definition 14, we have $\delta \leqslant \delta'$ and $\gamma' \leqslant \gamma$, as well as $\delta' \leqslant \delta$ and $\gamma \leqslant \gamma'$. Thus, $\delta' = \delta$ and $\gamma = \gamma'$. Therefore, $\blacktriangleright$ is antisymmetric. (iii) Suppose $\mathscr{D}_\gamma^\delta \blacktriangleright \mathscr{D}_{\gamma'}^{\delta'}$ and $\mathscr{D}_{\gamma'}^{\delta'} \blacktriangleright \mathscr{D}_{\gamma''}^{\delta''}$. Then we have $\delta \leqslant \delta' \leqslant \delta''$ and $\gamma'' \leqslant \gamma' \leqslant \gamma$ by Definition 14. Consequently, $\delta \leqslant \delta''$ and $\gamma'' \leqslant \gamma$. Thus, by Definition 14, $\mathscr{D}_\gamma^\delta \blacktriangleright \mathscr{D}_{\gamma''}^{\delta''}$. Therefore, $\blacktriangleright$ is transitive. □

The intuition underlying relation $\blacktriangleright$ is that if an argument meets a more demanding standard of defense, it satisfies a less demanding one as well.

Proposition 8. *Given* $\mathcal{AF} = \langle Arg, \rightarrow \rangle$ *and a set of arguments* $\Delta \subseteq Arg$. *If* $\mathscr{D}_\gamma^\delta \blacktriangleright \mathscr{D}_{\gamma'}^{\delta'}$ *then* $\mathscr{D}_\gamma^\delta(\Delta) \subseteq \mathscr{D}_{\gamma'}^{\delta'}(\Delta)$.

Proof. Suppose $\mathscr{D}_{\delta_\gamma} \blacktriangleright \mathscr{D}_{\delta'_{\gamma'}}$. We have $\delta \leqslant \delta'$ and $\gamma' \leqslant \gamma$ by Definition 14. Hence, $\mathscr{D}_{\delta_\gamma}(\Delta) \subseteq \mathscr{D}_{\delta'_\gamma}(\Delta)$ holds by Theorem 2. Again, by Theorem 2, it follows that $\mathscr{D}_{\delta'_\gamma}(\Delta) \subseteq \mathscr{D}_{\delta'_{\gamma'}}(\Delta)$. Consequently, we conclude that $\mathscr{D}_{\delta_\gamma}(\Delta) \subseteq \mathscr{D}_{\delta'_{\gamma'}}(\Delta)$. □

Example 7. To illustrates Proposition 8, we observe in Fig. 3a that $\mathscr{D}_{2/3_\gamma}^0(\Delta) = \{A\} \subseteq \mathscr{D}_{1/2_\gamma}^0(\Delta) = \{A, F\}$. Similarly, from Fig. 3b, it follows that $\mathscr{D}_{1_\gamma}^{2/5}(\Delta) = \{E\} \subseteq \mathscr{D}_{1_\gamma}^{3/5}(\Delta) = \{A, E\}$.

As $\mathscr{D}_{\delta_\gamma}$ is monotonic (see Proposition 5), its iteration converges to a limit by the Knaster-Tarski theorem. In finite argumentation frameworks, a limit is reachable in a countable number of steps and we can define the indefinite iteration of function: $\mathscr{D}_{\delta_\gamma}^*(\Delta) = \bigcup_{0 \leqslant i < \omega} \mathscr{D}_{\delta_\gamma}^i(\Delta)$. Then iterating the proportional defense function allows for the ranking of arguments with the following definition.

Definition 15 (Ranking arguments by proportional defense). *Given $\mathcal{AF} = \langle Arg, \rightarrowtail \rangle$ and a set of arguments $\Delta \subseteq Arg$. For $A, B \in Arg$, A is said to be at least as justified as B w.r.t. Δ according to the following relation:*

$$A \succeq_\Delta B \iff \forall \delta, \gamma \in [0,1], \text{ if } B \in \mathscr{D}_{\delta_\gamma}^*(\Delta) \text{ then } A \in \mathscr{D}_{\delta_\gamma}^*(\Delta).$$

Example 8. Consider Fig. 3a, $A \in \mathscr{D}_{0_{2/3}}^*(\Delta)$ while $F \notin \mathscr{D}_{0_{2/3}}^*(\Delta)$. Hence, according to Definition 15, $F \not\succeq_\Delta A$, i.e., F is not at least as justified as A w.r.t. Δ. However, $\forall \delta, \gamma \in [0,1]$, if $F \in \mathscr{D}_{0_{2/3}}^*(\Delta)$, then $A \in \mathscr{D}_{0_{2/3}}^*(\Delta)$. Therefore, by Definition 15, $A \succeq_\Delta F$, namely, A is at least as justified as F w.r.t. Δ.

4 Proportional Semantics

This section establishes proportional semantics in terms of the proportional defense function and the proportional neutrality function. These semantics can be regarded as variants of graded semantics [11]. We can rank arguments with proportional semantics.

Definition 16 (Proportional semantics). *Given $\mathcal{AF} = \langle Arg, \rightarrowtail \rangle$. For a set of arguments $\Delta \subseteq Arg$,*

(i) Δ is a $\tau\delta\gamma$-p-admissible extension of $\mathcal{AF}$ iff $\Delta \subseteq \mathcal{N}_\tau(\Delta)$ and $\Delta \subseteq \mathscr{D}_{\delta_\gamma}(\Delta)$;

(ii) Δ is a $\tau\delta\gamma$-p-complete extension of $\mathcal{AF}$ iff $\Delta \subseteq \mathcal{N}_\tau(\Delta)$ and $\Delta = \mathscr{D}_{\delta_\gamma}(\Delta)$;

(iii) Δ is a $\tau\delta\gamma$-p-preferred extension of $\mathcal{AF}$ iff Δ is a maximal $\tau\delta\gamma$-p-complete extension of $\mathcal{AF}$;

(iv) Δ is a $\tau\delta\gamma$-p-stable extension of $\mathcal{AF}$ iff $\Delta = \mathcal{N}_\delta(\Delta) = \mathcal{N}_\gamma(\Delta) \subseteq \mathcal{N}_\tau(\Delta)$.

(v) Δ is the $\tau\delta\gamma$-p-grounded extension of $\mathcal{AF}$ iff Δ is the least fixpoint of $\mathscr{D}_{\delta_\gamma}$.

These semantics can be viewed as generalizations of Dung's semantics [7] according to Proposition 1 and 4. A $\delta\gamma\tau$-p-admissible extension is a set of arguments that is $\delta\gamma$-p-self-defending and τ-conflict-free. A $\delta\gamma\tau$-p-complete extension is a set of arguments that is $\delta\gamma\tau$-admissible and $\delta\gamma$-reinstating. A $\delta\gamma\tau$-p-preferred extension is a set of arguments that is a $\delta\gamma\tau$-complete extension which has the maximality with respect to set inclusion. A $\delta\gamma\tau$-p-stable extension is a set of arguments that is the fixpoint of $\mathcal{N}_\delta$ and $\mathcal{N}_\gamma$, and τ-conflict-free. The $\delta\gamma\tau$-p-grounded extension is the least $\delta\gamma\tau$-p-complete extension.

The following theorem states that if a set of arguments is p-admissible, then the p-conflict-freeness is preserved by iterating the p-defense function.

Theorem 3. *Given $\mathcal{AF} = \langle Arg, \rightarrow \rangle$. Let $\Delta \subseteq A$ be such that $\Delta \subseteq \mathcal{D}_\delta^\gamma(\Delta)$ and $\Delta \subseteq \mathcal{N}_\delta(\Delta)$, and δ, γ be two real numbers such that $\gamma \geqslant \delta$. Then for any natural number k, $\Delta \subseteq \mathcal{D}_\delta^{k,\gamma}(\Delta) \subseteq \mathcal{N}_\delta(\mathcal{D}_\delta^{k,\gamma}(\Delta)) \subseteq \mathcal{N}_\delta(\Delta)$.*

Proof. First, to show $\Delta \subseteq \mathcal{D}_\delta^{k,\gamma}(\Delta)$, it suffice to show $\mathcal{D}_\delta^{k,\gamma}(\Delta) \subseteq \mathcal{D}_\delta^{k+1,\gamma}(\Delta)$ by induction on k. The base case $\mathcal{D}_\delta^{0,\gamma}(\Delta) \subseteq \mathcal{D}_\delta^{1,\gamma}(\Delta)$ holds by the assumption. For the induction step assume that $\mathcal{D}_\delta^{k,\gamma}(\Delta) \subseteq \mathcal{D}_\delta^{k+1,\gamma}(\Delta)$. We show that $\mathcal{D}_\delta^{k+1,\gamma}(\Delta) \subseteq \mathcal{D}_\delta^{k+2,\gamma}(\Delta)$, which amounts to $\mathcal{D}_\delta(\mathcal{D}_\delta^{k,\gamma}(\Delta)) \subseteq \mathcal{D}_\delta(\mathcal{D}_\delta^{k+1,\gamma}(\Delta))$. In light of the inductive assumption and the monotonicity of $\mathcal{D}_\delta$, it follows that $\mathcal{D}_\delta^{k+1,\gamma}(\Delta) \subseteq \mathcal{D}_\delta^{k+2,\gamma}(\Delta)$. Hence, $\Delta \subseteq \mathcal{D}_\delta^{k,\gamma}(\Delta)$ holds. Second, we prove $\mathcal{D}_\delta^{k,\gamma}(\Delta) \subseteq \mathcal{N}_\delta(\mathcal{D}_\delta^{k,\gamma}(\Delta))$ by induction on k. The base case $\mathcal{D}_\delta^{0,\gamma}(\Delta) \subseteq \mathcal{N}_\delta(\mathcal{D}_\delta^{0,\gamma}(\Delta))$ holds by the assumption $\Delta \subseteq \mathcal{N}_\delta(\Delta)$ where $\mathcal{D}_\delta^{0,\gamma}(\Delta) = \Delta$. For the induction step, assume that $\mathcal{D}_\delta^{k,\gamma}(\Delta) \subseteq \mathcal{N}_\delta(\mathcal{D}_\delta^{k,\gamma}(\Delta))$. We need to show that $\mathcal{D}_\delta^{k+1,\gamma}(\Delta) \subseteq \mathcal{N}_\delta(\mathcal{D}_\delta^{k+1,\gamma}(\Delta))$. Suppose for a contradiction that $\mathcal{D}_\delta^{k+1,\gamma}(\Delta) \not\subseteq \mathcal{N}_\delta(\mathcal{D}_\delta^{k+1,\gamma}(\Delta))$. Then according to the definition of $\mathcal{N}_\delta$, there is an argument $A \in \mathcal{D}_\delta^{k+1,\gamma}(\Delta)$, such that at least δ proportion of its attackers belonging to $\mathcal{D}_\delta^{k+1,\gamma}(\Delta) = \mathcal{D}_\delta(\mathcal{D}_\delta^{k,\gamma}(\Delta))$. By the assumption $\gamma \geqslant \delta$ and the definition of $\mathcal{D}_\delta$, there exist an A's attacker B such that there exists at at least δ proportion of the set of B's attackers belonging to $\mathcal{D}_\delta^{k,\gamma}(\Delta)$. Again, by the assumption $\gamma \geqslant \delta$ and the definition of $\mathcal{D}_\delta$, there exist an B's attacker C, such that $C \in \mathcal{D}_\delta^{k,\gamma}(\Delta)$ and C has at least γ proportion of the set of C's attackers belonging to $\mathcal{D}_\delta^{k,\gamma}(\Delta)$. Hence, $\mathcal{D}_\delta^{k,\gamma}(\Delta)$ is not γ-p-conflict-free by the assumption $\gamma \geqslant \delta$. Therefore, it contradicts the inductive hypothesis. Third, since $\mathcal{D}_\delta^{k,\gamma}(\Delta) \supseteq \Delta$ follows from the first claim and $\mathcal{N}_\delta$ is antitonic, it holds that $\mathcal{N}_\delta(\mathcal{D}_\delta^{k,\gamma}(\Delta)) \subseteq \mathcal{N}_\delta(\Delta)$. □

Dung's fundamental lemma states that if an admissible extension can defends an argument, then adding the argument to the extension is still admissible. A similar result holds for the proportional admissibility according to Theorem 3.

Lemma 1 (Proportional fundamental lemma). *Given $\mathcal{AF} = \langle Arg, \rightarrow \rangle$, a $\delta\gamma\tau$-admissible extension $\Delta \subseteq Arg$, and two arguments $A, A' \in Arg$ which are $\delta\gamma$-defended by Δ. If $\gamma \geqslant \delta$ and $\tau \geqslant \delta$, then (i) $\Delta' = \Delta \cup \{A\}$ is $\delta\gamma\tau$-admissible and (ii) Δ' $\delta\gamma$-defends A'.*

Proof. (i) Since $\Delta \subseteq \mathscr{D}_\delta^\gamma(\Delta)$ by the $\gamma\delta$-p-self-defense of Δ, and $A \in \mathscr{D}_\delta^\gamma(\Delta)$ by the assumption, then $\Delta \cup \{A\} \subseteq \mathscr{D}_\delta^\gamma(\Delta)$. Since $\mathscr{D}_\delta^\gamma(\Delta) \subseteq \mathscr{D}_\delta^\gamma(\Delta \cup \{A\})$ by the monotonicity of $\mathscr{D}_\delta^\gamma$, then $\Delta \cup \{A\} \subseteq \mathscr{D}_\delta^\gamma(\Delta \cup \{A\})$, namely, $\Delta \cup \{A\}$ is $\delta\gamma$-p-self-defending. On the other hand, according to Theorem 3, Δ is τ-p-conflict-free. We conclude that Δ is $\delta\gamma\tau$-p-admissible. (ii) The second claim follows from the monotonicity of the proportional function. □

We present the relationships among the proportional extensions in Definition 16 with the following proposition. Specifically, a $\delta\gamma\tau$-p-stable extension is a $\delta\gamma\tau$-p-preferred extension, and a $\delta\gamma\tau$-p-preferred extension is a $\delta\gamma\tau$-p-complete extension. Besides, a $\delta\gamma\tau$-p-complete extension is a $\delta\gamma\tau$-p-admissible extension.

Proposition 9. *Given $\mathcal{AF} = \langle Arg, \rightarrow \rangle$ and a set of arguments $\Delta \subseteq Arg$,*

(i) if Δ is a $\delta\gamma\tau$-p-preferred extension, then it is a $\delta\gamma\tau$-p-complete extension;
(ii) if Δ is a $\delta\gamma\tau$-p-stable extension, then it is a $\delta\gamma\tau$-p-preferred extension;
(iii) if Δ is a $\delta\gamma\tau$-p-complete extension, then it is a $\delta\gamma\tau$-admissible extension.

Proof. (i) The proof follows from Definition 16. (ii) Suppose that Δ is a $\delta\gamma\tau$-p-stable extension. Assume for the sake of a contradiction that Δ is not $\delta\gamma\tau$-p-complete, then there exists a $\delta\gamma\tau$-p-preferred Γ such that $\Delta \subset \Gamma$. Hence, there exists an argument $A \notin \Delta$ but $A \in \Gamma$. Therefore, there exists at least δ proportion of the set of A's attackers belonging to Δ, because Δ is $\delta\gamma\tau$-p-stable-extension. It follows that $A \notin \mathcal{N}_\tau(\Gamma)$. Hence, Γ is not τ-p-conflict-free. A contradiction arises. (iii) It follows from Definition 16. □

Besides, the $\delta\gamma\tau$-p-grounded extension can be reached by iterating $\mathscr{D}_\delta^\gamma$ according to the proportional fundamental lemma and the monotonicity of $\mathscr{D}_\delta^\gamma$.

Given an argumentation framework $\mathcal{AF} = \langle Arg, \rightarrow \rangle$, for a semantics $\mathbb{S} \in \{\delta\gamma\tau\text{-complete}, \delta\gamma\tau\text{-preferred}, \delta\gamma\tau\text{-stable}, \delta\gamma\tau\text{-grounded}\}$, $A \in Arg$ is *credulously* (resp., *skeptically*) *justified* w.r.t. $\mathbb{S}$, if A is in at least one (resp., all) of $\mathbb{S}$ extensions in $\mathcal{AF}$. For a given semantics, we can rank the justified statuses of arguments with respect to a given argumentation framework, similar to how it was done in Definition 15 for iterated proportional defense functions:

Definition 17 (Ranking arguments by proportional semantics). *Given $\mathcal{AF} = \langle Arg, \rightarrow \rangle$. For $A, B \in Arg$, and for $\mathbb{S} \in \{\delta\gamma\tau\text{-complete}, \delta\gamma\tau\text{-preferred}, \delta\gamma\tau\text{-stable}, \delta\gamma\tau\text{-grounded}\}$:*

$$A \succeq_{\mathcal{AF}}^{\mathbb{S}} B \iff \forall \delta, \gamma \in [0,1], \text{if } B \text{ is credulously (resp., skeptical) justified w.r.t.}$$
$$\mathbb{S}, \text{then } A \text{ is credulously (resp., skeptical) justified w.r.t. } \mathbb{S}.$$

5 Related Work

The approaches to rank arguments in abstract argumentation can roughly be divided into two categories. The first one includes those that diverge from Dung's notions while employing exogenous information (e.g., weights). Those approaches often propagate values across graphs to ranking arguments [9,13,17]. Another graph propagation approach involves ranking classical logic arguments using a categorizer function [3], which assigns high values to arguments attacked by low-valued arguments and lower values to those attacked by high-valued arguments. This function is extended in [5] to provide more intuitive results by transforming cyclic graphs. In [1], two ranking-based semantics, AB-b and AB-d, are introduced, focusing on the processing of attack paths, especially regarding the treatment of cyclic paths. The compensation-based semantics proposed in [2] rank all arguments within cycles and provide a unique solution for cyclic graphs.

To avoid relying on exogenous information, the second category includes approaches that are endogenous to the standard notions in Dung's theory to introduce a more nuanced concept of argument statuses. Our work falls into the second category, where the graded semantics [10,11] are the most closely related to our approach. The proportional semantics we have proposed can be seen as variants of the graded semantics, in the sense that the focus of the proportional semantics is on evaluating the statuses of arguments based on the proportion of attacks that are not counter-attacked, rather than on their absolute number. Solid semantics [14,15] also offer a high degree of acceptability based on proportionality, which is a special case of proportional acceptability. Some work in this category may not even require an explicit notion of graduality to distinguish arguments. For instance, using the standard notions in Dung's theory, [12] presents three argument statuses (accepted, rejected, and undecided), while [21] identifies six distinct justification statuses for arguments (strong accept, weak accept, strong reject, weak reject, undetermined borderline, and determined borderline). For a comparison of ranking-based semantics, see [4]. The key distinction of our work, compared to the aforementioned studies, is that we use proportionality to differentiate the justification statuses of arguments by generalizing the notions of Dung's theory (e.g., acceptability and extensions under the standard semantics). To the best of our knowledge, none of the works mentioned above have adopted such an endogenous approach that incorporates proportionality.

6 Conclusions and Future Work

In this paper, we propose the concept of proportional acceptability to differentiate the statuses of arguments. More specifically, inspired by the graded semantics proposed in [10], we present an endogenous approach (i.e., an approach that is closely based on Dung's theory) capable of differentiating argument statuses in terms of proportionality: an aspect not addressed by the graded semantics. The central idea is that an argument is considered proportionally defended by a set of arguments if there is not a significant enough proportion of its attackers such that there is not a significant enough proportion of the counter-attackers in the set. For example, it can capture that an argument is proportionally defended by a set of arguments if the argument does not have at least half of its attackers that do not have at least half of the counter-attackers in the set. Furthermore, we have introduced the proportional defense and proportional neutrality functions, which offer a structured approach to evaluating arguments by parameterizing their attackers and defenders, enabling the ranking of arguments. Last, we develop proportional semantics based on the proportional defense and proportional neutrality functions. These semantics are generalizations of Dung's semantics and variants of graded semantics. Moreover, we can rank the justified degrees of arguments using the proportional semantics.

In our future work, we will integrate proportional semantics with judgment aggregation, which is a branch of social choice theory. Given a single AF, where agents each contribute a set of arguments, recognized as an extension under a certain semantics, we investigate whether the aggregated result is still an extension under this semantics. A negative result in [6] shows that no quota rule preserves Dung's admissibility for any argumentation framework. But interestingly, a positive result in [15] shows that there exist quota rules that preserve solid admissibility for any argumentation framework. We have mentioned that solid semantics are special cases of proportional semantics. Hence, it would be interesting to investigate whether aggregating proportional extensions can yield a single proportional extension that represents the consensus of the agents. Another avenue is to integrate proportional semantics with graph aggregation [8]. We will aggregate multiple argumentation frameworks, each consisting of the same set of arguments, to obtain a single framework that reflects the agents' consensus. We seek to determine whether a set of arguments, when identified as a proportional extension in each individual framework, remains a proportional extension in the aggregated framework. Besides, it would be useful to explore which of the properties of ranking-based semantics proposed in [4] are satisfied by the proportional semantics. Additionally, a ranking-based semantics in [22] is based on the idea that sets of arguments can jointly attack an argument. It would be interesting to compare the semantics in [22] with the proportional semantics, as a set of arguments Δ proportionally defending an argument A can be seen as A's defenders in Δ jointly counter-attacking A' attackers. Finally, we would like to further investigate the properties of the ranking relation and apply, the relationship between the proportional semantics and the graded semantics.

Acknowledgments. This paper is an extended version of [16]. We are very grateful to Sylvie Doutre, Philippe Besnard, Jérôme Lang, Gabriella Pigozzi and the anonymous CLAR reviewers for their valuable comments and feedback. This paper was supported by the National Social Science Foundation of China (Grant No. 23CZX062).

References

1. Amgoud, L., Ben-Naim, J.: Ranking-based semantics for argumentation frameworks. In: International Conference on Scalable Uncertainty Management, pp. 134–147. Springer (2013)
2. Amgoud, L., Ben-Naim, J., Doder, D., Vesic, S.: Ranking arguments with compensation-based semantics. In: Fifteenth International Conference on the Principles of Knowledge Representation and Reasoning, pp. 12–21 (2016)
3. Besnard, P., Hunter, A.: A logic-based theory of deductive arguments. Artif. Intell. **128**(1–2), 203–235 (2001)
4. Bonzon, E., Delobelle, J., Konieczny, S., Maudet, N.: A comparative study of ranking-based semantics for abstract argumentation. In: Proceedings of the AAAI Conference on Artificial Intelligence. vol. 30, pp. 914–920 (2016)
5. Cayrol, C., Lagasquie-Schiex, M.C.: Graduality in argumentation. J. Artif. Intell. Res. **23**, 245–297 (2005)
6. Chen, W., Endriss, U.: Aggregating alternative extensions of abstract argumentation frameworks: preservation results for quota rules. In: Proceedings of 7th International Conference on Computational Models of Argument, pp. 425–436 (2018)
7. Dung, P.M.: On the acceptability of arguments and its fundamental role in nonmonotonic reasoning, logic programming and n-person games. Artif. Intell. **77**(2), 321–357 (1995)
8. Endriss, U., Grandi, U.: Graph Aggregation. Artif. Intell. **245**, 86–114 (2017)
9. Gabbay, D.M., Rodrigues, O.: An equational approach to the merging of argumentation networks. J. Log. Comput. **24**(6), 1253–1277 (2013)
10. Grossi, D., Modgil, S.: On the graded acceptability of arguments. In: Proceedings of the Twenty-fourth International Joint Conference on Artificial Intelligence. vol. 2015, pp. 868–874 (2015)
11. Grossi, D., Modgil, S.: On the graded acceptability of arguments in abstract and instantiated argumentation. Artif. Intell. **275**, 138–173 (2019)
12. Jakobovits, H., Vermeir, D.: Robust semantics for argumentation frameworks. J. Log. Comput. **9**(2), 215–261 (1999)
13. Leite, J., Martins, J.: Social abstract argumentation. In: Proceedings of 22nd International Joint Conference on Artificial Intelligence, pp. 2287–2292 (2011)
14. Liu, X., Chen, W.: Solid semantics and extension aggregation using quota rules under integrity constraints. In: Proceedings of the 20th International Conference on Autonomous Agents and MultiAgent Systems, pp. 1590–1592 (2021)
15. Liu, X., Chen, W.: Solid semantics for abstract argumentation frameworks and the preservation of solid semantic properties. In: Proceedings of 18th European Conference on Multi-Agent Systems, pp. 178–193. Springer (2021)
16. Liu, X., Chen, W.: On the proportional acceptability of arguments in abstract argumentation. In: Proceedings of 10th International Conference on Computational Models of Argument (COMMA 2024). Frontiers in Artificial Intelligence and Applications, vol. 388, pp. 355–356. IOS Press (2024)
17. Matt, P.A., Toni, F.: A game-theoretic measure of argument strength for abstract argumentation. In: European Workshop on Logics in Artificial Intelligence, pp. 285–297. Springer (2008)
18. Pollock, J.L.: How to reason defeasibly. Artif. Intell. **57**(1), 1–42 (1992)
19. Simari, G.R., Loui, R.P.: A mathematical treatment of defeasible reasoning and its implementation. Artif. Intell. **53**(2–3), 125–157 (1992)

20. Vreeswijk, G.A.: Abstract argumentation systems. Artif. Intell. **90**(1–2), 225–279 (1997)
21. Wu, Y., Caminada, M., Podlaszewski, M.: A labelling-based justification status of arguments. Studies in Logic **3**(4), 12–29 (2010)
22. Yun, B., Vesic, S., Croitoru, M.: Ranking-based semantics for sets of attacking arguments. In: Proceedings of the AAAI Conference on Artificial Intelligence, vol. 34, pp. 3033–3040 (2020)

Towards Assumption-Based Argumentation Mining in Hotel Reviews

Teeradaj Racharak[1,2](✉) ⓘ, Watanee Jearanaiwongkul[1,2] ⓘ,
Jiraporn Pooksook[3], and Kazuki Takashima[2]

[1] Advanced Institute of So-Go-Chi (Convergence Knowledge) Informatics,
Tohoku University, Miyagi, Japan
{racharak,watanee}@tohoku.ac.jp

[2] School of Information Science, Japan Advanced Institute of Science and Technology, Ishikawa, Japan
{racharak, kazuki.takashima}@jaist.ac.jp, watanee.j@gmail.com

[3] Department of Electrical and Computer Engineering, Faculty of Engineering, Naresuan University, Phitsanulok, Thailand
jirapornpook@nu.ac.th

Abstract. Argumentation mining (or argument mining) is the research area aiming at extracting human arguments and their relations (primarily) from text, with the ultimate goal to understand humans' arguments in argumentative texts. Nonetheless, the progresses thus far often ignore the computational models of structured argumentation formalisms which are well studied in the knowledge representation and reasoning (KRR) community. This means that there is a still big research gap if ones would like to automatically construct argumentation-based knowledgebase systems from text. In this paper, we investigate this problem and formally define important tasks for *argument mining* from the views of machine learning and KRR. Due to current progresses of KRR, there could be a plethora of tasks depending on targeted structured argumentation frameworks. This paper focuses on a well-known *assumption-based argumentation* (ABA) by defining relevant tasks for mining ABA from text and then accordingly build an annotated corpus in hotel reviews from Booking.com. Finally, we evaluate the in-context learning capabilities of large language models (i.e. GPT-4o) for an ABA's construction based on our annotated hotel reviews' corpus, demonstrating the proposed framework is promising in practice.

Keywords: Argumentation System · Automatic Knowledge Base Construction · Text Corpus · Machine Learning Pipeline

1 Introduction

We have an academic dream that one day machine learning (ML) researchers and knowledge representation and reasoning (KRR) researchers can sit down together at the table of a joint panel and discuss on how to progress and realize 'automated knowledge representation' systems from unstructured data such as natural language text. This similar dream was once stated in the work of [32, p. 5427] in the context of natural language processing (NLP) for ML and argumentation for KRR, which gives a nicely comprehensive survey of *argumentation mining* (or, shortly, argument mining) works.

Note that argument mining [18,32] is the research area aiming at automatically identifying and extracting the structure of inference and reasoning expressed as arguments presented in natural language. Grasping arguments' structure helps identify not only the stances that people take but also the reasons behind their opinions. This understanding offers valuable insights across various fields (see [32] for a review). Approaches towards this aim of argument mining was firstly introduced around 2010, showing techniques of mining (different connotations of) arguments from natural language. For example, [27] introduced a notion called *argumentative zoning* in scientific articles. [21] proposed an approach to detect legal arguments. Since these pioneering methods, the necessity for automating the extraction of arguments and their interconnections from natural language text was highlighted, though it received only limited attention. Currently, argument mining is well recognized as a sub-area of NLP that exploits philosophical/formal argumentation to deal with the automated representation, evaluation, and generation of arguments. For instance, [20] considered complex rhetorical moves in attacks or the presuppositions or value judgments in argumentation. Another example, [15] paid an attention to argumentative feedback systems in order to assist learners in improving the quality of their arguments.

Despite big progresses in argument mining, it is still relatively under-explored on how to deal with the automated representation, evaluation, and generation of arguments regarding the KRR's principles. Indeed, the NLP techniques disclosed in argumentation mining are not sufficient to mine arguments in computational forms. This problem could hinder diverse applications of formal argumentation, such as, Dung's argumentation [11], bipolar argumentation [4], and assumption-based argumentation (ABA) [2], in text documents. Note that there exist several studies aimed to fill this gap; however, formal argumentation formalisms are not still comprehensively explored. Exceptional works include [19] who developed an annotated text corpus for mining the bipolar argumentation, and [7] who studied NLP models to mine bipolar arguments.

To bridge the gap between computational models in KRR and ML, this paper specifically coins out a novel sub-field called *assumption-based argumentation mining* (ABA mining) in order to raise awareness on the lack of investigating NLP techniques for this purpose. Our main contributions are twofold as follows: **(1)** We introduce a novel annotation framework for mining ABA representation from text (cf. Section 3). **(2)** Accordingly, we develop a novel annotated corpus based on our framework in a context of Hotel Reviews [17] (cf. Section 4).

The remaining sections are structured as follows. Section 2 presents the basics of ABA. Section 5 shows our findings towards our ABA mining tasks by leveraging the in-context learning capabilities of large language models (i.e. GPT-4o). We relate the work in Sect. 7 and conclude in Sect. 8.

2 Preliminary: Assumption-Based Argumentation

Assumption-based argumentation (ABA) frameworks are 4-tuples $(\mathcal{L}, \mathcal{R}, \mathcal{A}, \overline{})$, where

- $(\mathcal{L}, \mathcal{R})$ is any deductive system with a language $\mathcal{L}$ and a set of inference rules of the form $l_0 \leftarrow l_1, \ldots l_n$ ($n \geq 0$ and $l_i \in \mathcal{L}$),
- $\mathcal{A} \subseteq \mathcal{L}$ represents a non-empty set of assumptions, and
- $\overline{} : \mathcal{A} \rightarrow 2^{\mathcal{L}} \setminus \emptyset$ is a total mapping such that $\overline{\alpha}$ represents a non-empty set of *contraries* of α.

Note that, in the original ABA framework [14], $\overline{}$ is a total mapping from $\mathcal{A}$ into $\mathcal{L}$; each assumption has a single contrary. This paper adopts an extension proposed in [14] as it better reflects the characteristics of raw data in our application domain, i.e., Hotel Reviews Booking.com (cf. Section 3).

For each rule $r \in \mathcal{R}$ of the form $l_0 \leftarrow l_1, \ldots l_n$, l_0 and the set $\{l_1, \ldots, l_n\}$ are referred respectively as the head and the body of r and denoted by $hd(r)$, $bd(r)$. We restrict ourselves to the flat ABA framework [2,14] such that the head of any inference rule cannot be an assumption, i.e., for any rule $r \in \mathcal{R}$, $hd(r) \notin \mathcal{A}$.

Any argument in ABA is in a tree structures represented by a deduction of a conclusion $c \in \mathcal{L}$ derived from a set of assumptions S with c at the root and S at the leaves. ABA is an instance of Dung's abstract argumentation (AA), and vice versa [9,10,28]. Hence, all semantic notions for determining the acceptability of arguments in AA are applicable to arguments in ABA, offering implementation methodologies for various application domains such as legal reasoning [12], medical reasoning [8], and decision theory [1]. Hence, it would be more worthwhile to have an automated labelling system to transform textual description of any application domain into such an ABA framework.

3 An Annotation Framework for ABA Mining in Text

To promote industrial impacts of ABA, we introduce a novel 'annotation framework' for ABA mining from text. In our framework, literals in $\mathcal{L}$ are represented by propositions due to its simplicity of developing machine learning-based mining platforms. For example, 'very helpful staff' in the raw data is converted into proposition 'helpful_staff' and 'option to have a good breakfast within the hotel save your time' is to proposition 'good_breakfast' (cf. Figure 1).

Since any ABA framework is the quadruple, we propose that any ABA mining platform must handle the following two problems which constitutes a sequential workflow of any ABA mining system.

1. *Inference rule mining*: requires obtaining a set of (inference) rules given that a document. Clearly, obtaining a rules' set allows to realize the components $(\mathcal{L}, \mathcal{R})$ and component $\mathcal{A}$ of the corresponding ABA framework.
2. *Contrary mining*: requires obtaining a contraries' set of any assumption a in $\mathcal{A}$ given that a document and the corresponding assumption set $\mathcal{A}$.

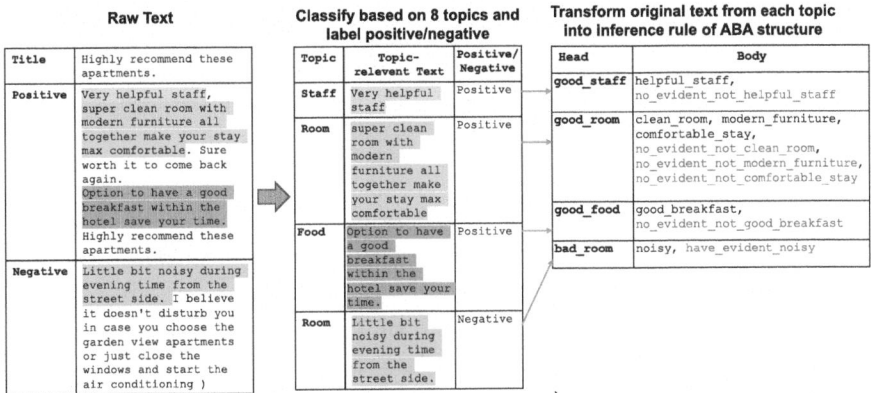

Fig. 1. Transforming raw hotel reviews in Booking.com into an ABA framework.

There could be various possible ways to address the above tasks, depending on the characteristics of raw data. In this paper, we aim at providing concrete methodologies including the annotated dataset and benchmark results using the state-of-the-art generative model (i.e. GPT-4o) for automatically constructing an ABA knowledge base system.

3.1 Raw Data: Hotel Reviews Booking.com

Our analysis is based on Hotel Reviews Booking.com in kaggle [17]. The dataset was scraped from La Veranda Hotel on Booking.com to contain 1,500 customer reviews for a hotel in Larnaca-Cyprus. These reviews provide the experiences of guests who stayed at the property during its first year of operation. Figure 1 (Raw Text) depicts example snapshots of the raw dataset. It consists of three parts: a title, a positive comment (labelled by 'positive'), and a negative comment (labelled by 'negative'); all parts were provided by the hotel's guests. Based on our analysis, the titles do not give valuable insights, compared to the others. Hence, we propose to mine the language and inference rules ($\mathcal{L}, \mathcal{R}$) from the positive and negative comments only.

The ABA-based corpus annotating framework proposed in this work has three annotating steps corresponding to each defined task (cf. Figure 2). Given any sentence in the raw data, the first step (corresponding to Task 1) is to annotate the *zoning* of each relevant text in the original sentence and label its corresponding *topic* and its *sentiment* (either 'positive' or 'negative'). Next, corresponding to Task 2, given a set of triples of the form (*topic, topic-relevant text, sentiment*), the second step is to annotate the *head* and the *body* of each corresponding inference rule. Clearly, the results of this annotating step yield ($\mathcal{L}, \mathcal{R}$) of ABA. The last step, which is corresponding to Task 3, is to label the *contraries* for each assumption in $\mathcal{A}$. This framework is analyzed based on the hotel review dataset mentioned in the above. Nevertheless, this framework is general

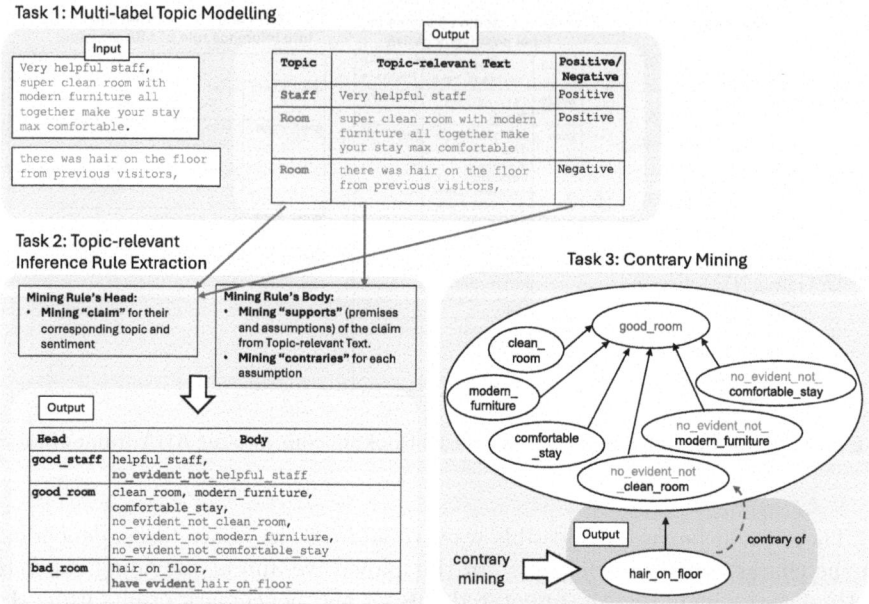

Fig. 2. Our ABA-based corpus annotating framework.

in a sense that it can be applied to other domains if the datasets include the topics, the positive comments, and the negative comments.

Figure 2 also shows the three corresponding tasks involved in our annotating framework: **(Task 1)** multi-label topic modelling, **(Task 2)** topic-relevant inference rule extraction, **(Task 3)** contrary mining. Indeed, Task 1 extracts (multiple) topics from an input document. Task 2 seeks for inference rules for all topics in the document. Task 3 extracts the contraries' set from the document. This design is agreed by two argumentation and one NLP researchers to ensure the applicability of any ABA reasoning engines (e.g. [14]) on the extracted ABA framework using the corpus. We detail all the tasks in the following subsections.

3.2 Task 1: Multi-label Document Typesetting

Definition 1. *Let T be a set of topics, D be a set of documents, Txt be a set of texts in D, and $S := \{0, 1\}$ be a set of boolean sentiments. We say that any multi-label topic modelling m is a function that maps from D into $D^{\downarrow}$, where $D^{\downarrow} \subseteq (T \times Txt \times S) \setminus \emptyset$ denotes a multi-label typeset document.*

Definition 1 outlines input-output representations for learning to label (multiple) topics in any input text. Learning such a multi-label topic modelling can be handled by various techniques, such as, unsupervised topic models and multi-label classification [3]. In this regard, our formal definition is general in a sense that it does not enforce any implementation techniques, but rather outlines how an annotated corpus should be created in order to enable the development of efficient models for mining ABA structure. Figure 2 (cf. Task 1) shows examples of the annotations, which can be seen as, for any document in D, there is a mapped triple consisting of a topic, its topic-relevant text, and its sentiment.

3.3 Task 2: Topic-Relevant Inference Rule Extraction

Given a set of topics, their corresponding relevant text, and the sentiments, we further extract inference rules and assumptions from the original document.

Definition 2. *Let $D^\downarrow$ be a multi-label typeset document, $\mathcal{R}$ be a set of inference rules, and $\mathcal{A}$ be a set of assumptions. We say that any* topic-relevant inference rule extraction *m is a function that maps from $D^\downarrow$ into $\mathcal{R} \times \mathcal{A}$.*

Like Definition 1, Definition 2 also outlines a general annotation framework for learning and evaluating inference rule extraction models. This work proposes to deal with this task by addressing two subtasks: **(1)** mining the rule's head and **(2)** mining the rule's body. Regarding the first subtask, we exploit sentiments of topics provided in $D^\downarrow$. If a sentiment is positive, the head is set to the topic's name prefixed by 'good_'. Otherwise, the topic's name is prefixed by 'bad_'. Furthermore, mining the rule's body can be viewed as a rewriting problem where a natural language text is rewritten as a sequence of semantic-identical premises with corresponding assumptions. These assumptions enables any deduction for claims to be 'undercut' as in the sense of ABA.

To ease the annotation, we use a rule-based procedure for generating assumptions. Indeed, if the sentiment is positive, each premise of the rule is a newly fresh proposition prefixed with 'no_evident_not_'. Otherwise, each premise of the rule is a newly fresh literal that prefixes its name with 'have_evident_'. Obviously, solving these two subtasks yield the output's representation as defined.

4 Corpus Creation for Hotel Reviews Booking.com

This section describes our data creation method of our annotated corpus for learning to mine an ABA framework from text, called *ABA-HotelReviews*, following the annotation framework outlined in Sect. 3. By following the proposed annotating framework, ABA-HotelReviews enables to learn machine learning models for extracting an ABA framework from the hotel reviews dataset.

Our main goal is to create an annotated corpus according to the theoretical framework of assumption-based argumentation. Thus, we start our process from investigating existing crawled datasets that requires least pre-processing for our annotation steps (cf. Section 3) based on the ABA's formalism. First, we select Hotel Reviews Booking.com in kaggle [17] (cf. Subsection 3.1) because the reviews contain arguments from customers by the domain's nature, and then proceed to creating different corpora for all the tasks proposed in Sect. 3. We use three domain experts to ensure the correctness of the annotated data for each task. All of them are familiar with knowledge representation and argumentation. We detail how the corpora for Task 1 and Task 2 are created below. We leave the creation for contrary mining as our future task. Figure 7 illustrates a visualization of the extracted ABA from the target dataset.

4.1 Creation of Multi-label Topic in Hotel Reviews

The scraped dataset from the La Veranda hotel in Booking.com contains 11 columns: Title, Positive Review, Negative Review, Score, Guest Name, Guest Country, Room Type, Number of Nights, Visit Date, Group Type, and Property Response. Our primary objective is to understand the arguments within this dataset. Therefore, we focus solely on the columns Positive Review and Negative Review, which detail what guests liked and disliked about the hotel.

Below is the pre-processing steps for preparing a multi-label topic dataset of La Veranda Hotel reviews:

1. **Remove unused data:** Since not all guests provided comments, some only rated a score (a satisfaction rating out of 10), then we removed rows without either a positive review or a negative review, resulting in 785 usable reviews out of 1500 total customer reviews (see Table 3).
2. **Determine topics:** We examined the dataset and agreed on classifying that each argumentative text is classified into eight potential topics: (1) room, (2) staff, (3) location, (4) food, (5) price, (6) facility, (7) check-in, (8) check-out. If the texts are outside these topics, they are classified as noises.
3. **Labeling rules:** For each review, we assigned a relevant topic to each phrase or sentence. Then, we corrected obvious typos appeared in the phrases and sentences, such as '5 lins away from the airport' to '5 mins away from the airport'. Sometimes, guests did not strictly write all positive experiences in the positive review and, similarly, all negative experiences were not written in the negative review. In such cases, we labelled sentences (or phrases) to the right sentiment. Tables 1 and 2 give examples of assigning topics to raw reviews that consist of both positive and negative comments.

In this study, we randomly selected 191 out of 785 customer reviews. As a result of the topic labeling, we obtained 381 rows of customer reviews categorized by topics and sentiments (see Table 3).

4.2 Creation of Topic-Relevant Inference Rules in Hotel Reviews

This subsection focuses on annotating inference rules from multi-label text yielded from Step 1 (Definition 1). As aforementioned in Sect. 2, any inference rule is composed of two parts called the head and the body of the rule. Since all the reviews have been classified into eight topics and labelled by binary sentiments, we created topic-relevant inference rules by the following three steps.

Table 1. Examples of positive and negative reviews from a customer

Positive Review	Negative Review
The food was very tasty (I didn't have breakfast but ate dinner at the restaurant), staff very helpful and friendly, very nice bathroom, and the room was well equipped and also smelled very nice.	It was a bit loud outside but that was just normal for summertime I guess.

Table 2. Examples of assigning topics to the relevant text and sentiment

Assigned Topic	Topic-relevant Text	Sentiment
Food	The food was very tasty	Positive
Staff	staff very helpful and friendly,	Positive
Room	very nice bathroom, and the room was well equipped and also smelled very nice.	Positive
Room	It was a bit loud outside	Negative
Noise	(I didn't have breakfast but ate dinner at the restaurant), but that was just normal for summertime I guess.	Positive

1. Generated the head of each rule by the topic and the sentiment (cf. Subsection 3.3), resulting in 16 fixed literals, i.e., good_room, bad_room, good_staff, bad_staff, good_location, bad_location, good_food, bad_food, good_price, bad_price, good_facility, bad_facility, good_check-in, bad_check-in, good_ check-out, bad_check-out. This step was handled by an automatic program for the head's generation.
2. Generated the supporting literals in the body of each inference rule by translating from the topic-relevant text. The translation was handled by two human annotators with an agreed template. One annotator played the role of the leading annotator and the other annotator was the reviewer who ensured the consistency. Note that any inference rule has two primary parts: the *supporting literals* and the *contrary literals*. The used translation template for creating the supports was as follows:
   (a) Removed articles (viz. a, an, the),
   (b) Changed either a phrase or a sentence to the present simple tense,
   (c) Changed to lowercase letters,
   (d) Replace each space by an underscore ('_'),
   (e) Restricted to use the vocabularies appeared in the original text,
   (f) Restricted to maintain short phrases or sentences (i.e. without adjectives and adverbs) unless they were not understandable. For example, "Service was great" was changed to 'great_service' and "Very helpful host showed us how nearby bus takes to town-centre" was changed to 'helpful_host',

Table 3. Statistics of the ABA-HotelReviews Dataset for Task 1

La Veranda Hotel	Number of customer review
Original customer review	1500
Customer review that contains comments	785
Customer review that contains comments (randomly selected)	191
Topic-relevant Text	381 (Positive: 261, Negative: 120)

Table 4. Statistics of the ABA-HotelReviews Dataset for Task 2

Classified Topic	Number of customer review	Positive	Negative
Room	148	79	69
Staff	78	75	3
Location	72	53	19
Food	42	34	8
Price	12	4	8
Facility	20	5	15
Check-in	9	7	2
Check-out	0	0	0
Total	381	257	124

  (g) Restricted to use noun phrases (if possible). For example, "The room was very clean" was changed to 'clean_room'.
3. Generated the contrary literals in the body of each inference rule by translating from each supporting literal and the topic-relevant text's sentiment (cf. Subsection 3.3). Indeed, there were two rules for creating contraries for positive and negative supports. For the positive support, we used the same word as presented in the supports but prefixed with 'no_evident_not_'. For the negative support, we prefixed it with 'have_evident_'. For example, if the text is "The restaurant area is nice and the staff very accommodating.", then the final generation contains four literals in the body of the inference rule as follows:
  (a) nice_restaurant_area (i.e. 'supporting literal')
  (b) accommodating_staff (i.e. 'supporting literal')
  (c) no_evident_not_nice_restaurant_area (i.e. 'contrary literal')
  (d) no_evident_not_accommodating_staff (i.e. 'contrary literal')

As a result, Table 4 summarizes the number of our annotated inference rules classified by all the eight topics (for both positive and negative sentiments). Note that in this study, our dataset contains zero row for the topic 'Check-out'. As always, all the annotations were agreed by three experts (two argumentation and one knowledge representation researchers) to ensure the appropriateness and applicability to use with argumentation reasoning engines in the future.

5 Experiments and Evaluations

Regarding our experiments for Tasks 1 and 2, we used the gpt-4o model from the OpenAI API[1] with temperature of 0 and top_p of 0.05. The API was configured with a low temperature and a low value for top_p to guarantee more predictable outputs (less creativity) and to control the vocabulary size in the generated outputs. Indeed, we considered only the top tokens to make the output as deterministic as possible. This configuration minimizes variability in the model's responses; thus it helps ensure the reproducibility.

In our experiments, each prompt was submitted five times. To ensure that the generated responses were not controversial, the results were selected based on the majority vote. If no majority responses appeared, we ran the prompt further (usually no more than nine times) until consistent responses could be generated. We designed prompts that could reflect and align with each task's objectives (see below).

Prompt 5.1
Please output the following [text] according to the [Constraints] in the [Output Format].

[Constraints] The output should only be in the [Output Format], and you must classify which part of the text corresponds to which Topic in the [Topics].
Additionally, determine whether each classified element is Positive or Negative. If there is no corresponding element, put Null for both 'text' and 'label'. The most important constraint is not to include any extra characters such as newline characters, 'json', or backticks, or any other unnecessary text outside of the [output format].
If there are two or more elements of the same Topic, number each so that they do not conflict when converted to json format data. However, if they have the same NegPos label, keep them in one Text as much as possible.

[Topics] Room, Staff, Location, Food, Price, Facility, Check-in, Check-out

[Output Format]
{ "Topics": { "Room":[{ "text": "test","label": "Positive"}],
"Staff":[{ "text": null,"label": null }],
"Location":[{ "text": "test","label": "Positive"}],
"Food":[{ "text": "test","label": "Negative"}],
"Price":[{ "text": "test","label": "Positive"}],
"Facility":[{ "text": "test","label": "Negative"}],
"Check-in":[{ "text": "test","label": "Positive"}],
"Check-out":[{ "text": null,"label": null}]}}

[Example]
"The room is big enough. But the room was a little bit dirty."
⇒ { "Topics":[{ "Room1":[{ "text": "The room is big enough.","label": "Positive"}],
"Room2":[{ "text": "the room was a little bit dirty.","label": "Negative"}],
"Staff":[{ "text": null,"label": null}],
"Location":[{ "text": null,"label": null}],
"Food":[{ "text": null,"label": null}],
"Price":[{ "text": null,"label": null}],
"Facility":[{ "text": null,"label": null}],
"Check-in":[{ "text": null,"label": null}],
"Check-out":[{ "text": null,"label": null}]}]}

[text]

---

[1] https://platform.openai.com.

5.1 Evaluation Metrics

Tasks 1 and 2 are kinds of information retrieval problems. Thus, it is inevitable to realize: **(1: micro-precision)** for each instance in the gold dataset, how precise can the GPT model respond to it?, and **(2: micro-recall)** for each instance in the gold dataset, how coverage can the GPT model deal with it? These two calculations are analogous to precision and recall, respectively; however, we attend to the scope of each individual review in the gold dataset instead. As these two measures give insights *locally*, it is natural to extend them for yielding *global* views. For this purpose, we also evaluate our implementations with two more aspects. **(3: average-precision)** on average, how precise can the model respond globally?, and **(4: average-recall)** on average, how coverage can the model respond globally?. These two values can be obtained by computing the average of all the micro-precisions and the average of all the micro-recalls, respectively.

5.2 Task 1: Creation of Multi-label Document Typesetting

Given 191 reviews, we executed 191 one-shot prompts independently to generate triples consisting of a topic, a topic-relevant text, and a sentiment corresponding to each input text. We designed one-shot prompt as illustrated in Prompt 4.2.1. As a result of its executions, we obtained 571 rows of topic-relevant text with 434 rows of positive, 135 rows of negative, and two rows of noises.

To evaluate the performance of our approach, we used the micro-precision and micro-recall as described earlier. Clearly, the total number of instances in the gold dataset and the generated responses are different. Therefore, these two metrics help measure "how precise and coverage can the model generate?" when compared with the gold dataset. Figures 3 and 4 present the total number of micro-precisions and micro-recalls. The responses achieved micro-precision of 1, 36.6%, micro-precision of 0.5, 12% and micro-precision of 0 is a little bit high at 16.8%. Furthermore, 63.4% achieved micro-recall of 1, while 16.8% achieved 0. For the global evaluation, Table 5 shows the averages of all the micro-precision and micro-recall's values for this task.

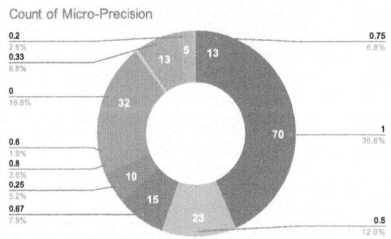

Fig. 3. Micro-precisions for Task 1

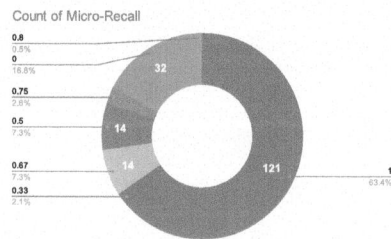

Fig. 4. Micro-recalls for Task 1

> **Prompt 5.2**
>
> Generate text in Assumption Based Argumentation (ABA) format from the **given text**. Use the following conditions carefully.
>
> 1. Claim is "good staff".
> 2. Supports are written in short words with no adjectives and no adverbs if it is not necessary for understanding.
> 3. For each support, use vocab from the original text. Do not provide synonyms. Check grammar. Do not provide further opinion.
> 4. Add a contrary for each support as a new support.
> 5. Each contrary must use the same word as presented in the support and each contrary starts with "no evident not".
> 6. Regarding the format of answer, provide a list of all supports and contraries. Do not separate supports and contraries into separated sections. Do not provide assumptions. Do not provide claims.
>
> [**Example**] The staff were exceptional. So helpful and friendly. Went out of their way for us. ⇒ exceptional, helpful, friendly, went_out_of_their_way_for_us, no_evident_not_exceptional, no_evident_not_helpful, no_evident_not_friendly, no_evident_not_went_out_of_their_way_for_us
>
> [**Text**] what will bring me back is the staff and the owners. Richard (the chef) is personally buying super fresh food for the restaurant. The owners have been super kind to me :)

5.3 Task 2: Creation of Topic-Relevant Inference Rules in Hotel Reviews

Task 2 is divided into two sub-tasks: (1) mining the rule's head and (2) mining the rule's body, in which the latter is also divided further: (3) mining the supporting literals and (4) mining the contrary literals.

For mining each rule's head, Subsect. 4.2 suggests an automatic procedure for the heads' generation. As this step did not involve the usage of any machine learning model, the evaluation metrics mentioned above were not used. Literally, given 381 labelled topics and their sentiments, our processing assigned the head directly based on the predefined 16 classes. For instance, the topic is 'room' and the sentiment is 'positive', then the head is 'good_room'. Otherwise, if the topic is 'room' and the sentiment is 'negative', then the head is 'bad_room'.

For mining each rule's body, given 381 topic-relevant texts, we executed 381 one-shot prompts (cf. Prompt 5.2) in accordance with the rules outlined in Subsect. 4.2. Note that some rules were not explicitly written in the prompt but were implicitly embedded in the one-shot's configuration.

To evaluate the performance of our approach, we compared all the 381 generated responses with the gold dataset and evaluate using the micro-precision and micro-recall. Figures 5 and 6 present these scores for all the individuals of each task, respectively. Indeed, 76.6% of the responses achieved micro-precision of 1, only 10.8% had micro-precision of 0.5. Furthermore, 88.2% achieved micro-recall of 1, while 3.7% had 0.67 micro-recall. Such high scores could be attributed by our relaxed threshold when comparing the responded text and the gold label in terms of structure, grammar, and semantic resemblance. Instead of requiring exact matches, we considered responses that conveyed similar concepts as valid. Here are examples that were considered equivalently: helpful and helpful_host, slow_elevators and slow_elevator, room_wasn't_clean and not_clean_room, badly_soundproofed and bad_soundproof, and quality_television_image_poor and poor_quality_television. On the other hand, the following are examples that were considered inequivalently: fresh_handmade and fresh_breakfast, fresh_ handmade and handmade_breakfast, food and good_food, small_side_street and location_in_small_side_street, and took_time and took_time_to_explain. Table 5 shows the average of all the micro-precision and micro-recall's values.

In order to achieve better results, we plan to refine our prompts by incorporating more shots and use advanced prompt techniques in the future work.

Table 5. Average of the micro-precisions and micro-recalls

Task Number	Average of Micro-Precisions	Average of Micro-Recalls
Task 1	0.61	0.75
Task 2	0.88	0.94

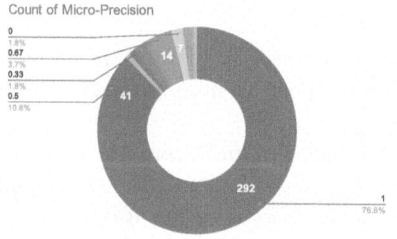

Fig. 5. Micro-precisions for Task 2

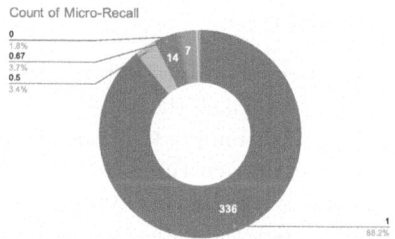

Fig. 6. Micro-recalls for Task 2

6 On Completion of ABA Mining: The Contrary Mining Task

As aforementioned in Sect. 2, this work adopts an extended ABA proposed by [14]. Thus, the notion of attack between arguments in ABA is defined in terms of the 'contraries' of assumptions, i.e., the set of assumptions is the set of assumptions from Task 2. The predicates beginning with 'no_evident_not' and 'have_evident_' are the mentioned assumptions.

Definition 3. *Let $\mathcal{L}$ be a language and $\mathcal{A}$ be a set of assumptions. We say that any* contrary mining *m is a function that maps from $\mathcal{A}$ into $2^{\mathcal{L}} \setminus \emptyset$.*

Like the above definitions, Definition 3 gives a general annotation framework for learning and evaluating the contrary mining task. For example, given that a premise set $\mathcal{L}$ and an assumption set $\mathcal{A}$, an annotated corpus for this task can be in forms of a pair set $\{(x_i, y_i) \mid i \in \mathbb{N}\}$ where $x_i \in \mathcal{A}$ and $y_i \subseteq 2^{\mathcal{L}} \setminus \emptyset$.

A similar idea could be employed for the contrary mining task. For example, given the vocabulary obtained from Task 2, we could use multiple LLMs for annotating the contrary relations among all the propositions; these results will be evaluated by the human experts to justify the validity, resulting in another dataset. It remains however to show whether this methodology produces acceptable results in practice.

7 Related Work

As aforementioned, it was once stated by [32] that argument mining was coined out to connect the research results between natural language processing and knowledge representation, especially argumentation. However, most existing works focus on the philosophical understanding of argumentation from the viewpoint of machine learning. A precise and clear definition was given by [16], saying that argument mining is "the general task of analyzing discourse on the pragmatics level and applying a certain argumentation theory to model and automatically analyze the data at hand".

A recent survey from [30] further concluded that recent progress of NLP has influenced the argument mining research area. Indeed, automatic recognition and identification of arguments have been enabled in various domains and various machine learning models for the analysis and representation of argumentative structure are developed. So far, the most common argument components are recognized to include claims, premises, rebuttal, etc., following the well-known Toulmin's argumentation model [29,31]. According to Toulmin, arguments should be composed of facts that support a claim such that the claim is not made in an irresponsible manner. A claim is the conclusion of an argument. In order to establish such a claim, an individual needs 'data' to justify it. Similarly, in order to support the relation between the data to the claim, such individual needs at least a 'warrant'. There are further models of argumentation that motivate the research in argument mining. These include many forms of argumentation schemes. For instance, the argument forms that represent inferential structures of arguments introduced by [6], and the forms of inferencing patterns from premises to a conclusion in human's dialogue introduced by [25]. A variety of machine learning models are studied to deal with these argumentation structure, such as, Naive Bayes [22], RNNs [23], pre-trained language models [5], and other supervised learning techniques [13].

Various heterogeneous datasets have been proposed since the beginning of research in argument mining. As the field lacks of clear definitions on the notions of arguments due to the adoption of diverse argumentation models, the datasets thus far have been annotated from different definitions of argument components and of the relations holding between them. For example, in [27], a rhetorical-level analysis of scientific articles is introduced. Data annotation is based on the typical argumentation to be found in scientific articles. In [33], an argumentation model and an annotation corpus for persuasive essays is studied following the work of [26], who define arguments' components for essays.

While there exist many progress on argument mining and philosophical models of argumentation, current results thus far are still not applicable to completely model structured argumentation frameworks in real world. A recent work by [24] investigated and showed that Toulmin's model of argumentation can be rewritten as a form of 2-tier argumentation system, where the first tier is Dung's abstract framework [11] and the second tier is any knowledge base which deduction is allowed. The main goal of [24] is to support the development of explainable AI systems in the real world by exploiting existing results in diverse areas of logic, e.g., formal argumentation, propositional logic, and the well-investigated proof procedures.

To the best of our knowledge, this is the first attempt that aims to fill a gap in connecting formal models of argumentation to natural language processing. We focus on the well-known ABA and introduce key machine learning tasks in order to transform raw data in the hotel reviews into an ABA framework.

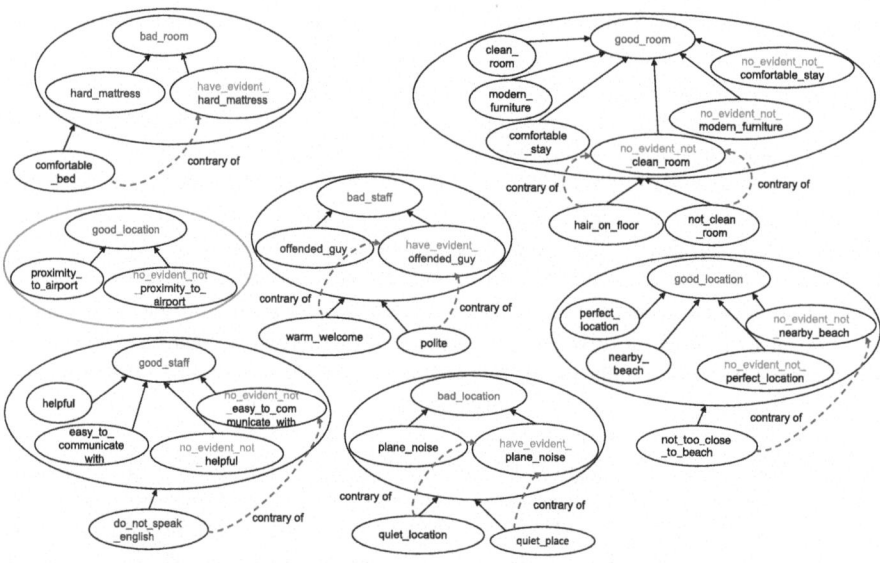

Fig. 7. A visualization of the extracted ABA knowledge base from the target dataset.

8 Conclusion

This paper introduces a novel research area called *assumption-based argumentation mining* (ABA mining) with our primary goal of connecting two mainstream areas in artificial intelligence: formal argumentation and natural language processing (NLP). To pursue this aim, we investigate hotel reviews in

Booking.com which contains arguments (positive and negative claims regarding customers' stays). Our analysis ensures that such data can be formalized in terms of ABA structure, allowing that the state-of-the-art ABA reasoners can be used to find further insights and gain understanding in the reviews. For example, by mining ABA structures from hotel reviews, one can realize which positive or negative claims are acceptable and explain why they are accepted or rejected.

Three novel tasks are formally defined and the dataset are annotated accordingly. We also experiment the applicability of our annotated corpus by leveraging the in-context learning capabilities of large language models in both Tasks 1 and 2. The findings show that in-context learning is promising. We aim to dive deeper into investigating further NLP techniques that could be useful for ABA mining.

Acknowledgement. This work was supported by JSPS KAKENHI Grant Numbers JP22K18004.

A Appendix A: Prompt Template

On the one hand, Prompt 4.2.1's template is static (i.e. an input to the prompt does not affect the template's content). On the other hand, the template of Prompt 5.2 could be dynamic in a sense that the content can be varied by the inputs. These inputs are parameters to the template, indicated by '{...}'.

Prompt A illustrates a parameterized content of the dynamic template of Prompt 5.2, where the parameters are 'good staff' and 'no evident not'. This template needs to be adjusted according to the 'rule's head'. Since the head is the 'claim' associated with each topic and sentiment, it is crucial to identify the specific claim used to mine its supports and contraries. Furthermore, the prefix used to the generated contraries also needs to be adjusted. This is to correct the meaning of generated contraries. For example,

- If the claim is 'good staff' (#1), the prefix will be 'no evident not' (#5).
- If the claim is 'bad staff' (#1), the prefix will be 'have evident' (#5).

B Appendix B: Additional Information

This section illustrates a graphical representation of our corpus for ABA mining. Figure 7 shows a visualization of the extracted ABA from the target dataset.

C Appendix C: Experiments and ABA-HotelReviews Datasets

Our experiments and ABA-HotelReviews datasets are accessible online at https://github.com/realearn-people/aba-mining-hotelreviews.

> **Prompt A: Dynamic Prompt Template**
> Generate text in Assumption Based Argumentation (ABA) format from the **given text**. Use the following conditions carefully.
>
> 1. Claim is {"good staff"}.
> 2. Supports are written in short words with no adjectives and no adverbs if it is not necessary for understanding.
> 3. For each support, use vocab from the original text. Do not provide synonyms. Check grammar. Do not provide further opinion.
> 4. Add a contrary for each support as a new support.
> 5. Each contrary must use the same word as presented in the support and each contrary starts with {"no evident not"}.
> 6. Regarding the format of answer, provide a list of all supports and contraries. Do not separate supports and contraries into separated sections. Do not provide assumptions. Do not provide claims.
>
> [Example] The staff were exceptional. So helpful and friendly. Went out of their way for us. ⇒ exceptional, helpful, friendly, went_out_of_their_way_for_us, no_evident_not_exceptional, no_evident_not_helpful, no_evident_not_friendly, no_evident_not_went_out_of_their_way_for_us
>
> [Text] what will bring me back is the staff and the owners. Richard (the chef) is personally buying super fresh food for the restaurant. The owners have been super kind to me :)

References

1. Berthold, M., Rapberger, A., Ulbricht, M.: Forgetting aspects in assumption-based argumentation. In: Proceedings of the International Conference on Principles of Knowledge Representation and Reasoning, vol. 19, pp. 86–96 (2023)
2. Bondarenko, A., Dung, P., Kowalski, R., Toni, F.: An abstract, argumentation-theoretic approach to default reasoning. Artif. Intell. **93**, 63–101 (1997)
3. Burkhardt, S., Kramer, S.: A survey of multi-label topic models. ACM SIGKDD Explor. Newsl **21**(2), 61–79 (2019)
4. Cayrol, C., Lagasquie-Schiex, M.C.: On the acceptability of arguments in bipolar argumentation frameworks. In: European Conference on Symbolic and Quantitative Approaches to Reasoning and Uncertainty, pp. 378–389. Springer (2005)
5. Chakrabarty, T., Hidey, C., Muresan, S., McKeown, K., Hwang, A.: Ampersand: Argument mining for persuasive online discussions. arXiv preprint arXiv:2004.14677 (2020)
6. Chesnevar, C., et al.: Towards an argument interchange format. The Knowl. Eng. Rev. **21**(4), 293–316 (2006)
7. Cocarascu, O., Toni, F.: Mining bipolar argumentation frameworks from natural language text. In: Bex, F., Grasso, F., Green, N.L. (eds.) Proceedings of the 17th Workshop on Computational Models of Natural Argument co-located with ICAIL 2017. CEUR Workshop Proceedings, vol. 2048, pp. 65–70. CEUR-WS.org (2017)
8. Čyras, K., Oliveira, T., Karamlou, A., Toni, F.: Assumption-based argumentation with preferences and goals for patient-centric reasoning with interacting clinical guidelines. Argument Comput. **12**(2), 149–189 (2021)
9. Dung, P.M.: Negations as hypotheses: An abductive foundation for logic programming. In: ICLP, vol. 91, pp. 3–17 (1991)
10. Dung, P.M.: An argumentation-theoretic foundation for logic programming. J. Logic Program. **22**(2), 151–177 (1995)

11. Dung, P.M.: On the acceptability of arguments and its fundamental role in nonmonotonic reasoning, logic programming and n-person games. Artif. Intell. **77**(2), 321–357 (1995)
12. Dung, P.M., Thang, P.M.: Towards an argument-based model of legal doctrines in common law of contracts. Proc. CLIMA IX **7** (2008)
13. Ein-Dor, L., et al.: Corpus wide argument mining-a working solution. In: Proceedings of the AAAI Conference on Artificial Intelligence. vol. 34, pp. 7683–7691 (2020)
14. Gaertner, D., Toni, F.: Computing arguments and attacks in assumption-based argumentation. IEEE Intell. Syst. **22**(6), 24–33 (2007)
15. Guerraoui, C., et al.: Teach me how to argue: a survey on NLP feedback systems in argumentation. In: Proceedings of the Workshop on Argument Mining. pp. 19–34 (2023)
16. Habernal, I., Gurevych, I.: Which argument is more convincing? analyzing and predicting convincingness of web arguments using bidirectional lstm. In: Proceedings of the 54th Annual Meeting of the Association for Computational Linguistics (Volume 1: Long Papers), pp. 1589–1599 (2016)
17. Hatab, M.: Hotel reviews booking.com: Reviews for an hotel in larnaca-cyprus (2023). https://www.kaggle.com/datasets/michelhatab/hotel-reviews-bookingcom/data, la Veranda Reviews on 2023-01-16 (Version 3)
18. Lawrence, J., Reed, C.: Argument mining:a survey. Comput. Linguist. **45**(4), 765–818 (2020)
19. Mestre, R., Milicin, R., Middleton, S.E., Ryan, M., Zhu, J., Norman, T.J.: M-arg: Multimodal argument mining dataset for political debates with audio and transcripts. In: Proceedings of the Workshop on Argument Mining pp. 78–88 (2021)
20. Mim, F.S., Inoue, N., Naito, S., Singh, K., Inui, K.: Lpattack: A feasible annotation scheme for capturing logic pattern of attacks in arguments. arXiv preprint arXiv:2204.01512 (2022)
21. Mochales, R., Moens, M.F.: Argumentation mining. Artificial intelligence and law **19**, 1–22 (2011)
22. Moens, M.F., Boiy, E., Palau, R.M., Reed, C.: Automatic detection of arguments in legal texts. In: Proceedings of the 11th International Conference on Artificial Intelligence and Law, pp. 225–230 (2007)
23. Niculae, V., Park, J., Cardie, C.: Argument mining with structured SVSM and RNNs. arXiv preprint arXiv:1704.06869 (2017)
24. Racharak, T., Tojo, S.: On the relationship with toulmin method to logic-based argumentation. In: Proceedings of ICAART, pp. 197–207. Springer (2021)
25. Reed, C., Walton, D.: Argumentation schemes in dialogue (2007)
26. Stab, C., Gurevych, I.: Annotating argument components and relations in persuasive essays. In: Proceedings of COLING 2014, the 25th International Conference on Computational Linguistics: Technical papers, pp. 1501–1510 (2014)
27. Teufel, S., Siddharthan, A., Batchelor, C.: Towards domain-independent argumentative zoning: Evidence from chemistry and computational linguistics. In: Proceedings of EMNLP, pp. 1493–1502 (2009)
28. Toni, F.: Reasoning on the Web with Assumption-Based Argumentation. In: Eiter, T., Krennwallner, T. (eds.) Reasoning Web 2012. LNCS, vol. 7487, pp. 370–386. Springer, Heidelberg (2012). https://doi.org/10.1007/978-3-642-33158-9_10
29. Toulmin, S.E.: The uses of argument. Cambridge university press (2003)

30. Vecchi, E.M., Falk, N., Jundi, I., Lapesa, G.: Towards argument mining for social good: a survey. In: Proceedings of the 59th Annual Meeting of the Association for Computational Linguistics and the 11th International Joint Conference on Natural Language Processing (Volume 1: Long Papers), pp. 1338–1352 (2021)
31. Verheij, B.: The Toulmin argument model in artificial intelligence: Or: how semi-formal, defeasible argumentation schemes creep into logic. Argumentation in artificial intelligence, pp. 219–238 (2009)
32. Villata, S., Cabrio, E.: Five years of argument mining: a data-driven analysis. In: 27th International Joint Conference on Artificial Intelligence (2018)
33. Wachsmuth, H., Al Khatib, K., Stein, B.: Using argument mining to assess the argumentation quality of essays. In: Proceedings of COLING, pp. 1680–1691 (2016)

A Dialogical Interpretation of Cut-Elimination and Its Application to Argumentation Theory

Ryo Takemura[✉]

Nihon University, Tokyo, Japan
takemura.ryo@nihon-u.ac.jp

Abstract. Towards an application of proof theory to argumentation theory, we investigate the framework of Lorenzen dialogue. Building on our previous studies on a sequent calculus representation of Lorenzen dialogue and a proof-construction style representation of cut-elimination, we propose a Lorenzen dialogical interpretation of cut-elimination. We then explore how Lorenzen dialogue for cut-elimination can be understood as a form of persuasion dialogue aimed at resolving conflicts of opinion between two individuals.

Keywords: Proof theory · Cut-elimination · Lorenzen dialogue

1 Introduction

The cut-elimination theorem, or more generally the proof-normalization theorem, is the most fundamental theorem in proof theory. It serves as the foundation for various proof-theoretical results and analyses. The cut-elimination theorem is typically proved by reducing a cut-formula to atoms, then by eliminating the atomic cut-formulas. (Cf. [7,13]) For example, by principal $\wedge$-reduction, *cut* on $A \wedge B$ on the following left is typically reduced to *cut* on A and on B on the following right.

$$\dfrac{\Gamma \vdash A \wedge B \quad A \wedge B, \Gamma \vdash}{\Gamma \vdash} (A \wedge B) \quad \triangleright \quad \dfrac{\Gamma \vdash B \quad \dfrac{B, \Gamma \vdash A \quad A, B, \Gamma \vdash}{B, \Gamma \vdash} (A)}{\Gamma \vdash} (B)$$

Such a reduction step can be regarded as the decomposition step of a given cut-formula. Generally speaking, *cut*-rule associates two sequents; the above $\Gamma \vdash A \wedge B$ and $A \wedge B, \Gamma \vdash$, as well as their proofs. If we identify the sequent $A \wedge B, \Gamma \vdash$ with $\Gamma \vdash \neg(A \wedge B)$, then *cut*-rule can be interpreted as associating two sequents with conflicting conclusions, $A \wedge B$ and $\neg(A \wedge B)$, as well as their proofs. Then, the cut-elimination process can be understood as a process to reduce the conflict between $A \wedge B$ and $\neg(A \wedge B)$ into conflicts between A and $\neg A$, and between B and $\neg B$.

From the perspective of argumentation theory, consider the following scenario: (1) Two individuals, the Proponent (P) and the Opponent (O), make conflicting claims, C and $\neg C$, respectively, within the same context. This situation can be expressed as $\Gamma \vdash C_P$ and $\Gamma \vdash \neg C_O$; (2) Both P and O possess their own arguments in their minds; (3) Through a dialogue, P and O collaboratively examine the conflict by tracing back the disagreement between C_P and $\neg C_O$. In [14], various types of dialogues are classified, and our dialogue can be regarded as a form of *persuasion dialogue*, in which two or more participants try to resolve a difference of opinion by arguing. See also [9]. Thus, *cut*-rule can be applied to represent a conflict between two individuals, and a cut-elimination process can be regarded as a persuasion dialogue aimed at resolving the conflict by reducing it to atomic conflicts.

To formalize this idea, we utilize the framework of Lorenzen dialogue. Lorenzen dialogue [5,6] was introduced as a dialogical interpretation of logical connectives, and it has also received attention from the perspective of argumentation theory as a formal dialectical system (cf. [14]). Lorenzen and his followers formulated rules for logical dialogue to characterize provability in intuitionistic/classical logic as the existence of winning strategies in the dialogue, cf. [1]. Herbelin [4] proved the correspondence between the winning strategies in Lorenzen dialogue and the cut-free proofs of a variant of sequent calculus. Similarly, Okada and Takemura [8] obtained essentially the same result by introducing a sequent calculus representation of Lorenzen dialogue.

However, these studies follow the proof-construction or proof-search paradigm, and cannot be directly applied to the study of cut-elimination. Thus, we adopt the proof-construction style representation of cut-elimination investigated in [10,11]. Sequent calculus mG3 for multi-sequents, which are sequences of the usual sequents, was introduced, and it was shown that a proof in mG3 represents a cut-elimination process. Thus, by combining the sequent calculus representation of Lorenzen dialogue presented in [8,12] with the proof-construction style representation of cut-elimination given in [10,11], we explore a dialogical interpretation of cut-elimination and its application to persuasion dialogue.

In Sect. 2, we provide a brief review of the usual sequent calculus G3, and illustrate a specific strategy for proving cut-elimination as presented in [10,11]. Then, in Sect. 3, we review sequent calculus mG3 for multi-sequents, and illustrate how a cut-elimination process is represented by the proof-construction in mG3. In Sect. 4, we review the sequent calculus representation G3D of Lorenzen dialogue from [8,12]. In Sect. 5, we introduce our Lorenzen dialogue mG3D for multi-sequents, which provides a dialogical interpretation of mG3. We discuss an application of our dialogue mG3D to the study of persuasion dialogue.

2 Sequent Calculus G3

We review sequent calculus G3 of [7,13]. We introduce the negation $\neg$ as a primitive connective instead of $\bot$. We consider classical logic, whose propositional connectives are $\neg$ and $\wedge$. Formulas, denoted by $A, B, C, \ldots$, are defined inductively as usual. Atoms are denoted by $Q, R, \ldots$. An atom or its negation is called a literal. A sequent is an expression $\Gamma \vdash \Delta$, where Γ and Δ are finite multisets of formulas. Γ is called the antecedent of the sequent, while Δ is called the succedent of the sequent.

Definition 1. **G3-rules** for $\neg$ and $\wedge$ are as follows.

$$\frac{\Gamma \vdash \Delta, A}{\neg A, \Gamma \vdash \Delta} \neg l \quad \frac{A, \Gamma \vdash \Delta}{\Gamma \vdash \Delta, \neg A} \neg r \quad \frac{A, B, \Gamma \vdash \Delta}{A \wedge B, \Gamma \vdash \Delta} \wedge l \quad \frac{\Gamma \vdash \Delta, A \quad \Gamma \vdash \Delta, B}{\Gamma \vdash \Delta, A \wedge B} \wedge r$$

An axiom is a sequent of the form $\Gamma, Q \vdash Q, \Delta$ or $\Gamma, Q, \neg Q \vdash \Delta$, where Q is an atom.

In each rule, Γ and Δ are collectively called the **context**. Contexts are denoted by $\Gamma, \Delta, \Pi, \Lambda, \ldots$. In the lower sequent of each rule, the formula not in the context is called the main formula. The abovementioned form of a rule whose main formula is C is referred by an **inference on** C. To investigate a correspondence between our sequent calculus and our dialogue, we here introduce axioms of the form $\Gamma, Q, \neg Q \vdash \Delta$.

A proof, which is denoted by $\pi, \pi_1, \pi_2, \ldots$, is a finite tree constructed using inference rules whose leaves are axioms. The height of a proof denotes the greatest number of successive applications of rules in it. A proof consisting only of an axiom has the height 0. See [7,13] for a formal definition.

The inversion, weakening, and contraction lemmas hold in G3 [7,13], and they are height-preserving.

G3 + *cut* is obtained by adding the following rule of *cut* to G3. We regard the following two expressions of *cut* equivalent.

$$\frac{\Gamma \vdash \Delta, C \quad C, \Gamma \vdash \Delta}{\Gamma \vdash \Delta} (C) \qquad \frac{C, \Gamma \vdash \Delta \quad \Gamma \vdash \Delta, C}{\Gamma \vdash \Delta} (C)$$

The set of the above two occurrences of formula C in the *cut*-rule is called the **cut-formula**. When a cut-formula is an atom, it is called a **cut-atom**. In an application of *cut*, we indicate the cut-formula in place of the name of the rule: By (C) with parentheses, we refer to an application of *cut* on cut-formula C.

In [10,11], a sequence of successive applications of *cut*-rule within a given proof is called a *cut-string*. By defining reduction rules not for a single application of *cut* but for the entire sequence of successive applications of *cut*, i.e., cut-string, the cut-elimination theorem of G3 + *cut* is proved. The following example illustrates a process of cut-string reduction.

Example 2. Assume that the following proof ending with *cut* is given, where A and B are atoms. Cut-formulas are indicated by $\boxed{}$.

$$\frac{\neg A \vdash \neg(A \wedge \neg B), \boxed{\neg A \wedge B} \quad \boxed{\neg A \wedge B}, \neg A \vdash \neg(A \wedge \neg B)}{\neg A \vdash \neg(A \wedge \neg B)} (\neg A \wedge B)$$

By assuming $\wedge l, r$-rules on $\neg A \wedge B$ with the inversion lemma, the above proof is reduced by principal $\wedge$-reduction as follows, where B^w is B obtained by the weakening lemma.

$$\cfrac{\neg A \vdash \neg(A \wedge \neg B), \boxed{B} \qquad \cfrac{\cfrac{\boxed{B^w}, \neg A \vdash \neg(A \wedge \neg B), \boxed{\neg A} \qquad \boxed{\neg A}, \boxed{B}, \neg A \vdash \neg(A \wedge \neg B)}{\boxed{B}, \neg A \vdash \neg(A \wedge \neg B)} (\neg A)}{\boxed{B}, \neg A \vdash \neg(A \wedge \neg B)} (B)}{\neg A \vdash \neg(A \wedge \neg B)}$$

By assuming $\neg l, r$-rules on $\neg A$ with the inversion lemma, the above proof is reduced by principal $\neg$-reduction as follows.

$$\cfrac{\neg A \vdash \neg(A \wedge \neg B), \boxed{B} \qquad \cfrac{\cfrac{\boxed{B}, \neg A \vdash \neg(A \wedge \neg B), \boxed{A} \qquad \boxed{A}, \boxed{B^w}, \neg A \vdash \neg(A \wedge \neg B)}{\boxed{B}, \neg A \vdash \neg(A \wedge \neg B)} (A)}{(B)}}{\neg A \vdash \neg(A \wedge \neg B)}$$

By assuming $\neg r$-rule on $\neg(A \wedge \neg B)$ with the inversion lemma, the above proof is reduced by auxiliary $\neg$-reduction as follows. Note that it is not the single *cut* on A but the cut-string involving both A and B as a whole that is reduced in a single step.

$$\cfrac{A \wedge \neg B, \neg A \vdash \boxed{B} \qquad \cfrac{\cfrac{\boxed{B}, A \wedge \neg B, \neg A \vdash \boxed{A} \qquad \boxed{A}, \boxed{B^w}, A \wedge \neg B, \neg A \vdash}{\boxed{B}, A \wedge \neg B, \neg A \vdash} (A)}{(B)}}{\cfrac{A \wedge \neg B, \neg A \vdash}{\neg A \vdash \neg(A \wedge \neg B)} \neg r}$$

Similarly, by assuming $\wedge l$-rule on $A \wedge \neg B$ and $\neg l$-rule on $\neg A$ with the inversion lemma, the above proof is reduced by auxiliary reductions as follows. Then, by eliminating cut-atoms A and B successively, we obtain a cut-free G3-proof.

$$\cfrac{A, \neg B \vdash A, \boxed{B} \qquad \cfrac{\cfrac{\boxed{B}, A, \neg B \vdash A, \boxed{A} \qquad \boxed{A}, \boxed{B^w}, A, \neg B \vdash A}{\boxed{B}, A, \neg B \vdash A} (A)}{(B)}}{\cfrac{\cfrac{\cfrac{\cfrac{A, \neg B \vdash A}{A, \neg B, \neg A \vdash} \neg l}{A \wedge \neg B, \neg A \vdash} \wedge l}{\neg A \vdash \neg(A \wedge \neg B)} \neg r}{}}$$

3 Sequent Calculus for Multi-sequents mG3

In [10,11], as a proof-construction style representation of cut-string reduction, sequent calculus mG3 for multi-sequents was introduced. A multi-sequent is a sequence of the usual sequents, serving as the sequential representation of a cut-string. When we distinguish the usual sequent from a multi-sequent, we refer to it as a **single sequent**.

We define the intersection among sequents as follows. $\bigcap(\Gamma_i \vdash \Delta_i) = \bigcap \Gamma_i \vdash \bigcap \Delta_i$, where $\cap$ in the right-hand side is the multiset intersection operation. For example, $\{A, A, B, B, C\} \cap \{A, A, B, D\} = \{A, A, B\}$.

Our multi-sequent is obtained, which begins from a single sequent, by connecting another single sequent individually.

Definition 3. A sequence of single sequents called a **multi-sequent** $\mathcal{M}, \mathcal{M}_1, \mathcal{M}_2, \ldots$, and cut-formulas thereof are inductively defined as follows.
- A single sequent $\Gamma \vdash \Delta$ is a multi-sequent, which has no cut-formula.
- Let $\mathcal{M}$ be a multi-sequent that consists of single $\Pi_1 \vdash \Lambda_1, \ldots, \Pi_n \vdash \Lambda_n$.
  - $(\Gamma \vdash \Delta, C \parallel \mathcal{M})_C$ is a multi-sequent if $\bigcap(\Pi_i \vdash \Lambda_i) = C, \Gamma \vdash \Delta$.
  - $(C, \Gamma \vdash \Delta \parallel \mathcal{M})_C$ is a multi-sequent if $\bigcap(\Pi_i \vdash \Lambda_i) = \Gamma \vdash \Delta, C$.

The **cut-formulas** of the multi-sequent $(\Gamma \vdash \Delta, C \parallel \mathcal{M})_C$ are, in addition to the cut-formulas of $\mathcal{M}$, the set of single occurrences of C in $\Gamma \vdash \Delta, C$ and in every $C, \Gamma \vdash \Delta$ shared by all single sequents of $\mathcal{M}$. Similarly for $(C, \Gamma \vdash \Delta \parallel \mathcal{M})_C$.

We assume $(\Gamma \vdash \Delta \parallel \mathcal{M})_C = (\mathcal{M} \parallel \Gamma \vdash \Delta)_C$. Each single sequent that constitutes a multi-sequent $\mathcal{M}$ is called as a **component sequent** of $\mathcal{M}$. By $\bigcap \mathcal{M}$, we mean $\bigcap(\Gamma_i \vdash \Delta_i)$ for all component sequents $\Gamma_i \vdash \Delta_i$ of $\mathcal{M}$.

We sometimes write a multi-sequent $(\Gamma \vdash \Delta \parallel \mathcal{M})_C$ as $(\Gamma \vdash \Delta \parallel \mathcal{M})$ without the subscription of its cut-formula. In what follows, when we write $(\mathcal{M}_1 \parallel \mathcal{M}_2)$, either $\mathcal{M}_1$ or $\mathcal{M}_2$ is a single sequent.

When $\mathcal{M} \equiv (\Gamma \vdash \Delta \parallel \mathcal{M}')$, the difference between $\Gamma \vdash \Delta$ and $\bigcap \mathcal{M}'$ is only in the (position of) cut-formula C. The same applies to every component sequent of $\mathcal{M}'$ by assuming $\mathcal{M}' \equiv (\Pi \vdash \Lambda \parallel \mathcal{M}'')$. Thus, $\bigcap \mathcal{M}$ is the single sequent obtained from any component sequent of $\mathcal{M}$ by deleting all cut-formulas of $\mathcal{M}$.

Example 4. In the following multi-sequent, the underlined C_1, C_2, C_3 are the cut-formulas of this multi-sequent.

$(\underline{C_3}, A \vdash C_1 \parallel (A \vdash C_1, \underline{C_2}, \underline{C_3} \parallel (\underline{C_2}, A \vdash C_1, \underline{C_1}, \underline{C_3} \parallel \underline{C_2}, \underline{C_1}, A \vdash C_1, \underline{C_3})_{C_1})_{C_2})_{C_3}$

Note that cut-formulas are occurrences; hence, the underlined occurrences of C_1 are cut-formulas, and the other occurrences of C_1 are not.

It is shown that our multi-sequent corresponds to the sequence of all upper sequents of a cut-string (i.e., a sequence of successive applications of *cut*). Given a multi-sequent $\mathcal{M}$, by indicating a multi-sequent $\mathcal{M}'$, which is a part of $\mathcal{M}$, and by abbreviating the other parts of $\mathcal{M}$ other than $\mathcal{M}'$, we denote $\mathcal{M}$ as $\mathcal{C}(\mathcal{M}')$. For example, the multi-sequent in Example 4 can be expressed as $\mathcal{C}(A \vdash C_1, C_2, C_3 \parallel \mathcal{M}')_{C_2}$ or $\mathcal{C}'(\mathcal{M}')$, where $\mathcal{M}' \equiv (C_2, A \vdash C_1, C_1, C_3 \parallel C_2, C_1, A \vdash C_1, C_3)_{C_1}$.

Our calculus is formalized in the proof-search style. In other words, given a multi-sequent, we apply our rule from bottom to top. The following mG3-rules are read from bottom to top. The lower sequent contains an expression like $\mathcal{M}_i \langle A \vdash B \rangle$ that describes the condition in which A occurs in the antecedent and

B occurs in the succedent of "all" component sequents of $\mathcal{M}_i$. If this condition is not satisfied, then the rule cannot be applied. The upper sequent contains an expression like $\mathcal{M}_i\{C, D \vdash E, F\}$ that expresses the multi-sequent obtained by replacing the occurrence of A, indicated in the lower sequent $\mathcal{M}_i\langle A \vdash B \rangle$, with C, D and the occurrence of B with E, F for all component sequents of $\mathcal{M}_i$. The abovementioned A, B, C, D, E, or F may be missing. When A (as well as B) is missing, C, D (resp. E, F), which may also be missing, is added to the designated place. When both C and D (resp. E and F) are missing, A (resp. B) is deleted from the designated place.

Definition 5. **mG3-rules** consist of the following principal and auxiliary rules.

Principal rules: Let $\mathcal{M}_1$ and $\mathcal{M}_2$ be multi-sequents such that $\mathcal{M}_1 \cap \mathcal{M}_2 = \Gamma \vdash \Delta$.

$$\frac{\mathcal{C}(\Gamma \vdash \Delta, D_2 \parallel (\mathcal{M}_2\{D_2^w \vdash D_1\} \parallel \mathcal{M}_1\{D_1, D_2 \vdash\})_{D_1})_{D_2}}{\mathcal{C}(\mathcal{M}_2\langle \vdash D_1 \wedge D_2 \rangle \parallel \mathcal{M}_1\langle D_1 \wedge D_2 \vdash \rangle)_{D_1 \wedge D_2}} \wedge$$

D_2^w is cut-formula D_2 called a **weakening formula**.

$$\frac{\mathcal{C}(\mathcal{M}_2\{D \vdash\} \parallel \mathcal{M}_1\{\vdash D\})_D}{\mathcal{C}(\mathcal{M}_2\langle \vdash \neg D \rangle \parallel \mathcal{M}_1\langle \neg D \vdash \rangle)_{\neg D}} \neg$$

Auxiliary rules:

$$\frac{\mathcal{M}\{\vdash B\}}{\mathcal{M}\langle \neg B \vdash \rangle} \neg l \qquad \frac{\mathcal{M}\{B \vdash\}}{\mathcal{M}\langle \vdash \neg B \rangle} \neg r \qquad \frac{\mathcal{M}\{B_1, B_2 \vdash\}}{\mathcal{M}\langle B_1 \wedge B_2 \vdash \rangle} \wedge l \qquad \frac{\mathcal{M}\{\vdash B_1\} \quad \mathcal{M}\{\vdash B_2\}}{\mathcal{M}\langle \vdash B_1 \wedge B_2 \rangle} \wedge r$$

An axiom of mG3 is a multi-sequent such that each of its component sequents is an axiom of G3 on an atom that is not a cut-formula.

The superscript ^{w} on a weakening formula D^w indicates that it is obtained by the weakening lemma to align contexts in the application of *cut*-rule in the corresponding cut-string reduction in G3. Cf. Example 2.

Every principal rule corresponds to a principal reduction of a cut-string, and every auxiliary rule corresponds to an auxiliary reduction. Every auxiliary rule has a form in which the usual G3-rule is applied to every component sequent of the given $\mathcal{M}$ simultaneously. In particular, when $\mathcal{M}$ in the rule is a single sequent, it is the usual G3-rule. The main formula of every auxiliary rule is not a cut-formula. The reason is that, by the condition described in the lower sequent, the main formula, such as $B_1 \wedge B_2$ of the $\wedge l$-rule, should appear at the designated place of every component sequent of the lower sequent $\mathcal{M}$. This condition is not satisfied by any cut-formula. In contrast, the main formula of every principal rule is a cut-formula, which is indicated by the subscription of the lower sequent.

Definition 6. An **m-proof** of $\mathcal{M}$ is a finite tree constructed using rules of mG3, whose root is $\mathcal{M}$, and leaves are axioms of mG3.

Example 7. The following m-proof is the mG3 representation of the cut-string reduction in Example 2.

$$\cfrac{\cfrac{\cfrac{\cfrac{\cfrac{(A,\neg B \vdash A, \boxed{B}\ \|\ (\boxed{B}, A, \neg B \vdash A, \boxed{A}\ \|\ \boxed{A}, \boxed{B^w}, A, \neg B \vdash A))}{(\neg A, A, \neg B \vdash \boxed{B}\ \|\ (\boxed{B}, \neg A, A, \neg B \vdash \boxed{A}\ \|\ \boxed{A}, \boxed{B^w}, \neg A, A, \neg B \vdash))}\ \neg l}{(\neg A, A \wedge \neg B \vdash \boxed{B}\ \|\ (\boxed{B}, \neg A, A \wedge \neg B \vdash \boxed{A}\ \|\ \boxed{A}, \boxed{B^w}, \neg A, A \wedge \neg B \vdash))}\ \wedge l}{(\neg A \vdash \neg(A \wedge \neg B), \boxed{B}\ \|\ (\boxed{B}, \neg A \vdash \neg(A \wedge \neg B), \boxed{A}\ \|\ \boxed{A}, \boxed{B^w}, \neg A \vdash \neg(A \wedge \neg B)))}\ \neg r}{(\neg A \vdash \neg(A \wedge \neg B), \boxed{B}\ \|\ (\boxed{B^w}, \neg A \vdash \neg(A \wedge \neg B), \boxed{\neg A}\ \|\ \boxed{\neg A}, \boxed{B}, \neg A \vdash \neg(A \wedge \neg B)))}\ \neg}{(\neg A \vdash \neg(A \wedge \neg B), \boxed{\neg A \wedge B}\ \|\ \boxed{\neg A \wedge B}, \neg A \vdash \neg(A \wedge \neg B))}\ \wedge$$

$\wedge$-rule represents the first $\wedge$-reduction in Example 2, where the change in the upper sequents of the cut-string is described by mG3-rule using multi-sequents. The same applies to the other rules.

As in G3, the inversion lemma holds in mG3 [10,11].

It is shown that every cut-string reduction is represented by an mG3-rule; thus, a cut-elimination process is represented by proof construction in mG3.

Proposition 8 ([10,11]). *If there exists a G3-proof π whose last is cut between $\Gamma \vdash \Delta, C$ and $C, \Gamma \vdash \Delta$, and no other cut is applied in π, then there exists an m-proof of $(\Gamma \vdash \Delta, C\ \|\ C, \Gamma \vdash \Delta)_C$ in mG3.*

Furthermore, from the following regular m-proof in mG3, by deleting cut-formulas, we obtain a cut-free G3-proof.

Definition 9. A **regular m-proof** is an m-proof, in which (1) the cut-formulas of every axiom are atoms, and (2) for every branch of the m-proof, there exists a unique multi-sequent $\mathcal{M}$ such that only auxiliary rules are applied above $\mathcal{M}$, and only principal rules are applied below $\mathcal{M}$.

Thus, a regular m-proof consists, from the bottom, of applications of principal rules followed by applications of auxiliary rules.

Definition 10. In any multi-sequent $\mathcal{M}$, the concatenation part of two single sequents $(\Gamma \vdash \Delta, C\ \|\ C, \Gamma \vdash \Delta)_C$ is uniquely determined. The cut-formula C of that part is called the **innermost cut-formula** of $\mathcal{M}$. An atom that is the innermost cut-formula is called the **innermost atom**. Let $\mathcal{C}(\Gamma \vdash \Delta, Q\ \|\ Q, \Gamma \vdash \Delta)_Q$ be a multi-sequent whose innermost atom is Q. By deleting the two occurrences of Q and by unifying the remaining Γ and Δ, a multi-sequent $\mathcal{C}(\Gamma \vdash \Delta)$ is obtained. We call this operation the **innermost atom deletion**.

Proposition 11 ([10,11]). *(I) Let π be a regular m-proof of non-single $\mathcal{M}$. For every multi-sequent in π, (1) apply the innermost atom deletion; (2) delete all non-single multi-sequents that do not contain any innermost atom. The resulting structure π' is then a regular m-proof of $\mathcal{M}'$ such that $\bigcap \mathcal{M} = \bigcap \mathcal{M}'$.*
(II) Any m-proof π of $\mathcal{M}$ is transformed into a cut-free G3-proof π' of $\bigcap \mathcal{M}$.

Example 12. Let us apply the innermost atom deletion to the m-proof given in Example 7. By deleting the innermost A, as well as the lower sequents of $\neg$-rule, which do not contain any innermost atom, we obtain the following m-proof on the left. Then, by deleting B, we obtain the following cut-free proof on the right.

$$\cfrac{\cfrac{\cfrac{(A, \neg B \vdash A, \boxed{B} \parallel \boxed{B}, A, \neg B \vdash A)}{(\neg A, A, \neg B \vdash \boxed{B} \parallel \boxed{B}, \neg A, A, \neg B \vdash)} \neg l}{(\neg A, A \wedge \neg B \vdash \boxed{B} \parallel \boxed{B}, \neg A, A \wedge \neg B \vdash)} \wedge l}{(\neg A \vdash \neg(A \wedge \neg B), \boxed{B} \parallel \boxed{B}, \neg A \vdash \neg(A \wedge \neg B))} \neg r \qquad \cfrac{\cfrac{\cfrac{A, \neg B \vdash A}{\neg A, A, \neg B \vdash} \neg l}{\neg A, A \wedge \neg B \vdash} \wedge l}{\neg A \vdash \neg(A \wedge \neg B)} \neg r$$

4 Sequent Calculus Representation of Lorenzen Dialogue

In this section, we review sequent calculus representation G3D of Lorenzen dialogue introduced in [8,12]. Lorenzen dialogue is defined as a two players' dialogue between *Proponent* (P) and *Opponent* (O). We use X, Y ($X \neq Y$) to denote P or O. The rule of Lorenzen dialogue is defined based on the following **argumentation form**, which describes how a composite formula may be attacked and, how, if possible, this attack may be defended. See [1–3].

In the following argumentation forms for $\wedge$ and $\neg$ (read from bottom up), Y's assertion is a formula C obtained previously by Y's defense on C or Y's attack on $\neg C$.

$\neg$-**argumentation form for** X

No defense is possible
X's attack by asserting A
Y's assertion of $\neg A$

$\wedge$-**argumentation form for** O

P's defense by asserting A_i
O's attack by choosing $i = 1$ or 2
P's assertion of $A_1 \wedge A_2$

$\wedge$-**argumentation form for** P

O's defense by asserting A_1 and A_2
P's attack on $A_1 \wedge A_2$
O's assertion of $A_1 \wedge A_2$

In [8,12], our sequent calculus representation of Lorenzen dialogue was introduced based on Kleene's sequent calculus GK. In this article, we introduce our G3D based on G3. Thus, we modify the $\wedge$-argumentation form for P so that it corresponds to a G3-rule instead of a GK-rule.

We introduce *d-sequents*, in which we distinguish formulas to be defended using brackets [ ] from formulas to be attacked. D-sequents simplify the definition of a dialogue, bringing it closer to the usual sequent calculus.

Definition 13. A **d-sequent** is of the form $[\Pi], \Gamma \vdash \Lambda, [\Delta]$ for any $\Pi, \Gamma, \Lambda, \Delta$.

$[\Pi]$ is formulas to be defended by O; Γ is formulas to be attacked by P; Λ is formulas to be attacked by O; and $[\Delta]$ is formulas to be defended by P.

Although we can define our G3D in the same way as [1–3], we here introduce our dialogue G3D in the style of sequent calculus. From the proof theoretical

A Dialogical Interpretation of Cut-Elimination and Its Application   299

viewpoint, a winning strategy corresponds to a proof, and a dialogue corresponds to a branch in the proof. Based on the correspondence, we define strategies prior to dialogues. Thus, in the following definition of moves, O's attack on $A_1 \wedge A_2$ ($Oa\wedge$) is defined including branching as it is in $\wedge r$-rule in G3.

Definition 14. (G3D) **Moves** of X's attack on $A_1 \wedge A_2$ ($Xa\wedge$), X's attack on $\neg A$ ($Xa\neg$), X's defense on A (Xd) are defined as follows.

$$\frac{[\Pi, A_1 \wedge A_2], \Gamma \vdash \Lambda, [\Delta]}{[\Pi], \Gamma, A_1 \wedge A_2 \vdash \Lambda, [\Delta]} \, Pa\wedge \qquad \frac{[\Pi], \Gamma \vdash \Lambda, [A_1, \Delta] \quad [\Pi], \Gamma \vdash \Lambda, [A_2, \Delta]}{[\Pi], \Gamma \vdash A_1 \wedge A_2, \Lambda, [\Delta]} \, Oa\wedge$$

$$\frac{[\Pi], \Gamma \vdash A, \Lambda, [\Delta]}{[\Pi], \Gamma, \neg A \vdash \Lambda, [\Delta]} \, Pa\neg \qquad \frac{[\Pi], \Gamma, A \vdash \Lambda, [\Delta]}{[\Pi], \Gamma \vdash \neg A, \Lambda, [\Delta]} \, Oa\neg$$

$$\frac{[\Pi], \Gamma \vdash \Lambda, A, [\Delta]}{[\Pi], \Gamma \vdash \Lambda, [A, \Delta]} \, Pd \qquad \frac{[\Pi], A_1, A_2, \Gamma \vdash \Lambda, [\Delta]}{[\Pi, A_1 \wedge A_2], \Gamma \vdash \Lambda, [\Delta]} \, Od\wedge$$

The above moves are read from the bottom up. If we ignore contexts, we find that the above moves correspond to the argumentation forms of Lorenzen dialogue: X's $\neg$-argumentation form corresponds to $Xa\neg$, and X's $\wedge$-argumentation form corresponds to the pair of moves $Xa\wedge$ followed by Yd.

Definition 15. A **strategy** for a sequent $\Gamma \vdash \Delta$ in G3D is a tree constructed using G3D-moves satisfying the following conditions.

1. The root of the strategy is the d-sequent $\Gamma \vdash [\Delta]$.
2. In each branch, the first (i.e., the bottom of the tree) is P's move, and thereafter, the moves of O and P alternately appear.
3. Pd on Q or $Pa\neg$ on $\neg Q$ for an atom Q is possible only when the given d-sequent is of the form $\Sigma, Q \vdash [Q, \Phi]$ or $\Sigma, Q, \neg Q \vdash [\Phi]$.

Every branch in a strategy is called a **dialogue**. A strategy is **winning** if it is finite, and every leaf thereof is of the form $\Sigma, Q \vdash Q, [\Phi]$ for an atom Q.

Example 16. The following is a winning strategy for $\neg A \vdash \neg(A \wedge \neg B)$, which read from bottom to top. (1) Pd: $\neg(A \wedge \neg B)$ holds. (2) $Oa\neg$: It does not hold since $A \wedge \neg B$ holds. (3) $Pa\wedge$: Does $A \wedge \neg B$ really holds? (4) $Od\wedge$: Yes, both A and $\neg B$ hold. (5) $Pa\neg$: Your assertion $\neg A$ does not hold since A holds as you affirmed it.

$$\frac{A, \neg B \vdash A}{\dfrac{A, \neg B, \neg A \vdash}{\dfrac{[A \wedge \neg B], \neg A \vdash}{\dfrac{\neg A, A \wedge \neg B \vdash}{\dfrac{\neg A \vdash \neg(A \wedge \neg B)}{\neg A \vdash [\neg(A \wedge \neg B)]} \, Pd} \, Oa\neg} \, Pa\wedge} \, Od\wedge} \, Pa\neg$$

The following is an essential property of dialogue G3D. Cf. [12].

Proposition 17. *In any strategy, the O's move is uniquely determined.*

In the same way as [8], we can show the correspondence between G3 and our G3D. Although the $\neg$-argumentation form in Lorenzen dialogue, where no defense is possible, requires slight modification of G3 sequent calculus proofs, there is a correspondence between every pair of P's and O's moves and a G3-rule. See [8,12] for the detail. In the strategy given in Example 16, $Pd; Oa\neg$ corresponds to $\neg r$-rule, and $Pa\wedge; Od\wedge$ corresponds to $\wedge l$-rule. Furthermore, in the same way as [12], it is shown that our G3D is Lorenzen dialogue; hence, we refer our G3D as Lorenzen dialogue in this article.

5 Dialogical Interpretation of Cut-Elimination

5.1 Lorenzen Dialogue mG3D for Multi-sequents

Our multi-d-sequent is obtained from a multi-sequent by adding brackets [ ] around certain formulas, as in a d-sequent. Hence, we denote a multi-d-sequent using the same notation $\mathcal{M}$ as a multi-sequent. However, in our dialogical counterpart of mG3-rules, we need to consider a sequent of the form $(\Gamma \vdash \Delta, A \parallel A \wedge \neg B, \Gamma \vdash \Delta)$, which is connected by cut-formulas A and $A \wedge \neg B$. The reason for this is that we decompose each mG3-rule into a sequence of moves of P and O. Thus, we extend multi-sequents by adding the following sequents.

Definition 18. If $\mathcal{C}(\mathcal{M}_2 \langle \vdash D_1 \wedge D_2 \rangle \parallel \mathcal{M}_1 \langle D_1 \wedge D_2 \vdash \rangle)_{D_1 \wedge D_2}$ is a multi-sequent with $\mathcal{M}_1 \cap \mathcal{M}_2 = \Gamma \vdash \Delta$, then $\mathcal{C}(\Gamma \vdash \Delta, D_2 \parallel (\mathcal{M}_2\{D_2 \vdash D_1\} \parallel \mathcal{M}_1 \langle D_1 \wedge D_2 \vdash \rangle)_{D_1 \wedge D_2})_{D_1 \wedge D_2}$ is a multi-sequent, whose cut-formulas are those of $\mathcal{C}, \mathcal{M}_1$ and $\mathcal{M}_2$, as well as the indicated occurrences of $D_1 \wedge D_2, D_1$, and D_2.

If $\mathcal{C}(\mathcal{M}_2 \langle \vdash \neg D \rangle \parallel \mathcal{M}_1 \langle \neg D \vdash \rangle)_{\neg D}$ is a multi-sequent, then $\mathcal{C}(\mathcal{M}_2 \{D \vdash \} \parallel \mathcal{M}_1 \langle \neg D \vdash \rangle)_{\neg D}$ is a multi-sequent, whose cut-formulas are those of $\mathcal{C}, \mathcal{M}_1$ and $\mathcal{M}_2$, as well as the indicated occurrences of $\neg D$ and D.

We call these forms of multi-sequents **irregular** when we need to distinguish them form the usual multi-sequents.

The irregular multi-sequents are exactly those that appear in the definition of our moves in mG3D. Note that the subscriptions of cut-formulas in the first form of an irregular sequent are $D_1 \wedge D_2$, and in the second form, it is $\neg D$.

Definition 19. A multi-d-sequent, **md-sequent** for short, is a sequence of d-sequents, from which the multi-sequent is obtained by removing all [ ]. Cut-formulas of an md-sequent are those of the underlying multi-sequent.

An md-sequent is **irregular** when the underlying multi-sequent is irregular.

The intersection on d-sequents is defined in the same manner as that on sequents. For $[\Pi_i], \Gamma_i \vdash \Lambda_i, [\Delta_i]$ with $1 \leq i \leq n$, $\bigcap([\Pi_i], \Gamma_i \vdash \Lambda_i, [\Delta_i]) = [\bigcap \Pi_i], \bigcap \Gamma_i \vdash \bigcap \Lambda_i, [\bigcap \Delta_i]$, where $\bigcap$ on the right-hand side is the multiset intersection.

Each principal mG3-rule is decomposed into four moves: one move for $\mathcal{M}_1$ and one move for $\mathcal{M}_2$, with each of these further decomposed into a pair of moves by P and O. The following moves are read from bottom up.

A Dialogical Interpretation of Cut-Elimination and Its Application   301

Definition 20. Moves of mG3D are the following principal and auxiliary moves.

Principal moves: Let $\mathcal{M}_1, \mathcal{M}_2$, and $\mathcal{M}_3$ be md-sequents such that $\mathcal{M}_1 \cap \mathcal{M}_2 = [\Pi], \Gamma \vdash \Lambda, [\Delta]$.

$$\frac{\mathcal{C}(\mathcal{M}_2 \parallel \mathcal{M}_1\{[D_1 \wedge D_2] \vdash\})_{D_1 \wedge D_2}}{\mathcal{C}(\mathcal{M}_2 \parallel \mathcal{M}_1\langle D_1 \wedge D_2 \vdash\rangle)_{D_1 \wedge D_2}} \, pPa\wedge \qquad \frac{\mathcal{C}(\mathcal{M}_2\{\vdash D\} \parallel \mathcal{M}_1)_D}{\mathcal{C}(\mathcal{M}_2\langle\vdash [D]\rangle \parallel \mathcal{M}_1)_D} \, pPd$$

$$\frac{\mathcal{C}([\Pi], \Gamma \vdash \Lambda, [D_2, \Delta] \parallel (\mathcal{M}_2\{D_2^w \vdash [D_1]\} \parallel \mathcal{M}_1)_{D_1 \wedge D_2})_{D_1 \wedge D_2}}{\mathcal{C}(\mathcal{M}_2\langle\vdash D_1 \wedge D_2\rangle \parallel \mathcal{M}_1)_{D_1 \wedge D_2}} \, pOa\wedge$$

$$\frac{\mathcal{C}(\mathcal{M}_3 \parallel (\mathcal{M}_2 \parallel \mathcal{M}_1\{D_1, D_2 \vdash\})_{D_1})_{D_2}}{\mathcal{C}(\mathcal{M}_3 \parallel (\mathcal{M}_2 \parallel \mathcal{M}_1\langle[D_1 \wedge D_2] \vdash\rangle)_{D_1 \wedge D_2})_{D_1 \wedge D_2}} \, pOd\wedge$$

$$\frac{\mathcal{C}(\mathcal{M}_2 \parallel \mathcal{M}_1\{\vdash D\})_D}{\mathcal{C}(\mathcal{M}_2 \parallel \mathcal{M}_1\langle \neg D \vdash\rangle)_{\neg D}} \, pPa\neg \qquad \frac{\mathcal{C}(\mathcal{M}_2\{D \vdash\} \parallel \mathcal{M}_1)_{\neg D}}{\mathcal{C}(\mathcal{M}_2\langle\vdash \neg D\rangle \parallel \mathcal{M}_1)_{\neg D}} \, pOa\neg$$

Auxiliary moves:

$$\frac{\mathcal{M}\{[B_1 \wedge B_2] \vdash\}}{\mathcal{M}\langle B_1 \wedge B_2 \vdash\rangle} \, Pa\wedge \qquad \frac{\mathcal{M}\{\vdash [B_1]\} \quad \mathcal{M}\{\vdash [B_2]\}}{\mathcal{M}\langle\vdash B_1 \wedge B_2\rangle} \, Oa\wedge$$

$$\frac{\mathcal{M}\{\vdash B\}}{\mathcal{M}\langle\neg B \vdash\rangle} \, Pa\neg \qquad \frac{\mathcal{M}\{B \vdash\}}{\mathcal{M}\langle\vdash \neg B\rangle} \, Oa\neg \qquad \frac{\mathcal{M}\{\vdash B\}}{\mathcal{M}\langle\vdash [B]\rangle} \, Pd \qquad \frac{\mathcal{M}\{B_1, B_2 \vdash\}}{\mathcal{M}\langle[B_1 \wedge B_2] \vdash\rangle} \, Od\wedge$$

Auxiliary moves are an extension of moves in Lorenzen G3D to those for md-sequents. In particular, when $\mathcal{M}$ consists of a single d-sequent in an auxiliary move, it is exactly a Lorenzen G3D-move. The principal moves are applied only to cut-formulas, which are specified in their lower sequents. Note that in $pPa\wedge$, cut-formulas of $\mathcal{M}_2$ may be D_1 or D_2 instead of $D_1 \wedge D_2$ by Definition 18. Similarly for the other principal moves. Principal $pPa\wedge$ can be considered a restriction of auxiliary $Pa\wedge$ to $\mathcal{M}_1$ only. The same applies to $pPa\neg, pOa\neg, pPd$, and $pOd\wedge$.

The definition of strategy is essentially the same as that of G3D. However, the winning condition is slightly different. Every mG3D-dialogue stops just short of the end of a Lorenzen G3D-dialogue in order to maintain the order of P and O. This is because some G3D-dialogues proceed in parallel in mG3D.

Definition 21. A **strategy** in mG3D is a tree constructed using mG3D-moves satisfying the following conditions.

1. The root of the strategy is an md-sequent whose component d-sequents are of the form $\Gamma \vdash [\Delta]$.

2. In each branch, the first is P's move, and thereafter, O's and P's moves appear alternately.
3. In principal pPd on D and $pPa\neg$ on $\neg D$, cut-formula D is not an atom; and in auxiliary Pd on B and $Pa\neg$ on $\neg B$, formula B is not an atom.

Every branch in a strategy is called a **dialogue**. A strategy is **ending** if it is finite and there is no possible move for P at every leaf of the strategy. An ending strategy is **winning** if every leaf thereof consists of d-sequents of the form $\Gamma, Q \vdash [Q, \Delta]$, or $\Gamma, Q, \neg Q \vdash [\Delta]$, where Q is an atom that is not a cut-formula.

Example 22. The following is a winning strategy for $(\neg A \vdash [\neg(A \wedge \neg B), \neg A \wedge B] \parallel \neg A \wedge B, \neg A \vdash [\neg(A \wedge \neg B)])_{\neg A \wedge B}$ in mG3D, which corresponds to the m-proof in Example 7. Cut-formulas are P-signed (resp. O-signed) in the left (resp. right) d-sequent of the given md-sequent, and their subformulas are uniformly signed as P or O. A P or O sign indicates that the formula is a claim of P or O.

$$
\begin{array}{c}
(\neg A, A, \neg B \vdash [B_P] \parallel (B_O^w, \neg A, A, \neg B \vdash [\neg A_P] \parallel \neg A_O, B_O, \neg A, A, \neg B \vdash)) \\
\hline
([A \wedge \neg B], \neg A \vdash [B_P] \parallel ([A \wedge \neg B], B_O^w, \neg A \vdash [\neg A_P] \parallel [A \wedge \neg B], \neg A_O, B_O, \neg A \vdash)) \quad Od\wedge \\
\hline
(\neg A, A \wedge \neg B \vdash [B_P] \parallel (B_O^w, \neg A, A \wedge \neg B \vdash [\neg A_P] \parallel \neg A_O, B_O, \neg A, A \wedge \neg B \vdash)) \quad Pa\wedge \\
\hline
(\neg A \vdash \neg (A \wedge \neg B), [B_P] \parallel (B_O^w, \neg A \vdash \neg (A \wedge \neg B), [\neg A_P] \parallel \neg A_O, B_O, \neg A \vdash \neg(A \wedge \neg B))) \quad Oa\neg \\
\hline
(\neg A \vdash [B_P, \neg(A \wedge \neg B)] \parallel (B_O^w, \neg A \vdash [\neg A_P, \neg(A \wedge \neg B)] \parallel \neg A_O, B_O, \neg A \vdash [\neg(A \wedge \neg B)])) \quad Pd \\
\hline
(\neg A \vdash [B_P, \neg(A \wedge \neg B)] \parallel (B_O^w, \neg A \vdash [\neg A_P, \neg(A \wedge \neg B)] \parallel [\neg A \wedge B_O], \neg A \vdash [\neg(A \wedge \neg B)])) \quad pOd\wedge \\
\hline
(\neg A \vdash [B_P, \neg(A \wedge \neg B)] \parallel (B_O^w, \neg A \vdash [\neg A_P, \neg(A \wedge \neg B)] \parallel \neg A \wedge B_O, \neg A \vdash [\neg(A \wedge \neg B)])) \quad pPa\wedge \\
\hline
(\neg A \vdash \neg A \wedge B_P, [\neg(A \wedge \neg B)] \parallel \neg A \wedge B_O, \neg A \vdash [\neg(A \wedge \neg B)]) \quad pOa\wedge \\
\hline
(\neg A \vdash [\neg(A \wedge \neg B), \neg A \wedge B_P] \parallel \neg A \wedge B_O, \neg A \vdash [\neg(A \wedge \neg B)]) \quad pPd
\end{array}
$$

The sequence of the first four moves $pPd; pOa\wedge; pPa\wedge; pOd\wedge$ corresponds to the principal $\wedge$-rule in mG3. In general, a sequence of four $POPO$ moves corresponds to a principal mG3-rule, and a pair of PO moves corresponds to an auxiliary mG3-rule. Thus, $Pd; Oa\neg$ corresponds to auxiliary $\neg r$-rule and $Pa\wedge; Od\wedge$ corresponds to auxiliary $\wedge l$-rule of mG3.

The following is an extension of Proposition 17 in Lorenzen G3D.

Proposition 23. *In any strategy, the O's move is uniquely determined.*

Proof. Beginning with an md-sequent whose component sequents are of the form $\Gamma \vdash [\Delta]$, P's possible move is $pPd, pPa\neg, pPa\wedge, Pd, Pa\neg$, or $Pa\wedge$. We examine principal moves. (1) By pPd or $pPa\neg$, we obtain an md-sequent some of whose component sequents are of the form $\Gamma' \vdash C, [\Delta']$. Then, the next possible O's move is only a $\wedge$ or $\neg$ attack on C; as such, we return to an md-sequent consisting of $\Gamma'' \vdash [\Delta'']$. (2) By $pPa\wedge$, we obtain $[C_1 \wedge C_2], \Gamma' \vdash [\Delta]$. The next possible O's move is only $pOd\wedge$, and we return to an md-sequent consisting of $\Gamma'' \vdash [\Delta]$. Auxiliary moves are similar. Thus, in a strategy, no choice of moves exists for O. ∎

5.2 Dialogue mG3D and Sequent Calculus mG3

We show the correspondence between our dialogue mG3Dand sequent calculus mG3. We first define the interpretation of multi-sequents.

Definition 24. A multi-sequent $\mathcal{M}$, whose component sequents are $\Gamma_i \vdash \Delta_i$, is interpreted as the md-sequent $\mathcal{M}^d$, whose component sequents are $\Gamma_i \vdash [\Delta_i]$.

We show that m-proofs of mG3 are transformed into winning strategies in mG3D.

Theorem 25. *Any m-proof of $\mathcal{M}$ in mG3 is transformed into a winning strategy for $\mathcal{M}^d$ in mG3D.*

Proof. In Lorenzen dialogue, O should immediately attack A after P attacks $\neg A$. This restriction indicates that, in mG3, an inference on A should be applied immediately after an application of $\neg$ or $\neg l$ on $\neg A$. Any m-proof in mG3 can be transformed into an m-proof that satisfies this restriction by using the inversion lemma of mG3 [11]. By assuming this modification of m-proofs, we prove the theorem by induction on the length of the given m-proof π of $\mathcal{M}$.
(Base step) Every component sequent of any axiom of π is of the form $\Gamma, Q \vdash Q, \Delta$ or $\Gamma, Q, \neg Q \vdash \Delta$, and is interpreted respectively as $\Gamma, Q \vdash [Q, \Delta]$ or $\Gamma, Q, \neg Q \vdash [\Delta]$, which satisfies the winning condition.
(Induction step) We provide the interpretation of every mG3-rule.
(Principal $\wedge$-rule) Let $\mathcal{C}^d(\mathcal{M}_2^d \langle \vdash [D_1 \wedge D_2] \rangle \parallel \mathcal{M}_1^d \langle D_1 \wedge D_2 \vdash \rangle)$ be the interpretation of the lower sequent of $\wedge$-rule with $\mathcal{M}_1^d \cap \mathcal{M}_2^d = \Gamma \vdash [\Delta]$. Then, we have the following strategy.

$$\cfrac{\cfrac{\cfrac{\cfrac{\mathcal{C}^d(\Gamma \vdash [D_2, \Delta] \parallel (\mathcal{M}_2^d \langle D_2^w \vdash [D_1] \rangle \parallel \mathcal{M}_1^d \langle D_1, D_2 \vdash \rangle)_{D_1})_{D_2}}{\mathcal{C}^d(\Gamma \vdash [D_2, \Delta] \parallel (\mathcal{M}_2^d \langle D_2^w \vdash [D_1] \rangle \parallel \mathcal{M}_1^d \langle [D_1 \wedge D_2] \vdash \rangle)_{D_1 \wedge D_2})_{D_1 \wedge D_2}} \; pOd\wedge}{\mathcal{C}^d(\Gamma \vdash [D_2, \Delta] \parallel (\mathcal{M}_2^d \langle D_2^w \vdash [D_1] \rangle \parallel \mathcal{M}_1^d \langle D_1 \wedge D_2 \vdash \rangle)_{D_1 \wedge D_2})_{D_1 \wedge D_2}} \; pPa\wedge}{\mathcal{C}^d(\mathcal{M}_2^d \langle \vdash D_1 \wedge D_2 \rangle \parallel \mathcal{M}_1^d \langle D_1 \wedge D_2 \vdash \rangle)_{D_1 \wedge D_2}} \; pOa\wedge}{\mathcal{C}^d(\mathcal{M}_2^d \langle \vdash [D_1 \wedge D_2] \rangle \parallel \mathcal{M}_1^d \langle D_1 \wedge D_2 \vdash \rangle)_{D_1 \wedge D_2}} \; pPd$$

We find that the uppermost sequent is the interpretation of the upper sequent of $\wedge$-rule. By Proposition 23, O's move is uniquely determined in the abovementioned interpretation. Hence, by the induction hypothesis, we obtain a winning strategy. Similarly for the other rules. ∎

To show the inverse of the above theorem, we slightly restrict P's move as follows. Cf. Definition 9.

Definition 26. A strategy is **regular** when (1) cut-formulas of every leaf are literals; (2) for every branch of the strategy, there exists a unique md-sequent $\mathcal{M}$ such that only auxiliary moves are applied above $\mathcal{M}$, and only principal moves are applied below $\mathcal{M}$; (3) $pPa\neg$ (and $pPa\wedge$) is applied together with $pOa\neg$ (resp. $pOa\wedge$) and is applied immediately after $pOa\neg$ (resp. $pOa\wedge$).

In the strategy given in Example 22, after the first two moves $pPd; pOa\wedge$, P can apply auxiliary Pd on $\neg(A \wedge \neg B)$ instead of $pPa\wedge$. However, such a strategy is not regular, even though it is winning.

By $|\mathcal{M}|$, we denote the underlying multi-sequent of an md-sequent $\mathcal{M}$ by removing all brackets [ ].

Theorem 27. *Let $\mathcal{M}$ be an md-sequent, which is not irregular, and which consists of d-sequents of the form $\Gamma \vdash [\Delta]$. Any regular winning strategy for $\mathcal{M}$ in mG3D is transformed into a regular m-proof of $|\mathcal{M}|$ in mG3.*

Proof. We examine the structure of a regular strategy. When the first P's move is a principal move, it is not $pPa\neg$ nor $pPa\wedge$, and it should be pPd on a cut-formula C by Definition 26 of the regular strategy. Then, by Proposition 23, the next is $pOa\neg$ or $pOa\wedge$ on C, and it is followed by $pPa\neg$ or $pPa\wedge$ by Definition 26 of the regular strategy. Then, again by Proposition 23, O's move is uniquely determined, and in the same way as the proof of Proposition 23, every component sequent returns to the original form $\Gamma' \vdash [\Delta']$.

When the first P's move is an auxiliary move, from Proposition 23, by a pair of P's and O's moves, every component sequent returns to the original form of $\Gamma' \vdash [\Delta']$.

Therefore, every regular strategy consists of the combination of pairs of auxiliary PO-moves and sequences of principal $POPO$-moves, and their translation is the inverse of that described in Theorem 25. ∎

By deleting cut-formulas from a regular winning mG3D-strategy in the same way as in Proposition 11([10,11]), we obtain a Lorenzen G3D-strategy.

Example 28. For the strategy given in Example 22, by the same way as the innermost atom deletion (Proposition 11), we obtain a G3D-strategy as follows.

By deleting cut-formula $\neg A$, we obtain the following strategy on the left. By further deleting cut-formula B, we obtain the following strategy on the right, which is essentially the same as the G3D-strategy in Example 16.

$$\dfrac{\dfrac{\dfrac{\dfrac{(\neg A, A, \neg B \vdash [B_P] \parallel B_O, \neg A, A, \neg B \vdash)}{([A \wedge \neg B], \neg A \vdash [B_P] \parallel [A \wedge \neg B], B_O, \neg A \vdash)}Od\wedge}{(\neg A, A \wedge \neg B \vdash [B_P] \parallel B_O, \neg A, A \wedge \neg B \vdash)}Pa\wedge}{(\neg A \vdash \neg(A \wedge \neg B), [B_P] \parallel B_O, \neg A \vdash \neg(A \wedge \neg B))}Oa\neg}{(\neg A \vdash [B_P, \neg(A \wedge \neg B)] \parallel B_O, \neg A \vdash [\neg(A \wedge \neg B)])}Pd \qquad \dfrac{\dfrac{\dfrac{\dfrac{\neg A, A, \neg B \vdash}{[A \wedge \neg B], \neg A \vdash}Od\wedge}{\neg A, A \wedge \neg B \vdash}Pa\wedge}{\neg A \vdash \neg(A \wedge \neg B)}Oa\neg}{\neg A \vdash [\neg(A \wedge \neg B)]}Pd$$

Thus, our dialogue mG3D is a natural extension of Lorenzen G3D in the sense that by deleting cut-formulas, as well as principal moves, from a regular winning mG3D-strategy, a winning G3D-strategy is obtained.

5.3 Cut-Elimination as Conflict-Elimination

In this section, we investigate an application of our mG3D to persuasion dialogue for resolving a conflict of opinions. For an md-sequent ($\Gamma \vdash [C, \Delta] \parallel C, \Gamma \vdash$

$[\Delta])_C$, we regard the cut-formula C in the left (resp. right) sequent as a P's (resp. O's) claim, and denote it as C_P (resp. C_O). We assume all subformulas of these cut-formulas are assigned the same P/O signature. We denote an X-signed formula as an X-formula, where X is P or O. Furthermore, by regarding O's claim as *not* C, we write it as $\sim C_O$. Then, the given md-sequent is written as follows: $(\Gamma \vdash [C_P, \Delta] \parallel \sim C_O, \Gamma \vdash [\Delta])_C$, which expresses a conflict between P's claim C_P and O's claim $\sim C_O$. Here, we intend that $\sim C_O, \Gamma \vdash$ is equivalent to $\Gamma \vdash \neg C_O$. However, the expression $\Gamma \vdash \neg C_O$ places the formula $\neg C_O$ in a position where it is to be attacked by O, though O's claim C_O should be attacked by P. Thus, to maintain the structure of a d-sequent, we express it as $\sim C_O, \Gamma \vdash$ by using $\sim$. In general, we assign $\sim$ to every cut-formula appearing in the antecedent of a given d-sequent. These signatures are always applied to the outermost of a formula, so parentheses are not necessary. By introducing $\sim$, as well as P/O signatures, mG3D-moves are essentially the same. The following are $pOd\wedge, pOa\neg$, and $pPa\neg$ with $\sim$ and P/O signatures. Other rules are similar.

$$\frac{\mathcal{C}(\mathcal{M}_3 \parallel (\mathcal{M}_2 \parallel \mathcal{M}_1\{\sim D_{1X}, \sim D_{2X} \vdash\})_{D_1})_{D_2}}{\mathcal{C}(\mathcal{M}_3 \parallel (\mathcal{M}_2 \parallel \mathcal{M}_1\langle [\sim D_1 \wedge D_{2X}] \vdash\rangle)_{D_1 \wedge D_2})_{D_1 \wedge D_2}} \; pOd\wedge$$

$$\frac{\mathcal{C}(\mathcal{M}_2\{\sim D_X \vdash\} \parallel \mathcal{M}_1)_{\neg D}}{\mathcal{C}(\mathcal{M}_2\langle \vdash \neg D_X \rangle \parallel \mathcal{M}_1)_{\neg D}} \; pOa\neg \qquad \frac{\mathcal{C}(\mathcal{M}_2 \parallel \mathcal{M}_1\{\vdash D_X\})_D}{\mathcal{C}(\mathcal{M}_2 \parallel \mathcal{M}_1\langle \sim \neg D_X \vdash\rangle)_{\neg D}} \; pPa\neg$$

From a regular winning strategy in mG3D, by deleting cut-formulas, i.e., conflicts between P and O, a winning strategy in Lorenzen G3D-dialogue is obtained, as seen in Example 28. We regard such a winning strategy in G3D as a representation of a dialogue leading to an agreement between P and O.

Let us further investigate strategies that are not winning. For a leaf in an ending strategy, when a component sequent $[\Pi], \Gamma \vdash \Lambda, [\Delta]$ thereof causes the given strategy to fail to be winning, we say that $[\Pi], \Gamma \vdash \Lambda, [\Delta]$ **is not winning**.

Example 29. By removing $\neg A$ from the md-sequent given in Example 22, we obtain an ending strategy for $(\vdash [\neg(A \wedge \neg B), \neg A \wedge B_P] \parallel \neg A \wedge B_O \vdash [\neg(A \wedge \neg B)])_{\neg A \wedge B}$ whose leaf is the following.

$$(A, \neg B \vdash [B_P] \parallel (\sim B_O^w, A, \neg B \vdash [\neg A_P] \parallel \sim \neg A_O, \sim B_O, A, \neg B \vdash)_{\neg A})_B$$

Since the leftmost $A, \neg B \vdash [B_P]$ is not winning, and it consists of P-formula B_P, we consider that P's claim is not justified in this case.

Example 30. By replacing $\neg A$ with B, and replacing $\neg(A \wedge \neg B)$ with $\neg A$ in Example 22, we obtain the following ending strategy for $(B \vdash [\neg A, \neg A \wedge B_P] \parallel \sim \neg A \wedge B_O, B \vdash [\neg A])_{\neg A \wedge B}$. Based on Proposition 23, we express every pair of P's and O's moves altogether.

$$\frac{\frac{\frac{(A, B \vdash [B_P] \parallel (\sim B_O^w, A, B \vdash [\neg A_P] \parallel \sim \neg A_O, \sim B_O, A, B \vdash))}{(B \vdash [\neg A, B_P] \parallel (\sim B_O^w, B \vdash [\neg A, \neg A_P] \parallel \sim \neg A_O, \sim B_O, B \vdash [\neg A]))}}{(B \vdash [\neg A, B_P] \parallel (\sim B_O^w, B \vdash [\neg A, \neg A_P] \parallel \sim \neg A \wedge B_O, B \vdash [\neg A]))}}{(B \vdash [\neg A, \neg A \wedge B_P] \parallel \sim \neg A \wedge B_O, B \vdash [\neg A])} \begin{array}{l} Pd; Oa\neg \\ pPa\wedge; pOd\wedge \\ pPd; pOa\wedge \end{array}$$

Although the middle sequent $\sim B_O^w, A, B \vdash [\neg A_P]$ is not winning, it consists of P-formula $\neg A_P$ and O-formula $\sim B_O^w$. However, $\sim B_O^w$ is a weakening formula, and it is shown that weakening formulas do not affect the provability of the given sequent. Thus, by disregarding the weakening formula $\sim B_O^w$, we consider that P's claim is not justified in this case.

Definition 31. A d-sequent is called an *X*-**sequent**, with X being P or O, if it contains only X-formulas, except for weakening formulas.

By examining every mG3D-move, we find that every component d-sequent of an md-sequent $\mathcal{M}$ in a strategy for $(\Gamma \vdash [C_P, \Delta] \parallel \sim C_O, \Gamma \vdash [\Delta])_C$ is either a P-sequent or an O-sequent.

We show that if an X-sequent is not winning in an ending strategy, then X's claim is not justified. To show this, we apply the usual truth-table semantics. The valuation v of formulas to be true T or false F is defined inductively as usual. For any multiset Γ of formulas, $v(\Gamma) = \mathsf{T}$ when $v(A_i) = \mathsf{T}$ for any $A_i \in \Gamma$, and $v(\Gamma) = \mathsf{F}$ when $v(A_i) = \mathsf{F}$ for some $A_i \in \Gamma$.

Definition 32. Let v be a valuation. For any sequent $\Gamma \vdash \Delta$, $v(\Gamma \vdash \Delta) = \mathsf{F}$ iff $v(\Gamma) = \mathsf{T}$ and $v(\Delta) = F$. For any multi-sequent $\mathcal{M}$, $v(\mathcal{M}) = \mathsf{T}$ iff $v(\Gamma \vdash \Delta) = \mathsf{T}$ for every component sequent $\Gamma \vdash \Delta$ of $\mathcal{M}$.

Lemma 33. *For any multi-sequent $\mathcal{M}$, if $v(\bigcap \mathcal{M}) = \mathsf{F}$ then $v(\mathcal{M}) = \mathsf{F}$ for any v.*

Proof. By induction on the length of $\mathcal{M}$.
(Base step) When $\mathcal{M} \equiv (\Gamma \vdash \Delta, C \parallel C, \Gamma \vdash \Delta)$, let $v(\Gamma \vdash \Delta) = \mathsf{F}$ for some v. Then, if $v(C) = \mathsf{F}$ then $v(\Gamma \vdash \Delta, C) = \mathsf{F}$, and if $v(C) = \mathsf{T}$ then $v(C, \Gamma \vdash \Delta) = \mathsf{F}$.
(Induction step) When $\mathcal{M} \equiv (\Gamma \vdash \Delta, C \parallel \mathcal{M}')_C$, let $v(\bigcap \mathcal{M}) = v(\Gamma \vdash \Delta) = \mathsf{F}$. Then, if $v(C) = \mathsf{F}$ then $v(\Gamma \vdash \Delta, C) = \mathsf{F}$, and if $v(C) = \mathsf{T}$ then $v(\mathcal{M}') = \mathsf{F}$ by the induction hypothesis for $v(\bigcap \mathcal{M}') = v(C, \Gamma \vdash \Delta) = \mathsf{F}$. ∎

Lemma 34. *In any branch of a strategy for $(\Gamma \vdash [C_P, \Delta] \parallel \sim C_O, \Gamma \vdash [\Delta])_C$, if a component X-sequent of $\mathcal{M}$ has value F with some v, then there exists a component X-sequent of its lower sequent $\mathcal{M}'$ that has value F with v.*

Proof. Based on the correspondence between strategies and m-proofs, we examine every mG3-rule to reduce the number of cases. For ∧-rule;

$$\frac{\mathcal{C}(\Gamma \vdash \Delta, D_{2X} \parallel (\mathcal{M}_2\{D_{2Y}^w \vdash D_{1X}\} \parallel \mathcal{M}_1\{D_{1Y}, D_{2Y} \vdash\})_{D_1})_{D_2}}{\mathcal{C}(\mathcal{M}_2\langle\vdash D_1 \land D_{2X}\rangle \parallel \mathcal{M}_1\langle D_1 \land D_{2Y} \vdash\rangle)_{D_1 \land D_2}} \land$$

(1) when a component Y-sequent $D_{1Y}, D_{2Y}, \Pi \vdash \Lambda$ of the upper $\mathcal{M}_1$ is F with some v, we have $v(D_{1Y}) = v(D_{2Y}) = v(\Pi) = \mathsf{T}$ and $v(\Lambda) = \mathsf{F}$. Thus, the component Y-sequent $D_1 \land D_{2Y}, \Pi \vdash \Lambda$ of the lower $\mathcal{M}_1$ is F with v.

(2) When a component X-sequent $D_{2Y}^w, \Pi \vdash \Lambda, D_{1X}$ of the upper $\mathcal{M}_2$ is F, we have $v(D_{2Y}^w) = v(\Pi) = \mathsf{T}$ and $v(\Lambda) = v(D_{1X}) = \mathsf{F}$. Thus, the component X-sequent $\Pi \vdash \Lambda, D_1 \wedge D_{2X}$ of the lower $\mathcal{M}_2$ is F.
(3) When $\Gamma \vdash \Delta, D_{2X}$ of the upper sequent is F, we have $v(\Gamma) = \mathsf{T}$ and $v(\Delta) = v(D_{2X}) = \mathsf{F}$. Then, $v(\Gamma \vdash \Delta, D_1 \wedge D_{2X}) = v(\bigcap \mathcal{M}_2) = \mathsf{F}$ for the lower $\mathcal{M}_2$. Thus, by Lemma 33, $v(\mathcal{M}_2) = \mathsf{F}$, that is, there exists a component X-sequent of the lower $\mathcal{M}_2$ which is F. Similarly for the other rules. ∎

Theorem 35. *For any regular ending strategy for* $(\Gamma \vdash [C_P, \Delta] \parallel \sim C_O, \Gamma \vdash [\Delta])_C$, *if a P-sequent is not winning, then* $v(\Gamma \vdash C_P, \Delta) = \mathsf{F}$; *and if an O-sequent is not winning, then* $v(C_O, \Gamma \vdash \Delta) = \mathsf{F}$ *for some valuation* v.

Proof. As seen in the proof of Theorem 27, every component sequent of a leaf of the given strategy is of the form $\Sigma \vdash [\Phi]$. Let a component P-sequent $\Sigma \vdash [\Phi]$ be not winning. We find that Σ consists of literals, and Φ consists of atoms, since otherwise, a P's move would be possible. Since it's underlying sequent is not an axiom, we are able to find a valuation v such that $v(\Sigma \vdash \Phi) = \mathsf{F}$. Therefore, by Lemma 34, we have $v(\Gamma \vdash C_P, \Delta) = \mathsf{F}$. The same applies to an O-sequent. ∎

In summary, beginning with a conflict $(\Gamma \vdash [C_P, \Delta] \parallel \sim C_O, \Gamma \vdash [\Delta])_C$, through an mG3D-dialogue, the conflict C is reduced to literals. By further mG3D-dialogue on the contexts Γ and Δ; (1) If a regular winning strategy is obtained, both P's claim C_P and O's claim $\sim C_O$ are justified. Thus, the conflict is considered as inessential, and it is removed. The resulting Lorenzen G3D-dialogue, without any conflict, leads to an agreement between P and O. (2) Otherwise, if an X-sequent is not winning, X's claim is not justified.

6 Future Work

As for Theorem 35, it seems that, from a non-winning regular ending strategy, we can extract a Lorenzen dialogue in which either P or O fails to be winning, in a manner similar to how a cut-free proof is obtained from an m-proof. We leave the syntactic proof of Theorem 35 as future work.

In [12], we apply *cut*-rule to formalize why-because dialogue, one of the most basic forms of dialogue. Along with the results in this article, we will investigate applications of *cut*-rule and cut-elimination to the formalization of more general dialogues, including rebuttals or counter-arguments.

References

1. Felscher, W.: Dialogues, strategies and intuitionistic provability. Ann. Pure Appl. Logic **28**, 217–254 (1985)
2. Felscher, W.: Dialogues as a foundation for intuitionistic logic. In: Handbook of Philosophical Logic III, Alternatives to Classical Logic, Reidel, Dordrecht, pp. 341-372 (1986)
3. Fermüller, C.G.: Dialogue games for many-valued logics - an overview. Stud. Logica. **90**, 43–68 (2008)

4. Herbelin, H.: Séquents qu'on calcule: de l'interprétation du calcul des séquents comme calcul de lambda-termes et comme calcul de stratégies gagnantes, PhD thesis (1995)
5. Lorenz, K., Lorenzen, P.: Dialogische Logik, Darmstadt (1978)
6. Lorenzen, P.: Ein dialogisches Konstruktivitätskriterium, in Infinitistic Methods, pp. 193–200. Pergamon Press, Oxford (1961)
7. Negri, S., von Plato, J.: Structural Proof Theory, Cambridge University Press (2001)
8. Okada, M., Takemura, R.: A New Proof-Theoretical View on an Old "Dialogue Logic". In: Essays in the Foundations of Logical and Phenomenological Studies, Keio University Press, pp. 153–167 (2007)
9. Prakken, H.: Formal systems for persuasion dialogue. Knowl. Eng. Rev. **21**(2), 163–188 (2006)
10. Takemura, R.: Another representation of cut-elimination. In: Proceedings of the 6th Asian Workshop on Philosophical Logic, pp. 264–278 (2024)
11. Takemura, R.: Proof construction style representation of cut-elimination. In: Exploring Negation, Modality and Proof, Sano, K., Ono, H., Hatano, R., (eds.), A Springer book series Logic in Asia: Studia Logica Library, to appear
12. Takemura, R.: A sequent calculus representation of Lorenzen dialogue extended with why-because dialogue, SAFA: Systems and Algorithms for Formal Argumentation 2024. CEUR Workshop Proceedings, pp. 90–103, 2024 (2024)
13. Troelstra, A.S., Schwichtenberg, H.: Basic Proof Theory, 2nd edition, Cambridge University Press (2000)
14. Walton, D., Krabbe, E.: Commitment in Dialogue: Basic Concepts of Interpersonal Reasoning, Albany, NY. State University of New York Press, USA (1995)

On SCC-Recursiveness in Quantitative Argumentation

Zongshun Wang[iD] and Yuping Shen[✉][iD]

Institute of Logic and Cognition, Department of Philosophy,
Sun Yat-sen University, Guangzhou, China
wangzsh7@mail2.sysu.edu.cn, shyping@mail.sysu.edu.cn

Abstract. *Abstract argumentation* is a reasoning model for evaluating arguments based on various *semantics*. *SCC-recursiveness* is a sophisticated property of semantics that provides a general schema for characterizing semantics through the decomposition along *strongly connected components* (SCCs). While this property has been extensively explored in various qualitative frameworks, it has been relatively neglected in quantitative argumentation. To fill this gap, we demonstrate that this property is well-suited to *fuzzy extension semantics*, which is a quantitative generalization of classical semantics in *fuzzy argumentation frameworks* (FAF). We tailor the SCC-recursive schema to enable the characterization of fuzzy extension semantics through the recursive decomposition of FAF along its SCCs. Our contributions are twofold. Theoretically, we show that SCC-recursiveness provides an alternative approach to characterize fuzzy extension semantics, offering a deep understanding and better insight into these semantics. Practically, our schema provides a sound and complete algorithm for computing fuzzy extension semantics, which naturally reduces computational efforts when dealing with a large number of SCCs.

Keywords: Abstract Argumentation · Quantitative Argumentation · SCC-recursiveness

1 Introduction

Argumentation serves as a process for reasoning and decision-making in conflict situations, garnering significant attention in the field of Artificial Intelligence [11, 27]. Its applications span diverse domains, including reasoning with inconsistent information [29], decision making [3], explainable AI [37], etc.

Dung's seminal work on *argumentation framework* [17] (AF) is a well-studied formalism in argumentation theory. It abstracts argumentation scenarios as a directed graph whose nodes represent arguments and arrows represent attacks among arguments. In recent years, Dung's AF has been extensively explored in quantitative settings, leading to significant developments such as Fuzzy AF [15, 25, 34], Probabilistic AF [23, 26] and Weighted AF [12, 18]. These quantitative frameworks enrich the expressive power of classical AF by associating numerical values with arguments or attacks to capture uncertain information.

The evaluation of arguments is a central topic in argumentation literature, commonly achieved through various *semantics* [4]. For instance, the well-known *extension semantics* [17] are proposed for Dung's AF to identify sets of jointly accepted arguments, while *gradual semantics* [1,15,32] are developed for quantitative frameworks to calculate the *acceptability degree* of arguments. Moreover, investigating the properties of semantics is crucial for their understanding, comparison and computation [2,6,9,30].

SCC-recursiveness [7] is a sophisticated property of semantics that relies on the graph-theoretical notion of *strongly connected components* (SCCs). Its significance lies in providing a general schema for characterizing semantics through the recursive decomposition of AF along its SCCs. Research on this schema has attracted extensive interest in the literature. First, it has proven to be one of the most efficient methods to reduce computational efforts [8,13,14,21]. Second, it has become a widely recognized property in principle analysis [20,30,31,35]. Third, many new semantics based on this schema have been proposed to address problematic behavior [7,19]. Finally, it has been extended to many other frameworks, such as *ADF* [22], *SETAF* [20], and *Unrestricted AF* [10].

Despite substantial contributions on this topic, almost all existing research on SCC-recursiveness has been restricted to qualitative settings. In contrast, research in various quantitative settings, such as probabilistic, fuzzy or weighted, remains *open* for investigation [28]. This limitation significantly restricts the applicability of SCC-recursiveness. It raises the question of how to define an SCC-recursive scheme to characterize semantics in quantitative settings. One underlying challenge is that, in these frameworks, arguments are often evaluated based on the degree to which they can be accepted, which seems incompatible with the schema.

In this paper, we show that SCC-recursiveness is well-suited to *fuzzy extension semantics*, introduced in [34] to generalize classical extension semantics within *fuzzy argumentation frameworks* (FAF). We tailor the existing SCC-recursive schema to enable the characterization of fuzzy extension semantics—including *admissible*[1], *complete*, *grounded* and *preferred*—through the recursive decomposition of FAF along its SCCs. Our contributions are twofold. Theoretically, we show that SCC-recursiveness provides an alternative approach to characterize fuzzy extension semantics, offering a deep understanding and better insight into these semantics. Our approach also paves the way for exploring SCC-recursiveness in other quantitative frameworks. Practically, our schema provides a sound and complete algorithm for computing fuzzy extension semantics, underpinned by several key theorems. As illustrated by examples, this algorithm naturally reduces computational efforts when dealing with a large number of SCCs, laying an implementation foundation for real-world applications.

The remainder of the paper is structured as follows. Section 2 reviews some basic concepts. Section 3 establishes the basic theory of SCC-recursiveness in FAF. Section 4 demonstrates the SCC-recursive characterization of fuzzy

---

[1] Following [5], we adopt the term 'admissible semantics' for the convenience of presentation, even though it is not considered as a semantics in Dung's original work.

extension semantics. Section 5 uses an example to illustrate the SCC-recursive schema. Section 6 discusses related work and concludes the paper.

2 Preliminaries

2.1 Fuzzy Set Theory

Definition 1. ([36]) *A* fuzzy set *is a pair* (X, S) *in which X is a nonempty set called the* universe *and $S : X \to [0,1]$ is the associated* membership function. *For each $x \in X$, $S(x)$ is called the* grade of membership of x in X.

For convenience, when the universe X is fixed, a fuzzy set (X, S) is identified by its membership function S, which can be represented by a set of pairs (x, a) with $x \in X$ and $a \in [0, 1]$. We stipulate that all pairs $(x, 0)$ are omitted from S. For any $X' \subseteq X$, we denote by $S|_{X'}$ the *restriction* of S to X': for any $x \in X'$, $S|_{X'}(x) = S(x)$, and for any $x \notin X'$, $S|_{X'}(x) = 0$.

For instance, the following are fuzzy sets with universe $\{A, B, C\}$:

$$S_1 = \{(A, 0.5)\}, S_2 = \{(B, 0.8), (C, 1)\}, S_3 = \{(A, 0.8), (B, 0.8), (C, 1)\}.$$

Note that $S_1(A) = 0.5, S_1(B) = S_1(C) = S_2(A) = 0$, and in S_3 every element has a non-zero grade. Evidently, S_2 is the restriction of S_3 on $\{B, C\}$, i.e., $S_2 = S_3|_{\{B,C\}}$.

A *fuzzy point* is a fuzzy set containing a unique pair (x, a). We may identify a fuzzy point by its pair. For example, S_1 is a fuzzy point and identified by $(A, 0.5)$.

Let S_1 and S_2 be two fuzzy sets. Say S_1 is a *subset* of S_2, denoted by $S_1 \subseteq S_2$, if for any $x \in X$, $S_1(x) \le S_2(x)$. Conventionally, we write $(x, a) \in S$ if a fuzzy point (x, a) is a subset of S. Moreover, we shall use the following notations:

- the *union* of S_1 and S_2: $S_1 \cup S_2 = \{(x, \max\{S_1(x), S_2(x)\}) \mid x \in X\}$;
- the *intersection* of S_1 and S_2: $S_1 \cap S_2 = \{(x, \min\{S_1(x), S_2(x)\}) \mid x \in X\}$.

In the above example, $S_1(x) \le S_3(x)$ for each element x, thus fuzzy point S_1 is a subset of S_3, written as $(A, 0.5) \in S_3$. Similarly, it is easy to check: (i) $S_2 \subseteq S_3$; (ii) $S_2 \cup S_3 = \{(A, 0.8), (B, 0.8), (C, 1)\}$; (iii) $S_1 \cap S_3 = \{(A, 0.5)\}$.

2.2 Fuzzy Argumentation Frameworks

In this paper, we focus on *fuzzy argumentation framework* and its associated *fuzzy extension semantics* introduced in [34].

Definition 2. *A* fuzzy argumentation framework *(FAF) over a finite set of arguments $Args$ is a pair $\mathcal{F} = \langle \mathcal{A}, \mathcal{R} \rangle$ in which $\mathcal{A} : Args \to [0,1]$ and $\mathcal{R} : Args \times Args \to [0,1]$ are total functions.*

In the definition, $\mathcal{A}$ and $\mathcal{R}$ are fuzzy sets of arguments and attacks. $\mathcal{A}$ can be denoted by pairs $(A, \mathcal{A}(A))$ and $\mathcal{R}$ can be denoted by pairs $((A,B), \mathcal{R}(A,B))$ or simply $((A,B), \mathcal{R}_{AB})$. Moreover, we denote by $Att(A)$ the set of all attackers of A, i.e., $Att(A) = \{B \in Args \mid \mathcal{R}(B,A) > 0\}$. For instance, we depict an FAF over $Args = \{A, B, C\}$ in Fig. 1, where

$$\mathcal{F} = \langle \{(A, 0.8), (B, 0.7), (C, 0.9)\}, \{((A,B), 0.8), ((B,C), 0.9)\}\rangle.$$

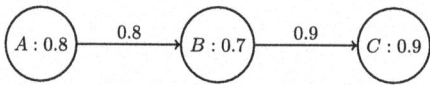

Fig. 1. A simple FAF

In the subsequent section, we apply a simple representation:

- (A, a) can be represented as A_a,
- $((A, B), r)$ can be represented as $A \xrightarrow{r} B$.

Therefore, the above FAF can be represented as

$$\mathcal{F} = \langle \{A_{0.8}, B_{0.7}, C_{0.9}\}, \{A \xrightarrow{0.8} B, B \xrightarrow{0.9} C\}\rangle.$$

While arguments with conflict cannot be accepted together in classical semantics, semantics in quantitative settings allow for a certain degree of tolerance for internal conflicts among arguments [15,18,23], enabling weak attacks to be ignored. We review the notion of *tolerable* attacks from [34].

Definition 3. *Suppose (A, a) attacks (B, b) w.r.t. $\mathcal{R}_{AB}$. Then the attack is tolerable if $a * \mathcal{R}_{AB} + b \leq 1$, otherwise it is sufficient. Here, $*$ is a shorthand s.t. $a * \mathcal{R}_{AB} = \min\{a, \mathcal{R}_{AB}\}$.*

Note that the degrees of the attacker and the attack relation are aggregated toward the attacker. Intuitively, a tolerable attack can be *ignored* and a sufficient attack *weakens* the attackee.

Definition 4. *Let (A, a) attacks (B, b) w.r.t. $\mathcal{R}_{AB}$. Then (A, a) weakens (B, b) to (B, b') where $b' = \min\{1 - a * \mathcal{R}_{AB}, b\}$, or precisely*

$$b' = \begin{cases} b & \text{if } a * \mathcal{R}_{AB} + b \leq 1, \\ 1 - a * \mathcal{R}_{AB} & \text{if } a * \mathcal{R}_{AB} + b > 1. \end{cases}$$

We say that S weakens (B, b) to (B, b') if $\exists (C, c) \in S$ weakens (B, b) to (B, b').

The notion of *weakening defence* and its associated characteristic function are reviewed below, indicating that a fuzzy set of arguments defends a fuzzy argument by weakening its attackers.

Definition 5. *A fuzzy set S weakening defends a fuzzy argument (A, a) iff, for any (B, b) that sufficiently attacks (A, a), S weakens (B, b) to $(B, b^{'})$ s.t. $(B, b^{'})$ tolerably attacks (A, a).*

Definition 6. *The characteristic function of an FAF $\mathcal{F} = \langle \mathcal{A}, \mathcal{R} \rangle$ is a function $F_{\mathcal{F}}$ from the set of all the subsets of $\mathcal{A}$ to itself, such that $\forall S \subseteq \mathcal{A}$, $F_{\mathcal{F}}(S) = \{(A, a) \in \mathcal{A} \mid S \text{ weakening defends } (A, a)\}$.*

The fuzzy extension semantics in [34] are reviewed as follows.

Definition 7. *Let $\mathcal{F} = \langle \mathcal{A}, \mathcal{R} \rangle$ be an FAF and $E \subseteq \mathcal{A}$ a fuzzy set.*

E is conflict-free *if all attacks in E are tolerable. Suppose E is conflict-free. Then we define:*

- *E is an* admissible *fuzzy extension if E weakening defends each element in E, i.e., $E \subseteq F_{\mathcal{F}}(E)$.*
- *E is a* complete *fuzzy extension if it is admissible and contains all the elements in $\mathcal{A}$ that E weakening defends, i.e., $E = F_{\mathcal{F}}(E)$.*
- *E is a* preferred *fuzzy extension if it is a maximal admissible fuzzy extension.*
- *E is the* grounded *fuzzy extension if it is the least fixed point of the characterization function $F_{\mathcal{F}}$.*

The set of fuzzy extensions under a given semantics $\mathcal{S}$ is denoted by $\mathcal{E}_{\mathcal{S}}(\mathcal{F})$.

As pointed out in [34], the stable and preferred fuzzy extensions coincide, so we omit the stable semantics. Intuitively, while classical extension semantics identify the arguments that can be accepted, fuzzy extension semantics quantify the degree to which arguments can be accepted—called the *acceptability degree*.

Example 1. *Continue considering the FAF depicted in Fig. 1. We compute a complete fuzzy extension E. Given that A has no attackers, we have $E(A) = \mathcal{A}(A) = 0.8$. Since B is weakened by A, it follows that $E(B) = 1 - E(A) * \mathcal{R}_{AB} = 0.2$. As B is weakened, C is weakening defended to the degree of 0.8, leading to $E(C) = 0.8$. Therefore, the acceptability degrees of A, B and C are 0.8, 0.2 and 0.8, respectively. Consequently, we obtain a complete fuzzy extension $\{(A, 0.8), (B, 0.2), (C, 0.8)\}$.*

3 SCC-Recursiveness in FAF

3.1 Graph Notations

The notion of SCC-recursiveness relies on the graph-theoretical notion of strongly connected components. To begin, we should integrate the graph notations into FAF.

Definition 8. *Let $\mathcal{F} = \langle \mathcal{A}, \mathcal{R} \rangle$ be an FAF over Args. Given an argument $A \in$ Args, we define the parent nodes of A as $par_{\mathcal{F}}(A) = \{B \mid \mathcal{R}(B, A) > 0\}$. A is called an* initial *node if $par_{\mathcal{F}}(A) = \varnothing$.*

Definition 9. *Let* $\mathcal{F} = \langle \mathcal{A}, \mathcal{R} \rangle$ *be an FAF over Args*, $A \in Args$ *and* $S, P \subseteq \mathcal{A}$. *We define that:*

- *S attacks A iff* $\exists B \in S$ *s.t.* $\mathcal{R}(B, A) > 0$;
- *A attacks S iff* $\exists B \in S$ *s.t.* $\mathcal{R}(A, B) > 0$;
- *S attacks P iff* $\exists A \in S$ *and* $\exists B \in P$ *s.t.* $\mathcal{R}(A, B) > 0$;
- $outpar_{\mathcal{F}}(S) = \{A \in Args \mid A \notin S \text{ and } A \text{ attacks } S\}$.

The notions of *path* and *path-equivalence* are defined as follows.

Definition 10. *Let* $\mathcal{F} = \langle \mathcal{A}, \mathcal{R} \rangle$ *be an FAF. We say that there is a* path *from A_1 to A_n iff there is a sequence* $\{A_1, A_2, ..., A_n\}$ *such that* $\mathcal{R}(A_i, A_{i+1}) > 0$ *for* $i \in \{1, ..., n-1\}$.

Definition 11. *Let* $\mathcal{F} = \langle \mathcal{A}, \mathcal{R} \rangle$ *be an FAF over Args. The binary relation of* path-equivalence *between nodes, denoted as* $PE_{\mathcal{F}} \subseteq Args \times Args$, *is defined as follows:*

- $\forall A \in Args, (A, A) \in PE_{\mathcal{F}}$;
- *given two distinct arguments* $A, B \in Args$, $(A, B) \in PE_{\mathcal{F}}$ *iff there is a path from A to B and a path from B to A.*

The notion of *strongly connected components* is defined as follows.

Definition 12. *Let* $\mathcal{F} = \langle \mathcal{A}, \mathcal{R} \rangle$ *be an FAF over Args. The equivalence classes under the path-equivalence relation are called* strongly connected components (SCCs) *of $\mathcal{F}$. We denote the set of SCCs of $\mathcal{F}$ by $SCCS_{\mathcal{F}}$. Given an argument $A \in Args$, the SCC that A belongs to is denoted as* $SCC_{\mathcal{F}}(A) = \{B \mid (A, B) \in PE_{\mathcal{F}}\}$.

We extend the notion of parents to SCCs, representing the set of other SCCs that attack a given SCC S as $sccpar_{\mathcal{F}}(S)$. Additionally, we introduce the concept of proper ancestors, denoted as $sccanc_{\mathcal{F}}(S)$.

Definition 13. *Let* $\mathcal{F} = \langle \mathcal{A}, \mathcal{R} \rangle$ *be an FAF and* $S \in SCCS_{\mathcal{F}}$. *We define*

$$sccpar_{\mathcal{F}}(S) = \{P \in SCCS_{\mathcal{F}} \mid P \neq S \text{ and } P \text{ attacks } S\}$$

$$sccanc_{\mathcal{F}}(S) = sccpar_{\mathcal{F}}(S) \cup \bigcup_{P \in sccpar_{\mathcal{F}}(S)} sccanc_{\mathcal{F}}(P)$$

An SCC S is called initial *if* $sccpar_{\mathcal{F}}(S) = \emptyset$.

For the purpose of decomposition, we introduce the notion of *restriction* of an FAF. Before the formal definition, consider attacks that are *always* tolerable. For instance, given an FAF $\mathcal{F} : A_{0.3} \xrightarrow{1.0} B_{0.2}$, it is evident that $\mathcal{A}(A) * R(A, B) + \mathcal{A}(B) = 0.3 * 1 + 0.2 \leq 1$, indicating that this attack is always tolerable in $\mathcal{F}$. We eliminate such always tolerable attacks when obtaining the restricted subframeworks from an FAF.

Definition 14. *Let $\mathcal{F} = \langle \mathcal{A}, \mathcal{R} \rangle$ be an FAF over Args and $\mathcal{A}' \subseteq \mathcal{A}$ a fuzzy set. The restriction of $\mathcal{F}$ to $\mathcal{A}'$ is the sub-framework $\mathcal{F}\downarrow_{\mathcal{A}'} = \langle \mathcal{A}', \mathcal{R}' \rangle$ where $\mathcal{R}'$ satisfies that*

- *if $\mathcal{A}'(A) * \mathcal{R}(A,B) + \mathcal{A}'(B) > 1$, then $\mathcal{R}'(A,B) = \mathcal{R}(A,B)$;*
- *otherwise $\mathcal{R}'(A,B) = 0$.*

For simplicity of discussion, we assume that the original FAF contains no always tolerable attacks in the subsequent discussion.

3.2 Basic Theory

While the idea behind SCC-recursiveness is intuitive and natural, the initial formalization of its required notions may seem quite complex due to its recursive nature. Therefore, we clarify its basic idea in this section.[2] In the following, we consider a generic FAF $\mathcal{F} = \langle \mathcal{A}, \mathcal{R} \rangle$ and a semantics $\mathcal{S} \in \{admissible, complete, preferred, grounded\}$.

To start, let us treat SCCs as single nodes. Then any FAF can be viewed as a directed acyclic graph; that is, the attack relation induces a partial order among the SCCs. Furthermore, we showed in [33] that the acceptability degree of an argument depends on its ancestor nodes under semantics $\mathcal{S}$. This implies that semantics can be computed following the sequence of SCCs. We begin by computing semantics for an initial SCC $\hat{S}$. To achieve this, we examine the sub-framework over $\hat{S}$ by restricting $\mathcal{F}$ to $\mathcal{A}|_{\hat{S}}$. The semantics of this sub-framework are processed by a *base function*, denoted as $\mathcal{BF}_\mathcal{S}$, which is defined to return the set of all fuzzy extensions under semantics $\mathcal{S}$.

Now, we arrive at the crucial problem: how to compute semantics for a given SCC S after computing its ancestor SCCs. Suppose $A \in S$ and $E \in \mathcal{E}_\mathcal{S}(\mathcal{F})$. Let $\max\limits_{B \in outpar_\mathcal{F}(S)} E(B) * \mathcal{R}_{BA} = \tilde{a}$. Then A is weakened to the lesser of $1 - \tilde{a}$ or $\mathcal{A}(A)$. Following Definition 5, only A's unweakened degree can influence its target arguments within S. This implies that we only need to consider a restricted sub-framework over S where arguments with the unweakened degree, e.g., the lesser of $1 - \tilde{a}$ or $\mathcal{A}(A)$ for A. Note that the relevant attacks may be suppressed when obtaining the restricted sub-framework, leading to the recursive decomposition of SCCs. Furthermore, an argument can be accepted to some degree only if it can be defended to that degree. Therefore, it is necessary to identify the degree to which an argument can be defended by E from outside S. Consequently, we can distinguish three components:

- *Weakened Component*, denoted as $W_\mathcal{F}(S,E)$, which represents the weakened degree of arguments in S by the ancestor SCCs.
- *Restricted Component*, denoted as $R_\mathcal{F}(S,E)$, which represents the unweakened degree of arguments in S.

---

[2] Referring to the example provided in Sect. 5 helps in understanding the concepts in this section.

- *Defended Component*, denoted as $D_{\mathcal{F}}(S, E)$, a subset of $R_{\mathcal{F}}(S, E)$ that represents the degree to which an argument can be defended by E from outside S.

Definition 15. *Let $\mathcal{F} = \langle \mathcal{A}, \mathcal{R} \rangle$ be an FAF, $E \subseteq \mathcal{A}$ and $S \in SCCS_{\mathcal{F}}$. We define that*

$$W_{\mathcal{F}}(S, E) = \{(A, a) \mid A \in S, a = \max_{B \in outpar_{\mathcal{F}}(S)} E(B) * \mathcal{R}_{BA}\}$$
$$R_{\mathcal{F}}(S, E) = \{(A, a) \mid A \in S, a = \min\{1 - W_{\mathcal{F}}(S, E)(A), \mathcal{A}(A)\}\}$$
$$D_{\mathcal{F}}(S, E) = \{(A, a) \mid A \in S, \forall B \in outpar_{\mathcal{F}}(S), E \text{ weakens } (B, \mathcal{A}(B)) \text{ to}$$
$$(B, b) \text{ that tolerably attacks } (A, a)\}.$$

From the above discussion, the computation of semantics over S depends on the restricted sub-framework $\mathcal{F}\downarrow_{R_{\mathcal{F}}(S,E)}$ and $D_{\mathcal{F}}(S, E)$. For the purpose of computation, we define a *generic function*, denoted as $\mathcal{GF}$, where

- input: a (possibly restricted) FAF $\mathcal{F} = \langle \mathcal{A}, \mathcal{R} \rangle$ and a fuzzy set C;
- output: a set of subsets of C.

We will use the notation $\mathcal{GF}(\mathcal{F}, C)$ for the generic function, which is defined as follows. If $\mathcal{F}$ consists of exactly one SCC, then $\mathcal{GF}(\mathcal{F}, C)$ coincides with a *base function* $\mathcal{BF}_{\mathcal{S}}(\mathcal{F}, C)$, which is defined to obtain the fuzzy extensions of $\mathcal{F}$ contained in C under semantics $\mathcal{S}$.[3] On the other hand, if $\mathcal{F}$ can be decomposed into several SCCs, then $\mathcal{GF}(\mathcal{F}, C)$ is obtained by recursively applying $\mathcal{GF}$ to each SCC of $\mathcal{F}$. Formally, this means that for any $S \in SCCS_{\mathcal{F}}$, $E|_S \in \mathcal{GF}(\mathcal{F}\downarrow_{R_{\mathcal{F}}(S,E)}, C')$, where C' represents the defended component. Note that C' is determined by considering both the attacks coming from outside $\mathcal{F}$ (as $\mathcal{F}$ is possibly restricted) and those coming from other SCCs within $\mathcal{F}$, yielding $C' = C \cap D_{\mathcal{F}}(S, E)$.

We now formally introduce SCC-recursiveness as a principle for fuzzy extension semantics.

Definition 16 (SCC-recursiveness). *A given semantics $\mathcal{S}$ is SCC-recursive iff for any FAF $\mathcal{F} = \langle \mathcal{A}, \mathcal{R} \rangle$, $\mathcal{E}_{\mathcal{S}}(\mathcal{F}) = \mathcal{GF}(\mathcal{F}, \mathcal{A})$, where for any $\mathcal{F} = \langle \mathcal{A}, \mathcal{R} \rangle$ and for any fuzzy set $C \subseteq \mathcal{A}$, the function $\mathcal{GF}(\mathcal{F}, C) \subseteq 2^{\mathcal{A}}$ is defined as follows: for any $E \subseteq \mathcal{A}$, $E \in \mathcal{GF}(\mathcal{F}, C)$ if and only if*

- *in case $|SCCS_{\mathcal{F}}| = 1$, $E \in \mathcal{BF}_{\mathcal{S}}(\mathcal{F}, C)$,*
- *otherwise, $\forall S \in SCCS_{\mathcal{F}}$, $E|_S \in \mathcal{GF}(\mathcal{F}\downarrow_{R_{\mathcal{F}}(S,E)}, D_{\mathcal{F}}(S, E) \cap C)$,*

where $\mathcal{BF}_{\mathcal{S}}(\mathcal{F}, C)$ is a function, called base function, *that, given an FAF $\mathcal{F} = \langle \mathcal{A}, \mathcal{R} \rangle$ s.t. $|SCCS_{\mathcal{F}}| = 1$ and a fuzzy set $C \subseteq \mathcal{A}$, gives a subset of $2^{\mathcal{A}}$.*

As noticed before, the generic function $\mathcal{GF}(\mathcal{F}, C)$ is recursively defined. The base of the recursion is given by the base function $\mathcal{BF}_{\mathcal{S}}(\mathcal{F}, C)$, which returns

---

[3] Note that this base function covers the previous case for computing the semantics of initial SCCs.

the results for $\mathcal{F}$ consisting of a single SCC. When $\mathcal{F}$ consists of more than one SCC, the recursive step involves a decomposition schema along its SCCs. Consequently, to show that a semantics is SCC-recursive, it suffices to identify its base function and demonstrate that it fits the decomposition schema.

The definition naturally provides a schema for computing SCC-recursive semantics. Consider a generic FAF $\mathcal{F} = \langle \mathcal{A}, \mathcal{R} \rangle$ over $Args$. First, for any initial SCC S, we have $R_\mathcal{F}(S, E) = D_\mathcal{F}(S, E) = \mathcal{A}|_S$. The restricted sub-framework over S is $\mathcal{F}\!\downarrow_{\mathcal{A}|_S}$, which clearly consists of a unique SCC. Then the base function $\mathcal{BF}_\mathcal{S}(\mathcal{F}\!\downarrow_{\mathcal{A}|_S}, \mathcal{A}|_S)$ is invoked, returning the set of fuzzy extensions of $\mathcal{F}\!\downarrow_{\mathcal{A}|_S}$ under semantics $\mathcal{S}$. The results are then utilized to identify the restricted sub-frameworks in subsequent SCCs. This procedure is recursively invoked and can be summarized as follows:

1. A (possibly restricted) FAF is partitioned into its SCCs; they form a partial order induced by the attack relation.
2. The set of fuzzy extensions over each initial SCC is determined using a semantic-specific base function.
3. For each fuzzy extension determined at step 2, the restricted and defended components within subsequent SCCs are identified; then the associated restricted sub-framework is taken into account.
4. The steps 1–3 are applied recursively on the restricted FAF obtained at step 3.

4 SCC-Recursive Characterization of Semantics

4.1 Generalized Fuzzy Extension Semantics

In order to develop an SCC-recursive characterization of semantics, it is necessary to redefine fuzzy extension semantics with reference to a specific subset C. In the following, we consider a generic FAF $\mathcal{F} = \langle \mathcal{A}, \mathcal{R} \rangle$ and a fuzzy set $C \subseteq \mathcal{A}$. The notion of admissible fuzzy extension in C is defined as follows.

Definition 17. *A fuzzy set $E \subseteq \mathcal{A}$ is an admissible fuzzy extension in C iff $E \subseteq C$ and $E \in \mathcal{AE}(\mathcal{F})$. The set of admissible fuzzy extensions in C is denoted as $\mathcal{AE}(\mathcal{F}, C)$.*

We introduce the notions of complete and preferred fuzzy extensions in C.

Definition 18. *A fuzzy set E is a complete fuzzy extension in C iff $E \in \mathcal{AE}(\mathcal{F}, C)$, and it contains all the elements in C that E weakening defend. The set of complete fuzzy extensions in C is denoted as $\mathcal{CE}(\mathcal{F}, C)$.*

Definition 19. *A preferred fuzzy extension in C is a maximal element of $\mathcal{AE}(\mathcal{F}, C)$. The set of preferred fuzzy extensions in C is denoted as $\mathcal{PE}(\mathcal{F}, C)$.*

The following proposition shows that preferred fuzzy extensions always exist for any FAF $\mathcal{F} = \langle \mathcal{A}, \mathcal{R} \rangle$ and for any $C \subseteq \mathcal{A}$.

Proposition 1. *Given an FAF $\mathcal{F} = \langle \mathcal{A}, \mathcal{R} \rangle$ and a fuzzy set $C \subseteq \mathcal{A}$, there is always a preferred fuzzy extension $E \in \mathcal{PE}(\mathcal{F}, C)$.*

Proposition 2 shows that a preferred fuzzy extension in C is also complete in C.

Proposition 2. *A preferred fuzzy extension in C is also complete in C.*

Definition 20. *The* characteristic function *of $\mathcal{F}$ in C is defined as follows:*

- $F_{(\mathcal{F},C)} : 2^C \to 2^C$
- $F_{(\mathcal{F},C)}(S) = \{(A,a) \mid (A,a) \in C, (A,a) \text{ is weakening defended by } S\}$.

It is easy to see that $F_{(\mathcal{F},C)}$ is monotonic w.r.t. fuzzy set inclusion. Then the grounded fuzzy extension in C can be defined in terms of the least fixed point of the characteristic function in C.

Definition 21. *The* grounded fuzzy extension in C, *denoted as $GE(\mathcal{F}, C)$, is the least fixed point of $F_{(\mathcal{F},C)}$.*

The following proposition demonstrates that the grounded fuzzy extension always exists and is unique for any FAF $\mathcal{F} = \langle \mathcal{A}, \mathcal{R} \rangle$ and any $C \subseteq \mathcal{A}$.

Proposition 3. *For any FAF $\mathcal{F} = \langle \mathcal{A}, \mathcal{R} \rangle$ and any $C \subseteq \mathcal{A}$, $GE(\mathcal{F}, C)$ exists and is unique.*

Proposition 4 states that the grounded fuzzy extension in C is also the least complete fuzzy extension in C.

Proposition 4. *$GE(\mathcal{F}, C)$ is the least complete fuzzy extension in C.*

Since the original version of fuzzy extension semantics is recovered by letting $C = \mathcal{A}$, the generalized definition covers the original ones.

4.2 SCC-Recursiveness of Fuzzy Extension Semantics

We first establish that admissible semantics fit the decomposition schema along SCCs. The characterization serves as the foundation for analyzing other semantics. This is achieved by Theorem 1, which requires two preliminary lemmas.

Lemma 1. *Let $\mathcal{F} = \langle \mathcal{A}, \mathcal{R} \rangle$ be an FAF and E be an admissible fuzzy extension. Suppose $(A, a) \in F_{\mathcal{F}}(E)$, denoting $SCC_{\mathcal{F}}(A)$ as S, then it holds that:*

- $(A, a) \in D_{\mathcal{F}}(S, E)$;
- (A, a) *is weakening defended by $E|_S$ in $\mathcal{F} \downarrow_{R_{\mathcal{F}}(S,E)}$.*

Lemma 2. *Given an FAF $\mathcal{F} = \langle \mathcal{A}, \mathcal{R} \rangle$, let $E \subseteq \mathcal{A}$ be a fuzzy set s.t. $\forall S \in SCCS_{\mathcal{F}}$, $E|_S \in \mathcal{AE}(\mathcal{F} \downarrow_{R_{\mathcal{F}}(S,E)}, D_{\mathcal{F}}(S, E))$. Then for any $\hat{S} \in SCCS_{\mathcal{F}}$ and any $(A, a) \in D_{\mathcal{F}}(\hat{S}, E)$, if (A, a) is weakening defended by $E|_{\hat{S}}$ in $\mathcal{F} \downarrow_{R_{\mathcal{F}}(\hat{S},E)}$, then (A, a) is weakening defended by E in $\mathcal{F}$.*

Theorem 1. *Given an FAF $\mathcal{F} = \langle \mathcal{A}, \mathcal{R} \rangle$ and a fuzzy set $E \subseteq \mathcal{A}$, it holds that: $\forall C \subseteq \mathcal{A}$, $E \in \mathcal{AE}(\mathcal{F}, C)$ if and only if $\forall S \in SCCS_\mathcal{F}$,*

$$E|_S \in \mathcal{AE}(\mathcal{F} \downarrow_{R_\mathcal{F}(S,E)}, D_\mathcal{F}(S,E) \cap C).$$

The following theorem shows that complete semantics also fit the decomposition schema.

Theorem 2. *Given an FAF $\mathcal{F} = \langle \mathcal{A}, \mathcal{R} \rangle$ and a fuzzy set $E \subseteq \mathcal{A}$, it holds that: $\forall C \subseteq \mathcal{A}$, $E \in \mathcal{CE}(\mathcal{F}, C)$ if and only if $\forall S \in SCCS_\mathcal{F}$,*

$$E|_S \in \mathcal{CE}(\mathcal{F} \downarrow_{R_\mathcal{F}(S,E)}, D_\mathcal{F}(S,E) \cap C).$$

Next, we demonstrate that preferred semantics also fit the decomposition schema, as shown by Theorem 3 based on the following lemma.

Lemma 3. *Let $\mathcal{F} = \langle \mathcal{A}, \mathcal{R} \rangle$ be an FAF, $E \in \mathcal{AE}(\mathcal{F})$ and $S \in SCCS_\mathcal{F}$. Then for any $\hat{E} \subseteq \mathcal{A}$, if $\hat{E}$ satisfies the following conditions:*

- *$E|_S \subseteq \hat{E} \subseteq D_\mathcal{F}(S, E)$, and*
- *$\hat{E}$ is admissible in $\mathcal{F} \downarrow_{R_\mathcal{F}(S,E)}$, i.e., $\hat{E} \in \mathcal{AE}(\mathcal{F} \downarrow_{R_\mathcal{F}(S,E)})$,*

then $E \cup \hat{E}$ is admissible in $\mathcal{F}$.

Theorem 3. *Given an FAF $\mathcal{F} = \langle \mathcal{A}, \mathcal{R} \rangle$ and a fuzzy set $E \subseteq \mathcal{A}$, it holds that: $\forall C \subseteq \mathcal{A}$, $E \in \mathcal{PE}(\mathcal{F}, C)$ if and only if $\forall S \in SCCS_\mathcal{F}$,*

$$E|_S \in \mathcal{PE}(\mathcal{F} \downarrow_{R_\mathcal{F}(S,E)}, D_\mathcal{F}(S,E) \cap C).$$

Finally, we prove that the grounded semantics also fit the decomposition schema, as shown by the following Theorem 4.

Theorem 4. *Given an FAF $\mathcal{F} = \langle \mathcal{A}, \mathcal{R} \rangle$ and a fuzzy set $E \subseteq \mathcal{A}$, it holds that: $\forall C \subseteq \mathcal{A}$, $E = GE(\mathcal{F}, C)$ if and only if $\forall S \in SCCS_\mathcal{F}$,*

$$E|_S = GE(\mathcal{F} \downarrow_{R_\mathcal{F}(S,E)}, D_\mathcal{F}(S,E) \cap C).$$

On the basis of the above theorems, we characterize that admissible, complete, preferred, and grounded fuzzy extension semantics are SCC-recursive by identifying the base functions in the theorem below.

Theorem 5 (SCC-recursive Characterization). *The admissible, complete, preferred and grounded semantics are SCC-recursive, characterized by the following base functions:*

- *$\mathcal{BF}_{\mathcal{AD}}(\mathcal{F}, C) \equiv \mathcal{AE}(\mathcal{F}, C)$;*
- *$\mathcal{BF}_{\mathcal{CO}}(\mathcal{F}, C) \equiv \mathcal{CE}(\mathcal{F}, C)$;*
- *$\mathcal{BF}_{\mathcal{PR}}(\mathcal{F}, C) \equiv \mathcal{PE}(\mathcal{F}, C)$;*
- *$\mathcal{BF}_{\mathcal{GR}}(\mathcal{F}, C) \equiv \{GE(\mathcal{F}, C)\}$.*

5 Illustrating Example for SCC-Recursive Schema

In this section, we use an example to illustrate the process of computing semantics using the SCC-recursive schema. Each FAF is recursively decomposed into many reduced sub-frameworks along the SCCs, enabling the efficient computation of the semantics of the original FAF based on these reduced sub-frameworks.

Example 2. *Consider an FAF $\mathcal{F} = \langle \mathcal{A}, \mathcal{R} \rangle$ depicted in Fig. 2, where*

$\mathcal{A} = \{A_{0.8}, B_{0.8}, C_{0.6}, D_{0.9}, E_{0.8}, F_{0.8}, G_{1.0}, H_{1.0}, I_{1.0}\}$

$\mathcal{R} = \{A \xrightarrow{1.0} B, B \xrightarrow{1.0} A, B \xrightarrow{1.0} C, C \xrightarrow{1.0} D, D \xrightarrow{1.0} E, E \xrightarrow{1.0} F, F \xrightarrow{1.0} C, C \xrightarrow{1.0} E,$
$D \xrightarrow{1.0} G, E \xrightarrow{1.0} I, G \xrightarrow{1.0} I, I \xrightarrow{1.0} G, G \xrightarrow{1.0} H, H \xrightarrow{1.0} G, I \xrightarrow{1.0} H\}$

In this example, we compute a preferred fuzzy extension E of $\mathcal{F}$. First, $\mathcal{F}$ can be partitioned into three SCCs: $S_1 = \{A, B\}$, $S_2 = \{C, D, E, F\}$, $S_3 = \{G, H, I\}$. Subsequently, we compute E following the sequence of these SCCs.

For the initial SCC $S_1 = \{A, B\}$, it is easy to see that

$$D_\mathcal{F}(S_1, E) = R_\mathcal{F}(S_1, E) = \{(A, 0.8), (B, 0.8)\},$$

yielding the first sub-framework by restricting $\mathcal{F}$ to $R_\mathcal{F}(S_1, E)$:

$$\mathcal{F}_1 = \mathcal{F} \downarrow_{R_\mathcal{F}(S_1, E)} = \langle \{A_{0.8}, B_{0.8}\}, \{A \xrightarrow{1.0} B, B \xrightarrow{1.0} A\} \rangle.$$

Since $|SCCS_{\mathcal{F}_1}| = 1$, the base function $\mathcal{BF}_{\mathcal{PR}}$ is invoked. There are many results for selection, which potentially lead to different decomposition. We choose $E|_{S_1} = \{(A, 0.2), (B, 0.8)\}$ for illustration.

Next, we consider the SCC $S_2 = \{C, D, E, F\}$. Given that S_1 attacks S_2 and $E|_{S_1} = \{(A, 0.2), (B, 0.8)\}$, we have

$$R_\mathcal{F}(S_2, E) = D_\mathcal{F}(S_2, E) = \{(C, 0.2), (D, 0.9), (E, 0.8), (F, 0.8)\}.$$

Evidently, the attacks from $(C, 0.2)$ to $(E, 0.8)$ and $(F, 0.8)$ to $(C, 0.2)$ are always tolerable, and therefore according to Definition 14, the restriction of $\mathcal{F}$ to $R_\mathcal{F}(S_2, E)$ is

$$\mathcal{F}_2 = \mathcal{F} \downarrow_{R_\mathcal{F}(S_2, E)} = \langle \{C_{0.2}, D_{0.9}, E_{0.8}, F_{0.8}\}, \{C \xrightarrow{1.0} D, D \xrightarrow{1.0} E, E \xrightarrow{1.0} F\} \rangle.$$

Then $\mathcal{F}_2$ can be recursively decomposed into four SCCs: $S_{2_1} = \{C\}$, $S_{2_2} = \{D\}$, $S_{2_3} = \{E\}$, $S_{2_4} = \{F\}$. It can be concluded that

- *for S_{2_1}*
  - $R_{\mathcal{F}_2}(S_{2_1}, E|_{S_2}) = \{(C, 0.2)\};$
  - $D_{\mathcal{F}_2}(S_{2_1}, E|_{S_2}) \cap D_\mathcal{F}(S_2, E) = \{(C, 0.2)\};$
  - $\mathcal{F}_{2_1} = \mathcal{F}_2 \downarrow_{R_{\mathcal{F}_2}(S_{2_1}, E|_{S_2})} = \langle \{C_{0.2}\}, \varnothing \rangle;$
  - $E|_{S_{2_1}} = \{(C, 0.2)\}.$
- *for S_{2_2}*

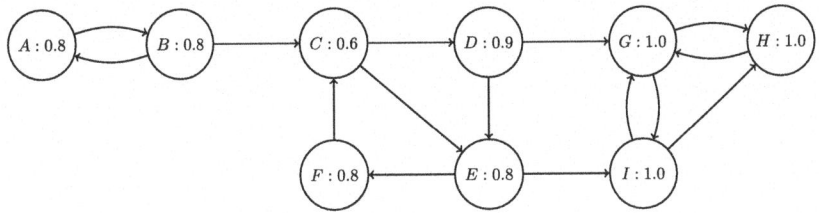
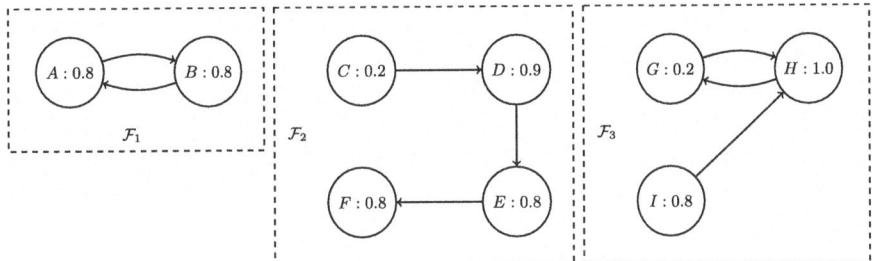
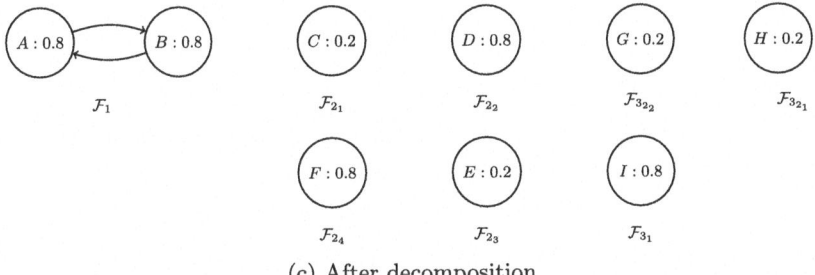

Fig. 2. SCC-recursive decomposition in Example 2

- $R_{\mathcal{F}_2}(S_{2_2}, E|_{S_2}) = \{(D, 0.8)\}$;
- $D_{\mathcal{F}_2}(S_{2_2}, E|_{S_2}) \cap D_{\mathcal{F}}(S_2, E) = \{(D, 0.8)\}$;
- $\mathcal{F}_{2_2} = \mathcal{F}_2 \downarrow_{R_{\mathcal{F}_2}(S_{2_2}, E|_{S_2})} = \langle \{D_{0.8}\}, \varnothing \rangle$;
- $E|_{S_{2_2}} = \{(D, 0.8)\}$.
- for S_{2_3}
  - $R_{\mathcal{F}_2}(S_{2_3}, E|_{S_2}) = \{(E, 0.2)\}$;
  - $D_{\mathcal{F}_2}(S_{2_3}, E|_{S_2}) \cap D_{\mathcal{F}}(S_2, E) = \{(E, 0.2)\}$;
  - $\mathcal{F}_{2_3} = \mathcal{F}_2 \downarrow_{R_{\mathcal{F}_2}(S_{2_3}, E|_{S_2})} = \langle \{E_{0.2}\}, \varnothing \rangle$;
  - $E|_{S_{2_3}} = \{(E, 0.2)\}$.
- for S_{2_4}

- $R_{\mathcal{F}_2}(S_{2_4}, E|_{S_2}) = \{(F, 0.8)\}$;
- $D_{\mathcal{F}_2}(S_{2_4}, E|_{S_2}) \cap D_{\mathcal{F}}(S_2, E) = \{(F, 0.8)\}$;
- $\mathcal{F}_{2_4} = \mathcal{F}_2 \downarrow_{R_{\mathcal{F}_2}(S_{2_4}, E|_{S_2})} = \langle \{F_{0.8}\}, \varnothing \rangle$;
- $E|_{S_{2_4}} = \{(F, 0.8)\}$.

Consequently, $E|_{S_2} = \{(C, 0.2), (D, 0.8), (E, 0.2), (F, 0.8)\}$.

As far as the SCC S_3 is concerned, from that S_2 attack S_3 and $E|_{S_2} = \{(C, 0.2), (D, 0.8), (E, 0.2), (F, 0.8)\}$, we derive that

$$R_{\mathcal{F}}(S_3, E) = D_{\mathcal{F}}(S_3, E) = \{(G, 0.2), (H, 1.0), (I, 0.8)\}.$$

Since the attacks between $(G, 0.2)$ and $(I, 0.8)$ are always tolerable, according to Definition 14, the restriction of $\mathcal{F}$ to $R_{\mathcal{F}}(S_3, E)$ is

$$\mathcal{F}_3 = \mathcal{F} \downarrow_{R_{\mathcal{F}}(S_3, E)} = \langle \{G_{0.2}, H_{1.0}, I_{0.8}\}, \{G \xrightarrow{1.0} H, H \xrightarrow{1.0} G, I \xrightarrow{1.0} H\} \rangle.$$

Similarly, $\mathcal{F}_3$ can be recursively decomposed into two SCCs: $S_{3_1} = \{I\}$, $S_{3_2} = \{G, H\}$.

- For S_{3_1}
  - $R_{\mathcal{F}_3}(S_{3_1}, E|_{S_3}) = \{(I, 0.8)\}$;
  - $D_{\mathcal{F}_3}(S_{3_1}, E|_{S_3}) \cap D_{\mathcal{F}}(S_3, E) = \{(I, 0.8)\}$;
  - $\mathcal{F}_{3_1} = \mathcal{F}_3 \downarrow_{R_{\mathcal{F}_3}(S_{3_1}, E|_{S_3})} = \langle \{I_{0.8}\}, \varnothing \rangle$;
  - $E|_{S_{3_1}} = \{(I, 0.8)\}$.

For S_{3_2}, since S_{3_1} attacks S_{3_2} and $E|_{S_{3_1}} = \{(I, 0.8)\}$, we obtain

$$R_{\mathcal{F}_3}(S_{3_2}, E|_{S_3}) = D_{\mathcal{F}_3}(S_{3_2}, E|_{S_3}) = \{(G, 0.2), (H, 0.2)\}.$$

Clearly the attacks between $(G, 0.2)$ and $(H, 0.2)$ are always tolerable, therefore, the restriction of $\mathcal{F}_3$ to $R_{\mathcal{F}}(S_{3_2}, E|_{S_3})$ is

$$\mathcal{F}_{3_2} = \mathcal{F}_3 \downarrow_{R_{\mathcal{F}_3}(S_{3_2}, E|_{S_3})} = \langle \{G_{0.2}, H_{0.2}\}, \varnothing \rangle.$$

Then $\mathcal{F}_{3_2}$ can be recursively partitioned into $S_{3_{2_1}} = \{H\}$ and $S_{3_{2_2}} = \{G\}$. Similar to the above analysis, we derive that

- for $S_{3_{2_1}}$
  - $R_{\mathcal{F}_{3_2}}(S_{3_{2_1}}, E|_{S_{3_2}}) = \{(H, 0.2)\}$;
  - $D_{\mathcal{F}_{3_2}}(S_{3_{2_1}}, E|_{S_{3_2}}) \cap D_{\mathcal{F}_3}(S_{3_1}, E|_{S_3}) \cap D_{\mathcal{F}}(S_3, E) = \{(H, 0.2)\}$;
  - $\mathcal{F}_{3_{2_1}} = \mathcal{F}_{3_2} \downarrow_{R_{\mathcal{F}_{3_2}}(S_{3_{2_1}}, E|_{S_{3_2}})} = \langle \{H_{0.2}\}, \varnothing \rangle$;
  - $E|_{S_{3_{2_1}}} = \{(H, 0.2)\}$.
- for $S_{3_{2_2}}$
  - $R_{\mathcal{F}_{3_2}}(S_{3_{2_2}}, E|_{S_{3_2}}) = \{(G, 0.2)\}$;
  - $D_{\mathcal{F}_{3_2}}(S_{3_{2_2}}, E|_{S_{3_2}}) \cap D_{\mathcal{F}_3}(S_{3_1}, E|_{S_3}) \cap D_{\mathcal{F}}(S_3, E) = \{(G, 0.2)\}$;
  - $\mathcal{F}_{3_{2_2}} = \mathcal{F}_{3_2} \downarrow_{R_{\mathcal{F}_{3_2}}(S_{3_{2_2}}, E|_{S_{3_2}})} = \langle \{G_{0.2}\}, \varnothing \rangle$;
  - $E|_{S_{3_{2_2}}} = \{(G, 0.2)\}$.

Consequently, $E|_{S_3} = \{(G, 0.2), (H, 0.2), (I, 0.8)\}$.

As a result, the combination fuzzy extension

$$E = \{(A, 0.2), (B, 0.8), (C, 0.2), (D, 0.8), (E, 0.2), (F, 0.8), (G, 0.2), (H, 0.2), (I, 0.8)\}$$

is a preferred fuzzy extension of $\mathcal{F}$.

6 Discussion and Conclusion

SCC-recursiveness was proposed in [7] as a powerful schema for characterizing semantics through the decomposition of AF along SCCs. This schema has been extensively studied in the literature.

First, it has proven useful in developing algorithms for solving semantics. Cerutti et al. designed an SCC-recursive algorithm for computing preferred semantics in [13] and further exploited the parallel computation in [14]. Baroni et al. proposed an incremental computation algorithm for solving semantics in the dynamics of AF based on the schema [8].

Second, this schema has facilitated the exploration of new semantics. In [7], Baroni et al. proposed *CF2* and *AD2* semantics by incorporating the concept of *conflict-freeness* and *admissibility* with the SCC-recursive schema. In [19], Dvořák and Gaggl proposed *stage2* semantics by combining stage semantics with the schema.

Third, the feasibility of SCC-recursiveness for various semantics has attracted considerable attention. In [31], Villata et al. proposed the so-called *attack semantics* and defined an SCC-recursive schema for this semantics using *attack labelings*. In [16], Dauphin et al. demonstrated that the SCC-recursive schema is inapplicable to *weakly admissible, weakly complete* and *weakly grounded semantics*, whereas Dvořák et al. confirmed its applicability to *weakly preferred semantics* in [21].

Finally, the schema has also been extended to various qualitative frameworks. In [10], Baumann and Spanring investigated the schema in *unrestricted AF*. In [35], Yu et al. examined the schema in *abstract agent AF*. In [22], Gaggl et al. studied the schema in *abstract dialectical frameworks*. In [20], Dvořák et al. explored the schema in *AF with collective attacks*.

Despite these substantial contributions, the exploration of SCC-recursiveness in quantitative frameworks remains relatively underdeveloped. Although Rienstra et al. [28] explored *SCC-decomposability* in probabilistic argumentation, proposing a factorization scheme aligned with SCCs, the principle of SCC-recursiveness has not been formally addressed in that setting.

In this paper, we demonstrated that SCC-recursiveness can be applied to characterize fuzzy extension semantics in FAF. To achieve this, we tailored the existing SCC-recursive schema, enabling the characterization of fuzzy extension semantics—including *admissible, complete, grounded* and *preferred*—through the recursive decomposition of FAF along its SCCs. Our contributions are twofold. Theoretically, we showed that SCC-recursiveness provides an alternative approach to characterize fuzzy extension semantics, offering a deep understanding and better insight into these semantics. Practically, we provided a sound and complete algorithm for computing fuzzy extension semantics. As illustrated by the provided example, this algorithm naturally reduces computational efforts when dealing with a large number of SCCs.

Future research can take several directions. First, it is worth investigating the development of specific algorithms for computing fuzzy extension semantics based on the SCC-recursive schema. Second, utilizing the schema to explore new semantics in fuzzy AF offers significant potential. Third, investigating SCC-recursiveness in other quantitative settings, such as probabilistic AF [24], is a desirable endeavor.

Acknowledgments. We would like to thank the anonymous reviewers for their helpful and thoughtful feedback. This work was supported by the Fundamental Research Funds for the Central Universities, Sun Yat-sen University Grant (24WKJC07).

Disclosure of Interests. The authors have no competing interests to declare that are relevant to the content of this article.

Appendix

A full version including proofs can be found at https://arxiv.org/abs/2006.08880.

References

1. Amgoud, L., Ben-Naim, J., Doder, D., Vesic, S.: Acceptability semantics for weighted argumentation frameworks. In: Proceedings of the 26th International Joint Conference on Artificial Intelligence, IJCAI, pp. 56–62 (2017)
2. Amgoud, L., Doder, D., Vesic, S.: Evaluation of argument strength in attack graphs: foundations and semantics. Artif. Intell. **302**, 103607 (2022)
3. Amgoud, L., Prade, H.: Using arguments for making and explaining decisions. Artif. Intell. **173**(3–4), 413–436 (2009)
4. Baroni, P., Caminada, M., Giacomin, M.: An introduction to argumentation semantics. Knowl. Eng. Rev. **26**(4), 365–410 (2011)
5. Baroni, P., Caminada, M., Giacomin, M.: Abstract argumentation frameworks and their semantics. In: Handbook of Formal Argumentation, vol. 1, pp. 159–236. College Publications (2018)
6. Baroni, P., Giacomin, M.: On principle-based evaluation of extension-based argumentation semantics. Artif. Intell. **171**(10–15), 675–700 (2007)
7. Baroni, P., Giacomin, M., Guida, G.: SCC-recursiveness: a general schema for argumentation semantics. Artif. Intell. **168**(1–2), 162–210 (2005)
8. Baroni, P., Giacomin, M., Liao, B.: On topology-related properties of abstract argumentation semantics. a correction and extension to dynamics of argumentation systems: a division-based method. Artif. Intell. **212**, 104–115 (2014)
9. Baroni, P., Rago, A., Toni, F.: From fine-grained properties to broad principles for gradual argumentation: a principled spectrum. Int. J. Approx. Reason. **105**, 252–286 (2019)
10. Baumann, R., Spanring, C.: A study of unrestricted abstract argumentation frameworks. In: Proceedings of the 26th International Joint Conference on Artificial Intelligence, IJCAI, pp. 807–813 (2017)
11. Bench-Capon, T., Dunne, P.E.: Argumentation in artificial intelligence. Artif. Intell. **171**(10–15), 619–641 (2007)
12. Bistarelli, S., Santini, F.: Weighted argumentation. J. Appl. Logics - IfCoLog J. Logics Their Appl. **8**(6), 1589–1622 (2021)

13. Cerutti, F., Giacomin, M., Vallati, M., Zanella, M.: An SCC recursive meta-algorithm for computing preferred labellings in abstract argumentation. In: Proceedings of the 14th International Conference on the Principles of Knowledge Representation and Reasoning, KR, pp. 42–51 (2014)
14. Cerutti, F., Tachmazidis, I., Vallati, M., Batsakis, S., Giacomin, M., Antoniou, G.: Exploiting parallelism for hard problems in abstract argumentation. In: Proceedings of the 29th AAAI Conference on Artificial Intelligence, AAAI, pp. 1475–1481 (2015)
15. da Costa Pereira, C., Tettamanzi, A., Villata, S.: Changing one's mind: erase or rewind? Possibilistic belief revision with fuzzy argumentation based on trust. In: Proceedings of the 22nd International Joint Conference on Artificial Intelligence, IJCAI, pp. 164–171 (2011)
16. Dauphin, J., Rienstra, T., van der Torre, L.: A principle-based analysis of weakly admissible semantics. Proceedings of the 8th International Conference on Computational Models of Argument, COMMA, vol. 326, pp. 167 (2020)
17. Dung, P.: On the acceptability of arguments and its fundamental role in non-monotonic reasoning, logic programming and n-person games. Artif. Intell. **77**(2), 321–357 (1995)
18. Dunne, P., Hunter, A., McBurney, P., Parsons, S., Wooldridge, M.: Weighted argument systems: basic definitions, algorithms, and complexity results. Artif. Intell. **175**(2), 457–486 (2011)
19. Dvořák, W., Gaggl, S.: Stage semantics and the SCC-recursive schema for argumentation semantics. J. Log. Comput. **26**(4), 1149–1202 (2016)
20. Dvořák, W., König, M., Ulbricht, M., Woltran, S.: Principles and their computational consequences for argumentation frameworks with collective attacks. J. Artif. Intell. Res. **79**, 69–136 (2024)
21. Dvořák, W., Ulbricht, M., Woltran, S.: Recursion in abstract argumentation is hard–On the complexity of semantics based on weak admissibility. J. Artif. Intell. Res. **74**, 1403–1447 (2022)
22. Gaggl, S., Rudolph, S., Strass, H.: On the decomposition of abstract dialectical frameworks and the complexity of naive-based semantics. J. Artif. Intell. Res. **70**, 1–64 (2021)
23. Hunter, A.: A probabilistic approach to modelling uncertain logical arguments. Int. J. Approx. Reason. **54**(1), 47–81 (2013)
24. Hunter, A., Polberg, S., Potyka, N., Rienstra, T., Thimm, M.: Probabilistic argumentation: a survey. In: Handbook of Formal Argumentation, vol. 2, pp. 397–441. College Publications (2021)
25. Janssen, J., De Cock, M., Vermeir, D.: Fuzzy argumentation frameworks. In: Proceedings of the 12th Information Processing and Management of Uncertainty in Knowledge-based Systems, IPMU, pp. 513–520 (2008)
26. Li, H., Oren, N., Norman, T.: Probabilistic argumentation frameworks. In: Proceedings of the 1st International Workshop on Theorie and Applications of Formal Argumentation, TAFA, pp. 1–16 (2011)
27. Rahwan, I., Simari, G.R.: Argumentation in Artificial Intelligence. Springer (2009). https://doi.org/10.1007/978-0-387-98197-0
28. Rienstra, T., Thimm, M., Liao, B., van der Torre, L.: Probabilistic abstract argumentation based on SCC decomposability. In: Proceedings of the 16th International Conference on Principles of Knowledge Representation and Reasoning, KR, pp. 168–177 (2018)
29. Simari, G., Loui, R.: A mathematical treatment of defeasible reasoning and its implementation. Artif. Intell. **53**(2–3), 125–157 (1992)

30. van der Torre, L., Vesic, S.: The principle-based approach to abstract argumentation semantics. IfCoLog J. Logics Their Appl. **4**(8), 2735–2778 (2017)
31. Villata, S., Boella, G., van der Torre, L.: Attack semantics for abstract argumentation. In: Proceedings of the 22nd International Joint Conference on Artificial Intelligence, IJCAI, pp. 406–413 (2011)
32. Wang, Z., Shen, Y.: Bilateral gradual semantics for weighted argumentation. In: Proceedings of the 38th AAAI Conference on Artificial Intelligence, AAAI, pp. 10732–10739 (2024)
33. Wang, Z., Shen, Y.: Fuzzy labelling semantics for quantitative argumentation. J. Logic Comput. **35**, **exaf009** (2025)
34. Wu, J., Li, H., Oren, N., Norman, T.: Gödel fuzzy argumentation frameworks. In: Proceedings of the 6th International Conference on Computational Models of Argument, COMMA, pp. 447–458 (2016)
35. Yu, L., Chen, D., Qiao, L., Shen, Y., van der Torre, L.: A principle-based analysis of abstract agent argumentation semantics. In: Proceedings of the 18th International Conference on Principles of Knowledge Representation and Reasoning, KR, pp. 629–639 (2021)
36. Zadeh, L.: Fuzzy sets. Inf. Control **8**(3), 338–353 (1965)
37. Čyras, K., Rago, A., Albini, E., Baroni, P., Toni, F.: Argumentative XAI: A survey. In: Proceedings of the 30th International Joint Conference on Artificial Intelligence, IJCAI, pp. 4392–4399 (2021)

Six Faces of Or-to-If

Xuefeng Wen(✉)

Institute of Logic and Cognition, Sun Yat-sen University, Guangzhou, China
wxflogic@gmail.com

Abstract. We examine the Or-to-If inference (also known as the Direct Argument), which infers $\neg\varphi \to \psi$ from $\varphi \vee \psi$. While this inference is valid in classical logic, it has sparked considerable debate in conditional logic. We advocate for a pluralistic conception of validity, arguing that our intuitions about validity are inherently ambiguous and can be systematically analyzed through distinct theoretical notions. The various notions of validity proposed arise from different treatments of premises (as beliefs, assertions, or assumptions), which yields three distinct forms of validity. Together with the differentiation between indicative and subjunctive conditionals, our semantic framework ultimately generates six variants of Or-to-If. We also show how the three notions of validity can be unified into one notion, by treating a logical consequence as a 4-ary relation, or by expressing the differently treated premises explicitly in the object language. This refined approach enables a precise characterization of the specific conditions under which Or-to-If holds or fails. While the paper focuses primarily on Or-to-If, the proposed pluralistic framework shows promise in reconciling the often-observed divergence between formal logical systems and concrete reasoning practices in natural language.

Keywords: Or-to-If · The direct argument · Conditional logic · Validity · Entailment · Logical consequence · Indicative conditionals · Subjunctive conditionals

1 Introduction

The Or-to-If inference, also known as the Direct Argument, is the rule that infers $\neg\varphi \to \psi$ from $\varphi \vee \psi$.[1] Although it is uncontroversially valid in classical logic, it has sparked considerable debate in conditional logic, especially when $\varphi \to \psi$ is intended to represent indicative conditionals in natural-language.

Motivated by the notorious paradox of material implication, conditional logic, pioneered by Stalnaker [17], Lewis [12], and Adams [1], aims to provide a nonclassical interpretation of conditionals, one that better reflects inference patterns in natural language. In conditional logic, the statement $\varphi \to \psi$ is not equivalent to the material conditional $\varphi \supset \psi$. Consequently, many principles and rules that hold for $\varphi \supset \psi$ do not extend to $\varphi \to \psi$. For instance, the inference $\psi \vDash \varphi \to \psi$ and $\neg\varphi \vDash \varphi \to \psi$ fail in conditional logic, which is arguably desirable, as we

---

[1] The label "Or-to-If" is attributed to Jonathan Bennett, possibly first used in [3].

usually do not regard a conditional as true merely because its consequent is true or its antecedent is false.

However, in disallowing these counterintuitive inferences, standard conditional logics also invalidate Or-to-If. This outcome appears to be an overcorrection, as Or-to-If is highly plausible. If we are presented with only two possibilities, then surely by excluding one we obtain the other. How can such a "direct" argument be invalid?[2]

From a formal perspective, conditional logic, aiming to provide a non-classical interpretation of conditionals, must invalidate Or-to-If. This stems from the fact that conditional logic validates Modus Ponens, namely $\varphi \to \psi, \varphi \vDash \psi$,[3] which in turn implies $\varphi \to \psi \vDash \varphi \supset \psi$. Or-to-If, together with Double Negation and Replacement of Equivalents, amounts to $\varphi \supset \psi \vDash \varphi \to \psi$. Consequently, accepting both Modus Ponens and Or-to-If collapse conditional implication into material implication. Since Modus Ponens is indispensable, Or-to-If has to be abandoned.

To address this tension between formal logic and intuitive reasoning, Stalnaker [18] proposes a pragmatic resolution by distinguishing between valid inferences and reasonable ones. He suggests that while certain inferences may not be formally valid, they can become reasonable when supplemented with appropriate pragmatic assumptions. Specifically, an inference is considered reasonable if, in any context where the premises can be asserted or assumed, a rational agent cannot consistently accept the premises while rejecting the conclusion. In this way, Stalnaker reconciles the tension by showing why Or-to-If, despite being formally invalid, remains intuitively compelling.

This paper proposes a purely semantic solution to the puzzle posed by Or-to-If. While Stalnaker maintains that semantics accommodates only one notion of validity, relegating intuitively compelling but logically invalid inferences to the realm of pragmatic reasonableness, we advocate for a pluralistic conception of validity. Our approach is motivated by the observation that our intuitions about validity are inherently ambiguous, a phenomenon that can be systematically analyzed through distinct theoretical notions of validity.

The various notions of validity we propose arise from different treatments of premises, as beliefs, assertions, or assumptions, which yields three distinct forms of validity. Furthermore, we differentiate between indicative and subjunctive conditionals, ultimately generating six variants of Or-to-If. This refined framework enables us not only to explain the apparent variability in the validity of Or-to-If, but also to precisely characterize the specific conditions under which it holds or fails.

While this paper focuses mainly on the specific inference form of Or-to-If, we contend that our pluralistic approach may provide a promising framework

---

[2] Note that Or-to-If is different from Disjunctive Syllogism, namely, $\varphi \lor \psi, \neg\varphi \vDash \psi$, which is valid in most conditional logics. Or-to-If would be valid if the deduction theorem holds. But the deduction theorem also fails in most conditional logics.

[3] Although Modus Ponens may fail in its general form in some conditional logics (e.g., [13]), it remains valid when both φ and ψ are Boolean formulas.

that could significantly reconcile the often-observed divergence between formal logical systems and concrete reasoning practices in natural language.

The rest of the paper is organized as follows. Section 2 gives some linguistic examples concerning the validity of Or-to-If and distinguishes three pre-theoretical notions of validity. Section 3 presents a formal semantics for both indicatives and subjunctives, based on which the three notions of validity are defined precisely. Section 4 applies the semantics, demonstrating that our semantic framework satisfies the linguistic desiderata of Or-to-If. Section 5 unifies the three notions of validity into a single one, by treating a logical consequence as a 4-ary relation. Section 6 extends the formal language so that differently treated premises in the meta-language can be expressed in the object language. Not only the six forms of Or-to-If can be reformulated in the new language, but a new form of Or-to-If can also be expressed in it. Section 7 concludes the paper and suggests some future work.

2 Linguistic Desiderata

Consider the following inference.

(1) Oswald killed Kennedy or someone else did it.
(2) Therefore, if Oswald did not kill Kennedy, then someone else did it.

Suppose we have not definitively confirmed Oswald's role in Kennedy's death, but rather believe that he killed Kennedy based on inconclusive evidence. Indeed, at this stage (imagine we are in the immediate aftermath of the incident), we cannot entirely rule out the possibility that Kennedy was not killed by anyone at all. Nevertheless, given our belief in Oswald's murder of Kennedy, we accept the truth of the premise (1). Does this imply that we should also accept the conclusion (2)? Obviously not.

In order to entertain the supposition that Oswald did not kill Kennedy, we must withdraw our previous belief. Under this supposition, we would have no grounds to maintain that Kennedy was killed by anyone, since our original belief in Kennedy's death was completely based on our belief in Oswald's involvement. Indeed, if Oswald did not kill Kennedy, it remains entirely possible that Kennedy was not killed at all. This is in principle the explanation why Or-to-If is invalid in standard conditional logics. In terms of Adams' notion of validity for conditionals [1], it is entirely possible that $\varphi \vee \psi$ has a high probability (or credence) while $\neg \varphi \rightarrow \psi$ remains low in probability (or credence).

But why do we find Or-to-If so compelling? The intuitive pull arises from treating the premise differently. Rather than viewing the premise as an uncertain belief, we regard it as a certain assertion. Under this reinterpretation, accepting (1) compels us to accept (2). After all, if we are certain that Kennedy was killed by someone, then it follows that, if the murderer was not Oswald, it must have been someone else.

Thus, the intuitive validity of Or-to-If stems from a distinct conception of validity, one that pivots not on the preservation of (contingent) truth or (uncertain) belief, but on the preservation of certainty. In other words, an inference is valid if, whenever we are certain of its premises, we must also be certain of its conclusion. This validity deviates from the standard truth-preservation one because we treat the premises as assertions. For clarity, let us denote these two notions of validity by Val_b (premises treated as beliefs) and Val_a (premises treated as assertions), respectively.

Let us now examine how the inference pattern changes when we reformulate our example using a subjunctive conditional.

(3) Oswald killed Kennedy or someone else did it.
(4) Therefore, if Oswald had not killed Kennedy, someone else would have done it.

As with the indicative case, this inference fails to be valid under Val_b. More interestingly, it is also invalid under Val_a, a notable distinction from its indicative counterpart. Even if we are absolutely certain of Kennedy's death as a historical fact, this occurrence represents a contingent event rather than a necessary one. When we entertain the counterfactual supposition that Oswald did not kill Kennedy, we must acknowledge the possibility that Kennedy might not have been killed at all.

This analysis reveals that the validity of Or-to-If depends not only on our chosen notion of validity but also on the type of conditionals employed in the inference. In the case of subjunctive conditionals, Or-to-If proves invalid under both Val_b and Val_a.

We now turn to examine how the validity of Or-to-If is affected when the premise is neither believed nor asserted, but rather assumed. Consider the following formulation.

(5) Suppose Oswald killed Kennedy or someone else did it.
(6) Then, if Oswald did not kill (had not killed) Kennedy, someone else did (would have done) it.

Remarkably, when the premise is treated as a supposition or assumption, as in (5), we find ourselves compelled to accept the conclusion, regardless of whether the conditional is formulated in the indicative or subjunctive mood. This observation leads us to introduce a third notion of validity, Val_s, which applies when premises are treated as assumptions.

The difference between supposition and beliefs or assertions is that the latter two are defeasible, whereas the former is not. In a context where we believed or asserted p, we could still consistently suppose $\neg p$. But in a context where we supposed p, we were no longer able to consistently suppose $\neg p$.[4] By supposing (5), even after introducing the antecedent of (6) as a new supposition, we are required to maintain the initial supposition, which forces us to the consequent of (6). This explains why Or-to-If is valid when the premise is assumed.

---

[4] Sometimes we may suppose p to derive q and suppose $\neg p$ to derive the same q. But the two suppositions are independent from each other, because they are not given in the same context. See [5, p. 538] for essentially the same differentiation between acceptance and supposition.

Through this analysis, we are about to establish a framework consisting of three distinct notions of validity (Val_b, Val_a, and Val_s) and two types of conditionals (indicative and subjunctive), yielding six forms of Or-to-If. Table 1 below summarizes which of these forms are intuitively valid or invalid.

Table 1. Linguistic Desiderata of Or-to-If

	Val_b	Val_a	Val_s
Indicatives	×	✓	✓
Subjunctives	×	×	✓

3 A Semantics for Conditionals

Given a set At of atomic formulas, our language $\mathcal{L}$ is given by the following BNF:

$$\mathcal{L} \ni \varphi ::= p \mid \neg\varphi \mid (\varphi \wedge \varphi) \mid (\varphi \vee \varphi) \mid (\varphi \rightarrow \varphi) \mid (\varphi \rightsquigarrow \psi),$$

where $p \in At$, $\varphi \rightarrow \psi$ and $\varphi \rightsquigarrow \psi$ represent indicative and subjunctive conditionals, respectively. The material conditional $\varphi \supset \psi$ is defined by $\neg\varphi \vee \psi$ as usual. A formula without indicatives or subjunctives is called Boolean.

Our semantic framework builds upon a slight modification of Stalnaker's selection models [17]. The core idea underlying our framework can be effectively implemented within alternative modeling frameworks, including Lewis' sphere systems [12]. To avoid introducing an "absurd world" as in Stalnaker's original semantics, we instead treat selection functions as partial rather than total mappings.

Definition 1. *A partial selection model is a triple* $\mathfrak{M} = (W, f, V)$, *where*

- $W \neq \emptyset$, *is a set of possible worlds;*
- $f : W \times \wp(W) \rightarrow W$, *is a partial function, satisfying the following conditions:*
  - **(id)** *if $f(w, X)$ is defined then $f(w, X) \in X$,*
  - **(cs)** *if $w \in X$ then $f(w, X) = w$,*
  - **(arr)** *if $f(w, X)$ is defined and $f(w, X) \in Y$ then $f(w, X \cap Y) = f(w, X)$;*
- $V : At \rightarrow \wp(W)$, *is a valuation function, mapping each atom to the set of worlds in which it is true.*

Unlike standard modal semantics, where evaluation takes place at a single point in a model, our approach evaluates formulas at a pointed model paired with a set of worlds representing the context, which will be updated or replaced by the antecedents of conditionals. Because the selection functions in our framework are partial, a formula may be neither true nor false, prompting us to introduce both truth and falsity conditions as follows.

Definition 2. *Given a partial selection model $\mathfrak{M} = (W, f, V)$, that φ is true (false, respectively) at (w, X) in $\mathfrak{M}$, denoted $\mathfrak{M}, w, X \Vdash \varphi$ ($\mathfrak{M}, w, X \dashv \varphi$, respectively), is inductively defined as follows.*

- $\mathfrak{M}, w, X \Vdash p$ iff $f(w, X)$ is defined and $f(w, X) \in V(p)$;
- $\mathfrak{M}, w, X \dashv p$ iff $f(w, X)$ is defined and $f(w, X) \notin V(p)$;
- $\mathfrak{M}, w, X \Vdash \neg\varphi$ iff $\mathfrak{M}, w, X \dashv \varphi$;
- $\mathfrak{M}, w, X \dashv \neg\varphi$ iff $\mathfrak{M}, w, X \Vdash \varphi$;
- $\mathfrak{M}, w, X \Vdash \varphi \wedge \psi$ iff $\mathfrak{M}, w, X \Vdash \varphi$ and $\mathfrak{M}, w, X \Vdash \psi$;
- $\mathfrak{M}, w, X \dashv \varphi \wedge \psi$ iff $\mathfrak{M}, w, X \dashv \varphi$ or $\mathfrak{M}, w, X \dashv \psi$;
- $\mathfrak{M}, w, X \Vdash \varphi \vee \psi$ iff $\mathfrak{M}, w, X \Vdash \varphi$ or $\mathfrak{M}, w, X \Vdash \psi$;
- $\mathfrak{M}, w, X \dashv \varphi \vee \psi$ iff $\mathfrak{M}, w, X \dashv \varphi$ and $\mathfrak{M}, w, X \dashv \psi$;
- $\mathfrak{M}, w, X \Vdash \varphi \to \psi$ iff $\mathfrak{M}, w, X \cap [\![\varphi]\!]_+^X \Vdash \psi$, where

$$[\![\varphi]\!]_+^X = \{u \in W \mid \mathfrak{M}, u, X \Vdash \varphi\};$$

- $\mathfrak{M}, w, X \dashv \varphi \to \psi$ iff $\mathfrak{M}, w, X \cap [\![\varphi]\!]_+^X \dashv \psi$;
- $\mathfrak{M}, w, X \Vdash \varphi \rightsquigarrow \psi$ iff $f(w, [\![\varphi]\!]_+^W)$ is defined and $\mathfrak{M}, f(w, [\![\varphi]\!]_+^W), [\![\varphi]\!]_+^W \Vdash \psi$;
- $\mathfrak{M}, w, X \dashv \varphi \rightsquigarrow \psi$ iff $f(w, [\![\varphi]\!]_+^W)$ is defined and $\mathfrak{M}, f(w, [\![\varphi]\!]_+^W), [\![\varphi]\!]_+^W \dashv \psi$.

According to the definition, an atomic proposition p is true (respectively, false) at a world w in a context X if and only if p is true (respectively, false) at the closest world to w within X. Boolean connectives are treated as usual. For an indicative conditional, $\varphi \to \psi$ is true (respectively, false) at w in X if and only if ψ is true (respectively, false) at w in the updated context obtained by intersecting X with the set of worlds where φ holds in X. Subjunctive conditionals are treated as in Stalnaker's original semantics.

The distinction between indicative and subjunctive conditionals lies in how they interact with context. Indicatives derive their truth values from previously established contexts, which are updated by the their antecedents. In contrast, subjunctives obtain their truth values independently of prior contexts, which are replaced by their antecedents. Consequently, propositions true in earlier contexts can influence indicatives, but not subjunctives.

We give the following abbreviations for brevity.

- $\mathfrak{M}, w, X \Vdash \Gamma \iff_{df} \mathfrak{M}, w, X \Vdash \varphi$ for all $\varphi \in \Gamma$.
- $\mathfrak{M}, X \Vdash \varphi \iff_{df} \mathfrak{M}, w, X \Vdash \varphi$ for all $w \in X$.
- $\mathfrak{M}, X \Vdash \Gamma \iff_{df} \mathfrak{M}, X \Vdash \varphi$ for all $\varphi \in \Gamma$.
- $\mathfrak{M} \Vdash \varphi \iff_{df} \mathfrak{M}, X \Vdash \varphi$ for all X in $\mathfrak{M}$.
- $\mathfrak{M} \Vdash \Gamma \iff_{df} \mathfrak{M} \Vdash \varphi$ for all $\varphi \in \Gamma$.
- $[\![\varphi]\!]_-^X =_{df} \{u \in W \mid \mathfrak{M}, u, X \dashv \varphi\}$.

The following lemma states that a formula cannot be both true and false, which is straightforward by induction.

Lemma 1. *For any partial selection model $\mathfrak{M}$ and X in $\mathfrak{M}$, for any $\varphi \in \mathcal{L}$, we have $[\![\varphi]\!]_+^X \cap [\![\varphi]\!]_-^X = \emptyset$.*

The following lemma indicates that Boolean formulas have the same truth and falsity conditions as atomic formulas.

Lemma 2. *Let* $\mathfrak{M} = (W, f, V)$ *be a partial selection model and* φ *be Boolean. Then*

(1) $\mathfrak{M}, w, X \Vdash \varphi$ *iff* $\mathfrak{M}, f(w, X), W \Vdash \varphi$
(2) $\mathfrak{M}, w, X \dashv\vdash \varphi$ *iff* $\mathfrak{M}, f(w, X), W \dashv\vdash \varphi$

Proof. By induction on φ.
Case 1: $\varphi = p$. Then $\mathfrak{M}, w, X \Vdash \varphi$ iff $f(w, X)$ is defined and $f(w, X) \in V(p)$ iff $f(w, X)$ is defined and $f(f(w, X), W) \in V(p)$ iff $\mathfrak{M}, f(w, X), W \Vdash p$, where the second 'iff' is by (cs). Analogously, we have $\mathfrak{M}, w, X \dashv\vdash p$ iff $\mathfrak{M}, f(w, X), W \dashv\vdash p$.
Case 2: $\varphi = \neg\psi, \psi \wedge \chi, \psi \vee \chi$. Immediate from the inductive hypothesis. □

The following lemma states that a context X updated first by φ and then by ψ is the same as that updated by $\varphi \wedge \psi$, provided that ψ is Boolean.

Lemma 3. *Let* $\mathfrak{M} = (W, f, V)$ *be a partial selection model and* ψ *be Boolean. Then*

$$X \cap [\![\varphi]\!]^X_+ \cap [\![\psi]\!]^{X \cap [\![\varphi]\!]^X_+}_+ = X \cap [\![\varphi \wedge \psi]\!]^X_+.$$

Proof. By Lemma 2 and (cs), we have

$$\begin{aligned}
X \cap [\![\varphi]\!]^X_+ \cap [\![\psi]\!]^{X \cap [\![\varphi]\!]^X_+} &= X \cap [\![\varphi]\!]^X_+ \cap \{w \in W \mid \mathfrak{M}, f(w, X \cap [\![\varphi]\!]^X_+), W \Vdash \psi\} \\
&= \{w \in X \cap [\![\varphi]\!]^X_+ \mid \mathfrak{M}, f(w, X \cap [\![\varphi]\!]^X_+), W \Vdash \psi\} \\
&= \{w \in X \cap [\![\varphi]\!]^X_+ \mid \mathfrak{M}, w, W \Vdash \psi\} \\
&= [\![\varphi]\!]^X_+ \cap \{w \in X \mid \mathfrak{M}, w, W \Vdash \psi\} \\
&= [\![\varphi]\!]^X_+ \cap \{w \in X \mid \mathfrak{M}, f(w, X), W \Vdash \psi\} \\
&= [\![\varphi]\!]^X_+ \cap \{w \in X \mid \mathfrak{M}, w, X \Vdash \psi\} \\
&= X \cap [\![\varphi]\!]^X_+ \cap \{w \in W \mid \mathfrak{M}, w, X \Vdash \psi\} \\
&= X \cap [\![\varphi]\!]^X_+ \cap [\![\psi]\!]^X_+ \\
&= X \cap [\![\varphi \wedge \psi]\!]^X_+
\end{aligned}$$

□

The following lemma states that if w is in the context, then Boolean formulas at w are context insensitive.

Lemma 4. *Let* $w \in X \cap Y$ *and* φ *be Boolean. Then*

(1) $\mathfrak{M}, w, X \Vdash \varphi$ *iff* $\mathfrak{M}, w, Y \Vdash \varphi$;
(2) $\mathfrak{M}, w, X \dashv\vdash \varphi$ *iff* $\mathfrak{M}, w, Y \dashv\vdash \varphi$.

Proof. For Item (1), we have $\mathfrak{M}, w, X \Vdash \varphi$ iff $\mathfrak{M}, f(w, X), W \Vdash \varphi$ iff $\mathfrak{M}, w, W \Vdash \varphi$, where the first 'iff' is by Lemma 2, and the second 'iff' is by (cs), since $w \in X$. Similarly, we have $\mathfrak{M}, w, Y \Vdash \varphi$ iff $\mathfrak{M}, w, W \Vdash \varphi$. Hence, $\mathfrak{M}, w, X \Vdash \varphi$ iff $\mathfrak{M}, w, Y \Vdash \varphi$. Item (2) can be proved analogously. □

The three notions of validity are defined as follows in the semantic framework.

Definition 3 (Validity). *The inference from Γ to φ is*

(1) *belief-valid, denoted $\Gamma \vDash_b \varphi$, if there are no $\mathfrak{M}$ and (w, X) with $w \in X$ such that $\mathfrak{M}, w, X \Vdash \Gamma$ and $\mathfrak{M}, w, X \dashv\vert \varphi$;*
(2) *assertion-valid, denoted $\Gamma \vDash_a \varphi$, if there are no $\mathfrak{M}$ and (w, X) with $w \in X$ such that $\mathfrak{M}, X \Vdash \Gamma$ and $\mathfrak{M}, w, X \dashv\vert \varphi$;*
(3) *supposition-valid, denoted $\Gamma \vDash_s \varphi$, if there are no $\mathfrak{M}$ and (w, X) with $w \in X$ such that $\mathfrak{M} \Vdash \Gamma$ and $\mathfrak{M}, w, X \dashv\vert \varphi$.*

Note that we adopt the *st*-validity proposed in Strict-Tolerant logic [6,16] rather than the standard notion of truth preservation. The *st*-validity treats an inference as valid if whenever the premises are true the conclusion is not false in a three-valued setting, which can be regarded as a formalization of Strawson entailment [19, pp. 176–177], according to which the inference from φ to ψ is valid if and only if ψ is true whenever φ is true and all presuppositions involved are satisfied. If we assume that a statement is neither true nor false if its presuppositions are not satisfied, and a statement cannot be both true and false, then it turns out that Strawson entailment and *st*-validity coincide. One merit of *st*-validity as shown by Strict-Tolerant logics is that when restricted to Boolean formulas, the semantics yields the same logical consequence as classical logic, unlike most three-valued logics, which are sublogics of classical logic.

Belief-validity, assertion-validity, and supposition-validity intend to formalize Val_b, Val_a, and Val_s introduced in Sect. 2, respectively. Beliefs are treated as local truths, assertions are treated as truths in contexts, and suppositions are treated as truths in models. The relation between the three notions of validity is as follows, which can be easily verified.

Proposition 1. *For all $\Gamma \cup \{\varphi\} \subseteq \mathcal{L}$, we have $\Gamma \vDash_b \varphi \Longrightarrow \Gamma \vDash_a \varphi \Longrightarrow \Gamma \vDash_s \varphi$.*

Armed with the three notions of validity, we can define three notions of equivalence.

Definition 4 (Equivalence). *We say that φ and ψ are*

(1) *belief-equivalent, denoted $\varphi \equiv_b \psi$, if $\varphi \vDash_b \psi$ and $\psi \vDash_b \varphi$;*
(2) *assertion-equivalent, denoted $\varphi \equiv_a \psi$, if $\varphi \vDash_a \psi$ and $\psi \vDash_a \varphi$;*
(3) *supposition-equivalent, denoted $\varphi \equiv_s \psi$, if $\varphi \vDash_s \psi$ and $\psi \vDash_s \varphi$.*

4 Application of the Semantics

Proposition 2 ((In)Validity of Or-to-If). *Or-to-If is (in)valid in the following forms.*

(1) $p \vee q \not\vDash_b \neg p \to q$
(2) $p \vee q \vDash_a \neg p \to q$
(3) $p \vee q \vDash_s \neg p \to q$
(4) $p \vee q \not\vDash_b \neg p \rightsquigarrow q$
(5) $p \vee q \not\vDash_a \neg p \rightsquigarrow q$
(6) $p \vee q \vDash_s \neg p \rightsquigarrow q$

Proof. For Item (1), let $\mathfrak{M} = (W, f, V)$, where $W = \{w, u\}$, $V(p) = \{w\}$, $V(q) = \emptyset$, $f(w, \{u\}) = u$. Then it can be verified that $\mathfrak{M}, w, W \Vdash p \vee q$ but $\mathfrak{M}, w, W \dashv\vdash \neg p \to q$.

For Item (2), suppose there exist $\mathfrak{M} = (W, f, V)$ and (w, X) with $w \in X$ such that $\mathfrak{M}, X \Vdash p \vee q$ and $\mathfrak{M}, w, X \dashv\vdash \neg p \to q$. By the latter, we have $\mathfrak{M}, w, X \cap [\![\neg p]\!]_+^X \dashv\vdash q$. By Lemma 2, $\mathfrak{M}, f(w, Y), W \dashv\vdash q$, where $Y = X \cap [\![\neg p]\!]_+^X$. By (id), $\mathfrak{M}, f(w, Y), X \Vdash \neg p$ and $f(w, Y) \in X$. By $\mathfrak{M}, X \Vdash p \vee q$ and $f(w, Y) \in X$, we have $\mathfrak{M}, f(w, Y), X \Vdash p \vee q$. Since $\mathfrak{M}, f(w, Y), X \Vdash \neg p$, it follows that $\mathfrak{M}, f(w, Y), X \Vdash q$, contradicting $\mathfrak{M}, f(w, Y), W \dashv\vdash q$, by Lemma 4.

Item (3) follows from Item (2) and Proposition 1.

Item (4) follows from Item (5) and Proposition 1.

For Item (5), consider $\mathfrak{M} = (W, f, V)$, where $W = \{w, u, v\}$, $V(p) = \{w\}$, $V(q) = \{u\}$, $f(w, \{u, v\}) = v$. Then it can be verified that $\mathfrak{M}, \{w, u\} \Vdash p \vee q$ but $\mathfrak{M}, w, \{w, u\} \dashv\vdash \neg p \rightsquigarrow q$. Hence, $p \vee q \not\vDash_a \neg p \rightsquigarrow q$.

For Item (6), suppose there exist $\mathfrak{M} = (W, f, V)$ and (w, X) with $w \in X$ in $\mathfrak{M}$ such that $\mathfrak{M} \Vdash p \vee q$ and $\mathfrak{M}, w, X \dashv\vdash \neg p \rightsquigarrow q$. By the latter, we have $\mathfrak{M}, f(w, [\![\neg p]\!]_+^W), W \dashv\vdash q$. By $\mathfrak{M} \Vdash p \vee q$, we have $\mathfrak{M}, f(w, [\![\neg p]\!]_+^W), W \Vdash p \vee q$. Then $\mathfrak{M}, f(w, [\![\neg p]\!]_+^W), W \Vdash p$. On the other hand, by (id), we have $\mathfrak{M}, f(w, [\![\neg p]\!]_+^W), W \Vdash \neg p$, contradiction. □

Note that uniform substitution does not hold in our semantics, as indicatives are context-sensitive. Some reasoning patterns that are valid for atomic and Boolean formulas may not extend to arbitrary formulas. For instance, although we have $p, p \to q \vDash_b q$, it is not the case that $p, p \to (q \to r) \vDash_b q \to r$, which explains McGee's famous counterexample to Modus Ponens [13]. In Proposition 2, we proved that the valid forms hold for atomic formulas, and these results can be easily extended to Boolean formulas. However, they may fail for arbitrary formulas. It remains open to us whether the valid forms of Or-to-If for Boolean formulas have counterexamples when generalized to arbitrary statements in natural language.

We summarize the (in)validity of six forms of Or-to-If in Table 2, which matches the linguistic desiderata summarized in Table 1.

Table 2. (In)Validity of six forms of Or-to-If

	belief-validity	assertion-validity	supposition-validity
Indicatives	✗	✓	✓
Subjunctives	✗	✗	✓

With Proposition 2, we can understand better about the relation between indicative (subjunctive) implication and material implication.

Proposition 3. *The following (in)equivalences hold.*

(1) $(p \to q) \not\equiv_b (p \supset q)$
(2) $(p \to q) \equiv_a (p \supset q)$
(3) $(p \to q) \equiv_s (p \supset q)$
(4) $(p \leadsto q) \not\equiv_b (p \supset q)$
(5) $(p \leadsto q) \not\equiv_a (p \supset q)$
(6) $(p \leadsto q) \equiv_s (p \supset q)$

Proof. Since we have $[\![\varphi]\!]_+^X = [\![\neg\neg\varphi]\!]_+^X$ and $[\![\varphi]\!]_-^X = [\![\neg\neg\varphi]\!]_-^X$, part of this proposition follows directly from replacing p by $\neg p$ and φ by $\neg\varphi$ in Proposition 2.

Item (1) follows from Item (1) of Proposition 2.

For Item (2), it suffices to show $p \to q \models_a p \supset q$, as the other direction has essentially been proved in Item (2). Suppose there exist $\mathfrak{M} = (W, f, V)$ and (w, X) with $w \in X$ such that $\mathfrak{M}, X \Vdash p \to q$ and $\mathfrak{M}, w, X \dashv\vert p \supset q$. By the latter, we have $\mathfrak{M}, w, X \Vdash p$ and $\mathfrak{M}, w, X \dashv\vert q$. By the former, we have $\mathfrak{M}, w, X \cap [\![p]\!]_+^X \Vdash q$. Note that $w \in X \cap [\![p]\!]_+^X$. It follows from Lemma 4 that $\mathfrak{M}, w, X \Vdash q$, contradicting $\mathfrak{M}, w, X \dashv\vert q$.

Item (3) follows from Item (3) of Proposition 2.
Item (4) follows from Item (4) of Proposition 2.
Item (5) follows from Item (5) of Proposition 2.

For Item (6), it suffices to show $p \leadsto q \models_s p \supset q$, as the other direction has essentially been proved in Item (6) of Proposition 2. Suppose there exist $\mathfrak{M} = (W, f, V)$ and (w, X) with $w \in X$ such that $\mathfrak{M} \Vdash p \leadsto q$ and $\mathfrak{M}, w, X \dashv\vert p \supset q$. By the latter, we have $\mathfrak{M}, w, X \Vdash p$ and $\mathfrak{M}, w, X \dashv\vert q$. By the former, we have $\mathfrak{M}, w, X \Vdash p \leadsto q$. Thus $\mathfrak{M}, f(w, [\![p]\!]^W), W \Vdash q$. On the other hand, by Lemma 4 and $\mathfrak{M}, w, X \Vdash p$, we have $\mathfrak{M}, w, W \Vdash p$. By (cs), it follows that $f(w, [\![p]\!]_+^W) = w$. Hence, $\mathfrak{M}, w, W \Vdash q$. By Lemma 4 again, we have $\mathfrak{M}, w, X \Vdash q$, contradicting $\mathfrak{M}, w, X \dashv\vert q$. □

Proposition 3 may explain why many authors advocate that indicative implication is no more than material implication in semantics (e.g. [7,9,11,15]). According to our semantics, although indicative implication is not belief-equivalent to material implication, the two implications are assertion-equivalent, meaning that asserting one amounts to asserting the other. They are also supposition-equivalent, supposing one amounts to supposing the other. Proposition 3 also aligns with the commonly accepted contention that subjunctive implication is not equivalent to material implication. They are not equivalent either as beliefs or as assertions.

With the three notions of validity, we can also understand better the notorious paradox of material implication.

Proposition 4. *The inferences underlying the paradox of material implication are (in)valid in the following forms.*

(1) $q \not\models_b p \to q$
(2) $q \models_a p \to q$
(3) $q \models_s p \to q$
(4) $q \not\models_b p \leadsto q$
(5) $q \not\models_a p \leadsto q$
(6) $q \models_s p \leadsto q$
(7) $\neg p \not\models_b p \to q$
(8) $\neg p \models_a p \to q$

(9) $\neg p \vDash_s p \to q$ \qquad (11) $\neg p \nvDash_a p \rightsquigarrow q$
(10) $\neg p \nvDash_b p \rightsquigarrow q$ \qquad (12) $\neg p \vDash_s p \rightsquigarrow q$

Proof. For Item (1), consider $\mathfrak{M} = (W, f, V)$, where $W = \{w, u\}$, $V(p) = \{u\}$, $V(q) = \{w\}$, $f(w, \{u\}) = u$. Then it can be verified that $\mathfrak{M}, w, W \Vdash q$ and $\mathfrak{M}, w, W \dashv\vdash p \to q$. Hence, $q \nvDash_b p \to q$.

Item (2) and Item (8) follow from Item (2) of Proposition 2.

Item (3) and Item (9) follow from Item (3) of Proposition 2.

For Item (4), consider the same counterexample as in the proof of Item (1).

For Item (5), consider $\mathfrak{M} = (W, f, V)$, where $W = \{w, u\}$, $V(p) = V(q) = \{w\}$, $f(w, \{u\}) = u$. Then it can be verified that $\mathfrak{M}, \{w\} \Vdash q$ but $\mathfrak{M}, w, \{w\} \dashv\vdash \neg p \rightsquigarrow q$. Hence, $q \nvDash_a \neg p \rightsquigarrow q$.

Item (6) follows from Item (6) of Proposition 2.

For Item (7), (10), and (11), consider the same countermodel as in the proof of Item (1).

For Item (12), suppose there exist $\mathfrak{M} = (W, f, V)$ and (w, X) with $w \in X$ such that $\mathfrak{M} \Vdash \neg p$ and $\mathfrak{M}, w, X \dashv\vdash p \rightsquigarrow q$. By the latter, we have $\mathfrak{M}, f(w, [\![p]\!]_+^W), W \dashv\vdash q$. Since $\mathfrak{M} \Vdash \neg p$, we have $[\![p]\!]_+^W = \emptyset$, whence $f(w, [\![p]\!]_+^W)$ is undefined, contradicting $\mathfrak{M}, f(w, [\![p]\!]_+^W), W \dashv\vdash q$. □

5 A 3-in-1 Notion of Validity

Consider the following comparison proposed in [4].

(7) If Lori were married to Kyle, then if she were married to Lyle, she'd be a bigamist. She is married to Lyle. Therefore, if she were married to Kyle, she'd be a bigamist.

(8) If Lori were married to Kyle, then if she were married to Lyle, she'd be a bigamist. Suppose she is married to Lyle. (Then) if she were married to Kyle, she'd be a bigamist.

Intuitively, (7) is invalid, because under the counterfactual supposition that Lori is married to Kyle, the most plausible scenario would be one in which she is no longer married to Lyle. In this case, she would not be a bigamist. By contrary, (8) is valid, because the supposition that Lori is married to Lyle remains in force and cannot be revoked by the counterfactual supposition introduced by the antecedent of the the conclusion. In this scenario, Lori would indeed be married to both Kyle and Lyle, thereby a bigamist.

In our current framework, while the invalidity of (7) can be captured through either $p \rightsquigarrow (q \rightsquigarrow r), q \nvDash_b p \rightsquigarrow r$ or $p \rightsquigarrow (q \rightsquigarrow r), q \nvDash_a p \rightsquigarrow r$, the argument (8) presents a challenge to our existing formalism. This is because its premises contain a hybrid of both belief and supposition, a combination our current theory cannot adequately accommodate. To properly analyze examples like (8), we require a more comprehensive theoretical framework capable of simultaneously handling multiple types of premises. This leads us to propose a unified definition that synthesizes the three existing notions of validity into a single, more versatile concept.

Definition 5 (3-in-1 Validity). *An inference from beliefs Γ, assertions Δ, and suppositions Σ to φ is valid, denoted $[\Gamma]_b, [\Delta]_a, [\Sigma]_s \vDash \varphi$, if there is no model $\mathfrak{M}$ and (w, X) with $w \in X$ such that $\mathfrak{M}, w, X \Vdash \Gamma$, $\mathfrak{M}, X \Vdash \Delta$, $\mathfrak{M} \Vdash \Sigma$, and $\mathfrak{M}, w, X \dashv \varphi$.*

The three notions of validity defined in Sect. 3 are just instances of the 3-in-1 notion of validity, as demonstrated in the following proposition, whose proof is straightforward.

Proposition 5. *Let $\Gamma \cup \{\varphi\} \subseteq \mathcal{L}$. Then*

(1) $\Gamma \vDash_b \varphi$ iff $[\Gamma]_b \vDash \varphi$
(2) $\Gamma \vDash_a \varphi$ iff $[\Gamma]_a \vDash \varphi$
(3) $\Gamma \vDash_s \varphi$ iff $[\Gamma]_s \vDash \varphi$

Armed with the new definition of validity, the contrast between argument (7) and (8) can be formulated and predicted by the following proposition.

Proposition 6. *For all $p, q, r \in At$, we have*

(1) $[p \rightsquigarrow (q \rightsquigarrow r)]_b, [q]_b \nvDash p \rightsquigarrow r$
(2) $[p \rightsquigarrow (q \rightsquigarrow r)]_b, [q]_a \nvDash p \rightsquigarrow r$
(3) $[p \rightsquigarrow (q \rightsquigarrow r)]_b, [q]_s \vDash p \rightsquigarrow r$

Proof. Item (1) follows from Item (2), Proposition 5, and Proposition 1.

For Item (2), consider $\mathfrak{M} = (W, f, V)$, where $W = \{w, u, v\}$, $V(p) = \{w, u\}$, $V(q) = \{u, v\}$, $V(r) = \{u\}$, $f(w, \{u, v\}) = v$, $f(v, \{u, w\}) = u$. Then it can be verified that $\mathfrak{M}, w, \{u, v\} \Vdash p \rightsquigarrow (q \rightsquigarrow r)$ and $\mathfrak{M}, \{u, v\} \Vdash q$, but $\mathfrak{M}, w, \{u, v\} \dashv p \rightsquigarrow r$. Hence, $[p \rightsquigarrow (q \rightsquigarrow r)]_b, [q]_a \nvDash p \rightsquigarrow r$.

For Item (3), suppose there exist $\mathfrak{M} = (W, f, V)$ and (w, X) with $w \in X$ such that $\mathfrak{M}, w, X \Vdash p \rightsquigarrow (q \rightsquigarrow r)$, $\mathfrak{M} \Vdash q$, and $\mathfrak{M}, w, X \dashv p \rightsquigarrow r$. By $\mathfrak{M}, w, X \Vdash p \rightsquigarrow (q \rightsquigarrow r)$, we have $\mathfrak{M}, f(w, [\![p]\!]_+^W), [\![p]\!]_+^W \Vdash q \rightsquigarrow r$. By $\mathfrak{M} \Vdash q$, we have $\mathfrak{M}, f(w, [\![p]\!]_+^W), [\![p]\!]_+^W \Vdash q$. By $\mathfrak{M}, w, X \dashv p \rightsquigarrow r$, we have $\mathfrak{M}, f(w, [\![p]\!]_+^W), [\![p]\!]_+^W \dashv r$. By the former two and (cs), we have $\mathfrak{M}, f(w, [\![p]\!]_+^W), [\![p]\!]_+^W \Vdash r$, contradicting $\mathfrak{M}, f(w, [\![p]\!]_+^W), [\![p]\!]_+^W \dashv r$. □

6 Making It Explicit

The three ways of treating the premises in the meta-language can be explicitly expressed by modal operators in the object language (cf. [20]). The extended language $\mathcal{L}_e$ is given by the following BNF:

$$\mathcal{L}_e \ni \varphi ::= p \mid \neg\varphi \mid (\varphi \wedge \varphi) \mid (\varphi \vee \varphi) \mid (\varphi \rightarrow \varphi) \mid (\varphi \rightsquigarrow \varphi) \mid \Box\varphi \mid \blacksquare\varphi,$$

where $\Box\varphi$ reads "φ is asserted" or "φ must be the case", and $\blacksquare\varphi$ reads "φ is assumed" or "φ is stipulated".

Definition 6. *Given a partial selection model $\mathfrak{M} = (W, f, V)$, the truth and falsity conditions for $\Box$ and $\blacksquare$ are given as follows.*

- $\mathfrak{M}, w, X \Vdash \Box\varphi$ iff $\mathfrak{M}, u, X \Vdash \varphi$ for all $u \in X$.
- $\mathfrak{M}, w, X \dashv\vdash \Box\varphi$ iff $\mathfrak{M}, u, X \dashv\vdash \varphi$ for some $u \in X$.
- $\mathfrak{M}, w, X \Vdash \blacksquare\varphi$ iff $\mathfrak{M}, Y \Vdash \varphi$ for all $Y \subseteq W$, i.e., $\mathfrak{M}, u, Y \Vdash \varphi$ for all $u \in Y \subseteq W$.
- $\mathfrak{M}, w, X \dashv\vdash \blacksquare\varphi$ iff $\mathfrak{M}, Y \dashv\vdash \varphi$ for some $Y \subseteq W$, i.e., $\mathfrak{M}, u, Y \dashv\vdash \varphi$ for some $u \in Y \subseteq W$.

Now we can recover the standard binary notion of validity as usual, except that we adopt the st-validity. More precisely, an inference from Γ to φ is valid, denoted $\Gamma \vDash \varphi$, if there is no model $\mathfrak{M}$ and (w, X) in $\mathfrak{M}$ such that $\mathfrak{M}, w, X \Vdash \Gamma$ and $\mathfrak{M}, w, W \dashv\vdash \varphi$. The following proposition is easily verified.

Proposition 7. Let $\Gamma \cup \{\varphi\} \subseteq \mathcal{L}_e$. Then

(1) $\Box\Gamma \vDash \varphi$ iff $\Box\Gamma \vDash \Box\varphi$
(2) $\blacksquare\Gamma \vDash \varphi$ iff $\blacksquare\Gamma \vDash \blacksquare\varphi$

Despite its simplicity, Proposition 7 sheds new light on the three notions of validity. It reveals that each type of validity, emerging from distinct treatments of premises, mirrors a specific form of truth preservation: validity under belief-based premises correspond to truth preservation across worlds; assertion-based premises correspond to truth preservation across contexts; and supposition-based premises correspond to truth preservation across models.

The proof of the following proposition is also straightforward.

Proposition 8. Let $\Gamma \cup \Delta \cup \Sigma \cup \{\varphi\} \subseteq \mathcal{L}$. Then

(1) $\Gamma \vDash_b \varphi$ iff $\Gamma \vDash \varphi$
(2) $\Gamma \vDash_a \varphi$ iff $\Box\Gamma \vDash \varphi$
(3) $\Gamma \vDash_s \varphi$ iff $\blacksquare\Gamma \vDash \varphi$
(4) $[\Gamma]_b, [\Delta]_a, [\Sigma]_s \vDash \varphi$ iff $\Gamma, \Box\Delta, \blacksquare\Sigma \vDash \varphi$.

Proposition 8 indicates that the three types of validity defined in the meta-language can all be reduced to the same basic notion – truth preservation across worlds. This reduction is achieved by explicitly expressing the differently treated premises in the object language using modal operators. Table 3 lists the six forms of Or-to-If with the premise explicitly expressed, using only one notion of validity.

Table 3. (In)Validity of Or-to-If With Explicit Premises

	Belief	Assertion	Supposition
Indicatives	$p \vee q \nvDash \neg p \to q$	$\Box(p \vee q) \vDash \neg p \to q$	$\blacksquare(p \vee q) \vDash \neg p \to q$
Subjunctives	$p \vee q \nvDash \neg p \rightsquigarrow q$	$\Box(p \vee q) \nvDash \neg p \rightsquigarrow q$	$\blacksquare(p \vee q) \vDash \neg p \rightsquigarrow q$

Although this theoretical reduction is appealing, the distinction between the three notions of validity in the meta-language remains illuminating in practical application. It provides a clearer explanation for why debates and divergent intuitions persist regarding the same inference patterns.

On the other hand, with the explicit modal operator, we can express another form of Or-to-If, illustrated by the following example.

(9) Either the butler or the gardener did it.
(10) Therefore, if the butler didn't (hadn't) do it, it must be (have been) the gardener.

The validity of the above inference is predicated by the following proposition.

Proposition 9 (Modal Or-to-If). *The modal Or-to-If is valid in the following forms.*

(1) $\Box(p \vee q) \vDash \neg p \to \Box q$
(2) $\blacksquare(p \vee q) \vDash \neg p \to \Box q$
(3) $\blacksquare(p \vee q) \vDash \neg p \rightsquigarrow \Box q$

Proof. For Item (1), suppose there exist $\mathfrak{M} = (W, f, V)$ and (w, X) in $\mathfrak{M}$ with $w \in X$ such that $\mathfrak{M}, w, X \Vdash \Box(p \vee q)$ and $\mathfrak{M}, w, X \dashv\!\vert \neg p \to \Box q$. By the latter, we have $\mathfrak{M}, w, X \cap [\![\neg p]\!]_+^X \dashv\!\vert \Box q$. Thus there exists $u \in X \cap [\![\neg p]\!]_+^X$ such that $\mathfrak{M}, u, X \cap [\![\neg p]\!]_+^X \dashv\!\vert q$. By Lemma 2, $\mathfrak{M}, f(u, X \cap [\![\neg p]\!]_+^X), W \dashv\!\vert q$. By (id), $f(u, X \cap [\![\neg p]\!]_+^X) \in X$ and $\mathfrak{M}, f(u, X \cap [\![\neg p]\!]_+^X), X \dashv\!\vert p$. By Lemma 4, $\mathfrak{M}, f(u, X \cap [\![\neg p]\!]_+^X), X \dashv\!\vert q$. Hence, $\mathfrak{M}, f(u, X \cap [\![\neg p]\!]_+^X), X \dashv\!\vert p \vee q$, contradicting $\mathfrak{M}, w, X \Vdash \Box(p \vee q)$.

Item (2) follows from (1), Proposition 1, and Proposition 8.

For Item (3), suppose there exist $\mathfrak{M} = (W, f, V)$ and (w, X) with $w \in X$ such that $\mathfrak{M} \Vdash p \vee q$ and $\mathfrak{M}, w, X \dashv\!\vert \neg p \rightsquigarrow \Box q$. Then $\mathfrak{M}, f(w, [\![\neg p]\!]_+^W), [\![\neg p]\!]_+^W \dashv\!\vert \Box q$. By $f(w, [\![\neg p]\!]_+^W) \in [\![\neg p]\!]_+^W$, then $\mathfrak{M}, f(w, [\![\neg p]\!]_+^W), [\![\neg p]\!]_+^W \dashv\!\vert q$. By Lemma 4, it follows that $\mathfrak{M}, f(w, [\![\neg p]\!]_+^W), W \dashv\!\vert q$. By $\mathfrak{M} \Vdash p \vee q$, we have $\mathfrak{M}, f(w, [\![\neg p]\!]_+^W), W \Vdash p$. On the other hand, by (id), we have $\mathfrak{M}, f(w, [\![\neg p]\!]_+^W), W \Vdash \neg p$, contradiction. □

Note that the modal Or-to-If is not valid for either material conditionals or subjunctive conditionals, even if the premise is asserted or assumed, as demonstrated by the following proposition.

Proposition 10. *The modal Or-to-If is invalid in the following forms, where* $> \in \{\supset, \rightsquigarrow\}$.

(1) $p \vee q \nvDash \neg p > \Box q$
(2) $\Box(p \vee q) \nvDash \neg p > \Box q$

Proof. By Proposition 1 and Proposition 8, it suffices to show Item (2). Consider $\mathfrak{M} = (W, f, V)$, where $W = \{w, u\}$, $V(p) = \{u\}$, $V(q) = \{w\}$, $f(w, \{w\}) = w$. Then it can be verified that $\mathfrak{M}, w, W \Vdash \Box(p \vee q)$, $\mathfrak{M}, w, W \dashv\!\vert \neg p \supset \Box q$, and $\mathfrak{M}, w, W \dashv\!\vert \neg p \rightsquigarrow \Box q$. Hence, $\Box(p \vee q) \nvDash \neg p \supset \Box q$. The case for $\rightsquigarrow$ follows from Item (5) of Proposition 2. □

Note that, as the language $\mathcal{L}_e$ is more expressive than $\mathcal{L}$, Or-to-If has more counterexamples in $\mathcal{L}_e$ than in $\mathcal{L}$. One notable counterexample is $\blacksquare(p \vee \Diamond p) \nvDash \neg p \to \Diamond p$ and thus $\Box(p \vee \Diamond p) \nvDash \neg p \to \Diamond p$. Even if you have assumed that there is p-world in the model, after updating the context by the antecedent $\neg p$ of the conditional of the conclusion, there is no more p-world in the model, whence the consequent $\Diamond p$ will be false. We leave the formal verification to the reader.

7 Conclusion

We distinguish three ways of treating the premises of an argument (as beliefs, assertions, or suppositions), which give rise to three corresponding notions of validity. By further differentiating indicatives from subjunctives, we obtain six forms of the Or-to-If inference rule, pinpointing precisely when it is valid or invalid. Unlike Stalnaker's approach, ours is purely semantic. It can also be reformulated using a single notion of validity, although this requires turning the binary relation of logical consequence into a quaternary one. Moreover, we extend our language so that premises treated differently in the meta-language can be explicitly represented in the object language, offering new insights into Or-to-If. While our primary focus is Or-to-If, our pluralistic perspective on validity has potential to address other related puzzles, bridging the gap between formal logic in theory and reasoning in natural language in practice.

Future work includes more applications concerning reasoning with conditionals and modals (e.g., the puzzle about the validity of Modus Ponens) and a full comparison to extant works, including Fitting's work on ternary consequence for modal logic [8] and other logics for conditionals and modals (e.g., [2,5,10,14]). Moreover, our logic validates $\varphi \to \psi \vDash \neg(\varphi \to \neg\psi)$ and $\varphi \to \neg\psi \vDash \neg(\varphi \to \psi)$, which makes it a weakly connexive logic [21]. Relating our work with connexive logic (especially connexive conditional logic [22,23]) might be desirable. Our logic also demands a proof theory, so that the logic can be better understood and compared to other logics.

Acknowledgments. This work was supported by National Social Science Foundation of China (Grant No. 23&ZD240). We thank the referees for their careful reading and helpful comments.

References

1. Adams, E.W.: The Logic of Conditionals: An Application of Probability to Deductive Logic. In: Reidel, D. (ed.) Synthese Library. Springer, Dordrecht (1975). https://doi.org/10.1007/978-94-015-7622-2
2. Baltag, A., Smets, S.: Conditional doxastic models: a qualitative approach to dynamic belief. Electron. Notes Theor. Comput. Sci. **165**, 5–21 (2006)
3. Bennett, J.: A Philosophical Guide to Condtionals. Oxford University Press (2003)
4. Carter, S.: A suppositional theory of conditionals. Mind **130**(520), 1059–1086 (2021)

5. Ciardelli, I.: Indicative conditionals and graded information. J. Philos. Log. **49**(3), 509–549 (2020)
6. Cobreros, P., Egré, P., Ripley, E., van Rooij, R.: Tolerant, classical, strict. J. Philos. Log. **41**(2), 347–385 (2012)
7. Dale, A.J.: A defence of material implication. Analysis **34**(3), 91–95 (1974)
8. Fitting, M.: Proof Methods for Modal and Intuitionistic Logics. Springer (1983). https://doi.org/10.1007/978-94-017-2794-5
9. Grice, H.Paul.: Studies in the Way of Words. Harvard University Press (1989)
10. Holliday, W.H., Mandelkern, M.: The orthologic of epistemic modals. J. Philos. Logic (2024). https://doi.org/10.1007/s10992-024-09746-7
11. Jackson, F.: On assertion and indicative conditionals. Philos. Rev. **88**(4), 565–589 (1979)
12. Lewis, D.: Counterfactuals. Harvard University Press (1973)
13. McGee, V.: A counterexample to modus ponens. J. Philos. **82**(9), 462–471 (1985)
14. Norlin, K.: Acceptance and certainty, doxastic modals, and indicative conditionals. J. Philos. Log. **51**(5), 951–971 (2022)
15. Rieger, A.: Conditionals are material: the positive arguments. Synthese **190**(15), 3161–3174 (2013)
16. Ripley, E.: Conservatively extending classical logic with transparent truth. Rev. Symbolic Logic **5**(2), 354–378 (2012)
17. Stalnaker, R.: A Theory of Conditionals. In: Rescher, N. (ed.) Studies in Logical Theory, pp. 98–112. Basil Blackwell Publishers (1968)
18. Stalnaker, R.: Indicative conditionals. Philosophia **5**(3), 269–286 (1975)
19. Strawson, P.F.: Introduction to Logical Theory. Wiley, Oxford, England (1952)
20. van Benthem, J.: Implicit and explicit stances in logic. J. Philos. Log. **48**(3), 571–601 (2018)
21. Wansing, H., Omori, H.: Connexive logic, connexivity, and connexivism: remarks on terminology. Stud. Logica. **112**, 1–35 (2024)
22. Wansing, H., Unterhuber, M.: Connexive Conditional Logic Part I. Logic Logical Philos. **28**(3), 567–610 (2019)
23. Wen, X.: Stalnakerian connexive logics. Stud. Logica. **112**, 365–403 (2024)

Relevance for Stability of Verification Status of a Set of Arguments in Incomplete Argumentation Frameworks

Anshu Xiong[1,2](✉) and Songmao Zhang[1]

[1] State Key Laboratory of Mathematical Sciences, Academy of Mathematics and Systems Science, Chinese Academy of Sciences, Beijing 100190, China
smzhang@math.ac.cn
[2] University of Chinese Academy of Sciences, Beijing 100049, China
xionganshu21@mails.ucas.ac.cn

Abstract. The notion of relevance was proposed for stability of justification status of a single argument in incomplete argumentation frameworks (IAFs) in 2024 by Odekerken et al. To extend the notion, we study the relevance for stability of verification status of a set of arguments in this paper, i.e., the uncertainties in an IAF that have to be resolved in some situations so that answering whether a given set of arguments is an extension obtains the same result in every completion of the IAF. Further we propose the notion of strong relevance for describing the necessity of resolution in all situations reaching stability. An analysis of complexity reveals that detecting the (strong) relevance for stability of sets of arguments can be accomplished in P time under the most semantics discussed in the paper. We also discuss the difficulty in finding tractable methods for relevance detection under grounded semantics.

Keywords: Abstract argumentation · Incomplete knowledge · Relevance · Computational complexity

1 Introduction

As a groundbreaking work for modeling argumentation, Dung's *Abstract Argumentation Framework* (AF) [9] represents attack relations among a group of arguments where justified sets of arguments can be computed under various types of semantics. Argumentation can be viewed as a dynamic process where not all arguments and attacks are known in advance. *Incomplete Argumentation Framework (IAF)* [6] is a prominent proposal for introducing qualitative uncertainty to AF for modeling dynamic argumentation settings. An IAF contains not only certain arguments and attacks but also uncertain ones whose existence is unknown at the moment. By investigating the existence of each uncertain element, various AFs can be reached called *completions* of the IAF.

Initially studied in [14,20], *stability* refers to that the question of interest has the same answer in any situation that will happen in the future, for instance any completion in the IAF setting. Given some semantics σ, issues about stability in IAFs have been concerned with different goals including stability of: justification of an argument a [5,12,15], which refers to acceptable status of a ranging over $\{sceptical, credulous\} \times \{in, out, undec\}$ under σ; verification of a set of arguments S [6,10], which tells whether S is a σ-extension; and the whole extensions [21], which refers to the set of all extensions under σ of an AF.

Practically, an IAF being stable means that there is no need to investigate the existence of the current uncertain elements. Meanwhile, the notion of stability also indicates that during the dynamics process from an IAF towards one of its completions, as long as we desire a fixed answer for the question of interest from the completion, then we need to resolve the current uncertainties until stability is reached. Therefore, it is of importance to explore how to resolve uncertainties in IAF so as to reach stability. Such a problem is recently studied in [15] where the notion of *relevance* is proposed. Relevance characterizes which uncertainties need to be resolved in order to reach stability. For instance, addition of an uncertain argument (or attack) e is said to be relevant w.r.t. IAF I if there exists an IAF 'specified' from I where the existence of all uncertain elements is decided except e, while the stability of interest is not reached yet and adding e will lead the reaching.

In [15], the relevance problem is discussed for stability of justification status of a given argument. We believe that relevance is worth exploring for other types of stability, and focus on stability of verification status of a given set of arguments in this paper. Essentially, this relevance is distinctive from the relevance in [15] due to the inherent differences across the two types of stability. Further, for an uncertain element whose addition or removal is relevant, it is also interesting to validate whether such an action is necessary to be done in any situation for reaching stability. We define such a stricter form as *strong relevance*. Generally, relevance reveals the need of resolutions in some situation for reaching stability, whereas strong relevance describes the necessity of resolutions in all situations.

The contribution of this paper consists of (1) extending the relevance problem proposed in [15] to relevance for stability of verification status of a set of arguments; and (2) proposing the notion of strong relevance for stability in IAFs. Specifically, we analyze the complexity for deciding two relevance problems under five common semantics including admissible, stable, complete, grounded and preferred semantics. For admissible, stable and complete semantics, we find tractable methods for detecting both relevance and strong relevance, showing that they are all in P complexity class. For preferred semantics, we give the upper bound and prove the lower bound of two relevance problems by constructing reductions from known problems in IAFs and SAT problems. The difficulty of finding tractable method for solving relevance problems under grounded semantics is also discussed. Overall our results show that deciding relevance for stability of verification of a set of arguments is simpler than that of justification of an argument, whose complexity is up to exponential level under all the common semantics as proven in [15].

The paper is organized as follows. In Sect. 2, we provide a brief, necessary introduction to basic definitions about AF, IAF and stability problems of verification in IAFs. In Sect. 3, we define and give a complexity analysis of the relevance problem for stability of verification status of a set of arguments. In Sect. 4, we introduce strong relevance and also study the complexity of its decision problems. Then in Sect. 5, the related work as well as related issues are discussed including the difficulty in tackling the relevance problem under grounded semantics. Lastly the paper is concluded in Sect. 6.

2 Preliminaries

Argumentation Framework (AF). An *abstract argumentation framework* [9] is a directed graph $F = \langle \mathcal{A}, \mathcal{R} \rangle$ where $\mathcal{A}$ represents a set of considered arguments and $\mathcal{R} \subseteq \mathcal{A} \times \mathcal{A}$ the set of attacks between arguments in $\mathcal{A}$. We say that a *attacks* b if $(a, b) \in \mathcal{R}$, a *attacks* $S \subseteq \mathcal{A}$ if $\exists b \in S, (a, b) \in \mathcal{R}$, and the meaning of S *attacks* a is analogous. Given a set of arguments $S \subseteq \mathcal{A}$, let $S_F^+ = \{a \in \mathcal{A} \mid S$ attacks $a\}$ and $S_F^- = \{a \in \mathcal{A} \mid a$ attacks $S\}$, and S is *conflict-free* iff $S \cap S_F^+ = \emptyset$. We say that S *defends* a if all the attackers of a are attacked by S and use the so-called *characteristic function* $\Gamma_F(S)$ [9] to denote all the arguments that S defends, i.e., $\Gamma_F(S) = \{a \in \mathcal{A} \mid S$ defends a in $F\}$.

Semantics of AF. A *semantics* σ is a function of which the input is an AF $F = \langle \mathcal{A}, \mathcal{R} \rangle$ and the output $\sigma(F)$ a set of subsets of $\mathcal{A}$, where every element of $\sigma(F)$ is called a σ-*extension* of F. The common semantics admissible, stable, complete, grounded and preferred semantics (abbr. **ad**, **st**, **co**, **gr**, **pr**) are originally proposed in [9] and defined as follows.

Definition 1. *Given an AF* $F = \langle \mathcal{A}, \mathcal{R} \rangle$ *and* $S \subseteq \mathcal{A}$,

1. $S \in \mathsf{ad}(F)$ *iff* S *is conflict-free and* $S \subseteq \Gamma_F(S)$;
2. $S \in \mathsf{st}(F)$ *iff* S *is conflict-free and* $S_F^+ = \mathcal{A} \setminus S$;
3. $S \in \mathsf{co}(F)$ *iff* $S \in \mathsf{ad}(F)$ *and* $\forall a \in \Gamma_F(S), a \in S$;
4. $S \in \mathsf{gr}(F)$ *iff* S *is* $\subseteq$-*minimal in* $\mathsf{co}(F)$; *and*
5. $S \in \mathsf{pr}(F)$ *iff* S *is* $\subseteq$-*maximal in* $\mathsf{ad}(F)$.

Given an AF F, a set of arguments S of F and semantics σ[1], the notion of *verification status* is defined as follows: (the verification status of) S is σ-*true* (resp., -*false*) iff $S \in \sigma(F)$ (resp., $S \notin \sigma(F)$).

Now we recall the notion of IAF expanding AF with qualitative uncertainty.

Definition 2 (Incomplete Argumentation Framework [6]). *An incomplete argumentation framework (IAF) is a quadruple* $\langle \mathcal{A}, \mathcal{A}^?, \mathcal{R}, \mathcal{R}^? \rangle$ *where* $\mathcal{A}$ *and* $\mathcal{A}^?$ *are disjoint sets of arguments and* $\mathcal{R}$ *and* $\mathcal{R}^?$ *disjoint subsets of* $(\mathcal{A} \cup \mathcal{A}^?) \times (\mathcal{A} \cup \mathcal{A}^?)$. $\mathcal{A}$ *(resp., $\mathcal{R}$) represents arguments (resp., attacks) that are known to certainly exist, while $\mathcal{A}^?$ (resp., $\mathcal{R}^?$) contains additional arguments (resp., attacks) whose existence is yet uncertain. An IAF is called an AtIAF (resp., ArIAF) if it has no uncertain arguments (resp., attacks).*

---

[1] In this paper we limit the semantics discussed to the five common semantics in Definition 1, and unless specifically stated otherwise the given semantics σ in context ranges over {ad,st,co,gr,pr}.

The *partial completions* [15] of an IAF I represent the possible IAFs that I can be specified to be, i.e., by remaining the certain parts and deciding some of the uncertain elements to be existent or not.

Definition 3 (Partial completion). *[15] Given an IAF $I = \langle \mathcal{A}, \mathcal{A}^?, \mathcal{R}, \mathcal{R}^? \rangle$, a partial completion is an IAF $I' = \langle \mathcal{A}', \mathcal{A}^{?'}, \mathcal{R}', \mathcal{R}^{?'} \rangle$ where:*

- $\mathcal{A} \subseteq \mathcal{A}' \subseteq \mathcal{A} \cup \mathcal{A}^?$;
- $\mathcal{R} \cap (\mathcal{A}' \cup \mathcal{A}^{?'}) \times (\mathcal{A}' \cup \mathcal{A}^{?'}) \subseteq \mathcal{R}' \subseteq \mathcal{R} \cup \mathcal{R}^?$;
- $\mathcal{A}^{?'} \subseteq \mathcal{A}^?$; and
- $\mathcal{R}^{?'} \subseteq \mathcal{R}^?$.

Note that $\mathcal{A}' \cap \mathcal{A}^{?'} = \emptyset, \mathcal{R}' \cap \mathcal{R}^{?'} = \emptyset, \mathcal{R}' \subseteq (\mathcal{A}' \cup \mathcal{A}^{?'}) \times (\mathcal{A}' \cup \mathcal{A}^{?'})$ and $\mathcal{R}^{?'} \subseteq (\mathcal{A}' \cup \mathcal{A}^{?'}) \times (\mathcal{A}' \cup \mathcal{A}^{?'})$ because I' is an IAF. We use $part(I)$ to denote the set containing all of the partial completions of I, and $cert(I) = \langle \mathcal{A}, \mathcal{R} \cap (\mathcal{A} \times \mathcal{A}) \rangle$ to denote the AF projected on the certain parts of I. We can see that by partial completion, the notion of *completion* [6] can be alternatively defined as that an AF F is a completion of an IAF I iff there is a partial completion I' of I such that $F = cert(I')$.

Given an IAF $I = \langle \mathcal{A}, \mathcal{A}^?, \mathcal{R}, \mathcal{R}^? \rangle$ and a set of arguments $S \subseteq \mathcal{A} \cup \mathcal{A}^?$, similarly to notations for AF, we give the following notations:

- $S_I^+ = \{a \in \mathcal{A} \cup \mathcal{A}^? \mid \exists b \in S, (b,a) \in \mathcal{R}\}$;
- $S_I^- = \{a \in \mathcal{A} \cup \mathcal{A}^? \mid \exists b \in S, (a,b) \in \mathcal{R}\}$; and
- $S_I^\sim = \{a \in \mathcal{A} \cup \mathcal{A}^? \mid \forall b \in S, (b,a) \notin \mathcal{R} \cup \mathcal{R}^?\}$.

Further, in order to concisely describe the changing of IAF I, given a set of attacks $\mathcal{R}_0 \subseteq \mathcal{R}^?$ or a set of arguments $\mathcal{A}_0 \subseteq \mathcal{A}^?$, let:

- $I + \mathcal{R}_0 = \langle \mathcal{A}, \mathcal{A}^?, \mathcal{R} \cup \mathcal{R}_0, \mathcal{R}^? \setminus \mathcal{R}_0 \rangle$;
- $I - \mathcal{R}_0 = \langle \mathcal{A}, \mathcal{A}^?, \mathcal{R}, \mathcal{R}^? \setminus \mathcal{R}_0 \rangle$;
- $I + \mathcal{A}_0 = \langle \mathcal{A} \cup \mathcal{A}_0, \mathcal{A}^? \setminus \mathcal{A}_0, \mathcal{R}, \mathcal{R}^? \rangle$; and
- $I - \mathcal{A}_0 = \langle \mathcal{A}, \mathcal{A}^? \setminus \mathcal{A}_0, \mathcal{R} \setminus \mathcal{R}', \mathcal{R}^? \setminus \mathcal{R}' \rangle$, where $\mathcal{R}' = \{(a,b) \in \mathcal{R} \cup \mathcal{R}^? \mid a \in \mathcal{A}_0$ or $b \in \mathcal{A}_0\}$, i.e., the set of attacks related to the arguments in $\mathcal{A}_0$.

Now we introduce the notion of stability of verification of a set of arguments, which is defined based on verification status. Given an IAF I, a set of arguments S and a verification status $j \in \{\mathsf{ad}, \mathsf{st}, \mathsf{co}, \mathsf{gr}, \mathsf{pr}\} \times \{true, false\}$, S is stable-j w.r.t. I iff the verification status of S remains j in any completion of I.

Definition 4 (Stability of verification in IAFs). *Given an IAF $I = \langle \mathcal{A}, \mathcal{A}^?, \mathcal{R}, \mathcal{R}^? \rangle$, a set of arguments $S \subseteq \mathcal{A} \cup \mathcal{A}^?$, and a verification status $j \in \{\mathsf{ad}, \mathsf{st}, \mathsf{co}, \mathsf{gr}, \mathsf{pr}\} \times \{true, false\}$, S is stable-j w.r.t. I iff for any completion F of I, S is j in F.*

The precise complexity results of verification stability problems can be obtained directly from the results of *PosVer* and *NecVer* problems given in [6,10]. For an IAF I, a set of arguments S and semantics σ, $PosVer_\sigma$ asks whether there is a completion F of I such that $S \in \sigma(F)$ whereas $NecVer_\sigma$

asks whether for any completion F of I, $S \in \sigma(F)$ always holds. Therefore, S is stable-σ-true w.r.t. I iff $NecVer_\sigma(I,S) = true$ and S is stable-σ-false w.r.t. I iff $PosVer_\sigma(I,S) = false$ holds. For $\sigma \in \{\text{ad}, \text{st}, \text{co}, \text{gr}\}$, both $PosVer_\sigma$ and $NecVer_\sigma$ problems are in P complexity class, while $PosVer_{\text{pr}}$ is Σ_2-c and $NecVer_{\text{pr}}$ is $coNP$-c [6,10]. These known results will be used subsequently in this paper.

Given semantics σ, we say that a set of arguments S is stable-σ w.r.t. an IAF I if S is stable-σ-true or stable-σ-false w.r.t. I, which means that S holds the same verification result under σ semantics in any completion of the IAF I.

3 Relevance for Stability of Verification

In this section, we define relevance for stability of verification status of a given set of arguments and then study the complexity of related computational issues.

3.1 Definitions for Relevance

First, we extend the notion of relevance to stability of verification. Given an IAF I, a set of arguments S, addition (resp., removal) of an uncertain element e is relevant for S to reach j verification status if there is a partial completion of I where e is the unique uncertain element not decided yet, and adding (resp., removing) e will lead S to become j whereas the opposite action will not.

Definition 5 (Relevance for stability of verification). *Given an IAF $I = \langle \mathcal{A}, \mathcal{A}^?, \mathcal{R}, \mathcal{R}^? \rangle$, a set of arguments $S \subseteq \mathcal{A} \cup \mathcal{A}^?$, a verification status j and an uncertain element $e \in \mathcal{A}^? \cup \mathcal{R}^?$, addition (resp., removal) of e is j-relevant for S w.r.t. I iff there exists an IAF $I' = \langle \mathcal{A}', \mathcal{A}'^?, \mathcal{R}', \mathcal{R}'^? \rangle \in part(I)$ satisfying that $\mathcal{A}'^? \cup \mathcal{R}'^? = \{e\}$, and S is j in $cert(I' + \{e\})$ (resp., $cert(I' - \{e\})$) while S is not j in $cert(I' - \{e\})$ (resp., $cert(I' + \{e\})$). We use $RE^+(I,S,j)$ and $RE^-(I,S,j)$ to respectively denote the uncertain elements whose addition and removal are j-relevant for S w.r.t. I.*

In other words, addition or removal of e is j-relevant for S if such an action is needed for S to reach j status in some situation. Since the verification status of S is either -$true$ or -$false$ in completions, we can see that the addition and removal are dual actions according to Definition 5, i.e., $RE^+(I,S,\sigma\text{-}true) = RE^-(I,S,\sigma\text{-}false)$ and $RE^-(I,S,\sigma\text{-}true) = RE^+(I,S,\sigma\text{-}false)$ always hold. This says that for any uncertain element, the -$true$ relevance of its addition or removal coincides with the -$false$ relevance of the opposite action.

If neither addition nor removal of e is σ-$true(false)$-relevant for S w.r.t. I, we say that e is σ-*irrelevant*. This means that there is no need to investigate e to reach stability, as in all situations, the existence of e has no influence on the verification result of S.

Example 1. Consider the IAF I_{ex} in Fig. 1. For the set of arguments $S = \{a,b\}$, $RE^+(I,S,\text{ad-}true) = \{(b,d)\}$ and $RE^-(I,S,\text{ad-}true) = \{d,(f,b)\}$. The uncertain attack (c,a) is ad-irrelevant, since c is necessarily attacked by $b \in S$ and

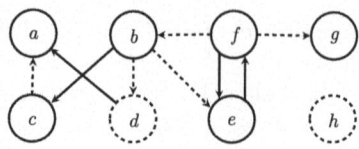

Fig. 1. An example IAF I_{ex} (uncertain arguments and attacks are depicted using dashed circles and lines, respectively)

S will be defended against the attacks from c in any completion. In contrary to (c,a), removal of d is ad-*true*-relevant for S w.r.t. I_{ex}, since when (b,d) is removed, there are no arguments in S attacking d and d is needed to be removed for S to be admissible. One can see that there is a partial completion $I'_{ex} = I_{ex} - \{(c,a),(b,d),(b,e),(f,b),(f,g)\} - \{h\}$ of I_{ex} such that S is not stable-ad w.r.t. I'_{ex} whereas S is stable-ad-*true* w.r.t. $I'_{ex} - \{d\}$.

Lastly in this subsection, we give a proposition that relates the identification of stability to detecting the existence of relevant elements.[2]

Proposition 1. *Given an IAF $I = \langle \mathcal{A}, \mathcal{A}^?, \mathcal{R}, \mathcal{R}^? \rangle$, a set of arguments $S \subseteq \mathcal{A} \cup \mathcal{A}^?$ and semantics σ, S is stable-σ w.r.t. I iff $\forall e \in \mathcal{A}^? \cup \mathcal{R}^?$, e is σ-irrelevant.*

3.2 Complexity Analysis of Relevance

In this subsection we study the computational complexity of decision problems for identifying the relevance of adding or removing an uncertain element for stability of verification status of a given set of arguments, which is formulated as follows.

---
j-RELEVANCE of action **a**

Given: An IAF $I = \langle \mathcal{A}, \mathcal{A}^?, \mathcal{R}, \mathcal{R}^? \rangle$, a set of arguments $S \subseteq \mathcal{A} \cup \mathcal{A}^?$, a verification status j, an action $\mathbf{a} \in \{\text{addition,removal}\}$ and an uncertain element $\mathbf{e} \in \mathcal{A}^? \cup \mathcal{R}^?$.
Question: Is **a** of **e** j-relevant for S w.r.t. I?

Next we give results for obtaining upper bounds of RELEVANCE problem. Directly according to Definition 5, we can conclude that for semantics σ whose verification problem is in C complexity, the relevance problem under σ is in NP^C. Thus we directly obtain an upper bound for various semantics as follows.

Corollary 1. *The following results hold:*

1. *for $j \in \{\text{ad},\text{st},\text{co},\text{gr}\} \times \{true, false\}$, j-RELEVANCE is in NP; and*
2. *pr-true(false)-RELEVANCE is in Σ_2^p.*

Although the above corollary tells an exponential upper bound for all semantics, in the next we will give characterizing conditions for ad,st and co semantics, all of which can be checked in polynomial time.

---
[2] Proofs of results of this paper are available in appendix at arxiv.

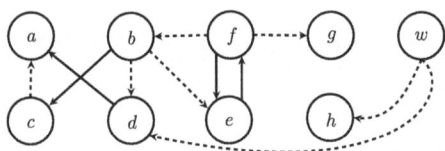

Fig. 2. The AtIAF I_{att} transformed from I_{ex} by Proposition 2

To obtain the complexity of RELEVANCE problem, we consider one of its specific problems which constrains the input IAF to have none uncertain arguments, i.e., the input being an AtIAF. The following proposition shows that the general RELEVANCE problem can be reduced to this specific form, which means that both of them hold the same complexity. The way in this proposition for constructing a related AtIAF from an IAF is borrowed from [13].

Proposition 2. *Given an IAF $I = \langle \mathcal{A}, \mathcal{A}^?, \mathcal{R}, \mathcal{R}^? \rangle$, a set of arguments $S \subseteq \mathcal{A} \cup \mathcal{A}^?$ and a verification status j, let w be an argument such that $w \notin \mathcal{A} \cup \mathcal{A}^?$ and $I_{att} = \langle \mathcal{A} \cup \mathcal{A}^? \cup \{w\}, \emptyset, \mathcal{R}, \mathcal{R}^? \cup \{(w, a) \mid a \in \mathcal{A}^?\} \rangle$. The following results hold:*

- *for each uncertain attack $e \in \mathcal{R}^?$, $e \in RE^+(I, S, j)$ (resp., $e \in RE^-(I, S, j)$) iff $e \in RE^+(I_{att}, S \cup \{w\}, j)$ (resp., $e \in RE^-(I_{att}, S \cup \{w\}, j)$); and*
- *for each uncertain argument $e \in \mathcal{A}^?$, $e \in RE^+(I, S, j)$ (resp., $e \in RE^-(I, S, j)$) iff $(w, e) \in RE^-(I_{att}, S \cup \{w\}, j)$ (resp., $(w, e) \in RE^+(I_{att}, S \cup \{w\}, j)$).*

Essentially, the uncertainty of the uncertain arguments can be replaced by the uncertainty of an attack from w to them, whereas the uncertainty of the uncertain attacks remains. This is because once an argument e is attacked by an argument not attacked by others, e is impossible to be accepted and can be regarded as absent.

Corollary 2. *Given a verification status j, j-RELEVANCE holds the same complexity with j-RELEVANCE problem constraining that the input IAF is an AtIAF.*

By Corollary 2, in the following we limit our discussion to RELEVANCE problem whose input IAF is an AtIAF. Recall that the σ-*true*-RELEVANCE of addition (resp., removal) essentially coincides with σ-*false*-RELEVANCE of removal (resp., addition), hence we just focus on σ-*true* RELEVANCE. Also, for the considered set of arguments which is already stable, the answer of RELEVANCE is trivial since all of the uncertain elements are irrelevant according to Proposition 1. Thus, we only need to study methods for finding relevance elements for a given, unstable set of arguments. Note that despite that the method by Proposition 2 gives a reduction to a specific AtIAF with an argument not attacked by others, the results we will give are about general AtIAFs.

Given an AtIAF I and a set of arguments S, since all semantics we discuss are based on conflict-freeness, the uncertain attacks between the arguments inside

S are necessary to be removed for reaching σ-true stability of S, thus removing each of these attacks is relevant whereas adding is not.

Except the uncertain attacks inside S, in the next we will give tractable methods to completely find all of the relevant attacks under ad, st and co, and we will show that both the addition and removal variants of RELEVANCE problem under these three semantics are all in P complexity class.

Firstly we discuss ad and st, under which verification of a set of arguments S is not influenced by those attacks whose neither attacker nor target is included in S. Hence, any uncertain attacks not related to S are irrelevant for verification of S under these two semantics and the relevant attacks are related to S.

Under ad semantics, an uncertain attack $r = (a, b)$ not inside S can become $true$-relevant in two cases: 1. $a \in S$ and b is a possible (necessary) attacker of S which is not attacked back by S, implying that r needs to be added when it is confirmed that b attacks S and no one else in S attacks b; and 2. $b \in S$ and a is not attacked by S, implying that r is unavoidable to be removed when all of the uncertain attacks from S to a are decided to be absent. Meanwhile, a does not attack other arguments in S except b, otherwise r turns out to be irrelevant. Therefore, we have the following proposition.

Proposition 3. *Given an AtIAF $I = \langle \mathcal{A}, \emptyset, \mathcal{R}, \mathcal{R}^? \rangle$ and a set of argument $S \subseteq \mathcal{A}$ such that S is not stable-ad w.r.t. I, for each attack $r = (a, b) \in \mathcal{R}^?$ s.t. $a \notin S$ or $b \notin S$,*

- *$r \in RE^+(I, S, \text{ad-}true)$ iff $a \in S, b \notin S_I^+$ and $S \not\subseteq \{b\}_I^{\sim}$; and*
- *$r \in RE^-(I, S, \text{ad-}true)$ iff $a \notin S_I^-, a \notin S_I^+$ and $b \in S$.*

Under st semantics, note that S is stable-st only when S is necessary or impossible to attack all of the other arguments, hence only the uncertain attacks from S toward the arguments which have not yet been attacked by S are relevant.

Proposition 4. *Given an AtIAF $I = \langle \mathcal{A}, \emptyset, \mathcal{R}, \mathcal{R}^? \rangle$ and a set of argument $S \subseteq \mathcal{A}$ such that S is not stable-st w.r.t. I, for each attack $r = (a, b) \in \mathcal{R}^?$ s.t. $a \notin S$ or $b \notin S$,*

- *$r \in RE^+(I, S, \text{st-}true)$ iff $a \in S$ and $b \notin S_I^+$; and*
- *$r \notin RE^-(I, S, \text{st-}true)$.*

Example 2. Figure 2 illustrates the AtIAF I_{att} transformed from I_{ex} in Fig. 1 by Proposition 2. For the argument set $S = \{a, b, f\}$, we have $RE^+(I_{att}, S \cup \{w\}, \text{ad-}true) = \{(b, d), (w, d)\}$ and $RE^-(I_{att}, S \cup \{w\}, \text{ad-}true) = \{(f, b)\}$ according to Proposition 3, and $RE^+(I_{att}, S \cup \{w\}, \text{st-}true) = \{(b, d), (f, g), (w, h), (w, d)\}$ according to Proposition 4. Then using Proposition 2, we transfer the results to the original input I_{ex} and S, and obtain $RE^+(I_{ex}, S, \text{ad-}true) = \{(b, d)\}$, $RE^-(I_{ex}, S, \text{ad-}true) = \{(f, b), d\}$, $RE^+(I_{ex}, S, \text{st-}true) = \{(b, d), (f, g)\}$, and $RE^-(I_{ex}, S, \text{st-}true) = \{h, d\}$. The reason why removing h, d is st-$true$-relevant lies in that h, d are impossible to be attacked by S once (b, d) is removed, so they must be removed so that S can attack all of the other arguments.

Proposition 3 and 4 imply that $RE^+(I, S, \sigma\text{-}true)$ disjoints with $RE^-(I, S, \sigma\text{-}true)$ under $\sigma \in \{\text{ad}, \text{st}\}$. However, under $\sigma \in \{\text{co}, \text{gr}, \text{pr}\}$, this property does not hold, and one can see a counterexample as follows.

Example 3. Let us consider the IAF $I = \langle \{a, b, c\}, \emptyset, \{(b,b), (b,c)\}, \{(a,b), (b,a), (a,c)\}\rangle$, $S = \{a\}$ and $\sigma \in \{\text{co}, \text{gr}, \text{pr}\}$. If (a,c) is removed, then (a,b) is needed to be removed for S to be a σ-extension, otherwise $c \notin S$ will be defended by S, hence $(a,b) \in RE^-(I, S, \sigma\text{-}true)$. On the other hand, if (b,a) is added, then (a,b) is needed to be added for S to reach $\sigma\text{-}true$ status, hence $(a,b) \in RE^+(I, S, \sigma\text{-}true)$.

Now we discuss co semantics. Before proposing a tractable method for identifying relevant attacks under co, we introduce an algorithm named *OutRel*. With input being an AtIAF I, a set of arguments S and an attack $r = (a,b)$ where $b \notin S$ is not necessarily self-attacked, $OutRel(I, S, r)$ determines if there exists a completion F such that $S \in \text{co}(F)$ and a is the unique attacker of b except the attackers attacked by S. If $r \in \mathcal{R}^?$ and $OutRel(I, S, r) = true$, then addition of r is co-*true*-relevant. This is because removing r from F will lead b defended by S and then S fails to be a co-extension. Algorithm 1 shows the details of *OutRel*. At first in line 1, we check whether there are attackers of b which are impossible to be attacked by S. If the answer is yes, then it is impossible for a to become the unique attacker of b except S_F^+ thus $false$ becomes the output of the algorithm. If the answer is no, we construct the partial completion I_1 of I by adding attacks from S to the certain attackers of b (line 2) and then removing all of the uncertain attacks to b except those from a (line 3). Finally, we check whether S is possible to become a co-extension from the IAF I_1, whose result is obtained as the output of the algorithm (line 4). It is obvious that the construction of I_1 in the algorithm can be done in polynomial time, and $PosVer_{\text{co}}$ has been proven in P [6,10], hence the complexity of algorithm *OutRel* is polynomial.

Algorithm 1: $OutRel(I, S, (a,b))$

Input: An AtIAF $I = \langle \mathcal{A}, \emptyset, \mathcal{R}, \mathcal{R}^?\rangle$, a set of arguments $S \subseteq \mathcal{A}$ and an attack $(a,b) \in \mathcal{R} \cup \mathcal{R}^?$ where $b \notin S$ and $(b,b) \notin \mathcal{R}$
Output: Whether there is a completion F of I such that $\{b\}_F^- \setminus S_F^+ = \{a\}$ and $S \in \text{co}(F)$

1 **if** $(\{b\}_I^- \setminus \{a\}) \cap S_I^\sim \neq \emptyset$ **then return** *false*
  $I_0 \leftarrow I + \{(s,v) \in \mathcal{R}^? \mid s \in S, v \in \{b\}_I^- \setminus \{a\}\}$
2 $I_1 \leftarrow I_0 - \{(u,b) \in \mathcal{R}^? \mid u \neq a\}$
3 **return** $PosVer_{\text{co}}(I_1, S)$

Now we present Theorem 1, which gives various tractable methods for identifying relevance for three different types of attacks that cover all of the possible attacks except attacks inside S: (1) attacks with both attackers and targets are outside S, (2) attacks whose targets are inside S, and (3) attacks whose attackers are inside S. Note that as the same as for ad and st semantics, the attacks whose both attackers and targets belong to S must be removed for satisfying conflict-freeness and then reaching co-$true$ status, so removing them is co-$true$-relevant whereas adding is not.

Theorem 1. *Given an AtIAF $I = \langle \mathcal{A}, \emptyset, \mathcal{R}, \mathcal{R}^? \rangle$ and a set of arguments $S \subseteq \mathcal{A}$ such that S is not stable-co w.r.t. I, for each attack $r = (a, b) \in \mathcal{R}^?$ s.t. $a \notin S$ or $b \notin S$, the following holds.*

(1) *If $a \notin S$ and $b \notin S$,*
  - $r \in RE^+(I, S, \text{co-}true)$ *iff* $(b, b) \notin \mathcal{R}$ *and* $OutRel(I, S, r) = true$; *and*
  - $r \notin RE^-(I, S, \text{co-}true)$.

(2) *If $a \notin S$ and $b \in S$,*
  - $r \notin RE^+(I, S, \text{co-}true)$; *and*
  - $r \in RE^-(I, S, \text{co-}true)$ *iff* $a \notin S_I^+$ *and* $PosVer_{co}(I - \{(s, a) \in \mathcal{R}^? \mid s \in S\}, S) = true$.

(3) *If $a \in S$ and $b \notin S$,*
  - $r \in RE^+(I, S, \text{co-}true)$ *iff* $(b, b) \notin \mathcal{R}$ *and* $OutRel(I, S, r) = true$, *or* $S \not\subseteq \{b\}_I^{\sim}$, $b \notin S_I^+$ *and* $PosVer_{co}(I + \{(a, b)\}, S) = true$; *and*
  - $r \in RE^-(I, S, \text{co-}true)$ *iff* $\exists v \in \mathcal{A} \setminus (S \cup \{b\})$ *s.t.* $(b, v) \in \mathcal{R} \cup \mathcal{R}^?$, $(v, v) \notin \mathcal{R}$ *and* $OutRel(I, S, (b, v)) = true$.

Proof (Sketch). (1) For $a \notin S$ and $b \notin S$, $r \in RE^+(I, S, \text{co-}true)$ iff there is a completion F of I where r is present and $S \in \text{co}(F)$ whereas removal of r will lead b defended by S then S fails to be a co-extension, which means that $\{b\}_F^{-} \setminus S_F^+ = \{a\}$. Hence $r \in RE^+(I, S, \text{co-}true)$ is equivalent to that $(b, b) \notin \mathcal{R}$ and $OutRel(I, S, r) = true$. And it is obvious that $r \notin RE^-(I, S, \text{co-}true)$.

(2) For $a \notin S$ and $b \in S$, $r \in RE^-(I, S, \text{co-}true)$ iff there is a completion F of I where r is absent and $S \in \text{co}(F)$ whereas addition of r will lead S not admissible, i.e., S is attacked by a but not attacking back, which is equivalent to that a is not necessarily attacked by S in I and S is possible to be a co-extension without attacking a, i.e., $a \notin S_I^+$ and $PosVer_{co}(I - \{(s, a) \in \mathcal{R}^? \mid s \in S\}, S) = true$. And it is obvious that $r \notin RE^+(I, S, \text{co-}true)$.

(3) For $a \in S$ and $b \notin S$, $r \in RE^+(I, S, \text{co-}true)$ iff there is a completion F of I where r is present and $S \in \text{co}(F)$ whereas removal of r will lead S to fail to be a co-extension in two cases: 1. b defended by S, which is equivalent to $(b, b) \notin \mathcal{R}$ and $OutRel(I, S, r) = true$; and 2. S fails to be admissible, i.e., S is attacked by b but r is the unique attack from S to b, which is equivalent to $S \not\subseteq \{b\}_I^{\sim}$, $b \notin S_I^+$ and $PosVer_{co}(I + \{(a, b)\}, S) = true$. In addition, $r \in RE^-(I, S, \text{co-}true)$ iff there is a completion F of I where r is absent and $S \in \text{co}(F)$ whereas addition of r will lead some new argument $v \neq b$ attacked by b defended by S, hence b is the unique attacker of v except the arguments attacked by S in F, thus $\exists v \in \mathcal{A} \setminus (S \cup \{b\})$ s.t. $(b, v) \in \mathcal{R} \cup \mathcal{R}^?$, $(v, v) \notin \mathcal{R}$ and $OutRel(I, S, (b, v)) = true$.

Example 4. Consider the IAF I_{att} in Fig. 2 and the set of arguments $S = \{a, b, w\}$. We can see that the co-*true*-relevant attacks for S are $(f, g), (f, b), (w, h), (b, d), (w, d)$ and (b, e), together covering all of the three conclusions listed in Theorem 1 when an uncertain element can be relevant under co: (1) $(f, g) \in RE^+$ since $OutRel(I_{att}, S, (f, g))) = true$; (2) $(f, b) \in RE^-$ since $f \notin S^+_{I_{att}}$ and $PosVer_{co}(I_{att}, S) = true$; (3) $(w, h) \in RE^+$ since $OutRel(I_{att}, S, (w, h)) = true$; $(b, d), (w, d) \in RE^+$ since d attacks S and S is possible to be a co-extension after addition of (b, d) or (w, d); and $(b, e) \in RE^-$ since $OutRel(I_{att}, S, (e, f)) = true$.

By Proposition 3, 4 and Corollary 2, we can conclude that deciding RELEVANCE for verification under ad and co semantics is in P. In Theorem 1, since *PosVer*, *OutRel* and other operations can all be done in polynomial time, deciding RELEVANCE under co is also in P.

Corollary 3. *For $j \in \{\text{ad}, \text{st}, \text{co}\} \times \{true, false\}$, j-RELEVANCE is in P.*

Finally, we give a method for proving Σ_2^p lower bound for pr-RELEVANCE, by giving a reduction from *PosVer* problem w.r.t. AtIAFs under pr, which is proven to be Σ_2^p-c in [6].

Proposition 5. *Given an AtIAF $I = \langle \mathcal{A}, \emptyset, \mathcal{R}, \mathcal{R}^?\rangle$ and a set of arguments $S \subseteq \mathcal{A}$, let $I' = \langle \mathcal{A} \cup \{w_1\}, \{w_2\}, \mathcal{R} \cup \{(w_2, s) \mid s \in S\}, \mathcal{R}^? \cup \{(w_1, w_2)\}\rangle$ where $w_1, w_2 \notin \mathcal{A}$.*

- *$PosVer_{pr}(I, S) = true$ iff $(w_1, w_2) \in RE^+(I' + \{w_2\}, S \cup \{w_1\}, \text{pr-}true)$; and*
- *$PosVer_{pr}(I, S) = true$ iff $w_2 \in RE^-(I' - \{(w_1, w_2)\}, S \cup \{w_1\}, \text{pr-}true)$.*

4 Strong Relevance for Stability of Verification

In this section we introduce the notion of strong relevance, which characterizes the necessity of resolution of relevant elements for reaching stability. Also, we define the related decision problem and give precise complexity results for each common semantics.

4.1 Definition of Strong Relevance

For a set of arguments where the j-stability can be reached, it is interesting to explore which elements are necessary to be added or removed in all partial completions where j-stability holds. Such elements are defined as follows to be *strongly j-relevant* for S w.r.t. the IAF.

Definition 6 (Strong relevance for stability of a set of arguments). *Given an IAF $I = \langle \mathcal{A}, \mathcal{A}^?, \mathcal{R}, \mathcal{R}^?\rangle$, a set of arguments $S \subseteq \mathcal{A} \cup \mathcal{A}^?$, a verification status j satisfying that there is at least one $I_p \in part(I)$ such* that S is stable-j w.r.t. I_p, and an uncertain element $e \in \mathcal{A}^? \cup \mathcal{R}^?$, addition (resp., removal) of e is strongly j-relevant for S w.r.t. I iff for each $I' \in part(I - \{e\})$(resp., $part(I + \{e\})$), S is not stable-j w.r.t. I'. We use $SRE^+(I, S, j)$ and $SRE^-(I, S, j)$ to respectively denote the uncertain elements whose addition and removal are strongly j-relevant for S w.r.t. I.

Obviously for each uncertain attack inside S, its removal is strongly -true-relevant since all the semantics we discuss require conflict-freeness. And for each uncertain argument belonging to S, its addition must be strongly -$true$-relevant since every argument of S should be present so that S can be an extension.

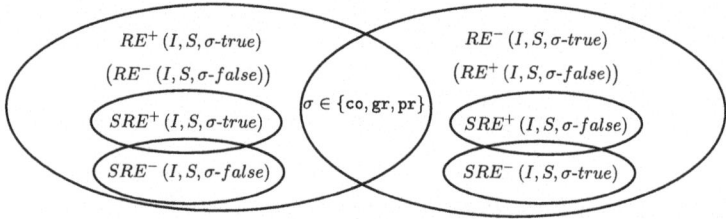

Fig. 3. Inclusion-relationships of sets of relevant and strong relevant elements, where an overlap of two ellipses means that the related sets may intersect under some semantics, and one ellipse within another indicates a subset under all semantics.

Figure 3 illustrates the inclusion-relationships of various relevant and strongly relevant sets of elements. It is obvious that a strongly relevant element is also relevant, i.e., $SRE^+(I, S, j) \subseteq RE^+(I, S, j)$ and $SRE^-(I, S, j) \subseteq RE^-(I, S, j)$. However, differently from relevance, -$true$ strong relevance of an action within {addition, removal} does not always coincide with -$false$ strong relevance of its opposite action. We give such instances in the subsequent example. Meanwhile, if addition of an element e is strongly σ-$true$(resp., $false$)-relevant, then it is trivial that removal of e is not σ-$true$(resp., $false$)-relevant.

Example 5. Continue with the IAF I_{ex} and the set of arguments $S = \{a, b\}$ in Fig. 1. We have $SRE^+(I_{ex}, S, \text{co}) = \{(f, g)\}$ and $SRE^-(I_{ex}, S, \text{co}) = \{h, (b, e), (f, b)\}$. For $\sigma \in \{\text{ad}, \text{co}, \text{pr}\}$, removal of (f, b) is strongly σ-$true$-relevant since it is impossible for S to be a σ-extension once (f, b) is present. Although being σ-$true$-relevant, removal of d is not strongly σ-$true$-relevant, since when (b, d) is added, d will no longer influence the verification of S, thus addition of d will not lead S to fail to be a σ-extension. One can see that $(f, b) \in SRE^-(I_{ex}, S, \text{ad-}true)$ but $\notin SRE^+(I_{ex}, S, \text{ad-}false)$. Moreover, $(f, g) \in SRE^+(I_{ex}, S, \text{co-}true)$ but $\notin SRE^-(I_{ex}, S, \text{co-}false)$. Therefore, addition and removal action do not hold the dual property in terms of strong relevance.

4.2 Complexity Analysis of Strong Relevance

Now we discuss the computational complexity for the decision problem of identifying strong relevance, which is formulated as follows.

j-STRONG-RELEVANCE of action a

Given: An IAF $I = \langle \mathcal{A}, \mathcal{A}^?, \mathcal{R}, \mathcal{R}^? \rangle$, a set of arguments $S \subseteq \mathcal{A} \cup \mathcal{A}^?$, a verification status j s.t. there is at least one $I' \in part(I)$ such that S is stable-j w.r.t. I', an action $\mathbf{a} \in \{\text{addition}, \text{removal}\}$, and an uncertain element $\mathbf{e} \in \mathcal{A}^? \cup \mathcal{R}^?$.

Question: Is a of e strongly j-relevant for S w.r.t. I?

We start with a proposition giving a reduction from STRONG-RELEVANCE problem to $PosVer$ and $NecVer$ problem. Directly according to the definition of stability, S can reach σ-$true$ stability only when $PosVer_\sigma(I, S) = true$, while S can reach σ-$false$ stability only when $NecVer_\sigma(I, S) = false$. Therefore, addition of an uncertain element e is strongly σ-$true$-relevant iff S is impossible to become σ-$true$ after the removal of e in I, i.e., $PosVer_\sigma(I - \{e\}, S) = false$.

Proposition 6. *Given an IAF $I = \langle \mathcal{A}, \mathcal{A}^?, \mathcal{R}, \mathcal{R}^? \rangle$, a set of arguments $S \subseteq \mathcal{A} \cup \mathcal{A}^?$ and semantics σ, if $PosVer_\sigma(I, S) = true$ (resp., $NecVer_\sigma(I, S) = false$), then for each uncertain element $e \in \mathcal{A}^? \cup \mathcal{R}^?$,*

- *$e \in SRE^+(I, S, \sigma\text{-}true)$ (resp., $e \in SRE^+(I, S, \sigma\text{-}false)$) iff $PosVer_\sigma(I - \{e\}, S) = false$ (resp., $NecVer_\sigma(I - \{e\}, S) = true$); and*
- *$e \in SRE^-(I, S, \sigma\text{-}true)$ (resp., $e \in SRE^-(I, S, \sigma\text{-}false)$) iff $PosVer_\sigma(I + \{e\}, S) = false$ (resp., $NecVer_\sigma(I + \{e\}, S) = true$).*

Using the complexity results of $PosVer$ and $NecVer$ in [6,10], we directly obtain the upper bounds of STRONG-RELEVANCE according to Proposition 6.

Corollary 4. *The following results hold:*

1. *for $j \in \{\text{ad}, \text{st}, \text{co}, \text{gr}\} \times \{true, false\}$, j-STRONG-RELEVANCE is in P;*
2. *pr-$true$-STRONG-RELEVANCE is in Π_2^p; and*
3. *pr-$false$-STRONG-RELEVANCE is in $coNP$.*

In order to prove $coNP$ completeness of pr-$false$-STRONG-RELEVANCE, we reduce from $NecVer$ problem w.r.t. AtIAFs under pr, which has been proven to be $coNP$-c in [6].

Proposition 7. *Given an AtIAF $I = \langle \mathcal{A}, \emptyset, \mathcal{R}, \mathcal{R}^? \rangle$ and a set of arguments $S \subseteq \mathcal{A}$, let IAF $I' = \langle \mathcal{A}, \{w\}, \mathcal{R}, \mathcal{R}^? \cup \{(w, w)\} \rangle$ where $w \notin \mathcal{A}$. The following results hold:*

- *$NecVer_{\text{pr}}(I, S) = true$ iff $w \in SRE^+(I' - \{(w,w)\}, S, \text{pr}\text{-}false)$; and*
- *$NecVer_{\text{pr}}(I, S) = true$ iff $(w,w) \in SRE^-(I' + \{w\}, S, \text{pr}\text{-}false)$.*

Next we show Π_2^p completeness of pr-$true$-STRONG-RELEVANCE by reducing from $\Pi_2 SAT$ problem. Given a pair of disjoint boolean variable sets X, Y and a formula φ in conjunctive normal form, $\Pi_2 SAT$ asks whether for any assignment τ_X for X, there always exists an assignment τ_Y for Y such that $\varphi[\tau_X, \tau_Y] = true$ holds. We translate a $\Pi_2 SAT$ instance to an IAF in Definition 7 based on the translation used in [5], which is illustrated in Fig. 4.

Definition 7. Let (φ, X, Y) be an instance of $\Pi_2 SAT$. And let $\varphi = \wedge_i c_i$ and $c_i = \vee_j \alpha_j$ where the α_j are the literals belonging to $X \cup Y$ that occur in clause c_i. We define the IAF $I_\varphi = \langle \mathcal{A}, \mathcal{A}^?, \mathcal{R}, \mathcal{R}^? \rangle$ as follows:

- $\mathcal{A} = \{\overline{x_i} \mid x_i \in X\} \cup \{y_i, \overline{y_i} \in Y\} \cup \{c_i \mid c_i \in \varphi\} \cup \{\varphi, w\}$;
- $\mathcal{A}^? = \{x_i \mid x_i \in X\}$;
- $\mathcal{R} = \{(x_i, \overline{x_i}) \mid x_i \in X\} \cup \{(y_i, \overline{y_i}), (\overline{y_i}, y_i) \mid y_i \in Y\} \cup \{(x_k, c_i) \mid x_k \in c_i\} \cup \{(\overline{x_k}, c_i) \mid \neg x_k \in c_i\} \cup \{(y_k, c_i) \mid y_k \in c_i\} \cup \{(\overline{y_k}, c_i) \mid \neg y_k \in c_i\} \cup \{(c_i, \varphi) \mid c_i \in \varphi\} \cup \{(c_i, c_i) \mid c_i \in \varphi\} \cup \{(w, x_i), (w, \overline{x_i}) \mid x_i \in X\} \cup \{(w, y_i), (w, \overline{y_i}) \mid y_i \in Y\} \cup \{(w, w)\}$; and
- $\mathcal{R}^? = \{(\varphi, \varphi), (\varphi, w)\}$.

The following proposition shows the reduction from $\Pi_2 SAT$ to pr-*true*-STRONG-RELEVANCE problem.

Proposition 8. *Given an instance (φ, X, Y) of $\Pi_2 SAT$, let I_φ be the IAF constructed by Definition 7. The following results hold:*

- $(\varphi, X, Y) \in \Pi_2 SAT$ iff $(\varphi, \varphi) \in SRE^+(I_\varphi + \{(\varphi, w)\}, \emptyset, \text{pr-}true)$; and
- $(\varphi, X, Y) \in \Pi_2 SAT$ iff $(\varphi, w) \in SRE^-(I_\varphi - \{(\varphi, \varphi)\}, \emptyset, \text{pr-}true)$.

In conclusion, despite the notion of strong relevance characterizes a stricter type of relevance, the complexity results show that its identification does not become a more difficult problem than identifying relevance.

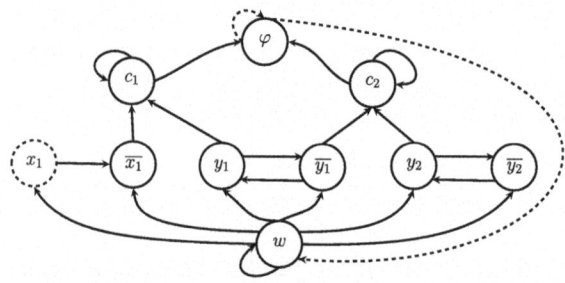

Fig. 4. The IAF created from the $\Pi_2 SAT$ instance $((\overline{x_1} \vee y_1) \wedge (\overline{y_1} \vee y_2), \{x_1\}, \{y_1, y_2\})$.

5 Related Work and Discussion

The notion of relevance is first proposed in [15] where relevance for stability of justification status of a given argument is studied. We follow that work and study the relevance for stability of verification status of a given set of arguments in this paper. Table 1 lists part of complexity results from [15] and our results about relevance and strong relevance. Compared with that all of the complexities for stability of justification are up to exponential level, we identify tractable methods for solving relevance problems for stability of verification under most considered semantics, showing that they are in P complexity level. Particularly, in Theorem 1 for deciding relevance for stability of a given set of arguments S under co-semantics, we divide the uncertain attacks into three separate parts, the attacks towards S, from S and not related to S, and then give methods accordingly to tackle the relevance problems. Such a dividing way may also benefit solving relevance problem of justification, for instance, in order obtain σ-*in-credulous(skeptical)*-relevant elements for a given argument a, one can divide the uncertain arguments and attacks into two parts, those that are able to reach a (through both certain and uncertain attacks) and those not. Then we can directly conclude that those not able to reach a are irrelevant as long as the semantics discussed satisfies *directionality* criterion [2]. Such a dividing intuition is also applied in [11] for reasoning in dynamic AFs.

Besides the distinction in complexity, the relevance problems discussed in [15] and this paper hold different properties. Recall that *-true*-relevance of addition coincides with *-false*-relevance of removal for verification of a set of arguments. Such a property does not hold for every two of *-in,-out* and *-undec-credulous(skeptical)*-relevance for justification of an argument, because for instance the status 'not in' does not coincide with either 'out' or 'undec'. Lastly, it is easy to see that the notion of strong relevance proposed in this paper can be adapted to justification of an argument. The preliminary results from a first attempt of ours show that the computational complexity of deciding strong relevance tends to be lower than relevance for justification of an argument, which will be elaborated in our future work. This is different from the verification of a set of arguments where relevance and strong relevance hold the same complexity in P for the most discussed semantics, as shown in Table 1.

We have not given the precise complexity result for gr semantics. It turns out to be difficult to find tractable methods for solving **gr**-RELEVANCE problem, especially for deciding the relevance of attacks related to a given set of arguments S. In order to decide the **gr**-RELEVANCE of an attack $r = (a, b)$ where $a, b \notin S$, we can use the same method for co in Theorem 1, i.e., $r \in RE^+(I, S, \text{gr-}true)$ iff $r \in RE^+(I, S, \text{co-}true)$. However, for attacks whose attackers or targets belong to S, the method of Theorem 1 cannot be used to decide **gr**-RELEVANCE. This is because gr semantics requires *strong admissibility* [2,7], characterizing that the accepted set S of arguments is able to be constructed from an initial set of arguments containing those in S that are not attacked by any other arguments, and then repeatedly merging the arguments defended by the current set until there are no arguments that can be merged. Such a strong admissibility requirement leads deciding relevance for attacks related to S under gr to be more difficult than under co. For instance, consider the IAF $I = \langle \{a, b\}, \emptyset, \{(a, b)\}, \{(b, a)\} \rangle$. We can see that removal of (b, a) is not co-*true*-relevant but **gr**-*true*-relevant for the set $\{a\}$. We leave the precise complexity of **gr**-RELEVANCE for future work.

Stability decision problem in IAFs is first proposed in [12] focusing on stability of acceptable status of an argument and related complexity results are given in [5]. Later a finer-grained acceptable status named justification status is introduced and the related stability problem is studied in [15]. Besides, *functionality* studied in [1] presents a more strictly acceptable status for a single argument, which specifies whether an argument can be firmly decided in any completion. The stability of verification can be viewed as possible and necessary verification problems studied in [6,10]. In addition to stability of an single argument and a set of arguments, in our previous work [21] we consider the stability of the whole extensions, i.e., an IAF is said to be stable for its extensions if any completion outputs the same extensions under certain semantics. Also focusing on the whole extensions of a semantics, [19] studies whether there exists a nonempty extension in some (or any) completion of an IAF. One can see that the notion of relevance and strong relevance can also be extended to these types of stability so as to solve their related problems about reaching stability.

Detecting relevance and strong relevance can be applied to *enforcement* problems [4], especially *general enforcement* proposed in [8], which asks how to add arguments or modify attacks in the current AF to enable a set of arguments to become an extension. A dynamic AF under constrained update can be modeled as an IAF, where uncertain arguments represent the new arguments allowed to be added and uncertain attacks represent the original (un)attacks which are questionable. One can see that if addition or removal of an element e is not -*true*-relevant for the desired set of arguments S w.r.t. the IAF, then such a modification is not included in any *minimal change* solution [8] for the enforcement of S. On the other hand, if addition or removal of e is strongly -*true*-relevant, then such a modification is necessary to be conducted in any minimal change. Also considering modification of one element e, the preservation problems [17,18] ask whether the verification status of an extension S will remain after modification of e. Although they appear similar to the concept of 'irrelevant' in this paper, they are essentially different because e being irrelevant means that S is preserved under modification of e in all of the possible situations that would occur in the future (i.e., all of the completions of the given IAF). In [3,16], an operation named σ-*kernel* on AFs is proposed, which essentially selects and removes attacks useless for semantics σ of an AF, i.e., the attacks whose modification has

Table 1. Complexity of various types of relevance in IAFs.

σ	relevance for justification [15]		relevance for verification	strong relevance for verification
	credulous-in	skeptical-in		
ad	Σ_2^p-c	trivial	P	P
st	Σ_2^p-c	Σ_2^p-c	P	P
co	Σ_2^p-c	NP-c	P	P
gr	NP-c	NP-c	in NP	P
pr	Σ_2^p-c	Σ_3^p-c	Σ_2^p-c	Π_2^p-c, $coNP$-c

no influence on the output of σ-extensions of the AF. Actually, the operations for different semantics proposed in [3,16] can be extended to IAFs and the attacks selected are irrelevant for verification of any set of arguments.

6 Conclusions

This paper explores the relevance and strong relevance problems for stability of verification status of a set of arguments in IAFs. A complexity analysis of the decision problems of both kinds of relevance is conducted and all of the common semantics are given precise complexity except gr semantics. Such relevance problems are distinct from the relevance for justification of an argument in [15], the original work where the relevance for stability is proposed and the study in this paper follows so as to tackle which uncertainties should be resolved to reach stability for verification. For future work, we will continue studying precise complexity for gr semantics, and extend the notion of (strong) relevance to other types of stability in IAFs including stability of the whole extensions.

References

1. Alfano, G., Greco, S., Parisi, F., Trubitsyna, I.: Incomplete argumentation frameworks: properties and complexity. In: AAAI Conference on Artificial Intelligence, AAAI 2022, vol. 36, pp. 5451–5460 (2022)
2. Baroni, P., Giacomin, M.: On principle-based evaluation of extension-based argumentation semantics. Artif. Intell. **171**(10–15), 675–700 (2007)
3. Baumann, R.: Normal and strong expansion equivalence for argumentation frameworks. Artif. Intell. **193**, 18–44 (2012)
4. Baumann, R., Brewka, G.: Expanding argumentation frameworks: enforcing and monotonicity results. In: Computational Models of Argument, COMMA 2010, pp. 75–86 (2010)
5. Baumeister, D., Järvisalo, M., Neugebauer, D., Niskanen, A., Rothe, J.: Acceptance in incomplete argumentation frameworks. Artif. Intell. **295**, 103470 (2021)
6. Baumeister, D., Neugebauer, D., Rothe, J., Schadrack, H.: Verification in incomplete argumentation frameworks. Artif. Intell. **264**, 1–26 (2018)
7. Caminada, M., Dunne, P.: Strong admissibility revisited: Theory and applications. Argument Comput. **10**(3), 277–300 (2020)
8. Coste-Marquis, S., Konieczny, S., Mailly, J.G., Marquis, P.: Extension enforcement in abstract argumentation as an optimization problem. In: Twenty-Fourth International Joint Conference on Artificial Intelligence, IJCAI 2015, pp. 2876–2882 (2015)
9. Dung, P.M.: On the acceptability of arguments and its fundamental role in non-monotonic reasoning, logic programming and n-person games. Artif. Intell. **77**(2), 321–357 (1995)
10. Fazzinga, B., Flesca, S., Furfaro, F.: Revisiting the notion of extension over incomplete abstract argumentation frameworks. In: Twenty-Ninth International Joint Conference on Artificial Intelligence, IJCAI 2020, pp. 1712–1718 (2020)
11. Liao, B., Jin, L., Koons, R.C.: Dynamics of argumentation systems: a division-based method. Artif. Intell. **175**(11), 1790–1814 (2011)

12. Mailly, J.G., Rossit, J.: Stability in abstract argumentation. In: NMR 2020 Workshop Notes, pp. 93–99
13. Mantadelis, T., Bistarelli, S.: Probabilistic abstract argumentation frameworks, a possible world view. Int. J. Approximate Reasoning **119**, 204–219 (2020)
14. Odekerken, D., Bex, F., Borg, A., Testerink, B.: Approximating stability for applied argument-based inquiry. Intell. Syst. Appl. **16**, 200110 (2022)
15. Odekerken, D., Borg, A., Bex, F.: Justification, stability and relevance in incomplete argumentation frameworks. Argument Comput. **15**(3), 251–308 (2024)
16. Oikarinen, E., Woltran, S.: Characterizing strong equivalence for argumentation frameworks. Artif. Intell. **175**(14–15), 1985–2009 (2011)
17. Rienstra, T., Sakama, C., van der Torre, L.: Persistence and monotony properties of argumentation semantics. In: Theory and Applications of Formal Argumentation: Third International Workshop, TAFA 2015, pp. 211–225. Springer (2015)
18. Rienstra, T., Sakama, C., van der Torre, L., Liao, B.: A principle-based robustness analysis of admissibility-based argumentation semantics. Argument Comput. **11**(3), 305–339 (2020)
19. Skiba, K., Neugebauer, D., Rothe, J.: Complexity of nonempty existence problems in incomplete argumentation frameworks. IEEE Intell. Syst. **36**(2), 13–24 (2020)
20. Testerink, B., Odekerken, D., Bex, F.: A method for efficient argument-based inquiry. In: Flexible Query Answering Systems, FQAS 2019, pp. 114–125. Springer (2019)
21. Xiong, A., Zhang, H., Zhang, S.: Stability of extensions in incomplete argumentation frameworks. In: International Conference on Scalable Uncertainty Management, SUM 2024, pp. 470–485. Springer (2024)

The A-BDI Metamodel for Human-Level AI
Argumentation as Balancing, Dialogue and Inference

Liuwen Yu[1(✉)] and Leendert van der Torre[1,2]

[1] University of Luxembourg, Esch-sur-Alzette, Luxembourg
liuwen.yu@uni.lu
[2] Zhejiang University, Hangzhou, China

Abstract. In this paper, we introduce A-BDI, the first metamodel for formal and computational argumentation. It contains three models, conceptualizing argumentation as balancing, argumentation as dialogue, and argumentation as inference respectively. Each model looks at argumentation from a different perspective, addressing its own concerns and using its own formal and computational methods. Whereas balancing is inspired by the scale metaphor and uses quantitative techniques typically found in theories in economics and neural computing, dialogue is developed in multiagent communication and interaction and uses chatbot and Large Language Models (LLMs) technology, and inference is derived from theoretical investigations in knowledge representation and reasoning and uses techniques from symbolic reasoning. By bringing together new and traditional Artificial Intelligence (AI) approaches, the A-BDI metamodel provides a formal and computational framework for human-level, neuro-symbolic, and hybrid AI.

Keywords: Metamodel for Argumentation · Methodology of Argumentation · Knowledge Representation and Reasoning · Hybrid Artificial Intelligence

1 Introduction

The research area of argumentation in Artificial Intelligence (AI) is highly diverse: there is natural, formal, and computational argumentation; there are various models of argumentation, and there is a diversity in the formal methods used [6,16,54]. To deal with this diversity, we are developing our A-BDI metamodel for formal and computational argumentation, which can be used in knowledge engineering of human-level AI systems. In this conference paper, we do not have the space to discuss the technical aspects of our A-BDI metamodel, but instead, our overall research question is: What are the motivation, methodology, and application of A-BDI metamodel? This overall question breaks down into the following questions:

1. What are the models and conceptualizations of argumentation used in traditional and new-generation AI?

2. What are the relations, similarities, and distinctions between the models?
3. How to use the A-BDI metamodel?
4. What are the motivations for a metamodel?

In our approach, the three models are BDI: balancing, dialogue, and inference. A metamodel provides a higher-level abstraction of how these models interrelate and can be integrated. Concretely, the metamodel we present uses extended Dung's abstract argumentation graphs to relate the models. These extended argumentation frameworks can be flattened into basic ones, demonstrating the universality of attack [54].

To answer the above four questions, we adopt the following approach, which also structures our paper.

1. We use the literature study underlying our chapter in the handbook to roughly delineate the three models of argumentation used in AI, and we illustrate all three approaches on a single example, highlighting their individual specifics.
2. We perform an analysis of the results obtained from the literature study.
3. As a first step towards a user guide for formal and computational argumentation in AI, we discuss how to choose a model for an application.
4. We use our work on the project Logics for New Generation Artificial Intelligence (LNGAI)[1] and workshop Causality, Agents and Large Models (CALM)[2] to provide motivations from a human-level, neurosymbolic hybrid AI.

Our aim in writing this paper and presenting it at CLAR is to receive feedback from the community on our proposal. In this sense, our paper is written as a discussion paper, with several questions and open issues identified. This paper builds on our work as editor of the handbook of formal argumentation, coPI of the logic for new generation AI projects in China, and creators of a new workshop series on causality and Argumentation using LLMs. Our vision for the shift in our work from traditional to current AI and from traditional argumentation methods to new ones resulted in thirteen challenges for formal and computational argumentation, as introduced and discussed in our chapter in the third volume of the handbook.

2 The Balancing, Dialogue, and Inference (BDI) Models

This section presents three models of argumentation. Each of them embodies a unique perspective on the construction and purpose of argumentation, a set of formal methods, and application across different disciplines and contexts. Table 1 provides an overview of the three models. We use a legal child custody case [53] to illustrate the three models.

---

[1] https://www.zlaire.net/lngai/.
[2] https://www.ciad-lab.fr/prima-causal-ai-workshop/.

Table 1. Three models of A-BDI

Models	Process	Theories and Formal Approaches	Application
Argumentation as balancing	Balancing pros and cons to reach a justified decision	Multi-criteria decision theory, case-based reasoning	Deliberative decision-making in law, ethics, and economics
Argumentation as dialogue	Dynamic verbal interaction between stakeholders to exchange information or resolve conflicts of opinion	Speech act theory, game theory, axiomatic semantics, operational semantics	Debating technologies, chatbots, recommender systems
Argumentation as inference	Logical structure and reasoning to derive conclusions from incomplete and inconsistent premises	Graph theory, nonmonotonic logic, computational logic, causal reasoning, Bayesian reasoning	Automated reasoning systems, knowledge representation, expert systems

2.1 Argumentation as Balancing

Argumentation as balancing is identified by Gordon [19]. It involves weighing the pros and cons of an issue in order to reach a balanced decision or judgment. It is applicable not only when resolving conflicts of opinion in persuasion dialogues but also, e.g., when deciding courses of action in deliberation dialogues [19]. In such a system, pro and con arguments for alternative resolutions of the issues (options or positions) are put forward, evaluated, resolved, and balanced. The formal methods used are multi-criteria decision theory and case-based reasoning, and they are applied in the realms of law, ethics, and economics.

One model of argumentation as balancing is the Carneades Argumentation System [20]. The conception of argument graphs in Carneades is similar to Pollock's conception of an inference graph. There are nodes in the graph representing statements (propositions) and links that indicate inference relations between statements. In particular, the system distinguishes between pro and con arguments. Semantically, con arguments are instances of presumptive inference rules for negating the conclusion. If the premises of a con argument hold, this justifies rejecting the conclusion or, equivalently, accepting its logical complement. With pro and con arguments, some statements need to be ordered or otherwise aggregated to resolve the conflict. Then there are several proof standards used to balance the pros and cons. Here are three examples:

SE (Scintilla of Evidence): A statement meets this standard iff it is supported by at least one defensible pro argument.

BA (Best Argument): A statement meets this standard iff it is supported by some defensible pro argument with priority over all defensible con arguments.

DV (Dialectical Validity): A statement meets this standard iff it is supported by at least one defensible pro argument and none of its con arguments are defensible.

We use a child custody example to illustrate how Carneades works, as visualized in Fig. 1.

Example 1 (Child custody in Carneades). Statements are depicted as boxes and arguments as circles. For the purpose of this discussion, we assume that all the premises are ordinary without distinguishing between different types of premises. Premises are shown as edges without arrowheads. Pro arguments are indicated by circle arrowheads while con arguments are shown with standard arrowheads. Argument a_1 asserts that the child knows what she wants and she wants to live with her mother, making it a pro argument for the statement "It is in the child's best interest that she lives with her mother". In contrast, argument a_2 argues that the mother is less wealthy than the father, serving as a con argument against that statement. In this scenario, a_1 is given priority over a_2. Consequently, according to the BA proof standard, the statement "It is in the child's best interest that she lives with her mother" is accepted.

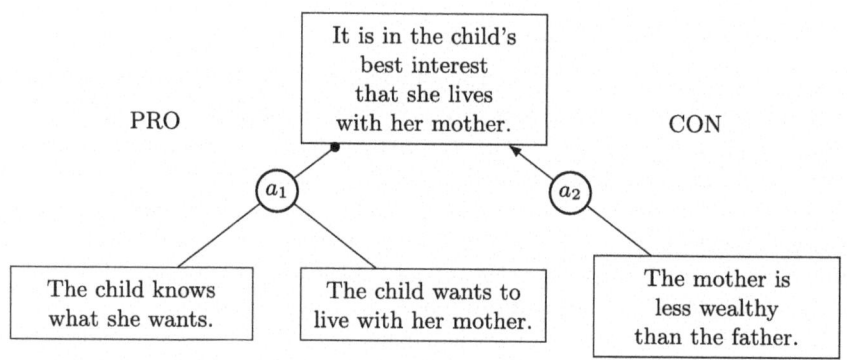

Fig. 1. Child custody case represented in Carneades argument graphs

Moreover, balancing extends beyond what Gordon proposed in Carneades, particularly in how the reason-based approach and balancing are gaining increasing importance in philosophical discussions. The fundamental metaphor of balancing is that reasons possess polarity (favoring or disfavoring an action) and weight (magnitude) [46], and these factors are aggregated to determine an act's deontic status, such as whether it is permissible, impermissible, or required. This metaphor is visualized as a balance scale [47], where reasons supporting an action push one side down while opposing reasons push the other side up, ultimately determining the normative outcome.

Particularly, there is a dispute on whether a reason's weight is context-sensitive. Atomists say no, while holists say yes. The former says that a reason in one context is a reason with the same polarity and weight in every other context; instead, the latter says that a reason in one context but, in some other context, has a different magnitude (weak vs strong) or polarity (for vs against) or is not a reason at all [13]. The moderate view [14] acknowledges that reasons have some context-independent weight, but their strength can be increased, reduced, or removed systematically through contextual considerations. Two key mechanisms shape this process: amplifiers (increase a reason's weight or attenuators that decrease it) and undercutters (nullify a reason's weight entirely), which modify the force of reasons, and two types of weights—the default weight, which represents a reason's initial strength, and the final weight, which accounts for contextual influences [46]. A major challenge in formal modeling is that existing frameworks fail to fully capture these nuances. A formal approach to this moderate view is proposed by Alcaraz et al. [1] and Streit [41] builds on weighted argumentation [3]. The model provides a normative structure that organizes the contextual considerations and their impact on the reasons. Example 2 illustrates the basic idea.

Example 2. Figure 2 represents the balancing scale model with undercutters, amplifiers, and attenuators graphically. The gray circles represent the two options for the child: living with the mother or the father, each placed on one side of the scale. Green and red circles stand for, respectively, positive and negative reasons. "Father is wealthy" is a positive reason for the child to live with the father, while "Father is busy" is a negative reason. "Child wants to live with the mother" is a positive reason for living with the mother. Blue, yellow, and purple circles represent, respectively, undercutters, attenuators, and amplifiers. "Father just went bankrupt" undercuts "Father is wealthy," nullifying its weight. "The Civil Code states that the judge must take into consideration the child's opinion" amplifies "Child wants to live with the mother," increasing its weight. "Public opinion states that ten-year-old children do not know what they want" attenuates "Child wants to live with the mother," reducing its weight.

There are more philosophical discussions on reasons and balancing. For example, Tucker distinguishes two kinds of reasons: justifying reasons and requiring reasons [46]. The difference can be illustrated by an example. There are two people trapped in a burning building. You can do nothing (save none), save one of them, or save both of them. If you save at least one, you will lose your legs. This scenario illustrates the tension between collective values (saving lives) and individual considerations (preserving one's health), and it raises the question of how to model and weigh these competing types of reasons. These two roles are distinct but complementary, highlighting the multidimensional nature of reasons. To model this interaction, Tucker introduces the Dual Scale model [46], which uses one scale to evaluate whether an action is permissible (based on the balance of justifying weight for the action and requiring weight for its alternative) and another scale to assess whether the alternative is impermissible.

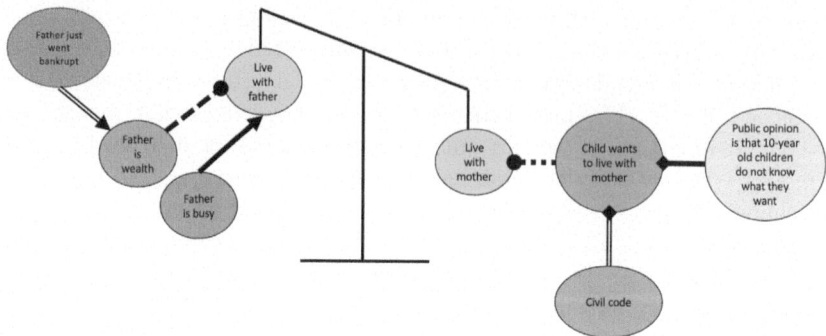

Fig. 2. A balancing scale model representing the child custody case with undercutters and modifiers

Interestingly, while "balancing" itself is not always explicitly mentioned, many theoretical approaches in formal argumentation often involve balancing, such as bipolar argumentation [11,51,53], weighted argumentation [8], and ranking-based argumentation [2]. Quantitative approaches in formal argumentation, often explored through extended abstract argumentation frameworks, bring a balancing perspective to reasoning. These models expand upon Dung's original framework by moving beyond binary notions of acceptance or rejection. Instead, they assign numerical scores, weights, or probabilities to arguments and their interactions. The question is: Which quantitative method in argumentation best serves the philosophical discussion of balancing?

2.2 Argumentation as Dialogue

Argumentation as dialogue conceptualizes argumentation as verbal interaction aimed at resolving opinion conflicts [37]. It involves defining argumentation protocols—rules governing the argumentation game—and strategic aspects that guide engagement. This approach draws on speech act theory, game theory, and both axiomatic and operational semantics. It is particularly suited for debates, chatbots, persuasion, and negotiation systems. We refer to the chapter by Black et al. for an overview of argumentation as dialogue [9]. For a comprehensive overview of argumentation as dialogue, we refer to the paper by Black et al. [9]. With recent advancements in LLMs and chatbot technology, this topic has gained renewed interest and presents promising opportunities for practical applications.

Chatbots are conversational software that seeks to understand input from human users and generate human-like responses [9]. In chatbot development, *questions* play a crucial role in enhancing the effectiveness of argumentation-based chatbots and building engaging conversations [27]. The use of *questions* allows chatbots to guide dialogues, challenge assertions, support critical thinking, and provide justifications. Below, we discuss how *question* mechanisms could be embedded into chatbots—justification-seeking questions defined by speech act theory.

Speech act theory, a subfield of pragmatics, examines how language conveys information and performs actions [5]. It has been formalized in the Foundation for Intelligent Physical Agents (FIPA) standards, widely used in computer science for agent communication [15]. A single utterance can serve multiple functions in dialogue [23], classified under basic types like assertions, questions, and commands, or complex ones like promises and declarations [39]. Unlike physical actions, speech acts primarily affect agents' mental and interactional states [45], shaping beliefs, desires, and intentions [17]. In human-like chatbots, speech acts structure interactions, with justification-seeking questions prompting explanations that enrich engagement and deepen understanding [21].

McBurney and Parsons [26] proposed an interaction protocol called Fatio comprising of five locutions for argumentation which can be considered as a set of speech acts.

F1: assert (P_i, ϕ): Speaker P_i asserts a statement ϕ, creating a dialectical obligation to justify ϕ if requested.

F2: question (P_j, P_i, ϕ): Speaker P_j questions a prior **assert**(P_i, ϕ), seeking justification. This act imposes no obligation on P_j.

F3: challenge (P_j, P_i, ϕ): Speaker P_j challenges **assert**(P_i, ϕ), both seeking justification and assuming an obligation to justify not asserting ϕ, e.g., by providing a counterargument. Thus, **challenge** is stronger than **question**.

F4: justify $(P_i, \Phi \vdash \phi)$: Speaker P_i, having asserted ϕ and been questioned or challenged, provides a justification $\Phi \in A$ for ϕ.

F5: retract (P_i, ϕ): Speaker P_i, having previously asserted or justified ϕ, withdraws it via **retract**(P_i, ϕ), removing any obligation to justify it.

Example 3 (Child custody dialogue). Alice and Lucy are talking about a divorce case, specifically whether it is in the child's best interest to live with her mother or with her father. They have the following dialogue.

Alice: It is in the ten-year-old child's best interest that she lives with her mother. (*assert*)
Lucy: Why? (*question*)
Alice: Because the child wants to live with her mother and the civil code states that the judge must take the child's opinion into account. (*justify*)
Lucy: A ten-year-old child does not know what she wants. (*challenge*)
Alice: Why? (*question*)
Lucy: Public opinion says that ten-year-old children do not know what they want. (*justify*)
Alice: Most ten-year-old children do know what they want. (*assert*)
Lucy: Why do you say that? (*question*)
Alice: Peter is a child psychologist, and Peter says that most ten-year-old children know what they want. (*justify*)

2.3 Argumentation as Inference

Argumentation as inference determines which conclusions can be drawn from an incomplete, inconsistent, or uncertain body of information. It defines a nonmonotonic notion of logical consequence through argument construction, attack, and evaluation, where arguments are structured as premises, conclusions, and inferences [37]. This approach employs formal methods such as nonmonotonic logic for commonsense reasoning, graph theory, computational logic, causal reasoning, and Bayesian reasoning. Its primary application is in knowledge representation and reasoning.

Most literature in formal argumentation focuses on argumentation as inference. Before Dung's 1995 paper, Pollock had already conducted extensive research on argument structure, defeasible reasons, the interplay between deductive and defeasible reasoning, argument strength, and different types of defeat [30–36]. He conceptualized reasoning as constructing arguments, where reasons serve as atomic links [31], and distinguished between defeasible (prima facie) and nondefeasible (conclusive) reasons [30]. While nondefeasible reasons logically entail their conclusions, defeasible reasons can be overridden by new information. He identified two types of defeaters: rebutting defeaters, which deny the conclusion, and undercutting defeaters, which challenge the link between reason and conclusion. To represent arguments, Pollock [31–33] introduced inference graphs, where nodes denote inference steps and arrows indicate defeasible inferences, deductive inferences, or defeat links [32].

Example 4 (Child Custody in an Inference Graph). The dialogue between Alice and Lucy can also be illustrated in the format of Pollock's inference graph, as shown in Fig. 3. Figure 3 illustrates two arguments rebutting the two opposite conclusions *"It is in the child's best interest that she lives with her father"*, and *"It is not in the child's best interest that she lives with her father"*. An undercutting argument, *"Public opinion is not reliable"*, defeats the argument *"Most ten-year-old children do not know what they want"*. In this figure, nondefeasible and defeasible inferences are visualized respectively with solid and dotted lines (without arrowheads). The arrows are defeat relations.

3 The Metamodel: Relations Between the BDI Models

A metamodel defines the structure and relationships between models, serving as a higher-level abstraction that standardizes their shared rules while allowing domain-specific variations. In software engineering, metamodels, e.g., Unified Modeling Language (UML) [29], enforce structural consistency by specifying syntax and constraints for models. In knowledge engineering, top-level ontologies, e.g., Basic Formal Ontology (BFO) [40], similarly ensure semantic consistency by providing foundational concepts and relationships for domain ontologies [42].

Table 1 in Sect. 2 might give the impression that the three approaches are distinct and that they have distinct application areas. We would like to point

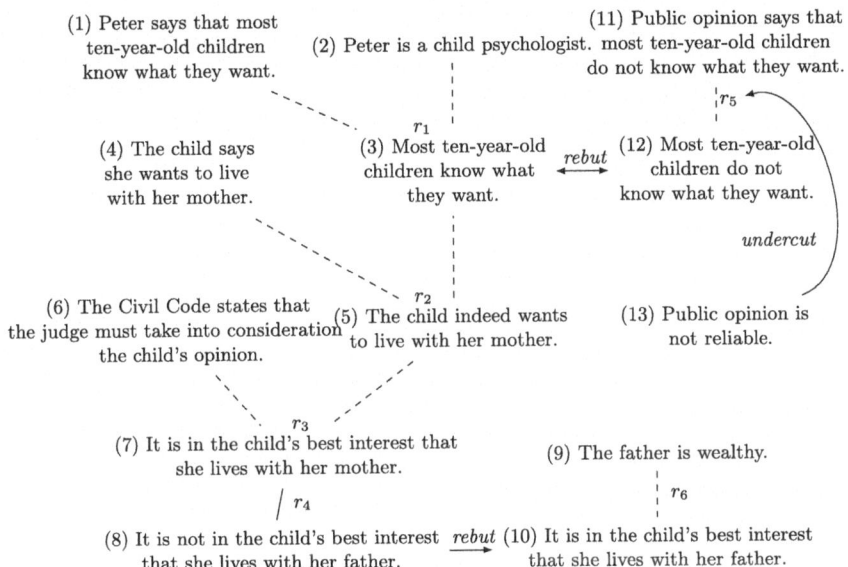

Fig. 3. The child custody case represented as a Pollock inference graph. The solid and dotted lines (without arrowheads) are nondefeasible and defeasible inferences respectively. The arrows are defeat relations.

out that this is not the case. The approaches (or types) of argumentation are not mutually exclusive or even incompatible. You can switch from one to another if you want to look at the same problem or situation from different angles, highlight different aspects, or select a modeling approach that is more suitable for a particular purpose. This also means that complex application areas like the legal domain can make very good use of each approach. Indeed, legal reasoning often engages with each of the three models—argumentation as inference, dialogue, and balancing—across different contexts and legal roles. Judges and attorneys may rely on one form of argumentation more than another, depending on the nature of the case and their specific role in the legal process. For instance, inference is commonly used by judges, attorneys, actually any type of lawyer, when applying legal rules to facts or deriving conclusions from incomplete or inconsistent premises. Dialogue plays a central role in courtroom exchanges between opposing parties. The structure of a trial often resembles a dialogue: each party presents their arguments and responds to those of the other while the judge oversees the process to ensure it follows legal procedures. Balancing is typically the domain of judges as they weigh multiple factors, conflicting interests, or values, to determine the most appropriate outcome. This is particularly important in discretionary decision-making where the law, instead of trying to provide detailed rules, assigns special power to judges so that they can make decisions based on their own evaluations. In such cases, judges exercise their judicial discretion by carefully balancing competing considerations within the framework of legal principles to reach a fair and just decision. Hence, these different modes of reasoning can correspond to and interact with one another, creating a comprehensive tool set for legal reasoning and decision-making.

Some papers in formal argumentation attempt to translate these different models from one to the other, for instance, from Carneades to ASPIC+ [18]. As mentioned in Sect. 2, Carneades uses varying proof standards and burdens of proof, reflecting a balancing perspective. It is mapped into ASPIC+ by treating assumptions as necessary axioms and modeling exceptions as undercutters. Another example is between ASPIC+ and dialogue, that is, ASPIC+ can be seen as at a fixed moment with a single agent in a dialogue. For example, Modgil uses ASPIC+ to define argument structures dynamically throughout a dialogue [28], establishing correspondences between the dialectical status of dialogue moves and argument acceptability.

4 The A-BDI Metamodel and Dung Style Abstraction

From the perspective of the A-BDI metamodel, each model—balancing, dialogue, and inference can be formally related through Dung's abstract argumentation graph at a higher level. Dung's framework is extended with—such as argument strength, bipolar relations, and multi-agent—to accommodate the specific methods and concerns of each model. We plan to discuss the universality of attack in greater depth in a separate paper, but the central point here is that these extensions are essential to unify all three models within the A-BDI metamodel without reducing one to another.

From the diversity of natural language arguments, there is a corresponding diversity of formal representations. The modern stage of formal argumentation identifies the diversity of argumentation and reasoning approaches a common core: Dung's theory of abstract argumentation. This paradigm shift in formal argumentation shows, roughly, how many forms of reasoning can be characterised at an abstract level as an instance of graph reasoning. Formal argumentation has been used since the mid-nineties as a general framework to classify reasoning methods, besides non-monotonic logic and logic programming also, for example, instances of game theory and social choice.

While the central notion of Dung's theory is the acceptability or non-acceptability of arguments based on attack and defense, Dung shows that non-monotonic logic is a special form of argumentation (more details in Sect. 3.2). It can be visualized as the commutative diagram in Fig. 4. There are two approaches to deriving conclusions from a knowledge base. The first is a direct approach where a given logic selects a set of rules with conclusions. The other is an indirect approach through argumentation, as shown in Fig. 4 (2–4). Structured argumentation studies the process that adds the structure that turns collections of rules into arguments and assigns attack relations (2) among arguments. This gives us abstract argumentation frameworks—directed graphs where nodes represent arguments, and arrows represent attack relations. Then argumentation semantics (3) determine the acceptance status of arguments and their conclusions. To represent a given logic by structured argumentation, eventually the conclusions from both approaches must be the same.

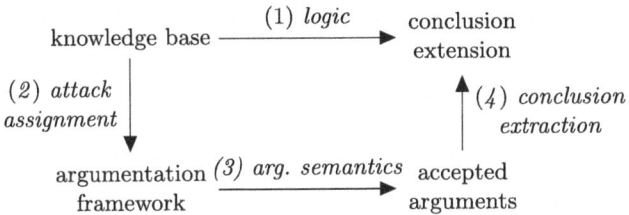

Fig. 4. Commutative diagram: two approaches to nonmonotonic inference: (1) logic systems; (2)–(4) argumentation systems. With appropriate choices on elements (2) and (3), one can obtain exactly the same conclusions as for the given logic (1).

Pre-existing ideas and methods, such as Pollock's argumentation-based inference, dialogue theories, and balancing, continue to persist and influence contemporary research. Rather than being rendered obsolete, these traditional theories are reinterpreted within the context of this new paradigm. On the one hand, Dung's theory provides a general framework that unifies diverse reasoning. On the other hand, it does not fully capture additional features important to dialogue, such as agents and strategies, or balancing, such as pros and cons with weights. Following this, there is a "reverse" diversity: various extended abstract argumentation frameworks and diverse semantics for (extended) abstract argumentation frameworks have been developed. For argumentation as dialogue, Abstract agent argumentation extends Dung's framework by associating arguments with agents [52]. Higher-order/meta-argumentation [10] introduces attacks on attack relations, reflecting real-life dialogues where arguments challenge other arguments and their relations. For instance, a lawyer may debate whether a suspect's argument effectively attacks another, or argue similarly about her own claims. For argumentation as balancing, examples are bipolar argumentation [11] that defines support and attack independently, weighted argumentation [8] that specifies a numeric value that indicates the relative strength of an attack, and value-based argumentation [4] defines values that are associated with an argument.

These examples illustrate how diverse extended argumentation frameworks build upon Dung's foundational concepts by introducing additional elements. We emphasize two points. The first is that the key reasoning ontology fundamentally relies on just two elements: arguments and attacks. Every utterance, be it a claim, an argument, or even an attack, can be modeled as an argument within these frameworks. Consequently, many of these extended frameworks can be *flattened* to basic ones, reinforcing the idea that attack graphs serve as a universal model of reasoning—much like how Turing machines serve as a universal model of computation. Second, while argumentation as inference has been extensively studied, the other two models have received relatively less attention.

5 Methodology

There is a gap between formal argumentation theories and applications of them. The main question is how to bridge these two. To address this, we need a "user guide" for argumentation that links theories to practical applications. However, creating such a user guide is challenging because of the diversity in natural, formal, and computational argumentation [54]. This diversity contrasts with the relative standardization found in fields like Answer Set Programming (ASP) and the Semantic Web. Understanding these differences is crucial to developing a "user guide" for argumentation.

First, we do not attempt to reduce one model to another. Instead, we assume that the three existing definitions or models exist for a reason, namely, they are developed for distinct concerns, and they represent distinct viewpoints on argumentation from stakeholders. To emphasize this point, we also call the models "conceptualizations". We do not exclude translation between these three models, but for our methodology, we believe it is too early to make commitments.

In Sect. 2, we take an example of child custody that seems to fit each conceptualization, and each conceptualization shows distinct aspects of the example. In this case, the judge must decide whether the child should stay with the father or the mother. This example is particularly illustrative because it involves inferential reasoning (e.g., drawing conclusions from legal and factual premises), structured dialogues among various parties (including parents, children, lawyers, and judges), and a final decision that cannot be strictly predetermined or automated. As the law emphasizes, the child's best interests must be balanced, making the decision process inherently complex and context-dependent.

The second step of the methodology we use in this paper is to compare the case study with other examples of reasoning in the literature. In Sect. 2, we focus on argumentation as balancing, as it is the least explored conceptualization within the COMMA community and the handbooks, despite extensive philosophical discussions. At the formal level, this means that we switch from qualitative approaches for inference and dialogue to quantitative approaches for balancing. Again, there is the problem of diversity, now the diversity of quantitative approaches, and the general problem of linking qualitative and quantitative approaches.

In the following, we present a preliminary step-by-step methodology for selecting a suitable model of formal argumentation. It is a structured process that considers the nature of the problem, the type of data and knowledge involved, and the stakeholders' objectives.

1. **Identify the problem context.** Determine the primary goal: Is the system intended to facilitate debates, persuasion, or negotiation? Is it meant to infer plausible conclusions from uncertain or conflicting information? Or is it balancing competing options and criteria?
2. **Define stakeholder requirements.** Elicit the needs and preferences of all parties involved. For instance, do stakeholders require a mechanism for real-time interaction, or do they need a computational approach to reason over

information? This helps to narrow down which model aligns best with practical constraints (e.g., time, resources, domain expertise).
3. **Map requirements to conceptual features.** Based on the considerations in Step 1 and Step 2, compare the required features to the characteristics of each model:
   – *Dialogue-oriented features:* Turn-taking rules, strategic discourse planning, and protocol definitions for dispute resolution.
   – *Inference-oriented features:* Focus on constructing and evaluating arguments in a nonmonotonic or probabilistic setting, emphasizing the derivation of conclusions from incomplete or contradictory information.
   – *Balancing-oriented features:* Mechanisms for weighing pro and con arguments, evaluating multiple criteria, and integrating ethical or legal considerations.
4. **Assess formal and computational methods.** Evaluate whether the domain demands specific formal tools:
   – *Dialogue-based* approaches typically rely on protocol design, strategic game-theoretic analysis, and speech-act formalization.
   – *Inference-based* approaches often require nonmonotonic reasoning techniques, graph-based argumentation frameworks, or probabilistic logic.
   – *Balancing-based* approaches commonly employ methods from decision theory, ethics, and multi-criteria or case-based reasoning.

   Choose the model whose formal toolkit matches your technical and theoretical requirements.
5. **Evaluate Scalability and Practical Feasibility.** Each model may come with different computational overhead, data requirements, and integration constraints. Determine whether the targeted system must handle large-scale reasoning tasks or real-time interactions, and ensure that the chosen model can be implemented with available resources.
6. **Validate Through Pilot Studies or Prototyping.** If feasible, implement a small-scale prototype or conduct a pilot study to confirm that the chosen model meets the desired objectives. Gather feedback from end-users or experts to identify any alignment issues or missing features.
7. **Iterate and Refine.** Refine your selection by revisiting earlier steps in the light of new insights. Adjust the chosen conceptual framework or explore a hybrid approach if the system requirements cross over more than one model.

6 Hybrid AI: Motivating the Metamodel

AI broadly encompasses two major paradigms: sub-symbolic and symbolic AI. Sub-symbolic methods, notably LLMs, excel at pattern recognition and natural language processing by learning complex statistical patterns from extensive datasets. Symbolic approaches, in contrast, rely on formal knowledge representation and reasoning (KRR) to provide rigorous frameworks for inference, explanation, and rule-based compliance. Both paradigms are well-established and applied across various fields such as law, ethics, and finance, yet each possesses distinct strengths and limitations.

A key objective in human-centered AI is to integrate these two paradigms so that the resulting systems can leverage the flexibility of data-driven methods while benefiting from the interpretability and critical thinking mechanisms inherent in symbolic logic. Data-driven technologies often struggle with transparency and accountability, issues that are particularly pressing in domains where decisions have legal or ethical consequences. Argumentation-based methods can mitigate these issues by guiding AI systems—especially large language models—to generate more interpretable explanations and engage in structured dialogue. Through argumentation schemes, speech act theory, and dialogical protocols, AI systems can reason about agents' beliefs, preferences, and intentions in ways that promote empathy, contextual awareness, and critical questioning.

Recent research has begun to demonstrate how formal argumentation frameworks can be integrated with LLMs to meet requirements in automated decision-making. For example, abstract argumentation and discussion games have been combined with prompt engineering to ensure that AI-generated explanations remain grounded in formal constraints [25]. This enables crucial legal safeguards such as the right to explanation or the right to challenge, making automated decisions more transparent and open to revision. Likewise, other proposals that integrate argumentation into new-generation AI appear in Distributed Argumentation Technology [50], which incorporates argumentation reasoning within multi-agent systems using distributed ledger technology. An instantiation of such is the IHiBO (Intelligent Human-Input-Based Blockchain Oracle). By placing argumentation structures and interactions on a blockchain, IHiBO affords decentralized, traceable, and secure decision-making processes, directly addressing concerns such as legal compliance, trust, and auditability.

In light of these developments, the A-BDI metamodel provides a structured perspective on formal and computational argumentation, clarifying how different models—balancing, dialogue, and inference. Each of these views can be integrated with LLMs and other AI technologies, depending on the specific requirements of an application. This highlights the need for a methodology that guides when and where formal and computational argumentation should be adopted, ensuring that its use is well-suited to the domain and objectives at hand.

7 Related Work

Methodologies from knowledge engineering, enterprise architecture, and formal logic offer valuable insights for the methodology of formal argumentation. For example, CommonKADS [48] emphasizes stakeholder analysis and knowledge modeling, which informs the identification of system users and the structuring of underlying knowledge in argumentation. LogiKEy [7], with its focus on logic-based knowledge engineering, highlights the role of formal verification, particularly in normative and legal reasoning. From an enterprise architecture perspective, ArchiMate [43], based on IEEE 1471-2000, demonstrates how diverse stakeholder concerns give rise to distinct viewpoints—an observation that aligns with the models of argumentation as inference, dialogue, or balancing. Similarly, in programming and decision theory, structured methodologies—ranging from test-driven development protocols to decision analysis frameworks [22,38]—provide systematic ways to transition from abstract theories to concrete implementations, reinforcing the value of methodical approaches in designing and applying formal argumentation systems.

Among the three models, balancing has received the least attention, yet it raises challenges in bridging philosophical discussions and formal models. At the formal level, balancing shifts from qualitative approaches to quantitative ones raises the challenge of linking these approaches and addressing the diversity of quantitative methods. For instance, quantitative argumentation considers both the strength of an argument and the attack relation itself, using fixpoints and multiplication methods [3], whereas Tucker's model focuses purely on the attack and employs addition methods. Tucker's model seems to offer a more sophisticated treatment of binary relations, going beyond the fixed structure of Dung's framework. The challenge remains to explore how ranking and gradual semantics in argumentation can further develop context-sensitive weighting mechanisms.

The burning-building example, where saving lives (a collective value) conflicts with preserving one's own health (an individual concern), illustrates a broader issue central to argumentation. In social sciences, this tension is known as the micro-macro dichotomy [12]. Micro-level reasoning focuses on an agent's individual judgments and choices, while macro-level approaches consider interactions among multiple agents, often within ethical or legal frameworks. In multi-stakeholder settings like Jiminy's ethical governor [24], bridging these levels requires merging norms or perspectives into a unified system. The challenge is how to formalize the balance between individual and collective considerations using argumentation tools.

8 Summary and Future Work

In this paper, we have introduced the A-BDI metamodel, the first metamodel for formal and computational argumentation. It contains three models, which conceptualize argumentation as balancing, dialogue, and inference. Each model addresses distinct concerns and employs its own formal methods, yet they have been discussed separately by extending Dung's abstract argumentation. By leveraging extensions that include argument strength, bipolar relations, and multi-agent dynamics, the A-BDI metamodel goes beyond a simple classification, enabling deeper relations and connections among diverse argumentation approaches. In complex real-world applications like child custody decisions, multiple models, or even all three, may be required. This raises further questions about whether additional models should be incorporated and whether existing ones should be further refined, for instance, by distinguishing between different types of dialogues [49]. With the increasing interaction between argumentation and LLMs and Generative Artificial Intelligence (genAI), the need for a well-defined methodology of formal argumentation has become more pressing. This is not a topic of one paper, but a change of focus of the whole community.

A key conclusion of this paper is that, in the past, the emphasis has been on argumentation as inference, but in the future, the emphasis will be on argumentation as dialogue and argumentation as balancing. There are three reasons. First, the advancement of chatbots and LLMs moves the field's center of attention from formal and computational argumentation to human-like, interactive dialogue systems. There is renewed interest in systems like Fatio, prompted by these new technologies. Second, argumentation on the web continues to grow in importance [44], consistent with earlier predictions by Gordon [19]. Third, deeper engagement with philosophical and ethical aspects of argumentation leads to more interaction between reason-based models and argumentation-based models, as illustrated by recent work in ethics and related areas [47].

In future work, several directions can be pursued. A key challenge is the methodology used to bridge the gap between formal theories and their application. Drawing inspiration from established frameworks such as CommonKADS, ArchiMate, and LogiKEy, this methodology will include steps for identifying stakeholders, selecting appropriate conceptual models, and validating implementations iteratively, tailored specifically to argumentation. Additionally, existing methodologies from knowledge-based systems (KBS) and related fields need to be adapted to accommodate the integration of LLM-based agents. As LLMs become more prominent in AI applications, understanding how formal argumentation interacts with their reasoning and decision-making processes will be essential. Finally, as discussed in Sect. 4, a crucial aspect of future research is the universality of attack. The question is how this principle can help relate the three conceptual models—balancing, dialogue, and inference—without reducing one to another. Rather than forcing a translation between them, we take inspiration from architecture methodologies such as ArchiMate, where different perspectives are systematically related while maintaining their distinct roles.

References

1. Alcaraz, B., Knoks, A., Streit, D.: Estimating weights of reasons using metaheuristics: a hybrid approach to machine ethics. In: Proceedings of the AAAI/ACM Conference on AI, Ethics, and Society, vol. 7, pp. 27–38 (2024)
2. Amgoud, L., Ben-Naim, J.: Ranking-based semantics for argumentation frameworks. In: Liu, W., Subrahmanian, V.S., Wijsen, J. (eds.) SUM 2013. LNCS (LNAI), vol. 8078, pp. 134–147. Springer, Heidelberg (2013). https://doi.org/10.1007/978-3-642-40381-1_11
3. Amgoud, L., Doder, D., Vesic, S.: Evaluation of argument strength in attack graphs: foundations and semantics. Artif. Intell. **302**, 103607 (2022)
4. Atkinson, K., Bench-Capon, T.: Value-based argumentation. In: Handbook of Formal Argumentation, Volume 2, pp. 397–441 (2021)
5. Austin, J.L.: How to Do Things With Words. Harvard University Press (1975)
6. Baroni, P., Gabbay, D., Giacomin, M., van der Torre, L. (eds.): Handbook of Formal Argumentation, vol. 1. College Publications (2018)
7. Benzmüller, C., Parent, X., van der Torre, L.: Designing normative theories for ethical and legal reasoning: LogiKEy framework, methodology, and tool support. Artif. Intell. **287**, 103348 (2020)

8. Bistarelli, S., Santini, F., et al.: Weighted argumentation. In: Handbook of Formal Argumentation, Volume 2 (2021)
9. Black, E., Maudet, N., Parsons, S.: Argumentation-based dialogue. In: Handbook of Formal Argumentation, Volume 2 (2021)
10. Cayrol, C., Cohen, A., Lagasquie Schiex, M.C.: Higher-order interactions (bipolar or not) in abstract argumentation: a state of the art (2021)
11. Cayrol, C., Lagasquie-Schiex, M.C.: On the acceptability of arguments in bipolar argumentation frameworks. In: Godo, L. (ed.) ECSQARU 2005. LNCS (LNAI), vol. 3571, pp. 378–389. Springer, Heidelberg (2005). https://doi.org/10.1007/11518655_33
12. Coleman, J.S.: Micro foundations and macrosocial behavior. Angewandte Sozialforschung anc AIAS Informationen Wien **12**(1–2), 25–37 (1984)
13. Dancy, J.: Ethics without principles (2004)
14. Drai, D.: Reasons have no weight. Philos. Q. **68**(270), 60–76 (2018)
15. FIPA: Communicative act library specification. http://www.fipa.org/specs/fipa00037 (2002)
16. Gabbay, D., Giacomin, M., Simari, G., Thimm, M. (eds.): Handbook of Formal Argumentation, vol. 2. College Publications (2021)
17. Georgeff, M., Pell, B., Pollack, M., Tambe, M., Wooldridge, M.: The belief-desire-intention model of agency. In: Müller, J.P., Rao, A.S., Singh, M.P. (eds.) ATAL 1998. LNCS, vol. 1555, pp. 1–10. Springer, Heidelberg (1999). https://doi.org/10.1007/3-540-49057-4_1
18. van Gijzel, B., Prakken, H.: Relating Carneades with abstract argumentation via the ASPIC+ framework for structured argumentation. Argument Comput. **3**(1), 21–47 (2012)
19. Gordon, T.F.: Towards requirements analysis for formal argumentation. Handbook Formal Argumentation **1**, 145–156 (2018)
20. Gordon, T.F., Prakken, H., Walton, D.: The Carneades model of argument and burden of proof. Artif. Intell. **171**(10–15), 875–896 (2007)
21. Hakim, F.Z.M., Indrayani, L.M., Amalia, R.M.: A dialogic analysis of compliment strategies employed by Replika chatbot. In: Third International conference of arts, language and culture (ICALC 2018), pp. 266–271. Atlantis Press (2019)
22. Keeney, R.L.: Decision analysis: an overview. Oper. Res. **30**(5), 803–838 (1982)
23. Kissine, M.: Speech act classifications. Pragmatics Speech Actions **173**, 202 (2013)
24. Liao, B., Pardo, P., Slavkovik, M., van der Torre, L.: The jiminy advisor: moral agreements among stakeholders based on norms and argumentation. J. Artif. Intell. Res. **77**, 737–792 (2023)
25. Liga, D., Markovich, R., Yu, L.: Addressing the right to explanation and the right to challenge through hybrid-AI: symbolic constraints over large language models via prompt engineering (2025). submitted to ICAIL 2025
26. McBurney, P., Parsons, S.: Locutions for argumentation in agent interaction protocols. In: van Eijk, R.M., Huget, M.-P., Dignum, F. (eds.) AC 2004. LNCS (LNAI), vol. 3396, pp. 209–225. Springer, Heidelberg (2005). https://doi.org/10.1007/978-3-540-32258-0_14
27. McBurney, P., Parsons, S., et al.: Argument schemes and dialogue protocols: Doug Walton's legacy in artificial intelligence. FLAP **8**(1), 263–290 (2021)
28. Modgil, S.: Towards a general framework for dialogues that accommodate reasoning about preferences. In: Black, E., Modgil, S., Oren, N. (eds.) TAFA 2017. LNCS (LNAI), vol. 10757, pp. 175–191. Springer, Cham (2018). https://doi.org/10.1007/978-3-319-75553-3_13

29. Pilone, D., Pitman, N.: UML 2.0 in a Nutshell. O'Reilly Media, Inc. (2005)
30. Pollock, J.L.: Defeasible reasoning. Cogn. Sci. **11**(4), 481–518 (1987)
31. Pollock, J.L.: How to reason defeasibly. Artif. Intell. **57**(1), 1–42 (1992)
32. Pollock, J.L.: Justification and defeat. Artif. Intell. **67**(2), 377–407 (1994)
33. Pollock, J.L.: Cognitive Carpentry: A Blueprint for How to Build a Person. MIT Press (1995)
34. Pollock, J.L.: Defeasible reasoning with variable degrees of justification. Artif. Intell. **133**(1–2), 233–282 (2001)
35. Pollock, J.L.: A recursive semantics for defeasible reasoning. In: Simari, G., Rahwan, I. (eds.) Argumentation in artificial intelligence, pp. 173–197. Springer, Boston (2009). https://doi.org/10.1007/978-0-387-98197-0_9
36. Pollock, J.L.: Defeasible reasoning and degrees of justification. Argument Comput. **1**(1), 7–22 (2010)
37. Prakken, H.: Historical overview of formal argumentation. In: Handbook of Formal Argumentation, pp. 73–141. College Publications (2018)
38. Raiffa, H.: Decision Analysis: Introductory Lectures on Choices Under Uncertainty. Addison-Wesley, Reading (1968)
39. Searle, J.R.: Expression and Meaning: Studies in the Theory of Speech Acts. Cambridge University Press (1979)
40. Smith, B.: BFO/MEDO: basic formal ontology (2003). https://basic-formal-ontology.org/. Accessed 16 Feb 2025
41. Streit, D.: From metaethics to machine decisions: formal models of normative reasons and their application in philosophy and machine ethics. Doctoral thesis, Université du Luxembourg (2024)
42. Sure, Y., Staab, S., Studer, R.: On-to-knowledge methodology (OTKM). Handbook on Ontologies, pp. 117–132 (2004)
43. The open group: ArchiMate forum. https://www.opengroup.org/archimate-forum (2025). Accessed 21 Jan 2025
44. Thieyre, J., Beynier, A., Maudet, N., Vesic, S.: Reassessing the impact of reading behaviour in online debates under the lens of gradual semantics. In: Fifth International Workshop on Systems and Algorithms for Formal Argumentation (SAFA-24), vol. 3757, pp. 119–133 (2024)
45. Traum, D.R.: Speech acts for dialogue agents. In: Foundations of rational agency, pp. 169–201. Springer (1999). https://doi.org/10.1007/978-94-015-9204-8_8
46. Tucker, C.: The Weight of Reasons: A Framework for Ethics. Oxford University Press, New York (forthcoming)
47. Tucker, C.: The Weight of Reasons: A Framework for Ethics (2024)
48. Waldner, J.B.: Principles of Computer-Integrated Manufacturing. Wiley (1992)
49. Walton, D., Krabbe, E.C.: Commitment in dialogue: basic concepts of interpersonal reasoning. State University of New York Press (1995)
50. Yu, L.: Distributed Argumentation Technology. Ph.D. thesis (2023)
51. Yu, L., Al Anaissy, C., Vesic, S., Li, X., van der Torre, L.: A principle-based analysis of bipolar argumentation semantics. In: Gaggl, S., Martinez, M.V., Ortiz, M. (eds.) European Conference on Logics in Artificial Intelligence, vol. 14281, pp. 209–224. Springer, Cham (2023). https://doi.org/10.1007/978-3-031-43619-2_15
52. Yu, L., Chen, D., Qiao, L., Shen, Y., van der Torre, L.: A Principle-based Analysis of Abstract Agent Argumentation Semantics. In: Proceedings of the 18th International Conference on Principles of Knowledge Representation and Reasoning, pp. 629–639 (11 2021). https://doi.org/10.24963/kr.2021/60

53. Yu, L., Markovich, R., Van Der Torre, L.: Interpretations of support among arguments. In: Legal Knowledge and Information Systems, pp. 194–203. IOS Press (2020)
54. Yu, L., van der Torre, L., Markovich, R.: Thirteen challenges in formal and computational argumentation. In: Gabbay, D., Kern-Isberner, G., Simari, G.R., Thimm, M. (eds.) Handbook of Formal Argumentation, Volume 3, pp. 890–976. College Publications (2024)

Author Index

A
Ågotnes, Thomas 185

B
Bentzen, Bruno 1

C
Chen, Chen 235
Chen, Wei 84
Chen, Weiwei 254
Chen, Yulin 1
Chen, Zixuan 17
Chi, Haixiao 1
Cui, Jianying 121

D
Doutre, Sylvie 34
Duy Hung, Nguyen 66

F
Fu, Xiaoxuan 53

G
Gabbay, Dov 1
Gao, Ziyi 235

H
Huynh, Van-Nam 66

J
Jearanaiwongkul, Watanee 272
Jiang, Lehuai 84
Ju, Fengkui 17

K
Kulicki, Piotr 104

L
Lagasquie-Schiex, Marie-Christine 34
Lan, Ting 121
Li, Hengfei 139
Li, Xu 150
Li, Yanjun 168, 185
Liang, Runcheng 201
Liao, Beishui 1, 235
Lindqvist, John I. 217
Liu, Siyi 235
Liu, Xiaolong 254

M
Mailly, Jean-Guy 34

P
Pooksook, Jiraporn 272

R
Racharak, Teeradaj 272
Ren, Jie 185

S
Shen, Yuping 309
Shi, Chenwei 217

T
Takashima, Kazuki 272
Takemura, Ryo 291
Trypuz, Robert 104

V
van der Torre, Leendert 361

W
Wang, Zongshun 309
Wen, Xuefeng 327
Wu, Jiachao 139

X
Xiong, Anshu 343

Y
Yao, Zelai 1
Yu, Liuwen 361

Yuan, Bo 1
Yuste-Ginel, Antonio 34

Z
Zhang, Songmao 343
Zhao, Zhiguang 53

The manufacturer's authorised representative in the EU is Springer Nature Customer Service Centre GmbH, Europaplatz 3, 69115 Heidelberg, Germany. If you have any concerns regarding our products, please contact ProductSafety@springernature.com

Printed and bound by CPI Group (UK) Ltd, Croydon, CR0 4YY

26/03/2026

02078968-0007